HOUSE OF LORDS

SESS

SELECT COMMITTEE ON
THE EUROPEAN COMMUNITIES

ENFORCEMENT OF
COMMUNITY COMPETITION RULES

REPORT WITH EVIDENCE

Ordered to be printed 7 December 1993

LONDON : HMSO
£27·50 net

(HL Paper 7)

CONTENTS

4

ORAL EVIDENCE

WRITTEN EVIDENCE

NOTE: pages of the report are numbered in bold type; pages of evidence are numbered in ordinary type. References in the text of the report are as follows:
(Q) refers to a question in oral evidence;
(p) refers to a page of written evidence.

FIRST REPORT

7 December 1993

By the Select Committee appointed to consider Community proposals, whether in draft or otherwise, to obtain all necessary information about them, and to make reports on those which, in the opinion of the Committee, raise important questions of policy or principle, and on other questions to which the Committee consider that the special attention of the House should be drawn.

ORDERED TO REPORT

ENFORCEMENT OF COMMUNITY COMPETITION RULES

PART 1 INTRODUCTION

1. A modern market economy requires legal rules whose object is to guarantee fair competition. To create a single market among several States with different legal systems it is essential to have common rules to prevent that market being fragmented or distorted by the conduct of private enterprises. The removal of state-imposed barriers to the free movement of goods and services across frontiers must be accompanied by prohibitions on enterprises to stop them agreeing to keep out of each others' national markets or to fix prices. Articles 85 to 89 of the EEC Treaty, which are reproduced in Appendix 3 to this Report, lay down the basic Community competition rules which regulate the conduct of private enterprises.[1] The prohibitions in Articles 85 and 86 are central to the common market and of all the provisions in the Community Treaties they are the most familiar to those outside government.

2. Article 85 prohibits agreements between undertakings, decisions by associations of undertakings and concerted practices which may affect trade between Member States and which have as their object or effect the prevention, restriction or distortion of competition within the common market. Prohibited agreements are automatically void. Paragraph 3 of Article 85 however provides for exemptions to be granted where the agreement (a term which will henceforth be used to include decisions by associations of undertakings and concerted practices) contains countervailing economic benefits in which consumers share. Article 86 prohibits abuse by an undertaking of a dominant position within the common market or in a substantial part of it, insofar as it may affect trade between Member States.

3. The EEC Treaty initially left it to Member States to enforce these rules, and permitted national authorities to grant exemptions under Article 85(3). The Commission had from the outset a general duty to ensure their application and on finding an infringement to propose appropriate measures to end it. The Council was however required by the Treaty to adopt appropriate regulations or directives to give effect to Article 85 and 86. These were to take into account "the need to ensure effective supervision on the one hand and to simplify administration to the greatest possible extent on the other". In 1962 the Council adopted Regulation 17, which conferred on the Commission strong powers to enforce the competition rules. Regulation 17 as amended is reproduced at Appendix 4 to this Report. Articles 85 and 86 were however provisions with direct effect, and the European Court later confirmed that they could also be relied on or enforced in proceedings before national courts. But the majority of Member States had until recently no established national competition authority, enterprises found it difficult to initiate actions before

---

[1] Articles 90 to 94 lay down parallel rules regarding state aids and the conduct of public undertakings which are outside the scope of this Report.

national courts in order to secure redress, and in practice most of the enforcement of the Community competition rules was taken over by the Commission.

4.   By 1982 the Commission was seriously overloaded with notifications of agreements and complaints of infringements which Regulation 17 required it to investigate and appraise. There was a backlog of thousands of cases. There was also wide concern about the efficiency and fairness of the Commission's procedures. The Advocate-General in the *Distillers* case[1] had said:

> "The Commission seems to me moreover to have overlooked that "justice must not only be done but must manifestly be seen to be done". Justice is not seen to be done if there is concealed from an undertaking, for no imperative reason, part of the text of a complaint made against it".

Against this background the Select Committee undertook an enquiry into the procedures of the Commission under Regulation 17, and considered to what extent the combination of administrative and judicial functions by the Commission endangered fairness of enforcement.

5.   The Select Committee's Report on *Competition Practice*[2] ("the 1982 Report") had an important influence on Commission procedures in competition cases. Virtually all the recommendations of the Committee which did not require amendment of Regulation 17 or of the Community Treaties were implemented within a short space of time. Undertakings were given greater access to the Commission's file on their case. The post of "Hearing Officer" was established within the Competition Directorate of the Commission, to supervise and preside over oral hearings of the parties and report on them prior to a Commission decision. The Commission began to make more use of block exemptions covering an entire class of agreements and of comfort letters giving informal assurances as to the Commission's attitude to a case. The latter two reforms were designed as ways of reducing the backlog of cases, and their implementation did this to some extent over the next few years.

6.   In recent years, however, there have been signs of renewed anxiety. In 1989 the Select Committee reported on proposals to confer on the Commission formal powers to appraise large-scale mergers with potential effects on competition in the Community. Doubts were expressed by witnesses as to the Commission's ability to discharge these new functions. The Committee in supporting the proposal made clear that its recommendations were conditional on improved procedures being incorporated in the new Regulation and additional qualified staff made available to the Competition Directorate of the Commission—conditions which were met when the merger control system came into effect in 1990. The Court of First Instance, which was established in 1988 with jurisdiction, *inter alia*, over competition cases, has delivered several judgments in which it has held that Commission procedures were flawed. Practitioners have continued to express serious concern that delays in disposing of notified agreements and complaints were an impediment to efficient conduct of business. Budgetary constraints have continued to deny the Commission sufficient staff to resolve the backlog of cases.

7.   The Commission has recently taken two important initiatives in response to these perceived difficulties. In December 1992 Sir Leon Brittan, then Commissioner in charge of competition, announced new procedures under which the Commission would apply administrative deadlines in order to guarantee prompt disposal—at least on an informal basis—of new cases. These would apply first to joint ventures—seen as resembling mergers which under the 1989 Merger Regulation now enjoy the benefit of short and legally binding procedural deadlines. Later, the self-imposed deadlines would apply generally. Secondly, and in part in response to the widespread debate on subsidiarity, the Commission in February 1993 published a Notice on co-operation between national courts and the Commission in applying Articles 85 and 86 of the EEC Treaty.[3] This is

---

[1]   Distillers Company v Commission [1980] ECR 2290.

[2]   8th Report, 1981-82 (HL 91), now out of print.

[3]   OJ 93/C 39/05, 13.2.93.

reproduced at Appendix 5 to this Report. The Notice has given rise to debate on the extent to which it is possible or appropriate for national courts, and for national competition authorities to assist the Commission in the enforcement of Community competition rules. Competition is an exception to the general principle that enforcement of rules of Community law against individuals and firms takes place at national level, and in the context of a general attempt to assess more rigorously the best level for all Community action it is right that the exception should be re-examined. A third element in the background to the enquiry was the requirement under the Merger Regulation that there should before the end of 1993 be a review of the criteria which determine whether a merger is appraised at Community level by the Commission or at national level by national authorities. At the outset of the enquiry it was widely supposed that the Commission would formally propose changes to these criteria so as to bring more prospective mergers within the scope of the Regulation and of Commission control. In the event this did not happen. But in-depth examination of the Merger Regulation and of the first three years of its operation carries important lessons for the enforcement of Article 85 and 86 of the EEC Treaty.

8.   Sub-Committee E (Law and Institutions) therefore decided to carry out a further enquiry into the enforcement of Community competition rules, with special reference to procedures and levels of decision making. As regards procedures, the enquiry began by examining the 1982 Report on *Competition Practice*, the changes made in response to its recommendations and the extent to which its recommendations where unimplemented remain valid. The question of the level of enforcement was examined against the background of the Commission's Notice on co-operation between national courts and the Commission and of the review of the Merger Regulation.

Structure of the Report and Evidence

9.   Part 2 of this Report sets out the recommendations in the 1982 Report against the underlying legal and factual background, describes the extent to which they have been implemented and gives the views of witnesses regarding the current position. Part 3 of the Report contains the Opinion of the Committee. Part 4 contains a Summary of Conclusions.

10.   Sub-Committee E (Law and Institutions) whose Members are listed in Appendix 1 received evidence from the witnesses listed in Appendix 2. The evidence, both written and oral, is printed with the Report. The Committee are most grateful to the witnesses for the exceptional quality of the evidence supplied for a complex and wide-ranging enquiry. Appendix 3 reproduces Articles 85 to 89 of the EEC Treaty. Appendix 4 reproduces Regulation 17 as amended. Appendix 5 contains the Commission's Notice on co-operation between national courts and the Commission in applying Articles 85 and 86 or the EEC Treaty. Appendix 6 contains a Commission summary of the enforcement of the competition rules, extracted from the publication EEC Competition Policy in the Single Market and last revised in 1989.

PART 2 BACKGROUND AND VIEWS OF WITNESSES

Separation of Enforcement Functions

11.   Article 89 of the EEC Treaty confers on the Commission the general duty to "ensure the application of the principles laid down in Articles 85 and 86". Council Regulation 17/62 sets out the functions and procedures of the Commission in applying these principles, and emphasises that Commission decisions are subject to review by the Court of Justice under the conditions specified in the Treaty. Because Regulation 17 confers wide powers on the Commission to collect information, to require termination of an infringement even on an interim basis, to impose administrative fines for established infringements, and sole power to grant exemptions under Article 85(3), most proceedings to enforce the competition rules of the Treaty are set in motion before the Commission or at the instance of the Commission. A summary of the current operation of the rules is in Appendix 6 to the Report. The largest category of proceedings consists of notifications of agreements by enterprises seeking negative clearance (no grounds of Commission action under Article 85(1)) or exemption on the grounds set out in Article 85(3) (contribution to improving the production or distribution of goods or to promoting technical or economic progress, while allowing consumers a fair share of the resulting benefits). Third parties—national authorities, individuals or enterprises—who can show a legitimate interest may bring anti-competitive behaviour to the attention of the Commission by way of complaint. In all these categories of proceeding the Commission is responsible for investigation (in liaison with national authorities), for giving interested parties the right to be heard and for making final recommendations or decisions. A basic question for consideration is whether it is appropriate "for the one body to be simultaneously the detective, the prosecutor, the negotiator and the decision maker".[1]

12.   The Joint Working Party on Competition Law of the Bars and Law Societies of the United Kingdom ("the Joint Working Party") pointed out that in 1982, during the Select Committee's earlier enquiry into *Competition Practice*, the Commission had described the division of responsibility between the investigators and the decision makers within the Commission's Directorate-General for Competition (DG IV). This separation of roles had been abandoned. "However well meaning the individual, this is bound to have an effect upon the conduct of the procedures and in particular upon the feeling of a defendant as to whether he has been given a fair hearing". The Court of First Instance had made clear in the *Shell*[2] case that it was not a breach of procedural rules for the same officials to be involved through successive stages. But if there was no-one coming in to the case at a later stage to bring a fresh mind to bear on the decision whether to carry the matter forward, the necessary level of objectivity would be lacking. The ideal solution would involve separation of the three functions of detective, prosecutor and decision maker, but the most important distinction was between investigation and the decision to proceed. As Mr David Vaughan QC put it on behalf of the Joint Working Party: "I would see a major need for a division between the inspector who comes round to your offices and the case handler" (p 61, QQ 194-198, 208-218).

13.   Mr Jeremy Lever QC also argued that it was essential for the Commission to revert to the division of functions earlier practised. In evidence given to the Select Committee's earlier enquiry into Merger Control, Mr Lever proposed "the establishment of a small Directorate General, separate from DG IV, that would be responsible for the formulation of Commission decisions in competition (and anti-dumping) cases, leaving DGIV to perform, after delivery of a Statement of Objections, only its present role of prosecution. The new Directorate General could comprise a small corps of senior officials with mixed legal and economic experience and having, in effect, the status of administrative law judges".[3] Mr Lever, in continuing to advocate this proposal in the present enquiry, maintained that while it might alter the results, it would not necessarily increase the man

[1]   The question was posed in these terms by the Monopolies and Mergers Commission in evidence to the Select Committee enquiry into *Merger Control*, 6th Report, 1988-89 (HL 31), at p 3.

[2]   Case T 11/89, *Shell v. Commission [1992] ECR II 757*.

[3]   6th Report, 1988-89, *Merger Control*, (HL 31), at pp 110-112.

hours required to be spent by Commission officials. Cases might be decided more quickly and with fewer appeals. If the Commission continued to resist such internal reform, "it then will become necessary to consider very seriously the establishment of a competition tribunal, and I think that that should be on the agenda in 1996" (QQ 539-545, 576-579, 581).

14. The Bundeskartellamt of the Federal Republic of Germany maintained that efficient implementation of competition would in the long run best be achieved by an independent European competition authority. "Short lines of decision would considerably shorten the process of decision-making and raise the efficiency of enforcement. The burden on the Commission would be eased if there was a separation of legislative tasks from administrative tasks. The European competition authority would be exclusively responsible for enforcement, but it would be subject to control by the Commissioner responsible for competition policy". The legislative power to issue block exemptions would remain with the Commission (pp 198, 202).

15. Other witnesses were however doubtful whether it was practicable, or even desirable, to alter the existing institutional framework in order to achieve formal separation of enforcement functions. For the Office of Fair Trading (OFT) the Director General, Sir Bryan Carsberg, accepted that a theoretically ideal procedure might be different, but the Commission was a living organisation "broadly on the right track" and it was not necessary to separate out the investigative, prosecuting and decision-making functions (QQ 309-312). The Confederation of British Industry (CBI) emphasised that establishment of an independent competition tribunal was not a realistic option at present (pp 191-193). The Monopolies and Mergers Commission (MMC) pointed out that under the United Kingdom system the MMC as the investigatory body was independent both from the organisation which recommended a reference of a prospective merger (the OFT) and independent from the body which decided on action and recommendations in the light of an MMC report (the Secretary of State for Trade and Industry). This separation avoided conflicts of interest and was a strength of the system—but other countries as well as the European Commission successfully employed an integrated system. Although the Bundeskartellamt were arguing in favour of a system with greater separation of functions, the German system was itself unitary (p 46, QQ 117-122, 129-130).

16. Mr Michael Reynolds of Allen & Overy, Solicitors, suggested that the argument for introducing an independent element into the Commission's competition procedures was now less strong in that the Court of First Instance had made a considerable difference to the application of the rules by providing a greater element of outside judicial control of the Commission. The unsatisfactory elements could be "remedied by measures which fall short of the wholesale re-writing of Regulation 17. Regulation 17 was once referred to by one of your Lordships as the 'Ark of the Covenant', but it is also regarded as a 'Pandora's box'". An independent review body might be no less political and would inevitably make procedures much longer (pp 6-7, QQ 3-4, 10-12, 17-18, 62).

17. For the European Commission Dr Claus-Dieter Ehlermann, Director-General of the Competition Directorate (DG IV), also emphasised the supervisory powers of the European Court in regard to Commission action. The old system of a separate inspection directorate within DG IV had proved inefficient—the importance of the facts was such that investigative and prosecution functions could not be separated without risk that the prosecutor would find certain facts lacking and would launch a further investigation. Separation of functions would not improve the quality of the statement of objections or of the decision and would not make the best use of limited resources. If there were more resources it would be better to have larger teams for complex cases, as had been done within the Merger Task Force. To establish an independent competition authority which would assume the decision-making functions of the Commission would require Treaty amendment, and although Germany had proposed such a change during negotiation of the Treaty of Maastricht, there had been no support from other delegations. He doubted whether the German system, based on a regard for the competition principle deeply rooted in national public opinion, could be transferred to the Community level. It could be more difficult for a small authority, separate from the Commission, to take courageous decisions, and the distribution of sensitive posts

among different nationalities could become acrimonious. Mr Joshua of DG IV added that "it would be misleading to draw an exact parallel between a body such as the Commission which is not a purely judicial body, and the straight courtroom model in a contentious case between two litigants. I do not think that there is anything repugnant in administrative law for a body which is given the task of performing a particular function to have, inside that function, an adjudicatory capacity provided that the procedure is fair" (p 106, QQ 403-406, 412-414, 416-418, pp 134-136).

Fundamental Rights of Defendants and Complainants

18.   Regulation 17 states in its Preamble that undertakings concerned must be accorded the right to be heard by the Commission and third parties whose interests may be affected by a decision must be given the opportunity to submit their comments beforehand. Article 19 sets out the substantive requirements in somewhat general terms. The details are spelt out in Commission Regulations, in particular Regulation 27 of 1962 and Regulation 99/63 which prescribes detailed rights of defence and regulates the conduct of oral hearings. In 1982 the Select Committee concluded that it was "essential that the recognised standards of natural justice should, as far as is possible, be applied in the adjudication by the Commission of contentious or disputed cases. Administrative convenience is no ground for lowering the standards of natural justice". The right to a fair hearing has been established as a general principle of Community law by successive decisions of the European Court. In his evidence, Dr Ehlermann stated that "the Commission is absolutely committed to ensure that it meets the highest standards in this respect. Not only is this stage of the Commission's procedure necessary to give effect to a fundamental principle of Community law, it is also of benefit to DG IV. Occasionally, the hearing of the parties makes it clear that some or all of our concerns are unfounded, or that it is necessary further to develop our arguments to ensure that they are watertight. Equally, on other cases, the exercise of trying to defend a clear infringement of the competition rules has led companies to accept the existence of the infringement, introducing, for example, a compliance programme". Dr Ehlermann submitted that over the last ten years there had been major improvements in the speed and legal security offered by Commission procedures in regard to notifications and complaints, and that the result, while open to further improvement "already stands favourable comparison with almost any other anti-trust system in the world" (pp 106, 120).

19.   Mr Reynolds suggested that the most severe problem facing complainants was that it could take the Commission several years to reach a final decision which might come too late. Although the Commission had the power to decide on interim measures, such a decision required many of the essential procedural steps of a full decision but in a much shorter time-frame. He argued that in view of the long time before a substantive Commission decision, the interim measures procedure should be streamlined. A complainant awaiting a decision had no formal right to a Commission decision which could be appealed, although in his experience the Commission was willing to give complainants a rejection decision which could be challenged before the European Court (pp 9-10, 17).

20.   The Commission is taking active steps to reduce the long delays experienced by complainants and defendants. In December 1992 Sir Leon Brittan, then the Commissioner responsible for competition, announced that changes would begin on 1 January 1993 which would "in the foreseeable future lead to every single case being dealt with in a fixed, predictable and reasonable period of time". Structural cases such as joint ventures would be tackled first—within two months from receiving complete notification the Commission would write either a comfort letter or a warning letter. A warning letter would enable companies to be aware of competition problems and to begin discussions with the Commission. Parties would be informed of the deadline by which the Commission intended to reach a final decision—these could not be standardised but would be as short as possible. Over a period of years the periods would be reduced and ultimately the Commission would be able to determine how to propose to the Council amendment of Regulation 17 to introduce binding deadlines for all structural cases. For other notifications and complaints a similar two-stage procedure, with self-imposed deadlines notified to the parties would be introduced from 1 April 1993. The Commission's Annual Report on Competition Policy would

henceforth contain a section devoted to procedure, including a detailed analysis of notifications and complaints, and the time taken to deal with them. (Press Release of 23.12.1992 annexed to Commission Memorandum, at p 121).

21. The Competition Law Association commented that the introduction of the Merger Regulation with its strict time limits for decisions had highlighted starkly the Commission's performance in other competition cases. Binding deadlines in the context of mergers had been part of the price of obtaining Community powers of control at all. But the procedural reforms announced by Sir Leon Brittan would be a welcome step forward—a half-way house between the present situation and binding deadlines (pp 9-10). The OFT believed the changes, backed by internal instructions, "would result in a greatly improved service from the Commission" (p 92).

22. The Joint Working Party gave as their first ground for concern about the Commission's procedures in contentious competition cases "the lack of respect for natural justice and the rights of defence and the absence of any interlocutory procedure to resolve disputes during contentious procedures so as to ensure that those rights are respected in the conduct of proceedings". It was not sufficient that the Court of First Instance could annul a final decision for a procedural defect which had occurred many years before. This violated the interests of the complainant and of others who had been affected by the conduct as well as those of the defendant. "A decision annulled for the failure of the Commission to carry out proper procedures is as much a denial of justice to those who suffer, as is the denial of rights of defence to the defendant". It was an essential requirement that the statement of objections should clearly set out the case against the defendant or defendants, but standards varied greatly between cases. In the *Woodpulp Case*[1] the major part of the Commission decision was annulled because of defects in the statement of objections, and in the *Cimenteries Case*[2], where there were over 70 separate defendants, it was alleged that the Commission by disclosing only part of the statement of objections to individual defendants, denied them an opportunity to consider the overall case against them (p 59). Mr Lever also stressed the waste of Community resources and prejudice to the wider Community interest which resulted from defects in enforcement procedures. He did not believe that the situation had improved in the last few years, and drew attention to the finding of serious misuse of evidence in the presentation of a case by the Commission in the *Italian Flat Glass Case*[3] (pp 163-164). Mr Ivo Van Bael of Van Bael & Bellis, a Member of the Brussels Bar, expressed concern that the Commission's discretion in choosing which cases to pursue was wide, its choices unpredictable and its settlement procedures (though settlement should be encouraged) were not amenable to public or judicial scrutiny. He argued that there was a need for more discipline and greater respect for law and procedure. On the credit side however was the performance of the Merger Task Force, the introduction of time limits by the Commission and other self-imposed procedural improvements (pp 220-221).

23. Mr Peter Duffy described the extent to which the Community institutions had come to accept the procedural safeguards of Article 6 of the European Convention on Human Rights as applicable to Commission procedures in competition cases. Article 6 provides that "In the determination of his civil rights and obligations or of any criminal charge against him, everyone is entitled to a fair and public hearing within a reasonable time by an independent and impartial tribunal established by law". Minimum rights of defence are set out for the benefit of those charged with a criminal offence. In the *Fedetab* case[4], the European Court of Justice stated that "The Commission is bound to respect procedural guarantees provided for by Community law [but] ... it cannot be classified as a tribunal within the meaning of Article 6 of the European Convention". In

[1] Joined Cases 89, 104, 114, 116, 117 and 125, *Ahlstrom Osakeyhtio v. Commission* [1988] ECR 5193, [1993] 4 CMLR 407.

[2] Joined Cases T10/92, T11/92, T 12/92 and T15/92 *SA Cimenteries CBR and Others v. Commission* [1993] 4 CMLR 243.

[3] Joined Cases T68, 77 and 78/89, *Societa Italiano Vetro Spa and others v. Commission*, not yet reported.

[4] Cases 209-215 and 218.78 [1980] ECR 3125.

the recent case of *Niemitz v. Germany*[1] however, the European Commission of Human Rights had unanimously held that a French company fined by a French court for anti-competitive behaviour faced a "criminal charge" within the meaning of the Convention. The Convention permitted use of administrative decisions concerning civil rights and obligations or investigative procedures concerning criminal charges, but only on condition that undertaking retained the right to due process before an independent tribunal. "The judicial control by the CFI and, in appropriate cases, the ECJ will only provide the judicial redress required under the Convention if all issues are fully considered and no discretionary reserve is shown in relation to Commission findings of fact and/or economic evidence". Recent decisions of the European Court and Court of First Instance had shown a robust approach to examination of evidence. In regard to the right against self-incrimination however, the approach taken by the European Court fell short of the standard of safeguard adopted in a more recent case before the European Court of Human Rights (pp 195-196). For the Joint Working Party Mr Vaughan said that "one of the things that the Court of First Instance has done is to make it very clear to everyone that whether they are a tribunal, a court, or whatever they are, they expect them to comply with Article 6 of the Human Rights Convention". The principles were clearly established—the problem lay in the practice (QQ 206, 231-239).

24.   The CBI stressed the need for vigilance as pressure to produce rapid decisions increased. The new time limits were welcome, but brought with them "a danger that rights of defence and procedural correctness will be sacrificed in order to meet the target time schedules". Competition law should be predictably enforced in accordance with fair and transparent procedures. It would be more appropriate to the penal nature of the remedies under Regulation 17 if new rules enshrined rights to:

"   — receive timely notice and adequate formulation of the legal and factual issues
         involved in the case;

         — present oral testimony, documentary evidence and argument;

         — rebut adverse evidence by cross-examination or other appropriate means;

         — appear with counsel;

         — have the decision based exclusively on matters introduced into the record;

         — have a complete record consisting of the transcript of the oral stage as well as the
         documentary evidence and other papers filed in the proceeding." (pp 191-192, 194-
         195).

Access to the File

25.   In its 1982 Report, the Select Committee suggested that "the Commission could effect a great improvement in its present system by allowing undertakings to have access, subject to necessary safeguards, to the whole of the Commission's file". The Commission responded promptly to this recommendation by announcing new procedures intended to permit undertakings to inspect the file on their case and so exercise their rights as complainants or defendants more effectively. According to the Department of Trade and Industry, "Undertakings are invited to consult the relevant documents on the Commission's premises (in the case where the undertakings wish to consult only a few documents the Commission may forward copies). The Commission informs the undertakings beforehand which documents they may examine and which are considered confidential. If the undertaking makes a justified request to see a document which is considered to be confidential, the Commission may make a non-confidential summary available" (p 142). The Commission duties regarding confidentiality derive from Article 20 of Regulation 17, which provides that "Without prejudice to the provisions of Article 19 and 21, the Commission and the competent authorities of the Member States, their officials and other servants shall not disclose

---

[1]   1993 16 European Human Rights Reports 97.

information acquired by them as a result of the application of this Regulation and of the kind covered by the obligation of professional secrecy".

26. The Joint Working Party said that the right of access to documentation which could be helpful to the defence was a fundamental human right. They acknowledged that following the 1982 Report the Commission had set out improved procedures in successive Competition Reports. But the Commission did not always provide full access to files, and individual procedures were not uniform. They pointed to a number of cases where rights of access had been found by the European Court or the Court of First Instance to be inadequate, contrasting in particular the position in the *Cimenteries Case*[1] with that in *BPB Industries and British Gypsum v. Commission*.[2] They suggested that the Commission had not done enough to reconcile the conflict between access to the file and confidentiality, and that it should be possible to explore such ideas as limited disclosure to lawyers or providing non-confidential summaries. Sometimes information had ceased to be truly confidential by the time the Commission took action. "However, in any event there can be no doubt that the rights of defence are a far superior right to the rights of confidentiality ... and problems of confidentiality in a particular case can never justify the failure to provide full rights of defence". The Hearing Officer should be given jurisdiction to deal with disputes over the rights of defence in the course of proceedings, particularly since the Court of First Instance could only act on an appeal against a final decision of the Commission.

27. In a Supplementary Memorandum, the Joint Working Party enlarged on the difficulties experienced by practitioners in gaining full access to Commission files. Appendix 1 to this Memorandum sets out the Commission rules developed in this context. The Twelfth Report on Competition Policy, where the rules were first formulated, made clear that the Commission regarded as confidential:

" (i) documents or parts thereof containing other undertakings's business secrets;

(ii) internal Commission documents, such as notes, drafts or other working papers;

(iii) any other confidential information, such as documents enabling complainants to be identified where they wish to remain anonymous, and information disclosed to the Commission subject to an obligation of confidentiality".

The Joint Working Party said that the main difficulties were that the Commission appeared to have no consistent view as to the meaning of "professional secrecy" in Article 20 of Regulation 17 or on the extent to which the confidential documents listed in the Twelfth Report came within it, and that the Commission was often unable to identify intrinsically confidential information. The Commission argued that where an undertaking considered that the file contained exculpatory documents, the onus was on that undertaking to identify the documents and request their production. The problem of production of incomplete evidence was in their view related to the problem of access—and in this connection they cited recent European Court cases and in particular the *Italian Flat Glass* case[3] (pp 60-61, QQ 236, 247, 256, pp 83-89).

28. Mr Lever endorsed these criticisms. Although the Commission objective was to disclose material which might assist the defence, officials had admitted that they found difficulty in identifying what material on the file fell into that category. Everything that was not a real business secret should be available to defendants. Real business secrets which could not be disclosed should not be used in evidence—but he did not suggest that they were. The need to rely on documents in translation also caused misunderstandings. It was not clear at what level decisions on confidentiality of documents were taken, and there was a compelling case for publication of rules of procedure

[1] Joined Cases T10/92, T11/92, T 12/92 and T15/92 *SA Cimenteries CBR and Others v. Commission* [1993] 4 CMLR 243.

[2] Cast T 65/89 *BPB Industries & British Gypsum v. Commission* [1993] 5 CMLR 32.

[3] Case T68/89, *Societa Italiano Vetro Spa and others v. Commission*, not yet reported.

which would clarify such matters (QQ 559-562). Mr Nicholas Forwood QC said that lawyers and officials from different backgrounds within Europe had different expectations as to what "access to the file" should mean. The Commission had failed adequately to clarify its practice, and so in different cases there was significant variation in the level of disclosure accorded by different Commission rapporteurs. It was unclear whether the extent of disclosure given would meet the requirements of the right of defence as developed in the jurisprudence of the European Commission and Court of Human Rights. Disclosure gave rise to particular problems in cases involving multiple defendants, who might have business secrets from one another (p 209).

29.   Other witnesses were less critical of the Commission's current practice. Mr Reynolds explained that in the *AKZO* case[1] the European Court of Justice had held that the Commission must provide the defendant with a full copy of a formal complaint made under Regulation 17. In the *Distillers* case[2] the Court endorsed the practice of omitting business secrets. Following issue of the statement of objections, which was accompanied by annexes setting out documentary evidence, the defendant might examine and copy all documents on which the Commission relied, except internal documents and those containing business secrets. A decision to disclose a document could be appealed immediately. Mr Reynolds did not think that full access was possible or desirable, but parties—including third parties with a legitimate interest—should have access to documents not relied on by the Commission (p 15, QQ 21-28). The MMC emphasised that there was no free exchange of information between itself and the Commission—the MMC was precluded from disclosure of material received in the course of their enquiries by section 133 of the Fair Trading Act 1973, and the Commission was similarly restrained by Regulation 17. The European Court had recently confirmed that enquiries had to be kept in watertight compartments. Mr Noel Ing, Senior Legal Adviser to the MMC, commented that there was a risk that permitting more disclosure between competition authorities would act as a deterrent to the original flow of information (p 45, QQ 140-145). The CBI laid emphasis on the need for partial access to the file to enable undertaking to challenge the Commission's evidence in a meaningful way, but offered no criticism of the balance now struck between disclosure and commercial confidentiality (p 192).

30.   For the Commission Dr Ehlermann set out the practice developed since the 1982 Report in the light of successive decisions of the European Court and the Court of First Instance. Since 1982 the Commission had adopted almost 90 final prohibition decisions and in only a handful of cases had there been conflict over access to the file. He believed that the Commission was "obliged to provide to the companies concerned documents that are manifestly exculpatory in relation to the allegations raised by the Commission". Preparing the file for examination involved checking every page—often thousands—to avoid inadvertent disclosure of business secrets or other confidential information. There were great difficulties in cartel cases with many defendants, where evidence derived almost exclusively from inspections under Article 14 of Regulation 17. "The companies concerned have, in many cases, claimed that all of the documents copied during such inspections were confidential in nature and should on no account be disclosed to third parties, particularly their customers and competitors. Once the Statement of Objections had been sent, however, the companies claimed that they should be given access to the whole of the Commission's file, including the documents of their competitors". Evidence which was central would be disclosed notwithstanding a claim for confidentiality. If the Commission allowed disclosure more generally, this could facilitate the behaviour it sought to detect and prohibit—price fixing and market sharing. There had been errors—for example in the *Italian Flat Glass* case, and since then additional safeguards had been introduced, with greater involvement of the Commission Legal Service. An internal manual of procedures was being drawn up for all rapporteurs. The mandate of the Hearing Officer should be enlarged so that he was available as a kind of ombudsman in case of difficult conflicts between access and protection of confidentiality. There should be a notice setting out the rules to avoid misunderstandings.

---

[1]   Case 53/85 *AKZO Chemi BV v. Commission* [1986] ECR 1965.
[2]   Case 30/78 *Distillers Co v. Commission* [1980] ECR 2229.

31. On the question of how "manifestly exculpatory" documents could be identified Mr Joshua of DG IV said that when a company asked for the opportunity to examine documents of its competitors on a speculative basis, they would be asked to identify a specific line of enquiry, and the Commission would then examine the documents in search of any document fitting the description. "I can assure you that we are extremely careful. We bend over backwards if there is a document which is relevant. If it is a question of the conflict between confidentiality and the right to be heard, we are very careful to make sure that the right to be heard is paramount" (pp 106-108, QQ 419-425, 430, 436).

The Oral Hearing and the Role of the Hearing Officer

32. The 1982 Report, accepting that wholly independent review of Commission handling of cases was not possible without Treaty amendment, suggested the creation of an additional post of Director in DG IV, to preside over the oral hearing and to assume responsibility within DG IV for the subsequent conduct of the case. The post of Hearing Officer was established in response to that recommendation, with the responsibility of ensuring proper conduct of the oral hearing.[1] According to the Department of Trade and Industry (the DTI), "In performing his duties he ensures that the rights of the defence are respected, while at the same time taking account of the need for effective application of the competition rules. He also ensures that in the preparation of draft Commission decisions in competition cases due account is taken of all the relevant facts, whether favourable or unfavourable to the parties concerned". To ensure his independence he has a right of direct access to the Member of the Commission with special responsibility for competition policy. For the DTI Mr Philip Bovey said "He is more like an ombudsman but at the moment a rather partial ombudsman because he is concerned only with the actual formal hearing". If he were to be given wider interlocutory functions, this would require an amendment of Regulation 17 so that he would prepare the ground for a final Commission decision. His role would then be like that of an American administrative law judge rather than an ombudsman. It would be more reasonable to use the Hearing Officer to decide on disclosure of a particular document than to request him to comb through an entire file to see if anything had been withheld. Mr Alan Cooper suggested that there was scope for enhancing the status of the Hearing Officer so that his view "is almost something which other officials will tremble at". It was in the Commission's interest to get things right, and a Hearing Officer with the necessary authority could improve the quality of the decision (pp 141-143, QQ 481-492, 497-499).

33. Mr Reynolds argued that the Hearing Officer should be given an enhanced status and wider functions. The preliminary hearing recommended in the 1982 Report had not been implemented, and the Hearing Officer should also have power to rule on matters such as time limits for replying to Statements of Objections and access to the file. Publication of his Report would enhance its importance and the Hearing Officer's status. At present the Hearing officer was independent from the Commission team and in regulating the conduct of hearings might prevent the Commission from pursuing an unfair line of questioning. He did not make formal decisions and so no appeal lay from his procedural decisions. Enlargement of his functions in the way suggested would make it necessary to have more than one Hearing Officer (pp 16, 17, QQ 11, 13, 29-48). All these suggestions were endorsed by the Joint Working Party, and they further argued that the Hearing Officer's Report should be made available to the Advisory Committee, to all the Commissioners with responsibility for the decision and to the Court of First Instance. Following any subsequent judgment of the Court of First Instance he should have power to make recommendations and his response should appear in the next annual Report on Competition Policy. An interlocutory decision by the Hearing Officer should be open to review by the Court of First Instance, but the Officer himself should remain within DG IV. As Mr Vaughan put it, "if he is the Master and the Court of First Instance is the Judge, he takes the run-of-the-mill decisions and then, if people do not like that, they appeal" (pp 59-62, QQ 207, 227-228, 240-263). Similar recommendations for enhancing the status and functions of the Hearing Officer were put forward by the Competition Law Association,

---

[1] Current terms of reference of the Hearing Officer are set out in the Commission's XXth Report on Competition Policy (1990) at p 273.

by the CBI and by Mr Van Bael. The Competition Law Association saw advantage in attaching the Hearing Officer to the Commission Legal Service instead of DG IV (pp 178, 192, 222).

34.   The OFT on the other hand, did not believe that there was a general need to give the Hearing Officer a much wider role, though they favoured greater publicity for his Report (QQ 340-349). From a different standpoint Mr Lever regarded the suggestion as "a kind of watered down version of my division of functions, my separate directorate-general". A more senior Hearing Officer without the power to take final decisions would be merely a tinkering with the present system (QQ 546-555).

35.   Dr Ehlermann considered the post of Hearing Officer to be a very valuable development and believed the appointment had increased the importance of the oral hearing. An additional Hearing Officer had been appointed to deal with merger cases, and he could chair hearings on Article 85 or Article 86 matters. In the absence of both Officers an *ad hoc* replacement would be made from among Advisors to the Director-General who did not deal with individual cases, so that in all cases a clearly impartial official would chair the hearing. Before the oral hearing a preparatory meeting to clarify the issues would be held at the request of any of the parties or if the Hearing Officer considered it useful. Dr Ehlermann was receptive to the suggestions made for enlarging the functions of the Hearing Officer (particularly regarding access to the file) and, subject to budgetary constraints, for giving him a higher formal status. He argued however that his function was advisory and did not envisage that it would be right for him to be able to take or recommend formal decisions which could be appealed. Nor did he accept that his Report should be made public. Decisions had to be attributable to the Commission and only to the Commission, but the independence of the Hearing Officer was crucial. "I will do everything to maintain his independence. I appreciate the advice of the hearing officer greatly in order to avoid the repetition of events which have aroused so much criticism, such as the *Flat Glass* decision" (pp 108-109, QQ 420, 425-429, 431-435, 437-442).

Investigations

36.   The Select Committee in the 1982 Report recommended that a Commission decision under Article 14 of Regulation 17 authorising a summary investigation into an undertaking or association of undertakings should be subject to the leave of the President of the European Court or a Judge of the Court nominated by him. Alternatively the Director to be appointed (later established as the Hearing Officer) could be given this responsibility. This change required amendment of Regulation 17, and has never been made. Dr Ehlermann was in favour of the change, while not regarding it as one of the Commission's highest priorities. At present, if an undertaking did not submit to a decision ordering an investigation, the Commission requested the assistance of the competent authority in the relevant Member State. National legislation under which the authority afforded the necessary assistance varied, but in some Member States a court order from a national judge enforcing the Commission decision was required. The European Court had made clear in the *Hoechst* case[1] that the national authority was entitled to review the Commission decision to verify that it was authentic and not arbitrary or excessive. Dr Ehlermann maintained that to require leave from a Judge of the Court of First Instance (which would require amendment to the Rules of Procedure of the Court and perhaps to its Statute) would have the advantage of underlining respect for fundamental rights within the Community legal system (pp 105-106, QQ 455-457).

37.   The DTI said that in 1982 the Commission had drawn up an explanatory memorandum on procedures to be followed during inspections, which set out the scope and limits of the inspectors and the rights of the undertakings concerned. In particular the memorandum explained that the undertakings were entitled to call in their legal advisers (as the Select Committee had recommended) and that they might draw to the attention of the inspectors factors favourable to themselves which might emerge from documents other than those requested. Dr Catherine Bell for the DTI said that although Regulation 17 enabled the Commission to request the competent

---

[1]   Joined Cases 46/87 and 227/88 *Hoechst v. Commission* [1989] ECR 2919.

authorities of Member States to undertake necessary investigations on its behalf, with or without the assistance of Commission officials, United Kingdom Ministers were wary of further use of that provision. They believed there was a danger that investigative powers would be more rigorous in those Member States with a well developed competition infrastructure (pp 141-143, 145-146, QQ 521-525). The OFT on the other hand believed that the Commission could make more use of the power to request investigations by national authorities. They had twice carried out unannounced investigations on behalf of the Commission, and Sir Bryan Carsberg said that he would welcome further use of the practice, though he did not regard this as a matter of great significance. Although not all Member States had equivalent procedures, the Commission could take account of the position at national level in its own procedures (p 93, QQ 371-372).

38.   The Joint Working Party expressed satisfaction with the current investigation procedures of the Commission and its application of rules of legal professional privilege. There had been a great improvement following the 1983 Report. Like DTI Ministers, they expressed reservations about greater delegation by the Commission of inspections to national authorities because of the possibility of differential results in different Member States. At present Commission investigators might carry out simultaneous searches in different Member States in close liaison. The results of these might determine who were defendants in the case, and it would be unfair if this were to depend on the efficiency of a national policy force (p 61, QQ 275-276).

39.   Other witnesses were less sanguine. Mr Van Bael said that although the Commission had imposed administrative disciplines on itself, in the *AKZO* case[1] none of the safeguards had been complied with. In the *Hoechst* case[2] the European Court ruled that the Commission must be assisted during a search by national authorities who must ensure that national safeguards are observed—but these differed from one Member state to another (p 222). Mr Reynolds stated that "It has been my experience that there is a great tendency for the inspectors to ask questions which go beyond the scope of the documents being examined. It is obviously difficult to regulate this type of on the spot investigation, but it remains an issue of some concern where a party, who may have had no previous knowledge of the Commission's interest in its affairs, is asked difficult questions under stressful conditions regardless of whether its legal advisers are present. This problem is compounded by the fact that the scope of the investigations as set out in the inspectors' mandate is often expressed extremely vaguely" (p 15, QQ 55-56). Mr Duffy suggested that the decision of the European Court in *Hoechst*[2] that Article 8 of the European Convention on Human Rights, requiring respect for private and family life, home and correspondence, did not extend to business premises required reassessment in the light of subsequent case law of the European Court of Human Rights. In a recent case the European Court of Human Rights had found that a search of a lawyer's office came within the scope of the Article, and rejected the German Government's reliance on the European Court of Justice case law. Mr Duffy suggested that in the light of this development "a welcome adjustment to EC competition procedures would be to subject EC Commission search and seizure powers to prior judicial authorisation by the CFI" (pp 196-197).

Comfort Letters

40.   One way in which the Commission has tried to alleviate the problems resulting from long delays before final decisions is by issuing informal indications of its view known as "comfort letters". Mr Reynolds explained these as follows: "In a typical comfort letter, DG IV writes to say that on the basis of the information available it is satisfied that an agreement does not fall within Article 85(1), or that it merits exemption under Article 85(3). The Commission will then close its file on the case. It has also become quite common for the Commission to issue 'discomfort' letters. In these letters the Commission says that the agreement does fall within Article 85(1) and does not merit an exemption...... The Commission seems to use discomfort letters frequently where it considers that a national court is better placed than the Commission to resolve a dispute and

---

[1]   Case 5/85 *AKZO Chemie v. Commission* [1986] ECR 2585.
[2]   Joined Cases 46/87 and 227/88 *Hoechst v. Commission* [1989] ECR 2919.

therefore may be more frequently used in the future as national courts play a greater role". Sometimes the issue of a letter was preceded by publication of a notice in the Official Journal, but although this added to its legal strength it could also lead to objections from third parties which might cause the Commission to change its view. He believed there was scope for improving the legal status of comfort letters by more publicity—before and after issue of the letter—and by giving fuller reasons. Before a national court a comfort letter did not have binding effect. A discomfort letter led to the closing of the Commission's file, but left the recipient in an anomalous position if the question came up before a national court. He acknowledged that "from the point of view of my clients, if you took an opinion poll, they would be happy with the system as it was and they would not want to do anything which slowed down or made it more difficult or more likely there would be a dispute between the Commission services or within the Commission which would delay the issuing of a comfort letter" (pp 9, 16, QQ 63-78).

41.   The Joint Working Party expressed broadly similar views and suggestions. Mr Vaughan said that "For the individuals they are very nice to have, they are very comforting. When you receive them you are very pleased to get them, I suspect, because it means that is the end of that problem for the moment. They are not very comfortable if you take a longer term view or if you are going to fall out later. They are probably disastrous from the point of view of third parties". The formal notice before a decision to grant an exemption opened up for third parties the possibility of attack (p 62, QQ 285-292). Mr Ian Forrester QC suggested that "If the letter is regarded institutionally, it looks like a blessing, but regarded legally it seems to be nothing very definite" and submitted that the uncertainty of such an important document was unsatisfactory (p 204). Mr Forwood said that the risk of challenge to a comfort letter by a third party in the event of a dispute was not insignificant. Comfort letters were "at best only a partial remedy, and at worst may prove to provide false comfort" (p 208). Mr Lever did not believe that a United Kingdom court could give judgment to enforce an agreement on the basis of a comfort letter when an exemption might subsequently be refused (p 161). The CBI suggested that if the status of a comfort letter were in issue, "Only in a very few cases is it likely to be manifestly clear that no exemption would be granted or that Article 85(1) does not apply at all. The likely result is a stay in national proceedings until the Commission reaches a decision" (p 193).

42.   The Competition Law Association suggested revision of Commission practice "so that it was clear from each letter whether the Commission, following a preliminary assessment, considered that the agreement notified was within Article 85(1) at all. If it did, the Commission should say so and also indicate whether it would be likely, on the facts known, for an Article 85(3) exemption to be forthcoming .... The Commission could issue a Notice on comfort letters stating the law and practice and developing the use of this instrument" (pp 179, 181).[1]

43.   For the DTI Dr Bell said "I think our broad view is pretty positive. They do speed up procedures. They have helped DG IV reduce the backlog of cases they need to deal with and they have a good record of reliability". The disadvantage in requiring more extensive reasoning was that the Commission might feel the need for a formal decision resolving legal issues (pp 137-138, QQ 512-520). Annex VI to the DTI Memorandum at p 147 shows in statistical terms how comfort letters and closure of files have reduced the backlog of cases by nearly half. Figures for 1992, published in the Commission's XXIInd Annual Report on Competition, showed a further big drop in the backlog, from 2287 cases on 31 December 1991 to 1562 cases on 31 December 1992.

44.   Dr Ehlermann said that the Commission viewed comfort letters "as a crucial tool that helps the Community's competition policy work in practice, and would only withdraw them in circumstances in which we would also withdraw the benefit of a formally granted exemption decision". Greater use of comfort letters since the 1982 Report had helped to reduce delays for companies dealing with DG IV. The Commission was examining whether each comfort letter could

---

[1]   In *Inntrepreneur Estates Ltd v. Mason* [1993] 2 CMLR 293 the English High Court had to determine what was meant by the term "comfort letter".

be followed up with a short but formal exemption or negative clearance decision. This was not procedurally possible at present, but he was optimistic that a simplified procedure, not involving adoption of a decision in nine languages, would be devised and applied in the future. The introduction of the self-imposed deadlines announced by Sir Leon Brittan was being monitored closely—particularly in order to see if it led to an increase in notifications. There would be a new notification form to ensure that companies provided all the necessary information reasonably available to them. The Commission had already decided to distinguish clearly in comfort letters whether they were a substitute for negative clearance or a substitute for exemption, and they were prepared to give them greater publicity (p 112, Q 444). Mr Forrester said that fuller detail and wider publicity would make comfort letters more convincing (pp 206-207).

Exemptions

45.   Article 85(3) of the EEC Treaty empowers the Commission to grant exemptions to any agreement or category of agreements

> "which contributes to improving the production of goods or to promoting technical or economic progress, while allowing consumers a fair share of the resulting benefits, and which does not
>
> (a)   impose on the undertakings concerned restrictions which are not indispensable to the attainment of these objectives;
>
> (b)   afford such undertakings the possibility of eliminating competition in respect of a substantial part of the products in question."

A formal decision by the Commission requires, under the terms of Regulation 17 prior publication in the Official Journal of a summary of the case, so enabling interested third parties to submit observations within a fixed time limit of not less than one month. An agreement duly notified to the Commission enjoys no provisional validity pending a final decision—if it infringes the competition rules it is automatically void until an exemption is granted. Formal exemptions following completion of Regulation 17 procedures are very few—according to Mr Forrester "the Commission rarely issues more than five specific exemptions in a year, and usually less than fifty each decade" (p 204).

46.   In their 1982 Report the Select Committee emphasised that they regarded the delays in exemption and negative clearance cases as unacceptable and said that it created intolerable problems in financing and initiating new trading ventures. We recommended that

> "So far as possible, the position should be improved by issues of guidance notices or block exemptions. But the Committee suggest that Community law should be altered so as to provide for an automatic exemption after the lapse of a suitable time from the application for exemption; the automatic exemption should last either for a fixed period or preferably until the Commission finally decides whether exemption is to be granted."

Block exemptions are the way in which the Commission by regulation exercises its Treaty power to grant exemptions to categories of agreement. The DTI said that block exemptions were used before the 1982 Report, but that since then the Commission had greatly increased its use of them in order to reduce its backlog of case work. In Annex VII to its Memorandum the DTI set out a complete list of block exemptions currently in force (p 148). The Commission had also adopted an "opposition procedure" to deal with grey zones in certain block exemptions. Under this procedure terms which were neither expressly exempted nor expressly prohibited might gain the benefit of the block exemption if they were notified and no objection was raised within the given time limit. The DTI attached importance to the Commission's monopoly on granting exemptions under Article 85(3), which had been important in establishing even-handed application of Community competition rules throughout the Member States, particularly as several Member States did not have until recently comprehensive national competition law or experience in handling investigations. Their witness, Dr Bell, made clear that they favoured improvements in speed of handling which would not require legislative change—in particular the self-imposed deadlines for joint ventures were welcome and had so far been met as promised. "I think if the text of Regulation 17 is opened, then a wider agenda is put in front of all the principal interests in the Member States and I believe that we should look at these administrative changes in the first instance to see what can be achieved in that area, and then take another appraisal". The DTI favoured further use of block exemptions, but since they were resource-intensive it was important that they should cover significant numbers of agreements. The opposition procedure also required careful watching to check that it was not being abused by enterprises looking for a way round the rules (pp 138-141, 147-149, QQ 462-480, 510-511).

47.   For the MMC Mr Daniel Goyder said that block exemptions were helpful to industry because they enabled commercial practice to be framed reliably and helpful to the Commission in that they relieved an intolerable workload. From the viewpoint of competition authorities block exemptions could pose problems because "inevitably, like most legislation, a block exemption represents a compromise. It is a compromise between competition authorities who want a tough law and industry who want a relatively liberal law". A block exemption might be put in place for ten or fifteen years, during which time the economics of the market would change. It was important that national competition authorities should themselves carry out investigations into the relevant sector so that their information and evidence could be used by the Commission in reassessing the position at the end of the block exemption period (p 45, QQ 132, 189-190). Sir Bryan Carsberg for the OFT also believed it was an important advantage of block exemptions that they were given for a short period of time and were then reviewable. Like the DTI, the OFT was inclined to believe that recent procedural reforms, in particular the self-imposed time limits, should be given a chance to show their effect before formal revision of Regulation 17 was undertaken. They were cautious about introducing a procedure allowing automatic exemption for notified agreements if no objection was made following publication—it was preferable to have a positive decision taken on good analysis. But the procedure could have value for some agreements which did not really have adverse effects on competition (pp 91, 92, QQ 306-310, 314, 317-323, 337-339).

48.   The Joint Working Party were also unenthusiastic about the possibility of introducing an automatic exemption procedure, which they thought could be unfair to the rights of third parties and of society as a whole. There would have to be publication, which would bring the procedure close to that under the opposition procedure included in later block exemptions. The effect might be that in practice the Commission would not let the time limits pass without taking positive action but if they did, the result would not be satisfactory (QQ 283, 293-303).

49.   Other witnesses however favoured introduction of an automatic or opposition procedure to overcome delay in obtaining formal exemptions. Mr Forwood suggested that a possible procedure would enable parties to notify agreements in the knowledge that unless the Commission or others raised objection within three months, for example, the agreement would receive an automatic exemption which might be for five years. "There can be no philosophic objection to such an arrangement—since such automatic exemptions are already in force in some sectors". Such a pragmatic approach would recognise that more harm may be done by withholding an individual exemption than by allowing automatic exemption to a large number of agreements not raising serious competition concerns (p 208). The Competition Law Association made a similar proposal, emphasising the need for adequate publicity through the Official Journal, and suggesting that a clearance for a limited period could be conditional on continuance of the underlying market conditions (p 181).

50.   Mr Reynolds maintained that the introduction of greater reliance on block exemption regulations, had been extremely useful, particularly for small and medium sized enterprises. There was scope for introducing block exemptions in other areas and for refining existing ones when they expired. Where individual decisions were required, internal deadlines could not be relied on unless they were made mandatory. Automatic exemptions would be a realistic option which had already been introduced in important areas such as aviation and maritime transport. Their effect could be

to make the Commission organise itself at an early stage to deal with the matter as efficiently as possible (pp 1, 11-12, QQ 85-91).

51.   Union des Confederations de l'Industrie et des Employeurs d'Europe (UNICE), supported by the CBI, welcomed the Commission's recent action to extend the scope of existing block exemptions on specialisation, research and development, know how and patent licensing agreements. The CBI suggested however that the problem of delay in obtaining exemptions should be dealt with by the Commission adopting a more realistic interpretation of Article 85(1) so as to concentrate on prohibiting agreements and practices likely to have seriously anti-competitive effects (pp 215-218, 193-194).

52.   Dr Ehlermann drew attention to new and extended block exemptions[1], and said that the Commission were actively examining the possibility of issuing more. But it was important that before formulating exemptions the Commission should have sufficient experience in the sector concerned. Trade mark licensing and software licensing were obvious candidates for block exemptions, but the Commission did not have sufficient experience. If there was excessive reliance on block exemptions there was a risk of "allowing too many agreements to be whitewashed". In principle Dr Ehlermann supported the recommendation for a non-opposition procedure allowing automatic exemptions, but given budgetary constraints and the priorities for DG IV he did not believe this option was realistic at the present time (pp 111-112, QQ 452-454).

53.   The possibility of delegating the power to grant exemptions under Article 85(3) to national authorities is dealt with below at paragraphs 81 to 85.

The Advisory Committee

54.   Article 10 of Regulation 17 sets out procedures for liaison with the authorities of the Member States. The competent authorities of the Member States are to be supplied with copies of applications, notifications and relevant documents, and the Commission are to carry out their functions under Article 85 of the EEC Treaty "in close and constant liaison" with them. An Advisory Committee on Restrictive Practices and Dominant Positions must be consulted prior to a decision on negative clearance or exemption. The Advisory Committee is composed of an official representative of each Member State. A report of the outcome of the consultation must be annexed to the draft decision submitted to the full Commission, but the report "shall not be made public". In the *Distillers* case[2] the Advocate-General expressed some concern that undertakings had no knowledge of what the Committee was told by the Commission or of the Committee's own report, suggesting that it might be open to question whether this secrecy was compatible with fundamental principles of Community law.

55.   The Select Committee in their 1982 Report were not persuaded that the confidentiality of the exchange of views between Member States and the Commission was wrong in principle. They recommended however that the undertakings under investigation should be informed of the documents submitted to the Committee, that the minutes of the oral hearing should always be submitted to the Committee, and that the report of the Committee should be communicated to the undertaking. Mr Reynolds said that "The proceedings of the Advisory Committee remain shrouded in secrecy, and the Report of the Committee is still not published. This situation is now highly anomalous since the Committee's Report is published in cases under the Merger Control Regulation. The Report should be published and should indicate the way in which each Member State voted". Nor had the other recommendations in regard to the Advisory Committee been implemented. His own impression was that certain Member States took the role of the Advisory Committee more seriously than others (pp 16, 17, QQ 49-54). The CBI and the Competition Law

---

[1]   A very recent example is in Commission Regulation 3932/92 of 21.12.1992 covering practices in the insurance sector such as establishment of common standard policy conditions, published in [1993] 4 CMLR 90.

[2]   *Distillers Co. Ltd. v. Commission* [1980] ECR 2229.

Association also argued that the Advisory Committee report should be published or at least made available to the parties (pp 192, 178, 182).

56.   The Joint Working Party believed that Member States did not treat the Advisory Committee seriously unless they saw an important national interest at stake. Their impression was that the report did not greatly influence the Commission's final decision. The Committee served a purpose in that it induced Member States to be represented at oral hearings. It did not help to safeguard due process, since the parties did not know what material was before them or how they had reported. Some Members of the Joint Working Party favoured making the report of the Advisory Committee available to the parties (p 62, QQ 264-274). Mr Van Bael argued that it would help to build expertise within national competition authorities if the views of the Advisory Committee were more seriously considered by the Commission. "Indeed, one has the distinct impression that the national authorities send no representatives at all or only junior representatives to Brussels because the feeling prevails that for the Commission Services, the consultation process is a mere 'ritual', without much impact on the further course of the proceeding" (p 221).

57.   The OFT said that in 1992, they had received notifications and documents in respect of more than 400 new cases under Articles 85 and 86 and the Merger Regulation. An official was always sent to take part in an oral hearing. Liaison was sometimes hampered by short notice given for meetings in Brussels and late despatch of documents. Sir Bryan Carsberg attached value to the Advisory Committee as a means of communication with the Commission and an opportunity to express views on conditions in the national market. He favoured publication of the Committee's report on grounds of the need for transparency regarding individual cases and the value of seeing the underlying economic analysis. Reports would be unlikely to reveal the positions of individual governments (pp 90, 93, QQ 356-365). The DTI took a similar line, saying that the Advisory Committee provided an independent review before a decision is finalised. Mr Alan Cooper suggested that "It gives an opportunity for Member States to raise questions if the case is not convincing and if the decision is not framed in a way which they think will stand up, either for legal reasons or on economic grounds". They favoured publication of the report, subject to their overriding reluctance to re-open Regulation 17 (QQ 500-509).

58.   Dr Ehlermann said that the Select Committee's recommendation that minutes of the oral hearing should be submitted to the competent authorities in the Member States had been accepted and applied. He pointed out that under the Merger Regulation the Commission was obliged to take the 'utmost account' of the opinion of the Committee and to inform the Committee of the manner in which its opinion had been taken into account. The Committee might recommend publication of its Opinion and so far all opinions had been published. He favoured similar transparency in regard to Article 85 and 86 proceedings, but this required amendment of Regulation 17 and had not been a priority for the Commission (p 109).

Fining Policy

59.   Articles 15 and 16 of Regulation 17 set out the Commission's power to impose fines or periodic penalty payments in order to enforce the competition rules in the Treaty and in the Regulation. The ceiling placed on fines for intentional or negligent infringement is one million ecu, or a sum in excess of that but not exceeding ten per cent of turnover in the preceding business year of each participating undertaking. Regard is to be had to the gravity and the duration of the infringement, and fines are not of criminal law nature. There is immunity from fines pending a Commission decision or "letter of discomfort". Similar powers are conferred by Article 14 of the Merger Regulation.

60.   In the *Pioneer* case[1] the European Court issued guidance on the factors to be taken into account by the Commission—these included the nature of the restriction on competition, conduct of the undertakings, their knowledge of the infringement and the profit derived from it, their market

---

[1]   *Musique Diffusion Francaise and Others v. Commission*, Cases 100-103/80 [1983] ECR 1825.

shares, importance of the product, threat to Community objectives, whether it was a repeat offence and the deterrent effect of a fine. The Court also said that the Commission might adjust the level of fines to the needs of policy.

61.   Mr Reynolds said that this judgment had "heralded the start of a more aggressive fining policy" on the part of the Commission. Annex II to his Memorandum set out a table showing how fines had increased dramatically in recent years. But the Commission had a wide discretion how it calculated fines or apportioned them in the case of a cartel. Where a Commission decision broke new ground or applied the rules for the first time in a particular sector, a low fine was usually imposed, but a recent case formed an exception to this. There were other cases where similar infringements had been punished by fines of a different level. Sometimes it appeared that some kind of plea bargaining had taken place. In the *Tetra Pak* case[1] a fine of 75 million ecu was imposed—without warning tripling the maximum fine imposed on one Swedish company. "I personally question whether the fine would have been of that level if it had been an Italian, French or British company with a Commissioner to speak up for it in the College of Commissioners". He suggested that there should be clear guidelines for the Commission and decisions which showed why lower fines were imposed in certain cases. The European Court and the Court of First Instance had made limited reductions in some fines (pp 2, 7-9, 16, 22-27, QQ 92-103). For the Joint Working Party Mr Vaughan also argued that the Commission should have to explain the amount of a fine, the period to which it related and the degree of involvement alleged against each enterprise (QQ 304-305). Mr Van Bael said that "the rule of proportionality and the principle of non-discrimination would seem to imply that a greater effort should be undertaken to streamline sanctions instead of following an 'à la carte' approach" (p 221).

62.   Dr Ehlermann agreed that the European Court had a tendency to reduce Commission fines, and was "looking forward to the day when the Court increases the fine". There had however only been one case where the Court had held that the reasons for a fine were insufficiently set out. He did not believe that it was possible or advisable to establish a tariff formula which one could calculate in advance. He suggested that "the risk of being caught is not that big and people would calculate whether they should or should not violate the law in view of the tariff". There had to be wide discretionary power to balance all the different elements. The Commission could give more reasons, and there was strong pressure for that from the Court, but the practice itself was not fundamentally flawed (QQ 450-451).

Structure and Quality of Commission Administration

63.   In its 1982 Report, the Select Committee noted that an internal review of competition procedures was being undertaken by the Commission, and suggested that this should cover the adequacy of the staffing of DG IV, arrangements for co-operation between DG IV and the other Directorates-General concerned, and the efficiency of the Commission's procedures for fact-finding and economic analysis.

64.   The Joint Working Party expressed concern at the lack of adequate direction and supervision over the fact-finding and decision-making processes of the Commission. Quite apart from the absence of independent control and of an interlocutory procedure by which to challenge procedural defects, they argued that there was a lack of consistency and uniformity in regard to the quality of statements of objections and in regard to access to the file. "At present the application of competition procedures appears to rely too much on the individual feelings (and abilities) of the Rapporteur". This had been highlighted by recent decisions of the European Court and the Court of First Instance. Insofar as delays in coping with notifications and exemptions was due to shortage of staff or budgetary constraints, "we would support any suggestion that the number of well qualified staff should be increased". Mr Vaughan suggested that although there were some very good people there, there was insufficient high level involvement with contested cases which might lead to large fines. There were not enough staff, and in particular not enough lawyers or economists.

---

[1]   Decision of 24.7.91, Case IV/31.043.

Nor was there sufficient independent review from the Legal Service. They suggested that there should be a senior member of the Legal Service, such as a Deputy Director-General, with overall supervisory responsibility. It might however be possible for the supervisory function to be exercised by the Hearing Officer, if there were a sufficient number of Hearing Officers. Seconding officials into DG IV from national authorities, as had been done for the Merger Task Force, would not help (pp 59, 61, 62, QQ 198-206, 216, 219-223, 260-263).

65.   Mr Reynolds said that although the 1982 Report had identified the lack of adequate staffing in DG IV as a major cause of delays, this was still a serious problem. DG IV had about 268 professional grade officials to deal with all competition matters including state aids, whereas the US Department of Justice had over 1000 to cover a similar area. Lack of manpower was not the only cause of delays. "The need for translation of key documents, the consultation process between the services of the Commission and frequent disagreements about policy which arise between them, together with DG IV's own hierarchical decision making structure have all added to the slowness of the procedure". There was a sharp contrast with the efficient working of the recently established Merger Task Force. There were administrative lessons which could be drawn from that. Secondment of officials from national administrations into DG IV would not only speed procedures but also improve communications between them (p 1, QQ 105-106). Mr Lever endorsed these criticisms, noting that in the *Automec* case[1] the Commission had confirmed to the European Court that its resources were inadequate to permit it to enforce the competition rules. He had long argued "that it was important to provide DG IV with adequate resources to cope with its pre-existing responsibilities rather than leave it in a chronic state of underprovision (pp 161, QQ 541, 559-562)."

66.   Similar views were expressed by many other witnesses. Mr Van Bael stressed the lack of effective supervision by the full Commission, whose adoption of competition decision by the "written procedure" without serious deliberation left casehandlers without much internal supervision or discipline. The Competition Law Association believed that matters might be improved if whenever the Commission were found wanting by the European Court or Court of First Instance they had to publish a statement setting out steps to be taken to guard against a repetition. Mr Forwood expressed concern at "economically dubious" reasoning in Commission decisions and apparent lack of respect for economic arguments. This pointed to a need for more economists within DG IV, at least where a firm believed that there were serious or complex economic issues (pp 220, 178, 209-210, 193).

67.   The OFT echoed the same criticisms, and in particular the weakness of economic analysis. But Sir Bryan Carsberg said that his own impression was that DG IV displayed a professional approach to competition policy, and that the shortcomings identified in recent court cases "must be assessed in the context of the many hundreds of cases dealt with by the Commission" (pp 92-93, QQ 315, 369). The DTI described the structural changes which had taken place in 1984 within the Commission in order to reduce administrative delays and ensuring consistency, objectivity and fairness in decision making. Annex VIII to the DTI Memorandum set out the current structure of DG IV and explained how organisation within the Merger Task Force differed from that in the other divisions in that merger teams were chosen for each case so as to provide a balance of specialists such as language skills, accountancy, law and economics. According to the Commission's XXIst Report on Competition Policy, on 31 December 1991, DG IV had a staff of 373, representing a 5 per cent increase on the figure a year previously. 46 per cent of those were occupied exclusively on Article 85/86 work and 14 per cent on merger control.[2] The Legal Service played an important role in competition cases, checking conformity of Commission procedures with the jurisprudence of the European Court (pp 141-143, 149-150).

---

[1]   Case T 24/90 *Automec Srl v. Commission* [1992] 5 CMLR 431.

[2]   A year later, DG IV had 407 staff, including national experts: a further increase of 9 per cent: XXIInd Report on Competition Policy, at p 80. The proportions in 85/86 work and in merger control work were slightly lower.

68.   Dr Ehlermann said that within the Commission efforts had been concentrated in recent years on improving the efficiency of procedures. The delays in granting negative clearances or exemptions so as to give companies adequate legal security could only hamper Community industry. Compliance with deadlines under the Merger Regulation had been possible because adequate resources were provided and because the Regulation itself established a procedure which enabled rapid decision-making. Case handlers on Article 85 and 86 cases were each dealing with many more cases than those in the Merger Task Force, and the Article 85/86 case involved a wider range of legal issues and problems and more complex fact finding "It is simply not realistic therefore, to expect the Commission to respect the same or similar deadlines in Article 85 and 86 cases that it achieves in merger cases". Nor was it realistic to expect increases in existing staff levels given the present budgetary restraints on the Commission. It was not true to say that the hierarchy was not involved in the work of the rapporteurs. "The hierarchy might also make mistakes, that is human, but the general assumption that the rapporteur might operate on his own is simply wrong, and I would like to reject that". The Legal Service was consulted on complex cases as often as possible (pp 109-112, QQ 403, 407-411, 415).

The Court of First Instance

69.   In 1982 the Select Committee recommended that "the European Court should, as a matter of urgency, examine its structure and responsibilities with a view to submitting to the Council proposals designed to improve the judicial review of competition cases". In 1986 the European Court sent to the Council, the Commission and the European Parliament proposal to set up a Court of First Instance which, subject to a limited right of appeal, would assume jurisdiction over certain matters, including competition. The Single European Act had already amended the Community Treaties by adding provisions which enabled the Council, acting unanimously, to attach to the Court of Justice a court with jurisdiction to hear and determine "certain classes of actions or proceedings brought by natural or legal persons". The Select Committee reported on the European Court's proposal in 1987, saying that "the most important advantage which a CFI would have over the present ECJ when dealing with cases of a technical or financial nature would be its ability to handle complex issues in specialised fields". The Court of First Instance was established in 1988.[1]

70.   Witnesses were unanimous in praising the contribution which had been made by the Court of First Instance to the enforcement of Community competition rules. The CBI said that the Court had the means and ability to investigate procedural matters and gave parties ready access to files. Their judgments had highlighted procedural irregularities of the Commission and it was "essential that the CFI continues to be adequately resourced so that failures by the Commission to follow appropriate procedures are remedied" (p 192). Mr Reynolds expressed similar views (QQ 4-9). The Joint Working Party said: "All of us who have had experience of the work of the CFI have nothing but praise for the way in which they tackle individual cases. The quality of preparation, the conduct of the hearing (in cases which frequently last for many days) and the quality of the judgments are of the highest order. We consider that this has been a development of great importance in judicial protection of individual rights" (p 63, Q 206). Dr Ehlermann said that the Court of First Instance was necessary and effective. "Not only does this have the effect of assuring companies that any Commission decision will be subject to a full review, it also clarifies for the Commission the standards of proof that it must respect in order to adopt an infringement decision in a contested case. I believe that this had led to an improvement in the standards applied by the Commission when adopting such decision and will continue to do so" (p 109).

71.   Mr Forwood said that the Court of First Instance was regarded as more willing to scrutinise details of the Commission's reasoning in competition cases. "Whether or not that view is justified, what is probably just as important is that the Commission appears to believe that its decisions will be more closely scrutinised". There were however areas where the CFI had not yet fulfilled expectations—delays between close of pleadings and oral hearing and between oral hearing and

---

[1]   By Council Decision 88/591/ECSC, EEC, Euratom, OJ No L 319, 25.11.1988, recently amended by Council Decision 93/350/Euratom , ECSC, EEC, OJ No L 144/21, 16.6.93.

judgment and reluctance on the part of the Court to appoint economic experts or to second guess economic assessments of the Commission (p 210).

72.   The *Cimenteries* or *Cement* case[1] arose from a statement of objections formulated by the Commission in respect of seventy-six undertakings in the cement industry. The full text of the notice was not served on each undertaking, and the Commission refused to forward the full notice or to allow the undertakings access to the file beyond the documents they had already been able to inspect. On appeal against these refusals, the Court of First Instance held that they did not amount to measures which could be challenged under Article 173 since they did not definitively alter the defendants' position. A number of witnesses expressed unhappiness at this result. The Competition Law Association said that the decision was "particularly unsatisfactory given that undertakings clearly have the ability to challenge certain interlocutory decisions by the Commission (eg decisions on interim measures, and the withdrawal of immunity from fines) there is no sense in denying them the ability to challenge equally important matters, such as rulings on requests for access to the file, whether the statement of objections is adequately framed and whether the timetable for response laid down is reasonable". One way of developing an adequate system of interlocutory proceedings would be to introduce a right of interlocutory appeal to the CFI, subject to a filtering process as with leave to appeal or judicial review proceedings in domestic law. These should be dealt with under an expeditious procedure similar to interim measures (p 178).

73.   Mr Lever believed that such a procedure could be useful in enabling procedural errors to be corrected swiftly instead of a final decision being overturned much later. "Even at the cost of letting guilty people off it may be worth the court striking down decisions where things have been done wrong in order to compel the Commission to do the thing right in the first place" (QQ 556-558). The Joint Working Party agreed that the Court of First Instance should have more power over interlocutory matters and that the jurisprudence of the Court should be reconsidered (QQ 224-228). The DTI, Mr Reynolds and the Commission however, while not opposed to the suggestion, emphasised that by introducing a fundamental appeal at an early stage it would greatly lengthen the proceedings and could lead to delaying tactics (QQ 14, 442-443, 493-496).

Co-operation Between National Courts and the Commission

74.   The Commission's 1989 guidance booklet EEC Competition Policy in the Single Market in its Chapter on Enforcement of the competition rules (printed in Appendix 6) points out that:

> "In practical terms it is now established that the Community competition rules create rights and obligations for private legal parties which may be raised in national legal proceedings. Accordingly, any company or individual who claims to have suffered injury as a result of action which was in breach of Community competition law has access, in principle to a national remedy, and is entitled to make a claim for damages. However, the exact legal nature of the claim and the level of damages available will vary according to local jurisdictional rules and procedures."

As was pointed out above in paragraph 3, most proceedings to remedy possible breach of the competition rules have been under Commission procedures. Recently, however, the Commission has sought to devolve more responsibility for enforcement onto national courts and national competition authorities. In February 1993 the Commission published a Notice on co-operation between national courts and the Commission in applying Article 85 and 86 of the EEC Treaty. The full text is printed in Appendix 5. The Notice recalls that the European Court has confirmed that Articles 85(1) and 86 have direct effect, and says that the Commission considers that the substantive provisions of an individual exemption decision are directly applicable. According to the European Court's jurisprudence this means that "individuals and companies have access to all procedural remedies provided for by national law on the same conditions as would apply if a comparable

---

[1]   Cases T10-12/92 and T15/92 *SA Cimenteries CBR and Others v. Commission* [1993] 4 CMLR 243.

breach of national law were involved".[1] Simultaneous application of national competition law raised no problem, subject to the precedence of Community law in the event of conflict. The Commission intended to concentrate itself on proceedings having "particular political, economic or legal significance to the Community". As the *Automec* case had confirmed, this condition would not be satisfied where the plaintiff had an adequate remedy before the national courts. The Notice underlined the procedural advantages of national actions—in particular the possibility of an award of damages. It then sets out extensive guidance for national courts in regard to notifications, Commission decisions, comfort letters, block exemptions and agreements and practices which existed before Regulation 17 was applicable to them. As the Notice acknowledges however, there are particular difficulties "where the practical application of Article 85(1) and Article 86 gives rise to legal or economic difficulties, where the Commission has initiated a procedure in the same case or where the agreement decision or concerted practice concerned may become the subject of an individual exemption within the meaning of Article 85(3)". In cases where an exemption might be granted by the Commission, the national court is invited to suspend proceedings, perhaps granting interim measures, seek a ruling from the European Court, or seek the assistance of the Commission under a procedure which is set out. Commission guidance, which would not be binding on the national court, could take the form of procedural information, legal or factual advice or an interim decision.

75. Dr Ehlermann stressed that enforcement at Community level was vital if the single market was to be a level playing field—otherwise different standards of competition policy could lead to investment decisions being based on considerations other than operational efficiency. In procedural terms, only the Commission had the linguistic tools and the discovery powers effectively to review cross-border agreements and practices. But the EEC Treaty reflected the subsidiarity test by limiting the Commission's jurisdiction to cases which affect trade between Member States. In procedural terms however the Commission had been examining the level at which Article 85 and 86 should be enforced. National courts had in some respects wider powers—either to award damages, to award immediate interim relief and to order positive action to remedy an infringement—than the Commission which could only impose fines. The *Automec*[2] case had given the Commission an important tool in promoting application of Articles 85(1) and 86 at national level. Dr Ehlermann, having described the terms of the Commission Notice, commented that it would give national judges the confidence to give judgment in cases concerning clear breaches of the competition rules. The new procedures were part of a wider effort to apply the subsidiarity principle in practice. There would in the future also be greater enforcement of Articles 85 and 86 by national competition authorities. It was for each Member State to adopt the necessary procedural rules, and he hoped that those who did not already have jurisdiction would adopt appropriate rules. But the power to grant exemption, which was "the very heart of the Community's competition policy", should remain a Commission monopoly. For these decisions it was essential to have access to a wide range of information and be able to "make a qualified judgment as to the interests of the Community as a whole". National powers to grant exemptions would lead to administrative and legal confusion, to differential standards, forum shopping and distortion of the single market. Dr Ehlermann said that the Notice was a consolidation of Commission thinking on subsidiarity which had evolved in the light of decisions of the court of First Instance (pp 112-117, Q 447).

76. The DTI welcomed the Commission Notice generally, but commented that while the Commission retained exclusive jurisdiction to grant exemptions under Article 85(3) it would not greatly reduce the Commission backlog of cases. Transfer of the power to exempt to national level would however threaten the even application of the rules. The DTI said that legal costs and jurisdictional limits were deterrents to national legal actions, and they suggested that United Kingdom courts would not be able to hear evidence from the Commission on points of law. There would also be a risk that the Commission could become bogged down in national proceedings,

---

[1] Case 158/80 *Rewe v. Hauptzollamt Kiel* [1981] ECR 1805, at para 44.
[2] *Automec v. Commission* (No 21) [1992] 5 CMLR 431.

28   FIRST REPORT FROM THE

which would defeat the object of decentralisation, or exercise too much influence over the national judge (pp 138, 145-146, QQ 526-534). The OFT shared these views (p 93).

77.   The Joint Working Party submitted a Memorandum they had prepared on the basis of the draft Notice (which was published unchanged). This expressed scepticism that the Notice would lighten DG IV's workload. They saw instead a possibility that difficult cases would be referred to the European Court, that harmless agreements which the Commission could otherwise endorse by letter would require a formal decision, that it would no longer be possible to modify borderline agreements in order to gain clearance and that differing national decisions would cause confusion. The Notice amounted to "changing the system without changing the rules". To decentralise enforcement to national courts and authorities would require major changes in the Community system and in the organisation and powers of national authorities. Mr Hall said he would prefer "to see the Commission adequately resourced, adequately staffed and performing properly the functions assigned to it under the Treaty" (pp 62-65, QQ 277-284).

78.   Mr Reynolds gave a detailed analysis of the comparative advantages between action with the Commission and action before national courts, in terms of cost, effectiveness and anonymity. The Commission had long been concerned by the differences in remedies available in national courts—in particular injunctions and damages, and had considered internally whether it would be appropriate to harmonise these by a directive. In the Delimitis[1] judgment the European Court had said that it would be appropriate for national courts to decide on cases where there was little risk of the Commission taking a conflicting decision—this had influenced the Commission's Notice. Complainants would now be under more pressure to proceed before national courts, or to show that this was not a viable option. Mr Reynolds thought that in theory the Commission's workload should be considerably reduced by application of the Notice, but that there was a risk of different application of the rules in different Member States. He agreed with other witnesses that there was also a risk of the Commission being overburdened by national requests and of its exercising undue influence in national courts without its evidence being properly tested (pp 12-14, Q 82).

79.   Mr Lever expressed reservations as to the basis on which a United Kingdom court could take the opinion of the Commission on Community law. Submissions by the Commission as amicus curiae might in fact be "the opinion of a relatively junior official with idiosyncratic views". It the national court gave judgment on the basis that a Commission exemption was "unlikely", its status would be uncertain if an exemption were in fact given. There were practical obstacles to invoking the competition rules in United Kingdom courts, and private litigation founded on Article 85 or 86 could not be an adequate substitute for administration of the Articles as rules of public law (pp 161-162, QQ 563-568). The Competition Law Association shared these reservations and objections, and believed that the Commission might have over-estimated the attraction of claims for damages—the principles of which remained uncertain under United Kingdom law. They feared that "to abandon those cases in which the Commission has little interest and to leave them to actions before national courts may be to leave undertakings without practical and effective remedies" (pp 179-180).[2] Mr Forrester came to a similar conclusion, pointing out that in the light of the obstacles to action before national courts it was "natural and understandable that the Commission is a more attractive interlocutor than a national judge" (pp 204-205). Other witnesses were also sceptical that the Notice would help the situation. UNICE argued that there was no clear dividing line between the powers of the Commission and those of national authorities and courts, that the decentralised application proposed might be a source of uncertainty to the legal security of undertakings (particularly as national judges were not yet sufficiently familiar with Community law) and that the Notice would not lead to much wider application of Articles 85 and 86 by national courts than was already the case (pp 218-219, 193, 199).

---

[1] Case C234/89 Delimitis v. Henninger Bräu [1992] 5 CMLR 210.
[2] The notice was applied by the English High Court in Inntrepreneur Estates Ltd v. Mason [1993] 2 CMLR 293, where the court took account of a Commission letter which fell short of being a comfort letter.

80.   A more positive approach to the Notice was taken by Mr Forwood, who suggested practical ways in which co-operation between the Commission and national courts could be assisted in order to overcome difficulties regarding obtaining evidence and the unfamiliarity of United Kingdom judges with the economic concepts of Community law. He acknowledged, however, that even with these improvements there would remain many cases where recourse to national courts was not a viable option (pp 210-212). Mr August Braakman, advocate and partner in Nauta Dutilh in Rotterdam maintained that the Notice "offers the possibility of a quick indication of the way in which the Commission feels that Article 85 or 86 applies and offers the much-needed legal certainty that the interlocutory ruling of the Judge President is in line with the Decision of the Commission which is yet to come". Mr Braakman described the way in which Community competition rules are enforced by Dutch courts—there had been 130 decisions involving Article 85 or 86 since the entry into force of the EEC Treaty and very few references to the European Court. In most cases applicants lodged a complaint with the Commission and at the same time interlocutory proceedings in the national court in order to secure provisional measures while the Commission prepared a decision. He cited two cases which illustrate the difficulties pointed out by other witnesses above. In one case a judgment was delivered and upheld on appeal on the basis that the Commission would not regard an agreement as a serious infringement of Article 85—the Commission later decided that it was and the earlier national rulings were withdrawn. In a later case the Judge at first instance followed the procedure set out in the Notice (then in draft form), but the Court of Appeal reversed the judgment and refused to approach the Commission for information. Some months later the Commission made clear that the agreements in issue seriously infringed Article 85(1) and that an exemption was excluded—thus obliging the complainants to start fresh interlocutory proceedings before the national courts. Dutch lawyers had also argued that an approach by Dutch courts to the Commission seeking legal arguments and facts was "a bridge too far" and might endanger the independence of the national judiciary. But Mr Braakman believed that these arguments were outweighed by the need for co-operation in the difficult task of applying Articles 85 and 86 at national level (pp 172-177).

The Powers of National Competition Authorities

81.   Dr Ehlermann made "a strong plea in favour of subsidiarity to have Article 85 and 86 made applicable not only by the judges but also by administrative authorities charged with the application of Community law". Although the Commission should retain a monopoly in regard to grant of exemptions under Article 85(3)[1], complaints under Article 85(1) should be shared out between DG IV and national competition authorities. For this to happen, national authorities would have to be given the necessary powers—but the majority of Member States were now able to do so. Only the United Kingdom, Ireland, Denmark and the Netherlands lacked powers (pp 112-113, 116-117, QQ 445-447). The DTI described the relationship between the Commission and United Kingdom competent authorities and the liaison between them on Article 85 and 86 cases. In a helpful Supplementary Memorandum[2] they set out a summary of domestic competition regimes in other Member States which showed those whose national competition authorities were enabled to apply Articles 85 and 86, or rules based closely on them, and the possible avenues of appeal from administrative decisions. Notwithstanding Article 9(1) of Regulation 17, in Spain a Court for the Protection of Competition had power—in wider terms than Article 85(3)—to authorise exemptions (pp 140-141, Q 460). Mr Reynolds suggested that the absence of a prohibition similar to Articles 85 and 86 in United Kingdom law could cause problems now that most other Member States—as well as EFTA and East European States—were modelling their national competition law on Articles 85 and 86 (QQ 111-115).[3]

---

[1] For the reasons set out above at paragraph ??.

[2] Not printed—available in the Record Office.

[3] The Government have announced their intention to amend United Kingdom competition law to introduce a prohibition which would be similar to Article 85. They do not at present intend to take parallel action to introduce a prohibition parallel to Article 86. See DTI Consultative Document Abuse of Market Power, Cm 2100, and Hansard HC 14 April 1993 at col. 844.

82.   The response of most witnesses was favourable towards the possibility of greater enforcement of competition rules by national competition authorities. The MMC and OFT believed that there was scope for leaving to national authorities more decisions of essentially national relevance. The MMC said that this "would have the advantage that authorities that had the closest understanding of the relevant markets would carry out some or all of the necessary functions, while also reducing the call on the European Commission's scarce resources and enabling it to focus more effectively on the more important cases". Mr Goyder said however that this would operate more smoothly if United Kingdom competition law were more closely approximated to Community law and that effective enforcement at national level would require resources, staff and the development of a tradition (pp 44-46, QQ 136, 146-147, 173-181, 188). OFT said that the question of application of Articles 85 and 86 by the Director-General was currently under discussion and that this "would make it easier for my Office and the Commission to share the casework between them, even though I would not have the power to apply Article 85(3)". Sir Bryan Carsberg was in favour of greater co-operation between the national authorities and the Commission and believed that this would continue to evolve. Reform of United Kingdom restrictive practices legislation would lead to a more efficient procedure (pp 90, 93, QQ 386-392, 396-399).

83.   The Competition Law Association said that the European Economic Area Agreement provided jurisdictional rules for allocating cases between the Commission and the new EFTA Surveillance authority and that these might offer a model for rules as between the Commission and national authorities. If national implementing rules were available, enforcement of Articles 85(1) and 86 at national level could offer the prospect of an improvement on the current situation, although with some risk of divergent practice. If national authorities were empowered to apply Article 85(3) the concern over divergence of approach would be greater (p 181). The CBI also was opposed to decentralised application of Article 85(3) as likely to lead to a fragmented policy (pp 193-194).

84.   Mr Lever maintained that United Kingdom public law did not provide adequate remedies for the victim of monopolistic abuse, and the Commission did not have the resources to deal adequately with complaints. The Commission "monopoly" should therefore be modified so that a national authority would be entitled to apply Article 85(1) and 86 in a case directly involving only citizens of the relevant Member State "unless within a limited period of time the Commission itself initiated a procedure and undertook to conduct that procedure with all good speed". Unless the Commission did so within the limited time available it would be precluded from doing so thereafter. A similar system could operate where citizens of more than one Member State were concerned provided that the relevant national authorities could agree on which should take the lead. The national decisions would be subject to judicial review, with the possibility of reference to the European Court, so safeguarding the internal consistency of Community law. As regards Article 85(3) the national authority could prepare a draft decision granting or refusing exemption—this would be passed to the Commission who would either adopt it as a Commission decision or produce a different decision within a limited period of time. Mr Lever argued that even if there were inconsistency between national decisions, the disadvantage would be less than the disadvantage of the present system (pp 162-163, QQ 569-573, 580).

85.   The Bundeskartellamt claimed that "the Commission at present seems to be willing to cede to Member States only 'run of the mill' cases, while dealing with all major cases itself. Under the circumstances it is hardly surprising that the national authorities are not too keen to apply EC competition law". Germany had assumed powers to apply Community competition rules in 1990 but had rarely applied them. There should be agreement between the Commission and the Member States in regard to delegation of tasks on the basis that the Commission should determine cases of substantial Community interest while other cases should be investigated by the national competition authority of the Member State whose territory was most affected by the infringement. National authorities would have to be assured that their decisions would stand. Before a national prohibition decision was granted there should be an understanding with the Commission that exemption would not be granted unless there was a change in the facts. Enforcement of competition law would be far more efficient if by amendment of Regulation 17 the national authorities were given the power to

grant exemptions, with arrangements to ensure uniform application of the Community rules by the Commission and the Member States. But general criteria for delimitation would be very difficult, and would presuppose fully operational authorities in all Member States. One possibility would be to leave priority with the Commission, which could delegate in accordance with the availability of willing and able national authorities and by consensus. Uniformity of approach could be ensured by requiring Commission consent to grant of an exemption—or at least providing for *ex post facto* notification of an exemption to the Commission who would then be entitled to initiate proceedings. Such decentralisation would require change only to Article 9 of Regulation 17 and would reflect the concept of an administration close to its citizens (pp 197-202).

Harmonisation of National Remedies

86.   Witnesses in favour of decentralised administration of the Community competition rules were agreed that to be effective this required that national authorities should be given jurisdiction to apply the substantive rules. The question which then arises is whether in addition it is necessary or at least desirable that there should be some approximation of remedies available at national level. Mr Reynolds said that "The lack of uniformity in such matters as how you assess quantum of damages, causation, limitation period, lawyers' costs, is enormous". The MMC believed that consistency in approach among national procedures was highly desirable, but that harmonisation of remedies was merely an ultimate aim (QQ 182-187).

87.   Although Dr Ehlermann regarded the more extensive remedies available at national level—to order interim measure, to award damages or to order positive measures to remedy an infringement for example—as an important reason for seeking to enforce competition rules at national level, he did not believe that it would be practical to impose harmonisation of remedies. "Particularly with respect to remedies, I see differences in our judicial systems which are due to profound historical differences and cultural attitudes". It was only necessary that the substantive Community rules—or equivalent national rules—should be capable of application at national level (pp 113-114, QQ 448-449).

Merger Control

88.   In 1989 the Select Committee reported on drafts of a Council Regulation on the control of concentrations between undertakings. In our Report on *Merger Control*[1], we agreed that it was a logical consequence of the establishment of the internal market that there should be some transfer to the Community of the power to block large-scale mergers. We said:

> "The central issues are: which mergers should be assigned to Community control? how should they be assessed? what powers should rest with Member States? and how should the Commission be staffed for its new functions?"

We recommended, *inter alia*, that the threshold of the Community regime should be set so high that the Commission would handle at first only the largest European mergers, but would be capable of reduction without unanimity in the Council, that appraisal at Community level should be carried out by the Commission and not by the Council or by any new Community body, that improvements in procedure over those applied to competition cases generally should be set out in the Regulation, that DG IV should be given sufficient additional staff (including some seconded from national competition authorities) and that the Regulation should provide "one-stop" control of mergers within its control. The Council adopted the Merger Regulation[2] on 21 December 1989, and the final version complied to the Committee's satisfaction with all these recommendations.[3]

---

[1] ·6th Report, 1988-89 (HL 31).

[2] Council Regulation (EEC) No 4064/89 on the control of concentrations between 1989-90, OJ No L 395/1, 30.12.89.

[3] See letter from Baroness Serota of 4 December 1989, printed in Correspondence with Ministers, 8th Report, 1989-90 (HL 28) at p 66.

89.   Article 1 applies the Regulation to all concentrations with a Community dimension as defined in paragraph 2. Paragraph 2 provides as follows:

"2.   For the purposes of this Regulation, a concentration has a Community dimension where;

(a)   the aggregate worldwide turnover of all the undertakings concerned is more than ECU 5000 million, and

(b)   the aggregate Community-wide turnover of each of at least two of the undertakings concerned is more than ECU 250 million,

unless each of the undertakings concerned achieves more than two-thirds of its aggregate Community-wide turnover within one and the same Member State"

Paragraph 3 requires a review of the thresholds laid down in paragraph 2 before 31 December 1993. At the outset of the current enquiry, Sub-Committee E were aware that the Commission was consulting widely prior to making proposals for revision of the Merger Regulation, and the procedural operation and possible revision of the Regulation was included within the scope of this enquiry.

90.   Witnesses generally believed that the Merger Regulation had worked well over its first three years and were enthusiastic about the performance of the Commission's Merger Task Force, which operates as a separate Division of DG IV. Mr Reynolds said that "the system set up at the beginning of 1990 has worked well and the efficient way that the Task Force has dealt with cases has been much praised by companies and their advisers". Clients were eager to bring transactions within the scope of the Regulation, and the tight time limits had been respected and brought legal certainty. The Task Force had been willing to give informal guidance at an early stage of preparing a formal notification, and to waive the requirement for unnecessary information. Settlements had often been on the basis of undertakings to the Commission to sell off part of an acquired business, for example, or to modify the terms of the proposed agreement. The Air France/Sabena agreement had been approved subject to conditions designed to prevent undue dominance of certain aviation markets. He emphasised that the Regulation had never been envisaged as a vehicle for prohibition of mergers. The Commission had applied a strict competition test as required by the Regulation, even in the face of strong governmental and sectoral lobbying. The case for a new decision-making body was not strong—this would be likely to lengthen procedures and make settlements more difficult. Mr Reynolds annexed to his Memorandum a complete list of cases under the Regulation showing dates of notification, clearance or final outcome. Decisions under the Regulation were better drafted, although shorter than Article 85/86 decisions (pp 1-6, 16, 18-21, QQ 104-105, 108-111). Mr Van Bael, noting that clearance had been so far refused in only one proceeding, said that "this user-friendly attitude is in contrast with the traditional approach of DG IV in the application of Article 86". He was however concerned that the favourable approach of the Commission might not continue and suggested more objective criteria to provide greater legal certainty (p 221). Sir Bryan Carsberg took the view that day-to-day procedures under the Regulation had worked well. "All deadlines have been met, and the liaison between my officials and the case officers in the Commission has worked smoothly despite the tight timetable" (pp 90-91). The DTI also said that the Regulation had been operated effectively, commenting that there was "a trade-off between establishing transparency and certainty against the need to provide decisions for business at minimum cost and delay" (pp 139, 144-145).

91.   The MMC shared the view that the Regulation had operated efficiently and effectively, although it had not yet been tested under pressure of numbers of mergers or highly controversial or opposed mergers. Performance had been in practice even better than required in terms of time limits—substantive consideration of a second stage procedure was being completed in far less than the four months allowed. Mr Goyder said however that the decisions were highly compressed and uninformative in comparison with an MMC report, particularly in regard to the underlying facts, which made them unhelpful to practitioners. The MMC described the residual powers of Member States in regard to mergers which fell within the Regulation. Under Article 9 a Member State could

request a proposed merger to be referred back for assessment, on the ground that it threatened to create or strengthen a dominant position significantly impeding competition in a distinct market in its territory—the United Kingdom authorities had made one successful application for a reference back in regard to the proposed Tarmac/Steeley merger.[1] There could be a split jurisdiction between the Community and the national authority if there was more than one bid for a company, but they saw no way of avoiding that entirely and did not regard it as serious (pp 44-46, QQ 124-129, 148-168).

92.   The review of the thresholds was begun by a survey conducted by the Commission with about three hundred of the Community's leading companies. The object was to identify the cases which would have come within the Regulation in 1991 and 1992 if the world-wide turnover threshold had been lowered from five to two billion ecu and the Community turnover threshold of each of at least two of the undertakings from 250 to 100 million. At the time of adoption of the Regulation the Commission declared that it envisaged subsequent threshold reduction on these lines. The survey showed that the lower thresholds would have roughly doubled the Commission's caseload of fifty to sixty cases per year. It also showed that the "two-thirds rule" had removed from Community jurisdiction important cases having a Community dimension and that perhaps a "three-quarters rule" would achieve a better balance between Community and national jurisdiction. Dr Ehlermann said that the survey had also indicated that general legal and economic considerations favoured increased Community merger control. "The advantages of a rapid 'one-stop' shop procedure combined with rapid decision-making has been widely appreciated by the business community". The single market was a driving force towards cross-border mergers. The Merger Regulation had spurred Member States which had lacked national merger controls to introduce legislation, so that where the Regulation did not apply there were more potential hurdles for companies to clear. If however thresholds were reduced there would be a greater risk of catching mergers with a primarily national impact and so there would be a need for more flexibility in Article 9 which allows referral of a merger by the Commission to national authorities, as well as in Article 22(3) which enables Member States to refer to the Commission a merger which falls outside the Regulation. Dr Ehlermann also identified a number of areas where the Regulation could be clarified to reflect practice or provide more transparency.

93.   After Dr Ehlermann gave oral evidence, the Commission completed its extensive consultations[2] and at the end of July announced that it did not intend to propose modification of the Regulation. Competition Commissioner Karel van Miert said that "while there were strong arguments for lowering the threshold in order to bring more cases under EC scrutiny, business was broadly in favour of the status quo .... The Commission acknowledged that without business support, any changes now would risk jeopardising the considerable consensus built up during the three years of the Regulation's operation. It called for a further review at the end of 1996". (p 117-120, QQ 458-459, Commission publication The Week in Europe, 29.7.1993). The formal Report from the Commission to the Council on the Implementation of the Merger Regulation[3], received by the Committee late in the enquiry, stressed the "widespread acceptance of and satisfaction with the existing arrangements for merger control by the Commission" as well as the strong level of commitment to ensuring that the Regulation is applied effectively. The Commission accepted that it would be prudent to acquire further experience of the working of the Regulation and of the impact of national merger control before proposing any revision. A number of improvements in transparency and legal certainty could be made by the Commission issuing guidance statements on the application of the Merger Regulation. On 27 September 1993 the Council took note of the Commission Report.

---

[1]   The facts were reported in [1993] 4 CMLR 28.

[2]   The Commission's Working Paper on the Review (revised version 17.05.1993) with an accompanying Technical Note was made available to the Committee and is available in the Record Office.

[3]   Document 8455/93; COM (93) 385 final.

94.   This cautious approach was in line with the recommendations of most of our witnesses. The DTI, although Ministers had not taken a final view, were "sceptical of the need for lower thresholds". Nor were they in favour of more referrals to national authorities of mergers notified to the Commission but mainly threatening competition within a distinct national market. This they believed might detract from a consistent approach to large scale mergers involving inter-State trade. Dr Bell said: "We think that the broad approach and the application by the Commission has been acceptable" (p 139, QQ 535-537). For the MMC Mr Odgers said "I think we would probably like to see the present system tested for a rather longer period than it has been tested so far" (QQ 153-156). The OFT was "not opposed in principle to a lowering of the thresholds" but thought it important to consider any package as a whole and favoured more reference back of mergers affecting only national markets (p 91, QQ 373-385). Mr Reynolds said "It was far from clear that the current review will result in a reduction of the thresholds" (p 6, Q 104). The Bundeskartellamt maintained that the thresholds should not be lowered for the time being, but that there should be development of Article 9 of the Regulation to enable more cases to be referred back to national authorities "which would give sufficient effect to the subsidiarity principle" (pp 199, 201-202). This view may have been conditioned by unsuccessful efforts to persuade the Commission to refer certain mergers back for Bundeskartellamt appraisal under Article 9 (Q 104).

95.   Only two witnesses favoured reduction in the thresholds. The Working Party supported reduction in principle, provided that the Merger Task Force had sufficient resources to deal with the increased number of notifications—"in addition to the benefit of 'one-stop shop review', such a reduction should result in more consistent treatment throughout the Community". They saw some merit in informal liaison between the Commission and a national authority to agree on which body should appraise both prospective mergers when the application of the thresholds would otherwise lead to split jurisdiction, and they supported greater transparency regarding these contacts (pp 65-66, 82). UNICE, while pointing out that the Community turnover threshold and the "two-thirds rule" did not need change for the time being, said that "the majority of UNICE's member federations consider that the threshold of ecu 5 billion [aggregate world-wide turnover] should be gradually lowered". They argued that this threshold discriminated against smaller undertakings which were subjected to multiple national controls, and that a single system for all mergers would take better account of the interests of the Community as a whole. They were opposed to widening the scope of Article 9 to provide for automatic reference to the competent authority in a Member State if the merger threatened to create or strengthen a distinct national market (pp 213-215).

PART 3 OPINION OF THE COMMITTEE

96.   The objectives of law enforcement are that it should be

   fair—justice must be done;

   transparent—justice must manifestly be seen to be done;

   swift—justice delayed is justice denied; and

   deterrent—the sword in the right hand, as well as the scales in the left.

These requirements relate to any system for enforcing national, Community or international law, and the first three of them are aspects of due process which for European States and for everyone within their jurisdiction has been elaborated in Article 6 of the European Convention on Human Rights. Beyond these, however, there is a further objective which relates to the competition rules of the Community. Effective enforcement of these rules requires the exercise of sound judgment in the interests of the Community as a whole. More than most areas of law, competition law requires not merely analysis of complex facts and legal interpretation of legislation and agreements, but also economic, industrial and even political judgment. The enforcement of competition law is very likely to involve activities in several Member States. This led to the appreciation among Member States in the early years of the Community's development that judgment of the interests of the Community as a whole could best be exercised at Community level, unlike most enforcement of Community law against individuals and private enterprises which takes place by contrast at national level.

97.   Regulation 17 therefore, having declared that

"Whereas, in order to establish a system ensuring that competition shall not be distorted in the common market, it is necessary to provide for balanced application of Articles 85 and 86 in a uniform manner in the Member States;"

continues as follows:-

"Whereas, in order to secure uniform application of Articles 85 and 86 in the common market, rules must be made under which the Commission, acting in close and constant liaison with the competent authorities of the Member States, may take the requisite measures for applying those Articles;".

There have over the years been many criticisms of the Commission's performance in enforcing the competition rules. But it cannot fairly be said that the Commission has failed to provide "balanced application of Articles 85 and 86 in a uniform manner in the Member States." In this central aspect of deciding cases and developing a competition policy in the interests of the Community as a whole, the Commission has justified the confidence placed in it by the Member States in 1957 and 1962.

98.   The criticisms made in 1982 and to some extent repeated to us in this enquiry related to the more basic elements of law enforcement—fairness, transparency and speed. The Commission of course has had to develop its practices outside the framework and the constitutional disciplines of a national law enforcement system. Few of the Member States had at the outset developed systems of competition law, far less procedural guarantees for those suspected of infringement, so that the Commission had no obvious model for its own procedures. The application of Article 6 of the European Convention on Human Rights to Commission procedures and practices has been established only in the last few years. The Member States who in 1962—ten years before United

Kingdom accession—allocated enforcement functions to the Commission failed to allocate adequate resources to carry them out properly. Throughout the seventies the backlog of cases pending before the Commission was over four thousand. The procedures laid down by the Council, together with the level of resources made available, were simply not capable of handling the number of applications and of notified agreements which arrived.

99.   The Commission has never been insensitive to criticism, and its reaction to the 1982 Report was immediate and constructive. Virtually all the recommendations in the 1982 Report which could be met without amendment of Regulation 17 or of the EEC Treaty were met to the best of the Commission's ability. The changes made— which are summarised in the Introduction to this Report and set out in detail in Part 2—improved the fairness and transparency of procedures and reduced the backlog of cases. Even the recommendation which in 1982 appeared the most ambitious—that the European Court should submit to the Council proposals designed to improve the judicial review of competition cases—has been met, and the Court of First Instance has been widely praised for the contribution it is making to protection of the rights of individuals and enterprises and to other aspects of effective enforcement of competition law.

100.   The revival of concern recently has in our view been mainly due to two factors. The first of these is rising burdens on and expectations of the Commission. With new Member States, greater awareness of the obligations imposed by competition law, growth of competition—and potential threats to that competition—in the single market, it is not surprising that the number of new cases continues to rise. Judgments from the Court of First Instance are perceived as enforcing discipline on Commission performance and clarifying guidelines for procedural disputes—but the short-term effect has been to reveal imperfections in the conduct of particular cases. In particular the Court of First Instance has made it clear that Commission procedures, which are essentially administrative in nature, are subject to the standards of due process imposed by Article 6 of the European Convention on Human Rights—standards which are gradually raised as well as clarified by the European Commission and Court of Human Rights. The successful first three years of operation of the Merger Regulation has shown that the Commission—with improved rules and adequately resourced—is able to deliver a high standard of service in carrying out important and sensitive new functions.

101.   The second factor is that the reforming tendencies in the Commission are now constrained by Regulation 17. The recent initiatives by the Commission to introduce deadlines and to encourage remedies to be pursued at national level in straightforward cases are to be welcomed—but these ideas could be carried forward much more effectively with the assistance of relatively modest changes to the structure of Regulation 17. At the time of its adoption Regulation 17 was bold and innovative and it has withstood the strains imposed on it for thirty remarkable years. Now that the Community Treaties themselves have been so frequently reviewed and revised, we see no reason to regard Regulation 17 as sacrosanct.

102.   The possibility of change to Regulation 17 would allow the problems to be addressed more constructively than has until now been possible. On the one hand it would allow the supervisory role of the Court of First Instance to be extended—thereby bringing in a greater degree of separation of functions. On the other hand it would open the way to more reference of cases for decision at national level as the Commission clearly wishes—but within a firm legal framework. Such flexibility would reflect in this context the principle of subsidiarity.

Separation of Enforcement Functions (paragraphs 11-17)

103.   In our 1982 Report we attached importance to the division of responsibility between investigators and decision makers which then existed within the Competition Directorate of the Commission, DG IV. The Joint Working Party and other witnesses made a powerful case for structural changes which ideally would separate the three functions of detection, prosecution and decision making. We are however not persuaded that structural change of this kind would be the right way forward. We agree with the Commission, and with the Court of First Instance[1], that continuous involvement of the same officials throughout the successive stages of investigation and appraisal is not wrong in principle. What is essential is that the procedure should be fair and transparent and that there should be the possibility of independent judicial control to guarantee this. The Court of First Instance is now in a position to provide this independent judicial control, and we shall recommend below that its role should be extended.

104.   Secondly, we do not consider it desirable to adopt the more radical changes which some have advocated. It is clear that there is little support at present among Member States for the establishment of a new competition authority separate from the Commission to be exclusively responsible for enforcement of Community competition rules. A number of new agencies which the Member States have agreed to establish in recent years have run into problems of location and financing which for some time prevented them from embarking on the tasks assigned to them. The record is not encouraging. Many of the staff for an independent agency would presumably have to be recruited from the ranks of DG IV, given the limited supply of lawyers and economists with the necessary understanding of the Community competition rules. Transfer to a new agency might neither increase their objectivity nor improve their morale. Nor are we convinced of the need for a new Directorate-General, separate from DG IV. Delays already occur because of the need to reach agreement among different Directorates-General, including the Legal Service. We therefore confirm the view we took in 1982 "that the strong administrative and policy content in the enforcement of the competition rules makes it right and inevitable that the function of enforcement should be principally entrusted to the Commission".

105.   Dr Ehlermann argued strongly that separation of detection, prosecution and decision-making functions within the Commission would not improve the quality of the procedures and would not make the best use of limited resources. Others however made a persuasive case for resorting to the earlier division of functions, particularly between investigation and the decision to launch proceedings. We do not find the suggested division of functions essential to fair and transparent enforcement, and we think that the other changes we shall recommend would deal with the perceived problems more effectively. We support the use of increased resources (to which we return below at paragraph 125) to form teams of case handlers for complex investigations. But we do not on balance recommend structural separation of the enforcement functions within the Commission.

Fundamental Rights of Defendants and Complainants (paragraphs 18-24)

106.   We welcome the emphasis which the Court of First Instance has laid on the need for Community institutions, including the Commission, to comply with the requirements of Article 6 of the European Convention on Human Rights. Article 6 gives everyone the right "to a fair and public hearing within a reasonable time by an independent and impartial tribunal established by law". For this purpose the European Court has accepted that it is the Court itself and the Court of First Instance which constitute the "independent and impartial tribunal". The Commission has

[1]   In Case T11/89, *Shell v. Commission* [1992] ECR II 757.

vested in it the Community's executive power in regard to competition matters and therefore lacks the independence from the executive which would be necessary. The right to a fair hearing from the Commission is not only established in Regulation 17 and accepted by the Commission as a fundamental commitment, but is now being effectively supervised by the Court of First Instance.

107.   The Court of First Instance is not however capable of enforcing speed of decision-making on the Commission. It has long been emphasised that it is unacceptable that the Commission should take several years to come to a decision on important cases, and in most cases should not come to a decision at all. The implementation of some of the recommendations we made in 1982 reduced but did not eliminate the backlog of unresolved complaints and notifications. The number of agreements left in a limbo of potential illegality and the general uncertainty for business enterprises remain unacceptable.

108.   The objective announced by Sir Leon Brittan—that every case should be dealt with in a fixed, predictable and reasonable period of time—is clearly right. The self-imposed deadlines are a welcome first step, and it appears that so far they have been observed. Mandatory time limits would however give defendants and complainants legal security in regard to speed of decision-making, which is one element of due process. We accept that uniform deadlines such as have been prescribed in the Merger Regulation are not feasible for all cases under Article 85 and 86, since the complexity of the facts and legal analysis is so varied. But we recommend that Regulation 17 should require the Commission, when it embarks on the procedure for a formal decision, to prescribe a timetable for each stage which would be mandatory. Extensions of time would require agreement between all the parties and the Commission. Article 10 of the Merger Regulation contains a number of elements of flexibility in regard to deadlines, and imposes discipline on the Commission by its final provision that where the Commission has failed to meet those deadlines, the merger "shall be deemed declared compatible with the common market", subject to the possibility of action by the competent authorities of a Member State. This sanction would often be inappropriate in Article 85 and 86 cases. If the mandatory timetable is not complied with, the other party concerned should have the right to apply to the Court of First Instance for such order as it considers appropriate—for example a fine or discontinuance of the proceedings.

Access to the File (paragraphs 25-31)

109.   There is some conflict between the practice of the Commission as described to us by Dr Ehlermann and the practice as described to us by some other witnesses with direct experience of the conduct of cases. We are not in a position to resolve this. On the principles to be applied it is common ground that defendants are entitled to a full copy of a formal complaint, documents relied on by the Commission and documents which are "manifestly exculpatory" in relation to the Commission's allegations. It is also common ground that they are not entitled to access to business secrets or to information given in confidence. The grey area between includes internal Commission documents[1]—which the Commission understandably wishes to protect to encourage frankness of analysis during the preparation of cases—and documents which do not appear to Commission officials to be either incriminating or exculpatory. There is clearly great difficulty where a case involves multiple defendants who may have business secrets from one another. English lawyers—with experience of a jurisdiction which gives discovery of documents on a very wide scale—seem to have wider expectations of access than those from other jurisdictions.

---

[1]   The Court of First Instance supported the Commission's position in regard to internal documents and some other disputed categories of documents in *BPB Industries and British Gypsum Ltd v. Commission*, Case T 65/89 [1993] 5 CMLR 32.

110.   We recommend three improvements to current procedures:-

(i)   an internal manual of procedures for all Commission rapporteurs;

(ii)   a Commission notice to be published in the Official Journal setting out the rules on access to the file established through practice, laying down time limits and incorporating rules approved in judgments of the Court of First Instance[1]; and

(iii) an extended mandate for the Hearing Officer to enable him to rule on conflicts between access and confidentiality.

These recommendations require no legislative change—and we believe that they should help to meet the criticisms and suggestions made by other witnesses.

The Oral Hearing and the Role of the Hearing Officer (paragraphs 32-35)

111.   At present the powers of the Hearing Officer are limited to the conduct of the oral hearing and the follow-up to the hearing, but within that narrow scope the successive Hearing Officers are generally regarded as having contributed greatly to the fairness and transparency of competition proceedings. A number of suggestions were made for giving the Hearing Officer a more authoritative status and extended interlocutory powers regarding the conduct of cases, and we accept most of these. We recommend that:-

(i)   the Hearing Officers should remain within DG IV, since they should be easily accessible for informal consultation by rapporteurs;

(ii)   the number of Hearing Officers should be increased in line with their wider responsibilities and they should have adequate support staff;

(iii) at least one Hearing Officer should be appointed at A2 grade, and all Hearing Officers should be irremovable except for serious professional misconduct;

(iv)   in addition to their present functions in regard to the oral hearing, and the conduct of the preliminary hearing where this is requested, they should have interlocutory powers to resolve procedural disputes between parties to a case, including the case handlers within DG IV, on access to the file, time limits and full disclosure of the case against a defendant;

(v)   the Hearing Officer's Report should be sent to the parties;

112.   Where either a party or the Director General for Competition is dissatisfied with an interlocutary ruling of a Hearing Officer, it seems to us that his decision should be capable of review eventually by the Court of First Instance. This could be done in one of two ways. The first is that the ruling of the Hearing Officer should be treated as a decision which could be appealed directly and speedily to a single judge of the Court of First Instance. The second is that the ruling of the Hearing Officer could be referred to the Commissioner responsible for competition, whose decision should be appealable to a judge of the Court of First Instance. We think that it is for the Commission to consider which of these two routes is administratively preferable. We prefer the first alternative.

---

[1]   In particular *Cimenteries v. Blue Circle Industries*, Case T 10 and 11/92 [1993] 4 CMLR 243, and *BPB Industries and British Gypsum Ltd v. Commission*, Case T 65/89 [1993] 5 CMLR 32.

Investigations (paragraphs 36-39)

113.   There was little criticism of the current investigation procedures of the Commission—most of the difficulties noted appeared to relate to matters which could be remedied by improved guidance to inspectors. While it is clearly right, for example, that an undertaking cannot oppose the carrying out of a search on the ground that its legal advisers cannot be found, it should be possible in such circumstances to postpone the asking of questions going beyond the whereabouts of documents until a legal adviser is there to protect the defendants' interests.

114.   In 1982 we recommended amendment of Regulation 17 so as to require leave of a Judge of the European Court before the Commission adopted a decision requiring an undertaking to submit to search of its premises, or alternatively that some other independent authority, such as the "independent person" who was later appointed as "Hearing Officer" should be required to give leave before a search took place. The case for requiring some form of judicial intervention before a Commission decision is executed at national level is accepted in principle by the Commission, and it has been strengthened by the recent decision of the European Court of Human Rights in *Niemitz v. Germany*.[1] In most national systems there appears already to be some procedure whereby leave of a national judge is required before a Commission decision ordering an investigation is carried out against the wishes of the undertaking. We recommend that Regulation 17 should be amended so as to make this a general requirement, and that it should be made clear that the lawfulness and proportionality of the decision to be enforced can be challenged at this stage.

115.   Witnesses were divided as to whether the Commission should be encouraged to make more use of the power under Article 13 of Regulation 17 to request the competent authorities of the Member States to undertake necessary investigations. Although this would be consistent with the desire to lighten the burdens on the Commission, there was some concern that wide delegation could lead to uneven enforcement as between different Member States. The vigour and thoroughness of an investigation might determine whether successful proceedings could be brought in respect of an infringement. It appears that little use has been made by the Commission of the facility of Article 13, and this may reflect the Commission's own judgment of the circumstances in which it would be appropriate to delegate. Article 13 is already cast in flexible terms, and allows Commission officials to assist national officials in the conduct of an investigation at the request of either side. An authorisation in writing from the national competent authority, specifying the subject matter and purpose of the investigation, is also required and must be produced by the officials carrying out a search. We do not recommend any change to Article 13 and we are content to leave it to the Commission to judge when delegation would be appropriate. It is however important that procedural guidance issued to national inspectors in regard to such matters as questioning should be identical with that issued to Commission inspectors. It should in addition be the usual practice that national officials carrying out an investigation should be assisted by at least one Commission inspector.

Comfort Letters (paragraphs 40-44)

116.   As we pointed out in paragraph 98, the decision-making procedures laid down in Regulation 17, together with the level of resources made available, were simply not capable of handling the number of cases which were lodged. Comfort letters are the method which the Commission has devised to reduce the backlog of notifications. Because they fail to take account of the interests of third parties whose interests may be affected, and do not comply with other

---

[1]   1993 16 European Human Rights Reports 97.

procedural requirements of Regulation 17, they are not capable of binding third parties. According to the Commission, it has never re-opened them except under circumstances where a binding decision would have been re-opened, and we received no evidence to the contrary. They have been effective in reducing the backlog of undecided cases, and parties to a notified agreement prefer them to the limbo in which their agreement would otherwise remain. Their use is likely to increase under the new practices announced by Sir Leon Brittan to assist in prompt disposal of cases.

117. As a first step, we agree with the improvements already in train or promised by the Commission—comfort letters should indicate whether the Commission's view favoured negative clearance or an exemption, and they should be given greater publicity both before and after the event, even although this cannot be done without risk of objection from interested third parties. The parties to an agreement cannot expect a result which carries more weight as against third parties without those third parties being given some opportunity to know what is afoot.

118. In the longer term, we believe that the right course must be amendment of Regulation 17 so that it permits a simpler and more expeditious procedure, leading to a final decision, for those cases which now end with a comfort letter or a simple closing of the file. We consider that in such cases there could be a final decision by a single Commissioner, under delegated powers. We would not however favour an automatic procedure under which, in the absence of third party objection or a decision by the Commission, the party notifying could rely on the negative clearance or exemption sought. Following the precedent of Article 20 of the Merger Regulation, which requires publication in the Official Journal only of the more significant Commission decisions, it should not be necessary to publish Article 85/86 decisions in simplified form, or to translate them into all Community languages.

Exemptions (paragraphs 45-53)

119. Block exemptions are the second most effective method, after comfort letters, which the Commission has employed in order to reduce the backlog of cases. While we are wholly in favour of further block exemptions in appropriate cases, we agree with the Commission policy of legislating to introduce block exemptions only when it has sufficient experience of the sector of industry involved. We agree also with the warning by the DTI that the non-opposition procedure (under which terms not expressly covered by a block exemption may be accorded cover under it if they are notified and meet with no objection) is helpful but requires monitoring to prevent abuse.

120. In 1982 we also recommended that individual applications for exemption under Article 85(3)—outside the context of block exemptions—should benefit from automatic exemption if no objection was raised within a given time limit after notification. The exemption was to last until the Commission took a final decision on whether to grant an exemption. Automatic exemption required amendment of Regulation 17 and the recommended change was never made. On balance, we now believe that automatic exemption is not right in principle. In the first place, we agree with the Office of Fair Trading that it is preferable to have a positive decision based on good analysis. Secondly, we have recommended other changes—both above (regarding simplified procedure) and below (reference to national authorities)—which if accepted and applied would lead to speedier decisions on applications for exemption.

The Advisory Committee (paragraphs 54-58)

121. The Advisory Committee introduces an element of independent supervision into Commission procedures prior to a formal decision in application of Article 85 or 86. This procedure also enables national authorities to express views on conditions in national markets. We are not, however, convinced that the Advisory Committee composed of representatives of the Member

States contributes in an important way to the fairness or transparency of the competition procedures as a whole.

122.   In the context of a simplified procedure for less important cases which we have recommended above, we see no need for the Advisory Committee to play a role. This would merely formalise existing practice under which the Advisory Committee are not involved in the issue of comfort or discomfort letters.

123.   Other cases to be decided by the Commission will by their nature raise important competition issues and for these we believe that Member States will wish to retain the Advisory Committee procedure. In these cases we recommend that the Advisory Committee Report should be made available to the parties and that, as in the Merger Regulation, the Committee should be able to recommend wider publication. We further recommend following the precedent of the Merger Regulation by requiring the Commission to "take the utmost account" of the opinion of the Advisory Committee and to inform the Committee of how it has done so.[1]

Fining Policy (paragraphs 59-62)

124.   The European Court gave clear guidance in the *Pioneer* case[2] on the factors to be taken into account by the Commission in assessing the amount of a fine. We see no reason to question these criteria, nor do we suggest that they should be codified so as to result in more predictable tariffs for particular infringements. In the interests of a deterrent system of enforcement of the competition rules, we do not believe that this would be a desirable or even a feasible approach. What is important is that the reasons for particular fines should be fully set out so that in particular they are open to challenge and review by the Court of First Instance. The Commission accepts the need for that, and we see no need for any further recommendation in regard to fines or penalty payments.

Structure and Quality of Commission Administration (paragraphs 63-68)

125.   In 1982 we recommended that the Commission's own review of competition procedures should cover the adequacy of the staffing of DG IV, arrangements for co-operation between Commission services and efficiency of Commission procedures for fact-finding and economic analysis. Concern was again expressed to us about a number of aspects of Commission administration. For some of the criticisms we have already suggested or approved remedies which we believe would assist.

126.   Adequacy of numbers continues however to be an almost universal concern. From the evidence given to us it emerges that the staffing provision given to the newly established Merger Task Force greatly exceeds, in relation to the number of cases, what is available for the handling of Article 85/86 cases. The widely admired performance of the Merger Task Force is not simply the result of streamlined procedures and high-powered, well-motivated staff, but is also the result of a structure in which case handlers have fewer cases and those cases are mostly less complex. The initiatives already taken by the Commission in regard to new procedures and co-operation with national courts have already diminished the backlog of unresolved cases, to judge from the latest published figures, and will certainly lead to further reductions. We ourselves have recommended further measures which in time could bring about a major reduction in DG IV's case load. Meanwhile, however, we urge the budgetary authorities in the strongest possible terms to provide

---

[1]   Merger Control Regulation Article 19 paragraph 6.

[2]   *Musique Diffusion Francaise & Others v. Commission*, Cases 100-103/80 [1983] ECR 1825.

additional staff to clear the backlog of cases. We strongly endorse the importance of providing DG IV with adequate resources to cope with its responsibilities.

127. It may be possible to second staff from elsewhere in the Commission. We have previously argued for greater flexibility of deployment of staff by Community institutions.[1] There is also room for new recruitment of economists in particular. And, drawing again on the experience of the Merger Task Force, we believe that short-term secondments of staff from national competition authorities may well bring in additional staff with the most relevant experience and in addition be of value in developing the links and mutual understanding which are essential if Community and national authorities are to co-operate in the most effective way in enforcing Community competition rules.

The Court of First Instance (paragraphs 69-73)

128. The final recommendation in our 1982 Report was the examination of the structure and responsibilities of the European Court with a view to improving the judicial review of competition cases. Although the establishment of a new court with jurisdiction over competition cases required amendment of the Community Treaties, this took place in the Single European Act in 1986. On the basis of our evidence, this appears of all the recommendations in the earlier Report to be the one which has been implemented to the greatest level of general satisfaction. We agree with the evidence we received that the operation of the Court of First Instance has given confidence to enterprises in the possibility of full review of decisions, has clarified for the Commission the standards of proof it must follow and will continue to lead to improved performance by the Commission in applying the competition rules. It is essential that the Court of First Instance continues to be given adequate resources to maintain the excellent quality of its analysis and judgments even under the burdens of the new jurisdiction recently conferred on it by the Member States.

129. The authority which the CFI has acquired among business and practitioners leads to the question whether even more use could be made of its resources. We have already suggested in making recommendations on the role of the Hearing Officer in paragraph 112 that there should be a new possibility of appeal to a Judge of the Court of First Instance from certain rulings by a Hearing Officer. As proposed by the Competition Law Association, the right of interlocutory appeal to the CFI would need to be subject to a leave procedure, to deter appeals without real substance and should be dealt with under an expeditious procedure similar to that employed for requests for interim measures. This change would require amendment of Regulation 17 to specify the matters subject to appeal through this new route (so as to avoid the limitation on admissibility established in the *Cimenteries* case[2] and is likely to require change in the rules relating to the Court. It would however would meet the criticism expressed by a number of witnesses that the absence of any interlocutory appeal to the European Court meant that a decision flawed by a procedural defect might be annulled many years later, so denying swift justice to all concerned as well as allowing waste of resources.

130. We believe that the combined effects of the improvements already made in response to judgments of the Court and under internal reforms made or agreed to be necessary by the Commission, together with other changes we are recommending in this Report should make it unlikely that excessive use will be made of this proposed new interlocutory appeal. But its existence

---

[1] *Staffing of Community Institutions,* 11th Report, 1987-88 (HL 66), at paragraphs 144, 151 and 188: "Sideways mobility of staff should be encouraged, and should not damage promotion prospects".

[2] Cases T10-12/92 and T15/92 *SA Cimenteries CBR and Others v. Commission.*

would help to impose stringent discipline on Commission officials in their procedural handling of contentious cases.

Co-operation between National Courts and the Commission (paragraphs 74-80)

131.   We accept that the Commission's Notice on co-operation between national courts and the Commission in applying Articles 85 and 86 of the EEC Treaty is a helpful summary of the jurisprudence of the European Court and Court of First Instance and that it will assist national courts to resolve in a more uniform and predictable manner cases brought before them in which plaintiffs seek remedies at national level. We do not believe that it will in itself make a substantial contribution to the alleviation of the backlog of cases awaiting Commission decision. It highlights the difficulties for litigants and for national courts resulting from the Commission's monopoly on the grant of exemptions coupled with the current failure to resolve applications within a reasonable time. No doubt there will be a few cases where a national court issues a decision on the assumption that the Commission will or will not grant an exemption and the guess is in the event proved to be wrong. These cases will have to be unscrambled later—as the case from the Netherlands[1] showed, it is possible for that to be done. If there are many cases where proceedings are suspended while the Commission takes a decision, this will increase pressure on the Commission to resolve these cases and will bring pressure on Member States generally for more effective remedies for the situation.

132.   The operation of the Notice will require to be carefully monitored. There may be some risk of development of divergent national approaches, although we do not believe that the Notice itself increases this—rather the contrary. We do not see objection to the Commission appearing as *amicus curiae* in a United Kingdom or other national court—indeed we have supported such a proposal in previous Reports.[2] But if the result of the Notice were to be diversion of Commission staff from their main responsibility of resolving cases under Regulation 17, there might then be a need for the Commission to reduce the number of occasions on which the Commission could provide assistance in national court proceedings.

The Powers of National Competition Authorities (paragraphs 81-85)

133.   It is clear that there is already a trend in favour of more application of Articles 85 and 86 by national competition authorities. Eight Member States now have domestic powers enabling their competition authorities to carry out the necessary fact-finding and decision-making. The United Kingdom is one of those which does not have the necessary domestic powers[3], but we were told by the Office of Fair Trading that changes are under discussion which would make it easier for the OFT and the Commission to share Article 85 and 86 cases between them. The Commission favours greater delegation of cases and looks forward to Member States providing the necessary powers to their own authorities. Greater decentralisation of the enforcement of competition rules is to be recommended. It offers a real prospect of reduction in the intolerable workload of DG IV.

---

[1]   Described in Mr Braakman's evidence and summarised in paragraph ?? above.

[2]   In our 12th Report, 1987-88, *Compliance with Public Procurement Directives* (HL 72) we said "The Committee accept that there may be cases in the public procurement field where it would be appropriate for the Commission, at the invitation or with the leave of the national court, to make submissions about the Community legislation, its interpretation by the European Court and the desirability or otherwise of making a reference to that court under Article 177 of the EEC Treaty. This would be consistent with the Commission's responsibility under Article 155 of the EEC Treaty to 'ensure that the provisions of this Treaty and the measures taken by the institutions pursuant thereto are applied'. These submissions would not be binding on the national court".

[3]   Neither the Fair Trading Act 1973 (c. 41) nor the Competition Act 1980 (c. 21) contain powers to apply Article 85 or 86 at national level. Possible changes are described in footnote 1 to paragraph 81.

134.   We agree with the Bundeskartellamt that there should be delegation of case investigation and assessment on the basis that the Commission should determine cases of substantial Community interest while other cases are handled by the national competition authority of the Member State whose territory was most affected. It would be extremely difficult to devise automatic criteria—such as exist under the Merger Regulation—for determining the division of jurisdiction between the Commission and national competition authorities. We consider that the criteria to be adopted throughout the Community should be established in discussion between the Member States and the Commission and incorporated in future Community legislation. For the time being however division of jurisdiction will have to be agreed between the Commission and the national competition authorities on a case by case basis, and if no agreement is reached in a particular case, the case must remain for decision by the Commission. Under the recent changes announced by Sir Leon Brittan, a notification or application is to be met within two months by a comfort letter or a warning letter from the Commission. Following amendment of Article 9 of Regulation 17, there should be a preliminary decision to be taken within two months as to whether a case: (a) should proceed towards full decision by the Commission; (b) should be determined under the simpler procedure which we have suggested above should replace comfort letters and closing the file; or (c) should be referred to a particular national authority.

135.   A key question to be determined is however whether national authorities should be permitted to grant exemptions under Article 85(3). Article 9.1 now gives the Commission sole power to grant exemptions, and this has been an important element in uniform enforcement of the competition rules throughout the Community. There are now signs of a wish on the part of some national authorities at least to decentralise the power again. The Bundeskartellamt suggested that the lack of power to grant exemptions was a deterrent to the exercise of assessment functions by national competition authorities. We do not favour giving national authorities an uncontrolled right to grant exemptions. We prefer the following system which is close to that suggested by Mr Lever. Where an exemption was sought in a case being determined by a national authority, that authority could reject it, without prejudice to the right of the applicant to apply to the Commission for the exemption. If however it considered that there was or might be a strong case for an exemption, it should refer the case back to the Commission for a decision to grant or refuse the exemption. For these "dual control cases", which would probably be relatively few, there would have to be provision for transfer of confidential information from the national authority to the Commission, if the Commission was not to re-open the entire procedure of investigation.

136.   We accept the warning given to us that effective enforcement at national level will require resources, trained staff and the development of traditions and experience. There would have to be mutual assistance provisions to assist in gathering evidence. There may be national variations in efficiency and in zeal, and national procedures will not necessarily be swifter, fairer or more transparent than those of the Commission. An approach which left discretion with the Commission in regard to reference to national authorities would however enable some account to be taken of the degree of national experience. It would be a condition of delegation that national administrative decisions would be open to some form of judicial review and thus ultimately to some degree of control by the European Court. We believe however that the number of cases requiring resolution under Community rules will continue to rise and that there is in the longer term no alternative to this form of decentralised administration.

Harmonisation of National Remedies (paragraphs 86-87)

137.   It will in the longer term be desirable to harmonise national remedies, particularly in regard to damages, injunctions requiring termination of unlawful conduct and interim measures. This would however inevitably be a complex exercise and should be kept separate from what we regard as the more pressing matter of modifying Regulation 17. Greater application of the competition rules by national courts, such as is likely to occur in consequence of the Commission's Notice on co-operation between national courts and the Commission, will provide useful comparative background against which the Commission might at a later stage make a proposal. By then it should also be possible to draw on the experience of the Directives which have approximated national remedies in the field of public procurement.

Merger Control (paragraphs 88-95)

138.   We believe that the Commission has made the right decision in postponing formal proposals to review the Merger Regulation for another three years. The procedures in the Regulation and the performance of the Merger Task Force have won general praise from business. Such criticisms as were expressed by our witnesses were relatively minor, and some of them can be addressed without the need for amendment of the Regulation. It may be possible, for example, for decisions to be somewhat more informative about the underlying facts without sacrifice of the highly important speed of result. There may well be room for greater flexibility in the application of the provisions which allow reference by national authorities to the Commission or by the Commission to national authorities. Where a single merger faces multiple national controls, or there is more than one bid for a company, for example, there may sometimes be a good case for a reference to allow appraisal by a single authority. What is of the greatest importance is that the Merger Task Force is regarded as "user-friendly", and that there is eagerness to bring prospective mergers within its reach. We have noted also that there will in any event be some gradual increase in the number of mergers handled, since the thresholds are not index-linked. If a further transfer of jurisdiction occurs at a later stage, it is likely to be demand-led.

139.   A further reason why we agree with the Commission's decision to defer review of the Merger Regulation for three years is that we regard it as much more urgent for the Member States to bring Regulation 17 up to date. The success of the Merger Regulation is due not only to the high motivation and lighter case-load of the staff of the Merger Task Force, but in large measure to the establishment of a framework which has set binding but attainable time-limits, provided in a number of ways for greater transparency than does Regulation 17 and achieved a realistic balance between appraisal at national and at Community level. The experience of the Merger Regulation has been an invaluable background to the necessary revision of Regulation 17, as has the work recently carried out among businesses and governments in order to re-appraise it. The Merger Regulation is clearly performing well and can be left to mature for a few years longer.

A Commission Vade Mecum

140.   We have already said that we regard the Commission's Notice on co-operation between national courts and the Commission as providing helpful guidance to national courts. There is room for similar general guidance for businesses and lawyers negotiating Commission competition procedures. Chapter IV of the Commission booklet "EEC Competition Policy in the Single Market" on Enforcement of the competition rules[1] is clearly presented, but having been last revised in 1989 does not describe the Court of First Instance or take account of its judgments. An updated Vade Mecum for business, describing the enforcement procedures in straightforward terms, as has been

---

[1]   Appendix 6.

done with the Community rules on public procurement, would be of great help. Practitioners may need something more detailed—a kind of "White Book"[1] which would set out procedures in difficult and complex areas in more detail, noting the European Court and CFI cases on which they are based. Information is now scattered throughout several Council and Commission Regulations, successive Commission Reports on Competition Policy and a growing number of European Court cases. Even the highly experienced practitioners who assisted us in our enquiry were not necessarily aware of all the elements of Commission practice as it emerged from the Commission's own account. It would clearly help to avoid controversy if practice on such matters as access to the file or preliminary enquiries were governed not simply be internal instructions to Commission rapporteurs, but by general rules publicly available and updated each year. The updated version could be prepared alongside the annual Report on Competition Policy.

Envoi

141. Returning to the basic objectives of fair, transparent, swift and deterrent enforcement of Community competition rules, we believe that there has been and continues to be substantial improvement since 1982. The European Court and the Court of First Instance have forced the pace. Reforms initiated by Sir Leon Brittan are clearly being carried forward by the current Commissioner and Director-General for Competition. The changes we have suggested would take this process further. An enhanced role for the Hearing Officer and ultimate control of interlocutory disputes by a Judge of the Court of First Instance would help to guarantee fairness and transparency. A simplified decision-making procedure and more references to national competition authorities would help to produce swift and final decisions—a more effective deterrent to anti-competitive behaviour than letters or the limbo in which hundreds of cases still lie. Most of these recommended changes do no more than reflect the improved procedures already in place under the Merger Regulation, while others would more accurately codify the practice which has developed without legislative backing. Effective implementation of the competition rules is central to the functioning of the single market, and we have noted in this context a number of highly relevant recommendations in the Sutherland Report[2]—the need to review the way in which rights of individuals to obtain redress for breaches of Community law are provided across the Community, administrative partnership between the Commission and the Member States in the application of rules and improvements in the quality of Community legislation.

142. We consider that Regulation 17 should not be regarded as incapable of change. It is not a Pandora's box, which will release all human ills if it is opened. Nor is it the Ark of the Covenant, within which is contained the law on tables of stone. If it is an ark, it is Noah's Ark, after thirty years needing refitting and a new coat of pitch to match its sister ship the Merger Regulation.

---

[1] "The White Book" is used to describe the Supreme Court Practice of England and Wales, including the heavily annotated Rules of the Supreme Court. For many years it was revised and re-issued each year, and is now re-issued at intervals of three years (with Supplements every six months).

[2] Council Document 9837/92 Report to the Commission by the High Level Group on the Operation of the Internal Market: "The Internal Market after 1992—Meeting the Challenge".

PART 4 SUMMARY OF CONCLUSIONS AND RECOMMENDATIONS

General Conclusions

143.   The objectives of all law enforcement are that it should be fair, transparent, swift and deterrent. Effective enforcement of Community competition rules requires in addition sound judgment in the interests of the Community as a whole and this the Commission has provided. Defects in fairness, transparency and speed of Commission practices are in part due to the procedures laid down by the Council and the inadequate level of resources made available (paragraphs 96-98).

144.   Virtually all the recommendations in our 1982 Report which did not require amendment of Regulation 17 or of the EEC Treaty were met, and these improved fairness and transparency of procedures and reduced the backlog of cases. The new Court of First Instance has been widely praised for its contribution to protection of individual rights and other aspects of effective enforcement (paragraph 99).

145.   Revival of concern is due to rising burdens on and expectations of the Commission, to the successful early operation of the Merger Regulation and to the constraints on reform imposed by Regulation 17. The possibility of change to Regulation 17 would allow the problems to be addressed more constructively (paragraphs 100-102).

146.   Structural change to separate the functions of detection, prosecution and decision making is not essential if procedure is fair and transparent and there is independent judicial control to guarantee this. We do not favour establishment of a new competition authority or division of functions within the Commission (paragraphs 103-105).

147.   The emphasis now laid on compliance with the European Convention on Human Rights helps to guarantee the right to a fair hearing from the Commission. But delays in making decisions on important cases remain unacceptable. The self-imposed deadlines announced by the Commission are a welcome first step (paragraphs 106-108).

Recommendations not Requiring Amendment of Regulation 17

148.   To improve access by parties to the Commission's file, we recommend:-

   (i) an internal manual of procedures for all Commission rapporteurs;

   (ii) a Commission notice setting out the legal and procedural rules; and

   (iii) an extended mandate for the Hearing Officer enabling him to rule on conflicts between access and confidentiality (paragraphs 109-110).

149.   To improve the conduct of proceedings, we recommend that:-

   (i) there should be more Hearing Officers, with adequate support staff;

   (ii) at least one Hearing Officer, within Directorate-General IV, should be appointed at A2 grade, and that all Hearing Officers should be irremovable except for serious professional misconduct;

   (iii) Hearing Officers should have wider powers to resolve procedural disputes on access to the file, time limits and full disclosure of the case against a defendant; and

   (iv) the Hearing Officer's Report should be sent to the parties (paragraph 111).

150.   Regulation 17 allows the Commission the right flexibility to delegate necessary investigations to competent authorities of the Member States. We recommend however that procedural guidance to national inspectors should be identical with that issued to Commission inspectors and that national inspectors should be assisted by at least one Commission inspector (paragraphs 113-115).

151.   To improve the usefulness and the status of comfort letters, we recommend that they should indicate whether the Commission favours negative clearance or an exemption and that they should be given greater publicity before and after issue (paragraphs 116-117).

152.   We favour further block exemptions in appropriate cases. We do not favour any procedure for automatic grant of exemptions (paragraphs 119-120).

153.   We recommend that the reasons for particular fines should be fully set out so that in particular they are open to review by the Court of First Instance (paragraph 124).

154.   We recommend provision of resources to Directorate-General IV adequate for its responsibilities. We favour new recruitment of economists and secondments from national competition authorities (paragraphs 125-127).

155.   It is essential that the Court of First Instance continues to be given adequate resources to maintain the excellent quality of its analysis and judgments (paragraph 128).

156.   The Commission's Notice on co-operation between national courts and the Commission in applying Articles 85 and 86 is a helpful summary of the Courts' decisions and will help national courts to provide remedies at national level in a more uniform way. It will not however help to reduce the backlog of cases, and must not be allowed to divert Commission staff from their main responsibility of resolving cases under Regulation 17 (paragraphs 131-132).

157.   The Commission was right to postpone proposals to review the Merger Regulation for three years. The Regulation is performing well (paragraphs 138-139).

158.   The Commission should issue an updated Vade Mecum describing competition procedures in straightforward terms, and for practitioners a "White Book" setting out practice in complex areas in more detail and updated each year along with the annual Report on Competition Policy (paragraph 140).

Recommendations for Amendment of Regulation 17

159.   The Commission, when it embarks on the procedure for a formal decision, should prescribe a timetable which would be mandatory, with extensions requiring agreement between all parties and the Commission (paragraph 108).

160.   There should be an interlocutory appeal from a ruling of a Hearing Officer (possibly through the Commissioner responsible for competition) whose decision (under delegated authority) would constitute a Commission decision appealable to the Court of First Instance. The procedure must be kept as simple and as expeditious as possible and it seems to us that such an appeal could be dealt with by a single judge of that Court (paragraphs 112 and 129-130).

161.   Before a Commission decision ordering an investigation is carried out against the wishes of the undertaking, the leave of a national judge should be required and the lawfulness and proportionality of the decision should be open to challenge (paragraph 114).

162.   For cases which now end with a comfort letter or closing of the file, there should be a simple and expeditious procedure leading to a final decision by a single Commissioner under delegated powers (paragraph 118). In these cases the Advisory Committee would not be involved (paragraph 122).

163.   Investigation and assessment of appropriate cases should be delegated to national competition authorities. Division of jurisdiction should be agreed between the Member States and the Commission on a case by case basis, with the case remaining with the Commission in the absence of agreement. In the longer term, criteria for division should be established at Community level. National authorities could reject requests for exemptions, without prejudice to the applicant's right to apply to the Commission for an exemption, but where they considered that there was, or might be, a case for granting an exemption, would have to refer cases to the Commission. National decisions would be open to judicial review and thus to ultimate control by the European Court (paragraphs 133-136).

164.   In the longer term, national remedies should be harmonised, particularly in regard to damages, injunctions and interim measures (paragraph 137).

Final Comment and Recommendation

165.   The changes we have suggested would carry forward the reforms begun in 1982. Most of them only reflect improved procedures for mergers while others codify practice. Effective implementation of competition rules is central to the functioning of the single market. Regulation 17 is not immutable and should be brought up to date (paragraphs 141-142).

166.   The Committee believe that this Report on the Enforcement of Community Competition Rules raises important matters of policy and principle to which the attention of the House should be drawn, and we make this Report to the House for debate.

APPENDIX 1

Sub-Committee E (Law and Institutions)

The Members of the Sub-Committee which conducted this enquiry were:

L. Allen of Abbeydale
L. Archer of Sandwell
V. Colville of Culross
B. Elles
L. Hacking
L. Holme of Cheltenham
L. Oliver of Aylmerton
L. Skidelsky
L. Slynn of Hadley (Chairman)
L. Wedderburn of Charlton
B. Williams of Crosby

APPENDIX 2

List of Witnesses

The following witnesses gave evidence. Those marked * gave oral evidence.

    Mr August J Braakman
*   Commission of the European Communities
    Competition Law Association
    Confederation of British Industry
*   Department of Trade and Industry
*   Director General of Fair Trading
    Mr Peter Duffy
    Federal Cartel Office
    Mr Ian Forrester QC
    Mr Nicholas Forwood QC
*   Joint Working Party on Competition Law
*   Mr Jeremy Lever
*   Monopolies and Mergers Commission
*   Mr Michael Reynolds
    UNICE
    Mr Ivo Van Bael

APPENDIX 3

Articles 85-89 of the European Community Treaty

Article 85

1. The following shall be prohibited as incompatible with the common market; all agreements between undertakings, decisions by associations of undertakings and concerted practices which may affect trade between Member States and which have as their object or effect the prevention, restriction or distortion of competition within the common market, and in particular those which:

(a)   directly or indirectly fix purchase or selling prices or any other trading conditions;
(b)   limit or control production, markets, technical development, or investment;
(c)   share markets or sources of supply;
(d)   apply dissimilar conditions to equivalent transactions with other trading parties, thereby placing them at a competitive disadvantage;
(e)   make the conclusion of contracts subject to acceptance by the other parties of supplementary obligations which, by their nature or according to commercial usage, have no connection with the subject of such contracts.

2. Any agreements or decisions prohibited pursuant to this Article shall be automatically void.

3. The provisions of paragraph 1 may, however, be declared inapplicable in the case of;

—   any agreement or category of agreements between undertakings;
—   any decision or category of decisions by associations of undertakings;
—   any concerted practice or category of concerted practices;

which contributes to improving the production or distribution of goods or to promoting technical or economic progress, while allowing consumers a fair share of the resulting benefit, and which does not:

(a)   impose on the undertakings concerned restrictions which are not indispensable to the attainment of these objectives;
(b)   afford such undertakings the possibility of eliminating competition in respect of a substantial part of the products in question.

Article 86

Any abuse by one or more undertakings of a dominant position within the common market or in a substantial part of it shall be prohibited as incompatible with the common market in so far as it may affect trade between Member States. Such abuse may, in particular, consist in:

(a)   directly or indirectly imposing unfair purchase or selling prices or unfair trading conditions;
(b)   limiting production, markets or technical development to the prejudice of consumers;
(c)   applying dissimilar conditions to equivalent transactions with other trading parties, thereby placing them at a competitive disadvantage;
(d)   making the conclusion of contracts subject to acceptance y the other parties of supplementary obligations which, by their nature or according to commercial usage, have no connection with the subject of such contracts.

Article 87

1. Within three years of the entry into force of this Treaty the Council shall, acting unanimously on a proposal from the Commission and after consulting the Assembly, adopt any appropriate regulations or directives to give effect to the principles set out in Articles 85 and 86.

If such provisions have not been adopted within the period mentioned, they shall be laid down by the Council, acting by a qualified majority on a proposal from the Commission and after consulting the Assembly.

2. The regulations or directives referred to in paragraph 1 shall be designed, in particular:

(a)   to ensure compliance with the prohibitions laid down in Article 85(1) and in Article 86 by making provision for fines and periodic penalty payments;

(b)   to lay down detailed rules for the application of Article 85(3), taking into account the need to ensure effective supervision on the one hand, and to simplify administration to the greatest possible extent on the other;

(c)   to define, if need be, in the various branches of the economy, the scope of the provisions of Articles 85 and 86;

(d)   to define the respective functions of the Commission and of the Court of Justice in applying the provisions laid down in this paragraph;

(e)   to determine the relationship between national laws and the provisions contained in this Section or adopted pursuant to this Article.

Article 88

Until the entry into force of the provisions adopted in pursuance of Article 87, the authorities in Member States shall rule on the admissibility of agreements, decisions and concerted practices and on abuse of a dominant position in the common market in accordance with the law of their country and with the provisions of Article 85, in particular paragraph 3, and of Article 86.

Article 89

1. Without prejudice to Article 88, the Commission shall, as soon as it takes up its duties, ensure the application of the principles laid down in Article 85 and 86. On application by a Member State or on its own initiative, and in co-operation with the competent authorities in the Member States, who shall give it their assistance, the Commission shall investigate cases of suspected infringement of these principles. If it finds that there has been an infringement, it shall propose appropriate measures to bring it to an end.

2. If the infringement is not brought to an end, the Commission shall record such infringement of the principles in a reasoned decision. The Commission may publish its decision and authorise Member States to take the measures, the conditions and details of which it shall determine, needed to remedy the situation.

APPENDIX 4

Regulation 17[1]

THE COUNCIL OF THE EUROPEAN COMMUNITY

Having regard to the Treaty establishing the European Economic Community, and in particular Article 87 thereof;

Having regard to the proposal from the Commission;

Having regard to the Opinion of the Economic and Social Committee;

Having regard to the Opinion of the European Parliament;

Whereas, in order to establish a system ensuring that competition shall not be distorted in the common market, it is necessary to provide for balanced application of Articles 85 and 86 in a uniform manner in the Member States;

Whereas in establishing the rules for applying Article 85(3) account must be taken of the need to ensure effective supervision and to simplify administration to the greatest possible extent;

Whereas it is accordingly necessary to make it obligatory, as a general principle, for undertakings which seek application of Article 85(3) to notify to the Commission their agreements, decisions and concerted practices;

Whereas, on the one hand, such agreements, decisions and concerted practices are probably very numerous and cannot therefore all be examined at the same time and, on the other hand, some of them have special features which may make them less prejudicial to the development of the common market;

Whereas there is consequently a need to make more flexible arrangements for the time being in respect of certain categories of agreement, decision and concerted practice without prejudging their validity under Article 85;

Whereas it may be in the interest of undertakings to know whether any agreements, decisions or practices to which they are party, or propose to become party, may lead to action on the part of the Commission pursuant to Article 85(1) or Article 86;

Whereas, in order to secure uniform application of Articles 85 and 86 in the common market, rules must be made under which the Commission, acting in close and constant liaison with the competent authorities of the Member States, may take the requisite measures for applying those Articles;

Whereas for this purpose the Commission must have the co-operation of the competent authorities of the Member States and be empowered, throughout the common market, to require such information to be supplied and to undertake such investigations as are necessary to bring to light any agreement, decision or concerted practice prohibited by Article 85(1) or any abuse of a dominant position prohibited by Article 86;

Whereas, in order to carry out its duty of ensuring that the provisions of the Treaty are applied, the Commission must be empowered to address to undertakings or associations of undertakings recommendations and decisions for the purpose of bringing to an end infringements of Articles 85 and 86;

Whereas compliance with Articles 85 and 86 and the fulfilment of obligations imposed on undertakings and associations of undertakings under this Regulation must be enforceable by means of fines and periodic penalty payments;

---

[1]   JO 1962, 204; OJ 1959-1962, 87; came into force 13 March 1962.

Whereas undertakings concerned must be accorded the right to be heard by the Commission, third parties whose interests may be affected by a decision must be given the opportunity of submitting their comments beforehand, and it must be ensured that wide publicity is given to decisions taken;

Whereas all decisions taken by the Commission under this Regulation are subject to review by the Court of Justice under the conditions specified in the Treaty; whereas it is moreover desirable to confer upon the Court of Justice, pursuant to Article 172, unlimited jurisdiction in respect of decisions under which the Commission imposes fines or periodic penalty payments;

Whereas this Regulation may enter into force without prejudice to any other provisions that may hereafter be adopted pursuant to Article 87;

HAS ADOPTED THIS REGULATION

Article 1

Basic provision

Without prejudice to Articles 6, 7 and 23 of this Regulation, agreements, decisions and concerted practices of the kind described in Article 85(1) of the Treaty and the abuse of a dominant position in the market, within the meaning of Article 86 of the Treaty, shall be prohibited, no prior decision to that effect being required.

Article 2

Negative clearance

Upon application by the undertakings or associations of undertakings concerned, the Commission may certify that, on the basis of the facts in its possession, there are no grounds under Article 85(1) or Article 86 of the Treaty for action on its part in respect of an agreement, decision or practice.

Article 3

Termination of infringements

1. Where the Commission, upon application or upon its own initiative, finds that there is infringement of Article 85 or Article 86 of the Treaty, it may by decision require the undertakings or associations of undertakings concerned to bring such infringement to an end.

2. Those entitled to make application are:

(a)   Member States;
(b)   natural or legal persons who claim a legitimate interest.

3. Without prejudice to the other provisions of this Regulation, the Commission may, before taking a decision under paragraph 1, address to the undertakings or associations of undertakings concerned recommendations for termination of the infringement.

Article 4

Notification of new agreements, decisions and practices

1. Agreements, decisions and concerted practices of the kind described in Article 85(1) of the Treaty which come into existence after the entry into force of this Regulation and in respect of which the parties seek application of Article 85(3) must be notified to the Commission. Until they have been notified, no decision in application of Article 85(3) may be taken.

2. Paragraph 1 shall not apply to agreements, decisions or concerted practices where:

(1)   the only parties thereto are undertakings from one Member State and the agreements, decisions or practices do not relate either to imports or to exports between Member States;

(2)   not more than two undertakings are party thereto, and the agreements only:

(a) restrict the freedom of one party to the contract in determining the prices or conditions of business upon which the goods which he has obtained from the other party to the contract may be resold; or

(b) impose restrictions on the exercise of the rights of the assignee or user of industrial property rights—in particular patents, utility models, designs or trade marks—or of the person entitled under a contract to the assignment, or grant, of the right to use a method of manufacture or knowledge relating to the use and to the application of industrial processes;

(3) they have as their sole object:

(a) the development or uniform application of standards or types: or
[(b) joint research and development;
(c) specialisation in the manufacture of products, including agreements necessary for the achievement of this;

—where the products which are the subject of specialisation do not, in a substantial part of the common market, represent more than 15 per cent of the volume of business done in identical products or those considered by the consumers to be similar by reason of their characteristics, price and use, and
—where the total annual turnover of the participating undertakings does not exceed 200 million units of account.

These agreements, decisions and concerted practices may be notified to the Commission].[1]

Article 5

Notification of Existing Agreements, Decisions and Practices

1. Agreements, decisions and concerted practices of the kind described in Article 85(1) of the Treaty which are in existence at the date of entry into force of this Regulation and in respect of which the parties seek application of Article 85(3) shall be notified to the Commission [before November 1, 1962].[2] [However, notwithstanding the foregoing provisions, any agreements, decisions and concerted practices to which not more than two undertakings are party shall be notified before February 1, 1963].[3]

2. Paragraph (1) shall not apply to agreements, decisions or concerted practices falling within Article 4 (2); these may be notified to the Commission.

Article 6

Decisions Pursuant to Article 85(3)

1. Whenever the Commission takes a decision pursuant to Article 85(3) of the Treaty, it shall specify therein the date from which the decision shall take effect. Such date shall not be earlier than the date of notification.

2. The second sentence of paragraph 1 shall not apply to agreements, decisions or concerted practices falling within Article 4(2) and Article 5(2), nor to those falling within Article 5(1) which have been notified within the time limit specified in Article 5(1).

Article 7

Special Provisions for Existing Agreements, Decisions and Practices

1. Where agreements, decisions and concerted practices in existence at the date of entry into force of this Regulation and notified [within the time limits specified in Article 5(1)][4] do not satisfy the requirements of Article 85(3) of the Treaty and the undertakings or associations of undertakings concerned cease to

---

[1] Amended by Reg. 2822/71.
[2] Substituted by Reg. 59, Art. 1(1). See also Art. 25, *post.*
[3] Added by Reg. 59, Art. 1(2).
[4] Added by Reg. 59, Art. 1(3).

give effect to them or modify them in such manner that they no longer fall within the prohibition contained in Article 85(1) or that they satisfy the requirements of Article 85(3), the prohibition contained in Article 85(1) shall apply only for a period fixed by the Commission. A decision by the Commission pursuant to the foregoing sentence shall not apply as against undertakings and associations of undertakings which did not expressly consent to the notification.

2. Paragraph 1 shall apply to agreements, decisions and concerted practices falling within Article 4(2) which are in existence at the date of entry into force of this Regulation if they are notified [before January 1, 1967].[1]

Article 8

Duration and revocation of decisions under Article 85(3)

A decision in application of Article 85(3) of the Treaty shall be issued for a specified period and conditions and obligations may be attached thereto.

2. A decision may on application be renewed if the requirements of Article 85(3) of the Treaty continue to be satisfied.

3. The Commission may revoke or amend its decision or prohibit specified acts by the Parties:

(a)   where there has been a change in any of the facts which were basic to the making of the decision;
(b)   where the parties commit a breach of any obligation attached to the decision;
(c)   where the decision is based on incorrect information or was induced by deceit;
(d)   where the parties abuse the exemption from the provisions of Article 85(1) of the Treaty granted to them by the decision.

In cases to which sub-paragraphs (b), (c) or (d) apply, the decision may be revoked with retroactive effect.

Article 9

Powers

1. Subject to review of its decision by the Court of Justice, the Commission shall have sole power to declare Article 85(1) inapplicable pursuant to Article 85(3) of the Treaty.

2. The Commission shall have power to apply Article 85(1) and Article 86 of the Treaty; this power may be exercised notwithstanding that the time limits specified in Article 5(1) and in Article 7(2) relating to notification have not expired.

3. As long as the Commission has not initiated any procedure under Articles 2, 3 or 6, the authorities of the Member States shall remain competent to apply Article 85(1) and Article 86 in accordance with Article 88 of the Treaty; they shall remain competent in this respect notwithstanding that the time limits specified in Article 5(1) and in Article 7(2) relating to notification have not expired.

Article 10

Liaison with the authorities of the Member States

1. The Commission shall forthwith transmit to the competent authorities of the Member States a copy of the applications and notifications together with copies of the most important documents lodged with the Commission for the purpose of establishing the existence of infringements of Articles 85 or 86 of the Treaty or of obtaining negative clearance or a decision in application of Article 85(3).

2. The Commission shall carry out the procedure set out in paragraph (1) in close and constant liaison with the competent authorities of the Member States; such authorities shall have the right to express their views upon that procedure.

---

[1]   Substituted by Reg. 118/63m Art.1. And see Art. 25, *post*.

3. An Advisory Committee on Restrictive Practices and Monopolies shall be consulted prior to the taking of any decision following upon a procedure under paragraph (1), and of any decision concerning the renewal, amendment or revocation of a decision pursuant to Article 85(3) of the Treaty.

4. The Advisory Committee shall be composed of officials competent in the matter of restrictive practices and monopolies. Each Member State shall appoint an official to represent it who, if prevented from attending, may be replaced by another official.

5. The consultation shall take place at a joint meeting convened by the Commission; such meeting shall be held not earlier than 14 days after dispatch of the notice convening it. The notice shall, in respect of each case to be examined, be accompanied by a summary of the case together with an indication of the most important documents, and a preliminary draft decision.

6. The Advisory Committee may deliver an opinion notwithstanding that some of its members or their alternates are not present. A report of the outcome of the consultative proceedings shall be annexed to the draft decision. It shall not be made public.

Article 11

Requests for information

1. In carrying out the duties assigned to it by Article 89 and by provisions adopted under Article 87 of the Treaty, the Commission may obtain all necessary information from the Governments and competent authorities of the Member States and from undertakings and associations of undertakings.

2. When sending a request for information to an undertaking or association of undertakings, the Commission shall at the same time forward a copy of the request to the competent authority of the Member State in whose territory the seat of the undertaking or association of undertakings is situated.

3. In its request the Commission shall state the legal basis and the purpose of the request and also the penalties provided for in Article 15(1)(b) for supplying incorrect information.

4. The owners of the undertakings or their representatives and, in the case of legal persons, companies or firms, or of associations having no legal personality, the persons authorised to represent them by law or by their constitution shall supply the information requested.

5. Where an undertaking or association of undertakings does not supply the information requested within the time limit fixed by the Commission, or supplies incomplete information, the Commission shall by decision require the information to be supplied. The decision shall specify what information is required, fix an appropriate time limit within which it is to be supplied and indicate the penalties provided for in Article 15(1)(b) and Article 16(1)(c) and the right to have the decision reviewed by the Court of Justice.

6. The Commission shall at the same time forward a copy of its decision to the competent authority of the Member State in whose territory the seat of the undertaking or association of undertakings is situated.

Article 12

Inquiry into sectors of the economy

1. If in any sector of the economy the trend of trade between Member States, price movements, inflexibility of prices or other circumstances suggest that in the economic sector concerned competition is being restricted or distorted within the common market, the Commission may decide to conduct a general inquiry into that economic sector and in the course thereof may request undertakings in the sector concerned to supply the information necessary for giving effect to the principles formulated in Articles 85 and 86 of the Treaty and for carrying out the duties entrusted to the Commission.

2. The Commission may in particular request every undertaking or association of undertakings in the economic sector concerned to communicate to it all agreements, decisions and concerted practices which are exempt from notification by virtue of Article 4(2) and Article 5(2).

3. When making inquiries pursuant to paragraph 2, the Commission shall also request undertakings or groups of undertakings whose size suggests that they occupy a dominant position within the common market or a substantial part thereof to supply to the Commission such particulars of the structure of the

undertakings and of their behaviour as are requisite to an appraisal of their position in the light of Article 86 of the Treaty.

4. Article 10(3) to (6) and Articles 11,13 and 14 shall apply correspondingly.

Article 13

Investigations by the authorities of the Member States

1. At the request of the Commission, the competent authorities of the Member States shall undertake the investigations which the Commission considers to be necessary under Article 14(1), or which it has ordered by decision pursuant to Article 14(3). The officials of the competent authorities of the Member States responsible for conducting these investigations shall exercise their powers upon production of an authorisation in writing issued by the competent authority of the Member State in whose territory the investigation is to be made. Such authorisation shall specify the subject matter and purpose of the investigation.

2. If so requested by the Commission or by the competent authority of the Member State in whose territory the investigation is to be made, the officials of the Commission may assist the officials of such authorities in carrying out their duties.

Article 14

Investigating powers of the Commission

1. In carrying out the duties assigned to it by Article 89 and by provisions adopted under Article 87 of the Treaty, the Commission may undertake all necessary investigations into undertakings and associations of undertakings. To this end the officials authorised by the Commission are empowered:

    (a)   to examine the books and other business records;
    (b)   to take copies of or extracts from the books and business records;
    (c)   to ask for oral explanations on the spot;
    (d)   to enter any premises; land and means of transport of undertakings.

2. The officials of the Commission authorised for the purpose of these investigations shall exercise their powers upon production of an authorisation in writing specifying the subject matter and purpose of the investigation and the penalties provided for in Article 15(1)(c) in cases where production of the required books or other business records is incomplete. In good time before the investigation, the Commission shall inform the competent authority of the Member State in whose territory the same is to be made of the investigation and of the identity of the authorised officials.

3. Undertakings and associations of undertakings shall submit to investigations ordered by decision of the Commission. The decision shall specify the subject matter and purpose of the investigation, appoint the date on which it is to begin and indicate the penalties provided for in Article 15(1)(c) and Article 16(1)(d) and the right to have the decision reviewed by the Court of Justice.

4. The Commission shall take decisions referred to in paragraph 3 after consultation with the competent authority of the Member State in whose territory the investigation is to be made.

5. Officials of the competent authority of the Member State in whose territory the investigation is to be made may, at the request of such authority or of the Commission, assist the officials of the Commission in carrying out their duties.

6. Where an undertaking opposes an investigation ordered pursuant to this Article, the Member State concerned shall afford the necessary assistance to the officials authorised by the Commission to enable them to make their investigation. Member States shall, after consultation with the Commission, take the necessary measures to this end before October 1, 1962.[1]

---

[1]   See Art. 25, *post.*

Article 15

Fines

1. The Commission may by decision impose on undertakings or associations of undertakings fines of from 100 to 5000 units of account where, intentionally or negligently:

(a) they supply incorrect or misleading information in an application pursuant to Article 2 or in a notification pursuant to Articles 4 or 5; or

(b) they supply incorrect information in response to a request made pursuant to Article 11(3) or (5) or to Article 12, or do not supply information within the time limit fixed by a decision taken under Article 11(5); or

(c) they produce the required books or other business records in incomplete form during investigations under Article 13 or 14, or refuse to submit to an investigation ordered by decision issued in implementation of Article 14(3).

2. The Commission may by decision impose on undertakings or associations of undertakings fines of from 1,000 to 1,000,000 units of account, or a sum in excess thereof but not exceeding 10 per cent of the turnover in the preceding business year of each of the undertakings participating in the infringement where, either intentionally or negligently:

(a) they infringe Article 85(1) or Article 86 of the Treaty; or

(b) they commit a breach of any obligation imposed pursuant to Article 8(1).

In fixing the amount of the fine, regard shall be had both to the gravity and to the duration of the infringement.

3. Article 10(3) to (6) shall apply.

4. Decisions taken pursuant to paragraphs 1 and 2 shall not be of criminal law nature.

5. The fines provided for in paragraph 2 shall not be imposed in respect of acts taking place:

(a) after notification to the Commission and before its decision in application of Article 85(3) of the Treaty, provided they fall within the limits of the activity described in the notification;

(b) before notification and in the course of agreements, decisions or concerted practices in existence at the date of entry into force of this Regulation, provided that notification was effected within the time limits specified in Article 5(1) and Article 7(2).

6. Paragraph (5) shall not have effect where the Commission has informed the undertakings concerned that after preliminary examination it is of opinion that Article 85(1) of the Treaty applies and that application of Article 85(3) is not justified.

Article 16

Periodic penalty payments

1. The Commission may by decision impose on undertakings or associations of undertakings periodic penalty payments from 50 to 1000 units of account per day, calculated from the date appointed by the decision, in order to compel them:

(a) to put an end to an infringement of Article 85 or 86 of the Treaty, in accordance with a decision taken pursuant to Article 3 of this Regulation;

(b) to refrain from any act prohibited under Article 8(3);

(c) to supply complete and correct information which it has requested by decision taken pursuant to Article 11(5);

(d) to submit to an investigation which it has ordered by decision taken pursuant to Article 14(3).

2. Where the undertakings or associations of undertakings have satisfied the obligation which it was the purpose of the periodic penalty payment to enforce, the Commission may fix the total amount of the periodic penalty payment at a lower figure than that which would arise under the original decision.

3. Article 10(3) to (6) shall apply.

Article 17

Review by the Court of Justice

The Court of Justice shall have unlimited jurisdiction within the meaning of Article 172 of the Treaty to review decisions whereby the Commission has fixed a fine or periodic penalty payment; it may cancel, reduce or increase the fine or periodic penalty payment imposed.

Article 18

Unit of account

For the purposes of applying Articles 15 to 17 the unit of account shall be that adopted in drawing up the budget of the Community in accordance with Articles 207 and 209 of the Treaty.

Article 19

Hearing of the parties and of third persons

1. Before taking decisions as provided for in Articles 2, 3, 6, 7, 8, 15 and 16, the Commission shall give the undertakings or associations of undertakings concerned the opportunity of being heard on the matters to which the Commission has taken objection.

2. If the Commission or the competent authorities of the Member States consider it necessary, they may also hear other natural or legal persons. Applications to be heard on the part of such persons shall, where they show a sufficient interest, be granted.

3. Where the Commission intends to give negative clearance pursuant to Article 2 or take a decision in application of Article 85(3) of the Treaty, it shall publish a summary of the relevant application or notification and invite all interested third parties to submit their observations within a time limit which it shall fix being not less than one month. Publication shall have regard to the legitimate interest of undertakings in the protection of their business secrets.

Article 20

Professional secrecy

1. Information acquired as a result of the application of Articles 11, 12, 13 and 14 shall be used only for the purpose of the relevant request or investigation.

2. Without prejudice to the provisions of Articles 19 and 21, the Commission and the competent authorities of the Member States, their officials and other servants shall not disclose information acquired by them as a result of the application of this Regulation and of the kind covered by the obligation of professional secrecy.

3. The provisions of paragraphs 1 and 2 shall not prevent publication of general information or surveys which do not contain information relating to particular undertakings or associations of undertakings.

Article 21

Publication of decisions

1. The Commission shall publish the decisions which it takes pursuant to Articles 2, 3 6, 7 and 8.

2. The publication shall state the names of the parties and the main content of the decision; it shall have regard to the legitimate interest of undertakings in the protection of their business secrets.

Article 22

Special provisions

1. The Commission shall submit to the Council proposals for making certain categories of agreement, decision and concerted practice falling within Article 4(2) or Article 5(2) compulsorily notifiable under Article 4 or 5.

2. Within one year from the date of entry into force of this Regulation, the Council shall examine, on a proposal from the Commission, what special provisions might be made for exempting from the provisions of this Regulation agreements, decisions and concerted practices falling within Article 4(2) or Article 5(2).

Article 23

Transitional provisions applicable to decisions of authorities of the Member States

1. Agreements, decisions and concerted practices of the kind described in Article 85(1) of the Treaty to which, before the entry into force of this Regulation, the competent authority of a Member State has declared Article 85(1) to be inapplicable pursuant to Article 85(3) shall not be subject to compulsory notification under Article 5. The decision of the competent authority of the Member State shall be deemed to be a decision within the meaning of Article 6; it shall cease to be valid upon expiration of the period fixed by such authority but in any event not more than three years after the entry into force of this Regulation. Article 8(3) shall apply.

2. Applications for renewal of decisions of the kind described in paragraph 1 shall be decided upon by the Commission in accordance with Article 8(2).

Article 24

Implementing provisions

The Commission shall have power to adopt implementing provisions concerning the form, content and other details of applications pursuant to Articles 2 and 3 and of notifications pursuant to Articles 4 and 5, and concerning hearings pursuant to Article 19(1) and (2).

[Article 25

1. As regards agreements, decisions and concerted practices to which Article 85 of the Treaty applies by virtue of accession, the date of accession shall be substituted for the date of entry into force of this Regulation in every place where reference is made in this Regulation to this latter date.

2. Agreements, decisions and concerted practices existing at the date of accession to which Article 85 of the Treaty applies by virtue of accession shall be notified pursuant to Article 5(1) or Article 7(1) and (2) within six months from the date of accession.

3. Fines under Article 15(2)(a) shall not be imposed in respect of any act prior to notification of the agreements, decisions and practices to which paragraph 2 applies and which have been notified within the period therein specified.

4. New Member States shall take the measures referred to in Article 14(6) within six months from the date of accession after consulting the Commission.[1]

[5. The provisions or paragraphs 1 to 4 above shall apply in the same way in the case of the accession of the Hellenic Republic, the Kingdom of Spain and of the Portuguese Republic.]]

This regulation shall be binding in its entirety and directly applicable in all Member States.

Done at Brussels, February 6, 1962.

---

[1]   Added by the Act of Accession, Annex I.

APPENDIX 5

Notice on Co-operation Between National Courts and the Commission
in Applying Articles 85 and 86 of the EEC Treaty[1]

I. Introduction

1. The abolition of internal frontiers enables firms in the Community to embark on new activities and Community consumers to benefit from increased competition. The Commission considers that these advantages must not be jeopardized by restrictive or abusive practices of undertakings and that the completion of the internal market thus reaffirms the importance of the Community's competition policy and competition law.

2. A number of national and Community institutions have contributed to the formulation of Community competition law and are responsible for its day-to-day application. For this purpose, the national competition authorities, national and Community courts and the Commission each assume their own tasks and responsibilities, in line with the principles developed by the case-law of the Court of Justice of the European Communities.

3. If the competition process is to work well in the internal market, effective cooperation between these institutions must be ensured. The purpose of this Notice is to achieve this in relations between national courts and the Commission. It spells out how the Commission intends to assist national courts by closer cooperation in the application of Articles 85 and 86 of the EEC Treaty in individual cases.

II. Powers

4. The Commission is the administrative authority responsible for the implementation and for the thrust of competition policy in the Community and for this purpose has to act in the public interest. National courts, on the other hand, have the task of safeguarding the subjective rights of private individuals in their relations with one another.[2]

5. In performing these different tasks, national courts and the Commission possess concurrent powers for the application of Article 85 (1) and Article 86 of the Treaty. In the case of the Commission, the power is conferred by Article 89 and by the provisions adopted pursuant to Article 87. In the case of the national courts, the power derives from the direct effect of the relevant Community rules. In *BRT v. Sabam*, the Court of Justice considered that 'as the prohibitions of Articles 85 (1) and 86 tend by their very nature to produce direct effects in relations between individuals, these Articles create direct rights in respect of the individuals concerned which the national courts must safeguard'.[3]

6. In this way, national courts are able to ensure, at the request of the litigants or on their own initiative, that the competition rules will be respected for the benefit of private individuals. In addition, Article 85 (2) enables them to determine, in accordance with the national procedural law applicable, the civil law effects of the prohibition set out in Article 85.[4]

7. However, the Commission, pursuant to Article 9 of Regulation No. 17,[5] has sole power to exempt certain types of agreements, decisions and concerted practices from this prohibition. The Commission may exercise this power in two ways. It may take a decision exempting a specific agreement in an individual case. It may also adopt regulations granting block exemptions for certain categories of agreements, decisions or concerted practices, where it is authorized to do so by the Council, in accordance with Article 87.

8. Although national courts are not competent to apply Article 85 (3), they may nevertheless apply the decisions and regulations adopted by the Commission pursuant to that provision. The Court has on several

[1]   OJ 1993 C39/6.

[2]   Case C-234/89, *Delimitis v. Henninger Bräu*, [1991] ECR I-935, paragraph 44; Case T-24/90, *Automec v. Commission*, judgment of 17 September 1992, paragraphs 73 and 85 (not yet reported).

[3]   Case 127/73, *BRT v. Sabam*, [1974] ECR 51, paragraph 16.

[4]   Case 56/65, *LTM v. MBU*, [1966] ECR 337; Case 48/72, *Brasserie De Haecht v. Wilkin-Janssen*, [1973] ECR 77; Case 319/82, *Ciments et Bétons v. Kerpen & Kerpen*, [1983] ECR 4173.

[5]   Council Regulation No. 17 of 6 February 1962: First Regulation implementing Articles 85 and 86 of the Treaty (OJ 1962 13, 204/62; Special Edition 1959-62, p. 87).

occasions confirmed that the provisions of a regulation are directly applicable.[1] The Commission considers that the same is true for the substantive provisions of an individual exemption decision.

9. The powers of the Commission and those of national courts differ not only in their objective and content, but also in the ways in which they are exercised. The Commission exercises its powers according to the procedural rules laid down by regulation No. 17, whereas national courts exercise theirs in the context of national procedural law.

10. In this connection, the Court of Justice has laid down the principles which govern procedures and remedies for invoking directly applicable Community law.

'Although the Treaty has made it possible in a number of instances for private persons to bring a direct action, where appropriate, before the Court of Justice, it was not intended to create new remedies in the national courts to ensure the observance of Community law other than those already laid down by national law. On the other hand . . . it must be possible for every type of action provided for by national law to be available for the purpose of ensuring observance of Community provisions having direct effect, on the same conditions concerning the admissibility and procedure as would apply were it a question of ensuring observance of national law'.[2]

11. The Commission considers that these principles apply in the event of breach of the Community competition rules; individuals and companies have access to all procedural remedies provided for by national law on the same conditions as would apply if a comparable breach of national law were involved. This equality of treatment concerns not only the definitive finding of a breach of competition rules, but embraces all the legal means capable of contributing to effective legal protection. Consequently, it is the right of parties subject to Community law that national courts should take provisional measures, that an effective end should be brought, by injunction, to the infringement of Community competition rules of which they are victims, and that compensation should be awarded for the damage suffered as a result of infringements, where such remedies are available in proceedings relating to similar national law.

12. Here the Commission would like to make it clear that the simultaneous application of national competition law is compatible with the application of Community law, provided that it does not impair the effectiveness and uniformity of Community competition rules and the measures taken to enforce them. Any conflicts which may arise when national and Community competition law are applied simultaneously must be resolved in accordance with the principle of the precedence of Community law.[3] The purpose of this principle is to rule out any national measure which could jeopardize the full effectiveness of the provisions of Community law.

III. The Exercise of Powers by the Commission

13. As the administrative authority responsible for the Community's competition policy, the Commission must serve the Community's general interest. The administrative resources at the Commission's disposal to perform its task are necessarily limited and cannot be used to deal with all the cases brought to its attention. The Commission is therefore obliged, in general, to take all organizational measures necessary for the performance of its task and, in particular, to establish priorities.[4]

14. The Commission intends, in implementing its decision-making powers to concentrate on notifications, complaints and own-initiative proceedings having particular political, economic or legal significance for the Community. Where these features are absent in a particular case, notifications will normally be dealt with by means of comfort letter and complaints should, as a rule, be handled by national courts or authorities.

---

[1] Case 63/75, *Fonderies Roubaix v. Fonderies Roux*, [1976] ECR 111; Case C-234/89, *Delimitis v. Henninger Bräu*, [1991] ECR I-935.

[2] Case 158/80, *Rewe v. Hauptzollamt Kiel*, [1981] ECR 1805, paragraph 44; see also Case 33/76, *Rewe v. Landwirtschaftskammer Saarland*, [1976] ECR 1989; Case 79/83, *Harz v. Deutsche Tradax*, [1984] ECR 1921; Case 199/82, *Amministrazione delle Finanze dello Stato v. San Giorgio*, [1983] ECR 3595.

[3] Case 14/68, *Walt Wilhelm and Others v. Bundeskartellamt*, [1969] ECR 1; Joined Cases 253/78 and 1 to 3/79, *Procureur de la Republique v. Giry and Guerlain*, [1980] ECR 2327.

[4] Case T-24/90, *Automec v. Commission*, judgment of 17 September 1992, paragraph 77 (not yet reported).

15. The Commission considers that there is not normally a sufficient Community interest in examining a case when the plaintiff is able to secure adequate protection of his rights before the national courts.[1] In these circumstances the complaint will normally be filed.

16. In this respect the Commission would like to make it clear that the application of Community competition law by the national courts has considerable advantages for individuals and companies:

— the Commission cannot award compensation for loss suffered as a result of an infringement of Article 85 or Article 86. Such claims may be brought only before the national courts. Companies are more likely to avoid infringements of the Community competition rules if they risk having to pay damages or interest in such an event,
— national courts can usually adopt interim measures and order the ending of infringements more quickly than the Commission is able to do,
— before national courts, it is possible to combine a claim under Community law with a claim under national law. This is not possible in a procedure before the Commission,
— in some Member States, the courts have the power to award legal costs to the successful applicant. This is never possible in the administrative procedure before the Commission.

IV. Application of Articles 85 and 86 by National Courts

17. The national court may have to reach a decision on the application of Articles 85 and 86 in several procedural situations. In the case of civil law proceedings, two types of action are particularly frequent: actions relating to contracts and actions for damages. Under the former, the defendant usually relies on Article 85 (2) to dispute the contractual obligations invoked by the plaintiff. Under the latter, the prohibitions contained in Article 85 and 86 are generally relevant in determining whether the conduct which has given rise to the alleged injury is illegal.

18. In such situations, the direct effect of Article 85 (1) and Article 86 gives national courts sufficient powers to comply with their obligation to hand down judgment. Nevertheless, when exercising these powers, they must take account of the Commission's powers in order to avoid decisions which could conflict with those taken or envisaged by the Commission in applying Article 85 (1) and Article 86, and also Article 85 (3).[2]

19. In its case-law the Court of Justice has developed a number of principles which make it possible for such contradictory decisions to be avoided.[3] The Commission feels that national courts could take account of these principles in the following manner.

1. Application of Article 85 (1) and (2) and Article 86

20. The first question which national courts have to answer is whether the agreement, decision or concerted practice at issue infringes the prohibitions laid down in Article 85 (1) or Article 86. Before answering this question, national courts should ascertain whether the agreement, decision or concerted practice has already been the subject of a decision, opinion or other official statement issued by an administrative authority and in particular by the Commission. Such statements provide national courts with significant information for reaching a judgment, even if they are not formally bound by them. It should be noted in this respect that not all procedures before the Commission lead to an official decision, but that cases can also be closed by comfort letters. Whilst it is true that the Court of Justice has ruled that this type of letter does not bind national courts, it has nevertheless stated that the opinion expressed by the Commission constitutes a factor which the national courts may take into account in examining whether the agreements or conduct in question are in accordance with the provisions of Article 85.[4]

21. If the Commission has not ruled on the same agreement, decision or concerted practice, the national courts can always be guided, in interpreting the Community law in question, by the case-law of the Court of Justice and the existing decisions of the Commission. It is with this in view that the Commission has,

---

[1] Case T-24/90, cited above, paragraphs 91 to 94.

[2] Case C-234/89, *Delimitis v. Henninger Bräu*, [1991] ECR I-935, paragraph 47.

[3] Case 48/72, *Brasserie de Haecht v. Wilkin-Janssen*, [1973] ECR 77; Case 127/73, *BRT v. Sabam*, [1974] ECR 51; Case C-234/89, *Delimitis v. Henninger Bräu*, [1991] ECR I-935.

[4] Case 99/79, *Lancôme v. Etos*, (1980) ECR 2511, paragraph 11.

in a number of general notices,[1] specified categories of agreements that are not caught by the ban laid down in Article 85 (1).

22. On these bases, national courts should generally be able to decide whether the conduct at issue is compatible with Article 85 (1) and Article 86. Nevertheless if the Commission has initiated a procedure in a case relating to the same conduct, they may, if they consider it necessary for reasons of legal certainty, stay the proceedings while awaiting the outcome of the Commission's action.[2] A stay of proceedings may also be envisaged where national courts wish to seek the Commission's views in accordance with the arrangements referred to in this Notice.[3] Finally, where national courts have persistent doubts on questions of compatibility, they may stay proceedings in order to bring the matter before the Court of Justice, in accordance with Article 177 of the Treaty.

23. However, where national courts decide to give judgment and find that the conditions for applying Article 85 (1) or Article 86 are not met, they should pursue their proceedings on the basis of such a finding, even if the agreement, decision or concerted practice at issue has been notified to the Commission. Where the assessment of the facts shows that the conditions for applying the said Articles are met, national courts must rule that the conduct at issue infringes Community competition law and take the appropriate measures, including those relating to the consequences that attach to infringement of a statutory prohibition under the civil law applicable.

2. Application of Article 85 (3)

24. If the national court concludes that an agreement, decision or concerted practice is prohibited by Article 85 (1), it must check whether it is or will be the subject of an exemption by the Commission under Article 85 (3). Here several situations may arise.

25. (a) The national court is required to respect the exemption decisions taken by the Commission. Consequently, it must treat the agreement, decision or concerted practice at issue as compatible with Community law and fully recognize its civil law effects. In this respect mention should be made of comfort letters in which the Commission services state that the conditions for applying Article 85 (3) have been met. The Commission considers that national courts may take account of these letters as factual elements.

26. (b) Agreements, decisions and concerted practices which fall within the scope of application of a block exemption regulation are automatically exempted from the prohibition laid down in Article 85 (1) without the need for a Commission decision or comfort letter.[4]

27. (c) Agreements, decisions and concerted practices which are not covered by a block exemption regulation and which have not been the subject of an individual exemption decision or a comfort letter must, in the Commission's view, be examined in the following manner.

28. The national court must first examine whether the procedural conditions necessary for securing exemption are fulfilled, notably whether the agreement, decision or concerted practice has been duly notified in accordance with Article 4 (1) of Regulation No. 17. Where no such notification has been made, and subject to Article 4 (2) of Regulation No. 17, exemption under Article 85 (3) is ruled out, so that the national court may decide, pursuant to Article 85 (2), that the agreement, decision or concerted practice is void.

29. Where the agreement, decision or concerted practice has been duly notified to the Commission, the national court will assess the likelihood of an exemption being granted in the case in question in the light

---

[1]   See the notices on:
   —   exclusive dealing contracts with commercial agents (OJ 1962 No. 139 2921/62),
   —   agreements, decisions and concerted practices in the field of cooperation between enterprises (OJ 1968 C75/3, as corrected in OJ 1968 C84/14),
   —   assessment of certain subcontracting agreements (OJ 1979 C1/2),
   —   agreements of minor importance (OJ 1986 C231/2).
[2]   Case 127/73, *BRT v. Sabam*, [1974] ECR 51, paragraph 21. The procedure before the Commission is initiated by an authoritative act. A simple acknowledgement of receipt cannot be considered an authoritative act as such; Case 48/72, *Brasserie de Haecht v. Wilkin-Janssen*, [1973] ECR 77, paragraphs 16 and 17.
[3]   Case C-234/89, *Delimitis v. Henninger Bräu*, [1991] ECR I-935, paragraph 53, Part V of this Notice.
[4]   A list of the relevant regulations and of the official explanatory comments relating to them is given in the Annex to this Notice.

of the relevant criteria developed by the case law of the Court of Justice and the Court of First Instance and by previous regulations and decisions of the Commission.

30. Where the national court has in this way ascertained that the agreement, decision or concerted practice at issue cannot be the subject of an individual exemption, it will take the measures necessary to comply with the requirements of Article 85 (1) and (2). On the other hand, if it takes the view that individual exemption is possible, the national court should suspend the proceedings while awaiting the Commission's decision. If the national court does suspend the proceedings, it nevertheless remains free, according to the rules of the applicable national law, to adopt any interim measures it deems necessary.

31. In this connection, it should be made clear that these principles do not apply to agreements, decisions and concerted practices which existed before Regulation No. 17 entered into force or before that Regulation became applicable as a result of the accession of a new Member State and which were duly notified to the Commission. The national courts must consider such agreements, decisions and concerted practices to be valid so long as the Commission or the authorities of the Member States have not taken a prohibition decision or sent a comfort letter to the parties informing them that the file has been closed.[1]

32. The Commission realizes that the principles set out above for the application of Articles 85 and 86 by national courts are complex and sometimes insufficient to enable those courts to perform their judicial function properly. This is particularly so where the practical application of Article 85 (1) and Article 86 gives rise to legal or economic difficulties, where the Commission has initiated a procedure in the same case or where the agreement, decision or concerted practice concerned may become the subject of an individual exemption within the meaning of Article 85 (3). National courts may bring such cases before the Court of Justice for a preliminary ruling, in accordance with Article 177. They may also avail themselves of the Commission's assistance according to the procedures set out below.

V. Cooperation Between National Courts and the Commission

33. Article 5 of the EEC Treaty establishes the principle of constant and sincere cooperation between the Community and the Member States with view to attaining the objectives of the Treaty, including implementation of Article 3 (f), which refers to the establishment of a system ensuring that competition in the common market is not distorted. This principle involves obligations and duties of mutual assistance, both for the Member States and for the Community institutions. The Court has thus ruled that, under Article 5 of the EEC Treaty, the Commission has a duty of sincere cooperation *vis-à-vis* judicial authorities of the Member States, who are responsible for ensuring that Community law is applied and respected in the national legal system.[2]

34. The Commission considers that such cooperation is essential in order to guarantee the strict, effective and consistent application of Community competition law. In addition, more effective participation by the national courts in the day-to-day application of competition law gives the Commission more time to perform its administrative task, namely to steer competition policy in the Community.

35. In the light of these considerations, the Commission intends to work towards closer cooperation with national courts in the following manner.

36. The Commission conducts its policy so as to give the parties concerned useful pointers to the application of competition rules. To this end, it will continue its policy in relation to block exemption regulations and general notices. These general texts, the case-law of the Court of Justice and the Court of First Instance, the decisions previously taken by the Commission and the annual reports on competition policy are all elements of secondary legislation or explanations which may assist national courts in examining individual cases.

37. If these general pointers are insufficient, national courts may, within the limits of their national procedural law, ask the Commission and in particular its Directorate-General for Competition for the following information.

---

[1]   Case 48/72, *Brasserie de Haecht v. Wilkin-Janssen*, [1973] ECR 77; Case 59/77, *De Bloss v. Bouyer* [1977] ECR 2359; Case 99/79, *Lancôme v. Etos*, [1980] ECR 2511.

[2]   Case C-2/88 Imm., Zwartveld, [1990] ECR 1-3365, paragraph 18; Case C-231/89, *Delimitis v. Henninger Bräu*, [1991] ECR I-935, paragraph 53.

First, they may ask for information of a procedural nature to enable them to discover whether a certain case is pending before the Commission, whether a case has been the subject of a notification, whether the Commission has officially initiated a procedure or whether it has already taken a position through an official decision or through a comfort letter sent by its services. If necessary, national courts may also ask the Commission to give an opinion as to how much time is likely to be required for granting or refusing individual exemption for notified agreements or practices, so as to be able to determine the conditions for any decision to suspend proceedings or whether interim measures need to be adopted.[1] The Commission, for its part, will endeavour to give priority to cases which are the subject of national proceedings suspended in this way, in particular when the outcome of a civil dispute depends on them.

38. Next, national courts may consult the Commission on points of law. Where the application of Article 85 (1) and Article 86 causes them particular difficulties, national courts may consult the Commission on its customary practice in relation to the Community law at issue. As far as Articles 85 and 86 are concerned, these difficulties relate in particular to the conditions for applying these Articles as regards the effect on trade between Member States and as regards the extent to which the restriction of competition resulting from the practices specified in these provisions is appreciable. In its replies, the Commission does not consider the merits of the case. In addition, where they have doubts as to whether a contested agreement, decision or concerted practice is eligible for an individual exemption, they may ask the Commission to provide them with an interim opinion. If the Commission says that the case in question is unlikely to qualify for an exemption, national courts will be able to waive a stay of proceedings and rule on the validity of the agreement, decision or concerted practice.

39. The answers given by the Commission are not binding on the courts which have requested them. In its replies the Commission makes it clear that its view is not definitive and that the right for the national court to refer to the Court of Justice, pursuant to Article 177, is not affected. Nevertheless, the Commission considers that it gives them useful guidance for resolving disputes.

40. Lastly, national courts can obtain information from the Commission regarding factual data: statistics, market studies and economic analyses. The Commission will endeavour to communicate these data, within the limits laid down in the following paragraph, or will indicate the source from which they can be obtained.

41. It is in the interests of the proper administration of justice that the Commission should answer requests for legal and factual information in the shortest possible time. Nevertheless, the Commission cannot accede to such requests unless several conditions are met. First, the requisite data must actually be at its disposal. Secondly, the Commission may communicate this data only in so far as permitted by the general principle of sound administrative practice.

42. For example, Article 214 of the Treaty, as spelt out in Article 20 of Regulation No. 17 for the purposes of the competition rules, requires the Commission not to disclose information of a confidential nature. In addition, the duty of sincere cooperation deriving from Article 5 is one applying to the relationship between national courts and the Commission and cannot concern the position of the parties to the dispute pending before those courts. As *amicus curiae*, the Commission is obliged to respect legal neutrality and objectivity. Consequently, it will not accede to requests for information unless they come from a national court, either directly, or indirectly through parties which have been ordered by the court concerned to provide certain information. In the latter case, the Commission will ensure that its answer reaches all the parties to the proceedings.

43. Over and above such exchange of information, required in specific cases, the Commission is anxious to develop as far as possible a more general information policy. To this end, the Commission intends to publish an explanatory booklet regarding the application of the competition rules at national level.

44. Lastly, the Commission also wishes to reinforce the effect of national competition judgments. To this end, it will study the possibility of extending the scope of the Convention on jurisdiction and the enforcement of judgments in civil and commercial matters to competition cases assigned to administrative courts.[2] It should be noted that, in the Commission's view, competition judgments are already governed by this Convention where they are handed down in cases of a civil and commercial nature.

---

[1] See paragraphs 22 and 30 of this Notice.
[2] Convention of 27 September 1968 (OJ 1978 L304/77).

VI. Final Remarks

45. This Notice does not relate to the competition rules governing the transport sector.[1] Nor does it relate to the competition rules laid down in the Treaty establishing the European Coal and Steel Community.

46. This Notice is issued for guidance and does not in any way restrict the rights conferred on individuals or companies by Community law.

47. This Notice is without prejudice to any interpretation of the Community competition rules which may be given by the Court of Justice of the European Communities.

48. A summary of the answers given by the Commission pursuant to this Notice will be published annually in the Competition Report.

ANNEX

BLOCK EXEMPTIONS

A. ENABLING COUNCIL REGULATIONS

I. **Vertical agreements** (see under B.I and B.II)

Council Regulation No. 19/65/EEC of 2 March 1965 on the application of Article 85 (3) of the Treaty to certain categories of agreements and concerted practices (OJ 1965-66 Spec. Ed. 35).

II. **Horizontal agreements** (see under B.III)

Council Regulation (EEC) No. 2821/71 of 20 December 1971 on the application of Article 85 (3) of the Treaty to categories of agreements, decisions and concerted practices (OJ 1971-III Spec. Ed. 1032), modified by Regulation (EEC) No. 2743/72 of 19 December 1972 (OJ 1972 Spec. Ed. 60).

B. COMMISSION BLOCK EXEMPTION REGULATIONS AND EXPLANATORY NOTICES

I. **Distribution agreements**

1. Commission Regulation (EEC) No. 1983/83 of 22 June 1983 concerning exclusive distribution agreements (OJ 1983 L173/1).

2. Commission Regulation (EEC) No. 1984/83 of 22 June 1983 concerning exclusive purchasing agreements (OJ 1983 L173/5).

3. Commission Notice concerning Commission Regulations (EEC) No. 1983/83 and (EEC) No. 1984/83 (OJ 1984 C101/2).

4. Commission Regulation (EEC) No. 123/85 of 12 December 1984 concerning motor vehicle distribution and servicing agreements (OJ 1985 L15/16).

5. Commission Notice concerning regulation (EEC) No. 123/85 (OJ 1985 C17/4).

6. Commission Notice on the clarification of the activities of motor vehicle intermediaries (OJ 1991 C329/20).

---

[1] Regulation No. 141/62 of the Council of 26 November 1962 exempting transport from the application of Council Regulation No. 17 (OJ 124 1962 2751/62), as amended by Regulations Nos. 165/65/EEC (OJ 210 1965 3141/65) and 1002/67/EEC (JO 306,1967 1): Regulation (EEC) No. 1017/68 of the Council of 19 July 1968 applying rules of competition to transport by rail, road and inland waterway (OJ 1968 L175/1); Council Regulation (EEC) No. 4056/86 of 22 December 1986 laying down detailed rules for the application of Articles 85 and 86 of the Treaty to maritime transport (OJ 1986 L378/4); Council Regulation (EEC) No. 3975/87 of 14 December 1987 laying down the procedure for the application of the rules on competition to undertakings in the air transport sector (OJ 1987 L374/1).

II. Licensing and franchising agreements

1. Commission Regulation (EEC) No. 2349/84 of 23 July 1984 concerning patent licensing agreements (OJ 1984 L219/15; corrigendum OJ 1985 L280/32).

2. Commission Regulation (EEC) No. 4087/88 of 30 November 1988 concerning franchising agreements (OJ 1988 L359/46).

3. Commission Regulation (EEC) No. 556/89 of 30 November 1988 concerning know-how licensing agreements (OJ 1989 L61/1).

III. Cooperative agreements

1. Commission Regulation (EEC) No. 417/85 of 19 December 1984 concerning specialization agreements (OJ 1985 L53/1).

2. Commission Regulation (EEC) No. 418/85 of 19 December 1984 concerning research and development agreements (OJ 1985 L53/5).

APPENDIX 6

ENFORCEMENT OF THE COMPETITION RULES[1]

Enforcement by the National Courts

As was stated in Chapter I, the European Community has, at its disposal, a number of instruments for applying and implementing Community policy. Community rules, in the form of regulations and decisions are directly applicable and binding in the Member States. Regulations are generally applicable, while decisions are binding on those to whom they are addressed. Treaty provisions and directives are also capable of conferring rights upon private litigants to the extent that they have direct effect as defined by the European Court of Justice.

In practical terms, it is now established that the Community competition rules create rights and obligations for private legal parties which may be raised in national legal proceedings. Accordingly, any company or individual who claims to have suffered injury as a result of actions which were in breach of Community competition law has access, in principle to a national remedy, and is entitled to make a claim for damages. However, the exact legal nature of the claim and the level of damages available will vary according to local jurisdictional rules and procedures.

To date, undertakings concerned about a possible breach of the competition rules have tended to use the Community's own complaints procedure (see the following section of this chapter) in preference to direct action against the alleged offenders in the national courts. This is despite the fact that the powers of the Commission and the Court of Justice, while extensive, do not include the award of damages to injured parties.

Where a person or company suffers loss, as a result of such an infringement, it may therefore, be appropriate to seek relief using available local remedies. In this connection, plaintiffs should be aware of the possibility, available to all national judges, of referring questions of Community law to the European Court of Justice for a preliminary ruling. Courts of final appeal are obliged to seek a preliminary ruling, where a decision on the question is necessary to enable it to give judgment.

Enforcement by the Commission

Running parallel to the possibility of such actions before national courts is an elaborate procedure of application of the competition rules by the Commission. In some ways, this procedure has further-reaching consequences for the firms involved than actions at national level, in that, for example:

(i)   the Commission has the power to impose administrative fines for infringement of the competition rules;

(ii) the Commission has extensive powers to collect the information it needs in order to determine whether an infringement is taking place;

(iii) only the Commission has the power to grant exemptions on the basis of Article 85(3);

(iv) the Commission can take interim measures to bring damaging behaviour to an immediate halt.

The procedure before the Commission cannot, however, culminate in an award of damages to the victim. Fines imposed are paid to the Commission, not to the injured party.

The Initiation of a Procedure

There are a number of ways in which a procedure before the Commission involving the competition rules can be set in motion:

(a)   notification, for negative clearance or for exemption;
(b)   complaints;
(c)   own-initiative action by the Commission;
(d)   sector investigations by the Commission.

---

[1]   This extract is Chapter IV of the Commission's Periodical 1/1989, EEC Competition Policy in the Single Market.

Notification

The Mechanism of Notification

Agreements between enterprises and decisions by associations (eg trade associations) may be submitted to the Commission to seek a decision from the latter that the agreement does not violate Article 85(1) at all (this is a negative clearance) or that the agreement does fall under Article 85(1) but meets the conditions for exemption under Article 85(3). Although the correct terminology is 'application for negative clearance' and 'notification for exemption', the term 'notification' is used for both possibilities. In fact, applicants will normally submit one notification to the Commission seeking negative clearance, or in the alternative, individual exemption.

Note: No notification is necessary when an agreement falls under one of the group exemptions.

Notification must be made in writing on an official form issued by the Commission (Form A/B). This form requires the applicant(s) to give detailed information relating to the parties to the agreement and the essential features and aims of the agreement. To avoid any possible misunderstanding, it is wise to attach a copy of the agreement in its entirety to the form.

Notification need not be made by all those concluding an agreement, but whoever takes it upon himself to notify must in any event be a party to the agreement. Officially authorised representatives are also committed to submit a notification.

Finally, enterprises should be aware of the importance of submitting accurate, complete and truthful information in their notifications. The Commission has the power to impose fines of up to ecu 5,000 where applicants intentionally or through negligence supply incorrect or misleading information in a notification.

Copies of Form A/B and the accompanying explanatory memorandum prepared by the Commission can be obtained from the Commission's Information Offices in each Member State and also outside the Community (a list of these addresses is given at the end of this brochure).

The Importance of Notification

There are three main reasons why notification can be very important to firms:

(i)   as a rule the Commission cannot grant negative clearance or an individual exemption with regard to any agreement which has not been notified to it in the proper manner;

(ii)   no administrative fines can be imposed by the Commission for activities which take place after notification and until the Commission reaches a decision, final or provisional, as to the applicability of Article 85(1) and/or Article 85(3), provided those activities do not go beyond those described in the notification;

(iii)   where the Commission has established an opposition procedure for 'borderline' cases, the operation of this procedure requires notification of the agreement.

The fines which can be imposed for actual violation of Articles 85(1) and 86 must be distinguished from the (more minor) fines which can be imposed where a notification intentionally or negligently contains misleading or untruthful information.

There are two exceptions to the general rule that, to obtain an exemption under Article 85(3), the agreement in question must be notified to the Commission:

(1)   agreements which fall under one of the group exemptions are automatically exempted (subject to notification, to qualify under the opposition procedure);

(2)   certain types of agreement do not have to be notified, and can nevertheless, if the case arises, be exempted by the Commission retrospectively to the date on which the agreement was concluded. In broad lines, the requirement to notify does not apply to:

  (a)   agreements between parties located only in one Member State and not relating to imports or exports, in other words, agreements which are purely domestic or local in scope;

(b)   agreements between two parties in which the sole restriction is a unilateral restriction on one of the parties as to prices and terms of resale or as to the exercise of industrial property rights or know-how;

(c)   agreements between two parties which have as their sole object:
   —   the development or uniform application of certain standards or types, or
   —   joint research and development, or
   —   specialization in manufacturing, where the market share is not more than 20% and aggregate annual turnover not more than ECU 500 million.

A caveat should be added:

(i)   in case any doubt exists as to whether a particular agreement falls under one of the categories for which notification is not required, the parties should not hesitate to notify;

(ii)   the advice 'when in doubt, do notify' is especially important because the benefit of immunity from fines is available only with respect to notified agreements and agreements covered by group exemptions.

Quick Checklist in Connection with Notification

When deciding whether or not an agreement should be notified to the Commission, undertakings should run through the following questions:

(i)   Does the agreement have any connection at all with competition? If not—for example, the agreement concerns a simple sale of goods—there is no need to contemplate notification.

(ii)   If the agreement does feature certain restrictions on competition, are the competition rules nevertheless inapplicable because, for example, the effects are minimal, or the activity is covered by one of the relevant Commission notices? If so, parties need not notify.

(iii) If the agreement seems likely to contain elements which are contrary to Article 85(1), but also appears to the parties to fulfil the requirements for exemption under Article 85(3), parties must determine:
   (a)   whether the agreement falls under one of the group exemptions. If so there is no need to notify. The agreement is safe and no fines can subsequently be imposed;
   (b)   whether the agreement is one of the types of agreement for which notification is not required. If so there is no need to notify, exemption can if necessary be obtained later, even in the absence of notification. One risk in not notifying is, however, that immunity from fines is not guaranteed.

If neither of the above applies, parties should make the proper notification on Form A/B as soon as possible after concluding the agreement (or even before). The importance of timely notification lies in the fact that fines may still be imposed for the period preceding notification.

Complaints

General

Anti-competitive behaviour can be brought to the attention of the Commission by way of a complaint.

Potential complainants should first carefully consider a number of questions:

(i)   Is the object of the complaint autonomous behaviour by undertakings or is the behaviour imposed by national legislation? In the latter case, the competition rules do not apply.

(ii)   Is there a transfrontier effect involved in the behaviour? If not, the matter would be one of national, not Community, competence.

(iii) Are all the other elements of either Article 85 or 86 fulfilled? For actions under Article 85, the complainant should check whether the agreement in question is perhaps *de minimis*. In that case, there is no point in complaining. For Article 86 cases, a dominant position is required—not always an easy requirement to prove—and there must be an abuse thereof.

(iv)   Would action before a national court be preferable in order to obtain damages?

In short to avoid wasting the time of all involved, complaints should only be submitted after careful consideration.

Who Can Complain?

Those entitled to submit complaints are Member State authorities, individuals or legal persons, such as companies or trade associations.

One essential requirement is that a complainant must have a legitimate interest in the termination of the objectionable behaviour. Parties to an agreement would in any event be deemed to have a legitimate interest. Furthermore, any third party who can show that the alleged anti-competitive behaviour is damaging—even potentially—to him, will normally have a legitimate interest.

Consequences

When a complaint is submitted by a party having a legitimate interest in the matter, the Commission will examine whether a violation of the competition rules is in fact taking place. If the complaint turns out to be well-founded, the Commission can then take the necessary measures to put an end to the infringement. If, on the other hand, the Commission, after examining the matter, find that the complaint is not justified, it must inform the complainant of its reasons for not pursuing the matter. The complainant must then be allowed a certain period of time to submit any further comments, after which the Commission will either continue its investigation, if new facts have come to light, or definitely reject the complaint.

Form and Contents of a Complaint

There are no specific requirements as to the form in which a complaint is made. However, given the fact that the Commission is only obliged to investigate a complaint by a party showing a legitimate interest in the matter, it is in the interest of the complainant clearly to present the facts involved in writing. A simple letter is sufficient. The complaint should in any even include:

(a) the name and address of the complainant;
(b) the identity of the undertaking(s) which are the subject of the complaint;
(c) evidence which support the complainant's claim to a legitimate interest in the matter;
(d) a clear description of the substance of the complaint and, if possible, the reasons why the complainant believes the behaviour in question constitutes an infringement of Article 85 and/or 86;
(e) if the complainant is signed by a representative, evidence of his authority to act on behalf of the complainant.

The party who is the subject of the complaint will be informed of the complaint against him and will be given the opportunity to present his views. In this context, the complainant would be well advised to indicate clearly which parts of his complaint are to be considered as confidential and thus not to be transmitted to the party in question.

Informal or Anonymous Complaints

The Commission also receives oral—sometimes anonymous—complaints. The difference with the 'formal' complaints described above is that the Commission is under no obligation to examine such so-called informal complaints, although it may of course do so if it wishes.

Therefore, where there is serious evidence that an infringement of the competition rules is taking place, any undertaking which is being harmed by the behaviour in question should contemplate the advantage of lodging a formal complaint in writing.

Own-initiative Intervention by the Commission

There is a variety of ways in which the Commission can become aware of possibly anti-competitive behaviour. These include questions raised in the European Parliament, articles in newspapers, information received from Member State authorities, or contacts with interest groups, such as consumer organizations. Although the Commission is not obliged to pursue matters which come to its attention in this way, it can decide on its own initiative to examine further, such cases and will definitely do so if the information it has received seems to point to a serious infringement of the competition rules.

Furthermore, the Commission has the power to conduct general inquiries into economic sectors where it feels competition is being restricted or distorted. Such inquiries have, for example, taken place in the brewery industry and the margarine industry.

Fact-finding by the Commission: Procedural Decisions

Where the Commission decides that commercial activities which have come to its attention seem to pose problems in the context of the competition rules, it will normally need more information to be able to reach a definite opinion on the legality of the behaviour in question.

There are two basic ways in which the Commission can obtain information from undertakings:

(i)   written requests for information;
(ii)   investigations.

Requests for Information

The Commission can send written requests (including telexes) for information, not only to undertakings which are suspected of infringements, but also to third parties who may be in a position to clarify certain matters. For example, where the Commission is examining the behaviour of a dominant firm, it may ask smaller firms who have dealings with that firm to indicate whether they have ever been subject to specific abusive treatment by it.

Requests for information involve the following consequences:

(i)   where the undertakings interrogated reply promptly, correctly and completely to the Commission's letter, no further complications need be feared (although the Commission may, of course, subsequently request additional information);

(ii)   if in their reply the undertakings concerned provide incorrect or incomplete information, the Commission has the right to impose fines of up to ECU 5000;

(iii) if the undertakings choose to ignore the initial request for information altogether, or if their reply is incomplete, the Commission may as a second step take a formal decision ordering complete information to be supplied. Failure to respond to this formal decision is not to be recommended, because daily default fines of up to ECU 1000 can be imposed by the Commission until a complete reply is finally received.

In sum, undertakings who receive a request for information from the Commission must seriously bear in mind:

(a)   that if they decide to reply, that reply must be correct and complete;
(b)   that if they do not reply to the first request for information, they stand the risk of subsequently being forced to reply anyway, if necessary, by means of daily default payments.

Investigations

The Commission has the power to send authorized officials to the premises of undertakings in order to gather the information it needs. The officials who make an inspection visit are entitled to examine the company's business records and documents, take copies of extracts thereof, request explanations and enter all premises, land or vehicles belonging to the company. Again, as in the case of written requests for information, undertakings who submit to such an inspection but produce the requested material in incomplete form run the risk of fines of up to ECU 5000.

Undertakings are not obliged to admit Commission officials who come on inspection, but the Commission may then proceed to take a formal decision ordering them to comply, if necessary reinforced by a daily penalty payment of up to ECU 1000 for each day the undertaking refuses to admit the Commission inspectors.

The Commission is not obliged first to give the undertaking concerned the opportunity to comply with an investigation based on a simple mandate before passing on to the more forceful instrument or ordering the undertaking to comply by a formal decision. Normally, the Commission will resort to an unannounced visit by decision at the outset where a serious risk exists that the undertakings, if forewarned of the inspection, will destroy any incriminating evidence.

Undertakings who receive a visit from Commission inspectors are allowed to ask for a legal adviser to be present, but the inspection can not be unduly delayed to await the arrival of such a person.

The Procedure Leading to a Final Decision

The three basic types of decisions which the Commission can take in application of Articles 85 and 86 are:

(i) decisions granting negative clearance;
(ii) exemption decisions pursuant to Article 85(3);
(iii) decisions ordering the termination of an infringement.

The procedural decisions which the Commission can take in connection with its powers of investigation, for example, ordering an undertaking to admit Commission inspectors, have been dealt with in the preceding paragraph.

Other measures which may occur when the Commission deals with a case are:

(a) interim measures;
(b) provisional decisions;
(c) informal settlements.

Negative Clearance

When an undertaking has made an application on Form A/B, seeking formal assurance from the Commission that its agreement or other commercial activities are not deemed to infringe the competition rules, the Commission must first give any other interested parties the chance to make their views on the matter known. This is done by publishing the main facts of the case in the *Official Journal*. Any interested parties are given a specific period of time to react to this publication and thus new facts may be brought to light which may cause the Commission to reconsider its position.

A second formality which must be observed before negative clearance can be given is consultation of Member States authorities, who meet for this purpose in the body referred to as the 'Advisory Committee on Restrictive Practices and Dominant Positions'.

If after these steps have been observed the Commission maintains the view that negative clearance is justified, a formal decision is taken which states that on the basis of the facts in its possession, there are no grounds for the Commission to take any action under Article 85(1) and/or Article 86 against the agreement or other commercial activity involved.

It is clear that if new facts subsequently arise or if the circumstances involved change substantially, the Commission retains the power to reconsider the matter. To date, however, no cases have occurred in which the Commission has gone back on a decision granting negative clearance.

Exemption

As in the case of negative clearances, a decision granting exemption must be preceded by publication in the *Official Journal* of the main elements involved, giving interested parties the opportunity to submit any observations, and by consultation of the Advisory Committee on Restrictive Practices and Dominant Positions.

The Commission's decision indicates why the agreement or other activity in question is deemed to violate Article 85(1) and what elements have been found by the Commission which fulfil all the requirements for justifying an exemption under Article 85(3).

Exemption is always granted for a fixed period of time, which can be extended. The decision may impose certain obligations on the undertakings involved and in some cases, the parties may be requested to modify certain aspects of their agreement before exemption can be granted at all.

Normally, exemption can only be granted as of the date of notification. Only in the case of certain types of agreement which need not be notified (as above) can exemption be granted as of the date on which the agreement was concluded.

Decisions Attacking an Infringement

(i)   Procedure

When a matter comes to its attention through a complaint, a notification or in any other way, the Commission may reach the preliminary conclusions that a violation of Article 85(1) or 86 is taking place and, in the case of notifications, that the conditions for granting an exemption under Article 85(3) are not present.

The Commission must give the parties concerned notice of its objections to their behaviour in the form of a written communication known as the 'statement of objections'. Annexed to the statement of objections is a list of the documents which constitutes the Commission's file in a particular case. In order to prepare their response, parties may examine the file on the Commission's premises, although documents of a confidential nature, for example, concerning other undertakings' business secrets or internal Commission notes, are normally not accessible. Parties are given a specific time-limit—normally one or two months, depending on the complexity of the case—to respond in writing to the Commission's objections.

After their written response, parties can also request an opportunity to argue their case orally. This 'oral hearing' is organized by the Directorate-General for Competition and is conducted by the Hearing Officer. This official ensures that the rights of the defence are respected and has the right to make observations to ensure that in the procedure leading to the Commission's decision, due account is taken of all the relevant facts, whether favourable or unfavourable to the parties concerned.

Following the oral hearing, the Commission must consult the Advisory Committee on Restrictive Practices and Dominant Positions.

Only after all these procedural steps have taken place can the Commission come to a final decision.

(ii)   Contents of the Decision

Where an infringement is found to exist, the Commission will order the undertaking involved to put an end to it forthwith, a so-called cease and desist order. Of course, where the parties have already terminated the infringement, for example, during the course of the procedure before the Commission, the decision may simply consist of a declaration that the behaviour in question constituted an infringement.

If appropriate, the Commission also has the power to order positive action by the undertakings involved. For example, where a dominant undertaking has been found to abuse its position by refusing to supply a customer, the Commission may require that firm to resume supplies within a specified period and ensure appropriate supply arrangements for the future.

(iii)   Fines

The Committee has the power to impose fines of up to ECU 1 million or 10% of the world annual turnover of the undertaking concerned in the previous business year (whichever of the two is greater), where undertakings are found to have infringed Article 85(1) or 86, intentionally or through negligence.

Whether or not a fine will be imposed, and the determination of the amount of the fine, will depend, among other things, on the seriousness of the behaviour, how long it went on and the size of the undertakings involved. A deliberate infringement will normally deserve a heavier fine than where undertakings can only be accused of negligence. Activities which have been frequently attacked by the Commission in the past will also warrant heavier fines, because such undertakings should realise, through the case-law built up by the Commission and the Court of Justice, that this behaviour is not permitted.

With respect to notified agreements, fines cannot be imposed for the period between the moment of notification and the Commission's decision, whether provisional or definite (see below).

Fines are, however, possible for the period during which the agreement was in force before notification.

Also, where the Commission refuses to grant an exemption, the result is that the agreement in question, whose illegality is thus confirmed, may give rise to actions in national courts, for example, for damages.

Interim Measures

Depending on the complexity of any given case, it may take the Commission one or two years or even more to reach a final decision. During that time, the behaviour in question may give rise to serious and irreparable damage to, for example, a complainant, whose very existence may be threatened, or it may be totally unacceptable in the general public interest. In such cases of urgency, the Commission has the power to take immediate action in the form of so-called interim measures to stop the objectionable behaviour. Such measures are of a temporary nature aimed at safeguarding the status quo and do not determine the final outcome of the matter being dealt with.

Provisional Decisions

The general rule is that once an agreement has been notified, no fines can be imposed with respect to the period after notification. This immunity from fines can, however, be lost where the Commission takes a provisional decision informing the parties that after preliminary examination, it is of the opinion that Article 85(1) applies and exemption under Article 85(3) is not justified.

If the parties disregard this warning, they run the serious risk of being fined in the Commission's final decision.

Informal Settlements—Administrative Letters

For the sake of expediency, many cases before the Commission are concluded by way of an informal settlement, notably where the undertakings involved voluntarily eliminate any objectionable practices. In fact, the Commission normally takes 20 or so formal decisions each year, whereas the number of informal settlements is usually several hundred.

In some cases, informal settlements take place by way of 'administrative letters' in which the Commission services inform the parties that it sees no reason to take any action under the competition rules and that the relevant file will therefore be closed. Such letters are administrative documents and do not have the legally binding effects of decisions, but may nevertheless be useful as guidance. Also, the Commission's recently instituted practice of publishing a notice of its intention to issue an administrative letter in certain cases, allowing third parties to react before it takes any further steps, enhances the value of such administrative letters.

Publicity

Decisions granting negative clearance, exemption or ordering the termination of an infringement, as well as interim measures and provisional decisions, must be published in the *Official Journal*. Procedural decisions, such as those formally requesting an undertaking to supply information, need not be published in the *Official Journal*, but the Commission may nevertheless decide to do so, for example in cases of general interest.

The Commission normally issues press releases regarding the decisions it has taken. Press releases can also be used to make the general public aware of informal settlements which for some reason contain important elements which are of general interest.

Finally, the Commission's monthly *Bulletin*, as well as the annual *Report on Competition Policy*, contain information on the decisions and informal settlements that have taken place.

Control Over the Commission by the European Court of Justice

The European Court of Justice has the following powers of review over decisions taken by the Commission:

(i)   the Court has the power to confirm, reduce, cancel or increase fines and penalty payments imposed by Commission decisions;

(ii)   all formal decisions by the Commission—negative clearances, decision granting or refusing exemption, orders to terminate infringements, decisions requesting information, orders to submit to an investigation and provisional decisions relating to the immunity from fines—can be reviewed and, if necessary, annulled or varied by the Court.

Furthermore, appeals can be brought before the Court where the Commission has failed to act, for example, failure to examine a formal complaint that has been submitted to it or to inform the complainant of its reasons for not pursuing the matter after preliminary examination.

Those entitled to bring actions before the Court are all natural or legal persons against whom a decision has been taken as well as any other parties who are directly and personally affected by a decision.

MINUTES OF EVIDENCE

TAKEN BEFORE THE EUROPEAN COMMUNITIES COMMITTEE
(SUB-COMMITTEE E)

WEDNESDAY 28 APRIL 1993

Present:

Boston of Faversham, L.   Oliver of Aylmerton, L.
Elles, B.   Slynn of Hadley, L. (Chairman)
Holme of Cheltenham, L.   Wedderburn of Charlton, L.

Memorandum by Mr Michael Reynolds, Head of EC Competition Group, Allen & Overy

INTRODUCTION

It is a great pleasure to have an opportunity to present evidence to the Select Committee on procedural aspects of the EC competition rules. The 1982 Report of the Committee played a major part in a number of important procedural changes being made which improved the rights of defence of parties involved in competition investigations and which helped reduce delay in Commission procedures. The introduction of a Hearing Officer to protect defendants' rights, the granting of access to the Commission's files, the greater use of comfort letters and block exemption regulations to cut down on the delay in Commission procedure are all examples. An important number of suggestions made in evidence to the Committee and accepted by the Committee itself were not taken up and are as relevant today as they were when they were made in 1982.

One of the most important problems identified in the 1982 Report was the long delay in dealing with claims for Article 85(3) exemptions or with an application for negative clearance and the lengthy nature of Commission proceedings generally. A number of causes were identified, particularly the lack of adequate staffing in DGIV. After 14 years in Brussels I still see this as one of the major problems in the application of the competition rules. It is a problem which deprives companies doing business in the Community of the legal certainty which they require. Much of the evidence presented to the Committee and the Committee's own conclusions recommended the alteration of Community law to provide for automatic exemption after the lapse of a suitable time from the application for exemption. It was suggested that this automatic exemption should last for a fixed period or until the Commission finally decided whether an exemption was to be granted. Unfortunately, this recommendation was never accepted by the Commission because it would require an amendment to Regulation 17, once described as the " Ark of the Covenant ". This possibility has also always been regarded by the Commission as the opening of Pandora's box. Other suggestions which were adopted, such as the increased use of block exemptions, did improve the position but fundamental problems remain for those who have to make an individual application for exemption because their agreement does not fit within the block exemption. The Commission is aware of these problems. Sir Leon Brittan, in his recent speech to the Centre for European Policy Studies (CEPS), acknowledged that the Commission's decision making process could hamper European industry in its attempts to compete on ever-widening markets. Sir Leon announced that every case would be dealt with in a fixed, predictable and reasonable period of time, and deadlines would be introduced first for structural cases and then for all other notifications and all complaints. It is too early to tell how effective these deadlines (which will be purely internal in nature) will be. They do not go as far as the 1982 Report's recommendations which would have given parties a firm legally binding automatic exemption once the specified period had been passed.

It is clear that delays in decision making are not only due to lack of manpower. There are other important factors. The need for translation of key documents, the consultation process between the services of the Commission and frequent disagreements about policy which arise between them, together with DGIV's own hierarchical decision making structure have all added to the slowness of the procedure. The evidence below attempts to illustrate the difficulties which this can cause for notifiers and complainants alike. The evidence considers how the situation might be improved by national courts playing a greater role, as was foreseen in the *Delimitis* judgment (Case C-234/89, *Delimitis* v *Henniger Bräu* [1991] ECR 935) and as further detailed in the Commission Notice on co-operation between national courts and the Commission (OJ C 39/60 of 13.2.93).

The procedures under the Merger Control Regulation are important since there have now been over 150 formal notifications to the Merger Task Force. In general, the system set up at the beginning of 1990 has worked well and the efficient way that the Task Force has dealt with cases has been much praised by companies and their advisers. However, some aspects of the Regulation require improvement. In particular, it is difficult to negotiate settlements with the Commission in the first one-month phase of proceedings which means that in some cases the proceedings often have had to go, perhaps unnecessarily, into the more complicated and drawn out " Phase Two ", which can last for a further four months before a settlement can be achieved.

The key question for the future of the Regulation is whether the thresholds for its application will be reduced. The Regulation was the child of compromise between the Commission and the Member States. Certain Member States wanted the thresholds to be even higher than they are now and the Commission wanted them to be lower. A review is currently in progress but it is not at all certain that the thresholds will be lowered as a result. This could mean that many significant mergers with cross-border effects may have to be dealt with on a country by country basis and will be deprived of the benefits of the " one-stop shop ". On the whole, companies prefer that their arrangements should fall within the Regulation since this means that their case is dealt with in a short time-frame and without the need to obtain clearances in a number of different Member States. The treatment of concentrations falling within the Regulation has to date compared favourably with that accorded to " co-operative " joint ventures which have been handled under Articles 85 and 86 where no time limits have applied. The Commission proposes to deal with these cases in future by a system of " internal " deadlines. This is a welcome step forward. These deadlines will be internal in nature, and it is hoped will contribute significantly to a speeding up of procedures.

The evidence covers other aspects of procedure and policy in the application of Articles 85 and 86. One particular area of concern is the current fining policy of the Commission. There are a number of points here. In the first place, the criteria and methods used by the Commission to calculate fines are not transparent. In recent years there has been a tendency to impose very heavy fines out of all proportion to those imposed in earlier years. There can be no doubt that this has been part of a deliberate policy of deterrence on the part of the Commission. An example is the fine of ECU 75 million imposed on Tetra Pak. This submission examines the consistency of the Commission's fining policy and the need for greater transparency.

The submission also considers the general question of transparency of Commission procedures and the Commission's power to obtain information.

There are three annexes. The first is a list of all Commission proceedings to date under the Merger Control Regulation, showing which cases have been cleared in one month or dealt with under the second phase of proceedings and describing the types of decision taken, products covered and the nationalities of the notifiers. The second annex is a table showing fines imposed for infringements illustrating the nature and length of the infringements, and the third shows the number of cases settled by final decision or comfort letter.

All views expressed in this submission are purely personal.

A.   PROCEDURES UNDER THE MERGER CONTROL REGULATION

On the whole, the experience of the procedures adopted under the Merger Control Regulation has been a good one. Indeed clients now often prefer transactions to fall within the Regulation than outside it. They would rather deal with the one-stop shop offered by the Merger Task Force than deal with a number of national merger control authorities in the Member States. The tight time limits which are laid down under the Regulation also offer greater legal certainty, particularly since they have been respected. We have even had cases where clients will not proceed with transactions unless they fall within the Regulation's thresholds. This is relevant to the question of whether the thresholds will be, or should be, reduced.

PRE-NOTIFICATION CONTACTS

One of the most satisfactory aspects of the operation of the Merger Task Force has been its willingness to engage in informal discussion with the parties before the deadline for notification arises under the Regulation. These meetings are easy to arrange and have a variety of uses. First, they enable the parties to have clear guidance as to whether the Regulation will apply to their transaction, which is particularly helpful in cases where the calculation of turnover is difficult or where it is necessary to decide whether the operation is concentrative or co-operative in nature. Early advice on questions such as these can save the parties a great deal of time and effort. Another important aspect of the pre-notification discussion is the help that it gives to completion of the notification Form CO. The Form is highly complex and requires the submission of a large amount of information. However, in practice, the Commission's implementing regulation permits the granting of a waiver in respect of information which will not really be necessary to the Task Force's enquiry if this is requested before notification. Through these preliminary discussions, it is possible to prepare the Form in such a way that difficulties will be avoided after it has been submitted. A further useful function of the pre-notification meeting is that it serves to identify possible areas of concern enabling the parties to adjust their transactions or the terms of any agreement before the notification is submitted. It is also possible at these early meetings to have an idea of whether the Commission officials are likely to have serious doubts as to the compatibility of the transaction with the Common Market, which might result in " Phase Two " proceedings being opened. We have quite often found that it is useful to attend these pre-notification meetings with a draft notification form which can be the object of early comments from the Commission officials. In our experience the pre-notification meetings with the Commission have taken place in strict confidence and there have been no leaks at Commission level.

NOTIFICATION

When the original draft Form CO was first introduced it was badly received. Representations were made to the Commission that the form was too complex and asked for a great deal of information which was unnecessary. I was involved in making submissions to the Commission on behalf of the Anti-Trust Committee of the International Bar Association of which I am Vice-Chairman. As a result of the many submissions which it received, the Commission modified Form CO considerably and was encouragingly responsive to the points raised. However, even after the extensive changes which were made, Form CO still asks for a large amount of very complicated information, some of which will not be in the possession of the notifier, especially in a contested bid situation. For example, under Section 6 " General Conditions in Affected Markets ", one is required to provide in relation to each relevant affected product market information about the distribution channels and service networks that exist in general (including those of competitors). Under Section 6.11, one is required to state the extent to which co-operative agreements exist in the affected markets, which again seems to assume a knowledge of arrangements between competitors. Notifiers are also required to provide a comparison of their prices and those prevailing in the EC, the United States, Japan and the EFTA countries which is often a difficult exercise.

Technically speaking, unless all sections are completed in full or good reasons are given explaining why it has not been possible to complete unanswered questions, the notification will be incomplete. Notifications only become effective on the date that complete information is received by the Commission. This has the consequence that time limits only begin to run once the Commission has received a notification which it considers complete. Several notifications have been returned to notifiers as incomplete.

This underlines the importance of pre-notification consultation with the Merger Task Force to discuss the extent to which information required by Form CO need not be provided. Where the Task Force consider they do not need particular items of information which would otherwise be required, they may waive the obligation to supply it. Those cases where notifications have been returned as incomplete have generally been those where the parties have not had any pre-notification meetings with the Commission and in general, notifications which have encountered problems have tended to be those where no serious advance consultation has taken place.

Even where extensive information is given in the notification form, this will not prevent the Commission sending lengthy requests for information which has to be supplied within short time limits. This has happened in a number of cases, particularly those where the Commission was considering the opening of Phase Two proceedings. To be bombarded with such lengthy requests for information to be supplied at short notice often puts a severe strain on companies and their advisers. However, this is probably an unavoidable problem if the Commission is to carry out thorough investigations of mergers within tight time limits.

One of the interesting features of the application of the Regulation has been its wide territorial reach. A graphic illustration of the Regulation's long reach is the *Kyowa/Saitama* case (Case IV/M 0069, decision of 14.3.91 OJ C 66/13). This concerned a domestic Japanese merger between Kyowa Bank and Saitama Bank who both enjoyed a strong position in Japan, being ranked 17th and 20th respectively, by equity. One tenth of the total assets of both parties amounted to ECU 20 billion and we are told that the amount of these assets attributable to the Community was sufficient to constitute a Community dimension under the special method of calculation contained in Article 5(3). Kyowa has two wholly owned subsidiaries in the United Kingdom and the Netherlands, a branch office in Frankfurt and representative offices in Amsterdam and Frankfurt. Saitama has wholly owned subsidiaries in the United Kingdom and Belgium and a representative office in Frankfurt. However, both banks concentrate on retail customers and small businesses lending in metropolitan Tokyo and the great majority of their business is done outside the Community, the main aim of their international business being to support and assist their domestic customer base. They have no retail banking network in the Community. Nevertheless, the parties were required to provide details of their main fields of activity in the Community wholesale banking sector. The banks' extremely low shares in the Community's financial markets resulted in a clearance.

The effect of the Regulation's long geographical reach is compounded where a concentrative joint venture is established outside the Community but notification needs to be made because the turnover of the joint venture's parents in the Community exceeds the threshold requirement that at least two of the parties do more than ECU 250 million worth of business within the Community, even where the activities in the EC have nothing to do with the joint venture. Thus theoretically, if two Japanese automobile manufacturers establish a concentrative joint venture in Hokkaido, covering their sales of motor bikes there, notification has to be made to Brussels because of the parents' sales of motor cars in the Community. The Commission might however apply a rule of reason in such a case as proceedings for non-compliance are discretionary.

This could cause companies outside the Community to overlook the notification requirement which is serious considering the heavy penalties for consummation of a non-notified merger. The solution may be the adoption of a *de minimus* notice dealing with such situations.

In fact, the Commission has shown itself remarkably lenient where notifications have been made late. In *Torras Sarrio* (Case IV/M 0166, decision of 5.3.92, OJ C 58/20), the main purchase agreement was signed on 7 February 1991 and notified in January 1992, that is with almost one year of delay. It was put into effect in breach of Articles 4 and 7 of the Regulation. In this case the Commission held that in view of the difficulty in calculating the turnover of bodies such as the Kuwait Investment Office, fines would not be appropriate. There have been other cases where the Commission has shown flexibility and leniency for a failure to submit a notification in time, particularly where it is a complex or novel case. We have also found that the Commission is willing to extend the one-week deadline for notification during the pre-notification discussions where a notification is proving exceptionally difficult to put together.

In the Form CO the parties are asked whether, if the Commission decides the notified transaction does not fall within the Merger Regulation, they wish the notification to be treated as an application under Article 2, or a notification under Article 4 of Regulation 17/62/EEC (for an exemption or negative clearance under Article 85 of the EEC Treaty). This is permitted by virtue of Commission Regulation 2367/90 (Article 5).

In the case of a joint venture it has proved sensible to answer this question in the affirmative. If the joint venture is concentrative but the thresholds are not met, the transaction effectively escapes the EC competition rules and can only be dealt with under national law. On the other hand, if the Merger Control Regulation is inapplicable only because the joint venture is not considered concentrative but co-operative, it will in many cases come within the scope of Article 85 of the EEC Treaty and be otherwise notifiable to the Commission under Regulation 17/62. Moreover, a co-operative joint venture which has been notified to the Commission on Form CO will, if the parties so request, be referred by the Task Force to the appropriate Directorate within DGIV, for consideration under those provisions. There are numerous examples where this has been done: *Koipe-Tabacalera/Elosua, EUREKO, Herba/IRR, Flachglas/Vegla, BSN-Nestlé-Cokoladovny, Appolinaris/ Schweppes, Elf/Enterprise, VTG/BPTL, Baxter/Nestlé-Salvia,* and *Mediobanca/Generali.* The disadvantage in such cases is that the Commission is not obliged to deal with the cases within any time limits, and parties may fall victim to the protracted decision making process. Our experience is that such "converted" notifications tend to receive speedier treatment than normal individual notifications on Form A/B.

If the parties wish the Form CO notification to be treated as a notification under Form A/B, this is usually subject to the provision within a time limit laid down by the Commission of any further information which may be required.

SETTLEMENTS IN MERGER CASES

All but two of the cases which have resulted in the opening of Phase Two proceedings have been settled. This has usually involved one or more of the relevant parties giving binding undertakings to the Commission to sell off part of their acquired business. Settlements have also been reached in the first phase although the Merger Control Regulation does not expressly provide for the Commission to attach conditions and obligations to clearance decisions in Phase One, unlike Phase Two. In several cases, transactions have been approved once the parties have agreed to make alterations to the terms of their proposed agreement or other business arrangements, effectively amending the notification. For example, the Commission approved the transaction in *Ford/New Holland/Fiat* (Case IV/31.400, decision of 15.12.92 OJ L 20/1) during Phase One, taking into account factors such as Fiat's declining market share, low prices for the relevant product (combine harvesters) and Ford's termination of an exclusive purchasing agreement.

In other cases, mergers have been approved during Phase One on the basis of undertakings given by the parties (and others). The Commission's favourable decisions in both *Air France/Sabena* (Case IV/M 0157, decision of 5.10.92 OJ C 272/5), and *British Airways/TAT* (Case IV/M 0259, decision of 27.11.92 OJ C 236/16) were based on various commitments entered into by the parties and the relevant air transport control authorities regarding future slot allocation and the entry of new carriers into the market, including interlining agreements and participation in frequent flyer programmes.

As mentioned above, a proposed merger can also be approved in Phase Two, with the approval being expressly conditional on the parties giving certain undertakings. The following are examples of Phase Two settlements.

In *Accor/Wagons-Lits* (Case IV/M 0126, decision of 28.4.92 OJ L 204/01), the Commission approved the acquisition by Compagnie Internationale des Wagons-Lits ("Wagons-Lits") of Accor SA ("Accor") following Accor's undertaking to sell the French motorway catering services of Wagons-Lits. As part of its investigation, the Commission questioned competitors of the two parties, trade associations and motorway operating companies.

These consultations indicated that the merged group would have an 89 per cent share of the French market for motorway catering as a whole, and would be 18 times the size of its nearest competitor. Even if the market was taken as that for light meals on French motorways, the merged group's market share would still have been 69 per cent. The Commission also found that barriers to entry were high, due to the long duration of motorway concessions, the limited number of existing motorways and the uncertainty of future motorway development in France.

Accor eventually reached agreement with the Commission that the merger would be declared compatible with the common market, provided that Accor gave an undertaking to sell Sogerba, the Wagons-Lits subsidiary responsible for the group's French motorway catering activities, within a definite (but undisclosed) timetable. In addition, Accor undertook that there would be no transfer of activity from Sogerba to Accor and that it would not alter the way in which Sogerba is operated commercially.

In the recent *Nestlé/Perrier* (Case IV/M 0190, decision of 22.7.92 OJ C 356/1), which also concerned the application of the Merger Regulation to oligopolies, the Commission's authorisation of the acquisition of Source Perrier SA by Nestlé was conditional on undertakings from Nestlé to sell a number of water sources to a strong independent third party.

In another recent case, *Du Pont/ICI* (Case IV/M 0214, decision of 30.9.92 OJ L 7/13), the Commission approved, subject to conditions, Du Pont's acquisition of ICI's nylon business as part of a swap deal in which ICI would acquire Du Pont's acrylics business in the United States. The Commission thought that as a result of the acquisition Du Pont would obtain a dominant position in the relevant market, which it held was the nylon carpet fibre market, and would be able to act independently of its customers and competitors. However, rather than blocking the deal outright, a compromise was reached, with the Commission insisting on certain detailed conditions being fulfilled.

Du Pont undertook to reserve 12,000 tonnes of the acquired carpet fibre production capacity for a third party competitor, drawn from a range of the business's products, and to manufacture under contract for five years according to that third party's specifications. One of ICI's research and development installations will be transferred to the third party which should be staffed by competent technicians at least half of whom should come from ICI's Oestringen installation. Moreover, Du Pont must provide adequate incentives for enough competent sales staff to transfer to the third party and must either transfer or license its "Timbrelle" trademark to the third party.

In all the above cases, a settlement was reached only after proceedings were opened. However, there have been cases where a settlement was reached during the first phase. In *Ford/New Holland/Fiat* the agreement under which Fiat took an 80 per cent stake in Ford's agricultural and earth-moving machinery business was notified in January 1991. The Commission announced one month later that the acquisition had been approved subject to conditions which would be announced at a later date, after the closing date of the agreement between Fiat and Ford. The conditions, which were announced in May 1991, required Fiat to end its exclusive supply arrangements with a national group of 72 farmers' co-operatives, and to allow former Ford New Holland dealers a 15-day option in which to decide whether to remain with New Holland or end their current distribution contracts. This case was a "mixed" case since the exclusive supply arrangements were dealt with under Article 85.

Similarly, in *Air France/Sabena,* the Commission approved the agreement within the initial one month period, subject to conditions designed to prevent domination on certain European and African routes. Both the airlines and their respective governments gave undertakings to the Commission. The conditions imposed on the two airlines included a limitation on take-off and landing slots at Zaventem airport in Brussels, so that competitors would have access to at least 25 per cent of the slots in any given hour. In order to prevent Air France and Sabena from dominating the market on some routes, the airlines had to agree that one of them would stop operating that route should a rival airline decide to begin offering a service. In addition, if traffic to certain other destinations increased, opportunities for competitors to carry some of the passengers would have to be provided.

In his speech to the Fordham Institute in 1991, Colin Overbury, the former Director of the Task Force, endeavoured to explain the Commission's settlement policy. At the same time he defended the Commission against the charge that, in his own words, "it had acted in an interventionist manner in forcing companies to enter into settlements based on arbitrary positions and to modify their business plans in order to accommodate the Commission's wishes as the price of a clearance decision". The Task Force, he said, was under a great deal of pressure from notifying parties to find solutions to problems revealed in a notified transaction during Phase One, in order to avoid Phase Two. The reason for this was that many companies believed that once Phase Two proceedings were opened, the proposed merger was heading for disaster. This he put down to a misinterpretation of the "serious doubts" raised as to a proposal's compatibility with the common market and the issuing of "objections" by the Commission. According to Colin Overbury, prohibition is not the aim of merger control.

In any event, this is the pressure the Task Force is under from notifiers who wish to negotiate settlements with the Commission. The Merger Task Force succeeds in fulfilling this demand by distinguishing between undertakings as to future behaviour and structural modifications to the notified transaction proposed by the parties. The Task Force's view appears to be that settlements in general may be reached as long as they involve accepting undertakings from the parties to modify the structure of the proposal as opposed to conditions or undertakings as to future behaviour. The Task Force's position is both practical and in tune with its interpretation of the Regulation. Undertakings as to future behaviour are unlikely to remedy effectively a structural problem in a proposed merger and, moreover, would be difficult to supervise.

Technically the Regulation does not permit the Commission to suggest or impose any modification in the structure of the proposed operation or extract undertakings from the parties, either during Phase One or Phase Two. However, the parties may offer to modify the operation as notified to the Commission. That is why any modifications to the structure of a merger must be portrayed as emanating from the notifying party and, obviously, any undertakings should not resemble quasi-conditions as to future behaviour. Whilst it is no doubt true that if parties want to reach a settlement during Phase One, then the onus is on them to propose substantive modifications in order to obtain a favourable decision from the Commission; this does not, however, prevent the Commission from informally indicating to the parties what amendments it considers could result in an acceptable solution all round, once the parties have indicated a willingness to compromise. Settlements have been reached during Phase One as indicated above, but only where irrevocable structural changes were made by the parties.

The pressure on the Commission to reach settlements within Phase One would be considerably lightened if Phase Two proceedings were made to seem less forbidding. Phase Two still bears a strong resemblance to Regulation 17/62 proceedings after a Statement of Objections has been issued. The requirement that the Commission should open Phase Two proceedings when the Commission has "serious doubts" about the compatibility of a transaction with the common market emphasises the negative nature of Phase Two proceedings. If Phase Two could be made less intimidating, companies might not be so insistent on achieving settlement solutions within the one month period.

B.   THE MERGER CONTROL THRESHOLDS

As the Committee will be aware, a review is in progress within the Commission of the level of the thresholds which govern the application of the Merger Control Regulation. This review also covers the operation of Articles 5, 9, 19 and 22 of the Regulation. Many in the Commission consider that the thresholds are set at too high a level to reflect the purpose of the Regulation. It is true that we advise on many mergers which are below the thresholds and which produce effects in more than one Member State. In many cases the companies concerned would prefer to deal with just one authority, the Commission, instead of having to notify and seek clearances in a number of Member States, particularly now that a number of Member States which previously did not have effective domestic merger control have recently introduced it. It is often the turnover requirement that at least two companies must have a minimum turnover within the Community of ECU 250 million that is not met, rather than the worldwide turnover figure of ECU 5 billion which is met in a surprisingly high number of cases. Lowering the Community turnover limit to ECU 100 million would cause many more mergers to fall within the Regulation.

It is far from clear that the current review will result in a reduction of the thresholds. This will mean that many significant transactions with cross-border effects will escape the Commission's jurisdiction and parties will be deprived of the benefit of the "one-stop shop". The problem with having to make notifications in a number of different jurisdictions is that national merger control rules and procedures are far from being harmonised. The same transaction will therefore be analysed under a variety of different rules with the parties being asked a variety of different questions. This can make a merger transaction highly complicated or even frustrate it altogether. As mentioned above, many companies prefer to deal with one authority acting within one specific set of time limits, rather than having to lodge applications in a number of Member States.

The lowering of thresholds need not mean that there would be less respect for the subsidiarity principle. At present, the thresholds are so high that few concentrations which affect only one Member State fall within the Commission's jurisdiction. Sir Leon Brittan in his CEPS speech made clear that the Commission would refer more cases back to national authorities under Article 9 if the thresholds were lowered, and might seek an amendment to the Merger Control Regulation to allow the passing of the Commission file to a national authority at an early stage. At present, very few references to Member States under Article 9 are made. As indicated above the operation of Article 9 is being reviewed in any event. Three requests from the German authorities have been refused. A referral back was made to the United Kingdom authorities in the *Steetley/Tarmac* case (Case IV/M 0180, decision of 12.2.92 OJ C 50/25). Any lowering of thresholds should be accompanied by a greater use of the referral procedure where a merger produces pronounced effects in one Member State.

AN INDEPENDENT MERGER REVIEW BODY

There have been several suggestions that an independent European mergers authority should be created to decide on merger cases. It has been argued that this would provide a more objective analysis of the compatibility of mergers with the common market. The proposal, as I understand it, is that matters would be referred to this body for examination under Phase Two much in the same way that mergers in the United Kingdom are referred to the Monopolies and Mergers Commission by the Secretary of State.

My own view is that it would be quite difficult to create such a body within the present legislative framework. Its members would presumably be drawn from the Member States in some way. It is difficult at first sight to see how this body would be more immune from lobbying than the Commissioners themselves.

So far the Commission has applied a strict competition test as the Regulation requires. This has been the case even in the face of strong governmental and sectoral lobbying in cases such as *De Havilland* (Case IV/M 0053, decision of 2.10.91 OJ L 334.42). On its record to date therefore the case for replacing the present decision making structure with some kind of new body is not made out. It is likely that the insertion of such a new body into the procedure would only serve to lengthen the decision making process and might even make it difficult to meet the present time limits laid down by the Regulation. It would also make more difficult and cumbersome to achieve settlements by the giving of undertakings which has been an important feature so far of cases when Phase Two proceedings have been opened.

C. EC COMMISSION FINING POLICY

The Commission has formidable powers to sanction breaches of Articles 85 and 86 of the EEC Treaty, which are contained in Article 15 of Regulation 17/62. Article 15 provides that the Commission may, on each of the companies involved, impose fines from 1,000 to 1 million units of account *or* an amount in excess thereof but not exceeding 10 per cent of turnover in the preceding business year. Article 15(2) provides that in fixing the amount of the fine, regard should be had to the gravity and the duration of the infringement. Similar powers are conferred by Article 14 of the Merger Regulation.

In the *Pioneer* case (*Musique Diffusion Française & Others* v *Commission*, Cases 100–103/80 [1983] ECR 1825) the European Court of Justice said that in assessing the gravity of an infringement, regard must be had to a large number of factors, the nature and importance of which may vary according to the type of infringement in question and the circumstances of the case. These factors include:

(i) knowledge of the parties;

(ii) nature of the restrictions on competition;

(iii) conduct of each of the undertakings;

(iv) role played by each of them;

(v) profit which they were able to derive from the infringement;

(vi) number and size of the companies concerned, their respective market shares and market situation at the time the infringement was committed;

(vii) importance of the product;

(viii) whether it is a repeat offence;

(ix) the threat which the infringements pose to objectives of the Community; and

(x) deterrent effect of a fine.

Prior to 1969 no fines were imposed, but in a number of cases since then particular types of infringements have been the subject of heavy fines. The table in Annex II shows how fines have increased dramatically in recent years. It is also striking that the method for establishing the level of fines remains a largely secret process. Some cases involving the same or similar infringements have resulted in fines which differ widely.

In the *Pioneer* case the Court upheld the general power of the Commission to increase the level of fines. The fact that the Commission in the past imposed fines of a certain level for certain types of infringement did not mean that it was stopped from raising the level (within the limits of Regulation 17) if that was necessary to ensure the implementation of Community competition policy. On the contrary, the Court held that the proper application of the competition rules requires that the Commission may at any time adjust the level of fines to the needs of policy. This heralded the start of a more aggressive fining policy.

One of the problems is that Article 15(2) does not prescribe a tariff of fines, but merely specifies an upper and lower limit. High fines, however, have never come near the ten per cent level. In *Pioneer*, the Commission fixed fines ranging from two to four per cent of turnover, although this was reduced by the Court having regard to the question of duration. There was a shorter duration relating to the partial annulment of the decision (which had purported to deal with infringements of a longer duration than those mentioned in the Statement of Objections). The purpose of the limits is to prevent fines being imposed which are disproportionate to the size of the undertaking; apart from this they seem to have little practical effect. Another problem is that Article 15 does not specify whether it is total (world-wide) turnover in all products that is pertinent or whether it is only turnover in relevant products in the Community.

The *Pioneer* case made clear that it is permissible to have regard to the total world-wide turnover of the undertaking which indicates its size and power, and also to the proportion of the turnover accounted for by the goods in respect of which the infringement was committed.

In reality the Commission does seem to operate on the basis of a percentage of turnover in the products involved in the infringement in the Community. That percentage appears to be anything between two and four per cent. It then has regard to the other factors such as mitigating factors and the situation of the industry. On this basis it seems that a proposal on the amount of the fine is made by DGIV to the Commissioner for Competition. His discretion is enormous although the final amount of the fine is decided by the full College of Commissioners. Precisely how the Commission apportions fines in the case of cartels involving a number of undertakings is also not totally clear. A fine appears to be imposed on each defendant in respect of all the substantive infringements it is found to have committed.

The Commission looks at what is a reasonable percentage of sales for each defendant and applies this to sales in products and markets concerned by the infringement. In *Polypropylene* (Case IV/31.149, decision of 23.4.86, OJ L 230/1) fines averaged four per cent of the defendants' European sales of the relevant product. In *Tipp-Ex* (Case C–279/87 *Tipp-Ex* v *Commission* [1990] ECR 293) the ECJ upheld a fine of three per cent of EC turnover in a case involving vertical restraints to prevent parallel imports. Some indication of the approach adopted was given in the report of the pleadings in the appeal of the *Anseau* decision (*NAVEWA* v *Commission* Cases 96–102, 104, 105, 108 and 110/82 [1983] ECR 3369). Anseau attracted the largest fine because it played the leading role in the certification system for washing machines which the Commission found made impossible or more difficult the importation of washing machines and dishwashers into Belgium.

It is clear that on some occasions the Commission has also taken into account the profits of the infringement. In *United Brands* (Case 27/76 *United Brands* v *Commission* [1978] ECR 207) the Commission said that it had taken into account " the high profits achieved by this undertaking as a result of its pricing policy ". In *Kawasaki* (Case IV/29.430, decision of 12.12.78, OJ L 16/9) the Commission linked quite closely the amount of the fine with the higher prices paid by the consumers in the Community and in particular in Germany as a result of the export ban imposed by the United Kingdom distributors on dealers in the United Kingdom. The Commission took the view that without the obstruction of parallel imports, prices on the German market would have been lower.

The profit consideration was clearly important in the *Tetra Pak* case (Case IV/31.043, decision of 24.7.91, OJ L 72/1) where a fine of ECU 75 million was imposed. The Commission was greatly helped here by the fact that Tetra Pak was a one-product company which had succeeded in achieving a high Community turnover in a number of years.

The infringements were very serious and had continued for a long time and covered all Member States. However, the fine itself was much greater than previous fines imposed on other companies in respect of similar conduct. The fact that Tetra Pak is a one-product company undoubtedly eased the calculation of the fine. One wonders whether a fine of this level would have been imposed had Tetra Pak been an EC company perhaps commanding more support within the Commission. On the other hand, Tetra Pak had very significant turnover within the Community.

There are several other anomalies in the Commission's fining policy. In some cases no fine or a low fine has been imposed because the Commission's decision has broken new ground or because it is the first time that the competition rules have been applied in the sector concerned. For example, in *Peugeot* (Case IV/31.143, decision of 25.9.86, OJ L 295/19), the Commission did not fine Peugeot for a systematic refusal of supplies within a distribution system because the necessary clarification of the obligations on dealers was not given until the Court's judgment in *Ford*. Again, in the *Italian Flat Glass* case (Case IV/31.906, decision of 7.12.88, OJ L 33/44) no fine was imposed under Article 86 because new legal ground was being broken. It is all the more striking that in the case involving the *French West African Shippers Committee* (Case IV/32.450, decision of 1.4.92, OJ L 134/1) where Regulation 4056/86 was being applied to infringements for the first time, very high fines totalling ECU 15 million were imposed. This was the first time that the competition rules had been applied through the imposition of fines in this sector and new legal ground was being broken.

There are other cases where similar infringements which have lasted for similar periods of time have been punished with fines of a different level. For example, Dunlop Slazenger *(Newitt/Dunlop Slazenger,* Case 32.290, decision of 18.3.92, OJ L 131/32) was recently fined ECU 5 million for imposing an export ban on a distributor for seven years. However, the Japanese company Toshiba was fined only ECU 2 million for a similar infringement even though the infringement lasted longer and Toshiba's turnover greatly exceeded that of Dunlop Slazenger. The only distinguishing feature appears to be that Toshiba did not contest the Commission's finding and adopted a compliance programme whereas Dunlop did seek to contest the Commission's findings. This does not seem to be an objectively justifiable reason for the imposition of a much higher fine.

In some cases it seems that some kind of plea bargaining has taken place when the Commission has imposed lower fines in return for not contesting a finding of infringement as in *Zinc Producer Group* (Case IV/30.350, decision of 6.8.84, OJ L 220/27) and *Cast Iron and Metal Rolls* (Case IV/30.064, decision of 17.10.83, OJ L 317/1) or when undertakings are given as to future conduct. Sometimes, as in the *Zinc* case, the lower fine is explained on other grounds such as the difficult situation existing in the industry. The Commission denies formally that plea bargaining takes place but it acknowledges that the " attitude of companies involved in a proceeding is important in the assessment of fines ". Blatant plea bargaining is a matter of concern and clear miscarriages of justice might occur where parties agree not to contest Commission findings in return for a lower fine. There is always a danger that the less sophisticated or less blameworthy may suffer by agreeing to submit in this way. In *Woodpulp* (Case IV/29.725, decision of 19.12.84, OJ L 285/1) those companies which offered unilateral undertakings as to their future conduct escaped with a lesser fine.

Clearly the Commission has enormous discretion in the way fines are calculated. No doubt it believes that fines have a strong deterrent effect and in practice it is clear that high fines are a strong deterrence to anti-competitive conduct. However, it is submitted that the fining policy of the Commission should be both coherent and transparent. Fines themselves should be proportionate and not set at an astronomically high figure simply to make an example in one case. When low fines are imposed because, for example, a company or industry is in difficulty, this should be made clear.

D.   THE USE OF COMFORT LETTERS

The Commission has over the years made increasing use of comfort letters to deal with cases. This has been designed to help deal with the delay in exemption and negative clearance cases which the Committee in its 8th Report considered unacceptable. This has enabled the Commission to provide far more rapid and flexible responses to particular problems. In a typical comfort letter, DGIV writes to say that on the basis of the information available it is satisfied that an agreement does not fall within Article 85(1), or that it merits an exemption under Article 85(3).

The Commission will then close its file on the case. It has also become quite common for the Commission to issue " discomfort " letters. In these letters the Commission says that the agreement does fall within Article 85(1) and does not merit an exemption. This means that the agreement may be in whole or in part null and void. The Commission does not take a decision and closes its file on the same terms as in a comfort letter. Technically the Commission could re-open its file in the event of a complaint or if economic circumstances change. The Commission seems to use discomfort letters frequently where it considers that a national court is better placed than the Commission to resolve a dispute and therefore may be more frequently used in the future as national courts play a greater role. The issue of a comfort letter is quite often preceded by the publication of a notice in the Official Journal. These notices may solicit comments from third parties causing the Commission to alter its favourable attitude expressed in the comfort letter. This was seen recently in *Proctor & Gamble* (Case No IV/33.697 P&G/Finaf, OJ C 3/2 of 7.1.92 and Commission Press Release IP(92)496 of 22.6.92). The Commission published a notice announcing its intention to adopt a favourable position on a joint venture. The comments of third parties were invited. Comments were received from competitors, national authorities and BUEC, the European Consumers' organisation. These comments caused the Commission to change its mind.

Even though publication of an intention to issue a comfort letter adds to its legal strength, particularly before a national court, the *Proctor & Gamble* case indicates the risk that parties may run in consenting to such publication. In some cases the Commission will insist on publication whatever the parties say.

It is often said that comfort or discomfort letters, particularly the latter, leave companies in limbo and uncertain of their legal position. In fact, in practice in both cases, companies often prefer the informal letter to having to wait for a formal decision. Companies would rather have a written statement of the Commission's position than the uncertainty of a seemingly interminable examination of a notification. They tend to feel secure in the knowledge that the Commission has closed its file, feeling probably with good reason that files once closed are not lightly re-opened. This gives greater security than the Commission having taken no position at all which could mean that a file could suddenly spring to life without warning.

The great attraction of the comfort or discomfort letters is the speed with which they are issued. Companies appreciate having a clear statement in writing by the Commission of its position and are prepared to accept the uncertainty of the legal status of such letters. They are usually prepared to accept responsibility for decisions and action taken based on comfort letters, and will usually prefer to forego prior publication where possible. On the other hand it would be more satisfactory if the legal status of comfort letters be improved, for example by making them more reasoned, provided that this would be done without slowing down the process whereby they are issued.

E.   THE POSITION OF COMPLAINANTS

An indication of the volume of complaints which the Commission receives each year is given in Annex III.

Usually the lodging of a formal complaint is preceded by one or more informal meetings with the Commission officials who are normally quite open about the merits of the case and give helpful guidance about particular points which need to be stressed and which aspects of a particular case are likely to give rise to difficulty. Quite often complaints are not lodged as a result of these meetings because it is clear that the complaint will not be taken up by the Commission.

In general the Commission requires a large amount of information before taking up a complaint and opening proceedings, and this is not a step which parties should enter into lightly. It is settled law that the Commission's reasoned but provisional letter issued under Article 6 of Regulation 99/63 stating that it does not consider that there is sufficient information to open proceedings is not appealable (see *Automec* v *Commission,* Case T-64/89 [1990] ECR 367). Once the Commission has issued such a letter it has in reality taken a strong position which it is difficult to overturn by further arguments or submissions, although Article 6 provides that complainants have a right to lodge these with the Commission. In some cases Article 6 letters have been formalised by publication in the Official Journal, for example *GEC/Siemens/Plessey* (Case IV/33.018, decision of 1.9.90, OJ C 239/2). Only a final decision can be appealed to the Court of First Instance and the right of unsuccessful complainants to institute proceedings appealing a rejection of a complaint is now firmly recognised (*BAT and RJ Reynolds* v *Commission,* Joined cases 142/84 and 156/84 [1987] ECR 4487). It is also clear that a complainant has no formal right to a decision which can be so appealed. It is our experience,however, that the Commission will give complainants a decision on the rejection of their complaint which can be appealed to the Court.

We have often found that these decisions contain new arguments which were not dealt with in the Article 6 letter. These new arguments do not necessarily result from submissions made by the complaint pursuant to the letter but appear often to be additional thoughts which the Commission has had. This was certainly the case in *BAT and RJ Reynolds* v *Commission.* The complainant can only deal with these new arguments in the appeal to the Court. It is submitted that any additional arguments should be put to complainants before the final decision on the complaint is taken so that the complainant has an opportunity to comment on them to the Commission and perhaps thereby influence the decision which the Commission ultimately takes.

The most difficult problem confronting complainants is the length of time required by the Commission to examine their complaints and open proceedings. This problem is compounded by the difficulty in obtaining interim measures from the Commission and by the inadvisability of requesting such measures, commented on below. We have experienced cases where it has taken the Commission up to three years to decide whether to open proceedings. We have, however, noticed lately that the Commission has acted more speedily. In a complex case in which we were involved recently, the Commission was about to issue a Statement of Objections about one year after the complaint was lodged. In fact, the Statement was never issued because in the meantime our client has been forced through its deteriorating economic circumstances to enter into a settlement agreement. This highlights one of the difficulties with complaints to the Commission particularly when the complainant is a small company with limited resources, complaining, for example, against a much larger company about an abuse of a dominant position. Quite often the complainant does not have the means to continue the fight during the very long investigation period the Commission seems to need. This means that they may be forced into disadvantageous settlements to resolve the matter, or risk being eliminated from the market.

F.   INTERIM MEASURES

The most severe problem facing complainants is that it may take the Commission several years to reach a final decision and eventual action by the Commission in the form of the issuing of a Statement of Objections or adoption of a decision may come too late. Complainants and their advisers frequently agonise over whether to include an application for interim measures in the complaint. They are often deterred by a number of factors. First, there is the apparent reluctance of the Commission to grant interim measures. Since the *Camera Care* case (Case 92/79R [1980] ECR 119) in 1980, interim measures have only been granted in five cases. It is true that the Commission has issued interim measures Statements of Objections in other cases (*Hilti, British Sugar, Irish Distillers*) resulting in undertakings being given to cease the alleged infringement until the Commission has reached a final decision.

Why is it so difficult to obtain interim measures? It is not so much the difficulty of satisfying the criteria for interim measures which were laid down in the *Camera Care* case. The real problem again comes down to internal procedures and lack of adequate staff within DGIV. The taking of an interim measures decision requires many of the same essential procedural steps as a substantive decision although these have to be accomplished in a much shorter time-frame. Even when undertakings are given by the party or parties concerned, avoiding the need for a full decision, this only happens after a Statement of Objections has been issued, and for the Commission to take matters as far as this is a relatively cumbersome and lengthy procedure. Commission officials at preliminary meetings frequently advise complainants against requesting interim measures pointing to the difficulty in obtaining them. They also sometimes refer to the fact that all the resources of the case team will be devoted to examining the interim measures application rather than looking at the issues raised in the substantive complaint. There is considerable room for streamlining the whole interim measures procedure and it is important that this should be done in view of the long time it takes the Commission to take action on the substantive complaint.

G. BLOCK EXEMPTIONS

Since the 1982 Report of the Select Committee, the Commission has continued to rely heavily on the use of block exemptions.

The Committee's 1982 Report recognised the value of block exemption regulations in helping to circumvent the delays in treatment of individual notifications. At that time, only three had been adopted (Regulation 67/67, exclusive dealing, and Regulations 2779/72 and 2903/77 for certain types of specialisation agreements). The aim of introducing block exemption regulations in a number of other areas has been to provide legal security on a wider basis and help overcome the bottle-neck problem caused by the cumbersome notification process. Since the Committee's 1982 Report, a number of block exemptions have been introduced which are set out at the end of this section.

Wide use of these regulations is made by companies and their advisers and they have done much to introduce legal certainty in the administration of the competition rules, particularly in areas such as patent and know-how licensing which were, and in some respects still are, highly controversial. Block exemptions are of particular help to small and medium sized enterprises when agreements can be brought within them. They also help to reduce the Commission's workload and allow limited manpower resources to be devoted to the examination of individual notifications.

Many of the block exemption regulations contain an opposition procedure whereby agreements are exempted automatically if the Commission does not raise objections within a certain deadline. However, it is striking that the opposition procedure has not been used very much in practice. The opposition procedure was really designed for those clauses in agreements which fall into a "grey" area and where it is not totally clear whether they fall within the exemption provisions of the regulation or not. Companies and their advisers seem loathe to rely on the opposition procedure, mainly because it, in some way, draws particular attention to an agreement and, of course, it does require a notification. Companies would prefer to be certain that their agreement fits the block exemption through informal discussions with the Commission rather than by making an opposition procedure notification. The Commission itself does not seem to have encouraged recourse to the opposition procedure which may also explain why there have been so few cases where it has been invoked.

Significant issues of interpretation are still arising requiring clarification in Commission decisions and case law. For example, the concept of intermediary in Article 3(1) of Commission Regulation 123/85 in the motor vehicle block exemption was seriously disputed in a case involving Peugeot (*Peugeot* v *Commission* Case T-23/90 Judgement of 12 July 1991) in a case which is currently before the Court of Justice on appeal from the Court of First Instance. This further case law has often served to enhance the usefulness of block exemptions.

There is some speculation as to whether the block exemption for selective distribution in the motor vehicles sector will be continued past its expiry date in 1995. It is to be hoped that it will, although there is definite scope for improvement in its drafting. Motor manufacturers and dealers, who have organised their distribution and servicing agreements on the basis of a block exemption regulation in the sector for a number of years, are entitled to the legal security that this or a similar regime will be continued and will not disappear overnight. Many of the problems in this regulation stem from the attempt to combine selective and exclusive distribution within the regulation. The answer is to improve the regulation not to dispose of it altogether.

On 31 December 1994 the block exemption for patent licences will expire. It is hoped that the opportunity is taken to amalgamate the patent licensing and the know-how licensing block exemption which expires on 31 December 1999. This would do much to add clarity to a confused area of the law, particularly since so many agreements cover both patents and know-how.

There are a number of types of agreement not covered by block exemptions which would benefit from them. It does not seem logical to have block exemptions for patent and know-how licensing but not for trade mark agreements or copyright licences. These agreements give rise to similar types of provisions which often require notification to the Commission. At present, this has to be done on an individual basis. Computer software licences could also benefit from the introduction of a block exemption regulation although disagreements between DGIV and other Directorates General within the Commission over the contents of such a block exemption could make its introduction difficult. There seems to be no good reason for failing to introduce block exemption regulations in respect of these categories of agreements. If the Commission feels it lacks the necessary " vires " to do so it can perhaps seek specific new " vires " from the Council, as was done in the case of a block exemption for the insurance industry where a specific Council enabling regulation was adopted (Council Regulation 1534/91), or in the case of the regulation for shipping consortia.

The following is a list of the block exemption regulations currently in force.

Vertical Agreements
Regulation 1983/83—Exclusive Distribution
Regulation 1984/83—Exclusive Purchasing
Regulation 123/83 —Selective Distribution and Servicing of Motor Vehicles
Regulation 4087/88—Franchising

Horizontal Agreements
Regulation 417/85 —Specialisation
Regulation 418/85 —Research and Development
Regulation 3932/92—Insurance

Intellectual Property Agreements
Regulation 2349/84—Patent Licensing
Regulation 566/89 —Know-how Licensing

Transport
Regulation 84/91 —Scheduled Air Services and Slot Allocation
Regulation 83/91 —Computer Reservation Systems
Regulation 82/91 —Ground Handling Services
Regulation 479/92 —Liner Shipping Consortia

The following section considers how the above problems facing notifiers and complainants may be alleviated by the greater decentralisation of the competition rules with national courts playing a greater role in their application.

H. ACTIONS IN NATIONAL COURTS

THE NOTICE ON CO-OPERATION BETWEEN NATIONAL COURTS AND THE COMMISSION

Until now the application of Community competition law has been to a large extent by the Commission rather than by national cartel authorities or national courts. Although it has been clear for a long time (since Case 127/73 *BRT* v *Sabam* [1974] ECR 51) that national courts and tribunals are competent to deal with Articles 85 and 86, the Commission has remained the main forum for competition disputes. At the same time, the cumbersome nature of its own procedures, an ever increasing workload and the lack of adequate staff has led to the problems which have been identified above both for notifiers and complainants. Despite these problems there has been a marked reluctance to seise national jurisdictions with EC competition law questions.

There are many reasons for this. First and foremost, while both national courts and the Commission can exercise parallel jurisdiction under Articles 85(1), 85(2) and 86, only the Commission has jurisdiction under Article 85(3) to grant an exemption. It is clear, however, that national courts can apply the block exemption regulations. This limits the relief which a national court can offer an aggrieved plaintiff. It is often argued that it is cheaper and more informal to complain to the Commission. It is even said sometimes that Commission procedures are " free of charge " whereas national procedures are very costly. It is true that complaining to the Commission can be done cheaply and informally. However, complaints are more likely to be acted on if they are well documented. Complaints are often preceded by meetings with Commission officials for which briefings have to be prepared. Once made, complaints often have to be followed by persistent contact with the Commission officials. In the case of a complex complaint with many issues, it may not necessarily be the case that it is cheaper for the client than pursuing the matter before a national court. Once the Commission takes up the complaint and pursues it actively it is true that this will cost the client less than court proceedings, but it is still often necessary for a complainant to participate in the proceedings and, for example, comment on the Statement of Objections and appear at the oral hearing.

There are other advantages in complaining to the Commission. The Commission has significant powers to obtain documents and information which, if fully used, would be more likely to produce valuable evidence of an infringement than discovery or the equivalent procedure in many national courts. It will often be difficult to obtain evidence under national procedural rules particularly where the complainant plaintiff has to gather evidence outside the territory where he brings proceedings. An interim measures decision is valid throughout the Community, whereas an injunction from a national court will have little effect outside the State where it is granted. However, as has been seen, it is very rare for the Commission to adopt such a decision. An unsuccessful complainant before the Commission cannot be ordered to pay the defendant's costs.

Another factor especially in Article 86 proceedings is that the identity of the complainant may remain unknown to the party against which the allegations are made at least during the initial stages of the investigation. This may be important for a small operator dependent for its business on a dominant undertaking against which it wishes to pursue a complaint. It may be the case that a national jurisdiction may not be familiar with Community law and not as acquainted with Community rules as the Commission. The Commission proposes in its Notice on co-operation to deal with this (see paragraphs 38-43). The Commission in applying the competition rules often has regard to the wider aspects of Community policy. This may mean that the Commission is more flexible and creative than a national judge who will simply apply the law as he finds it without bearing in mind wider concerns of competition policy or Community objectives generally.

Weighed against these there are disadvantages in complaining to the Commission and advantages in pursuing national court proceedings. As has been seen earlier, the Commission proceedings can be extremely protracted and it may take two years or more to get the Commission to open proceedings and issue a Statement of Objections in a case. It is also difficult to get interim measures from the Commission. Some national courts may be able to grant temporary injunctions more quickly.

The most important reason for choosing national proceedings must be that a national court can award compensation which the Commission has no jurisdiction to do. However, our experience is that victims of anti-competitive behaviour are often principally concerned to have that behaviour stopped by the most effective means available. They are less concerned about recovering compensation for loss which they have suffered, which can be difficult both to quantify and to prove to the necessary standard. In addition, a successful complainant who wins before a national court may be able to recover his legal expenses. It is also possible to combine a claim under national anti-trust law with a claim under Community law in a national court. In general, where it appears that a claim can be satisfactorily dealt with by a national court and an adequate remedy obtained, the Commission will be less likely to deal with it. This will be more so in the future as the Notice on Co-operation makes clear.

The Commission has been anxious for several years to overcome the difficulties in bringing proceedings before national courts so that it can devote its scarce resources to the really important cases which involve cross-border issues which are particularly important for the Community. Nine years ago in the 13th Report on Competition Policy, the Commission stated:

" Improved and more intense contact between national courts and the Commission would help tighten up enforcement . . . Another definite step forward in the enforcement of Community competition law by national courts would be to develop the existing practice whereby the court asks the Commission to give an opinion on issues arising from cases before it, since such clarifications can only be conducive to a good administration of justice. "

The Commission was at that time concerned, and has been ever since, by the differences in remedies available in national courts, in particular by the availability of injunctions and damages. The relevant national laws have considerable differences on points such as the measure of damages, causation and the nature of the injury which can be claimed for, limitation periods, national law requirements for permanent or temporary injunctions, rules relating to claims or injunctions against the State in a case of breach of Article 90, indemnity and contribution between defendants, discovery rules and limitations on the duty to disclose documents, recovery by a plaintiff of his lawyers' fees. The Commission has considered internally whether differences in national laws would have to be harmonised by a directive or a regulation under Article 87.

In the *Delimitis* judgment, the Court made clear that the Commission's competence to apply Articles 85(1) and 86 is shared with the national courts. The Court admitted that this would lead to the risk of national courts taking decisions which conflict with those taken or envisaged by the Commission in implementation of Articles 85(1) and 86. The Court considered that it was safe for the national court to act if (i) it is clear that the conditions of Article 85(1) are not satisfied and there is little risk of the Commission taking a different decision or (ii) it is clear that the agreement is incompatible with Article 85(1) and clearly could not benefit from an Article 85(3) decision. In cases where an agreement has been notified for an exemption or is capable of exemption, the Court suggests that the national court may stay proceedings and consult the Commission to find out whether an agreement has been notified and the state of any procedure the Commission may have set in motion. The Court envisaged that there should be a stay of proceedings where there is a risk of conflict between the decision of the national court and the Commission. In paragraph 53 of its judgment, the Court referred to the possibility of co-operation between the Commission and national courts. It said that where the application of Articles 85 and 86 raised particular problems the national court could contact the Commission to obtain " the economic and legal information which that institution can supply to it ". The *Delimitis* judgment was delivered while the Commission was working on its draft Notice on Co-operation and had a considerable influence on the final version.

The Notice draws attention to the fact that the Commission has sole power to exempt agreements under Article 85(3) (paragraph 7). National courts, however, can apply the decisions and regulations adopted by the Commission under Article 85(3) even though they cannot themselves grant an exemption under that Article. The Commission makes clear that in future it will concentrate on notifications, complaints and own initiative proceedings having " particular political economic or legal significance for the Community ". The Notice goes on to point out that where adequate remedies are available before national courts, the Commission will not consider there is a sufficient interest in examining the case, and states that national proceedings have certain advantages for individuals and companies, in particular the possibility for national courts to award damages. This makes clear that the Commission intends to deal with certain types of case. Already we have noticed this policy being applied in practice, with the Commission refusing to take up complaints which clearly fall within Articles 85 and 86 leaving complainants with no choice but to take national proceedings. It is clear from the *Automec* case (Case T–24/90, Judgment of 18 September, 1992) that the Commission is perfectly within its rights in adopting this attitude. The Court made clear that the Commission had no obligation to take a decision in respect of complaints submitted to it and had no *duty* to carry out an investigation into a complaint. In addition, the Court made clear that the Commission had the right to award priority to certain types of cases which may be of special importance for the development and enforcement of Community competition policy. This is without prejudice to rights of complainants to receive a reasoned rejection of their complaint under Article 6 of Regulation 99/63, and ultimately a decision which can be appealed to the Court. In view of the principles enunciated in the *Automec* judgment, it will be difficult to overturn such a decision before the Court.

Thus in future complainants who in the past had the option of the Commission taking up their complaint, with the various advantages which that entailed, will now be constrained to proceed before national courts or demonstrate to the Commission that this is not a viable option. Part IV of the Notice gives guidance on the application of Articles 85 and 86 by national courts, and Part V on co-operation between the Commission and national courts seeks to avoid some of the disadvantages associated with national proceedings as outlined above. Part IV seeks to clarify what will happen in cases which are being examined by the Commission for an exemption under Article 85(3) and are also the subject of proceedings before national courts.

It is too early to say how all this will work in practice. However, the following observations can already be made at this stage about the combined effect of the *Delimitis* judgment and the Notice:

(i) The workload of the Commission should theoretically be considerably reduced. At present it receives about 350 complaints a year. It is thought that a considerable number of these will now be rejected on the grounds that national court proceedings are more appropriate. It is to be hoped that this will translate into a much speedier process for those complaints which are judged to be within the priorities of the Commission, and a greater possibility of obtaining interim measures from the Commission in such cases.

(ii) There is likely to be a lessening of the role played by Article 85(3) as national courts play a greater part in deciding on the application of Article 85(1), probably taking a broader view than the Commission and adopting more of a " rule of reason " approach.

(iii) There is a very considerable danger that Community competition rules could have a different application in different parts of the Community, which may not be totally mitigated by the co-operation arrangements foreseen in the Notice or by resort to the preliminary rulings under Article 177.

(iv) The Notice indicates that where there is a possibility that the Commission could exempt an agreement under Article 85(3), proceedings should be suspended and the Commission asked for a provisional opinion on the likelihood or not of an exemption being granted. It is obviously important that in such cases the Commission should react speedily otherwise great delays will be occasioned to the national court proceedings, possibly greater than currently occur in proceedings before the Commission. It will be interesting to see how quickly the Commission will be able to react in reality, particularly in controversial cases where there are substantial differences of view within DGIV or between the Commission's services. In view of the delays which could result, it is encouraging to note that the Notice provides that the national court remains free to adopt any interim measures it deems necessary where proceedings are suspended.

(v) The same point applies to the consultation and co-operation provisions contained in Part V of the Notice. Where national courts consult the Commission on points of procedure or law, it is essential that a quick reaction is given or great delay could result in the national court proceedings. Initial indications are that such requests are handled quickly, possibly even within two weeks. It is understood that they will be handled by officials within Directorate A of DGIV. It remains to be seen how this system works when there are a large number of requests, some of which may raise controversial issues which the Commission has trouble resolving internally. How will the Commission deal in practice with questions formulated by national courts which are not sufficiently clear?

(vi) The effect of *Delimitis* and the Notice may be that in certain instances cases will be decided at national level on the basis of " economic and legal information obtained from the Commission " (*Delimitis*) or " statistics, market studies and economic analyses " (Notice, paragraph 40). There is a danger that in making this type of information available the Commission will in effect be passing an informal judgment on an agreement or course of conduct. Studies or analyses handed down to the national court in this way will inevitably have the imprimatur of Commission approval. It is certainly likely that the Commission's response could have a prejudicial effect on the parties to the national litigation without those parties having the opportunity to test the reliability of the Commission's " evidence " or the veracity of the facts that are communicated to the Court. Much will depend on the weight which national courts are prepare to give to information of this nature emanating from the Commission.

I. ACCESS TO THE FILE

In its 1982 Report, the Committee recommended that parties should be allowed access to the whole of the Commission's file on their case, subject to necessary safeguards for the protection of business secrets and the protection of the identity of a complainant to shield it where appropriate from any possible retaliation. Some commentators hoped that making available Commission paperwork would assist in dispelling mistrust towards the Commission.

Regulation 17/62 does not require the Commission to inform a company that a complaint against it has been received. If this approach was strictly followed, the first time a company would be aware of the existence of the complaint would be when it received the Commission's Statement of Objections. In *AKZO Chemi BV* v *Commission*, Case 53/85 [1986] ECR 1965 the European Court of Justice held that the Commission must provide the "defendant" with a full copy of a formal complaint made against it under Article 3 of Regulation 17, that copy omitting only business secrets as permitted following the judgment in the *Distillers* case (*Distillers Co* v *Commission* Case 30/78 [1980] ECR 2229). The Commission usually sends a copy of the complaint minus business secrets about three to four weeks after it has been lodged with the Commission.

Following the issue of the Statement of Objections, the defendant may now examine and copy all documents on the Commission file on which the Commission relies, with the exception of internal documents and those containing business secrets. This ability to access information is in addition to the documentary evidence which is already provided in the form of annexes to the Statement of Objections. The purpose of the annexes is to keep the Statement concise. The problem is that there may be other documents on the file which are helpful to the defendant's arguments but which are not disclosed because the Commission does not rely on them. In this sense there is not full access to the file.

Access to Commission internal working documents is still not given, as it is thought that it would restrain officials from freely expressing their opinions during work on a case. In Joined Cases 142 and 156/84 *BAT and RJ Reynolds* v *Commission*, the Court rejected an application for sight of the Commission's internal file. It held that the only time when it might be willing to grant such an application was if there was substantive evidence that the Commission had acted for concealed motives. Providing access to internal documents would clearly cause significant administrative problems for the Commission. On the other hand it is often difficult to verify whether the Commission has acted improperly in a case unless certain key documents on the Commission's file are made available.

Information provided during the investigation of a complaint may only be used for the purposes of that particular enquiry. The Commission will agree not to disclose business secrets, provided these are genuine business secrets. Since the decision in *AKZO*, the disclosure of documents has been an immediately appealable act which does not require the aggrieved party to wait until the final decision on the entire investigation. The Commission is generally receptive towards the parties' arguments as to what might constitute a business secret, but as it is the Commission which finally decides whether a fact qualifies as a business secret, that decision is by its very nature appealable.

J. INSPECTIONS

Article 14(3) of Regulation 17/62 empowers the Commission to make on the spot investigations, known as "dawn raids", without prior notification or warning to the party to be the subject of the inspection. These investigations, if they are to be mandatory, must be authorised by a Commission decision, which should indicate the nature of the suspected infringement of the competition rules. In *National Panasonic* v *Commission*, (Case 136/79 [1980] ECR 2033), the Court held that the Commission had a wide discretion as to the format which the investigation was to take. The Commission is not required to give reasons for its choice of an Article 14(3) investigation over any other method of obtaining information.

During an investigation the Commission, in addition to examining and copying documents, may ask questions. It has been my experience that there is a great tendency for the inspectors to ask questions which go beyond the scope of the documents being examined. It is obviously difficult to regulate this type of on the spot investigation, but it remains an issue of some concern where a party, who may have had no previous knowledge of the Commission's interest in its affairs, is asked difficult questions under stressful conditions regardless of whether its legal advisers are present. This problem is compounded by the fact that the scope of the investigation as set out in the inspectors' mandate is often expressed extremely vaguely.

In the 1982 Report, it was suggested that independent prior authorisation for an Article 14(3) investigation, perhaps granted by a judge from the European Court of Justice, should be required. The current backlog of proceedings at the Court suggests that this is still not a practical solution. The requirement for a Commission decision remains the sole prior authorisation needed to carry out a dawn raid. The 1982 recommendation that an independent Commission official should be appointed to oversee the investigation remains outstanding.

K. HEARING OFFICER

The position of Hearing Officer was introduced in 1982 to ensure that all parties would be given a fair opportunity to state their case, and that due account would be taken of their submissions when the final decision came to be made. The Hearing Officer is not involved in the preparation or conduct of the case, and presides at the oral hearing. He presents his views in the form of an Opinion.

It has been our experience, however, that the Commission does not attach great weight to this Opinion when formulating its decision. The Hearing Officer does not have a very high status. His Opinion is not made public and he appears to have no independent staff or secretariat. Among the suggestions in the 1982 Report was the introduction of a preliminary meeting to be held between the issue of the Statement of Objections and the date of the oral hearing, which would serve to clarify the factual basis of the complaint and identify the issues which were actually in dispute between the parties. The Report recommended that an independent person within the Commission should be appointed to oversee both the new preliminary hearing and the oral hearing. The preliminary hearing would also have served as an opportunity to give directions for the oral hearing.

This recommendation for a preliminary hearing has not been implemented by the Commission, not least because of the staffing limitations discussed earlier in this paper. The introduction of the Hearing Officer, although an official of limited power within the decision-making hierarchy, has still been of value to the parties given his role as a relatively independent regulator of the case whose purpose is to protect the interests of the defendants throughout the administrative procedure. The job of Hearing Officer has been assiduously carried out by the incumbents of that post and it has been clear at oral hearings that he has often protected defendants from unfair questioning by the Commission.

A major problem is that the Hearing Officer is only brought into a case at the stage of oral proceedings. It would be a great improvement if the Hearing Officer played a role at the stage of written proceedings to give rulings on matters such as access to the file or time periods for replying to Statements of Objections. This might involve increasing his staff or even the appointment of an additional Hearing Officer. A further improvement would be the publication of the Hearing Officer's Opinion. There seems to be no valid reason why this is not made public. Publication would enhance the Opinion's importance and the Hearing Officer's status.

L. THE ADVISORY COMMITTEE

The proceedings of the Advisory Committee remain shrouded in secrecy, and the Report of the Committee is still not published. The situation is now highly anomalous since the Committee's Report is published in cases under the Merger Control Regulation but not in other competition cases. There seems to be no valid reason for this distinction. The Report should be published and should indicate the way in which each Member State voted. In Merger Control cases this is still not revealed, and the Report is only published once the final decision has been taken. It would greatly add to the transparency of Merger proceedings if the Report were published before the final decision was adopted.

. M. CONCLUSIONS AND RECOMMENDATIONS

1. The operation of the Merger Control Regulation has been exceptionally smooth owing to the very high motivation of the Task Force staff and the sensible internal procedures established to ensure that the time limits would be met. Decisions were shortened and consultations were streamlined. Computers have been widely used and an efficiently functioning, well managed machine has been created. It would be welcome if this could be repeated elsewhere within the Commission. There is scope for improvement to the Merger Control procedures. The thresholds should be reduced so that more transactions receive the benefit of the " one-stop shop ". It is thought unlikely that this will happen.

2. There is still much to be said in favour of an alteration in Community law to provide for legally binding automatic exemption once a certain time period has elapsed, as suggested by the Committee in 1982. It is not yet clear whether the non-binding internal time limits proposed by the Commission in non-concentration cases will in reality have the desired result of shortening delays, although this is definitely a step in the right direction.

3. There needs to be greater transparency in the way fines are calculated. There is a feeling in industry and amongst practitioners that the Commission's method of setting the level of fines is arbitrary and inconsistent.

4. Comfort and discomfort letters continue to play a great role in overcoming the protracted decision making process within the Commission. Despite their uncertain legal status, clients prefer to have a written statement of the Commission's position.

5. There is greater scope for the use of block exemption regulations which have also helped circumvent the bottle-neck caused by the cumbersome notification process. The patent and know-how block exemptions should be combined, and regulations introduced covering trade mark agreements, copyright licences and licences for computer software.

6. It is still difficult to obtain interim measures from the Commission and the processing of complaints still takes a very long time. Nevertheless, there are still significant advantages in making a complaint to the Commission as opposed to taking national court proceedings. It remains to be seen whether the effects of the *Delimitis* judgment and the Commission's Notice on Co-operation between the Commission and national courts will redress this balance.

7. The Hearing Officer has been of value to parties to Commission proceedings, although the Commission does not always seem to attach great weight to his Opinion in formulating its decision. The status of the Hearing Officer needs to be enhanced and he should be brought into proceedings at the early written stage. His Opinion should be published.

8. The Report of the Advisory Committee should be published to add greater transparency to proceedings.

28th April 1993

Annex I

MERGER CONTROL REGULATION CASES TO 23 APRIL 1993

	Notified	OJ C	Parties	Cleared	OJ C	Proceedings opened	Result	OJ L
1.	04.10.90	254/3	Renault/Volvo	06.11.90	281/2			
2.	19.10.90	268/8	AG/Amev	21.11.90	304/27			
3.	30.10.90	278/15	ICI/Tioxide	28.11.90	304/27			
4.	08.11.90	285/18	Arjomari Prioux/ Wiggins Teape	10.12.90*	321/16			
5.	15.11.90	290/16	Promodes/Dirsa	17.12.90	321/16			
6.	20.11.90	293/8	Cargill/Unilever	20.12.90	327/14			
7.	26.11.90	300/8	Mitsubishi/Union Carbide	04.01.91	5/7			
8.	03.12.90	307/2	Matsushita/MCA	10.01.91	12/15			
9.	07.12.90	310/23	AT&T/NCR	21.01.91	16/20			
10.	10.12.90	315/13	Alcatel/Telettra	21.01.91		21.01.91	12.04.91†	122/48
11.	10.12.90	315/14	Magneti-Marelli/CEAC	21.01.91		29.01.91	29.05.91†	222/38
12.	21.12.90	5/7	BNP/Dresdner Bank (Hungary)	04.02.91	34/20			
13.	04.01.91	7/3	Baxter/Nestlé/Salvia	06.02.91‡	37/11			
14.	07.01.91	8/7	Fiat/Ford New Holland	08.02.91†	118/14			
15.	21.01.91	18/13	ASKO/Omni	21.02.91	51/12			
16.	23.01.91	18/14	Aérospatiale/MBB	25.02.91	59/13			
17.	22.01.91	18/15	Digital/Kienzle	05.03.91	56/16			
18.	06.02.91	36/15	Tetra Pak/Alfa Laval			18.03.91	22.07.91	290/35
19.	06.02.91	36/15	Kyowa/Saitama	07.03.91	66/13			
20.	22.02.91	51/5	OTTO/Grattan	21.03.91	93/6			
21.	25.02.91	55/4	Varta/Bosch			12.04.91	31.07.91†	320/26
22.	22.03.91	84/7	Usinor-Sacilor/ASD	29.04.91	193/34			
23.	22.03.91	84/8	Elf/Ertoil	29.04.91	124/13			
24.	25.03.91	87/10	La Redoute/Empire	25.04.91	156/10			
25.	09.04.91	100/18	ASKO/Jacobs/ADIA	16.05.91	132/13			
26.	25.04.91	118/14	Conagra/IDEA	30.05.91	175/18			
27.	29.04.91	119/12	Renault/Volvo/Heuliez	03.06.91				
28.	30.04.91	119/13	VIAG/Continental Can	06.06.91	156/10			
29.	03.05.91	123/28	Sanofi/Sterling	10.06.91	156/10			
30.	13.05.91	126/7	Elf/Occidental	13.06.91				
31.	13.05.91	128/13	Aérospatiale-Alenia/ de Havilland			12.06.91	02.10.91§	334/42
32.	16.05.91	132/12	Elf/BC/CEPSA	18.06.91	172/8			
33.	21.05.91	135/15	Péchiney/Usinor-Sacilor	24.06.91	175/18			
34.	22.05.91	137/18	Apollinaris/Schweppes	24.06.91‡	203/14			
35.	27.05.91	142/10	Nissan/R.Nissan	28.06.91	181/21			
36.	27.05.91	142/11	Dräger/IBM/HMP	28.06.91	236/6			
37.	10.06.91	156/9	Lyonnaise des Eaux/ Brochier	11.07.91	188/20			
38.	14.06.91	162/10	ICL/Nokia Data	17.07.91	236/6			
39.	18.06.91	162/11	EDS/SD Scicon	17.07.91	237/44			
40.	21.06.91	166/16	Elf/Enterprise	24.07.91‡	203/14			
41.	28.06.91	172/9	BP/Petromed	29.07.91	208/24			
42.	04.07.91	175/19	Eridania/ISI	30.07.91	204/12			
43.	18.07.91	189/25	Kelt/American Express	20.08.91	223/38			
44.	24.07.91	198/27	BNP/Dresdner Bank (Czech)	26.08.91	226/28			
45.	30.07.91	206/9	Digital/Philips	02.09.91	235/13			
46.	07.08.91	209/17	ABC/Compagnie Générale des Eaux/ Canal‡/W.H. Smith TV	10.09.91	244/5			
47.	09.08.91	213/20	Delta Air Lines/Pan Am	13.09.91	289/14			
48.	22.08.91	223/39	Mannesman/Boge	23.09.91	265/8			
49.	11.09.91	242/7	Metallgesellschaft/ Feldmühle	14.10.91	276/4			

	Notified	OJ C	Parties	Cleared	OJ C	Proceedings opened	Result	OJ L
50.	16.09.91	245/16	Paribas/MBH	17.10.91	277/18			
51.	20.09.91	250/31	Thomson/Pilkington	23.10.91	279/19			
52.	23.09.91	251/10	BankAmerica/ Security Pacific	24.10.91	289/14			
53.	04.10.91	265/7	Metallgesellschaft/ Safic Alcan	08.11.91	300/22			
54.	07.10.91	264/12	UAP/Transatlantic/ Sun Life	11.11.91	296/12			
55.	28.10.91	284/23	TNT/Post Offices	02.11.91	322/19			
56.	30.10.91	288/13	Cereol/Continentale	27.11.91*	7/7			
57.	05.11.91	292/16	Alcatel/AEG Kabel	18.12.91	6/23			
58.	06.11.91	293/11	Lucas/Eaton	09.12.91	328/15			
59.	12.11.91	297/10	Mannesmann/VDO	16.12.91				
60.	14.11.91	298/23	Accor/Wagons-Lits			17.12.91	28.04.92†	204/01
61.	15.11.91	300/21	Eurocom/RSCG	18.12.91	332/16			
62.	19.11.91	302/19	Campsa	19.12.91	334/23			
63.	19.11.91	304/18	Courtaulds/SNIA	19.12.91	333/16			
64.	19.11.91	304/19	Ingersoll-Rand/Dresser	18.12.91	86/15			
65.	19.11.91	304/20	Gambogi/Cogei	19.12.91	334/23			
66.	19.11.91	306/17	VIAG/EB Brühl	19.12.91	333/16			
67.	27.11.91	312/23	Sunrise	13.01.92	18/15			
68.	27.11.91	310/35	Mediobanca/Generali	19.12.91‡‖	334/23			
69.	29.11.91	314/24	Saab/Ericsson Space	13.01.92	17/10			
70.	05.12.91	320/12	Volvo/Atlas	14.01.92	17/10			
71.	10.12.91	325/26	Inchcape/IEP	21.01.92	21/27			
72.	11.12.91	329/23	Ericsson/Kolbe	22.01.92	27/14			
73.	16.12.91	331/19	Schweizer Rück/Elvia	14.01.92	27/14			
74.	20.12.91	1/13	Steetley/Tarmac	12.02.92¶	50/25			
75.	20.12.91	6/21	SPAR/ Dansk Supermarked	03.02.92	29/18			
76.	06.01.92	6/22	Grand Metropolitan/ Cinzano	07.02.92	47/23			
77.	10.01.92	11/10	James River/Rayne	13.02.92	43/19			
78.	16.01.92	16/15	BSN-Nestlé/Cokoladovny	17.02.92‡	47/23			
79.	22.01.92	21/26	Torras/Sarrio	24.02.92	58/20			
80.	30.01.92	27/15	Ifint/EXOR	02.03.92	88/13			
81.	20.02.92	52/16	Henkel/Nobel	23.03.92	96/23			
82.	25.02.92	53/19	Nestlé/Perrier			25.03.92	22.07.92†‖	
83.	05.03.92	62/3	Generali/BCHA	06.04.92	107/24			
84.	11.03.92	68/21	Flachglas/Vegla	13.04.92‡	120/30			
85.	13.02.92	70/19	Banesto/Totta	14.04.92	107/244			
86.	17.03.92	72/24	BSN/EXOR	01.04.92**				
87.	20.03.92	75/12	Thorn EMI/Virgin Music	27.04.92	120/30			
88.	20.03.92	75/13	Eureko	28.04.92‡	113/12			
89.	24.03.92	77/15	Herba/IRR	29.04.92‡	120/30			
90.	26.03.92	82/11	Solvay/LaPorte-Interox	04.05.92*	165/26			
91.	07.04.92	92/12	Mondi/Frantschach	12.05.92	124/19			
92.	14.04.92	103/22	Eucom/Digital	18.05.92	140/20			
93.	21.04.92	107/22	Scott/Mölnlycke	18.05.92**	135/20			
94.	21.04.92	107/23	Volvo/Lex	21.05.92	142/18			
95.	22.04.92	109/10	ABB/BREL	26.05.92	142/18			
96.	23.04.92	113/11	HSBC/Midland	21.05.92	157/18			
97.	30.04.92	116/13	Du Pont/ICI			03.06.92	30.09.92†	
98.	25.05.92	139/17	Bibby/Finanzauto	29.06.92	275/8			
99.	27.05.92	142/17	Mannesmann/Hoesch			14.07.92	12.11.92	
100.	05.06.92	151/14	Ericsson/Ascom	08.07.92	201/26			
101.	12.06.92	152/23	Promodes/BRMC	13.07.92	232/14			
102.	12.06.92	153/18	GECC/Avis Lease	15.07.92	201/26			
103.	16.06.92	154/29	Thomas Cook/LTU/ West LB	14.07.92	199/12			

	Notified	OJ C	Parties	Cleared	OJ C	Proceedings opened	Result	OJ L
104.	24.06.92	161/31	Elf Atochem/ Rohm and Haas	28.07.92	201/27			
105.	08.07.92	177/20	Rhone-Poulenc/SNIA	10.08.92	212/23			
106.	10.07.92	181/21	Pechiney/VIAG	10.08.92	307/7			
107.	10.07.92	181/22	Matra/Northern Telecom	10.08.92	240/15			
108.	(did not appear)		Eurocard/ Eurocheque-Europay	13.07.92*	182/19			
109.	17.07.92	185/17	Koipe-Tabacalera/Elosua	28.07.92‡	227/10			
110.	15.07.92	186/31	BTR/Pirelli	17.08.92	265/5			
111.	13.07.92	187/18	PepsiCo/General Mills	05.08.92	228/6			
112.	03.08.92	200/18	Elf Aquitaine-Thyssen/ Minol	04.09.92	232/14			
113.	03.08.92	204/14	Avesta/British Steel/NCC	04.09.92	258/9			
114.	07.08.92	207/19	Allianz/DKV	10.09.92	258/9			
115.	12.08.92	208/11	Volvo/Lex (2)	04.09.92	239/11			
116.	24.08.92	225/14	CCIE/GTE	25.09.92	258/10			
117.	28.08.92	226/8	Ahold/Jerónimo Martins	10.10.92	261/10			
118.	26.08.92	227/9	Siemens/Philips Kabel	11.11.92**	300/14			
	11.11.92	300/14	(resubmitted)	16.01.93**	11/5			
119.	27.08.92	227/10	Linde/Fiat	28.09.92	258/10			
120.	07.09.92	232/15	Air France/Sabena	21.10.92†	272/5			
121.	09.09.92	240/14	VTG/BPTL	12.10.92*	279/8			
122.	10.10.92	261/9	Fortis/La Caixa	05.11.92	297/4			
123.	23.10.92	283/10	British Airways/TAT	27.11.92†‖				
124.	23.10.92	288/6	Rhone Poulenc/SITA	26.11.92	319/6			
125.	09.11.92	298/10	Del Monte/Royal Foods/ Anglo American	09.12.92	331/13			
126.	18.11.92	307/7	Waste Management Int/ SAE	21.12.92	10/5			
127.	23.11.92	312/8	Sextant/BGT-VDO	21.12.92	9/3			
128.	25.11.92	315/2	Pepsico/KAS	21.12.92	8/2			
REQ.	30.11.92	328/4	British Airways/Dan Air	17.02.93	68/5			
129.	01.12.92	322/16	Credit Lyonnais/ BFG Bank	11.01.93	45/18			
130.	08.12.92	329/2	KNP/Buhrmann- Tetterode/URG			19.01.93?		
131.	08.12.92	331/14	Philips/Thomson/Sagem	18.01.93‡	22/2			
132.	23.12.92	4/2	Tesco/Catteau	04.02.93	45/18			
133.	23.12.92	5/3	Volkswagen (VWAG)/ VAG (UK)	04.02.93	38/12			
134.	06.01.93	9/3	Sarah Lee/ BP Food Division	08.02.93	39/12			
135.	21.01.93	27/3	CEA Industrie/France Télécom/Finmecanica SGS Thomson	22.02.93	68/5			
136.	12.02.93	46/10	Sanofi/Yves St Laurent	15.03.93	89/3			
137.	11.02.93	48/9	Ericsson/Hewlett-Packard	12.03.93	83/4			
138.	16.02.93	52/5	Matra/Cap Gemini Sogeti	17.03.93	88/8			
139.	24.02.93	53/10	SITA-RPC/Scori	19.03.93	88/9			
140.	19.02.93	55/11	Kingfisher/Darty	22.03.93	87/8			
141.	01.03.93	64/3	Zürich/MMI	02.04.93	112/4			
142.	01.03.93	64/3	Fletcher Challenge/ Methanex	31.03.93	98/12			
143.	04.03.93	66/14	Degussa/Ciba-Geigy	05.04.93	104/10			
144.	04.03.93	67/12	GEHE AG/OCP SA	05.04.93				
145.	08.03.93	71/7	Thomson/Shorts					
146.	11.03.93	75/11	Alcan/Inespal/Palco					
147.	12.03.93	79/5	Ahold/Jerónimo Martins/ Inovaçäo					
148.	25.03.93	88/9	Procordia/Erba					

	Notified	OJ C	Parties	Cleared	OJ C	Proceedings opened	Result	OJ L
149.	24.03.93	91/5	Schweizerische Kreditanstalt/ Schweizerische Volksbank					
150.	24.03.93	91/6	Harrisons & Crosfield/ AKZO					
151.	02.04.93	104/16	DASA/Fokker					
152.	02.04.93	105/4	Wacker/Hoescht					

Key

*	Regulation inapplicable—no Community dimension
†	Cleared subject to conditions
‡	Regulation inapplicable—not a concentration, article 85 applies
§	Prohibited
‖	Decision appealed to ECJ
¶	Referred back to national authorities
**	Notification withdrawn
REQ	Concentration not notified—for copy of notice, see file 1C1D (vol I)

STATISTICS: MERGER CASES

		From To	01/01/90 31/12/90	01/01/91 31/12/91	01/01/92 31/12/92	01/01/90 31/12/92
1.	Notifications		12	63	60	135
2.	Final decisions					
	Total		7	60	61	128
	6(1)(a) outside scope		2	5	9	16
	6(1)(b) no serious doubt		5	50	47	102
	8(2) simple clearance		0	1	1	2
	8(2) clearance with conditions		0	3	3	6
	8(3) prohibition		0	1	0	1
	9 referral		0	0	1	1
3.	Opening of proceedings		0	6	4	10
4.	Non referral decisions		0	2	2	4
5.	Other decisions					
	7(2) suspension		0	4	3	7
	7(4) derogation to suspension		1	1	2	4

STATISTICS: MERGER CASES

Breakdown of notifications to 15 April, 1993 according to nationality of companies involved

Belgium	7
Denmark	2
Germany	42
Greece	0
Spain	14
France	58
Ireland	1
Italy	19
Luxembourg	1
Netherlands	13
Portugal	3
United Kingdom	48
EFTA	26
USA	30
Japan	4

Annex II

TABLE OF FINES FOR INFRINGEMENT OF EEC AND ECSC COMPETITION RULES

Case	Commission decision	Infringement	Duration of infringement	Fine
Quinine	16 July 1969	Article 85: Horizontal market sharing, quota arrangements, and price fixing	6 years	Between ECU 10,000 and 210,000 Total: ECU 500,000 **Reduced to ECU 435,000 by the ECJ**
Dyestuffs	24 July 1969	Article 85: Horizontal price fixing	4 years	Between ECU 40,000 and 50,000 Total: ECU 490,000
Raffinerie Tirlemontoise	November 1971	Article 15(1)(c) of Regulation 17/62: Incomplete production of records during investigation	—	ECU 5,000
Pittsburgh Corning Europe	23 Nov 1972	Article 85: Discriminatory pricing to restrain parallel imports	1½ years	ECU 100,000
Commercial Solvents	14 Dec 1972	Article 86: Refusal to Supply	2 years	ECU 200,000
WEA-Filipacchi	22 Dec 1972	Article 85: Verticle export ban	4 months	ECU 60,000
Sugar	2 Jan 1973	Article 85: Horizontal market sharing, price fixing and collusive tendering; Article 86: Exerting pressure to restrict intra-Community trade	3–4 years	Between ECU 100,000 and 1.5 million Total: ECU 9 million **Reduced to ECU 1.59 million by the ECJ**
Deutsche Philips	5 Oct 1973	Article 85: Vertical export ban	5 years	ECU 60,000
Belgian Wallpaper	23 July 1974	Article 85: Horizontal aggregated rebate cartel and collective boycott	3 years	Between ECU 36,000 and 135,000 Total: ECU 358,500 **Quashed by the ECJ**
General Motors	19 Dec 1974	Article 86: Obstructing parallel imports by overcharging for conformity certificates	4 months	ECU 100,000 **Quashed by the ECJ**
French-Taiwanese Mushroom Packers	8 Jan 1975	Article 85: Horizontal export quotas and price fixing	—	Between ECU 2,000 and 32,000 Total: ECU 100,000
United Brands	17 Dec 1975	Article 86: Vertical customers restrictions, discriminatory pricing and refusal to supply	8 years	ECU 1 million **Reduced to ECU 850,000 by the ECJ**
Hoffman-La Roche	9 June 1976	Article 86: Fidelity rebates and exclusive dealing arrangements	5 years	ECU 300,000 **Reduced to ECU 200,000 by the ECJ**
Miller International	1 Dec 1976	Article 85: Vertical export ban	4 years	ECU 70,000

Case	Commission decision	Infringement	Duration of infringement	Fine
Theal-Watts	21 Dec 1976	Article 85: Vertical prevention of parallel imports; Article 15(1)(a) of Regulation 17/62: Supplying false information in notification	4 years	2 × ECU 10,000
Hugin/Liptons	8 Dec 1977	Article 86: Refusal to supply spare parts	2½ years	ECU 50,000
Vegetable Parchment	23 Dec 1977	Article 85: Horizontal market sharing and co-ordination of price increases	16 months	Between ECU 10,000 and 25,000 Total: ECU 115,000
BMW Belgium	23 Dec 1977	Article 85: Vertical export ban	5 months	Between ECU 1,000 and 150,000 Total: ECU 203,500
Kawasaki	12 Dec 1978	Article 85: Vertical export ban	1 year	ECU 100,000
Floral	28 Nov 1979	Article 85: Horizontal joint selling arrangements	10 years	3 × ECU 85,000 Total: ECU 255,000
Pioneer	14 Dec 1979	Article 85: Vertical export ban	3 months to 2 years	Between ECU 300,000 and 4,350,800 Total: ECU 6,950,000 **Reduced to ECU 3.2 million by the ECJ**
Fabbrica Pisana	20 Dec 1979	Article 15(1)(c) of Regulation 17/62: Incomplete production of records during investigation	—	ECU 5,000
Fabbrica Sciarra	20 Dec 1979	Article 15(1)(c) of Regulation 17/62: Incomplete production of records during investigation	—	ECU 5,000
French and German special steel producers	27 March 1980	Article 65 ECSC: Quota arrangements and price fixing	6 years	ECU 900,000
Johnson & Johnson	25 Nov 1980	Article 85: Vertical export ban	4 years	ECU 200,000
Michelin	7 Oct 1981	Article 86: Tying by means of discount and rebate scheme to prevent imports of competing products	6 years	ECU 680,000 **Reduced to ECU 300,000 by the ECJ**
Comptoir Commercial d'Importation	17 Nov 1981	Article 15(1)(b) of Regulation 17/62: Supplying false information in reply to discovery request	—	ECU 5,000
Telos	25 Nov 1981	Article 15(1)(b) of Regulation 17/62: Supplying false information in reply to discovery request	—	ECU 5,000
Möet & Chandon	27 Nov 1981	Article 85: Vertical export ban	2 years	ECU 1.1 million
National Panasonic (Belgium)	11 Dec 1981	Article 15(1)(b) of Regulation 17/62: Supplying false information in reply to discovery request	—	ECU 5,000

Case	Commission decision	Infringement	Duration of infringement	Fine
National Panasonic (France)	11 Dec 1981	Article 15(1)(b) of Regulation 17/62: Supplying false information in reply to discovery request	—	ECU 5,000
Hasselblad	2 Dec 1981	Article 85: Vertical prevention of parallel imports, influence on dealers' prices	6 years	Manufacturer: ECU 560,000 Distributors: ECU 165,000 and 3 × ECU 10,000 Total: ECU 755,000 **Reduced to ECU 670,000 by the ECJ**
Anseau	17 Dec 1981	Article 85: Horizontal prevention of parallel imports by means of conformity labelling	3 years	Between ECU 9,500 and 76,500 Total: ECU 935,000
AEG-Telefunken	6 Jan 1982	Article 85: Vertical restraints on dealers' pricing; discriminatory exclusion of dealers	3½ years	ECU 1 million
SSI (Dutch Cigarettes)	15 July 1982	Article 85: Horizontal price fixing	Three periods of 3–5 months	Between ECU 100,000 and 425,000 Total: ECU 1,475,000 **Reduced to ECU 1.425 million by the ECJ**
FNICF	27 Oct 1982	Article 15(1)(c) of Regulation 17/62: Incomplete production of records during investigation	—	ECU 5,000
National Panasonic	7 Dec 1982	Article 85: Vertical export ban	3 years	ECU 450,000
Rolled Zinc	14 Dec 1982	Article 85: Horizontal market sharing arrangement	3 years	ECU 400,000 and 500,000 **Quashed by the ECJ**
BNIC (Cognac)	15 Dec 1982	Article 85: Horizontal price fixing	3 years	ECU 160,000
Toltecs/Dorcet	15 Dec 1982	Article 85: No-challenge clause in trade mark agreement	7 years	ECU 50,000 **Quashed by the ECJ**
Windsurfing	11 July 1983	Article 85: Restrictions in patent licence agreements	4 years	Licensor: ECU 50,000 Licensees: Between ECU 5,000 and 15,000 Total: ECU 95,000 **Reduced to ECU 70,000 by the ECJ**
Cast Iron and Steel Rolls	17 Oct 1983	Article 85: Horizontal price fixing and market sharing	12 years	Between ECU 8,000 and 111,000 Total: ECU 1,250,000
IPTC (Anseau III)	5 Dec 1983	Article 85: Horizontal prevention of parallel imports	1½ years	ECU 5,000

Case	Commission decision	Infringement	Duration of infringement	Fine
Polistil/Arbois	16 May 1984	Article 85: Vertical prevention of parallel imports	3 years	2 × ECU 30,000
British Leyland	2 July 1984	Article 86: Obstruction of parallel imports by offences in connection with conformity certificates	3 years	ECU 350,000
Benelux Flat Glass	23 July 1984	Article 85: Horizontal marketsharing and price fixing	4 years	Between ECU 765,000 and 1,450,000 Total: ECU 4 million
Zinc Producer Group	6 Aug 1984	Article 85: Horizontal price fixing and market sharing	13 years	Between ECU 350,000 and 950,000 Total: ECU 3.3 million
Peroxygen	23 Nov 1984	Article 85: Horizontal price fixing and market sharing	10 to 20 years	Between ECU 500,000 and 3 million Total: ECU 9 million
John Deere	14 Dec 1984	Article 85: Vertical export ban	7 years	ECU 2 million
Wood Pulp	19 Dec 1984	Article 85: Horizontal price fixing	7 years	Between ECU 50,000 and 500,000 Total: ECU 4.125 million **Reduced to ECU 130,000 by the ECJ**
ECS/Akzo	14 Dec 1985	Article 86: Predatory pricing	4½ years	ECU 10 million **Reduced to ECU 7.5 million by the ECJ**
Sperry New Holland	16 Dec 1985	Article 85: Vertical export ban	10 years	ECU 700,000
Siemens/Fanuc	18 Dec 1985	Article 85: Horizontal market sharing	8 years	2 × ECU 1 million
Polypropylene	23 April 1986	Article 85: Horizontal price fixing and quota arrangements	6 years	Between ECU 500,000 and 11 million Total: ECU 57.85 million **Reduced to ECU 54,562,500 by the ECJ**
Balasco	10 July 1986	Article 85: Horizontal price and quota arrangements	6½ years	Between ECU 15,000 and 420,000 Total: ECU 1 million
Peugeot	25 Sept 1986	Article 15(1)(b) of Regulation 17/62: Supplying false information in reply to discovery	—	ECU 4,000
Meldoc	26 Nov 1986	Article 85: Horizontal price fixing and quota arrangements	6 years	Between ECU 425,000 and 3,150,000 Total: ECU 6,555,500
Fatty Acids	2 Dec 1986	Article 85: Horizontal exchange of information on sales	3 years	3 × ECU 50,000 Total: ECU 150,000
Tipp-Ex	10 July 1987	Article 85: Vertical obstruction of parallel imports	4 years	ECU 10,000 and 400,000

Case	Commission decision	Infringement	Duration of infringement	Fine
Sandoz	13 July 1987	Article 85: Vertical export ban	22 years	ECU 800,000 **Reduced to ECU 500,000 by the ECJ**
Fisher-Price	18 Dec 1987	Article 85: Vertical export ban	3 years	ECU 300,000
Konica	18 Dec 1987	Article 85: Vertical prevention of parallel imports	5 months	2 × ECU 75,000
Hilti	22 Dec 1987	Article 86: Tying and discriminatory practices	5 years	ECU 6 million
Hoechst	26 May 1988	Article 16(1)(d) of Regulation 17/62: Comtempt fines for refusal to submit to investigation	55 days	ECU 55,000
British Dental Trade Association	11 July 1988	Article 85: Discrimination against foreign exhibitors at trade fairs	5 years	ECU 100,000
British Sugar	18 July 1988	Article 86: Predatory conduct towards competitor	1 year	ECU 3 million
Hudson's Bay/DPF	28 Oct 1988	Article 85: Horizontal exclusive dealing arrangements	10 years	ECU 500,000
Sabena	4 Nov 1988	Article 86: Refusal to allow smaller competitor access to computerised booking system	2 months	ECU 100,000
British Plasterboard	5 Dec 1988	Article 86: Exclusive dealing to prevent imports	1 year	ECU 3 million and 150,000
Italian Flat Glass II	7 Dec 1988	Article 85: Horizontal price fixing and quota arrangements; Article 86: Collective unfair pricing	3–5 years	ECU 7, 4.7 and 1.7 million Total: ECU 13.4 million **Reduced to ECU 1,671,428 by the ECJ**
PVC	21 Dec 1988	Article 85: Horizontal price fixing and quota arrangements	4 years	Between ECU 400,000 and 3.5 million Total: ECU 23.5 million **Quashed by the ECJ as no decision made by the Commission**
LdPE	21 Dec 1988	Article 85: Horizontal price fixing and quota arrangements	7 years	Between ECU 100,000 and 5.5 million Total: ECU 37 million*
Welded Steel Mesh	2 Aug 1989	Article 85: Horizontal price fixing and market sharing	5 years	Between ECU 13,000 and 4.5 million Total ECU 9.5 million*
Bayo-N-Ox	13 Dec 1989	Article 85: Export ban	3½ years	ECU 500,000
Stainless Steel Cartel	18 July 1990	Article 65 ECSC: Quota arrangements	8 years	ECU 425,000

Case	Commission decision	Infringement	Duration of infringement	Fine
Secrétama	19 Dec 1990	Article 16(4) of Regulation 4056/86: Supplying false information in reply to discovery request	—	ECU 5,000
Soda Ash: Solvay/ICI	19 Dec 1990	Article 85: Market sharing	17 years	ECU 7 million each*
Soda Ash: Solvay/CFK	19 Dec 1990	Article 85: Quota arrangement	1 year	ECU 1 and 3 million*
Soda Ash: Solvay	19 Dec 1990	Article 86: Exclusionary discounts	6 years	ECU 20 million*
Soda Ash: ICI	19 Dec 1990	Article 86: Exclusionary discounts	6 years	ECU 10 million*
Baccarat	15 March 1991	Article 16(1)(c) of Regulation 17/62: Contempt fines for refusal to supply information	43 days	ECU 10,000
Gosme/Martell-DMP	15 May 1991	Article 85: Vertical prevention of parallel imports	1½ years	ECU 300,000 and 50,000
Viho/Toshiba	5 June 1991	Article 85: Vertical prevention of parallel imports	14 years	ECU 2 million
Tetra Pak II	24 July 1991	Article 86: Tying and exclusive maintenance and supply	15 years	ECU 75 million
Dutch Construction Industry	5 Feb 1992	Article 85: Horizontal price fixing	12 years	Between ECU 38,250 and 4,792,500 Total: ECU 22.5 million
Aer Lingus	26 Feb 1992	Article 86: Refusal to supply interlining facilities	3 years	ECU 750,000
Dunlop Slazenger Intl/AWS	18 March 1992	Article 85: Vertical prevention of parallel imports	7 years	ECU 5 million and 150,000
Eurocheque: Helsinki Agreement	25 March 1992	Article 85: Horizontal price fixing and restrictive practices	7½ years	ECU 5 and 1 million
French-West African Ship-owners Committee	1 April 1992	Article 85: Horizontal market sharing; Article 86: Predatory conduct towards competitor	5 years	Between ECU 2,400 and 11,628,000 Total: ECU 15,306,200
UKWAL	6 April 1992	Article 18(3) of Regulation 4056/86: Refusal to submit to an investigation	—	ECU 5,000
Viho/Parker Pen	15 July 1992	Article 85: Vertical export ban	2½ years	ECU 40,000 and 700,000*

*Indicates that an appeal is pending.

Annex III

COMPETITION PROCEEDINGS BY THE COMMISSION

Date	Cases Pending	Arising from			Settled by		
		Complaints	Applic/Not	Commission's Initiative	Decision	Informally	Comfort Letter
31.12.92	1,562	*	*	*	*	*	*
31.12.91	2,287	328	1,732	227	13	676	146
31.12.90	2,734	345	2,145	244	47	547	171
31.12.89	3,239	359	2,669	211	26	382	46
31.12.88	3,451	357	2,909	185	44	419	36
31.12.87	3,427	344	2,919	166	27	334	57
31.12.86	3,522	330	3,032	160	38	283	3
31.12.85	3,313	296	2,878	139	24	1,185	2
31.12.84	4,194	314	3,708	72	25	211	3
31.12.83	4,138	283	3,654	201	22	343	*
31.12.82	4,199	259	3,715	225	22	385	*
31.12.81	4,365	250	3,882	233	22	121	*
31.12.80	4,203	233	3,775	195	9	183	*
31.12.79	4,095	200	3,724	171	6	276	*
31.12.78	4,131	159	3,829	143	14	200	*
31.12.77	4,117	135	3,862	120	17	263	*
31.12.76	4,129	109	3,917	103	9	326	*
31.12.75	4,274	93	4,078	103	14	272	*
31.12.74	4,353	65	4,200	88	11	56	*
31.12.73	4,213	45	4,052	116	7	392	*
31.12.72	2,873	*	*	*	14	1,882	*
31.12.71	4,556	*	*	*	12	2,873	*
31.12.70	7,336	46	7,209	81	15	2,098	*
31.12.69	9,407	71	9,266	70	13	13,832	*

*Indicates that this information is not available.

Examination of witness

MR MICHAEL REYNOLDS, Allen & Overy, Brussels called in and examined.

Chairman

1. Mr Reynolds, we are grateful to you for coming to help us in this enquiry into the enforcement of competition rules. The Members of the Committee have received the written report which you prepared for us, and we are very grateful to you for having done so; it has obviously involved a great deal of work and we much appreciate that you have given up the time to do it. Perhaps, for the record, I should say that you are a partner in Allen & Overy, and you are the partner in charge of the Brussels office. Your time there in the last 14 years has been very largely concerned with, broadly speaking, anti-trust matters, mergers and, in particular, Articles 85 and 86 of the EC Treaty. Is that the substantial work of the Brussels office?

(Mr Reynolds) Yes, predominantly, competition rules and trade work; but predominantly competition work and dealing with the European Commission's Competition Directorate-General on questions of Articles 85 and 86.

2. I think you are also Vice-Chairman of the Anti-Trust Committee of the International Bar Association, and you have pretty wide experience of the sort of matters with which we are concerned today. Can I ask you, first, about something that the Select Committee said in its 1982 Report, with which I think you are familiar?

A. Yes.

3. The Select Committee said then that it was right and inevitable that the function of enforcement should be principally entrusted to the Commission, and that the Commission should also have certain judicial powers. Do you think that was a valid conclusion at the time by the Select Committee; do you think we should revise that view?

A. I certainly think that it is inevitable that the Commission has almost the monopoly in applying the competition rules in the Community and has judicial as well as administrative powers; that is really established in the Treaty and in Regulation 17. I think the likelihood of making amendments to the Treaty and indeed to Council Regulation 17 on these points would be extremely difficult as a matter of practice, and very difficult politically. Having said that, I have always been concerned with the fact that in competition cases one is dealing with a body that is the investigator, the administrator and, at the end

[Chairman *Contd*]

of the day, the judge. There are many who have said that, bound up in that process, we should have an independent body or person to help supervise the way the Commission administers the competition rules. As I say, that would be very difficult to do without any amendment to the Treaty and the Regulation. This is also relevant now under the Merger Control Regulation.

4. Leaving aside the possibility of improving the way in which matters are investigated, and leaving aside the possibility of improving the judicial element of the enquiry, do you think in principle the situation is such that these two functions should now be separated?

A. I think, probably now that we have the Court of First Instance, in principle the system can work adequately, provided certain more limited amendments are made, because the Court of First Instance, as I will come on to say, has made a considerable difference in the way the competition rules are applied, and does provide for a greater element of judicial control by a body outside the Commission.

5. Would you like to elaborate on that? In what ways have you seen that the Court of First Instance has, as it were, helped the effective working of the competition rules?

A. The Court of First Instance, first of all, has had the means and the ability to go into greater detail in competition cases on the factual side. It has also shown itself able to deal with procedural matters, and several procedural matters have gone to the Court of First Instance, and in a sense it has provided a more ready access for an appeal related to procedural matters before one gets to the final stage of decision. For example, on the question of access to the file there have been some appeals to the Court of First Instance in cases currently before the Commission where parties feel they have not had adequate access to the file.

6. Apart from errors of law or interpretation by the Commission in particular cases, or cases where it is said the Commission has in some way come to a wholly unreasonable decision, has the Court of First Instance made so far (because it has not had much time) a contribution towards revealing errors of procedure by the Commission, and has it done anything to put errors right, apart from access to the files?

A. The main case I was thinking of was the case of access to the file, where the parties in the *Italian Flat Glass* case, for example, had an extract from a document that was cited which was proved to have been wrongly cited. The document should have been cited in full, and the Court of First Instance considered that that was a serious procedural infringement. In the current *Cement* proceedings, which are going on before the Commission, there have been appeals to the Court of First Instance on disclosure of documents in other parts of the case relating to other parties. I think already the Court of First Instance, although it is early days, has proved itself a body where it is perhaps more possible to

make appeals on these matters of procedure; but there still are, of course, fundamental problems of admissibility at the early stages of the administrative proceeding.

7. I know in the early days of the Court of First Instance they were quite clearly willing to go into the facts and into the merits of the case far more than the Court of Justice ever had time to do. Do you get the feeling that approach is continuing?

A. I do, indeed, my Lord Chairman. I think the Court of First Instance is devoting a lot of time and resources to the examination of cases.

8. When people talk about transferring a great deal of work to the Court of First Instance, they must be careful not to impinge on the availability of time for competition cases?

A. Not to overload it.

9. What about appeals from the Court of First Instance to the Court of Justice on procedural questions, have there been many of those?

A. The Commission is appealing, I believe, the decision relating to the *Polypropylene* case on the defective adoption of decisions where it was alleged that matters were inserted into the text after a decision had been adopted by the Commission. I think that is a case which is being appealed from the Court of First Instance to the full Court.

10. Do the improvements which come as a result of the Court of First Instance mean that you would now accept that the Commission should continue to have enforcement and judicial functions, or do you think that the problems are still such that the Community should look at separating those powers? I know there was at one stage a great deal of criticism about the fact that the Commission was both prosecutor and judge in these cases. Is that criticism still extensive or do you think it is no longer fully justified?

A. The criticism is still there. I think myself it can be to some extent remedied by measures which fall short of the wholesale re-writing of Regulation 17. Regulation 17 was once referred to by one of your lordships as the " Ark of the Covenant ", but it is also regarded as a Pandora's Box.

11. I find that an interesting conjunction of phrases! That an Ark of the Covenant could also be a Pandora's Box!

A. Changing Regulation 17 could result in changing the fundamental ways in which Community competition law has been administered in the last 30 years. All sorts of matters can come out of the woodwork and become open to political debate. When we come on to talk about the institution of the Hearing Officer, which has been a valuable contribution, I think there are several aspects in the role of the Hearing Officer which could be increased and emphasised in a way which would make the Hearing Officer a more valuable and solid institution to protect defendants' rights, and that may be a more realistic way of providing for an internal system of checks and balances on what the Commission does.

[*Chairman Contd*]

12. I think to improve the procedure is something we want to go through, but we have to face the question at this stage, after 30 years' experience, do we think the basic structure is wrong or basically acceptable subject to improvements. What is your position on that?

A. My position is that if you were starting completely from scratch, all over again, it might have been better to have had some independent tribunal or regulatory body which was able to check what the Commission did at various stages of the administrative procedure, for example at the stage of investigation, and at the stage of access to the file before one got to the oral hearing. One of the great problems we find in Brussels is that when you have a case, by the time you get to the oral hearing the Commission has investigated the matter, it has written a Statement of Objections and the views of the officials often become very, very entrenched. It is extremely difficult to over-turn the line and attitude which the Commission takes in the Statement of Objections, even though it is only meant to be a provisional document. The reality is that it is extremely difficult to change what is said in the Statement of Objections. If you look at Statements of Objections and the decisions which ultimately follow, they are often extremely similar. One hopes that the Commission does take full account of what is pleaded before them on oral hearing.

13. You said if you were starting from scratch you would have separate functions, but we are not starting from scratch so should we tear it up or amend it?

A. I think I would be in favour of improving the administrative procedure through strengthening the office of the Hearing Officer, giving him a much more important role, making his hearing report available——

14. We will come on to the detail in a moment. You mentioned the Statement of Objections. The European Court held it really did not have the function of examining the validity or procedural correctness of the Statement of Objections. Do you think there should be some amendment to the rules or Treaty in order to allow the Court to get into the act at an earlier stage, particularly with the First Instance tribunal in existence? Or do you think the present procedures before the Court hearing are sufficient? In other words, you only look at the final stage when there is a real decision reached. I have in mind the *IBM* case, as you know.

A. Yes. Of course by allowing appeal of the Statement of Objections, which is meant to be a provisional document, one would be greatly lengthening the process and introducing a fundamental appeal at an early stage.

15. Unless you knocked it out? Unless you said the Statement of Objections was so vitiated by error that the enquiry should go on further?

A. Yes, if you could do that, that might well be a useful innovation.

16. Would it be a desirable innovation in your experience

A. I do not think myself it would necessarily be a desirable innovation. I think I would rather see greater importance being given to the oral hearing and perhaps the Commission being more responsive to pleadings which are put before it in the oral hearing.

17. If we come to the same conclusion, it will be a great relief to the Court of Justice! You mentioned merger control being an extra facet of this. Are there special considerations here in relation to enforcement and adjudication?

A. It is really at the second stage of procedure under the Merger Control Regulation. It has been suggested that once the Commission, having carried out its investigation, feels that there are serious doubts in its mind on the compatibility of a merger with the Common Market, that the second stage of the investigation should perhaps be entrusted to an independent body because that independent body would be less inclined to be subject, for example, to political lobbying and would present a more objective view of a merger case and would examine it in a more objective way. The ex-President of the German Federal Cartel Office, Professor Kartte, has suggested there should be an independent mergers review body which, as I understand it, would operate as a sort of European Monopolies and Mergers Commission. The problem of course with that proposal is again that it would require an amendment of the Treaty. There is no evidence that it would necessarily be less political in its nature because it is an independent body. It would still have to be composed, presumably, of representatives from individual Member States. The other problem of course about the insertion of another body is that it will make the procedures inevitably, in my view, much longer. For the business community, as we will come on probably to discuss when we look at the Merger Control Regulation in more detail, one of the present advantages of transactions which fall within the Regulation is the speed with which they are dealt. There is no doubt the insertion of a European MMC would lengthen the procedures.

18. I think we must look at the proposal of the German Federal Cartel Office. Anyway the result is that you would not go along with the suggestion, as I understand it?

A. I would not go along with that suggestion myself, no.

19. So far as the Court of First Instance is concerned, have they played a role yet in the merger control procedures?

A. There has been certainly one appeal to the Court in the *British Airways/TAT* case where Air France has appealed that decision to the European Court. In a sense it has been too early for the Court of First Instance to play a major role.

20. So in principle you accept the structure subject to amendments?

A. Yes.

[Chairman *Contd*]

21. You mentioned the question of access, in the 1982 enquiry there was considerable discussion about the question whether parties had sufficient right of access to the Commission's files. Since 1982 what, if any, changes or improvements have there been?

A. The main change following the 1982 report is that the parties to competition proceedings are allowed access to the Commission file. They are not allowed access to the full file, in the sense that they are not simply given the file to look at. There are a number of important exceptions; they are not allowed access to documents for which business secrets are claimed, they are not allowed access to the Commission's internal working documents, but they are allowed access to the documents on which the Commission relies in its Statement of Objections, and those are listed in schedules prepared by the Commission, and one depends on those schedules in examining the file to see what documents are available. So it is not full access to the file. For example, if there were documents in a case which might be of help to a defendant but were not relied on by the Commission, those would not be necessarily available to a defendant, for want of a better word, to competition proceedings. There is no doubt a change has been made. The Competition Directorate has reorganised its whole documentation system to take account of the need to protect confidentiality and to provide access. It is not, however, full access in the sense that one would possibly have in mind.

22. Perhaps full access—giving "full access" the fullest meaning of the phrase—is probably neither possible nor desirable.

A. I think that is probably right.

23. Are there areas where at the moment access is denied, where you think access should be possible?

A. I think the parties to competition proceedings should have a chance to see documents from the Commission's file which are not necessarily relied on, or the Commission does not allege that it relies on in the proceedings, which might be helpful to the parties in the protection of their rights of defence, and in enabling them to be heard properly during the administrative proceedings. That is not the case at present.

24. Is that a peculiarly English attitude? The Germans, for example, find that rather surprising looking at the procedure in civil law countries. Here it is perfectly normal that you disclose things which may help the other side, but in other countries it is not the practice.

A. I think it probably is an English viewpoint.

25. It is unlikely, therefore, that if we made too wide a recommendation that it would have any chance of being accepted?

A. Also, of course, the Commission's view has been endorsed by the Court.

26. What about people other than parties to the actual proceedings? There was an attempt made by the representative groups—I have in mind the consumers, the European BEUC—who applied to see documents and were told they had no right to see documents. Has that generated any dissatisfaction amongst other consumer representative groups, manufacturing representative groups, on the basis that there should be a right of access in order that they can make representations at enquiries?

A. I have not myself been aware of a major demand from consumer groups to have access to files.

27. BEUC was very dissatisfied when it was told it could not see the documents.

A. Yes. My own view is that if there is a party to proceedings which has established that it has a legitimate interest in the proceedings, I cannot see why that party cannot have access to the file, subject, of course, to the protection of confidential business secrets.

28. Perhaps for the record we had better say that BEUC is the Bureau Européen des Unions de Consommateurs.

A. The European Consumers' Association.

29. You mentioned the oral hearing and there might be improvements there. What do you think still needs to be done to improve the oral hearing? Perhaps you could tell us what changes have taken place and if anything is outstanding.

A. The main change that has taken place is that the hearing is presided over by a Hearing Officer. This was a post that was created after the 1982 Report. The Hearing Officer reports directly to the Commissioner responsible for competition. He is, in a sense, slightly outside the normal apparatus of the Competition Directorate-General. The meeting is now presided over by the Hearing Officer, who governs the questioning, prepares the hearing and who puts and summarises the essential legal and factual matters that the hearing is considering. The other Commission participants at the oral hearing tend usually to be only the Head of Division and the rapporteur dealing with the case, and perhaps representatives from elsewhere in the Commission, such as the Legal Service. As I said earlier, the problem is that often by the time one has got to the oral hearing the views of the Commission team dealing with the case are strongly entrenched.

30. Do you regard the Hearing Officer as being part of the Commission team?

A. No, I do not regard him as being part of the Commission team.

31. Is he part of DG IV, or is he separate outside?

A. He is part of DG IV, but directly answerable to the Commissioner without going through the normal hierarchy. He is an official of DG IV.

32. What kind of official is appointed to this sort of job?

A. Usually an official of DG IV. The holders of the post to date have been Heads of Division at A3 level who have become Hearing Officers.

33. How many of them are there?

A. There is only one Hearing Officer at a particular time. The Hearing Officer only becomes involved at the stage of the oral hearing. He does not become involved earlier on, when in my view it would

[Chairman *Contd*]

be extremely useful to have a more independent view outside the case team; so with procedural issues (such as access to the file, disclosure of documents and time limits for making replies to Commission Statements of Objection) which arise at the written stage of the proceedings, it would be helpful if the Hearing Officer was involved earlier. As it is, he is involved at the oral hearing stage.

34. Does he, in any sense, occupy the prosecution team, or does he occupy a wholly judicial function?
A. No, he does not occupy so much a *judicial* function, he is the chairman of the meeting. He runs the meeting; he regulates the questioning, and I have been present where the Hearing Officer has prevented the Commission from pursuing what one could have regarded as an unfair line of questioning. He provides someone who is outside the case dealing with the team, to whom defendant parties can complain if they feel that the Commission is riding roughshod over their arguments and not paying attention to particular arguments they are making. He regulates the conduct of the hearings.

35. Where do we find his powers and functions set out?
A. His functions are not set out in a Regulation; you will find them summarised in one of the Reports on Competition Policy which was adopted shortly after the 1982 Report.

36. Is there any appeal from a decision of his to anybody else?
A. No, he does not actually make formal decisions.

37. Procedural decisions. If he takes a procedural decision that the Commission may use something which a party regards as wholly unfair, is there anywhere they can go to complain about his decision?
A. No, having presided over the hearing, he prepares a report on the hearing. That report is not made available to the parties. I think that is a great mistake, because the Hearing Officer is there to help, at any rate to protect the rights of defence of the parties; but they never actually see the report he makes, because his duties extend beyond the oral hearing to what happens subsequently. He is meant to ensure, for example, that the minutes of the hearing are accurate; that the Commission has not been selective in the way that the minutes are put together. I think, there, the Hearing Officer has made a major difference. We now get fairer minutes of oral hearings than was the case before. We never see the report of the Hearing Officer. In other words, parties never see what he has to say about the way he might have had to defend their interests after the hearing has taken place, or indeed at the hearing. I see no reason why that report should be made the subject of secrecy. Dr Johannes, who was the Hearing Officer at the Fordham Conference two years ago, himself made the observation that he could see no reason why his report as Hearing Officer should not be made available to parties. I think it would add to the transparency of proceedings if that report was made available.

38. Would you recommend that any other powers be given to him, or any other obligations be imposed on him to make him more effective to protect the defendants's rights?
A. Yes, I would like to see him brought into the proceedings right at the beginning, even at the stage where the Commission has to conduct an investigation. I would like to see the Hearing Officer brought into the case right at the beginning of the written proceedings, so that parties with procedural problems have someone to go to, other than the rapporteur or the Head of Division or the Director who is prosecuting the case. If, for example, the Commission issues on Christmas Eve a time deadline for replying to a Statement of Objections of twenty days (which I am afraid has been my experience and does happen somewhat frequently, I would say) then one actually has an independent person outside the team to go to and make a ruling about the fairness or justice of that type of ruling. On questions such as access to the file, if you felt, for example, that documents were being withheld from you that you should have access to, a ruling from an independent Hearing Officer would be very helpful. I think he is brought into the proceedings far too late.

39. That is the kind of decision I had in mind when I asked you if there was anywhere else to go if the Hearing Officer was against the defendant for adjudication.
A. At the moment there is no appeal because the Hearing Officer does not actually make any formal decision which you could even appeal to the European Court.

40. If he decides twenty days is right, you might want to go somewhere else?
A. Yes. That is something which should be considered. There is no appeal.

41. The status of the Hearing Officer is quite a senior status. I remember when Dr Johnanes was appointed, he was a man of considerable experience in the Commission and of standing. Do you think the status is right or should it be someone more evidently judicial?
A. I think for the Hearing Officer to be taken more seriously in the Commission the status does need to be improved. I do not think he is sufficiently highly regarded by the Commission officials, and I think there is scope for improving his status, perhaps by extending his functions in a greater way. Also making his report public one would have the effect of enhancing his status.

42. Extending his functions to cover what kind of ruling or activity?
A. I think rulings at the early administrative stage.

43. Only that?
A. Primarily that. At the moment he makes his report to the Commissioner. There is of course the point that his hearing report could be made available to the full body of Commissioners who ultimately take the decision. At the moment there is no immediate link between the full body of Commissioners, who have no information apart

[Chairman *Contd*]

from what is presented to them by the Commissioner responsible for competition, and the other Commissioners in the College of Commissioners, who will not have been present at the oral hearing and have no way of seeing what was presented at the oral hearing.

44. Although you do not see the report, do you know what is the object of the report? What is in general terms the content of the report? What sort of matters does he report on?

A. As I have never seen one——

45. What is the object of the report if he is not part of the prosecution?

A. The object of the report is to make sure that the interests of the defendants have been taken into account, that matters which they have pleaded are properly reported and made available to those who ultimately take the decision. In reality what happens is that the report is made available to the Commissioner responsible for competition at the time that he has to take a decision as to whether or not the matter should ultimately be adopted as a full decision.

46. One of the complaints made frequently about the competition procedures in the Community is that the number of people dealing with enquiries and complaints is too small. Do you need more than one Hearing Officer? Is his staff adequate for the function? I suppose you say not if you enlarge the function?

A. Not if you enlarge the function.

47. At present?

A. At present he has no staff and I think it would add possibility to his status if one gave him even a secretariat of his own. He depends very much administratively on the help he gets from the Competition Directorate-General, and of course he still works in that building and is part of that organisation even though he has a slightly separate status. Giving him his own staff independently of the hierarchical DG IV system would increase his independence.

48. Perhaps in more concrete terms, do you need more that one Hearing Officer?

A. At present simply to conduct the actual hearings you probably do not need more than one Hearing Officer, if he had greater administrative back-up. If you enlarge his functions in the way I have suggested, so he is brought in at the written stage of the procedure—because not every case which starts with the written procedure ends up with an oral procedure as some case are settled before then—you would have more cases at the written procedure stage, and therefore duties would become much heavier. If you did that you would need more than one Hearing Officer and you might need one responsible for the written procedure stage and another responsible for the oral procedure stage. You could divide functions in that way.

49. Can we turn to the Advisory Committee set up under Article 10 of Regulation 17? Before the Commission decision is announced, an Advisory Committee has to be consulted. At the time of the last enquiry the Select Committee had very much in mind the criticism of the Advocate General in the *Distillers* case, that the workings of the Advisory Committee were too shrouded in secrecy. Has that improved at all?

A. No, my Lord Chairman, it has not. The workings of the Advisory Committee and the report of the Advisory Committee remain shrouded in secrecy. I have to say I was a *stagiaire* with the European Commission and therefore I have had the unique privilege amongst practitioners of having been present at a meeting of the Advisory Committee, because the Commission allows its *stagiaires* to sit in on meetings of the Advisory Committee. I have actually witnessed a meeting of the Advisory Committee. Normally those procedures are entirely secret and the opinion is secret.

50. So the opinion of the Committee, their report, is not communicated to the undertaking?

A. No, and it is not published.

51. Do you know what the Advisory Committee sees, what it is given?

A. We have no knowledge at all of what the Advisory Committee sees, although it is known they of course see the draft decision which the Commission proposes to adopt. That is common knowledge. As to what else they see, the parties and their lawyers have no knowledge.

52. In the last report the Select Committee recommended that the undertaking should be informed of the documents submitted to the Advisory Committee, that the minutes of the oral hearing should be submitted to the Advisory Committee, that the Advisory Committee's report should be communicated to the undertaking. From what you say, none of those three recommendations was accepted?

A. None of those three recommendations was accepted. What is extremely relevant now is that the Commission has accepted under the Merger Control Regulation that the opinion of the Advisory Committee, in cases under that Regulation, is published. It seems to me totally anomalous that the opinion of the Advisory Committee is published in merger cases, albeit at the time the decision is taken, but not published in cases under Articles 85 and 86, and I can see no justification at all for making that distinction.

53. But one of the objects of the Advisory Committee is that Member States should be aware of what is going on and what the Commission is proposing to do. Do you have the feeling, from your experience, that Member States attach any importance to the Advisory Committee, to what it does? Do they take it seriously?

A. I think there are certain Member States which take the role of the Advisory Committee more seriously than others. As I say, as one is never present at the hearing of the Committee it is very difficult to judge, but you can observe at the oral hearing that

[Chairman *Contd*]

there are some Member States which are consistently not represented, and there are other Member States which are always represented and always play an active part in the questioning, so it depends really on the Members States concerned. I myself would advocate the Advisory Committee's opinion being published, and I think it should be made clear exactly how the vote of the particular Member States went. Even under the Merger Control Regulation, all we are told at the moment is that a majority took one view and a minority took another view, we are not told which Member State voted which way. I can see no reason for this matter being kept secret.

54. Perhaps I should have got on the record at the beginning, the Advisory Committee consists of one representative, an official, from each Member State?
A. Yes, from the national competition authorities.

55. Can we turn to another Article of Regulation 17, and that is Article 14. If the Regulation is the Ark of the Covenant, this is a very important steering mechanism, if arks have steering mechanisms. Would you like to tell us about the way in which Commission investigations are now carried out under this? Do you think the Commission adequately carries out its investigations? Are there defects in the way it does so?
A. I think that this is also one of the bees which might fly out of Pandora's Box, if Regulation 17 was going to be amended. The investigation procedure is unsatisfactory in a number of respects. At present, when investigators arrive, either for a surprise visit under Article 14(3) or in an announced way under Article 14(2), because there are two types of investigation, their mandate to investigate is accompanied by an explanatory memorandum which proposes to detail the scope of the enquiry. One of the problems is that the scope of the investigation is usually extremely vaguely worded, and the Commission appears to be under no obligation to state precisely what it is investigating. That, for companies and their advisers, makes life extremely difficult. The other aspect which I have found in my experience of investigations, when I have been called suddenly to attend them, is that the Commission inspectors do have a tendency to ask very wide ranging questions which are not limited to the documents which they are inspecting. Under Regulation 17 their questions are supposed to be confined to oral explanations of the documents they are examining. In reality and in practice, and I am sure several of my fellow practitioners will bear this out, the range of questioning extends often far beyond those documents. Of course, company executives who are faced with this question may find that rather confusing, and it is a difficult situation to deal with. That is why it is important, I think, that their legal advisers are present with them at all stages of the investigation. I think those are the two main problems that we have at the moment with investigations.

56. One of the parts of Article 14 which initially was thought to be very important was that if the undertaking involved opposed an investigation by the Commission, Member States should be required to give the necessary assistance to the Commission in order to enable it to pursue its investigation. Do you have any experience as to the way in which this is actually carried out, and its obligation is carried out by Member States? Does the Commission get full co-operation? Does it vary from State to State? Are there some defaulters amongst Member States in this respect?
A. I have to say, my own experience has been confined to investigations which have taken place within the United Kingdom; I find it difficult, therefore, to comment on investigations which have taken place in other Member States. My own experience in the United Kingdom is that an official of the competition authority is part of the team which investigates, but in my experience does not play a very active role in the investigation at all. I would describe it more as a passive role. I have never been present at any investigation where the company opposed the entry of the investigators.

Baroness Elles

57. Might I come back, if I may, to the first question which is, I think, fundamental to our enquiry. I think you will accept, Mr Reynolds, that a few changes were brought into competition proceedings as a result of the 1982 proposals from this Committee, and clearly some have improved procedures and some have fallen slightly by the wayside. The fact, for instance, that a legal adviser does now attend investigations under 14(3) must be an improvement. Insofar as some of the matters have not been improved, I was wondering whether you really think it would be difficult to produce a new Regulation after 30 years of the 1962 Regulation 17. Would the Commission, in view of the comments that Sir Leon Brittan made in a very interesting article, be helped by having some kind of modified procedural notice at least, even if not a formal regulation. It could cover timetables, the role of the Hearing Officer, what his powers are, the transparency of the decisions. I wonder if you would think it might be possible, in perhaps some modified form, to make some improvements?
A. I think it would. Of course, one must bear in mind that Regulation 17 has effectively been modified by the Merger Control Regulation.

58. As far as that is concerned?
A. As far as that is concerned; it has actually been amended, in fact, in relation to mergers. In that sense one can no longer regard it as sacrosanct. Other procedural amendments, for example, connected with exemptions (and I think we ought to come on to that) have been made in certain areas, such as airlines and in relation to maritime transport automatic exemptions, which everyone had said could not be done because it required amendment of Regulation 17, have been introduced in block exemption regulations in those sectors. Therefore, I think the arguments for saying that we can never tamper with the entire mechanism, because it will all down if we do, may be slightly less valid now. I do think that some of these other matters to which I have

[Baroness Elles *Contd*]

alluded could usefully be included even in an amending Regulation. I think you will find there is enormous resistance to that within the Council of Ministers and within parts of the Commission itself. There is no doubt that there is scope for formalising more matters, such as the role of the Hearing Officer, access to the file and the conduct of oral hearings.

Chairman] It could well be that this sort of thing will have to wait for the signing of Maastricht.

Baroness Elles

59. There are some things which are clearly unacceptable still, are there not? The role of the Advisory Committee is totally unacceptable; the role of the Hearing Officer, and the fact that his report to the Commissioners is not seen by anybody, is totally unacceptable, particularly when it is very often the Commissioner himself who has to make the decision. Although the Commission as a whole, as a collegiate body, are meant to take the decision, in the majority of cases, as I understand it, they do not take a formal part in the decision, and they rely on the Commissioner responsible. Basically, at the end of the day, they are relying on the statement of the case handlers when you work downwards. I just wondered from a political point of view, now that the Court of First Instance plays a role in dealing with appeal cases, whether it might not be beneficial for the Commission to make its own position clearer in regard to the procedures, because its position has moved from the administrative role it used to have in 1962 to a much more judicial role, in view of the number of cases and the importance of the competition policy of the Community?

A. I think the other point to bear in mind, is that the Court of Justice has now made a whole number of procedural rulings, for example, on the rights of complainants, and whether or not letters rejecting complaints are appealable and whether you are entitled to a final decision. A whole range of matters have been ruled on since Regulation 17's adoption in 1962, or 1963 when the hearing Regulation 99/63 was adopted. I think there is a good case for saying that this is no longer so sacrosanct that we cannot amend it. As I say, it has effectively been amended.

Chairman

60. I think your view is that all these things can be done by amendment without tearing up the basic structure?

A. Yes. It is politically more feasible to suggest that, than to suggest a radical re-writing of the whole structure.

Lord Wedderburn of Charlton

61. Could I just ask a different question as an appendix to that. I appreciate that you have mainly dealt with United Kingdom cases, but the sorts of points which have been made in our questions to you so far are, I will not say " typically English " because that cuts out north of the border, but they are things to which lawyers in these jurisdictions tend to respond, and that is natural. You must have had

many, many conversations and discussions with people from other jurisdictions. Do you have to approach any of these points as though you have to be defensive about being very English, or are there chords which are struck elsewhere?

A. I think if you talk to German, French, and Belgian anti-trust lawyers they will share a large number of the concerns that I have mentioned. A large number of these points concern all companies from the Community who have been involved in competition proceedings, and their advisers. I do not think that any of these points are peculiarly of appeal just to English lawyers. I think the points Lady Elles has mentioned in particular are matters of common concern. I do not know whether your Lordships are going to receive evidence from any non-United Kingdom practitioners, but if you are I am sure you will find that they bear out a lot of these concerns.

Chairman

62. Even the anxiety about the basic structure having the same body being both the enforcer and the adjudicator is shared not just by English lawyers but by lawyers from Holland as well. Is that your experience?

A. That is my experience.

Lord Holme of Cheltenham

63. Following Lady Elles's question, if I understand it about 20 cases are settled by informal settlements for every one that goes forward into a full judicial process on competition. Similarly, the majority of merger cases are settled in phase one. That is a process of negotiation, of horse trading, if one wants to be pejorative, cutting a deal with which the Commission can live and with which the company concerned can live. Naturally, with distinguished lawyers and a legal focus, we are very much concerned with the judicial end of the process, but I would simply like to raise the question, and you mentioned getting the Hearing Officer more upstream in the whole process, whether the way that process happens, (which in fact is the normative one—the normative one is the negotiation rather than the adjudication and that is what happens in most instances), is a) in accordance with the rules of natural justice, and b) quasi-judicial, or is it administrative? I am not myself clear about that— my own ignorance, My Lord Chairman. Are there ways in which it may be made more transparent, more user-friendly? Would it be right that it should be? This is a large question, I am afraid.

A. It is a large question, my Lord. I think one does have to make the distinction between what I call contentious cases, where the Commission is taking formal proceedings, and where all the issues you have mentioned relating to the rights of defence therefore become more important, and cases which have a far more administrative nature. There is no doubt, and I think we will probably come on to this, that for industry, and for companies, the comfort letter mechanism is extremely welcome, and I do not think those companies would really welcome anything which made it more difficult or complicated and

[Lord Holme of Cheltenham *Contd*]

formalised the ability they have of reaching deals, as you put it, with the Commission. Because in fact in industry this is regarded as a perfectly acceptable way of proceeding and it gets over the enormous problems of getting formal decisions and exemptions and negative clearances from the Commission. Therefore I think myself that bringing the Hearing Officer into the proceedings earlier on would really only be relevant to what I call the contentious proceedings. I do not see by doing that you would necessarily make it more cumbersome for a notification to be dealt with by a comfort letter via negotiation with the case team by the simple fact that you had a Hearing Officer involved. Probably in that sort of case you would not need to involve the Hearing Officer because you are not in a contentious situation *vis-a-vis* the Commission, although it could turn into a contentious proceeding and the fact the Hearing Officer could be involved might be helpful.

64. I suppose my concern, my Lord Chairman, is that it is by not agreeing the Commission's deal that your case becomes contentious, to put it crudely.
A. Yes, it is not exactly a negotiation between equals.

Chairman

65. If 20 cases do get negotiated, for every one that goes through there must be some benefit in the negotiation process?
A. And, as I say, it is greatly welcomed.

66. As Lord Holme has indicated, the more you formalise, the greater the length of time you are going to take over cases, and the more we encourage Hearing Officers to get involved, the greater the risk of delay. Is delay in getting a decision a problem for the business community at the moment? Or do you think the timescale in the Commission broadly speaking is acceptable?
A. I think the timescale for obtaining formal clearances and exemption decisions is totally unacceptable, and I think the timescale for those who wish to complain about the anti-competitive activities of others is unacceptable. Any case which proceeds to a full decision can take as much as three to five years, particularly when there are disagreements within and between the Commission services. The fact is that for a full decision to be taken, there are something like 22 procedural steps which need to be taken. I was told in the preparation of a full decision, approximately 123 people can be involved at the various stages of it. Therefore the delays are extremely difficult to justify but they are caused by a variety of factors. The ability to find a short-cut through this, by getting a letter of comfort from the Commission, however doubtful its legal status may be in a national court, the simple fact you have a statement from the Commission of its position which is unlikely to be totally discarded—once you have a comfort letter from the Commission, in my experience, very rarely does it re-open the file to over-turn its comfort letter—that gives executives in industry comfort in the sense they feel they are able to proceed with transactions on that basis. On the whole

they would rather do that than go through the whole hoop of getting a formal decision.

67. Is there scope for more use of comfort letters, in your view?
A. Yes, I think there is, and I think what needs to be done with comfort letters is that their legal status needs to be improved by more advanced publication, more publication after they have been issued, and making them more reasoned—at the moment they are very bald sometimes in what they say. Somewhere I think there is a compromise between the speed of administration and efficiency and having something which has slightly more legal status than comfort letters do at the moment.

68. It really raises two questions. Is there a delay which can be criticised in the issue of the comfort letters once proceedings start on the administrative basis, or do they come reasonably quickly?
A. You can get a comfort letter really quite speedily from the Commission because the comfort letter can be issued from within Directorate-General IV. In a simple case it can be issued without the need to consult the legal service, and it is of course at the stage of consultation that a lot of delay occurs, particularly when there is a difference of view. So in general comfort letters come extremely speedily, in my experience.

69. How desirable is it to push the comfort letter procedure on to a more formalistic basis? If you ask for reasons and the Commission officials hear the reasons, they will have to be open to challenge and they will be slower in issuing comfort letters, and, perhaps even more undesirable, more reluctant perhaps to issue comfort letters? Is it not enough for businessmen to be given comfort rather than to know why?
A. I think my natural lawyer's caution, my Lord, leads me to desire greater legal comfort in the comfort letter, but from the point of view of my clients, if you took an opinion poll, they would be happy with the system as it is and they would not want to do anything which slowed down or made it more difficult or more likely there would be a dispute between the Commission services or within the Commission which would delay the issuing of a comfort letter.

70. When you say "more legal comfort" do you mean to have the status more clearly defined?
A. Yes, by making it more reasoned.

71. Enforceable? Is that what you are after when you talk about legal status?
A. The problem at the moment is that before a national court the Commission's comfort letter does not have binding effect. The degree to which it has persuasive effect depends on what is in it, and one must also bear in mind that the Commission has now taken to issuing what it calls the discomfort letter. A discomfort letter is where the Commission says that it has examined your case, it thinks that Article 85(1) applies, it is not minded that this is eligible for an exemption but it is closing the file, which leaves you in an extremely anomalous position, and if the matter

[Chairman Contd]

comes up before national courts that is a very vague situation to be left in legally.

72. So the comfort letter is really, as far as the Commission and the court, I imagine the First Instance court, are concerned is probably satisfactory. Your anxiety is over the use of comfort letters if, as the Commission wishes, they are to be increased in the future?
A. I had in mind the Notice on Co-operation between national courts and the Commission which we will no doubt be discussing.

73. Would it be the best solution for either Regulation 17 to be amended to state the legal effect of a Commission's comfort letter, or for the Court of Justice to be asked to rule in order to assist national courts or to bind national courts?
A. The problem of course is that any step like that, which does formalise the nature of the letter more, may make it harder to receive a comfort letter.
Chairman] This is my anxiety. We do not want to rock the boat in regard to comfort letters as they are at the moment.
Lord Holme of Cheltenham] I think, my Lord Chairman, when we talk to the MMC and the DTI we might pursue the British analogies to this.
Chairman] Yes.
Lord Holme of Cheltenham] Where there are comparable situations where they say things like, " You are probably all right " in more legal language.

Chairman

74. Do you have any experience of a British court accepting or not accepting a comfort letter as being decisive of the issue?
A. I have had no experience of it being accepted as decisive.

75. Or being rejected?
A. No direct experience.
Chairman] We may be able to ask the Bar Advisory Committee on that.

Baroness Elles

76. Do you foresee that with the development of the single market and the far greater number of contracts between businesses throughout the Community, and with the establishment of the European Economic Area, there might be more difficulty with regard to comfort letters, because it does not validate the contract, does it, vis-a-vis the Commission? Do you think that, therefore, there must be some kind of position taken, not necessarily going as far as recognising that it guarantees the legality of the contract, but do you think there is some kind of improvement in which way you could give legal certainty to firms which embark on an extension of their activities outside their own Member State?
A. In relation to the first part of the question, it is going to become more and more of a problem as companies do business in more and more jurisdictions. I think we come on to talk about the decentralisation of the application of Community

law when there are going to be more of these opinion letters handed down to national courts, and it becomes a major problem because the reality is that, increasingly, companies, and not only multinational companies but small companies, do business in a whole variety of jurisdictions across the Community. If they are now going to be told the Commission will not be dealing with their matters and they have to seek redress and deal with questions of Article 85 and 86 in national courts, it clearly is going to be a greater problem. If the guidelines are going to have any beneficial effect one really does need to address what the precise status the opinions, which the Commission will increasingly be called on to give, will have.

Lord Wedderburn of Charlton

77. Would one of the responses of the Commission—to cut down the size of it—be to make more use of discomfort letters, to keep its options open without having to do any more work? What is the response of the client if you tell him that he has a discomfort letter? Does he sleep more, or less?
A. Clients in general prefer to have anything which is a firm statement of the position. The result of both a comfort and a discomfort letter is that the Commission closes the file. Quite often the best news you can give a client is that the file has been closed, because he knows, wisely, that bureaucrats have an in-built reluctance to re-open files that have been closed. As the effect of both comfort and discomfort letters is that the file get closed, they welcome both. Obviously someone prefers to have a letter which says that the Commission is minded to take an exemption rather than one which say it is minded not to take an exemption.

Chairman

78. That is all right in the Community. The anxiety of course is when these documents, be they comfort or discomfort, are produced from a national judge?
A. Particularly in the case of discomfort letters.

79. Yes, a discomfort letter could have a very adverse effect. You mentioned the guidelines: were you referring to the recent anti-trust enforcement guidelines, or something else?
A. I was referring to the Notice on co-operation between the Commission and the national courts.

80. What about the anti-trust enforcement guidelines issued by the Commission recently, do you know about them?
A. I was thinking of the Notice on co-operation.

81. There is a document called the anti-trust enforcement guidelines which is meant to assist the national courts in carrying out their own investigations. We shall have to consider whether they are going to be sufficient to ensure that the rules are followed, and that legal certainty is given to undertakings. Do you have any views about that, or is it perhaps too early to have formed an impression about them?

[Chairman *Contd*]

A. I must confess, my Lord Chairman, I am not aware of any other guidelines. I have studied the Notice of co-operation.

82. Do you have any comment on that, as far as national courts are concerned?

A. I do have a number of comments. I think it is very early to see how that Notice is going to work in practice, not only in the United Kingdom courts but in courts throughout the Community. The Notice envisages that the Commission can be consulted by national courts for its opinion on cases which may also be before it, or which concern the same subject matter as proceedings before a national court. The Commission will be called upon to give an opinion as to its position, and will be called upon to give, effectively, a legal opinion as to the case. The Notice also foresees that the Commission will make available statistics and economic evidence. Put baldly like that, I think it begs an awful lot of questions. There is the problem that parties, once these matters are introduced directly by the Commission (and not by them) in national court proceedings, will have very little opportunity to contest the factual or legal elements that the Commission introduces into the proceedings. I think that possibly in a number of Member States in the Community, the actual admissibility of Commission opinions and evidence which the Commission is putting in, if it is evidence, will also cause a significant problem, even in the United Kingdom.

83. I think what you refer to as a " Notice " and I refer to as the " anti-trust enforcement guidelines " is the same document which was issued in 1991, and indicates the way in which the court should co-operate?

A. Yes. I think it is the same document.

84. It obviously does raise very serious questions for national courts?

A. Yes.

85. As Lord Wedderburn reminded us, we have to think of it not just in terms of the United Kingdom judges but judges in other countries. You have talked about exemptions: do you think that the Commission makes sufficient use of block exemptions in dealing with cases? If they made more use of it, it is inevitable, I suppose, that would be very advantageous from the point of view of delays; there would be more certainty and less delay?

A. I think the introduction of greater reliance on block exemption regulations, which I listed in the course of my submission, has been extremely useful, particularly for small and medium sized enterprises. Although sometimes they are difficult to interpret, they do introduce a great degree of certainty. They do, of course, avoid the need, if you come within them, to make an individual notification. I think there are other areas where the Commission could introduce block exemption regulations. For example, we have a block exemption for patent licences but we do not have one for trademark licences; we do not have one for computer software licences; so I think there are other areas where you could have block exemptions. My experience is that,

on the whole, they have been another tool that has enabled companies to avoid protracted proceedings of formal notifications.

86. Is there a great deal of lobbying for further block exemptions, or is it something which is rather left to the Commission's initiative?

A. I have a feeling, my Lord Chairman, that the Commission is reluctant to introduce further block exemption regulations. In fact, it may even be minded not to extend one or two of those that expire. I have in mind, for example, the block exemption for selective distribution in the motor industry, which expires in 1995, and there are indications that the Commission may be considering not renewing it. I think that would be strongly opposed by manufacturers and dealers who currently benefit from the legal certainty that that Regulation affords.

87. Is it your view that this is a useful tool which is under-employed, or is that overstating it?

A. No, I think it could be employed more.

88. That is thinking in terms of delays and lack of certainty for undertakings. The other matter which arises is the laying down of procedural deadlines. Sir Leon Brittan indicated that certain time limits would be followed for Article 85 and 86 cases. Do you think that these are going to be effective unless they are made mandatory, either as part of Regulation 17 or in some other way? Secondly, do you think there is anything to be learned from the Merger Control Regulation which could be introduced into the Articles 85/86 proceedings in this context?

A. My Lord Chairman, I trust I do not sound cynical, but in my experience in dealing with a bureaucracy, if a deadline is not mandatory then it is not a deadline. The proposed changes, which were announced by Sir Leon and have been confirmed by the Commission, would of course only apply to one sector of activity, and that is joint ventures at the moment where certain internal deadlines are proposed. There is no doubt in my mind that those internal deadlines will have nothing like the same effect as the guillotine that exists under the Merger Control Regulation where, if the Commission does not take a position within one month, the merger is deemed valid and cleared. The reality is that in the past, where the Commission has suggested such internal deadlines and, for one reason or another, they have slipped by, there is precious little the parties can do to enforce them. Indeed, in dealing with the Commission you will often not want to antagonise the Commission official dealing with the case by pointing out to him that the internal deadline, which is not a guillotine, has been passed. There are so many reasons the Commission can give for a deadline not being met, for example that it is the fault of another Directorate-General and not the Directorate-General for Competition, or the legal service, that it is very difficult to enforce them effectively. I think it is a step in the right direction and greatly to be welcomed that the Commission is aware of the problem. I think it is very difficult to justify two systems living side by side—if you have a merger falling under the Merger Control Regulation you

[Chairman *Contd*]

have clear guillotine deadlines of one month and four months, and if your transaction happens for whatever reason, which may be a very technical reason, to fall outside the Merger Control Regulation there are no time limits and theoretically at the moment the case could take, as has happened, five years. That is very difficult to justify. So any step in the direction of overcoming that, my own view is that unless you have firm guillotine——

89. Mandatory?
A. —mandatory deadlines—and I repeat, it can only be a deadline if it is mandatory—I do not think you will greatly improve the situation for enterprise.

90. Another suggestion made was that there should be an automatic exemption for agreements which have been waiting a Commission decision for a particular period. Is that a realistic suggestion?
A. I think it is realistic. It has in fact, as I have already mentioned, been introduced in two important sectors in relation to certain aspects of agreements concerning airlines and in maritime transport. If it can be applied there, I do not see why it cannot be applied in other sectors. It does give, of course, much greater legal certainty because you know if the Commission passes the due date without having taken a position, it can only re-open the proceedings by applying to the Court, so it makes the Commission organise itself at an early stage to deal with the matter as efficiently as possible. That the Commission can do that is evidenced in the case of Articles 85 and 86 in relation to airlines and sea transport, and in relation to Merger Control the Commission has had no problems in organising itself to deal with these very complex merger cases within the tight deadline.

91. Why maritime transport and air transport particularly? There was a lot of lobbying for the maritime sector, I seem to remember. I may be wrong. Was it as a result of lobbying, or are there special conditions there?
A. I have no idea. I can see no reason on paper why the 90 day deadline, which is the deadline in those two cases, should not apply in other areas. I cannot think, off-hand, why it is particularly important in airline and maritime matters and not in other very important sectors of industry where companies need early legal certainty for their transactions, particularly when they are joint ventures.

92. Let us move to the other end of the process. If there is a breach of Articles 85 and 86, can you help us with the way the Commission deals with fining? Is it consistent? Is it clear on what basis fines are calculated and imposed?
A. There are, my Lord Chairman, no clear guidelines as to the way in which fines are actually calculated in particular cases. The Court of Justice in the *Pioneer* case set out the sort of factors the Commission should take into account. Regulation 17 itself is extremely silent on the subject; it sets a maximum limit of 10 per cent on the worldwide turnover of an undertaking and it sets a minimum level. The whole process is in fact shrouded in

secrecy. From studying the cases, one can see in reality that the Commission does take into account as its starting point a percentage of turnover in the Community, although theoretically it can base its fine on the worldwide turnover, as the Regulation says—it has the freedom to do that. The *Pioneer* case makes it clear it can take a number of factors into account, such as whether it is a repeat offence——

93. Whether it was deliberate?
A. —whether it was deliberate or not——

94. Do you accept those standards? You have to as a matter of law.
A. I think those two standards are quite legitimate to take into account. I think there have been a number of companies which over and over again have been guilty of serious infringement of the competition rules.

95. But in the *Pioneer* case the court also said the Commission can change its competition fining policy without warning. Did that cause any problems?
A. I do not know whether that case caused it, but the effect has been in recent years that suddenly the Commission has substantially increased its fines. I have in mind the fine of 75 million units of account which was imposed on the Tetra Pak company. Without any warning the Commission suddenly and dramatically effectively tripled the maximum fines which it imposed on one company. Tetra Pak is a one-product company, it had been engaged in allegedly serious infringements, a matter which is subject to appeal at the moment, in a number of Member States of the Community. Nonetheless one has to have regard to the fact it was not an EC company. I personally question whether the fine would have been of that level if it had been an Italian, French or British company with a Commissioner to speak up for it in the College of Commissioners. If you study the fining decisions, and I set out in my submission all the fines which have ever been imposed, giving the durations and the nature of the infringements, you will see some striking anomalies. I compare, for example, the recent case of *Toshiba*, a Japanese company, and *Dunlop Slazenger*, both accused of the same infringement. Dunlop Slazenger received more than double the fine of Toshiba and the only difference I can detect is that Dunlop questioned and contested the Commission's findings whereas Toshiba accepted them and put in a compliance programme. The Commission itself has said that the attitude of the company is important; nonetheless if that actually leads effectively to plea-bargaining, I think there are enormous dangers. I would appreciate some clear guidelines which make clear, and also decisions which made clearer, why the Commission was imposing lower fines in certain cases.

96. In anticipation or after the event?
A. Both. I would like to have clear guidelines, in a sense almost a tariff of fines, and I would like to see it made clear in the decision whether a fine was imposed on a company because it was in a crisis industry, because that is not always the case.

Lord Wedderburn of Charlton

97. But you would not mind a deterrent element so long as you knew when it was likely to appear?
A. Yes. I can give another example—the French shipping case where the cartel was fined a total of 15 million ecu. Now it was the first time that the competition rules had been applied in that sector under a new Regulation relating to maritime transport. In other cases, where the Commission has applied Article 86 in a new sector or in a new way which represented virgin legal territory, the Commission has reduced the fine, but in that case they imposed a very heavy fine. There is no clear approach.
Chairman] There have been quite a number of cases involving that and we will have to see what Dr Ehlermann says about the policy.

Baroness Elles

98. In relation to fines, from what you are saying it seems clear compliance by an undertaking with the finding of the Commission does seem to effect in some way and influence the size of the fine. If this is the kind of conduct of the Commission, rightly or wrongly, it is going to influence, I would assume, complainants and others going to the Commission rather than to national courts where, of course, you would not get the same treatment when it comes to fining. Would you see here a great difficulty unless there is some kind of clear guideline set by the Commission and standards whereby companies can be certain of the kind of fines they might be expected to pay?
A. The policy of the Commission has had its desired effect of great deterrence, and it has also had the effect that complainants see the Commission as the more likely body to help them protect their position and their rights.

Chairman

99. Is not an element of surprise a useful weapon in deterrence? If people know what the fine is likely to be, they calculate whether it is worth violating the rules. If they do not know what it is going to cost them, they are less likely to break the rules? This is the argument, is it not?
A. That, my Lord Chairman, is the argument which the Commission would put to justify its ability suddenly to introduced out of the blue very large fines. If you compare the behaviour of the Commission with other anti-trust bodies, it is not consistent with what the other anti-trust bodies in the world do. I do not know of any other anti-trust body which has imposed a fine in the way the Commission did in the *Tetra Pak* case—there may be some but I certainly do not know of an instance where suddenly, almost overnight, a fine on a single company was imposed which was three or four times as great as had previously been the case.

100. Has the Court of First Instance done anything about fines? I remember in the Court itself we did not make very substantial reductions, as far as I remember. I think in *Pioneer* there were some reductions?

A. There have been limited reductions.

101. What about the Court of First Instance, is that following the same policy?
A. I think that any reductions may have been slightly greater but not dramatically greater.

102. Do you have a feeling that people on the whole tend to appeal from the Commission to the Tribunal or the Court of Justice because of the fine rather than because of the finding of breach?
A. I think when a company has been fined, given all the negative publicity concerned, often given the position of individual executives of the company concerned, there is strong pressure to try and vindicate the company's position in some way, and to make appeals to the Court, even though those companies may be advised that they have very little chance of success on the substance.

103. To get the fine down, I suppose, which is something of a triumph in itself?
A. Not so much for the money, but for whitening the otherwise black book.
Chairman] Perhaps if the Court of First Instance reduces the fine it reduces the risk of people going further to the Court of Justice.
Lord Holme of Cheltenham] I am conscious that time runs on, my Lord Chairman, but I wonder whether we are planning to get to the very specific subject which Mr Reynolds covered of merger thresholds?
Chairman] Yes. We have got three or four questions on mergers and then two general questions. Would you like to say something about it.

Lord Holme of Cheltenham

104. I read your evidence with great interest and, indeed, what Sir Leon Brittan had to say, and one can see from the single market the case for lowering the threshold is very considerable. If it is a single market why are mergers not dealt with as a whole within the market? At the same time we are clearly going to have, approaching the 1966 IGC, great talks about subsidiarity, and one can equally see the conflicting principle, because if a merger affects two companies within one country only, why should that not be dealt with within that country whatever the level? So that the question in a way seems less one of levels and more one of the market in which the companies operate if it is primarily a competitive issue. I think the doubts in this country that arise about lowering the threshold come because we have now established very clearly that there is only one criterion on mergers, which is competition. The doubt, inferred form one of our questions, about the Commission's merger policy is that it might take in other elements: and the European interest, European champions, and the European industrial policy are just three examples. The fact that only one merger has been turned down might mean that if there were Commissioners who were less competition minded and in a block trading world were more minded to look at the strength of European industries and were less concerned with intra-competition than extra competitiveness, then the prejudice of the European

[Lord Holme of Cheltenham *Contd*]

merger authorities would not be so clearly rooted in competition in a pure way. The question I am therefore asking, is whether you think we are building on a firm rock in saying, yes, let us bring the thresholds down and let us have what industry would prefer, which is the single stop and the single European position, and whether that is necessarily going to be as clearly biased towards the criterion of competition as the British merger policy now is?

A. That is a very comprehensive question. It raises a number of extremely interesting issues. First of all, on the subsidiarity issue, if the thresholds came down as the Commission suggested in the note it published at the same time as the Regulation, that they would like to see thresholds of 2bn ecu worldwide turnover and 100m ecu turnover within the Community, that would indeed catch many more cases. We have an awful lot of cases that fall between the 2bn and the 5bn figure which currently fall outside the Regulation, and that means for our clients that they now have to go and get clearances in Dublin, Berlin, Paris and London according to a number of different merger rules with different criteria, with different thresholds and they are asked different questions. For companies across the 12 Member States this is a serious problem, putting them, I would submit, at a competitive disadvantage to Japanese or American companies, so I think there is a major problem. If the thresholds were to come down, and I have to say I am very doubtful whether they will, my own view is that that should be accompanied by a strengthening of the provisions that allow referral to be made back to Member States under Article 9, where the Commission can refer back to a Member State a competition case which falls within the Regulation but, nonetheless, produces its effect primarily in one State. So far Article 9 has been operated in a very restrictive manner. I believe five requests have been made, and only one reference has been made back in the *Streetley/Tarmac* case, and all the rest, which were request from the Bundeskartellamt in Germany, have been refused. The Commission has adopted an extremely restricted approach. One of the problems is the way that Article 9 is drafted. It makes it very difficult for a Member State to establish that it has the jurisdiction to deal with the matter. Of course, it has also to be borne in mind that the third limb of the jurisdiction requirement, that where the Community turnover is more than two-thirds achieved by both companies in one and the same Member State, the matter will not fall within the Regulation and will remain so, as I understand it, even though the thresholds may come down. The sort of case you had in mind might well fall within that. I think it would also be necessary, and the Member States would almost certainly demand it, to have a strengthening of the referral procedure. Turning to your second point about the fact that there has only been so far one prohibition, I think I would say this: first of all, I do not think this Regulation was ever envisaged as a vehicle necessarily for prohibition; its aim was to help the Commission approve mergers. One of the problems we had before the Regulation was that there were no means for the Commission to actually approve mergers under Article 86. Secondly,

there would have been ten prohibitions if, in the cases where proceedings were opened, the companies had not come forward with restructuring and structural undertakings to the Commission. Those would probably, almost certainly, have been prohibited by the Commission if a solution had not been found. That is certainly what the Commission has made clear. In the one case that was prohibited, the decision was taken on purely competition grounds, despite extremely heavy lobbying, and the Commission did not in that case take into account the very substantial European industry arguments that were put to it. My own view on the political bargaining that takes place on the reduction of the thresholds, is that the Member States would almost certainly demand a number of quid pro quos. One would be an improvement of the referral back, but another would almost certainly be the insertion into the Regulation of an industrial policy exception to make it less rigid, because certain EC governments, probably not the United Kingdom, think that the system is too rigid. Of course, in that their views are shared by the European Parliament, as was evidenced in the resolution Parliament passed at the time of the *de Havilland* case. I think the other thing again is that one must look at the Commission's record compared with other anti-trust agencies. For example, over an equivalent period, if you look at the cases examined by Department of Jusitce, you see that there are about 1,500 cases that were examined and that proceedings were only opened in ten. If you look at the record of the German cartel office, over exactly the same period, you can see that 2,000 cases were examined and only one prohibited. The Commission's record is not necessarily strongly out of line with other authorities, except perhaps the United Kingdom where the criteria, nonetheless, are much wider under public interest. I personally do not attach an enormous amount of significance to the fact that only one case has so far been prohibited.

Chairman

105. There is no doubt that the way the Task Force has worked in DG IV has been very much praised by many people, and DG IV as a whole has probably been felt to be more effective in relation to merger control than in some other areas. Are there any changes or improvements, without amending the Merger Control Regulation, which could be made to the procedures or processes of DG IV in relation to mergers?

A. In relation to mergers, I think there are one or two changes which could be made, although I have to say, as I say in my submission, most of the changes would involve an amendment of the Regulation particularly in relation to the settlement procedure. I think it would be possible to publish the opinion of the Advisory Committee before the decision is taken, and require the Commission to motivate any difference in its decision from the Advisory Committee's opinion, so one could introduce a little more sunlight into the proceedings. At the moment after you have had an oral hearing before the Commission, in a case where proceedings have been

[Chairman *Contd*]

opened, it is very difficult to find out what is going on and usually there is a lot on in terms of lobbying and consultation between the Member States and the Commission. If one had access at an earlier stage to the Advisory Committee's opinion, that would increase the transparency of the proceedings. So that is something which could be done without amending the Regulation. I think possibly the Commission could adopt a sort of a *de minimis* notice. At the moment a number of cases are caught which have no possible interest to the Commission. I give an example in my submission of two Japanese motor manufacturers who may set up a concentrative joint venture on the island of Hokkaido to run a Sushi restaurant, and if they do more than the required turnover in the Community and their worldwide turnover as motor manufacturers passes the limit, they will have to notify that to Brussels. There is absolutely no effect in the Community, there is not interest, it is a waste of time the Commission devoting its resources to examining that sort of case. I think the introduction of that sort of case of a *de minimis* notice would make life easier for both companies, particularly those outside the Community, as well as the Commission. There have been a number of cases which have been caught almost accidentally by the way the turnover thresholds are defined, particularly in the case of joint ventures. The idea would be to re-draft Article 5 of the Regulation, but you could do that without introducing a notice. If I could say one word about the comparison and the way merger cases are dealt with, and the way DG IV is organised, again without making fundamental changes one could introduce the sort of administrative changes within DG IV which had to be put into effect to deal with the tight timetables of the Regulation in relation to cases under Articles 85 and 86. It is not so much a matter of more manpower. One hears the Commission is under-staffed; well it is under-staffed but that is not the only problem. The real reason in my view that those who set up the Task Force achieved an enormous success, was in streamlining various procedures, in eliminating much of the delay in consultation by effectively introducing an opposition procedure *vis-a-vis* other services in the Commission. One of the biggest causes of delay is disagreements between services in the Commission in my experience, it is not necessarily just lack of manpower. That is a problem; the use of nine languages is also a problem, but so is the consultation process. That was streamlined under the Merger Control Regulation. Other improvements were introduced such as the shortening of decisions and the waiving of the need to use nine languages at various stages in the procedure, and also the installation of proper computer facilities enabling matters to be put on a computer data base network. I see no reason why those sort of changes which the Commission had to introduce to comply with the guillotine time limits could not be introduced to speed up procedure in other cases. I think another improvement which the founders of the Task Force introduced which was invaluable was the secondment into the Commission of officials from national anti-trust administrations. That could be done in relation to those parts of DG IV which do not deal with mergers and would greatly speed up the proceedings and would also help overcome the manpower problem and improve communications between the Commission and national authorities.

106. You accept that even with these changes, DG IV is under-staffed?
A. It has about 268 A officials to handle the whole range of competition infringements, and that includes state aids which is increasingly important. The Department of Justice has well over 1,000 officials covering an area which is approximately the same. What DG IV has to deal with is far more complex. It is tremendously under-staffed, as indeed is the Commission as a whole.

107. You mentioned the decisions being shorter. Without giving away any argument you might want to adduce before the Court in later cases for specific clients, one has heard a lot of criticism about the actual drafting of the decision (it is said that the reasons are not always comprehensible and not full); as a general statement do you think the Commission's decisions are, give and take, reasonably well-drafted and well-presented?
A. Do you mean decisions under the Merger Control Regulation?

108. Under Articles 85 and 86 particularly, but both.
A. I find the decisions under the Merger Control Regulation are often easier to follow and understand and are better drafted, even though they are of course much shorter than the rather lengthy decisions which one gets under Articles 85 and 86. There have certainly been decisions under Articles 85 and 86 where one has the impression it has been the work of several hands which do not seem to have a clarity which makes them consistent and easy to understand.

109. Is it surprising, in view on the amount of paper involved, the amount of money involved?
A. It is not surprising, and if the decisions were too short we would say they were not properly reasoned and appeal them on that basis, so I think the Commission is quite justified in a way in having lengthy decisions, but sometimes the decisions seem to be far too long and have parts in them which seem to me superfluous. I think there is a middle way, somewhere, that you could have decisions sufficiently well-motivated, and the Merger Control Regulation proves this, without necessarily being 60 pages long.

110. The formal decision is a very important part of the procedure?
A. Yes.

111. We may need to say something about that. I think we shall probably be very much interested and very much concerned by the policy of delegating to national authorities the implementation of anti-trust policy in the Community through the national agencies and through the national courts. Do you see considerable difficulties here in achieving uniformity throughout the Community and achieving similar procedures and similar fines and consistent policy?

[Chairman *Contd*]

Or do you think this is an attainable aim? I have great anxiety about it, whether it will be consistently and uniformly applied. I do not know whether you have any feeling about it?

A. I share, my Lord Chairman, your anxiety. What the Sutherland Report has highlighted in relation to the application of the Community law as a whole, is not just a problem which affects competition but which affects claims for damages for non-implementation of Directives, along the lines of *Francovitch* and a whole range of other areas. The lack of uniformity in such matters as how you assess quantum of damages, causation, limitation period, lawyers' costs, is enormous.

112. *Francovitch* raises a hundred questions which will have to be tested by the Court in due course, and in the meantime there will be discrepancy particularly in relation to competition where the Commission's desire is that the national authorities should be far more involved?

A. One of the great problems is going to be that granting the exemption under Article 85(3) will remain the monopoly of the Commission, and it will be difficult therefore to get national authorities to apply Article 85 in its fullest sense, because national authorities themselves have the power to apply Articles 85 and 86 now. They are remarkably reluctant to do so.

113. Exactly. Probably essential regulation should be involved even in the national courts, by evidence and by advice, whatever.

A. And to appear in person.

114. In the area of public procurement, for example, an attempt is being made to produce harmonised remedies. It is a very much less complicated question than we have in relation to anti-trust matters?

A. I think that is right. In the case of the procurement remedies, which the Commission is dealing with by Directive of course, there are fewer issues that have to be harmonised. In the case of enforcement of anti-trust it would be necessary to cover a whole wider range of matters, such as remedies. There is also the problem of the national competition laws which, of course, still differ particularly now between the United Kingdom and the rest of the Community. We have an interesting situation that will arise because the United Kingdom Government has announced that it will not make a radical change in the national competition laws. We

will not have a prohibition which is similar to Articles 85 and 86 in United Kingdom law. I think that is going to raise major problems, because most of the other Member States of the Community are modelling their national competition law on Articles 85 and 86, as are other countries in EFTA and, indeed, Rumania, Poland, the Czech Republic and Hungary, and the United Kingdom will remain a country which has a national anti-trust law which make it very difficult for individuals to pursue their claims either before national courts relying on the national law, or before national authorities. At the same time the Commission is refusing to handle cases, and will not give priority to cases, which are predominantly national. At the moment one advises clients to go Brussels in a case which predominantly affects the United Kingdom, because in Brussels there is the remedy, for example, for abuse of market power. We are not going to have that in our national legislation. We are going to go to Brussels with a complaint, but Brussels will say, "You must deal with this before the national insurances", but the means to do that, my Lord, will not be there if the Government pursues its intention of not seriously modifying the existing legislation and modelling it more on Articles 85 and 86.

115. The relevant question will then be whether an Article 169 proceeding or a 177 reference gets to Luxembourg first?

A. That would be an interesting question.

116. Is there anything else you would like to add? You have gone through a long barrage of questions.

A. Only to say what a great pleasure it has been. I do feel, my Lord, that the work of this Committee is invaluable. The changes that were made after the 1982 Report, insofar as they were made, were extremely helpful to practitioners and to companies who had to deal with the Commission and are subject to the application of these rules. I know that the Committee's Report had an enormously high place in the priority of the Commission and those ultimately who decide what changes will be made.

Chairman] The Committee is extremely fortunate to have someone of your experience and standing who is prepared to come and devote so much time to assisting it. We very much value your authoritative statements in answer to our questions. If we have any supplementaries at a later stage, when we have heard other people, we will perhaps write to you. In the meantime, I would thank you most warmly for coming.

WEDNESDAY 12 MAY 1993

Present:

Allen of Abbeydale, L.   Slynn of Hadley, L. (Chairman)
Elles, B.   Wedderburn of Charlton, L.
Colville of Culross, V.

Memorandum by the Monopolies and Mergers Commission

INTRODUCTION

1. The Monopolies and Mergers Commission (MMC) is a statutory body whose principal role, upon a reference to it, is to investigate and report on the effects on the public interest, actual and potential, of merger and monopoly situations and anti-competitive practices, the performance of public sector bodies and the regulation of certain privatised industries. References are principally made by the Secretary of State for Trade and Industry, the Director General of Fair Trading, or the privatised industry regulators. The MMC is independent of Government, and of other regulatory authorities, both in its conduct of inquiries and in its conclusions and recommendations.

2. Since its original formation in 1948 the MMC's investigatory and judgmental role has progressively developed. In 1956, its original responsibility for restrictive trade practices was hived off leaving it only with investigations into monopoly situations in the supply of goods and certain general references. In 1965 investigations into mergers and monopoly situations in the supply of services were added to its responsibilities, and general references were redefined. In 1973 the MMC's work was consolidated by the Fair Trading Act, provision was made for references concerned with certain labour practices, and the office of the Director General of Fair Trading (DGFT) was created with powers to refer monopoly situations to the MMC. In 1980 the Competition Act gave the DGFT new powers to refer to the MMC anti-competitive practices, and to the Secretary of State to refer for investigation and report questions relating to the efficiency of the nationalised industries. In 1984 and subsequent years privatisation legislation for the telecommunications, gas, airports, electricity and water industries has given the MMC an important role in the regulation of these industries. Further responsibilities were added under the Broadcasting Act 1990; and it is proposed that in the future there will be functions under revised restrictive practices legislation.

3. The duties and procedures of the MMC are conveniently summarised in the attached *The Role of the Commission* booklet, and details on recent MMC activity in the *Annual Review 1992*. Also attached for information on the type of issue tackled by the MMC is a booklet on *Assessing Competition*[1].

IMPACT OF EC COMPETITION REGULATION

4. The work of the MMC is increasingly affected by EC competition regulation. First, as a result of the implementation of the EC Merger Regulation in September 1990, all mergers above a certain threshold fall for consideration at the Community level rather than the national: the effect of this on the MMC workload is not thought however to be great. More generally, and effective since the United Kingdom joined the Community, is the need for the MMC, in meeting its statutory obligations to report on a specific reference, to take account of, for example, the Treaty of Rome, Community legislation, and the jurisprudence of the European Court; this includes ensuring that it does not make recommendations, either of principle or of detail, which might cause the Secretary of State to breach EC law.

(a) *Merger control*

5. The EC Merger Regulation (Regulation 4064/89) entered into force on 21 September 1990 and provides for mergers involving concentrations or mergers "with a Community dimension" to be subject to the exclusive jurisdiction of the European Commission (save for limited exceptions). Broadly this means that mergers involving parties with a combined world-wide turnover of more than five billion ecu are subject to the control of the European Commission, provided that the EC turnover of each of at least two companies involved exceeds 250 million ecu and the companies concerned do not have at least two-thirds of their EC turnover from the same Member State.

[1]The three booklets are not printed but are available in the Public Record Office.

6. Mergers which are not caught by the EC Merger Regulation remain subject to national competition law. There are however some circumstances in which jurisdiction over mergers with an EC dimension may revert to the national competition authorities. A Member State can intervene under Article 21(3) of the Regulation on grounds of public security, prudential controls or diversity of the media to prevent a merger which the European Commission would otherwise have cleared. It may also request the European Commission under Article 9 to refer a merger back for assessment by the national competition authorities. For such an application to succeed the member state must demonstrate to the European Commission that the concentration threatens to create or to strengthen a dominant position significantly impeding competition in a distinct market in its territory. In such a case the European Commission decides, after preliminary inquiries, whether to deal with the matter itself or to refer issues arising under it to these national authorities. So far there has only been one successful application for national jurisdiction under these provisions: the proposed joint venture between Steetley plc and Tarmac plc which the European Commission referred back to the United Kingdom in March 1992 in respect of certain specific regional and national product markets. In the event this was referred to the MMC but parties withdrew and the reference was laid aside.

(b) *Articles 85 and 86*

7. The principal competition provisions of the Treaty of Rome are Articles 85 and 86. Article 85(1) prohibits all agreements which have as their object or effect the prevention, restriction or distortion of competition within the EC. Exemptions can be granted by the European Commission under Article 85(3). Article 86 prohibits any undertaking with a dominant position from abusing that position; under both articles there has also to be an effect on trade between Member States. The procedures of the European Commission in exercising its general powers to enforce Articles 85 and 86 are laid down by Regulation 17 of 1962. Although the MMC does not normally deal with the assessment of restrictive agreements, various regulations have been enacted by the European Commission giving group (or block) exemptions under Article 85(3) to certain types of agreements, such as selective distribution agreements for motor cars, and exclusive purchasing agreements for beer and petrol, which have had to be taken into account in the course of recent monopoly references. In framing their recommendations in references involving such agreements the MMC must therefore take account of such EC exemptions and their relevance to any suggested changes to practices within the United Kingdom.

MMC/European Commission Liaison

8. Liaison between the MMC and the European Commission in the course of an investigation can occur for a number of reasons, for example: to establish any limitations upon MMC jurisdiction arising from Community law so as to ensure (as far as is appropriate) consistency in the event of parallel jurisdiction; in order to be aware of European Commission activities or plans; or to seek views on the interpretation of Community legislation.

9. All such liaison is however subject to legal constraints which determine the limits of dialogue between the two bodies. The MMC is bound by section 133 of the Fair Trading Act 1973 and section 19 of the Competition Act 1980 (and by similar provisions in the privatisation Acts), the effect of which is that no information obtained under or by virtue of the provisions of the Acts about a particular business may be disclosed in the absence of consent. Disclosure may, however, be made if it is for the purpose of facilitating the performance of any of the functions of the MMC or of other named authorities (eg the Director General of Fair Trading, the Secretary of State for Trade and Industry) or pursuant to a Community obligation or for certain legal proceedings. Similarly the European Commission's powers to disclose information to the competent authorities of Member States are constrained by Article 20 of Regulation 17/62 and Article 17 of Regulation 4064/89. Information acquired as a result of the application of either Regulation may only be used for the purpose of the request, investigation or hearing for which it was obtained. Business secrets which are not also subject to the professional secrecy obligation may be disclosed in certain limited circumstances but only after the business concerned has been given an opportunity to challenge such disclosure, if necessary before the European Court of Justice. Competent authorities of Member States are bound by similar constraints if they receive such information from the European Commission.

Subsidiarity

10. It is right that the European Commission should be the decision-maker on those competition matters with a real and substantial EC-wide dimension. It is however for consideration whether matters of essentially national relevance should be either left to national authorities or partially delegated to them. This would have the advantage that authorities that had the closest understanding of the relevant markets would carry out some or all of the necessary functions, while also reducing the call on the European Commission's scarce resources and enabling it to focus more effectively on the more important cases.

11. Two cases have already brought into prominence the question of split jurisdiction as between the United Kingdom and the EC. Both the Hong Kong and Shanghai Banking Corporation and Lloyds Bank made bids for the Midland Bank. The HSBC bid fell within the EC Merger Regulation and was cleared by the initial procedure in Brussels as not raising competition concerns at a Community level. By contrast, the Lloyds bid fell within the United Kingdom's jurisdiction and was referred to the MMC as raising potential competition issues. Lloyds abandoned the merger after about two weeks. HSBC's bid was subsequently successful.

12. A second case, in which the question of split jurisdiction arose was the proposed Tarmac/Steetley merger (referred to above). Here a bid by Redland for Steetley came under the United Kingdom's jurisdiction while the proposed Tarmac/Steetley merger came under that of Brussels. However, at the request of Her Majesty's Government this case was referred back to the United Kingdom under Article 9 of the EC merger regulation, the first time this has been successfully invoked. The grounds were that the competition considerations were primarily within the United Kingdom and some of its regions. This bid was also abandoned soon after being referred to the MMC.

13. In the event that the European Commission should pursue the policy of subsidiarity and greater delegation of competition regulation, the MMC would be ready to take on such additional work as might be appropriate. This applies not only to mergers, but also to abuse of market power cases which might arise under Article 86.

PROCEDURES AND LEVELS OF DECISION-MAKING IN EC COMPETITION REGULATION

14. The following sections are concerned with areas where the MMC believes the United Kingdom system has particular strengths and where European Commission procedures and levels of decision-making differ. The comments should not be interpreted as criticism of the European Commission performance but rather to highlight some areas which may need to be reviewed, particularly in the merger field when experience has been gained of operating in a time of high merger activity and in handling controversial and contested cases. There is in any case room for consultation both with the European Commission and with competition authorities in Member States, with a view to learning how our own procedures can be improved. Similarly some identity of approach to competition issues between Member States and the European Commission would assist the development of consistency.

(a) *Separation of powers*

15. In the United Kingdom, the MMC, as the investigatory body, is independent from the organisation which decides upon or recommends a reference (generally the DGFT), and independent from the body deciding upon the action to be taken upon its report and recommendations (generally the Secretary of State). This separation of powers, and the inherent checks and balances thereby provided within the system, avoids conflicts of interest and is, the MMC believes, a strength of the United Kingdom system, particularly when coupled with the transparency of the system (see below). On the other hand, it is not the only system and other countries as well as the European Commission successfully employ an integrated system.

(b) *Transparency*

16. A further strength, the MMC believes, of the United Kingdom system, is that the MMC, as the independent investigatory body, is able to establish its own procedures to ensure fairness to all, not only the main parties involved, in an investigation. Moreoever, its procedures and decision-making is transparent in that it is required by statute to produce reports giving reasons for the conclusions reached and the remedies recommended. In this way, while some may disagree with the conclusions reached the facts on which the conclusions are based and the reasoning behind these conclusions are clear for all to see. Moreover, if the Secretary of State decides to override an adverse finding, or to modify the remedies to be applied, this is evident and reasons for the different course of action are given.

GENERAL

17. Overall interface between the European Commission and MMC will increase and EC law will have a greater impact on MMC work. Relations at working level between the respective institutions are good and constructive and whatever changes may occur in the operation of Community competition regulation (eg changes in thresholds, institutional arrangements) we confidently expect this to continue.

April 1993

Examination of witnesses

MR GRAEME ODGERS, Chairman, MR DANIEL GOYDER, Deputy Chairman, MR NOEL ING, Senior Legal Adviser and MR STEPHEN BURBRIDGE, Secretary, Monopolies and Mergers Commission, called in and examined.

Chairman

117. On behalf of the Sub-Committee, may I first thank you, Mr Odgers, Mr Goyder, Mr Ing and Mr Burbridge for coming to help us today. This is an enquiry to which we attach very great importance in the operation and enforcement of Community competition rules. We would be very grateful for any advice that you can give us in relation to mergers and perhaps more broadly. For the record, can I say Mr Graeme Odgers is the Chairman of the Monopolies and Mergers Commission; Mr Goyder is a Deputy Chairman; Mr Noel Ing is the Senior Legal Adviser and Mr Stephen Burbridge is the Secretary. Mr Odgers, I am afraid we have asked you to come rather shortly after you have assumed captaincy of the ship, if that is an appropriate term. We can perhaps offer you our congratulations on the appointment. Thank you very much for having come. Before we go through the various questions we would like to ask you, would you like to say anything by way of introduction?

(Mr Odgers) I wonder if I might say a very few words. You have identified the members of the team. It is important, I think, from the point of view of the conduct of this particular session, that you do recognise I am very much the new boy here, only having been here for three weeks, so I will very much rely on my colleagues here to answer many of the more detailed questions. Having said that, if I could just say one or two things about the Commission, if I may; first of all, it is a commission of independent people, that is the members. All except for the Chairman, that is myself, are part-time. All are independent of government. They come from various disciplines, various backgrounds. The members are supported by a multi-disciplinary staff of about a hundred people, consisting of economists, accountants, industrial advisers and general administrators. The MMC itself does not initiate its own investigations. It only acts after a formal reference is made to it, for example, by the President of the Board of Trade. In that instance the President would normally be advised by the Director General of Fair Trading, currently Sir Brian Carsberg. Other references would come from the Director General of Fair Trading himself and yet other references might come from the respective regulators of the privatized industries. That is where they initiate from; we do not actually initiate our own investigations. The MMC is not involved therefore in reference policy as such, nor in the decision to make references on individual cases. We do get involved in recommendations for action as a result of our reports but the enforcement of those actions is not for us. This is for other people. Thus the MMC is free, and is seen to be free, from external pressures in the objective conduct of its enquiries. In the context of the MMC and the European situation, we cooperate with DGIV as far as we can but we work within the relevant provisions of the United Kingdom competition legislation

relating specifically to disclosure of information. We might want to talk about that later on. With those preliminary remarks, may we open it up for questions?

Chairman] Thank you very much. We do appreciate your giving us this introductory explanation. We appreciate your personal position. I am sure your three colleagues, Mr Goyder, Mr Burbridge and Mr Ing, will help. Mr Goyder's reputation in the competition world and merger world, both as a writer and as a practitioner, is very high. I am sure we will have a great deal of help from all of you.

Viscount Colville of Culross

118. On that matter, they are neither the initiator, am I right in thinking, nor ultimately the decision-maker because the Commission makes a recommendation. It is the President of the Board of Trade who ultimately makes the decision, is it not, whether to implement that recommendation?

(Mr Odgers) I will ask my colleagues to come in in a moment. There are varying situations. For instance, we have just recently had the case in the broadcasting field, under the Broadcasting Act, where the final decision was actually made by ourselves but this was rather rare, as I understand it. Broadly speaking, it is as you have said. I do not know if any of my colleagues want to speak on this.

Chairman

119. Is that as a matter or practice or as a matter of obligation or a matter of law that you do not take the decision?

(Mr Burbridge) Perhaps I could expand on that. If one takes a merger case, if we clear the merger, then the Secretary of State has no alternative but to accept our decision. If we find adverse effects in a merger, then he is able to overturn our findings, and indeed he can vary the recommendations even though he does not overturn the findings. In practice, I think he has only overturned the finding once in the last, say, fifteen years. Somewhat more frequently, but not very often, he has changed the recommendations.

(Mr Ing) May I add two brief codas to that? As a general answer, and not only in merger cases, unless adverse effects are found by the Commission, then no action would follow from the report. The other point that I would make purely for completeness is this. Our Chairman has said that references under the Broadcasting Act are determinative; the Commission takes the decision. There is also one instance under the privatization legislation relating to water charges where the same is the case.

120. Mr Goyder, do you want to add anything?
(Mr Goyder) No; that fully states the position.

121. One of the reasons why we have undertaken this enquiry is that anxiety has been expressed by practitioners in the competition field in general that

[Chairman *Contd*]

the Commission should have so many different functions in applying Articles 85 and 86. We notice that when you very kindly came to give evidence to this sub-committee in 1988, on the Merger Control Regulation, you said, and I quote: " Is it appropriate for the one body to be simultaneously the detective, the prosecutor, the negotiator and the decision-maker? " Do you still think that it is wrong for the Commission to have all these function?

(Mr Odgers) I think that we would take the view now that we would not make the statement that it is wrong for the Commission to have all these functions. I think what we would say is that we do it rather differently. We see great advantages in doing it the way that we do it and that there is a case for the Commission to think about alternatives but I do not think we should say that it is wrong because there are other authorities, in Germany as I understand it, for instance, which work on a unitary system similar to the Commission and it works very effectively. I think our general feeling is that if you have a situation where there is a large number of mergers, particulary if there are contested mergers and controversial mergers, the unitary system is likely to be more difficult to operate without undue pressure, maybe political pressure, on the actual decision-making than a system such as we ourselves adopt where we are immunised, as it were, from those kinds of pressures and also where the decision-making becomes a transparent process because of the way in which we report on the individual cases.

122. That in some ways is more a question for the practitioners to say now whether they find this satisfactory. You said that maybe your system has some advantages which the European system does not have. What about your methods or your structure? Do you think it could be followed, adopted, by the European Commission?

(Mr Odgers) I do not actually think it is for us to say what we think the European Commission should do. I will ask my colleagues whether they disagree with that. Basically we are not in the policy-making game as such.

(Mr Burbridge) So far as procedure is concerned, we do think, apart from the separation of powers question, which Mr Odgers has mentioned, there is a considerable benefit to be gained from the transparency of our system. We do, in fact, reach, and indeed are required by the Act to reach clear conclusions and to show sufficient reasons to justify the conclusions. I think the wording of the Act is to have such a survey of the facts so that the reasoning can be understood.

123. But the Commission has to give reasons?

(Mr Burbridge) That is so but I think possibly my colleagues would know a little more about the degree of that.

124. I would like you to make clear where you think your system is more transparent than the Community system. I think Mr Goyder would certainly have something to say on that.

(Mr Goyder) I think the main difference is that if you look at an equivalent merger report—and this may be anticipating later questions but I think it is responsive to the question—from the Commission at the second stage, that is, one of the controversial and difficult cases as opposed to a routine clearance, you find, of course, a lot of detailed reasoning carried out in a very competent manner. What you do not find is any information about the parties beyond a bare four or five lines, nor any evidence in a proper summarized form approved by the parties so that you know accurately it represents what that company or department or other authority actually said about the consequences of the merger. You can read between the lines sometimes but it is very difficult, I imagine, for a practitioner, asked to advise by a large company, " Will we get our merger through the Brussels investigation? ", to answer it by reading the previous judgments. That is what worries a number of lawyers, and certainly myself.

125. Is this criticism limited to mergers or does your comment apply also to decisions by the Commission under Articles 85 and 86?

(Mr Goyder) I think it applies much more to mergers, partly because of the time pressures. One accepts that the European Commission has enormous problems because of the time it takes to translate and so on. I do not think my comment is simply a criticism. It is more an observation.

126. I was thinking of the Nestlé decision which had everything you say about the description of the parties, what they did and so on.

(Mr Goyder) Yes, I would say in the Article 85 and Article 86 cases by and large the Commission produce a report which would be of value to the practitioners in that way but if one goes to, say, the Aérospatiale case or the Nestlé/Perrier case, both immensely complex, and controversial cases, and you want to find out, as you would do if you were an adviser, what those companies are doing, how many people they employ, all the financial and other statistical information, it is just not there. It is in some annex which is not produced. Equally, the full evidence is not published, even in summary. One accepts that business secrets are very important and one accepts therefore that not everything can be published. I am concerned however (and I have not yet had a satisfactory answer from a Commission official, or indeed practitioner), as to why there cannot be a greater degree of transparency.

127. In reasoning, you mean?

(Mr Goyder) In information; in a sense the reasoning is maybe all very well but the difficulty is if it is not based on facts stated.

128. Your comments so far—I will not say criticisms —have been related only to the actual form of the decision. Mr Burbridge referred to more transparency here. Does that comment apply, other than the actual document and decision?

(Mr Goyder) I am afraid it does. I do not want to get too far away from your question. If you are assessing a merger there are two ways of doing it. One

[Chairman Contd]

is the way in which the Office of Fair Trading would
do it here, which is, if you are proceeding under the
1989 Companies Act procedure of acceptance of
undertakings, that they are entitled and authorised to
do a deal with the parties to the merger. In other
words, to look at the effects of the merger and say
such and such adverse consequences follow, but they
will not refer you and will tell the Secretary of State
not to refer you, if he agrees with the judgment,
because you will give certain undertakings that will
remove those adverse effects. The bidder for example
will dispose of a couple of factories or some brands,
or something of that kind. That is a perfectly
legitimate way of dealing with the case, so long as
everybody knows that the OFT is in this situation a
deal-making organisation. The MMC, of course, is at
the other pole. We are not allowed to, and the courts
have said we must not negotiate; we must simply
write a report and record the evidence and arguments
and then that goes to the Secretary of State.

129. The concept is fundamental?
(Mr Goyder) Yes. This is blurred at the European
Commission second stage level because it is quite
clear that the decision one reads is read as a legal
decision. It does not discuss negotiations. It is equally
clear, however, if one ever talks to lawyers involved
in the process, that it is a deal-making process. It is
that lack of clarity, that ambiguity, which causes
concern, which is not a problem of the MMC.
Baroness Elles] My Lord Chairman, would it be
too much trouble to ask the witnesses, when referring
to the MMC or the European Commission, to make
clear, of which they are speaking.
Chairman] That is a very good suggestion.

Viscount Colville of Culross

130. May I pick up one point, Mr Odgers? You
said you would not have answered the first question
in quite the same way now as before. You referred to
the German equivalent or parallel system. Is it right
that the European Commission system is basically
based upon the German model because it happened
in 1962, before we ever came anywhere near the EC?
Are there other countries which have the same sort of
model, so that if one wanted fundamentally to
change it, you would be up against a tremendous
amount of existing precedent in various countries in
Europe which would make it very difficult?
(Mr Odgers) I do not know the answer to that. My
colleagues can deal with that.
(Mr Goyder) It is actually very interesting,
although I am sure the Chairman of the Sub-
Committee knows a great deal more about the
German approach than I do. My impression is that
although the German system is unitary, the German
competition authorities would be very happy to see
the Commission operating in merger cases in a way
which is more similar to the United Kingdom system;
in other words, with an independent authority.
Heads of the German cartel authority (BKA) have
made public statements to that effect in recent years.

I do not think, therefore, there is any enormous
national or political barrier to that which flows from
the nature of the national system. I think different
Member States do take different views. I would
certainly say the United Kingdom is not the only
Member State that does have difficulties with the
present situation under the Merger Regulation.

Chairman

131. This sort of comparison with other countries
is obviously very important on the basis that
everything human can be improved. Do you,
yourselves, compare what happens in other countries
to see whether we can improve, or do you make
suggestions to the Commission as to how they might
improve the procedures which are involved?
(Mr Odgers) Certainly, I think it is incumbent on
the MMC to examine itself from time to time. We are
in the process of looking at our own procedures. We
will be going through the quinquennial review in a few
months time. Our own procedures will be looked at. I
think more than that, we need to be in constant touch,
I think, with our relevant counterparts, whether they
are in the OFT, for instance, or in the Department of
Trade and Industry, or indeed within the European
Commission, just to make sure that we are aligning
our procedures, our arrangements, our thinking, in a
way which makes most sense in terms of the effective
handling of the matters that come before us. I would
certainly seek, under my Chairmanship, to ensure that
there is a lot of contact, a lot of discussion and ideally
that there will be continuous improvement in terms of
the way in which we handle our affairs and, hopefully,
the other parties will get some benefit as well.

132. National courts are now increasingly having
to be conscious of Community law and Community
rules. How far do you find yourselves in the MMC
having to apply Community rules and Community
law?
(Mr Goyder) Perhaps I could deal with this. It will
take a moment or two. Obviously the Community
law, being part of our national law and in cases of
conflict with supremacy over it, is a very important
part of the background to our work. We are not a
court of law. Though we do not therefore have the
problem of direct application of European law, we
have to take both specific regulations and directives
and general legal principles into account in all our
cases where there is a Community element. These, of
course, are far more (as a proportion of our work)
than used to be the case, and sometimes, surprisingly
so. Sometimes also when you do not expect there to
be a European element, one turns up. I think there is
both a negative and a positive aspect to what we have
to do in this area. We have to take care negatively
that we do not make recommendations in our reports
that either in principle or in detail might cause the
Secretary of State to act in a way that would itself be
in breach of his Community obligations. For
example, we could not say of a particular merger,
"We think this merger should not be allowed

[Chairman *Contd*]

because the bidder is a foreign company controlled by nationals of another Member state ". Clearly that would be contrary to the rules of the Community. That is a very obvious example but there are many more that could be found. Although Article 85 would not appear at first sight to be relevant, dealing as it does with restrictive trade practices and cartels, in practice we find that in Monopoly inquiries dealing with subjects like beer or cars, where there is complex block exemption legislation, dealing with that industry, we have to deal in some detail with the prohibitions and exemptions of that legislation and try to ensure that whatever we recommend to the Secretary of State is itself not going to get him into difficulties in terms of the changes that he would wish to make. We have to give a lot of careful thought to the working of our recommendations in the light of Community law. On a more positive note, I think we try to keep fully abreast of the jurisprudence of the European Court, and the Court of First Instance, particulary under Article 86. It is unlikely that we actually have to apply it directly but it is important to be aware of particular practices that have been the subject of important decisions and ensure that we are not going to put things into our reports that seem to fly in the face of established jurisprudence.

133. No doubt equally there are decisions of the Commission which do not reach the Court?

(Mr Goyder) Yes. I think decisions of the Commission are a little bit more difficult, particularly, of course, where they are under appeal to Luxembourg because there one is slightly in limbo. I think particularly of the Plasterboard case, where the final decision of the European Court has only just been announced, and which, in fact, at the time we had the enquiry into Plasterboard, was only a Commission decision. At the time I think we took the view—Mr Ing will correct me if I am wrong—that we could rely on the findings of the Commission in that particular case which, of course, were relevant to our own findings.

(Mr Ing) I think that covers the legal aspect of what we do, what we have to bear in mind very thoroughly. There may be one other point that perhaps is worth making, though in a sense perhaps it shades into later questions. Of course, it is by no means uncommon for the European Commission to be formally consulted in the course of an enquiry to give its views and for those views to be included, as with the views of any parties or witnesses who appear before us, in our reports. That is a very different point from taking into account Community law but it is certainly an example of being thoroughly aware of the Community and the part it plays.

134. Outside specific enquiries, is there much cooperation or liaison with the European Commission from your side?

(Mr Goyder) We are not of course an executive body. In a sense, although we are not a court, we are closer probably in what we are required to do to a court and therefore we do not have quite that continuing volume of what one might call ordinary business that, shall we say, the OFT have.

135. You do not hobnob regularly with the Commission?

(Mr Odgers) I think I should ask Mr Burbridge to answer on that because there are regular contacts.

(Mr Burbridge) The previous Chairman of the MMC did have not frequent but a continuing contact with the three successive competition Commissioners. Indeed, at my level and at other levels we do keep in touch but I cannot pretend that it is very frequent.

136. Does it need to be more frequent?

(Mr Burbridge) I think it does, really following up one of your earlier questions, my Lord Chairman, because you were asking whether we should get more consistency, as it were, in approach with the Commission. Perhaps I could just add to Mr Odgers' answer there. I think we do believe that it makes sense that if we are all looking at competition, and obviously cross-border competition enters into the national consideration as well as that in Brussels, then it makes sense that we should work towards a greater consistency of approach. Indeed, we have discussed this only in recent weeks with the Head of the Merger Taskforce, whom we met. I have, in fact, sent one of my staff not only to Brussels, but to Germany, France, Italy and the United States, as it happens. We agreed to pay even more attention in the next few weeks to how they do things in Brussels.

137. The concept of a single market may become even more necessary?

(Mr Burbridge) Absolutely.

Baroness Elles

138. I just wanted to ask whether you would agree that some of your reports, in particular one or two, are the subject sometimes of questioning by the European Commission, such as the case of British Airways some time ago where the Commissioner of the day—I think it was Peter Sutherland—did seek to impose conditions, presumably under Article 86, the fear of dominant position, which was not evident from your original report. Presumably, you do keep in touch to some extent with the thinking of the European Commission when producing your reports.

(Mr Burbridge) I think we have to answer that one a little cautiously because the fundamental principle is that we give no other institution an inside track, as it were, in the conduct of our enquiries; that includes HMG for that matter, because if they want to influence our enquiries, then they do have to give evidence to us in an open way in which we can report or summarise in our reports. In that particular case of British Airways, as I recall it, there was some discussion, both by the parties and other people, about the actual timing of our investigation. I think some of the parties argued that the European Commission should look at it first and we second. As it happened, it worked the other way round. In that particular case, I think they did not give evidence, as I recall it, but they certainly had our report as the basis for their continuing enquiry.

[Baroness Elles *Contd*]

139. I think they imposed conditions in that particular case, did they not, as a result of your report and as a result of an appeal by one of the companies affected by the report, if I remember rightly?

(Mr Burbridge) That is right.

(Mr Goyder) I was a member of that reference team. I think our report suggested that there should be some routes divested by BA and the European Commission suggested there should be some additional route divestments. It was not a totally new remedy but an extension of our remedies that were proposed.

Chairman

140. Just to go back to the communication between the MMC and the Commission, is there in practice any problem about exchange of confidential information or is it accepted as a firm rule that you do not supply the Commission with confidential information and they do not supply you? Do you think there should not be this sort of embargo on the exchange of confidential information?

(Mr Ing) This is a rather difficult question because, of course, it has to be seen in the context of our ability to disclose and our duty to protect information generally. I think we have touched on that in some little detail in paragraph 9 of our written evidence. I do not want to trouble you, my Lord Chairman and your colleagues, in overmuch detail, but the basic principle, and it stems from Section 133 of the Fair Trading Act 1973, which is broadly repeated in the statutes governing the other areas of our work, is that we are prohibited from disclosing information about a particular business which we have received—I paraphrase—for the purposes of our enquiry unless with the consent of the person carrying on the business or for certain particular purposes which, if I may, I will come to in a moment. In practice the prohibition under Section 133 applies to the greatest part of the information which MMC receives in any enquiry. I think, to deal with a point that arose earlier, it would be almost impossible sensibly to discuss conclusions with any other body or individual, apart from other problems, without contravening that particular prohibition. There are exceptions to that. The MMC is permitted, is held harmless from the criminal consequences of disclosing prohibited information, no consent having been given by the person providing the information, if that is in order to facilitate the purposes of its own enquiry which enables it in some cases to put information to other parties to the enquiry, if that is necessary for our enquiry or for fairness. In at least one instance, it enabled us to put information to the European Commission, because we did not feel that their comments to us, which we needed, would be sensible, helpful, unless they knew something of the background. But that, of course, was to assist our enquiry. With one possible exception, what the provisions of Section 133, which exempt from the prohibition, do not permit is disclosure in order to facilitate the purposes of the European Commission. No doubt, if it was thought right, an exception for the purpose could be introduced. At the moment it does not. Unless we have the consent of the providers of the information, the Commission would be in the position of committing a criminal offence by disclosing information purely for the purposes of the European Commission.

Lord Allen of Abbeydale

141. Could I ask if you have had any awkwardness as a result of the lack of that power? You are arguing for a change in the law, are you not?

(Mr Ing) I am sorry, I may have expressed myself badly. I am not arguing for a change in the law. I was merely saying that if it was thought right, as a matter of policy, that we should be able to assist the European Commission with information of this kind, a change in the law would be necessary. We have had discussions about this area with representatives of the Commission. I think it is fair to say that those discussions have been amicable and we have respected each other's position because, of course, it is the case—and we referred to this in our written evidence—that the European Commission is itself under a prohibition in competition and no doubt other matters. I think it is a provision of Regulation 17, which is rather comparable to others. To take one instance of this, suppose, for the sake of argument, it was, as a matter of policy, thought right to confer on MMC, and perhaps other authorities, the power to provide information for the benefit of the European Commission's activities, as Community law stands, as I understand it, the European Commission would not be in a position normally to reciprocate. I would, as it were, ask Mr Goyder to correct or amend that proposition which perhaps I have expressed too bluntly, but in general terms that is how I understand it.

(Mr Goyder) I think the Spanish Banks case of the European Court quite recently has confirmed that one has to keep enquiries in their own watertight compartment, by and large, although a national competition authority can always start again with its own enquiries if it has been tipped off by something the Commission has told it. If there may be a problem under national law, you cannot use that Commission information directly. You have got to make your own enquiries and start again.

Chairman

142. I think the Commission normally is fairly jealous about protecting confidential information. Suppose, as the Commission has indicated and as everyone is now expecting, that more of the Commission's enforcement powers are passed on to national authorities to deal with, is that going to become a greater problem? There is a problem, is there not?

(Mr Ing) I think the problem would presumably be no less, unless there was a change in the law. I have left one point in the question unanswered which perhaps I should deal with, and that is whether the principle of the thing is right or wrong. I would have said—and I think my colleagues would broadly agree with me here, though they will be able to speak for themselves—that there are really two sides to this. On

[Chairman *Contd*]

the one hand, it could be said to be very good sense that competition authorities, the European Commission no less, should be able to exchange information reasonably freely. One can see that argument. The other argument—and I think it is one that perhaps has to be looked at not only from the point of view of the parties concerned but from the point of view of the future conduct of the work of a body like MMC—is that the risk is that the more that disclosure is permitted, the greater is the deterrence to the free flow of information to a body like MMC. I think on the whole the MMC's feeling on this is that the balance at the moment is in favour of the protection rather than the free exchange.

143. For a number of different reasons?
(Mr Ing) Indeed, yes.

Viscount Colville of Culross

144. I wondered whether it was going to work the other way round too. I read paragraph 9 of the evidence with great interest. I understand the prohibitions but also the prohibitions on the European Commission. Are they likely to find that they would get into difficulties if they were to disclose information to other competition authorities in the EEC countries in the same way that you have just suggested that you might yourselves? In other words, if the constraints upon them under the two articles that you quote, two sets of regulations, were in some way modified, would that in itself be likely to cause them difficulty about getting hold of the information in the first place?
(Mr Goyder) I think they have quite extensive powers under Regulation 17 and the equivalent merger regulation to get the information they want. Indeed, the MMC also has statutory powers, though I think the point is, as so often is the case, you do much better, if you have statutory powers, not always to be threatening their use; cooperation always tends to produce a better response than something exacted by threat of legal proceedings or subpoenas. I think, therefore, that it is not just a question of changing the law to give more freedom, although if the balance of enforcement were to change, then clearly it would be sensible to look and see if the status quo was sufficient or whether the rules could be liberalised. Although it has never yet been exercised to my knowledge, under another sub-section of Section 133 of the Fair Trading Act there is such a thing as "a Community obligation" under the 1972 European Communities Act if the Commission were legally to order an appropriate authority to produce such information within this category, then there would be a legal obligation to disclose it. Clearly, that is not the way that either the European Commission or the national authorities want things conducted.

Chairman

145. If you had an arrangement for a reciprocal exchange of information between you and the Commission, where it was clear that the Commission was entitled to pass on to you information obtained from other national authorities, and conversely you to pass on to them information, once you start to move away from watertight compartments of confidentiality and barriers to exchanging confidential information, it opens up a tremendous area of difficulty.
(Mr Burbridge) This is obviously an extremely important legal constraint that we have to bear in mind throughout but I think it would be wrong to give the impression that this makes all our enquiries completely watertight from influence of some kind from Brussels. That is to say, with the agreement of the parties, it is possible, as we have done on six or eight cases which have registered in our reports, to invite in the European Commission to have some sort of comment in our enquiries. For example, in beer and in cars where there was the exemption and there have been various jurisdictional problems that we felt we had to raise with the Commission. These again are chronicled in our reports. They are not entirely watertight, as long as we observe the important legal constraint.

146. We talked about derogation of the national authorities. If enforcement powers are to be used more by national authorities, what is going to be the effect of that in the United Kingdom? Will we have to revise our remedies or revise our competition law or can we just go on keeping the two separate? What will be the effect of that?
(Mr Goyder) I think it is a very difficult question. In a sense one would want to know firstly exactly what are the substantive changes. I think as a general principle one would want to say it would be perhaps a smoother system if the remedies could be tailored to meet the new substantive situation. Clearly the more closely United Kingdom competition law approximated to Community competition law, the easier and smoother the relationship would be. Since it looks from recent Government statements that they are not keen on introducing Article 86 into domestic law (although of course much of that ground is covered by either the Fair Trading Act or the Competition Act) and since therefore we will not, as it were, have the whole of Article 86, it does not look as if we are likely to have an absolute parallel system.

147. Perhaps you would prefer not to comment. From your experience as MMC, would you prefer the two were harmonised and were made the same?
(Mr Goyder) No, because I think actually we have some advantages in that the Fair Trading Act allows us to investigate some situations where Article 86 does not reach. Our jurisdictional threshold is lower, for example, at 25 per cent of the market for goods or services, than under Article 86.
(Mr Odgers) I think we did make some representation when we were looking at the abuse of dominant position question when we really went along with the basic thesis of the government, that we probably would want to retain our present flexible arrangements through a slight extension of our

[Chairman *Contd*]

existing legislation rather than moving towards the adoption of 85 and 86, certainly on that particular aspect of competition policy.

(Mr Burbridge) That is indeed correct because in fact we have a pretty wide array of remedies which one can bring to bear under the Fair Trading Act to meet the particular adverse effect we find in the particular circumstances.

148. Perhaps we can move on to the merger control regulation. We have heard some evidence about the way in which that is being operated through the Taskforce and so on. Do you have any comments as to how effective the merger control regulation has been?

(Mr Odgers) I think our general view would be that it seems to have worked efficiently, and I think probably effectively as well, if there is a distinction between effectiveness and efficiency. I think we would say, however, that it is still relatively early days. I am not sure whether the existing arrangements have been fully and properly tested in a situation where there is a great pressure in terms of numbers of mergers, in terms of the kind of mergers, for instance, highly controversial or opposed mergers or ones where there could be a significant political input. I think it is when those kinds of situations occur that there may be some pressure on the system that is being applied at the present time. I think so far it has worked reasonably well. That would be our general view.

149. I think the evidence we have had so far is really consistent with that. It is still useful to know whether you can see in the review of the regulation which is anticipated that there should be some changes made, some improvements to your greater independence.

(Mr Odgers) I think our view would be that we would advise that they consider alternative systems, rather than just say that their existing system is entirely proven to be the best one.

150. Have you positive proposals which you would wish to put forward for the amendments of the regulations?

(Mr Odgers) No, we have not.

Baroness Elles

151. I wonder if the MMC would agree that the timescale which has been imposed on the European Commission by the Merger Control Regulation has, in fact, broadly worked rather successfully, or would you say not?

(Mr Goyder) I think actually they deserve every credit for making the system work as well as it does. In fact, the official time limits are a bit misleading. Bearing in mind the quantity of translations that have to take place, particularly at the second stage, and the other bureaucratic formalities needed because of the very nature of the European Commission, actually it may take three weeks or a month to get the first stage done, but it is far less than four months for the substantive consideration of the second stage procedure to be carried out. I think it is

actually more like six to seven weeks. From talking to Commission officials, I get the impression that is about the length of time they have for the substantive consideration, which is a lot shorter than the equivalent time we have at MMC, and of course, they are covering the whole Community, whilst we are only covering one jurisdiction.

152. Would the MMC consider that this timescale within the present merger regulation is really very limited and should be extended or do you think the way it works should be left as it is?

(Mr Goyder) Knowing the pressures we are under at MMC to get mergers considerd and reported on in three months, without the language problem, I am quite sure they have great difficulties, and indeed there is always a trade-off between the time you have to do a complex investigation and the clarity and completeness, of the published report and recommendations at the end of the day.

Chairman

153. The other matter to be reviewed is the thresholds. What are your views about changes, if any, in the thresholds in the Merger Control Regulation?

(Mr Odgers) I do not think it really is up to us to say we would, as the MMC, recommend one thing or another.

154. What would you like to see happen?

(Mr Odgers) I think we would probably like to see the present system tested for a rather longer period than it has been tested so far.

Baroness Elles

155. Presumably the devaluation of the pound must have made quite a considerable difference to the threshold, 25 per cent, in relation to the Ecu over the last six months. That again must affect, therefore, the five billion Ecu threshold in terms of sterling.

(Mr Odgers) Indeed, but it is at the margin rather than a fundamental change.

156. 25 per cent is quite a big figure.

(Mr Odgers) It is still at the margin.

Chairman

157. Is there a problem where you get two bids for a company where one bid is below the threshold and the other above it, so you get a split jurisdiction?

(Mr Odgers) I think we can have a split jurisdiction under almost any system you like to name. We have cases of a split jurisdiction within the United Kingdom in terms of some of the contested mergers that are put to us where one party is to be considered by the MMC, whereas another merger or acquisition situation for the same target company could fall outside the reference for the MMC. You get that kind of situation occurring locally in the United Kingdom. I can see it happening elsewhere. I am not sure there really is an answer to that. Perhaps Mr Burbridge has some views on that.

[Chairman *Contd*]

(Mr Burbridge) I do not have any views. There have been cases, for example in 1990, when the Associated British Foods' bid for British Sugar was not referred but Tate and Lyle's was. As I understand government policy, it is their policy not to refer purely on the grounds of equality of treatment.

158. The existence of split jurisdiction does not bother you too much in that case? That is the impression you give, or is there a way in which it could be avoided?
(Mr Odgers) I think it is difficult. I think that is what we are suggesting. It could be very difficult to avoid all cases.
(Mr Goyder) I think there are two kinds of split. There is the kind of split which is purely jurisdictional.

159. I was speaking about thresholds.
(Mr Goyder) Yes, such as those between the European Commission and the MMC; you get a different kind of split, of course, within the United Kingdom where one proposed bid for a company has competition consequences and another one made at the same time has rather less competition consequences. People can claim unfairness in the second case as well as in the first.

160. Certainly; my question is really directed to the first of the two. I understand the second one. May I ask you about Article 9? I think you referred to the reference back of the proposed Tarmac/Steetley merger to the United Kingdom authorities. Have there been other attempts to have proposed mergers referred back to national jurisdiction which have not succeeded?
(Mr Burbridge) I am not sure, my Lord Chairman. The only successful one has been the Tarmac one which we have mentioned. I understand the German Government has made several attempts, I think three, if I am correct.

161. There has been none which the United Kingdom has asked to be referred back which have been refused?
(Mr Burbridge) As far as I know, none.

Viscount Colville of Culross

162. We have a memorandum from the DTI on this. They say, in what I read to be a pleased tone, that the only time that they have tried it they were successful but I wonder whether, in fact, the machinery is successful if the Germans have three times failed. I wonder if our witnesses have got any views about this.
(Mr Goyder) I have a view. May I speak not on the basis of my experience with the MMC but simply as an academic lawyer interested in the topic. I think a great deal depends on whether the particular case can be truly be described only to affect a local market. I think the reason why the European Commission turned down the German requests was that in each of those cases they saw them as having also a major consequence in another Member State, be it Spain or France. I think on the merits, therefore, perhaps the

German cases were not strong as the Tarmac/Steetley case, where really the merger only affected two regions of the United Kingdom and it was really difficult to argue to the contrary.

Chairman

163. What ought to be the criteria for deciding whether something should be sent back for national rather than Community appraisal?
(Mr Goyder) I think the present regulation, if objectively administered, represents a perfectly fair balance because there must clearly be a merger which has its anti-competitive effects, if any, in a particular region of that country. Thus in such a case it is likely the local competition authority will have a greater ability to get the relevant facts quickly and deal with the issues in the case which after all affect that Member State much more than anyone else.

164. You would not want to amend Article 9 to introduce any specific criteria?
(Mr Goyder) I did make the qualification "so long as it is objectively administered". I think there is always a risk that an authority, such as the European Commission, may be very protective, especially in the early days, of its own jurisdiction. Therefore, if there were in the future a lot of examples of reasonable applications being refused, then one might need to spell out the criteria more fully.

Lord Wedderburn of Charlton

165. There has not been a great difficulty with that concept in Article 9, the distinct market?
(Mr Goyder) I do not think that is a difficult concept. It is quite a familiar concept. It is a matter that reasonable men can disagree about but equally can be considered in an objective and logical way. It is not a totally subjective matter.

Chairman

166. There is one other question on the Merger Control Regulation. To what extent have Member States used or tried to use Article 21(3) to intervene on grounds of public security and so on? Is this being much used? You mentioned one successful application. Have there been others?
(Mr Odgers) I do not think there have been any successful applications.
(Mr Goyder) I do not think our written submission actually said that.
(Mr Burbridge) I think the *Tarmac/Steetley* case under Article 9 is the one to which we are referring.

167. Again, and it is not the same point as the Article 9 point, have there been any unsuccessful attempts, as far as the MMC knows?
(Mr Burbridge) I just do not know.
(Mr Goyder) I do not think that in the United Kingdom there have been.

168. Do you think this provision allowing Member States to intervene should be widened? Do you think it is sufficiently wide at the moment?

[Chairman *Contd*]

(Mr Goyder) I can answer on the same academic basis as before. I think from the viewpoint of the European Commission there would be a danger in having this too broadly drafted because it could become really such a glaring exception to the " one stop shop principle " that it defeated the main objects of the Regulation. It is probably right to say that the three examples given in Article 21(3) and the very restrictive ability to extend the principle any further is a fair balance. After all, banking, the media and defence are the three very sensitive areas that most governments would agree they wanted to retain a degree of control over. Of course, it is a limited power; it is only allowing the Member State to stop a merger that would otherwise be cleared. It does not allow them to clear a merger that the Community is minded to stop under the Regulation.

169. We have been looking at the guidelines and the notice on cooperation with a previous witness. Will that affect you at all in the application of Article 85 and 86?

(Mr Ing) I think we would not expect it to do so. The notice seems to be addressed primarily to what I might call courts proper. Of course, the MMC does not have the functions of a court. It is a body which is concerned with reporting on and, in a few cases, determining the public interest. Having looked again at the notice in the context to today's hearing, it did not seem to me clear that we were intended, the MMC was intended, to come within it. At the moment we would not.

170. One question which has been raised is whether it is really satisfactory for a national court to go to the Commission to ask for legal guidance, which would be something which is not binding on it. Should that be tightened up? Should be regarded as binding or should it take the opposite line and say, " You do not go for guidance at all "?

(Mr Ing) I think that is something that the MMC itself would have no view on. The MMC's concern with the courts has been a happy one, in the sense that, as a recipient of judicial review, we have been generally successful, but I do not think our experience assists us on that.

Viscount Colville of Culross] The reason, surely, is that there would be no difficulty in the MMC getting advice from a source like that because you are not bound by rules of evidence, whereas the courts might find grave difficulty. Therefore, in so far as you have got a view, you would not be troubled by it.

Chairman] It would not be so much evidence as an opinion from the Commission as to the law.

Viscount Colville of Culross

171. It would be some local standing of some sort perhaps.

(Mr Ing) I suppose that it would be a possibility that in some cases, irrespective of the notice, that the MMC could consider. I suspect that there might be argument from the parties as to whether that could be regarded by the MMC as binding in the course of its enquiry.

Chairman

172. Mr Goyder told us that Article 86 comes before you rather more than Article 85 as a matter of direct concern, as I understood it.

(Mr Goyder) Yes, as it involves the principles of monopoly, and monopolistic practices rather than restrictive practice and agreements.

173. I meant that. I think you accept in your written evidence that you could take on the 86 cases in this country.

(Mr Ing) I think it was rather that if arrangements for delegation were made and we were required to do so, then, as the MMC regards itself as a can-do organisation, to deal with what is referred to it, then, given appropriate changes in the law, the MMC would, of course, be prepared to do that.

174. Rather than leaving it to the courts to do it?

(Mr Ing) I suppose to say " horses for courses " would not be appropriate in this context. One might say that the courts are there to determine issues basically between parties. The MMC is more concerned with the public interest.

175. I think you are entitled to say you have a great deal of expertise in this area which not every judge perhaps has. " Horses for courses " is not entirely inappropriate.

(Mr Goyder) I think that in Article 86 cases there is normally a great deal of factual information that you need to find out about particular companies and about what is happening in that particular market. The MMC has a staff experienced in carrying out investigations in this area which, of course, a court does not have. A court is dependent on the parties to bring that evidence themselves before it.

Baroness Elles

176. I was wondering, if there were to be a passing on of cases from the European Commission to the MMC, would you find any conflict in deciding what was in the public interest as far as the United Kingdom was concerned and what would be the Community interest on which presumably European decisions are made? There must be some conflict.

(Mr Ing) I am afraid I seem to be establishing a kind of monopoly in this group of questions which perhaps ought not to be the case. I think in principle there might be a difficulty. At the moment the MMC operates under a very wide-ranging test, Section 84 of the Fair Trading Act. I am thinking of the general type of competition case, which I think is structured towards the United Kingdom domestic position, though, of course, capable of taking account of Community law. I think that if one were considering the question, as it were, of delegation, not on Article 9 but on a larger scale, then it would be for consideration whether the test ought, in fact, to be amended in someway, just as the test under the Broadcasting Act is a purpose-made one based on Community law. I think it is fair to say that in so far as we were able to look at the Tarmac/Steetley

[Baroness Elles *Contd*]

reference before the abandonment, it was clear that we were required to confine our consideration of the public interest under Section 84 to competition issues. So far so good but I think ultimately, whether the public interest test would be adequate for the purpose would depend on the nature and scope of the delegation. If one is imagining what I might call Article 9A or an Article 21A going further, then it might be that in the light of what was there proposed, one would feel that Section 84 in its present form was not quite adequate for the purpose. I am afraid here I am going into the realms of speculation.

Chairman

177. It is an interesting answer. This is perhaps an even more elementary question. We have a division as to what the Commission should do and what national authorities should do in relation to mergers by the threshold. What would be the criteria for dividing up the Article 86 cases? How would you say which had to go to Community and which had to stay here.
(*Mr Goyder*) This is well away from current MMC jurisdiction but, to be responsive to your question——

178. If you have to take on 86 you say in your evidence you would be willing to do it. What sort of cases do you think would be most appropriate to come to you? What would be the criteria?
(*Mr Goyder*) The MMC deals at present both with large cases and very small cases.

179. So a financial threshold, as with mergers, would not be appropriate?
(*Mr Goyder*) That really would not seem to be the appropriate one. I think the important question is: Do the issues primarily affect, and are the relevant sources of evidence in the United Kingdom? Is it, therefore, more likely that an effective enquiry and a report could be carried out here on the issues concerned. Assuming that they do affect mainly enterprises or undertakings in the United Kingdom, those are really the major considerations. One must also ask who is affected by it. Is it consumers and others in the United Kingdom or has it a broader effect? Those seem to me the important considerations.

180. So you would tailor it, as it were, in a national or geographical test rather than any other test, or as the first, the primary test, rather than to take types of case under Article 86?
(*Mr Goyder*) That would be my feeling. I would have thought also if there are very substantive, interested parties in the case in other European countries, it would be more difficult for us to handle that type of case. If the bulk of the interests, however, in relation to this particular case were locally based, then clearly this is our normal jurisidiction. If we had to get however, a lot of evidence from German companies, from French consumers, et cetera, that would be much more difficult for us to handle.

181. I think what we were really wondering was whether, apart from taking the test as to whether the activities were centred in or concerning the United Kingdom solely or more than anywhere else, there were any other criteria for defining which cases should be dealt with nationally here and which should go to Brussels. As I understand it, you take the national interest, the national effect rather than anything else. Is that correct?
(*Mr Goyder*) It is a combination of the practical issues, of where the evidence is to be found, with the consideration of the location of the effects of the practice.

182. Another thing we have got to think about is whether, if some competition enforcement is going to be delegated to national authorities in the different Member States, we ought to have a system of harmonised remedies throughout the Communities, as is happening in other area. Do you think that would be feasible or are our remedies in the various countries—and I know some countries do not have any procedures virtually—in Germany or here so disparate that it would be impossible to harmonise the rules and the remedies?
(*Mr Odgers*) I think that is a difficult question. The whole question of remedies is difficult enough within the context of our own MMC situation.

183. It is a very common problem everywhere in the Community. There was a recent decision in the court that damages can be awarded for failure to carry out a Community obligation. That is a very major question now: should the damages be assessed on a national basis or should they be assessed on a Community, autonomous basis?
(*Mr Odgers*) I think it would certainly be highly desirable that there would be some kind of harmonisation, both in terms of the thinking and the kind of amounts, if one was talking in terms of fines or those kinds of remedies. That is just a personal view. I do not know if anyone else has any views on this.

184. It is a very difficult problem. It may be too difficult to achieve.
(*Mr Burbridge*) I see it as an ultimate thing to seek. It is an ultimate aim, following on from what I was attempting to say earlier, that one does need some consistency in approach, at least so far as procedures are concerned. If you are able to achieve something along those lines, then, hopefully, rationalisation across borders will follow.
(*Mr Odgers*) I think we would need to be careful not to be put in a straightjacket in the sense of being forced along certain lines which one did not feel comfortable with in the particular case. I think that is the only point I was making.

Baroness Elles

185. In talking about the question of national enforcement, would not some Member States be in some difficulty, those that do not have, if I may say, the excellent set up such as the MMC. Some countries had no merger systems until 1988 and even

[Baroness Elles *Contd*]

now they are probably not very effective or efficient. You would presumably come across some great difficulties where you are trying to introduce national enforcement in certain cases.

(Mr Goyder) I would agree very much with that.

Viscount Colville of Culross

186. I wanted to leave aside for the moment the question of fines which Mr Odgers raised. That is a difficult question in itself. Where would one go to get an idea of what remedies there are available in other EEC countries so that one could start to get a comparison or see what it might be that others should adopt from us and vice versa?

(Mr Goyder) You are thinking of remedies for anti-competitive behaviour?

187. Yes.

(Mr Goyder) There are comparative law textbooks and encyclopaedias, some produced in the United States, some produced here in Europe, which give you a country by country account. They are all fairly lengthy, and contain the particular details of the local law. There obviously are some common themes between those countries with a fairly developed system over decades and those who are pretty recent in having any kind of competition law at all. The information is available, though with the laborious task to assemble it.

(Mr Burbridge) I did mention some of the studies that we were doing, as time allowed, in other countries. I was interested to read our study on the system in Germany. What was quite interesting was the great emphasis that they put on merger control. The whole emphasis was on merger control. Really, the number of cases that were dealt with under Article 86 type legislation were relatively few and far between. That was one point, I recall. The other thing is that in Germany they are much more interested in the structure of the market, getting the structure right and then not caring too much about prices, profit levels and so on, and letting the market flow. I think that as you look at each country, you will find different emphases of that type. It is a pretty complicated system to bring all together.

Chairman

188. I think the idea of rushing into harmonisation is probably quite impossible and wrong. Like so many things in the Community, " Slowly slowly " should be the motto. Do you think if there is a delegation to national authorities that there is any risk or any likelihood of a risk the competition rules would be less rigorously enforced than they have been by the Commission? Would some Member States tend to be a bit soft on this? I do not suggest you would.

(Mr Goyder) It is partly a question of developing a tradition of applying one particular law. You do not achieve an effective competition law simply by passing a competition statute. You have got to provide the necessary resources and staff trained in all the different disciplines. It is bound to take time. Even in the United States with its very long

experience of anti-trust, it took a long time, many decades, to get an effective system operative.

189. It is up to the Commission to make sure people carry out the Community rules. The final question, as far as I am concerned, is this. We had some comment from a witness who is a practitioner that they would like to see more use of block exemptions than perhaps the Commission has done so far. Perhaps it is not entirely a matter for the Monopolies Commission. Do you have a view on that? Is there really realistically scope for more views on exemptions?

(Mr Goyder) I think it depends whose viewpoint you are talking from.

190. I am asking from your viewpoint.

(Mr Goyder) From the viewpoint of industry, they are fairly helpful because they allow you to frame your commercial practice in a way that will probably guarantee to keep you outside the scope of Article 85(1). From the viewpoint of the Commission as an administrative body, they are essential because it means the workload is not as intolerable as otherwise would be the case. From the viewpoint of competition authorities, they are valuable in some ways. They delineate the area where people can safely proceed but they can also pose problems, as we have discovered in sectors like beer and cars where what has happened is that inevitably, like most legislation, a block exemption represents a compromise. It is a compromise between competition administrators who want a tough law and the industry who want a relatively liberal law. A compromise is negotiated over a period of time. Sometimes it takes many years. Sometimes it happens fairly quickly. It is put in place for ten or fifteen years. Inevitably the economics of that market change. Perhaps one finds that a regulation is not quite as satisfactory when it gets to the end of its life as it was when it began. I believe that it is valuable to the Community that authorities in Member States, both in the United Kingdom and elsewhere, should themselves carry out investigations that may touch upon these subjects and provide useful information and evidence, so that when it comes to the end of the block exemption period, the European Commission can utilise that work and can have another look. It is important to remember that block exemptions are not permanent legislation. They are valuable to cover a period of time but then have to be reexamined in the light of all that has happened since they first came into effect.

191. Do any members of the Committee have any other questions? Would you like to add anything to take up new topics that you think we ought bear in mind when we come eventually to write our report?

(Mr Ing) I have one small factual point, my Lord Chairman, simply for the record. At an earlier stage in the discussion, I think it was question one or two, my colleague, Mr Goyder, referred, correctly of course, to the courts having discouraged the MMC from negotiating with parties. Just to point up the reference, it is in the unreported Judicial Review case of Air Europe against the Monopolies and Mergers Commission in December 1987. It appears in the

[Chairman *Contd*]

judgment of Lord Justice Lloyd. If, my Lord Chairman, you yourself or your Legal Adviser would like the transcript, that can be sent to you.[1]

192. That is very kind of you. We would be very glad to see that. I do remember it. I think it was mentioned in the newspapers at the time. Are there any other topics you would like to mention?

---

[1] The judgment of the Divisional Court No. Co/1914/87 of 18 December 1987 was supplied to the Committee and is available in the Public Record Office.

(Mr Ing) No. I merely want to thank you, my Lord Chairman, for your patience in listening to my views on these various points.

Chairman] We are all extremely grateful to you. We are very lucky that the four of you were able to come. Obviously there are different aspects to this which we cannot expect one man or woman to deal with entirely alone. You obviously all have great experience and knowledge of these matters. We are very much indebted both for your written evidence and for the answers you have given us today.

WEDNESDAY 26 MAY 1993

Present:

Elles, B.   Slynn of Hadley, L. (Chairman)
Holme of Cheltenham, L.

Memorandum by the Joint Working Party on Competition Law

The written submission which follows is made by the Joint Working Party on Competition Law of the Bars and Law Societies of the United Kingdom to Sub-Committee E of the House of Lords Select Committee on the European Communities, in connection with their enquiry into the enforcement of Community competition rules, with special reference to procedures and levels of procedure making.

1. The Joint Working Party has, for some time, felt considerable concern about the Commission's procedures in contentious competition cases. In essence these concerns centre around:

(1) the lack of respect for natural justice and the rights of defence; and the absence of any interlocutory procedure to resolve disputes during contentious procedures so as to ensure that those rights are respected in the conduct of proceedings;

(2) the lack of any adequate direction and supervision over the decision-making process of the Commission, from the Statement of Objections to the taking of the actual decision. This includes the fact-finding processes;

(3) the lack of any independent control over many of these processes and the considerable disappointment at how the position of the Hearing Officer, as specified in his Terms of Reference, has fallen far short of what was expected when this proposal was first mooted.

(1) NATURAL JUSTICE AND THE RIGHTS OF DEFENCE

2. Natural justice and the rights of defence have always been regarded by the Court of Justice as being of paramount importance. This has been reinforced by recent decisions of the Court of First Instance, and probably, even more importantly in the long term, by the Decision of the Commission for Human Rights in *Stenuit* v *France* (1992) 14 EHRR 509, where the French competition procedures were held to fall within the provisions of Article 6 of the Human Rights Convention, and accordingly to require the fullest procedural protection.

3. It is not sufficient that many defects can be remedied by the Court of First Instance or the Court of Justice by annulling—often after many years—a final decision. The interests involved do not only concern the defendant in such a case, but the complainant and/or others who allegedly suffered as a result of the conduct. Both these latter categories have an interest in seeing that justice is done, as do the general public. A decision annulled for the failure of the Commission to carry out proper procedures is as much a denial of justice to those who suffer, as is the denial of rights of defence to the defendant.

4. Commission procedures should be clearly and publicly expressed, so that all concerned know what are their duties and expectations. That is certainly not the position in many of the Commission procedures, which are often obscure in their statement and obscure in their application.

5. The areas in which the absence of natural justice and rights of defence can be most clearly seen are:

(i) the requirement that the Statement of Objections should clearly set out the case against the defendant or defendants;

(ii) the requirement that the defendants should have full access to the relevant documents in the Commission's file.

(i) *Statement of Objections*

6. The standard of the Statement of Objections shows great variations between cases. In *Woodpulp*, Judgment of 31 March 1993 (ECJ) the defects in the Statement of Objections were such that the major part of the decision of the Commission was anulled by the Court of Justice. In recent cases, where the number of potential defendants has been great (for example *Cement*, where there are over 70 separate defendants), there have been many complaints, particularly by smaller producers, that the case against them was woefully inadequately stated and, more generally, that by disclosing only part of the Statement of Objections to individual defendants the Commission denied them an opportunity to consider the overall case being made against them. There is clearly a great need that the Statement of Objections be clearly drafted, so that all the defendants (and indeed the complainants) should know what is the case being made out by the Commission.

The Hearing Officer at present plays no part in resolving disputes as to the particularity of the Statement of Objections, and we propose that his Terms of Reference should be enlarged to give him power to resolve disputes on allegations of lack of particularity in the Statement of Objections.

(ii) *Access to the file*

7. In the 1982 Report of the House of Lords Select Committee on Competition Procedures, it was stated that general access to the file was the single most important matter of competition procedure which required improvement. It states that "no single reform could do more to dispel distrust and dissatisfaction in the business community". We wholeheartedly agree. The right to access to documentation which could be helpful to the defence is a fundamental human right (see *Edwards* v *United Kingdom,* European Court of Human Rights, Series A at 247 B, judgment of 16 December 1992). Community law in the past had provided for only limited access to the file, and in particular only access to documents actually used by the Commission to support its claim.

8. The 1982 Report was very influential and led to the Commission in successive Competition Reports setting out improved procedures (see 11th Report at paragraphs 22–25, 12th Report at paragraphs 34–35, 13th Report at paragraph 7(b), 14th Report at paragraph 46). However the Commission does not always provide full access to its files and the procedures adopted in individual cases are far from uniform. See in particular Case 49/88 *al-Jubail* [1991] ECR 3187 and the Opinion of Darmon A–G, and also see Case T1–4, 6–15/89 *Polypropylene* [1992] 4 CMLR 84, CFI and Opinion of Judge Vesterdorf. In *PVC,*the Commission refused to give general access to the file to the defendants and in *Soda Ash (ICI/Solvay)* the Commission even refused to provide a list of documents on the file. In case T-10-12/92, *Cimenteries* [1993] 4 CMLR 259 the CFI, in a case where again the Commission had refused general access to the file, repeated its insistence on the crucial importance of such a right so as to respect the rights of defence and the right to be heard. On the other hand, in Case T-65/89 *BPB Industries and British Gypsum* v *Commission,* Judgment of 1 April 1993 (CFI) the Commission had given full access to the file on the lines of its commitments in the 12th Report on Competition Policy and gave the defendant a list of 2,095 documents in its file broken down according to the nature of the documents, and specifying whether it was accessible to the defendant, partly accessible or not accessible. In that case the CFI again stressed the crucial importance of a defendant being given such rights.

9. Little or no attempt has been made by the Commission to resolve the issue of reconciling the "dual imperatives" of access to the file and confidentiality. Mr Advocate-General Darmon in *al-Jubail* (Opinion at paragraph 114–120), suggested that, as in the USA, procedures for limited disclosure to lawyers could be introduced. However, this does not necessarily provide a full answer for in many cases the information provided will mean little to the lawyer without obtaining instructions from his client. Further there should be no difficulty in providing non-confidential summaries (as in dumping cases). Notwithstanding that Opinion, the Commission appears to have done little or nothing to resolve this problem. In any event the problem of confidentiality can often be exaggerated, because, in many cases by the time the Commission takes action, the information (often names of customers or prices) has lost all trace of true confidentiality. However, in any event there can be no doubt that the rights of defence are a far superior right to the rights of confidentiality (see Case 264/82 *Timex* [1984] ECR 849 at paragraphs 29–30) and problems of confidentiality in a particular case can never justify the failure to provide full rights of defence.

10. In a recent matter before the Commission, the Commission contended that in the case of confidential business information, it was entitled to use that information to support an allegation of infringement of the competition rules, but it was precluded by Regulation 17 from disclosing confidential information on which it does not rely, even though it may be of assistance to the defence against the same allegations of an infringement. We consider such an attitude conflicts with the right to be heard in a totally unacceptable way.

11. In the 20th Report on Competition Policy the Commission stated that:

"The Commission has always allowed undertakings the right of access to the file so as to allow them to present their arguments in full knowledge of the facts before any decision having immediate effect is taken against them" (Paragraph 89).

In the experience of the Working Party this is unfortunately far from being correct. We consider that the Hearing Officer should have jurisdiction to deal with issues relating to access to the file, to ensure that full access is given, to deal with questions of confidentiality which might arise (if necessary preparing, or supervising the preparation of, non-confidential summaries), and generally supervising all matters relating to access to documentation.

12. All this points to a real need for the Hearing Officer to have powers to deal with disputes relating to the rights of defence in the course of proceedings. At present such disputes cannot effectively be dealt with by the CFI at the interlocutory stage (see *IBM* [1981] ECR 2639 (ECJ), see *Cimenteries CBR* [1993] 4 CMLR 259 (CFI) and can only be dealt with by appeal against the final decision of the Commission.

(2) LACK OF DIRECTION AND SUPERVISION

13. The Working Party consider that many of the problems which arise have arisen out of a failure by the Commission to exercise proper direction and supervision and control over the conduct of competition cases. The proper supervision would ensure a reasonably uniform standard of Statement of Objections, and a consistent policy on access to the file. At present the application of competition procedures appears to rely too much on the individual feelings (and abilities) of the Rapporteur. This is irrespective of our proposals for an increased role of the Hearing Officer.

14. This lack of direction applies not only to the procedures leading to the issue of the Statement of Objections (including the fact-finding procedures), but also to the matters which take place after the Statement of Objections (and in particular access to the file). The policy with regard to the presentation of documentation to the Advisory Committee also seems very haphazard (and are in any event very difficult to investigate). The recent decision of the CFI in *PVC*, (Joined Cases T-79 etc/89, Judgment of 27 February 1992) has highlighted the fact that this lack of direction and supervision extends also to the finalising of the draft Decision, and the actual taking of the decision by the Commissioners (and including allowing subsequent alterations after the decision has been taken by the Commissioners). Whatever the result of the Commission's appeal to the ECJ in *PVC*, all these procedures clearly need improvement and proper direction.

15. The fact-finding procedures also need considerable direction and supervision. Again its quality is extremely variable. *Woodpulp* shows what happens when cases are not properly directed and supervised. In *Italian Flat Glass* (Cases T-68, T-78/89 *Societe Italiano Ventro SpA* v *Commission*, Judgment of 10 March, 1992 (CFI)) documents were altered, and passages from documents were excluded so as to change their meaning. This could never have happened with proper supervision. Nor is it known whether there has been any change of procedures or internal direction following the decision of the ECJ and the CFI in such cases. Cases yet to be decided by the CFI also raise similar complaints of " doctoring " of documents and non-disclosure of relevant documents. As at present complaints as to denial of access to the file do not fall within the remit of the Hearing Officer, complaints to him can do little. In any event, when the Hearing Officer has reported that the procedures require considerable improvement (as apparently he did in *PVC*), there is little evidence that this has had any subsequent effect on such procedures. We make proposals below for extending the Hearing Officer's Remit to cover these matters, but these would only deal with individual cases, and the real problem is the lack of overall direction and supervision.

16. In 1982, when this Committee first reported, on Competition Procedures, the Commission defended its procedures on the basis that there was a division of responsibility between the investigators and those who were in charge of the decision-making process. This separation of roles was subsequently abandoned and now the investigators who inspect documents are often in charge of the preparation of the case and the drafting of the decision. (As to the CFI's position on this see Case T-11/89 *Shell v Commission*, Judgment of 10 March 1992.) However well meaning the individual, this is bound to have an effect upon the conduct of the procedures and in particular upon the feeling of a defendant as to whether he has been given a fair hearing. We have considerable reservations about combining this role, but if it is to be combined, it must be combined with much greater and effective supervision, and a much greater role for the Hearing Officer. However we would prefer DG IV to revert to the earlier regime under which investigations of alleged infringements and subsequent prosecution were conducted entirely separately.

17. In this respect we should say that the investigation procedures, as they are now applied, and the application of the Rules of Legal Professional Privilege, have presented no particular problems. There has certainly been a great improvement on investigation procedures following the 1982 Report of the Select Committee. As far as we are aware the absence of recognition by the Court of legal professional privilege to opinions of legally qualified in-house lawyers have not presented any particular problems, probably because the Commission inspectors are prepared to deal with this contentious issue in a sensitive manner. Nevertheless the position of employed lawyers does need to be resolved.

18. The Commission has power under Article 13 of Regulation 17 to call upon the competent authority of a Member State, in addition to its duty of assistance under Articles 11 and 14 of Regulation 17, to carry out an investigation on the Commission's behalf. We do not know of any case (even where a Member State has adopted legislation to give effect to this requirement) where the Commission has made use of such powers. We would have considerable reservations, if such a procedure were to be used, not least because of the differential results this would give in different Member States. As far as we are aware, there is no legislation in force in the United Kingdom to give effect to this duty under Article 13.

(3) THE HEARING OFFICER

19. Successive Hearing Officers have been unduly hampered by the restrictive effects of their Terms of Reference. The Terms of Reference *exclude:*

  (i) rulings on matters relating to disclosure of documents,

  (ii) rulings on questions such as whether the time limits for submitted defences to the Statement of Objections are reasonable,

(iii) rulings on whether the Commission should make its Statement of Objections more particular, either generally or in relation to individual defendants,

(iv) any power in relation to the actual drafting of the decision, and any input as to the attitude the Commission should take with regard to a particular case.

This is not just our view, but reference should also be made to a useful and constructive paper by the present Hearing Officer, Mr Johannes in (1989) Fordham University School of Law publication on " 1992 and EEC/US Competition and Trade Law".

20. The Hearing Officer is principally responsible for the conduct of the hearing, and in this the Hearing Officer has in most cases performed difficult tasks of organising complicated hearings with considerable tact and skill. Thus, in the very large *PP, PVC, LDPE,* hearings, the parties had nothing but praise for the conduct of the Hearing Officer, given his limited terms of reference. However, those hearing were conducted by the permanent Hearing Officer, and other hearings, conducted by ad hoc Hearing Officers (often without the tradition of independence which the Hearing Officers have been rightly proud to emphasise) have been less successful and sometimes given the impression that the individual appointed Hearing Officer for a particular case is part of the prosecution team. If it is so, it is unforgivable. Ad hoc Hearing Officers are not acceptable. If necessary a deputy should be appointed on permanent basis.

21. Following the Oral Hearing, the chief responsibility of the Hearing Officer is preparing the minutes. This has generally been well done, although in cases where the Commission seem particularly keen to produce a decision urgently (sometimes seemingly more connected with the terms of office of the Commissioner than anything else), the minutes could not have been approved before they were considered by the Advisory Committee. It is difficult to know what documents are actually placed before the Advisory Committee, and we consider that it would be helpful for these documents to be identified publicly, so that the parties know what they were. In this respect we do not consider that a Report of the Advisory Committee needs to be published or produced to the parties, and it would only be in very rare cases that such a report would be of any particular advantage. The procedures in Merger cases, where there is a requirement for the publication of such a Report, take place in a very different situation to that in an ordinary competition case.

22. The Hearing Officer's Report is not made public and is not available to the parties (see *ICI* v *Commission* [1987] 2 CMLR 500). If he makes a report he can insist that it be referred to the Commissioner with particular responsibility for Competition Matters. However, it is not made available to the Advisory Committee and is only made available to the Commission as a body if the individual Commissioner responsible for competition matters considers it is appropriate.

23. We consider that there is a real need to enlarge the Terms of Reference of the Hearing Officer, to include procedural matters (including access to the file) both before and after the Statement of Objections. Thus he would have power to deal with issues which arise out of the Statement of Objections. He should also produce a report on the hearing, dealing with both procedural and substantive matters, and this should be made available to the Advisory Committee, to all the Commissioners annexed to the draft decisions, and should be made available to all the parties (including complainants and the Court of First Instance). We consider that this will do much to improve the procedural and substantive problems adverted to in these Submissions, and will do much to improve the status of the Hearing Officer. The Hearing Officer's remit moreover should not end upon the taking of a particular decision. He should also have power to make recommendations on a particular case, in which he presided, in the light of any subsequent decision of the CFI and/or ECJ. Equally in this respect the Commission in its annual Competition Report should set out the correcting steps that he has taken in the light of any decisions of the Court of First Instance and/or the ECJ, and, if no steps are taken, why this was not considered appropriate.

(4) OTHER MATTERS

24. We consider that other matters relevant to the Committee's investigation into Competition Procedures are (i) national procedures, upon which we attach a copy of our paper to the Department of Trade and Industry in June 1992, (ii) mergers, upon which we enclose a copy of our paper to the Department of Trade and Industry dated 31 March 1993. For the reasons set out in the former paper we do not consider it likely that national procedures by national courts and national authorities will have any substantial effect upon the work-load of DG IV.

25. It is too early to decide whether any of the procedures mentioned by Sir Leon Brittan QC in relation to the exclusive delays in the conduct of non-contentious procedures in notifications and exemption cases will have any effect. Such a move is long overdue. For many undertakings, a comfort letter is a perfectly adequate (although not complete) protection, although it can be no real substitute for a legally binding decision.

26. In so far as the Commission's inability to cope with notifications and exemptions may arise from shortage of qualified staff or budgetary constraints, we would fully support any suggestion that the number of well qualified staff should be increased. The clearing of backlogs and the expeditious handling of such matters are important for the wellbeing of Community industry. Obviously staff shortages, or budgetary constraints, can never justify failure to respect the rights of defence in contentious matters.

27. Finally, although not actually relevant to Competition Procedures, we would like to make clear our great admiration for the work of the CFI in Competition Procedures. All of us who have had experience of the CFI have nothing but praise for the way in which they tackle individual cases. The quality of preparation, the conduct of the hearing (in cases which frequently last for many days) and the quality of the judgments are of the highest order. We consider that this has been a development of great importance in judicial protection of individual rights. We only wish that there was more evidence that the Commission took notice of the comments (and frequently strictures) of the CFI in procedural matters.

10 *May* 1993

Joint Working Party on Competition Law

THE DRAFT " NOTICE ON THE APPLICATION OF ARTICLES 85 AND 86 OF THE EEC TREATY BY NATIONAL COURTS "

1. This Memorandum is submitted in response to a request from the Department of Trade and Industry for comments on the Commission's draft Notice on the Application of Articles 85 and 86 of the EEC Treaty by National Courts.

2. On one level, it could be said that the draft Notice does no more than state the existing position. Articles 85 and 86 are part of the laws of the United Kingdom; they are not infrequently pleaded, especially in the form of the " Eurodefence "; and the United Kingdom courts are not finding very much difficulty in dealing with them. There is some doubt about the remedies available, and in particular the decision in *Bourgoin* must be regarded as questionable in the light of *Francovitch,* but it could be said that the Notice would make no difference to the legal position in the United Kingdom. Indeed, it could not do so, since it has no legally binding effect.

3. However, the Commission apparently intends that practice should change, in that more of the " routine " application of Articles 85 and 86 should be done by the national courts, (*v* paragraph 11 of the draft), though it does not make it clear how this is to be brought about. At the moment, most people who want to obtain redress for an alleged infringement of Article 85 or 86 complain to the Commission. One can only guess at the motives which impel potential plaintiffs to do this rather than to sue in the national courts, though the most obvious possibilities are the much lower cost of a complaint, the very powerful methods of discovery open to the Commission, and the fact that there is no risk of a penalty in costs if the claimant's suspicions prove unjustified. Whatever the reasons, the fact remains that people prefer to complain rather than sue, and it is not clear from the paper how these complainants are to be diverted to the national courts. It has till now been assumed that the Commission is obliged either by Article 89 of the Treaty or Article 9 of Regulation 17 to deal with all infringements of Articles 85 and 86 which come to its notice, and an unanswered complainant is clearly entitled to bring an action for " failure to act " under Article 175 of the Treaty. The amount of action required of the Commission is not great, but it is unlikely that a complete refusal to consider the merits of the complaint would qualify.

It might be possible for the Commission to inform a complainant that it would deal with his complaint when it had time to do so, but that might not be for several years, and that in the interim he might wish to take action in the national courts, but this is likely to be open to challenge before the ECJ.

4. If the Notice were to result in a significant number of cases being diverted to the national courts, new problems would be created and existing problems which now are purely theoretical would take on practical importance. The draft either ignores these, mentions them briefly without resolving them, or answers them in a legally questionable manner:

4.1 A substantial increase in the number of EC competition cases before national courts is very likely to generate a comparable increase in the number of Article 177 references to the European Court of Justice— the more so since the sort of cases which go to national courts will be those where what is alleged to have been done may or may not be caught by Article 85 or 86. The Commission will no doubt want to retain jurisdiction, and the power to fine, in cases where the activity alleged is clearly prohibited. It is not clear whether the Court was consulted about the draft, but it hardly seems a sensible allocation of resources to transfer any of the burden of resolving private disputes about the applicability of Articles 85 or 86 from DG IV to the ECJ— already overloaded as it is with cases about Sunday trading and milk subsidies.

4.2 Cases about Articles 85 and 86 are likely to have an international element, because the agreement or abuse has to affect trade between Member States to be caught. Although the framers of the Brussels Convention probably did not have competition actions in mind, they presumably fall somewhere within it, and so there may well be situations where potential litigants will have a choice of forum. Procedural and evidential matters are very important in competition cases, and there are wide differences in these matters between the various legal systems in the Community. In particular, the procedure of discovery appears to be confined to the British Isles. Since the nearest thing to an invariable rule under the Brussels Convention is that a defendant may be sued in the place where he is domiciled, a Continental litigant wishing to allege an infringement of Article 85 or 86 against a British or Irish defendant will be in a much stronger position than an Irish or British litigant wishing to do the same against a Continental one.

The draft Notice mentions " powers of national courts " in its list of matters to be discussed in the promised booklet, but does not suggest that they will be harmonised. Indeed, it seems from the quotation from *Rewe v Hauptzollamt Kiel* in paragraph 5 that there is no power to require such harmonisation.

4.3 Since the Commission has no power to redirect a case to the national courts, the final decision on whether to go to the national courts will have to be taken by the complainant. It is therefore quite possible that cases in which the Commission would like to interest itself will be taken to the national courts. It seems from Article 9.3 of Regulation 17 that the Commission will be able to intervene in such cases and oust the jurisdiction of the national courts, apparently at any stage of the proceedings. Is this acceptable?

4.4 Another question which will sooner or later arise if Articles 85 and 86 are to be enforced in national courts is the extent to which a decision of a national court is binding in the courts of other Member States and against the Commission, and conversely whether a refusal to act by the Commission bars access to the national courts. Two actions between the same parties on the same facts are presumably excluded by the Brussels Convention, but if the courts of country A have decided in litigation between X and Z that the agreement between X (domiciled in A) and Y (domiciled in B) is not caught by Article 85, can another plaintiff sue Y in country B? The " effect of *res judicata* of national court decisions " is again listed for the explanatory booklet as part of the section on " authority of Commission decisions ", but nothing is said about the Commission's likely attitude. The problem will be especially serious for decisions under Article 86, because the concept of " abuse " involves policy decisions like those on the application of Article 85(3), and so it is more likely that different national courts will come to different conclusions.

4.5 The draft Notice attempts to deal with the objection to the enforcement of Article 85 in national courts, that those courts cannot apply Article 85(3), by suggesting that the courts should be free to decide that there is no possibility that the Commission would apply Article 85(3) and that in other cases the court should suspend the case and consult the Commission. If the Commission gives it as its " provisional opinion " that exemption is unlikely, the court should proceed to judgment and prohibit the agreement. If the Commission does not give such an opinion, the case presumably remains suspended and the Commission will " endeavour to give priority " to the matter.

This proposal raises one constitutional and two practical problems. The constitutional problem is that it assumes that decisions not to apply Article 85(3) are not subject to Regulation 17, and that it is only decisions to exempt by applying Article 85(3) which have to be taken by the Commission in the manner laid down in Regulation 17. This is a novel and artificial reading of the Regulation.

The first practical problem is that this procedure will if operated as described increase rather than reduce the workload on DG IV. There is a substantial class of agreements which DG IV would regard as harmless or beneficial but which could be said to be within Article 85(1). If a complaint is made about such an agreement today, the Commission can reject it by a simple letter: but if the matter comes from a national court under the proposed system the Commission will have to go through the full procedure under Regulation 17. Since it is generally believed that with its present manpower and the procedures of Regulation 17 the Commission cannot take more than 20 decisions a year, this will lead to even more congestion and delay not only in DG IV but also in the national courts.

The second practical problem is that it is today possible to notify a slightly doubtful agreement in the knowledge that if the Commission are unhappy with some parts of it those parts can be amended before a final decision is taken. The new system would give no room for amendment.

5. This last point is an illustration of the general point that what is proposed is a change from an almost purely administrative system to one where some cases are dealt with by administrators and some by courts. The difference between the two is fundamental. Administrators have policies, which can change; courts have rules and precedents. Administrators can be negotiated with; courts have to deal with the facts before them. Administrators can sometimes give acceptable security in informal ways, such as a statement that in the view of the appropriate official, a certain agreement falls within a block exemption; courts have to produce formal decisions. This is not to say that administrators are better or worse than courts, only that they are different; and the system as it has developed is essentially administrative.

6. The draft Notice does not draw any clear distinction between those elements of Community " law " which are binding on national courts and those which are not, lumping together (in paragraph 26) the " case law of the Court of Justice, decisions taken by the Commission, the implementing and block exemptions regulations, the notices and the annual reports on competition policy " as " elements of secondary legislation or guidelines which may assist the national courts in examining individual cases ". If the national courts are to play a larger part in applying Articles 85 and 86, the Commission will have to accept that they are capable of distinguishing between law and Commission policy, and that they may choose not to follow the latter.

7. The Commission may have over-estimated the extent to which their proposals would reduce their work-load. Complaints in recent years have averaged between one-third and one-quarter of the cases raised with the Commission or commenced by it (not counting mergers). If all the complaints were handled by national courts, the Commission would still have to handle about two hundred notifications and as many own-initiative procedures as it chose to commence in any year, and it might well be that companies would be less ready to accept a comfort letter or a simple closure of the file if actions by third parties were a serious risk.

8. In sum, we welcome the Commission's recognition of the fact that it " has neither the physical nor the human resources to intervene in all cases where an infringement may have been committed ", and we sympathise with its attempt to lighten the load. However, we do not think that the problem can be solved in the manner proposed in the draft Notice, which amounts to changing the system without changing the legislation. We do not believe that the Commission's proposals as written will succeed in transferring any significant part of its case-load to the national courts, and we do not believe that the resulting system would be workable or equitable if it did. There are good arguments for saying that enforcement of many cases under Article 85 (and perhaps 86) should be " hived down " to national courts and competition authorities, but in our view this cannot be done without major changes in the EC system and in the organisation and powers of national authorities.

June 1992

Joint Working Party on Competition Law

REVIEW OF THE EC MERGER REGULATION (ECMR)

1. In his letter dated 11 March, Mr Alty invited the Joint Working Party to give its views on possible amendments to the ECMR as regards:

- the significance of multiple jeopardy;

- the practicability or desirability of increased referrals from the EC to national competition authorities; and

- the inter-relationship between national and EC merger control procedures under Articles 9 and 21, ECMR.

(i) SIGNIFICANCE OF MULTIPLE JEOPARDY

2. Reduction in the level of thresholds in the ECMR, envisaged by the Commission at the time of its adoption, will result in many more mergers benefitting from " one-stop shop " review—an important justification for adopting the ECMR. On grounds of cost and convenience alone, the Working Party welcomes the avoidance of multiple proceedings. Any widening of the gateways for reference back under Article 9 can only detract from the most important advantage otherwise derived from the Regulation.

3. However, it should be recognised that, seemingly consistent with the text of the ECMR, there is latitude in the interpretation and application of the threshold rules which can result in a merger falling for review by the Commission or, alternatively, remaining a matter for the national authorities. As a result of lack of clarity in the drafting of the ECMR—or perhaps because of lack of procedural transparency—there seems to be scope for " tinkering " with threshold figures in order to get a merger to come within, or escape from, the scope of the ECMR. Contrast the position, for example, relating to:

- Midland Bank and the competing interests of HSBC and Lloyds Bank. Calculation of turnover in other Member States enabled HSBC's bid to fall for review by the EC, whereas the proposals of Lloyds Bank remained a matter for the United Kingdom. Lloyds Bank has made it clear that it was unclear how HSBC was able to demonstrate satisfactorily that it had at least one third of its Community turnover in a Member State other than the United Kingdom.

- Dan Air and BA's acquisition of control of its non-charter business. In Case T-3/93 (OJ C45/20, 17.2.93), Air France claims that the EC was wrong to declare it had no power to consider the merger arising from BA's takeover of Dan Air on the ground that it lacked Community dimension because the charter business, which Dan Air had voluntarily given up prior to the concentration, had been excluded in the calculation of Dan Air's Community turnover.

In the view of the Working Party, the rules relating to determination of relevant thresholds should be clarified and made more precise as a matter of urgency.

4. As regards cases in which multiple jurisdiction is exercised, the impression to date of members of the Working Party is that, for all the inconvenience of additional expense, different procedures and timetables, in practice it remains reasonably easy to cope with the varying requirements of national authorities. However, as Member States which have not hitherto had merger control powers adopt new measures (most recently, for example, Belgium, following Spain and Italy), it is inevitable that a " one-stop shop " approach for mergers with significant transnational characteristics will become increasingly attractive.

5. The most significant difficulty resulting from the exercise of multiple jeopardy relates to the bid timetable, especially where, because of City Code requirements or contractual commitments, it is not possible to obtain all necessary domestic consents by the required date; in such cases, it is necessary to make completion of the transaction conditional upon receipt of final clearance, etc. Special timetable difficulties can be expected where, for example, a transaction involves contemporaneous procedures in France and the Republic of Ireland as well as in other Member States.

(ii) PRACTICABILITY OR DESIRABILITY OF INCREASED REFERRALS FROM THE EC TO NATIONAL COMPETITION AUTHORITIES

6. Accommodation of the principle of subsidiarity is of little interest to undertakings and their advisers if it detracts from achievement of " one-stop shop " control under the ECMR. To this extent, the Working Party sees no reason why, in the event that the current thresholds are reduced, there should be increased pressure on the Commission to widen the gateways for reference back to Member States. Such a move is likely to exacerbate the problems of delay, expense etc, referred to in paragraphs 4 and 5 above.

7. In addition, if the result of referring back to Member States mergers that would otherwise fall to be reviewed by the Commission is that there is an increased risk of divergence of assessment and application of merger rules Community-wide, the benefit of the ECMR is undermined. It may suit individual undertakings in some circumstances to derive commercial benefit from the operation of more liberal regimes available in some Member States as compared with others, but, to the extent that they are able to do so, this merely detracts from the value of the ECMR.

(iii) INTER-RELATIONSHIP BETWEEN NATIONAL AND EC MERGER CONTROL PROCEDURES UNDER ARTICLES 9 AND 21

8. Overall, the Commission has, in the view of the Working Party, applied the ECMR procedures with a much greater degree of efficiency and in a more " user-friendly " fashion than had been expected at the outset; to this extent, early concerns (based to some extent on the experience of dealing with DG IV) about the approach of the Commission have been misplaced. There remains, nevertheless, concern about the way in which some provisions of the ECMR have been interpreted and applied, and the overtly political nature of decisions adopted in a small number of cases.

9. As regards Articles 9 and 21, problems have been experienced because of the lack of transparency in Commission procedures especially in the case of contested bids and, more so, where there are competing bids and conflicting jurisdictions (eg Steetley/Redland/Tarmac; Midland/HSBC/Lloyds). For example, the parties remain largely ignorant of the nature and scope of exchanges between the Commission and Government Departments and the OFT in the United Kingdom in relation to Article 9(3) and Article 21(3); yet the characteristics of the market for the products or services involved, or the geographical markets concerned, are critical in determining whether it is appropriate for Community or domestic merger control procedures to operate in a particular case. Both the Commission and the national authorities should, in the view of the Working Party, operate (both under domestic rules and the ECMR) as transparently as possible and with the close involvement of the parties in determining which authority is to exercise jurisdiction under the respective provisions.

CONCLUSION

10. The Working Party endorses the undoubted benefits of " one-stop shop " review, and is concerned that the introduction of " more flexibility " in Article 9 will tend to undermine the benefits deriving from the ECMR.

31 *March* 1993

Examination of witnesses

Mr DAVID HALL, English Solicitor, Mr DAVID VAUGHAN, QC, English Barrister, MISS VIVIEN ROSE, English Barrister, Mrs KATHERINE HOLMES, English Solicitor, Mr DAVID FLINT, Scottish Solicitor, Mr RONALD MACKAY, Faculty of Advocates and Mr CHRISTOPHER PARKER, BACFI, called in and examined.

Chairman

193. May I, first of all, welcome you all to this meeting of Sub-Committee E and thank you for coming. The Committee is rather small in number today. Do not think that we are the only three who will consider the evidence which you give. It will be considered in considerable detail by all the members of the Committee. It is unfortunate there are a lot of clashes. May I also thank you very much for the very helpful paper which you have jointly produced and which we have all read and for which we have already expressed considerable admiration. It may be we will want to ask you a few supplementary questions about it. For the record, would you like to identify yourselves.

(Mr Hall) I am David Hall, a solicitor in private practice. I am Chairman of the Joint Working Party of the Bars and Law Societies concerned with competition law. To my left is David Vaughan, QC, then Miss Vivien Rose of Counsel and Mr Parker, a lawyer in industry. To my right is Mrs Katherine Holmes, a solicitor in private practice, Mr Ronald Mackay, from the Faculty of Advocates and Mr David Flint a lawyer in private practice. We also have on our Working Party representatives of the Northern Ireland Bar and Law Society but, unfortunately, we do not have anyone from that jurisdiction present here this afternoon.

194. When we put the questions, one of you perhaps could reply principally and then, if anyone else wants to add anything, you may. I do not think we can go down the line seven times on every question. Otherwise we may still be going when all the others turn up for next week's meeting! May I start with the opening part of your paper before us. It begins with some fairly trenchant criticisms of the way in which the Commission applies and enforces competition rules. I do not know whether there is anything in those criticisms you would like to elaborate at this stage on the complaints about lack of respect for natural justice and adequate direction and independent control. If not, perhaps you could tell us whether you think that any of these defects, and if so which, comes from the fact that the Commission seems to be both the investigator, the prosecutor and decider of competition matters. In the earlier report in 1982, and very many times since, people have criticised the fact the Commission has this multiplicity of roles. Do you think any of your criticisms stem directly from an amalgam of functions?

(Mr Vaughan) I have drawn this question. I think our criticisms do come from this amalgam of functions. A lot of the problems come from that. Equally, if you had a wonderfully divided system, you could have a large number of problems. It is very difficult to say if we change that system we would automatically get to a perfect system. I do not think

that would happen. Equally, the problems get much worse because of this unitary system that they have and because of that there is the greater need for supervision, which we deal with later on. There are no checks and balances within the Commission to deal with this sort of particular question. We see it being something that comes from that but, if that were rectified, that would not necessarily answer all the problems but, because there is a unitary system, many of the other problems which we highlight become more acute.

195. It might be said that the unitary system provides for a greater degree of control. The problem is that it is not independent control. That is your real criticism of it.

(Mr Hall) When some of us were here in 1981 before your Committee, it was put to the Committee by the witnesses from the Commission that there are a significant number of checks and balances that operate within the Commission to ensure that those administering Articles 85 and 86 are subject to various contracts, and that these checks and balances ensure that concerns or difficulties of a procedural or other nature are ironed out, so that at the end of the day the fact that the Commission is the detective, prosecutor, negotiator and decision-maker does not actually work adversely as regards the parties to the proceedings. Unfortunately, we I think the experience of members of this Working Party at least is that these checks and balances do not appear to work in practice.

196. Because it does not follow, the fact that the Commission is the detective, prosecutor, negotiator and decision-maker, natural justice should not be respected; it is perfectly possible for the unitary system to ensure that people do know the case against them and do have access to documents, files and so on.

(Mr Vaughan) I think the basis of our paper assumes that, apart from minimal changes within the Commission, there would not be a complete structural change. When we were giving evidence in 1981 and 1982, we were advocating having a different decision-maker so that the decision as to whether somebody is guilty or not would be taken by a third party, by the hearing officer. That has not happened. I think the basis of our paper really is that probably would not happen now because that would need perhaps a change in the Treaty.

197. Much of your paper—and we will come on to it later—really goes to increasing the powers and responsibilities of the hearing officer, which is obviously something we must go into in detail.
(Mr Vaughan) Yes.

198. Leaving that aside, if you split up the decision-making from the investigation and split off the negotiator, where would you see the control of direction and supervision of procedures lying? Who

[Chairman *Contd*]

would you envisage would provide this independent control?

(Mr Vaughan) I think we would be quite happy that it was within the Commission, DG IV, but there ought to be somebody at a very senior level who, as it were, is ultimately responsible for what happens.

199. Someone other than the hearing officer?

(Mr Vaughan) The hearing officer cannot deal with the quality of the decision, as things are at he moment. He is there to see fair play. A lot of our complaints are that the quality of the statement of objection is not adequate; the fact-finding is not adequate. That simply has got to come from within DG IV itself and should not be left to the policeman and the person who happens to have the files to have the ultimate say.

200. It goes to improving quality rather than changing the nature of the proceeding: is that your real complaint?

(Mr Vaughan) Yes, I think it is quality. I think it is quite scandalous at the moment; the quality of the stated objection and quality of the decision is not really good enough.

(Mr Hall) There is an apparent lack of accountability of those within the Commission services responsible for administering the rules, when errors of practice or procedure are identified, either as a result of concerns expressed by the parties during the course of the administrative procedure or as a result of cases taken to the Court.

201. But if you are going simply to seek to improve the quality, how do you go about it? Does it mean the personnel are wrong or that they are not getting the right sort of directions as to what to do or what? What lies behind your complaint about quality?

(Mr Vaughan) I think the individuals go about it as well as they can, given that they probably have a big case load and some of the cases are very big anyhow.

202. Are the people doing the job of the right calibre? That is the question, I suppose?

(Mr Vaughan) I think there are some very good people there but I suspect that there is not enough involvement at a high level in DG IV with the contested cases. I suspect most people are spending their time dealing with block exemptions and mergers and things like that and not enough people are really interested in seeing that these very importance cases, where people have been fined £50 million, or whatever it is, are really prepared properly. I think there are too many people who are saying, " That is just a contentious case and they can be dealt with at a relatively low level ".

203. That is it; there are two initial things. Are the people of the right calibre and are there enough of them? One witness has already told us that he thinks the problem does not lie in simply increasing the number of people dealing with these cases. The number is not the real criticism.

(Mr Hall) I think that that point of view may be sustainable if responsibility for applying the rules is either pushed down to national authorities or courts on the one hand or, alternatively, greater use is made of comfort letters. We are going to come on to that. However, if the Commission is going to do the job that is assigned to it by the Treaty, including operating and applying 85(3) in the way it was originally envisaged with all the implications that that has, I am not sure I agree that there is a sufficient number of people doing the job. It appears actually to be an issue involving the budget.

204. I am interested to hear you say that, because I was surprised when we were told that the number of people was not the real problem. I always had the impression that one of the great complaints, both within the Commission and outside it, was that there were not enough people dealing with these cases. You tell us they can only deal with something like twenty cases a year at the moment. That does not sound as if they have enough staff.

Baroness Elles

205. Do you think one of the problems has been that up to 1982 the Commission regarded its role entirely as administrative and not to do with the results of a judicial tribunal, which is, in fact, its role when it has to make decisions and apply what have become very big fines? Therefore, I wonder if the problem does not lie in the basic organisation of DG IV, recognising that they have a judicial role as well as an administrative role, because in some of the cases I am sure your members will have come across when it comes, for instance, to assessing economic aspects of competition, they have to bring in outside people? They do not have the people within DG IV to do the economic assessments which, of course, are involved? I wondered if there is not some fundamental flaw in the conceived role of DG IV in the light of Regulation 17 and Article 85.

(Mr Hall) I think it is certainly our impression that there is either a lack of economists within DG IV, or a reluctance to use them. Also, one has noticed in recent years that once proceedings get under way, the Commission has used outside lawyers to assist them, whereas in the earlier years it would have confined itself to the use of the Legal Service. The other comment I would make is that the Commission certainly asserts that it is conducting entirely administrative proceedings and does not appear to accept in any sense that in applying Articles 85 and 86 it is performing a judicial function. Regarding that, it is entirely a matter for the Courts.

206. Would you say that is, in fact, a basic flaw really in the structure of the way DG IV handles competition cases and its present role as now conceived?

(Mr Vaughan) That could well be said. I think one of the things that the Court of First Instance has done is to make it very clear to everyone that whether they are a tribunal, a court, or whatever they are, they

[Baroness Elles *Contd*]

expect them to comply with Article 6 of the Human Rights Convention. I think that clearly will lead the Commission, if they continue on that jurisprudence, to think very carefully about whether in fact their structures are right to deal with this question and whether they should not have a better system for arriving at the right answer.

Lord Holme of Cheltenham

207. To follow Lady Elles's question, you are all distinguished lawyers and therefore naturally the concentration is on those cases which ultimately become, as it were, justiciable. Presumably as a normative system—and maybe this bears on the administrative point—a lot of it is in the earlier negotiation phase; lots of issues are settled, most issues are settled, and it is the exception which moves into the zone that is giving you concern. One of the questions I would like to ask is: Is your perception that the Commission, which still operates primarily with an administrative system, uses in any way the threat or the possibility of judicial proceedings as a sanction to try and get people to agree at an earlier stage, so that it does not reach that point, so that in a sense their implicit weight is brought to bear? You could argue that would therefore make them semi-adversarial in any putative proceedings that ended up being taken. It is a complicated question but I know what I mean. I hope you do.

(Mr Hall) The way I would answer it is this. Until September 1989 I would have said that there might be some force in that argument; of course, since the Merger Regulation came into operation, with the Merger Task Force assessing and appraising qualifying mergers under the rules, there is quite good evidence, even in mainly non-contentious circumstances, of corners being cut or interpretations adopted which do not appear to be consistent with the requirements of the Regulation. I do not think it is only that many round this table have been involved in anti-trust infringement proceedings. I think essentially what we are now saying reflects what we were saying in the early 1980s, namely that the appointment of the hearing officer, which was put forward by the Commission as a way of meeting the criticisms that were being expressed by those outside the administrative system, has not really solved the problems that we referred to then.

Chairman

208. One of the things you mentioned in paragraph 16 of your working paper, and it is perhaps relevant to this, is that in 1982, when the Committee first reported, the Commission defended its procedures on the basis that there was a division of responsibility between the investigators and those who were enshrined in the decision-making process. This separation of roles was subsequently abandoned and now the investigators who inspect documents are often in charge of the preparation of the case and the drafting of the decision. The

Commission, on the other hand, appears to say that there is a distinction between investigation and decision-making. When did this change take place?

(Miss Rose) I think that in the *Shell* case that was one of the arguments put forward by the applicant, the change in the procedures, which meant that there was no longer the distinction in function, and that this has led to a lack of impartiality in the Commission's deliberations. In that case on the facts the Commission attempted to refute that by stating that in that particular case, the case being so large, a large number of Commission officials had been involved in the procedure, so that in fact different officials had dealt with different stages. The Court of First Instance was very clear there that in any event it was not a breach of procedural rules for the same officials to be involved. That being the case, it is clearly now open to officials within the Commission to adopt both functions. As far as the calibre of the people involved in the Commission's operations, it is not necessarily simply a matter of calibre because a person can be a very good investigator and yet that would not be a suitable person, however good at that role they are, to play a part in the later aspects of the case. The difficulty with the lack of distinction of function is that there is then not necessarily somebody who comes to the case at a later stage and brings a fresh mind to bear on whether in fact this is an appropriate case to be taken forward to the next stage of proceedings because the people who have investigated it may be too closely involved in that to be able to bring the level of objectivity that is really needed to bear in the next stage of the procedure.

209. Without necessarily incurring a great deal of delay because you had to have a rather more formalised quasi-judicial procedure?

(Miss Rose) Sometimes delay is necessary.

210. Is it a proposal of your group then that the Commission's structure should change to this extent, that the investigation and the decision-making can be quite separate, quite distinct departments of DG IV, or do you not go as far as that?

(Mr Hall) I think the Commission removed the very safeguards that were trailed eight or nine years ago as ensuring observance of due process; we believe this was around 1984 or 1985, at about the time the hearing officer was first appointed. We think, given the way the hearing officer is performing, that this change was a retrograde step. It might at least put things back to where we had understood them to be if this division was maintained. It is quite clear, I think from the information that was provided to your Committee in 1981/82, and from the evidence the Commission supplied about how DG IV was then structured, that the inspectors were a separate team within DG IV from those conducting the proceedings. I have a copy here of DG IV's current internal telephone directory. The inspectors are now dotted all round the various directorates. They are certainly not separate. I believe around this table we have experience of the inspectors actually working on

[Chairman *Contd]*

the file to the point of preparation of the Statement of Objections and beyond.

211. You would have a separate department of DG IV dealing with the actual decision-making? The other three categories which were mentioned said that the Commission is detective, prosecutor and negotiator. How many of those can be done by the same people—detective and prosecutor, together, the same people?

(Mr Vaughan) I rather wonder whether, in fact, the distinction should not be between the detective and then the rest where the detective gathers information, makes the file or dossier, and then the rest is handed over to the Crown Prosecution Services, as it were. Then they carry on'with the rest.

212. Including the decision?

(Mr Vaughan) Including the decision, but that the quality should be better supervised from within DG IV and the hearing officer should play a real part.

213. I am surprised you say that the actual prosecution and decision-making should be done by the same person. Do you think the function is such that it really is not comparable with a judicial enquiry?

(Mr Hall) This is where the members of the Working Party speak in an individual capacity and show their preferences one way or another.

214. Perhaps someone would like to tell us. Would Mr Mackay like to add something on this?

(Mr Mackay) I think the fundamental and most important distinction is really between the investigator and the decision to proceed. I think one knows, and from my experience in other fields, that the investigator, especially on a large case, very often regards his work as being an extraordinary investment and he is very reluctant to see it being discarded and matters not taken further. That applies even if the results of the investigation show quite clearly that it ought not to go further. For my part I would also wish to see a distinction between, as it were, the officials presenting the case and the man who actually takes the final decision. I regard the former, the first distinction, as being perhaps the more important. I am conscious that my views may not be shared by the others.

215. The view you have expressed is the one I was putting, that the person who takes the decision and perhaps negotiates should be separate from the person who is presenting the case. Perhaps " prosecution " is the wrong word. Would some of you at any rate agree that the actual investigation and what has been called the prosecution should go along together? " Prosecution " is an odd concept in some ways.

(Mr Vaughan) One of the problems is that there is not really a prosecution. What happens at an oral hearing is that somebody gets up and says, " Nod, nod, they are guilty, are they not? " Then they have to defend themselves against the statement of objection. Then a few questions may or may not be asked of the witnesses, or whoever presents the case. There is very little, as it were, prosecuting, once the statement of

objection has been drafted. That is what you have to defend yourself against. The problem with having a further division later on is that it makes what you actually say to the tribunal, or whatever it is, even more remote, unless the hearing officer is going to be the decision-maker in a particular case, because ultimately it is the Commissioners who decide in theory, whom you are never going to see. Then the next stage is who then takes the decision below that. One of the arguments against the hearing officer that was phrased at the time was, " Are you not better off having the Director General or the Director who you are actually addressing in charge of the contentious cases and taking the decision, rather than having a hearing officer ", so the Director was never there at these hearings.

Baroness Elles

216. From the point of view of a practitioner, and I know you are all practitioners in this field, is it not easier perhaps to deal with one case handler dealing with a specific case than to have to talk to the investigator on one aspect of the case, and then talk to the next stage to find another official and go through the whole process again to make your point and to make your arguments? I think it is true to say that a lot of the competition cases are not exactly a negotiation between legal advisers but nevertheless there is a contact between lawyers and the Commission and a lot of the work is based on that negotiation process between the two. I wonder, from a practical point view, how easy it is to separate those two issues of investigator and the decision-making, apart, of course, from going up to the Commissioner where there is actually argument. It seems to me it is normally done by the case handler and it is perhaps at that level where the problem arises, that he does not ensure that natural justice, as my Lord Chairman was referring to, is actually guaranteed. This would be where the hearing officer, and that is more important in a way possibly, should be the one who should come in much earlier on in the case. You could go to a hearing officer to have your rights protected for access to files and follow the judicial procedures, rather than trying to divide the investigator and the decision-maker within the Commission's officials.

(Mr Hall) I have to say I think this brings you back to the issue of accountability. Certainly in my time at the Commission, the Legal Service played a significant role in reviewing what DG IV did. The decision-taker, ie the Commissioner responsible for competition, had yet a further role. Increasingly one senses that the actual decisions from start to finish are taken within DG IV and that what is produced from then on tends to be rubber-stamped.

Chairman

217. That is the whole point. I believe the structural question is very important, as to whether you want to have a dividing up of functions or

[Chairman *Contd*]

whether you think it is quite enough to have one person handling it as long as he obeys the rules. I have always understood the objection was that the structure of it was wrong and that you should have a different person, whether you call him the handler or the prosecutor or investigator it does not matter. Then somebody should have the case put to him to take the decision, subject to it going up to the Commission. Is this what you are recommending or not, some division of function? You do not seem to be entirely agreed.

(Mr Vaughan) Part of it is what is practical and what is theoretically sound. I would see a major need for a division between the inspector who comes round to your offices and the case handler. That seems to me to be very important, so that there should be somebody other than the policeman who decides whether to prosecute effectively and how strong the case is and how to put the case, other than the policeman who had been round. After that, from my point of view, it seems to me that matters then could be left with one person with better supervision but with a hearing officer protecting the rights at that stage and with a much greater role for him at that stage.

218. Is that the view of everybody?

(Mr Flint) From a Scottish standpoint, I think there is a distinction between the detective, the prosecutor and the decision-maker. In an ideal world you have three separate functions and you would not actually have the person prosecuting being the same person who did the detective work. That is because that is largely to some extent that system to which we are used. I think a lot of it comes back to the point which your Lordship made earlier on lack of personnel of a suitable calibre and quantity within the Commission. Certainly, given that they only appear to be able to come to a decision in some twenty cases a year, there appears to be an over-eagerness on the part of officials, having started a proceeding, to get it to some conclusion. A number of the apparent procedural short-cuts which have taken place over the last few years appear largely to have stemmed from a belief by the officials at certain levels, and probably at junior levels, that it did not matter what they did, as long as they got the result which they were attempting to achieve at the end of the day. That goes against he whole principle of natural justice. I think that again is a reason for separation of functions, someone looking over their shoulder simply to say, " No, I know what you are trying to achieve but the defence "—if that is in fact what it is—" have rights ".

219. Supervising one person doing all the functions is a very different concept from having, at any rate, a division between two people, the investigator and the decider.

(Miss Rose) There is also the point as far as separation of functions is concerned as between the policeman who goes round the premises and the later stages on the question of privileged documents and the sight that the investigators have of documents which at a latter stage it is determined ought not to be relied upon by the Commission in arriving at their findings. Again, the unitary system that presently operates seems to make no provision for that distinction to be made, which arguably rather detracts from the privilege which attaches to documents, whether on the basis of legal privilege or self-incrimination or whatever.

(Mr Vaughan) The point Mr Hall made, which I think is a very valid point and which we have not made in our paper, was the role of the legal service. In the good old days there were very senior members of the legal service who had very great experience of competition law, who were quite formidable characters and a decision had to be put through and past them. Nowadays the legal service moves very quickly from one area to another and you do not get the tendency to have a very senior person in that role saying, " You cannot say that ". I think there may be a watering down of the role of the legal service in this way. There also have been other things, that the member of the legal service who tends to watch a particular case will probably become the advocate for the case at the court. So he will be defending the position at the court. He gets brought in to the whole team. I think there is less distinction than there used to be between which of the legal services you used to be very proud of, that they were wholly distinct, and if the legal service said " no ", then that was it.

220. It sounds as if the two events would adapt, to use Mr Flint's phrase. It sounds as if they were out not to get what they want at the end of the day but out to get what they want at the beginning of the day. We will pass on from this. Whether there is a structural change is one question. You all seem to agree that there should be some form of supervision to ensure that rights of the defence, et cetera, are protected. Who should do the supervision? You cannot just say that the Head of DG IV should do it. He cannot possibly be watching everybody in his team doing all these cases. What sort of person should do it? Should it be a member of the legal services staff or a member of DG IV with a special responsibility for keeping an eye on people?

(Mr Vaughan) It came back to the point I was making that there should be a senior member of the legal service, who is a Deputy Director General or something in the legal service, who should be given the role of ensuring that these matters are dealt with properly.

(Mr Hall) If I might add, where we originally came from in the late seventies and early eighties was that the decision-making function or the decision-makers responsible for applying 85 and 86 actually ought to be independent of the Commission. The hearing officer emerged as a solution because it was possible to achieve that within the rules and within Treaty requirements. If one is circumscribed, if you like, by what changes can be made, it does seem that this supervisor of what is going on in DG IV has to be someone within the Commission structure. That is

[Chairman Contd]

not to say that some of us would not actually support the appointment of an outside body, perhaps answerable to the Commissioner along a dotted line or whatever, having that sort of role. We are told, however, that it is not achievable.

221. I do not think we can say there should be supervision without having some idea as to what would constitute the supervision. Should it be the head of the department whose job is simply to keep an eye on the others?; should it be a lawyer within the Commission? What does he do? Does he intervene of his own motion? Does he wait for problems to be put to him? Do you have somebody outside? What is his function? Does he interfere and keep abreast with what is going on? One has to have a very clear idea of what you mean by supervision.

(Mr Hall) He is actually a very superior form of a hearing officer; unfortunately, what we have at the moment does not actually achieve the task.

222. Could the hearing officer's function be adapted to cover the supervision?

(Mr Hall) I would have thought it could, if he had the status and a sufficient degree of independence.

223. And a sufficient number of hearing officers?

(Mr Hall) Absolutely, and a sufficient number of hearing officers.

(Mr Flint) I think the problem comes back to the whole structure of the Commission within the Community's legal order in general. Whereas in a national system, such as there is in the United Kingdom, there would be a government Minister who is responsible for the actions of his officials, ultimately answerable to Parliament, and if there were serious mistakes, then he would have to answer for those before Parliament and, if appropriate, resign his position. There is no one within the Commission who is in fact subject to the same political or public scrutiny with any checks and balances. At the end of the day somebody somewhere knows he is answerable to some outside body. Even at the Commissioner level the Commission is not answerable in the same way as a national government official is.

224. Is this kind of supervision of the interlocutory stages a matter which ought to be expressly given to the Court of First Instance? Obviously the Court of Justice in the IBM case restricted very much its control of the early stages of enquiry and the Advocate General very reluctantly. Should the Court of First Instance be given more power over interlocutory matters?

(Mr Hall) I think the view of this Working Party is yes, and that the jurisprudence that developed in and following IBM requires to be reconsidered.

(Miss Rose) I think when the Court of First Instance was established it was certainly the hope among some practitioners that that was the role that it would take on to play, the role of intervening to ensure that the procedure kept along the right track in a manner with which we are very familiar in the English courts. That is, the Master's jurisdiction and the judge in chambers who deals with a large number of interlocutory matters to make sure that the matter is then properly dealt with at trial. In the recent Cement decision, in the Court of First Instance, that was the clearest possible example in my view of where interlocutory proceedings would usefully have been brought and a decision could easily be made where the question was whether the totality of the statement of objection should have been served on each of the defendants or whether the partial disclosure of the statement of objections was lawful. The Court of First Instance, following IBM, declined to say, on the grounds that at the end of the day that could be one of the grounds of challenge of the decision. That leaves a situation where the seventy-odd defendants and the Commission now have to devote a huge amount of time and resources in pursuing the proceedings to the end. If a decision results, and is taken on appeal, the whole of that time and resource may prove to have been wasted because the statement of objections was invalid.

225. The court in the IBM decision did slightly leave the door open and nobody has ever tried to push it, I think. You would have to give the Court of First Instance in that case very specific but very different procedures from the ones that exist today, would you not? You would have to have something expeditious like a Master dealing with the matter, or would you not?

(Miss Rose) The Cement case was brought on fairly expeditiously.

226. Would you not have to devise some much less formalised procedure to allow interlocutory things to be challenged quickly so that the case could get on, or do you think that is not necessary?

(Miss Rose) I think the difficulties with that are the reliance on the written procedure which is inevitable, given the language difficulties. It is hard to see how that can be short-circuited. In the context of an investigation like Cement or like any of the other cartel investigations, from the initial Article 14 investigation until the date of the final decision is usually a very long timescale. Even current interlocutory timescales of bringing proceedings before the Court of First Instance are not wholly unrealistic.

227. You would be quite happy to have supervision by the Court of First Instance, broadly speaking under existing procedures with existing timescales, would you, or would you think it desirable to have some new type of procedure to deal with fairly short points where it was said that natural justice had not been observed?

(Mrs Holmes) I think this was why we suggested that there should be enhanced powers for the hearing officer, as it may well be possible for a dispute which arises during the course of a hearing to be settled if the hearing officer is sufficiently independent and senior to deal with it. Then only if the matter is not resolved to the satisfaction of one's clients the matter might move an appeal to the CFI.

[*Chairman Contd*]

228. The CFI would then not be the first line of approach if something was going wrong in an interlocutory way. You want somebody in the Commission, like a hearing officer, to deal with the sort of judicial review or appeal to the Court of First Instance?
(*Mr Vaughan*) The hearing officer would deal with privilege disputes on the first basis,without having to go to the court under the AMS procedures. He could deal with that sort of thing as well.

229. One thing that has caused a lot of anguish has been the difficulty about getting access to the file. The Court of First Instance has done something about that. Perhaps you could tell us, for the record, what, if any, changes have been produced by the Court of First Instance and the Commission's practice.
(*Mr Vaughan*) Nothing; there is no difference in the practice. Following on from your Lordships' report, then the procedures in theory got extremely good but in the large cases the Commission has gone back to its previous practice. In *Polypropylene* they gave complete access, or virtually complete access, to the file. In *PVC* they did not; they gave us access, but not complete access. In *LDPE* I think it was same. In *Soda Ash* they refused any access, even to a list of the documents on the file. Things have got worse and worse.

230. Forgive me if I interrupt you. Is that all compatible with what the Court of First Instance said or has the Court of First Instance not given them enough direction?
(*Mr Vaughan*) The Commission has not made its position clear since *Polypropylene* or *PVC*. I have forgotten which is the first one where they really made it clear what the duties were. The Commission had not given any indication it was going to change its procedures. In the 20th Report the Commission said there were no problems, which is just not correct.

231. Would the procedures and principles laid down by the Court of First Instance be acceptable and satisfactory from your point of view if they were followed?
(*Mr Vaughan*) Yes, if they were worked out properly and if the question of confidentiality can be dealt with too.
(*Mr Hall*) I think the problem is that the Commission states its position very fully and what it says appears to be very reasonable, measured and so on, but for those around this table the proof of the pudding is in the eating. The reality is that frequently the quality of approach adopted varies from case officer to case officer. In some instances there is a failure to communicate sufficient information as to what is being withheld and why. The Court has made clear on a number of occasions now what obligations the Commission is subject to, and the Commission tells us repeatedly it is taking account of those obligations, but it does not do so.

232. That is for someone to challenge with the Court.
(*Mr Hall*) By which time we are eight to ten years down the line. One can cite *Woodpulp* as an example. This goes back to the previous question. The Statement of Objections was found in that case to be riddled with errors and wholly inadequate; it took eight years between the time of the oral hearing at the Commission and actually getting judgment from the Court. That is possibly the sort of delay you are going to face in cases of the sort that have just been cited.

233. There were one or two legal issues in *Woodpulp*!
(*Mr Hall*) Yes.

Baroness Elles

234. It is quite clear there is room for procedural improvement all down the line. I am wondering whether the question of access to the file could not be resolved internally by a set of rules which are recognised by DG IV as being binding to those within the Directorate, and of which lawyers will be aware, saying at what stage you have right of access to the file, what are the grounds for confidentiality, which documents you can see. I think you will all have had cases, and I have got examples here, where the person named in the complaint is requested to comment on the complaint from the moment the informal investigation process is started. In other cases you are not given access for a long time down the road. Is that really just a matter again of internal administration that could resolve this problem without having to have something laid down by the Court of First Instance?
(*Mr Vaughan*) The rules are very clear in the competition reports. They are pretty clearly set out.

235. They are not observed.
(*Mr Vaughan*) They are not observed, no.

Chairman

236. Apparently you say that the principles are also clearly set out in what the Court of First Instance is saying but it is not observed?
(*Mr Vaughan*) Yes.
(*Mr Hall*) May I give you an example, my Lord? Documents withheld form part of the file; they are withheld on the grounds of confidentiality. The documents are numbered in sequence; a party will be told that documents, say 100 to 150, are confidential. You have no idea what is in that file. The documents withheld may be documents relating to your case; they may make references to you. You have to assume that there is nothing there that is either supportive of the position of the company involved or, alternatively, that the confidentiality is well claimed. There is no way of checking.

237. It is perhaps important that we should state that as far as you are concerned the Court of First Instance has laid down the principles and rules and

[Chairman *Contd*]

they are simply not being followed. If followed, they would be satisfactory. One or two people have made references to the Convention on Human Rights. It is a little bit difficult for us to suggest that the Commission should observe the Convention on Human Rights when the Select Committee has just ordered that the Community should not accede to it!

Baroness Elles] My Lord Chairman, we did not say they should not observe the Convention.

Chairman

238. No. Suppose the Commission were to accept it, were a tribunal and the principles of Article 6 were to be followed, would that be sufficient?

(*Mr Vaughan*) I think, having spent a lot of time worrying about the problems, the Court of First Instance has taken the jurisprudence quite a lot further forward recently. It is pretty clear that the Court of First Instance will expect people to comply with Article 6 as regards knowing what the case is, knowing the documents, even if they are for or against you, and will follow the cases in the Court of Human Rights. I think that problem does not require a constitutional decision. I think the Court of First Instance seems to be working on the assumption that it is bound by Article 6.

239. The Court itself has held often enough that principles in the Convention on Human Rights have their parallels in Community law. It would be very easy for the Court of First Instance to follow the same line very strictly in relation to Article 6. You think that would be satisfactory?

(*Mr Vaughan*) Yes.

240. Let us go back to the hearing officer. Is there any room for a link between the hearing officer and the Court of First Instance? Should he remain a part of the Commission or should he be a wholly separate person?

(*Mrs Holmes*) We have tried to be pragmatic in our suggestions. We believe, therefore, that the hearing officer is better placed within DG IV because it is the procedures of DG IV that we are concerned about. I think if he was, for instance, linked to the Court of First Instance, it might be a rather less expeditious procedure than we would like to see.

241. Would anyone else like to comment?

(*Mr Vaughan*) The other point is the point we made earlier, that in a way if he is the Master and the Court of First Instance is the Judge, he takes the run-of-the-mill decisions and then, if people do not like that, they appeal.

242. You would give him first jurisdiction to decide any kind of interlocutory point that arose at the point it arose?

(*Mr Vaughan*) Yes, and that would be a "decision", in quotes, under Article 173.

243. Reviewable by the Court of First Instance?

(*Mr Vaughan*) Yes.

244. That would give him one function. If we were writing a job specification, what else do we put in it?

(*Mr Vaughan*) Great tact to cope with a lot of very difficult lawyers!

245. You cannot always be tactful and decisive.

(*Mr Vaughan*) I think the problem at the moment is that they just have not got enough authority. The first hearing officer had a terrible shock when he was told he did not have the powers he thought he had. The second hearing officer has been complaining particularly about his lack of powers.

246. He has always been very insistent about his independence and he seeks to act as quasi judicial or as a judicial person.

(*Mr Vaughan*) Yes, very judicial, both of them.

247. If we are going to say his power should be increased or his authority should be increased, we have to be fairly specific about it. Is there anything else, in addition to giving him jurisdiction positively to decide interlocutory disputes, we should add, in your view?

(*Mr Vaughan*) There has got to be an increase of his jurisdiction anyhow to include areas which are not covered at the moment, like access to the file. He does not deal with access to the file. You complain to him about this and he says, " I entirely agree with you. It is monstrous you do not have these documents but I cannot do anything about it ".

248. You mentioned some ways in your written paper in which you think his powers should be increased. Are there any ways in which you think he should have further powers?

(*Mrs Holmes*) In addition to decisions on interlocutory matters, we think it is obviously important that the reports that he makes on the case should be available to the parties. That would be quite a significant change to the existing rules.

(*Mr Vaughan*) And also, as a matter of course, his report should go to the Commissioner. At the moment it does not go to the Commissioners as a matter of course. It goes only if the Commissioner wants it to go.

249. And nobody sees his report?

(*Mr Vaughan*) Nobody sees his report. In the *ICI* case the Court said we should not see it.

250. Do you think that should be changed?

(*Mr Vaughan*) Yes.

(*Mr Flint*) If the hearing officer's report were to be made public we think it would add to the status and importance of a hearing officer's position. He would cease to be able to be marginalised by the Commission when they eventually came to take the decision if there were, in fact, a report from the hearing officer who, in accordance with our suggestions, would be a more senior Commission official than at present and with greater powers. If there were a reported decision or report by him which was published, it could build up a useful jurisprudence to which reference could be made as to

[Chairman Contd]

how Commission procedures were developing and to add to the checks and balances which we would be imposing.

251. Would he report once at the end of a case or would he publish his report from time to time during the progress of the case? What would the report include?
(Mr Flint) I think it would depend largely on the progress of the case.
(Mrs Holmes) The most important report possibly would be the hearing officer's report following the oral hearing. I think that is the most important report people would wish to see.

252. Setting out his conclusions on the matters that arose?
(Mrs Holmes) Yes.

253. And a reasoned opinion, a reasoned report?
(Mrs Holmes) Yes.

254. It would be made public to the parties and available?
(Mr Vaughan) And to the Court.

255. The public quite generally?
(Mr Vaughan) Yes. There is no reason why not.

Lord Holme of Cheltenham

256. It has been suggested to us by Professor Lauwaars of the University of Amsterdam that the hearing officer should have positions similar to that of the administrative law judge in Federal Trade Commission procedures under US Federal Anti-Trust law. I do not know whether that model is familiar to any of your committee but it is an interesting suggestion. I think it bears on the status and position more than the powers.
(Mr Hall) As I understand it, under equivalent US procedures, it is a sine qua non that the full file, subject to confidentiality, is made available to the parties. It contains all documents, whether they are supportive of the FTC's position or not.

257. That is the key point.
(Mr Hall) That to me is the key point. In a sense that is half the battle. Then the hearing officer has a status, independent of those prosecuting the case, which further ensures that, as I say, there is due process.

Chairman

258. Would anyone else like to comment on that?
(Mr Vaughan) I think in 1982 we were advocating the administrative law. We were saying it would be a good thing but the hearing officer came in as a compromise. The problem with that is that it would require a change in the Treaty because it would be a different person who took the decision.
(Mr Mackay) I would like perhaps to go back for a minute to the status of the hearing officer and his decision. If one envisages that his decision is capable of challenge in the Court of First Instance, then it

might well be said that there are disadvantages in that, because one would find a considerable number of interlocutory appeals. But that does not mean to say that one should not perhaps extend his role, nonetheless, to encompass such matters as access to the file and the sufficiency of the detail given in the statement of objection because, as I think Mr Vesterdorf in his opinion in one of the cases, Polypropylene stated, the function of the hearing officer is also to give to those in the Commission who are dealing with the case, as it were, a separate and independent point of view. For that reason, I would be in favour of the extension of his jurisdiction, even if it were decided that there were disadvantages in having his decisions challengeable before the Court of First Instance at the interlocutory stage.

259. How would you limit it, as far as you do, by the Court?
(Mr Mackay) I think it would have to be of the view that all that he was doing was giving advice on the question of the disputed confidentiality to the competition Commissioner as to what course the Commission should adopt, but that may in itself resolve a number of problems.
(Mr Vaughan) If one went down that route, it would have to be public, so you would have to know; it would have to be a document that was shown to people as to what the nature of the decision was, what the effect of the decision was.

260. How many hearing officers are we going to need to carry out all these extra functions? You say one is not enough. Do you envisage two or five or ten?
(Mr Vaughan) Two or three, I should have thought. I would have thought that the number of hearings going on simultaneously is not very great. There are obviously some which are so big, like Cement, like the Petrochemical alleged cartels, that they may need full-time work by somebody. In the run-of-the-mill case, I doubt if they have many overlapping. The run-of-the-mill cases are pretty short. They would take a day or less, I suspect.

261. I think it is implicit in what you say that more staff would be needed to carry out these, apart from the actual hearing officer himself?
(Mr Vaughan) Yes.

262. Is there anything to be learnt from the experience of the Merger Task Force which would be relevant in this area of controlling what happens inside the Commission in relation to Articles 85 and 86?
(Mr Hall) I think the key lesson to be learnt from the Regulation and its operation is the adherence to strict time limits. I do not think one can draw a direct parallel between the effect of the work under the Regulation and proceedings under Articles 85 and 86 in the sense that infringement proceedings clearly are quite different from the assessment and appraisal of mergers, the vast majority of which do not raise problems in terms of merger control. Nor do I think that under the Merger Regulation we learn much in

[*Chairman Contd]*

terms of staffing. I do not think seconding officials into DG IV from national authorities is going to help us with regard to Articles 85 and 86.

263. Mrs Holmes, do you agree with that?

(Mrs Holmes) Yes, I do. On the question of the number of hearing officers, we have suggested tasks in addition to controlling the oral hearing. There would, as you suggest, be a number of interlocutory matters which would go to him. I agree with David Vaughan that probably no more than a handful of people need to be added. It is something that would have to be kept under review.

264. Would anyone like to comment on the hearing officer point, changes or control in procedures, before we pass on? If not, we would like to have your views on the Advisory Committee. We have had a certain amount of evidence on its utility and effectiveness. What are your views about the Advisory Committee?

(Mr Mackay) I think I drew the straw on this one! In our report we indicated we did not think there was any need for the Advisory Committee's report to be published or produced to the parties. I think that was on the view that the general impression was that the report of the Advisory Committee did not contribute to, or influence a great deal, the ultimate decision. That said, I think the feeling is that the Advisory Committee does perform a useful function in having representatives from the Member States present at the oral hearing. I do not think we would suggest that the Committee's presence at the hearing should in any way be done away with. On the question of publishing or producing the report, I do not think we have particularly strong feelings. On reflection, I think some of us think that there might be advantages in it being made available to the parties, perhaps for a similar reason as Mr Flint indicated earlier, that it would enhance the status of the Advisory Committee.

265. But published in the fullest sense or only to the parties or made public?

(Mr Mackay) I think made public in the fullest sense.

Baroness Elles: Would the witnesses agree that Member States would almost certainly not approve of a report coming out of the Advisory Committee being published or even notified to the parties because the way the Advisory Committee is run, as you will know, is that one never quite knows what documents are even before them or in what languages or even if all the Advisory Committee is there. I think, rather than revealing all these details, I would have thought their activities should be kept silent rather than published! I do not know if the witnesses would agree.

Chairman

266. It is obvious, as Lady Elles says, the chances of Member States agreeing to publish is one thing. What we want to know from you is whether it is

desirable that it should be published and, if so, what we should say about it, or do you share the views that the less it is seen, the better?

(Mr Flint) I think Baroness Elles has raised an interesting point and one on which the committee has certainly been concerned, the calibre of persons who are sitting on the Advisory Committee. There is a general feeling that in certain cases where there is not perceived to be a particularly important national interest at stake, perhaps the calibre of persons sent by the national governments to the particular meetings may not be at as high a level as it might be in other cases, to put it kindly. I think for that reason there may be an argument against publishing. I think the parties are entitled to know that instead of sending a senior Principal Under-Secretary they have sent somebody who was on a youth training secondment and who was the only person in the office who was not doing anything that day. I think that is important. The other point which Baroness Elles made, the question that the parties do not even know what papers are coming before the Advisory Committee, again is one which I think is important. Our view on that would be that the parties should be told what documents are going to the Advisory Committee. Given that the Commission, wearing its various hats, is also the person that decides ultimately what papers they are sending to the Advisory Committee, it is possible that the advice which they ultimately give, even if it were to be published, would be based on an incomplete understanding of the facts because documents which the parties believe to be critical to their argument might simply not be before them.

267. Is your position that you think the Advisory Committee does fulfil a useful purpose or that you know so little of what it does that you do not know whether it fulfils a useful purpose, or that you do know if fulfils no useful purpose?

(Mr Hall) If I may add one supplemental point, picking up on my earlier comments about the Merger Regulation; there the views of the Advisory Committee can be published if the Committee requests it. I think, as a matter of practice, in phase two investigations they are always published. I do not think the fact that information is available has caused any problems to the Commission or to the Mergers Task Force. I suspect there is a considerable degree of doubt on this side of the table about how valuable a function and role the Advisory Committee performs in Article 85/86 procedures. There is no evidence that it plays any relevant part whatever as regards due process.

Baroness Elles

268. Perhaps the witnesses would agree that the role of the Advisory Committee is really just to guard the national interest of Member States represented? After all, as far as the Commission is concerned, the Commission takes almost no account, I think is the wording of what they say, and that can be interpreted

[Baroness Elles *Contd*]

in many ways. Their view is not binding in any way. Therefore, I wonder what value legally any published report would actually have.

(*Mr Hall*) It certainly does not appear to have had much impact as regards safeguarding due process.

(*Mr Vaughan*) I think it does perform a function in so far as the Member States are present at oral hearings. I think it is important that Member States should be entitled to be there for oral hearings. I think it is important from the companies' point of view, whether they are complainant or defendant. It is comforting to know there is somebody outside who is watching what is happening.

269. What happens in practice? Does the representative from the Member State from which the company comes appear and nobody else, or do you get a side representation at an important oral hearing?

(*Mr Vaughan*) The recent ones I have done have all been ones where somebody from almost every Member State has been in attendance. There have been quite a lot of people turning up.

270. Is that the practice, that if the company under review comes from one or two Member States, it is just the representatives of those Member States who come, or would they come from everywhere?

(*Miss Rose*) I think the cases in my experience are the cases where there is an important legal issue involved, whether that is a substantive or a procedural issue. Then there will be fairly wide representation from the Member States.

271. You get twelve people coming into the room with everybody else?

(*Miss Rose*) And they sometimes ask them searching questions which may be more difficult to answer than those asked by the members of the Commission.

272. That might mean there is a useful function in that particular respect.

(*Mrs Holmes*) In terms of the rights of the defence, there is a procedure under which the Commission consults the Advisory Committee and it is very difficult to see how the rights of defence can be fully respected if the defence does not know what happened and what was the consequence of that discussion. There might be some scepticism about the usefulness of the Advisory Committee. I would argue very strongly the report ought to be made available to the parties. However, in procedures under Articles 85 and 86, there are some doubts as to whether the Advisory Committee reports ought to be made available to the public, as distinct from the merger reports, because of the different nature of the proceedings.

(*Mr Hall*) Perhaps I should add that I would not want my remarks to be interpreted as suggesting that United Kingdom participation in these procedures is not considerable in the sense that representatives of the competent authority do attend these meetings, and do the best they can within the parameters of what is achievable.

273. That is to ensure proper conduct of the proceedings.

(*Mr Hall*) Yes, so far as they can to ensure proper conduct. I entirely agree with Baroness Elles: If they have not got the relevant papers and are not told what is happening in sufficient time to read the material to know what has been going on, it is difficult for the national authorities really to play an effective role.

274. It is doubly difficult for the parties if they do not know what the Advisory Committee representatives have got.

(*Mr Hall*) Yes. It is a catch-22 situation.

(*Miss Rose*) That is particularly the case, given currently the position of whether the Court of First Instance or the European Court is at the end of the day one of the parties relying as a ground of appeal on a procedural defect. It is up to the party to show that that defect made some difference to the result and that the breach of the rights of the defence had some impact on the ultimate decision. Given that burden is placed on the parties, it becomes all the more important, in my view, that the parties have access to these documents.

275. We mentioned the Member States and their representatives. Perhaps we could ask you a few questions about the role of Member States which it is thought might become more important. Let us stick with the present procedures to begin with. You seem to have reservations about the idea of Member States carrying out investigations on behalf of the Commission. What is the basis of your reservations?

(*Mr Vaughan*) This is really dealing with the position of the carrying out of the police aspect, the investigation on the site, as it were, under Article 13 of Regulation 17. Our main reservation I think is that, first of all, this is the Member State doing it entirely itself and not helping the Commission in the course of its investigation, which is the normal procedure. We have some reservations about it because it will mean that where you have a case involving lots of different Member States, at the moment the Commission investigators go in and carry out very often simultaneous searches in different countries, knowing what they are going to look for, and liaise and talk to each other during the course of those investigations. That is an efficient way and does provide a lot of ammunition for the Commission in those investigations. The problem is going to happen if that is delegated to Member States' competent authorities to deal with and then that, when necessary, resulted in inequality of treatment in different Member States. One could imagine in, say, two countries, the United Kingdom and Germany, the police investigation may be very efficient. In other Member States it may not be and who are going to be the defendants in a particular case may well depend on the efficiency of the national police force effectively, the competition police force. We think that would be very unfair.

[Baroness Elles Contd]

276. How far does the Commission go to other Member States to ask for investigations to be carried out? We have been told, as you know, there have been some examples here. Is it very widespread?

(Mr Vaughan) We, in fact, had not heard of any under Article 13. We had heard of cases under Article 14 where there had been assistance but we were not aware of any under Article 13 where they had actually delegated the roles. No doubt they have done it very efficiently. I think it is the disparity of treatment that worries us more, not merely the delegating itself but the disparity of treatment you might get. One factor is that it is not just the incriminating documents but it is getting all the relevant documents. If you found, to take an example, the Spanish authorities did not produce many documents in their searches, it may be if they had produced a bigger investigation, they would have produced more documents which may help the other defendants put forward their defence. The documents produced by the inspectors are not just incriminating documents; there are often bound to be, or one would hope there would be bound to be as a lawyer defending the company, some documents which are helpful.

277. For the future, is the suggestion that national authorities should play a more direct part in the enforcement of the Community competition rules? We have read your own paper replying to the draft notice on the application of these Articles by national courts. You have obviously perceived considerable difficulties inherent in this in your paragraph 4. Is there any way in which you could delegate enforcement and avoid these difficulties, or do you think they are inherent in the fact of delegation, or do you feel there should not be delegation? The Commission is very keen that national courts and national authorities should play a much more active part. Do you think this is wrong in principle or do you think it is right in principle but it needs some safeguards?

(Mr Hall) If consistency of approach and equality of treatment are the key factors to be borne in mind, it is very difficult to see how that is to be achieved if national authorities are to have responsibility for applying 85(1) and 86, whether it be at the investigatory stage or through to the point at which decisions are taken in applying those Articles. I have to say the preferred solution, as far as I am concerned, would be to see the Commission adequately resourced, adequately staffed and performing properly the functions assigned to it under the Treaty.

278. Rather than to delegate?

(Mr Hall) Rather than to delegate. Whether this proposed delegation is suggested as a means of achieving some degree of subsidiarity, or whether the Commission does not want to be responsible for dealing with insignificant complaints and so suggests Member States should do them, I do not know.

279. As I understand it, it began in the first place outside the context of subsidiarity simply on the basis the Commission was not coping and it wanted other people to take on some of this work. It is quite a long time ago when this idea was first mooted.

(Mr Hall) It does not seem to be coping because it does not seem either to be adequately resourced or find it within itself responsibility for following through cases involving Articles 85 and 86 to a conclusion. In the latest annual report that has just been published it is extraordinary, to me at least, that reference is made there to some hundreds of files being closed. One reason given is that some of the agreements concerned have expired. Some of these proceedings seem to take years to run their course. Perhaps delegation to the Member States is a means of sloughing off responsibility because the Member States are better resourced. I do not know.

280. It is perhaps not necessarily sloughing off responsibility. It is just trying to get the thing done in a speedier and more efficient way. Can you rely on that in the various Member States?

(Mr Hall) Unfortunately not, because of the difficulty of achieving consistency of approach.

281. And the difference in experience in Member States. Obviously, if you look at the German system, it is very different from the systems which obtain, if they obtain at all, in some of the other Member States which I had better not mention.

(Mr Hall) And the extent to which any of the findings have any value by way of precedent.

282. We are also troubled about the remedies. It is not just the actual process of investigation. Can you have applied by national courts a harmonised system of remedies or do you have to leave it to the national courts to apply their own remedies or are the problems so great that only the Commission should carry out these functions and control their energies?

(Miss Rose) I think, if I may say, there are two very distinct kinds of delegation that we are discussing. The first is the delegation of the kind of equivalent to a Regulation 17 type of procedure which is carried out in an inquisitorial manner by the competent authority. That is a very different matter from the exercise of directly effective treaty rights in the national courts. The Commission in another two has indicated that it regards the exercise of directly effective rights in some circumstances as being an adequate substitute, in a way, for the Commission launching its own investigation. I think that the two types of procedure are very distinct, not only in the manner in which they are carried out but in their aim and function. I think that with regard to some problems they arise in both forms of delegation and other problems only arise in one or the other. The main difficulty that arises in both at present is the lack of delegation as far as the application of Article 85(3) is concerned. That is, in my view, the major sticking point, particulary in relation to the notice on the co-operation between national courts and the Commission. That difficulty of the national

[Baroness Elles Contd]

authorities coming up against the question of whether Article 85(3) applies then leads one on to the separate but related problem of comfort letters and their status in national proceedings which really creates a whole raft of difficulties which stand in the way.

283. Would you be happy to leave the Member States with delegated authority to deal with Article 85(3) or would you not get again great disparity?

(Miss Rose) You would and that is the balancing act that has to be addressed. At the moment it is not being addressed. The Commission in a way is trying to get the best of both worlds to try and conserve its resources and delegate, but without delegating that ultimate decision-making power. The vehicle by which it does that, namely the increased number of comfort letters, I think we are all agreed is an unsatisfactory vehicle.

284. Did you ever get a reply to your document on the guidelines?

(Mr Hall) Not from the Commission, no. I have to say that the CCBE[1]—and I am the United Kingdom delegate on the Competition Committee in my capacity as Chairman of this Working Party—also put in representations to the Commission in response to its draft. Not only did the comments that it made not result in any response, but the CCBE was told that there was to be a further text produced reflecting the views that had been put forward. In the event the document simply emerged as the final text, so there was no real consultation whatever as far as the CCBE was concerned.

285. Miss Rose mentioned comfort letters. It has been suggested to us the Commission is favouring more use of comfort letters. Is this a good or a bad thing?

(Miss Rose) I think that the Court of First Instance in the PVC judgement was very clear about the dangers that there are in failing to follow the procedures that are laid down for the decision-making process, the dangers of uncertainty of the legal position of undertakings. I think that those dangers which were enumerated by the court in that decision apply all the more so to comfort letters. The inability of parties to know the seniority of the person who took the decision to issue the comfort letters and the facts on which that decision were based obviously apply particularly with regard to such letters.

286. The danger is much less if you have a centralised system. The difficulties really multiply if you delegate the power to take decisions under Articles 85 and 86 to national authorities and the Commission has issued a comfort letter. It leads to a great deal of discussion as to what in principle is their effect on national proceedings, and even in relation to national restrictive practice or anti-trust legislation; not only principle, but the detail of any particular case may raise very difficult issues.

(Miss Rose) Yes. That is the comfort letters in addition to the new procedure that is suggested in the notice of co-operation of the national court consulting Commission officials in the event that a comfort letter has not been issued. The status of that kind of advice, of course, is subject to the same difficulties. It has been suggested that one way out of the problem is if the Court of Justice were to determine what the status of the comfort letter was and to give it some greater status.

287. In practice, when comfort letters have been issued, does anyone subsequently become uncomfortable or by and large does the Commission follow the comfort letters? Do they ever depart from the comfort letters and start proceedings?

(Miss Rose) There is one case at the moment, the Apple case, where both parties applied for exemption and were given a comfort letter and then one party fell out and one of them made a complaint. I think an investigation was launched. It arose in interlocutory proceedings in the English High Court.

288. Have there been cases where the status of a comfort letter in relation to national laws and procedures has been raised directly?

(Mr Vaughan) It has in the Perfume cases, I think. The other point is a third party position. If you have, as it were, a networking agreement which has a wide effect throughout the Community but does not directly affect anyone immediately, the problem is they might go off, get a comfort letter, then somebody complains about this practice and the other side say, "Oh, we got a comfort letter from the Commission". The person who then, if he had known about the letter, would have complained before, is faced with the position of deciding to go to court against the possibility of a comfort letter and may well find it very difficult to complain in that situation. At least if there had been an exemption he would have known what the position was; he could have attacked exemption and he could have made representations to the Commission when the 19(3) notice was published.

289. On balance is it your view comfort letters cause more problems than they solve?

(Mr Vaughan) For the individuals they are very nice to have; they are very comforting. When you receive them you are very pleased to get them, I suspect, because it means that is the end of that problem for the moment. They are not very comfortable if you take a longer term view or if you are going to fall out later. They are probably disastrous from the point of view of third parties.

290. On balance should we recommend that they be kept or that they be abandoned?

(Mr Vaughan) I think they need looking at. They had the idea at one stage of publishing brief details of what they were intending to comfort, so that people could at least know and make representations. That never happened.

---

[1] Note by witness: Council of the Bar and Law Societies of the European Community.

[Baroness Elles *Contd]*

291. Shall we say keep comfort letters with certain modifications? What are the modifications?

(Mr Vaughan) I think details ought to be briefly published to allow people to make representations.

(Mrs Holmes) There are, as usual, complications in all these things. There are two kinds of comfort letters, and even in some cases interim comfort letters. There are comfort letters which are unofficial statements from the Commission officials in DG IV. Then, there are other comfort letters which are publicised in the Official Journal. It is in any case where you fear there might be contention unsatisfactory to have to receive a comfort letter. The Commission sometimes does refuse requests that it should take a formal decision. That is clearly unsatisfactory.

292. Mr Vaughan mentioned exemptions as contrasted with comfort letters. One thing that we have heard a little bit about is the use of block exemptions. Some people seem to think the Commission could make more use of block exemptions. Is that your view, that it would be desirable the Commission should make more use of comfort letters?

(Mr Hall) I think it is desirable in this sense, that, subject to the undertaking concerned complying with the terms of the block exemption regulation, an exemption from 85(1) is available. I personally remain very unhappy about the status accorded to comfort letters by the Commission. I understand all the administrative problems they have. I understand the administrative convenience of issuing these things. Because they have no legal status as between the parties and third parties, and their status in national proceedings is an issue which can give rise to difficulties, I cannot, for my part, see why, given that under the Merger Regulation, for example, the Commission has been able to produce decisions on quite complex, difficult issues in a clear short form, it should not be possible in 85(3) cases for the Commission to produce a similar document which has a legally binding status as between the parties, even if it is not in the detailed form of an 85(3) exemption of the sort that has been issued in the past. I do not think it is a solution simply to issue a comfort letter and then close the file. Sooner or later the issue is going to be litigated.

293. Do you think that is in practice on the ground that making a block exemption will avoid these difficulties in relation to comfort letters to any substantial degree or is it really dealing with a wholly separate problem?

(Mr Hall) As I said at the outset, I think it does provide that legal degree of comfort which you do not get with a comfort letter.

(Miss Rose) There is the curious practice of issuing comfort letters to agreements which purport to have been drafted within a block exemption but which, in fact, do not fit within a block exemption. Clearly, some of the block exemptions have an opposition procedure which allows for agreements which do not fit full square within the exemption to be treated as exempt, if no contest is made. For example, I have represented brewery tenants in a number of cases in litigation in the High Court, challenging the time of the agreement, which we have said did not fulfil the criterion in the block exemption but it became clear at one point that the brewer was nevertheless in the course of receiving a comfort letter from the Commission, it not being clear whether that was being issued on the basis that in the Commission's view the agreement did fall within the block exemption or that it did not but it was nevertheless entitled to an individual exemption. It seems to me that if a block exemption is issued, then agreements should fall within that exemption. If they do not, then it is difficult to see why there should be room for a comfort letter in those circumstances. I think that blurs the ambit of the ability to challenge the agreement. People think that they know what needs to be in the agreement and in fact they do not.

294. Would anyone else like to comment on that? It raises a very practical problem. The problem about delays has been apparently thought about in the Commission. Sir Leon Brittan announced his procedural deadlines. Are they going to have any effect at all on this unless they are made obligatory or mandatory?

(Mr Hall) There is already one example of a co-operative joint venture benefiting from this new, accelerated procedure. I only know of the one case. Naturally, the proof of the pudding is going to be in the eating. It may be a one-off, or it may be this is now going to become the norm.

295. We do not really have any experience to comment on it. Has anyone ever brought a 175 case, failure of the Commission to get on and deal with things?

(Mr Vaughan) The first time I met Mr Hall we were on opposite sides in a case called *National Carbonizing* in the seventies, I think it must have been. We were both very young!

296. Have you done one since?

(Mr Vaughan) We have done it since. I think the case settled.

297. Does that mean it is not effective?

(Mr Vaughan) We got into terrible complications and the whole thing settled anyhow.

(Mr Hall) It was under the Coal and Steel Treaty, my Lord, which of course has slightly different rules.

298. Is it used in practice as a threat?

(Mr Vaughan) It is used as a threat.

299. Does it work as a threat?

(Mr Vaughan) Not really, I do not think, because they know they do not have to take a decision. All they have to do is take a position. We are busy thinking of the position.

300. That is the problem.

26 May 1993]   *[Continued*

[Baroness Elles *Contd]*

301. I thought you would say it was not very likely.
(Miss Rose) One of the aspects of the *Asia Motor* case was that the applicants had brought 175 proceedings and then the Commission had taken a position and the applicants tried to change the proceedings into a 173 challenge to the position taken. It was felt that was not a possible course. In fact, the Commission at any stage in 175 proceedings seems to be able to bring them to a shuddering halt by taking a position and then you have to start again.

302. 175 has been used so little it has almost ceased to be a tool in the Treaty. Would not the alternative be to go on to automatic exemption when cases have been hanging around for a certain period without a decision? Does that really stick as a suggestion?
(Mr Flint) The view one would take on that suggestion would depend on which side of the fence one happened to be. Obviously from an applicant's point of view it would be very nice to know that six months or a year, or whatever period was fixed after sending the papers, you would get an automatic exemption. It is not quite clear how long that would be for, whether it would be for the whole period of the agreement or for some lesser period. I think it raises very important issues regarding the rights of third parties and of society as a whole. If parties have notified an agreement to the Commission who, for whatever reason, had not dealt with it and it has important effects on the rights of third parties on a global distribution system or networking system of some sort, and there is no publication and no way in which such an agreement would come to the attention of third parties who might actually or potentially be affected by that, it would obviously, from a legal point of view, be wrong for them to be bound simply because of the Commission's inactivity during a particular period. There would require to be some publication procedure, something akin to the opposition procedure which exists in some of the later block exemptions. I have a feeling personally that if you were going to have an automatic publication procedure, then that would in fact stop any of the automatic exemptions happened on the basis that if the Commission actually had to do something, they might as well do the whole thing properly rather than just publish it.

303. That is an interesting point of view.
(Miss Rose) I think it works if the result of it is that the Commission in fact does not allow the time to elapse, which seems to be what has happened with the merger regulation. The problem arises if the result is the Commission does allow time to elapse and then these deemed exemptions come into effect.

304. I want to ask you a few brief questions on the merger control regulation before asking a final point on the general 85/86 position. We have heard suggestions made that the Commission ought to explain more its policy on fining and reveal more the way in which it applies the fine. Do you agree with that or do you think it is perfectly reasonable that the Commission should be allowed to fine without explaining? In the *Musique Diffusion* case, of course, it changed its policy without giving notice.
(Mr Vaughan) I think there are two sorts of cases. One is just when there is one defendant. The other is where there are lots of defendants. I can deal with that point where there is a balance between the different defendants. Certainly in the *PVC* case, it was absolutely clear the Commission tried to explain their fining policy. It was quite clear that they had assumed people were involved in the cartel in periods when they were not making any allegations. By giving more transparency to that, it became clear it gave a right of defence which did not otherwise exist. Otherwise you would just be saying that eight or ten million is too high. I have forgotten the figure in that case. When one saw the breakdown of the figures, it became absolutely clear they had got it wrong. If the Commission win the appeal it will come back on fines. From that point of view I think it is very important in those cases where you have got to compare one person's involvement with another.

305. Is this a general problem or is it a one-off?
(Mr Vaughan) No. In *Woodpulp* it was certainly a problem as to what the right of the fines were and how they were calculated. I think it is important when there are lots of defendants that they should say not necessarily the decisions but defend in the court the amount of the fine and the period for which it relates and the base of the degree of involvement which they allege against each person. Other people have different views on other parts, I think.
Chairman] May I, on behalf of the Committee, thank you all very warmly for the evidence you have given today. You have obviously given all these matters a great deal of thought and you all have very great experience, which will be very useful to us. We are very indebted to you for having given up the time to come.

Supplementary Memorandum by the Joint Working Party on Competition Law

WRITTEN RESPONSE TO QUESTIONS 16–20 NOT DEALT WITH
AT THE HEARING HELD ON 26 MAY 1993

The written response of the Joint Working Party to questions relating to the EC Merger Regulation (ECMR) is as follows:—

Question 16: How would you suggest revising the ECMR so as to reduce the likelihood of split jurisdiction where there is more than one bid for a company?

At the outset, the Working Party wishes to make clear that it does not seek to suggest that, in the event of competing bids, both should necessarily be subject to Phase 2 review under the ECMR or, alternatively, investigation by the Monopolies and Mergers Commission. It has long been made clear for example that, as regards competing bids within the scope of the Fair Trading Act ("FTA"), each bid is considered on its merits, and reference of one bid to the Monopolies and Mergers Commission does not trigger off an automatic bid of the other.

The concern of the Working Party arises because different rules of assessment arise under the ECMR and the FTA, and different timetables apply—a matter of particular concern in the case of mergers governed by City Code requirements.

The scope for harmonising FTA requirements with those of the ECMR is probably unrealistic (although this possibility is worthy of further consideration). The only alternative would appear to be for the EC and national authorities to agree that, in the event of split jurisdiction, responsibility for evaluating the competition implications of *both* bids should be undertaken *either* by the Mergers Task Force *or,* alternatively, by the Office of Fair Trading (or by whichever relevant competent national authority is concerned). By this means, competing bids would at least benefit from review and evaluation by a single regulatory body under identical terms and on an equivalent basis.

Question 17: Would more review of prospective mergers at national level be likely to lead to less vigorous enforcement or to intrusion of narrow concepts of public interest?

Review at national level is conducted in accordance with requirements of domestic legislation, not the ECMR; on the face of things, therefore, review by Member States should not result in less vigorous enforcement etc than at present. The longer term objective should be for closer alignment of domestic merger control rules with the ECMR in order to align timetable requirements and the criteria governing assessment.

Question 18: What suggestions would you like to make to the Commission concerning revision of the existing thresholds in the ECMR?

The Working Party supports in principle a reduction in the threshold levels, provided that the Merger Task Force has sufficient resources to deal with the increased number of notifications that would result; in addition to the benefit of "one-stop shop review", such a reduction should result in more consistent treatment of mergers throughout the Community.

Question 19: You suggest a need for greater transparency in the contacts between the Commission and national authorities which may determine whether a prospective merger is appraised at Community or at national level. Would you favour greater precision in the demarcation rules or merely close involvement of the parties?

Both, especially for the reasons set out in paragraphs 3 and 9 of the Working Party's paper to the Department of Trade and Industry dated 31 March 1993 (referred to in paragraph 24 of the Written Submission of the Working Party).

Question 20: Are you content with the operation of Article 21 of the ECMR?

The test applied under the ECMR is solely concerned with competition issues. The public interest considerations set out in Section 84(1), FTA, are concerned with a number of matters which are unrelated to competition. Article 21 enables Member States to apply their non-competition related domestic legislation to mergers otherwise falling to be assessed by the Commission under the ECMR.

The Working Party understands that the Department of Trade and Industry reviews qualifying mergers as a matter of course to determine whether concerns relating to legitimate interests in the reserved areas (public security, plurality of the media and prudential rules) arise. The circumstances in which any other public interest aspect under Article 21(3) might fall for domestic review are far from clear, and the Working Party feels that there has been insufficient experience to date to assess whether Member States are under-utilising the opportunity to scrutinise mergers on such grounds. The issues of additional guidance notes in this area would be welcome.

13 July 1993

Supplementary Memorandum by the Joint Working Party of the United Kingdom Bars and Law Societies on Competition Law

I. INTRODUCTION

1.0 The Working Party attaches particular importance to adequate access to files in the possession of the Commission, and the need for full disclosure to the parties of all relevant evidence to which they are entitled during the course of the administrative proceedings.

1.1 This submission summarises the current position relating to file access, and how the rules are often applied in practice; it then provides some examples of cases in which DG IV has produced, and relied on, misleading or incomplete evidence. Finally, it comments on aspects of current Commission procedure of greatest concern to the Joint Working Party.

II. ACCESS TO THE FILE

2.0 Until the early 1980s and in the absence of set rules, DG IV seemingly had an ambivalent attitude to the need to make any part of its files available to the parties. It relied on the notion that adequate disclosure was made by attaching documents of its own selection to the Statement of Objections, and no more. When, in 1981, the Statement of Objections was issued in the *Woodpulp* proceedings, the Case Officer told one of the parties that the Commission " was under no obligation under Regulation 17 to make any files available ", but then informally permitted the party to review the dossier confined to the documents that the undertaking and its European agents had previously supplied to the Commission. Another party in the same case was so incensed by the procedure adopted by the Case Officer that it wrote to the Director General of DG IV as follows:

> " . . . we requested an opportunity to examine ' the file '. That opportunity has been given to us, but upon terms that made it impossible for us to do more than carry out the most cursory review. To offer an opportunity to consider over 5000 documents, but to restrict the time for review to parts of two days, was . . . quite unreasonable. The opportunity has to be . . . not merely to skim a mass of documents. The size of the file itself is such that if any adequate commentary is to be made, it cannot be made within the constraint of a three month period after receipt of the Statement of Objections. "

2.1 The Commission first published rules governing access to the file in 1983, in its Twelfth Competition Report for 1982; these rules were subsequently elaborated in the Thirteenth and Eighteenth Reports. Relevant extracts from these Reports are set out in Appendix I.

2.2 Access to the file is currently subject to:—

● the obligation on the part of the Commission to observe the professional secrecy of documents required by Article 20, Regulation 17; and

● the self imposed rules adopted by the Commission in its Twelfth Report, as elaborated, which excludes from disclosure:—

—documents containing business secrets;

—internal working papers of the Commission;

—other confidential documents.

2.3 Cartel cases involve detailed appraisal of a mass of facts, often contained in numerous, seemingly unrelated, documents; full and proper access to the file is thus of crucial importance in the administrative proceedings if a proper response to the Statement of Objections is to be given. It is in relation to the documents withheld, and the Commission's interpretations of the rules referred to in paragraph 2.2 above, that significant difficulties arise in practice; more particularly, the Commission

● appears to have no consistent view as to the meaning to be attached to " professional secrecy " under Article 20, Regulation 17, and the extent to which " other confidential documents " referred to in the Twelfth Report come within the scope of this Article;

● maintains that it is often unable to identify whether information contained in all or part of a document is intrinsically confidential.

2.4 The Court of First Instance has confirmed on a number of occasions (most recently in Case T-7/89, *Hercules* v *Commission* judgment dated 17 December 1991, not yet reported; Case 7-10/92, *SA Cimenteries CBR and others* v *Commission* judgment dated 18 December 1992, not yet reported) that the Commission may not depart from the rules that it has imposed on itself, and also that it

> " . . . has an obligation to make available to the undertakings involved in Article 85(1) proceedings all documents, whether in their favour or otherwise, which it has obtained during the course of the investigation . . . ".

2.5 In the experience of practitioners, in relation to exculpatory documents in its possession, the Commission displays extreme reluctance to interpret its rules in a manner that takes proper or fair account of defence rights. Whilst understandably not prepared to grant undertakings full and free access to all the files in its possession because of the requirements of Article 20, Regulation 17, it nevertheless maintains that it is not in a position to work out correctly which documents might be favourable to an undertaking, or in what manner; it further asserts that it cannot be expected to anticipate what the undertaking's arguments will be. The Commission considers that the limit of its obligation is to produce to a party documents which

- are relied on by it in the Statement of Objections;

- have been found at an undertaking's premises; or which

- are in the public domain.

It was suggested by the Commission, in the *Cimenteries* case, that one can reasonably expect it to be able to recognise documents containing references to an undertaking, and that it provides adequate access to the file by producing such documents to the undertaking concerned; it must be said that practitioner members of the Working Party simply do not recognise such a practice as having been adopted by the Commission in proceedings with which they have been concerned.

2.6 As regards any other documents in its possession, the Commission interprets ground 55 of the *Hercules* judgment as imposing an obligation *on the undertakings* to show that the Commission has "selected" documents in such a way as to prevent them from answering the Statement of Objections. In short, if an undertaking considers that the files contain exculpatory documents, the onus is on that undertaking to provide the Commission with an indication of the existence of particular documents, and to request its production. The Commission asserts that for its part it has no responsibility in the matter.

2.7 The current practice, therefore, is that the Statement of Objections is (usually) accompanied by an annex which summarises all the documents on the Commission file which indicates, by reference to a key, which documents may be given to the parties in whole or in part. The recent experience of a solicitor regarding access to the file is described in Appendix II; as will be seen, the information provided by the Commission, whether in writing or at the time of inspection of the file, left the solicitor uncertain in the case in question that he had been provided with access to all the documents he considered he was permitted to see. Unfortunately, his experience seems to be all too typical; further, as noted in paragraph 13 of the earlier written submission of the Working Party, application of the procedure appears too often to be a matter of individual inclination of the Case Officer concerned.

III. PRODUCTION OF INCOMPLETE EVIDENCE

3.0 This issue, which is closely related to that of adequate access to the file, concerns what can only be described as the production by the Commission of partially complete evidence. Two examples of cases which were the subject of subsequent appeal to the European Courts will suffice to illustrate the point:—

(i) *Pioneer*

The case was concerned, *inter alia,* with restrictions on the parallel imports of hi-fi equipment from the United Kingdom and Germany to France. The case illustrates the manner in which material written evidence was misused by the Commission by means of selective deletions or the late production of evidence to the parties. Relevant extracts from the case report and judgment of the Court of Justice are contained in Appendix III:—

(a) the Commission, which had obtained a signed statement from a material witness, provided a copy of the statement to Pioneer GB having blanked out most of statement: the Commission claimed that the deleted text was confidential. The text that was omitted in fact confirmed that the company of which the witness was manager had in fact only limited commercial opportunities to export hi-fi equipment from the United Kingdom. The Commission, which disclosed the full text of the statement for the first time to the Court in the appeal proceedings, based part of its decision on the contents of the statement;

(b) handwritten notes of interviews with two other witnesses, which had been conducted by the Inspector, were disclosed for the first time by the Commission in its Rejoinder to the Court. The notes, which had the appearance of having been extracted from formal statements, were not dated, signed or approved by the persons to whom they were attributed. The Commission maintained before the Court that these notes, the existence of which Pioneer GB was not even aware at the time of the administrative proceedings, comprised admissible statements that supported the Commission's finding of infringement.

The Court held in both cases that the Commission was wrong to have based its decision on the contents of the documents.

(ii) *Italian Flat Glass*

The Commission concluded that a number of Italian glass makers had acted together contrary to Articles 85(1) and Article 86, relying heavily on documents obtained from the files of the parties concerned. On appeal, the Court of First Instance established (relevant extracts from the judgment are contained in Appendix IV) that:—

(a) a number of documents obtained by the Commision during the course of its investigation into the case, and produced to the parties during the administrative proceedings prior to adoption of the contested decision, were in incomplete form;

(b) passages had been deliberately deleted or omitted from these documents, even though the passages deleted were not such as to constitute business secrets such that deletion was necessary in order to comply with the provisions of Article 20, Regulation 17;

(c) no indication was given in the documents concerned that words or passages had been deleted;

(d) the sense of the documents was changed completely by the deletions that had been made;

(e) seemingly, not all departments of the Commission were in possession of the same set of documents;

(f) the omissions would not have come to light but for the vigilance of the Juge Rapporteur responsible for the case; and

(g) the Commission was unable to provide any objectively justifiable explanation for at least one of the deletions.

3.1 The Working Party is aware of other instances in which evidence has been rendered incomplete or misleading in a similar manner as in the *Italian Flat Glass* case; there is at least one case currently before the Court of First Instance involving such issues.

IV. COMMENT

4.0 All the issues identified above relate to maintenance of recognised and acceptable standards of natural justice applicable in the Commission's administrative proceedings; in particular:—

● *access to the file*: although there has been some improvement in the procedure that previously operated, the present arrangements are still applied in an insufficiently transparent manner, eg:—

—the list of documents provided by the Commission contains inadequately detailed information to enable the recipient to identify what documents are being withheld, and why;

—the procedure is not applied uniformly by Case Officers, who appear not to understand fully the meaning of due process, or the meaning or scope of confidentiality under Regulation 17; or the obligation incumbent on the Commission to make all documents available, whether or not favourable to the party concerned;

—the onus imposed by the Commission on undertakings to identify exculpatory evidence is unreasonably high, is not readily achievable and denies the parties access to all non-confidential documents that are relevant to their case;

—there is no mechanism presently available by which to challenge before the Court of First Instance deficiencies encountered at the administrative stage of the proceedings.

● *absence of adequate checks and balances within the Commission*: the Terms of Reference of the Hearing Officer exclude rulings on matters relating to disclosure of documents and, as the *Italian Flat Glass* proceedings demonstrate, neither the Legal Service nor the Commissioner (or his Cabinet), in exercise of the checks and balances that are said to exist, was seemingly in a position to recognise that evidence relied upon by DGIV had in fact been suppressed or altered.

● *alteration of evidence by the Commission*: suppression of evidence by the Commission Services is itself unacceptable as falling below any recognised standard of natural justice. The alteration of evidence simply should not occur. Adoption of an internal manual of procedures, and greater involvement of senior officials of DGIV and the Legal Service with the work of rapporteurs, should contribute to ensuring that defence rights are better observed. However, the key protection lies in the transparency of the procedure adopted, and a more clearly defined role for the Hearing Officer in this area is to be welcomed. It is to be hoped that the internal manual and the revised terms of reference of the Hearing Officer will be published.

4.1 The Commission's Twenty-second Report on Competition (May 1993) comments (paragraph 321) in relation to the *Italian Flat Glass* proceedings the " there is an(other) important lesson to be learned from [the] judgment, namely the extreme importance of *documentary evidence and the way it is presented in a Commission decision* " (emphasis added). That the enforcement agency can make such a remark beggars belief, and merely confirms its apparent misunderstanding of the purpose of due process: it is the presentation of evidence *to the parties in the administrative proceedings*, and *not in the Commission decision*, that is essential to ensure that rights of defence are adequately, and fairly, protected.

6 *July* 1993

Appendix I

ACCESS TO THE FILE: COMMISSION RULES

COMMISSION'S TWELFTH REPORT ON COMPETITION POLICY (1982/83) (pp 40, 41)

The Commission:

". . . permits the undertakings involved in a procedure to inspect the file on the case.

. . . Undertakings are informed of the contents of the Commission's file by means of an annex to the statement of objections or to the letter rejecting a complaint, listing all the documents in the file and indicating documents or parts thereof to which they may have access.

They are invited to come and consult these documents on the Commission's premises. If an undertaking wishes to examine only a few of them the Commission may forward copies.

However, the Commission regards the documents listed below as confidential and accordingly inaccessible to the undertaking concerned:

(i) documents or parts thereof containing other undertakings' business secrets;

(ii) internal Commission documents, such as notes, drafts or other working papers;

(iii) any other confidential information, such as documents enabling complainants to be identified where they wish to remain anonymous, and information disclosed to the Commission subject to an obligation of confidentiality.

Where an undertaking makes a justified request to consult a document which is not accessible, the Commission may make a non-confidential summary available ".

COMMISSION'S THIRTEENTH REPORT ON COMPETITION POLICY (1983/84) (pp 63, 64)

The Commission:

". . . does not offer access to its file before formal proceedings are started. This means that undertakings do not have a possibility of access until they have received a formal statement of objections from the Commission. To the statement of objections is annexed a list of the documents in the Commission's file, with an indication of the degree of access.

Whether or not the reports prepared by the Commission inspectors are accessible depends on the type of report concerned. Reports drawn up after an inspection visit and containing a purely factual account thereof are accessible to the firm which was subject to the investigation. Statements made by employees or officers of undertakings during an investigation may be recorded in a separate minute. To the extent that they constitute evidence of an infringement and figure in the statement of objections, such minutes will normally be made available to all parties concerned.

Inspectors' final assessment reports are considered to be internal Commission documents and thus not accessible "

COMMISSION'S EIGHTEENTH REPORT ON COMPETITION POLICY (1988/89) (pp 58, 59)

". . . The Court's judgments in the 'AKZO/professional secrecy' and 'BAT/Commission' cases oblige the Commission to take particular care in handling confidential information. After careful examination of this problem, the Commission has come to the conclusion that the principles underlying the existing arrangement should be maintained. However, it is necessary to afford confidentiality to any document of an undertaking the disclosure of which might be likely to have a significant adverse effect upon the supplier of such information. This includes documents containing business secrets but may also include other proprietary documents belonging to an undertaking which it may not wish to be made accessible to third parties or to parties involved in the proceedings. In particular, confidential (sensitive) information provided by third parties in the course of investigations should, in principle, not be made accessible to parties involved in the proceedings.

In cases where proceedings are instituted against several competing firms the Commission, for reasons of public interest, must ensure that the access to files does not lead to an exchange of commercially sensitive information between the undertakings which are the subject of the proceedings. This rule applies even if the undertakings agree to waive confidentiality for such information on a reciprocal basis. This recognition of extensive protection for confidential information is, however, subject to an important exception justified by the public interest in the enforcement of the EEC competition rules. The confidential nature of documents does not preclude their disclosure where the Commission relies upon the information in question as necessary evidence of an alleged infringement of the EEC competition rules. This applies both to its own proceedings and in court proceedings. When deciding whether such disclosure should occur the Commission will take into account the legitimate interests of the undertaking providing the information, and the rights of defence of the parties who are the subject of the proceedings.

Documents or information can be made accessible to parties to proceedings, either by access to the file or by the sending of copies, according to the circumstances. "

Appendix 2

ACCESS TO THE FILE AND RELATED ISSUES: ONE SOLICITOR'S RECENT EXPERIENCE

In a major cartel case, the Commission attached to the Statement of Objections documents which it categorised as follows:

    (i) Annexes.

    (ii) " Further relevant documents from the following files ", which were the individual files of a number of producers involved in the alleged infringements.

    (iii) " Other accessible documents from the following files " again being extracts from the individual files of various producers involved in the alleged infringements.

    (iv) A so-called " sommaire " (the language of the case was in fact English, not French) which contained manuscript notes under the following headings: " page, date, nature du document, classification ". This was no doubt intended to be some sort of index but is quite incomprehensible. No entries were made under the " classification " heading. The " nature du document " was in each case a number between one and ten; no key was provided, although it is likely that, for example, " one " meant " letter ", " two " meant " price list " and so on.

On any view, this was not a full indication of the papers in the Commission's possession against which the parties could verify that the documents which had been supplied with the Statement of Objections disclosed all relevant evidence, including possibly evidence favourable to the parties.

The letter accompanying the Statement of Objections extended an invitation to inspect the file in Brussels. When the Solicitor telephoned the Case Officer to avail himself of this opportunity, he was told it would be pointless since the Case Officer had already sent the Solicitor copies of all documents which he could see. The Solicitor nevertheless said that he would wish to see the file for himself. When he visited DG IV's offices to inspect the file, he was only shown the file relating to his client and not the parts of other producers' files which the Commission said were accessible to him. The Case Officer assured the Solicitor that he had already supplied him with everything which he was entitled to see and no purpose would be served by further inspection.

Appendix 3

JOINED CASES 100–103/80
MUSIQUE DIFFUSION FRANCAISE AND OTHERS *v* COMMISSION (1983 ECR 1825)

EXTRACT FROM THE REPORT OF FACTS AND ISSUES (at pp 1856–1857)

" Pioneer GB considers that its right to a proper hearing has been infringed because the Commission disclosed only a wholly irrelevant part of Mr Mason's statement before the adoption of the decision. In fact, by letter of 9 October 1978 the Commission disclosed paragraphs 1 and 2 of the statement and the signature. The relevant paragraphs, namely numbers 3, 4 and 5, were disclosed to Pioneer GB by Comet on or about 21 November 1978 (the date of the hearing at the Commission). The Commission disclosed the full text only in its letter to the Court of 6 April 1981.

. . .

Pioneer GB also considers that its right to a proper hearing has been infringed because the report which the Commission's inspector drew up regarding his visit to Comet and the other evidence, including Comet's invoices upon which the Commission relied for its statement that Comet had ceased to export following Mr Todd's letter, were not disclosed to it before the adoption of the decision.

. . .

According to the Commission, Audiotronic replaced Comet as regards supplies to Euro-electro, as soon as Comet had discontinued exporting Pioneer equipment . . . the Commission relies upon the oral statements made to its inspectors by Mr Keighley and Mr Smith of Audiotronic. One of the Commission's inspectors also checked Audiotronic's export invoices for the period in question.

The statements made by Mr Keighley and Mr Smith are reproduced in the final report of the Commission's inspectors.

. . .

The hand written notes which the inspector in question took during his meeting with Messrs Smith and Keighley were disclosed for the first time in the Commission's letters to the Court dated 6 April 1981 and 11 June 1981.

Pioneer and Pioneer GB ask the Court to declare the statements of Messrs Smith and Keighley inadmissible as evidence since they did not make written statements, the inspector's notes were not disclosed until after service of the rejoinder and they are not dated, signed or approved by the person to whom they are attributed. In the event of the Court's considering that the notes in question are admissible as evidence, Pioneer submits that their content does not support the Commission's allegations referred to above.

The Commission considers that the statements of Messrs Smith and Keighley are admissible as evidence and that they support the conclusions drawn from them.

Pioneer GB also claims that its right to a proper hearing was infringed in so far as the abovementioned notes, the report of the Commission's inspector on his visit to Audiotronic and all the other evidence on which the Commission relies for its allegation that Audiotronic stopped exporting Pioneer equipment following Mr Todd's letter were not disclosed to it before the adoption of the decision. "

EXTRACT FROM THE JUDGMENT (at pp 1884–1885)

" The failure to disclose documents

24. First, Pioneer and Pioneer GB maintain that, despite their requests to that effect, the Commission did not transmit to them, in due time, the documents on which it based its findings as regards the effects of the letters sent by Mr Todd of [Pioneer GB] to the directors of Comet and Audiotronic.

25. On that point the Commission asserts, in paragraph (50) of its decision, that it was established that, as a result of [Pioneer GB's] intervention, Comet ceased to export Pioneer equipment for resale. According to the decision, Audiotronic replaced Comet in supplying one of its customers, Euro-electro in Brussels; in March 1976 Audiotronic received large orders but was able to carry out only a part of them owing to difficulties caused by [Pioneer GB].

26. Since the period to be taken into consideration in assessing the duration of the infringements must, as has been stated above, be confined to late January and early February 1976 and since the Commission's findings relating to the effects on Audiotronic's exports relate specifically to a later period, the Court's examination of this part of the submission may be restricted to Comet's situation.

27. As far as the latter undertaking is concerned, the Commission relied essentially on a written statement by Mr Mason, a director of Comet, and on the reports of its inspectors on visits to Comet and Euro-electro and on accounting documents relating to Comet.

28. Mr Mason's statement was communicated to the applicants by the Commission on 9 October 1978, but only in part. The Commission refused to divulge the pertinent points of the statement, invoking their confidential nature, which did not however prevent Mr Mason himself from sending the applicants, at their request, a complete copy of the statement.

29. Although, as a result of their own diligence, the applicants thus gained knowledge of the whole of the statement made by Mr Mason just before the hearing, it is not disputed that they were not acquainted or were only partially acquainted with the other documents mentioned above before the Commission adopted its decision. Therefore they did not have the opportunity, in due time of making known their views on the contents and the scope of those documents or of obtaining and putting forward, where appropriate, evidence to the contrary. It follows that the Commission was wrong to base its decision on the contents of those documents. "

Appendix 4

CASES T–68/89
SOCIETA ITALIANO VETRO SPA AND OTHERS v COMMISSION (JUDGEMENT OF
10 MARCH 1992, NOT YET REPORTED)

EXTRACT FROM THE JUDGMENT

" 41. At that meeting, the Judge-Rapporteur explained that he intended, in order to facilitate examination of the files and the conduct of the hearing, to submit to the Chamber, following the informal meeting, Reports from the Hearing whose content could be accepted by each of the parties as a complete and detailed summary of its position, and a single common file of documents for all the cases containing all the documents which the parties considered important for consideration of their cases. He asked the parties to send him their observations on the draft Reports for the Hearing which he communicated to them, and on the list of documents to be included in the common file. He also asked the Commission to produce, in the original form in its possession, the documentary evidence on which it relied for the adoption of its decision.

89. With regard to the second plea in law, which concerns the findings of fact and the evidence, a point must be mentioned at this stage which came to light only when, as was stated above (paragraph 41), the Commission was called upon to place in the file, in the original form in its possession, the documentary evidence on which it relied when adopting its decision.

. . .

90. Under Article 14(1)(b) of Regulation No 17, in the course of the investigations which it carries out at the premises of undertakings, the Commission is authorised only to take copies of or extracts from the books and business records. In the present case, a large number of the documents to which the Commission refers in its statements of objections, and which it communicated to the undertakings in the form of photocopies, are handwritten notes, sometimes scarcely legible, in Italian. In some cases, it was clear from the form of the document communicated by the Commission to the undertakings that the document in question was only part of the original document. Other documents were internal memoranda of the undertakings or their subsidiaries. Once again, it was clear from the form of the document that, in some cases, the documents in question were merely part of the original. In other cases, the fact that the document was an extract was not evident from the document communicated.

91. It emerges from the inquiry carried out by the Court that when the Commission prepared the documentary evidence with a view to communication to the undertakings, certain relevant passages were deliberately deleted or omitted, even though they did not relate to business secrets. In particular, nine words were deleted without trace in a handwritten note from SIV of 30 January 1985 (#374).

. . .

93. The Court considers that it is self-evident and indisputable that the tenor of the note is changed completely by the omission of those nine words. With those nine words the note could be taken as clear evidence of a competitive struggle between SIV and FP on the one hand and VP on the other. At the hearing, the Commission tried in vain to supply an objectively justifiable reason for the deletion of those words.

94. The Court must record that that is not the only example of such a proceeding, other examples of which will be commented upon below (see in particular paragraphs 214, 215, 224, 236 and 246 below). The Court also observes that SIV's note of 30 January 1985, cited above, and another note of SIV of 24 June 1985 (#715) appear in the list of documents referring expressly or implicitly to VP supplied to the Court by the Commission, as making implicit reference to VP, whereas it emerges from the full version of those notes that they make express mention of VP. That fact would appear to indicate that the full versions of those documents were not available to all departments of the Commission.

95. Accordingly, the Court considers that it is incumbent on it, in assessing the applicants' second general pleas, to check meticulously the nature and import of the evidence taken into consideration by the Commission in the decision. . . ."

WEDNESDAY 9 JUNE 1993

Present:

Allen of Abbeydale, L.	Holme of Cheltenham, L.
Colville of Culross, V.	Skidelsky, L.
Elles, B.	Slynn of Hadley, L. (Chairman)

Memorandum by the Director General of Fair Trading

INTRODUCTION

1. This memorandum considers the procedures of the European Commission in relation to competition cases and the experience which my Office has gained in participating in those procedures. The cases include those brought under Articles 85 and 86 of the Treaty of Rome as well as mergers which fall under the European Community Merger Regulation (ECMR).

2. Under Regulation 17/62 (the Regulation which implements Articles 85 and 86) the Commission is required to act "in close and constant liaison with the competent authorities of the Member States. In the United Kingdom, I am designated as a competent authority together with the Secretary of State for Trade and Industry. In relation to cases under the Merger Regulation, the Commission is under an identical obligation to liaise with the Member States and for the purposes of that Regulation the Monopolies and Mergers Commission is also designated as a competent authority. In general, my Office is responsible for the handling of individual cases, and the Department of Trade and Industry has overall responsibility for wider policy issues including new Community legislation.

ARTICLES 85 AND 86 CASEWORK

3. My Office handles the United Kingdom contribution on individual cases and therefore has day-to-day contact with officials in the Commission's Directorate General for Competition (DG IV). The Office has built up a close working relationship with DG IV which works to our mutual benefit.

4. My Office receives copies of all important documents sent to the Commission on individual cases. The Commission is required to send copies of certain documents to the competent authorities of Member States under Article 10(1) of Regulation 17. The purpose of this is, first, to inform Member States of the Community procedures concerning undertakings situated in their territory, and secondly, to allow the competent authorities to give their views to the Commission. My Office thus receives copies on behalf of the United Kingdom of all notifications of agreements and complaints made to the Commission together with copies of the most important documents in the case as the investigation proceeds. In 1992, notifications and documents in respect of more than 400 new Article 85 and 86 and ECMR cases were received by the Office.

5. The investigation of cases is a matter for the Commission but under Articles 13 and 14 of Regulation 17 (or their equivalent in certain transport regulations) the competent authorities of Member States may be asked to assist the Commission in its investigations. When Commission officials visit companies in the United Kingdom, including those visits made without prior notice, they are always accompanied by officials from my Office. On two occasions the Office has itself carried out the visits unaccompanied, at the request of the Commission, as is provided for in the regulations.

6. Where, following an assessment and investigation of a case, the Commission finds that there has been an infringement of the competition rules and intends to take a formal decision to that effect, it issues a Statement of Objections. In response to this the party or parties concerned may comment in writing and ask for an oral hearing. Competent authorities may appoint an official to take part in the hearing and my office always does so. Parties to Commission investigations frequently get in touch with the Office. The Office is receptive to such approaches as it can enable my officials to have a better understanding of the issues (although the Office does not act as an advocate for the parties).

7. Subsequently to an investigation, and hearing (if held), Articles 10.3 and 10.4 of Regulation 17 (or the equivalent in transport cases) require the Commission to consult an Advisory Committee which is made up of officials of the Member States. My Office provides the United Kingdom representative for this Committee. In preparing the line to take, the Office consults the Department of Trade and Industry and other Departments who might have a special interest in a particular case. This is the stage at which the Commission formally consults the Member States but my officials will have been in touch with the DG IV case officers during the investigation.

MERGERS CASEWORK

8. The European Community Merger Regulation which came into effect in September 1990, gave the Commission the powers to investigate large mergers with cross-border effects (ie those mergers which have a "Community dimension" as defined in the Regulation).

9. The ECMR lays down tight timescales in which the Commission must reach a decision on a proposed merger. Copies of notifications of proposed mergers are sent by the Commission to Member States within three days of their receipt. Member States have a limited time, as noted below, in which to submit their views. The Commission must take a decision within one month of a notification as to whether a merger falls within the scope of the ECMR. If so, the Commission has to decide whether it is compatible with the Common Market, according to criteria set out in Article 2 of the Regulation or whether there are serious doubts as to compatibility, and that proceedings should therefore be initiated to allow further investigation. The one-month period is further increased by two weeks if a request is received (under Article 9) from a Member State for the case to be referred to the national authority. If the Commission decides to open proceedings it has a further four months in which to make a final decision. If it fails to reach a decision within the deadlines set, the concentration is then deemed to have been declared compatible with the Common Market.

10. Member States' involvement in merger cases is similar to that in Article 85 and 86 cases under Regulation 17. In the United Kingdom my Office receives from the Commission a copy of the notification made by the parties to a proposed merger. The Office examines the jurisdictional and competition aspects of the case and sends a preliminary view to the Department of Trade and Industry, and a final view is taken which the Office transmits to the European Commission. This is an informal procedure and the aim is to give the Commission the United Kingdom view of the particular case within two weeks of receiving a copy of the notification so as to have a realistic possibility of influencing the Commission's decision taken at the end of the one month allowed by the Regulation. If the Commission decides to open proceedings and go into the second stage, the procedure is similar to that under which competition cases under Articles 85 and 86 are handled, with a written Statement of Objections, a hearing, and Member States' views being given at a meeting of an Advisory Committee.

ADMINISTRATION OF MERGER CASES

11. Since the introduction of the ECMR in September 1990, the Commission has dealt with 156 mergers (as at end April 1993). One hundred and twenty of these were cleared within the one-month timescale laid down in the ECMR. Fifteen fell outside the ECMR and 11 went to full proceedings. Five notifications have been withdrawn and currently five decisions are pending. Only one merger has been blocked (Aerospatiale/Alenia joint acquisition of de Havilland), and one merger referred to a national authority under the provisions of Article 9 of the ECMR (the Tarmac/Steetley joint venture which was referred back to the United Kingdom).

12. As far as the Commission's operation of day-to-day procedures on merger cases is concerned, I take the view that the system has worked well. All deadlines have been met, and the liaison between my officials and the case officers in the Commission has worked smoothly despite the tight timetable.

REVIEW OF THE ECMR

13. Under the provisions of Article 1 of the ECMR, the turnover thresholds must be reviewed before the end of 1993. The Commission has previously stated a view that the turnover thresholds should be lowered; this would have the effect of bringing more mergers (out of those which are currently dealt with by those Member States with merger legislation) under the Commission's jurisdiction. The Commission sees the main advantage of such a change as strengthening the common regime across the Community. Article 9, under which mergers can be referred back to Member States, is also to be reviewed before the end of the year. I am not opposed in principle to a lowering of the thresholds although I think it is important to consider the complete package of amendments to the Regulation as a whole. There may be scope for the referral back to Member States of a larger number of mergers which affect competition in national markets. I would also welcome a development of the Commission's procedure which would allow the Member States to play a more active role in the Commission's investigation of the effects of a merger on national or sub-national markets in the Member State concerned and I would hope to see the Member States contribution reflected in the Commission's formal decision. However, I appreciate the difficulties which are posed by the timescale of a merger investigation.

GENERAL OBSERVATIONS ON THE OPERATION OF COMMISSION PROCEDURES

14. Generally speaking the Commission's procedures work well. This is particularly so in the case of the operation of the European Community Merger Control Regulation where the Commission has an obligation to make its assessment of concentrations in a very tight timescale. With Article 85 and 86 cases there is some concern about the time that may be taken before a decision is reached by the Commission.

15. Subsequently to the Select Committee's report in 1982 the Commission instituted certain procedures to improve the administrative handling of cases. These changes include:

(a) the increased use of block exemptions for certain categories of agreements several of which have an opposition procedure which guarantees clearance within a set timescale if there are no objections;

(b) the use of administrative letters ("comfort letters"), which, although not giving complete legal certainty, advise companies that the Commission considers, on the basis of facts to hand, that there are no grounds for action under Article 85(1), or that an agreement fulfils the conditions for an exemption under Article 85(3);

(c) greater access for the parties to Commission files and willingness on the part of the Commission to enter into discussions (even after the issuing of a Statement of Objections);

(d) the appointment of a hearing officer who, although a Commission official, is a member of a separate directorate not directly connected with the work of the DG IV section conducting an investigation;

(e) the reorganisation of the case handling in DG IV (in 1984) into trade/industry sections which deal with all aspects of a case rather than making certain enquiries and then passing a case on to another section for investigation;

(f) improvements in documentation, documentation handling concerning professional secrecy, and the institution of more open procedures when Commission officials conduct on-the-spot investigations; and

(g) the publication of an increased number of Commission notices in the Official Journal which indicate how the Commission is likely to treat particular kinds of agreements or aspects of competition—these include notices dealing with agreements of minor importance, exclusive distribution and purchasing agreements, assessment of joint ventures and the application of Articles 85 and 86 in national courts.

16. More details on these initiatives are given in Annex 1 and a brief description of the structure of DG IV is to be found in Annex 2. (Both of these documents also appear in the memorandum submitted by the Department of Trade and Industry).[1]

17. While the changes in procedures have improved the Commission's efficiency and provided benefits for companies involved in the procedures, certain areas for concern remain. These fall into two broad groupings—the time taken to handle cases, and administrative procedures.

DELAYS IN THE COMPLETION OF CASES

18. The Commission does not publish statistics on the time taken to deal with cases overall but an average can be computed for the time taken to reach formal decisions from the Commission's published text of decisions. In 1991 this was 2·5 years. There may be some justification in the timescale where the parties have entered into protracted negotiations with the Commission but the average period appears to be excessive. Timescales cannot be computed (without extensive research into many hundreds of files) for the cases which are settled by less formal means but it is clear that many take an inordinate time to complete.

19. The Commission is, however, aware of the problem and in a speech in December 1992 the then Commissioner for competition, Sir Leon Brittan, announced to the Centre of European Policy Studies that from 1 January 1993 the Commission would deal with joint ventures which are notified under Article 85 (and where all the necessary information has been provided) within a "fixed, predictable and reasonable period of time". The Commission issued a press release on 23 December 1992 in which it announced that internal instructions had been issued providing for a speed up in the handling of structural joint venture cases under Article 85. Within two months of receiving a complete notification, the Commission will inform the parties whether the agreement concerned gives rise to serious doubts as to its compatibility with the EC competition rules. Sir Leon also stated that from 1 April a similar system will enter into force for all other notifications and all complaints.

20. The Commission is clearly aware therefore of the shortcomings in its administration and procedures and I welcome this commitment to their improvement. While fully recognising the difficulties when cases vary so much in their complexity, the Office has for some time encouraged the Commission to set targets for Article 85/86 cases in line with the procedures used in merger cases. The introduction of a quick, first-level assessment of Article 85/86 cases and complaints and the commitment to provide firm timetables for the processing of "second-stage" cases without endangering the thoroughness of the investigation would result in a greatly improved service from the Commission. This could be achieved by means of internal instructions or failing that, by amending Regulation 17 to include time limits as in the Merger Regulation.

ADMINISTRATIVE PROCEDURES

21. The Committee will be aware that the Court of First Instance has criticised the Commission in certain recent judgments where procedures have been disregarded. In *PVC*[2] the Court of First Instance found that procedures followed by the Commission in adopting and disseminating a decision were flawed and the resultant measures were not merely void but actually non-existent in law. In *Flat Glass*[3] the Court criticism included the fact that the Commission had wrongly assessed the facts, concluding that there was collusion where there was none, and that there were improprieties in the treatment and presentation of evidence against

---

[1] Annex 1 is identical to Annex II in DTI evidence (printed at p. 141) and Annex 2 is identical to Annex VIII (printed at p. 149).

[2] *BASF and Others* v. *Commission*. Judgement of 27 February 1992.

[3] *SIV and Others* v. *Commission*. Judgement of 10 March 1992.

the applicant companies. In *Wood Pulp*[1] the Court of First Instance found, *inter alia*, that the Commission's finding of concertation on transaction prices was based on evidence requested by the Commission *after* it had heard the producers. Community law requires the Commission to communicate its conclusions based on that new evidence by a new Statement of Objections before any decision is taken which is based on the new evidence. This was not done.

22. The shortcomings of procedures in these three cases must be assessed in the context of the many hundreds of cases dealt with by the Commission. Certainly there is a need for a detailed appraisal by the Commission of how the shortcomings in these cases came about and for steps to be taken to avoid any recurrence.

23. On less serious issues, the work of my Office has been hampered on occasions by the short notice given for meetings in Brussels and the late despatch of certain documents. It is appreciated that there are 12 Member States involved and a need for document translations and interpreters at meetings but as far as the Office is concerned it leads to inefficient use of scarce staff resources with the need to study papers at short notice and cancel other engagements. These aspects have been brought to the notice of the Commission and some improvement has been noted, but the problem continues.

DECENTRALISATION AND SUBSIDIARITY

24. In the speech noted in paragraph 21 above Sir Leon stated that although Article 3b of the Maastricht Treaty will formally confirm the subsidiarity principle as one of the basic principles of Community law, the Community's competition policy has always been underpinned by the subsidiarity principle in that Articles 85 and 86 are only applicable to agreements or practices that have an appreciable effect on trade between Member States. The Commission see the turnover thresholds of the European Community Merger Regulation and the provisions allowing referral of certain mergers to be considered by Member States (Article 9 and 23 (3)) as other examples of the subsidiarity principle.

25. The Commission has published a Notice on co-operation between national courts and the Commission in applying Articles 85 and 86, and I agree in principle that there may be more scope for using national courts to decide on the application of Articles 85(1) and 86. This would, however, have limited benefits in practice. National courts do not possess all of the powers available to the Commission to pursue cases, particularly in the obtaining of evidence. There would also be a problem in the United Kingdom courts in relation to the admissibility of opinions (such as the Commission's) on the application of EC law. The United Kingdom advised the Commission to be cautious in advising complainants to take their cases to national courts. Furthermore, there is a limit as to how far a judicial body (such as a national court) can take on the work of an administrative body (such as the Commission).

26. Nevertheless, subject to resource constraints I share the Commission's stated aim of a greater involvement of Member States where cases have a particular national interest. On occasion the Commission will refer a case back to me if it can be dealt with more effectively under United Kingdom law, and I encourage the Commission to continue with and further develop this approach.

27. I would suggest that another option to consider would be for the Commission to develop the practice of involving Member States' competent authorities in its investigations, while retaining the final authority to make decisions. For example, the Commission could take more advantage of its powers to authorise Member States to carry out investigations under Article 13 of Regulation 17 (or its equivalent in transport regulations). I have twice carried out unannounced visits on behalf of the Commission and would welcome further use of this practice.

28. Whereas the Office can apply domestic competition law to cases which might be referred to it by the Commission, United Kingdom competition authorities do not have the power to apply Articles 85 and 86. Although this matter is currently under discussion, no decision has yet been taken by the Government on whether I should be empowered to apply those Articles. An advantage of my being so would be that it would make it easier for my Office and the Commission to share the casework between them, even though I would not have the power to apply Article 85(3). There would of course be resource implication of any increase in the caseload of my Office which I would need to consider. Aside from the questions about who makes decisions or takes formal action, is the need to ensure that the application of Articles 85 and 86 takes account of market conditions in each part of the Community. As I suggested above in relation to mergers, there may be scope for greater involvement of the Member States in the Commission's investigation of national or sub-national markets.

Sir Bryan Carsberg
Director General of Fair Trading
May 1993

---

[1] *Ahlströhm and Others* v. *Commission*. Judgement of 31 March 1993.

Examination of witnesses

SIR BRYAN CARSBERG, Director General, MR EDWARD WHITEHORN, Head of International Section, and
DR MARTIN HOWE, Director of Competition Policy Division, Office of Fair Trading, called in and examined.

Chairman

306. Sir Bryan, Mr Whitehorn and Dr Howe, may
I thank you for coming to give evidence before us and
for your very helpful memorandum. As you know,
we are looking into the competition practices of the
Community and the way in which competition rules
are enforced. We regard this as a very important
subject and one that is obviously very relevant to
your Office, so we appreciate your coming. May I ask
you first about the general position in the
Commission's procedures. A number of people have
criticised them fairly severely. The criticism last time
the Committee reported and the criticism that one
has always heard in the last ten years is that it was
quite wrong for the Commission to be the
investigator, the prosecutor, the decision maker and
the judge and that there should be some separation.
In addition there were a lot of detailed criticisms
about failure to notify people of reasons, failure to
give information, failure to give access to the file and
that sort of thing. We should very much like to know
what the reactions of the Office of Fair Trading are to
criticisms of this kind?
   (Sir Bryan Carsberg) Thank you, my Lord
Chairman. Our view is that the Commission has
made good progress in recent years in improving its
procedures; the establishment of the hearing officer
and the intention to be more open about information
and various things of that kind have been steps in the
right direction. We think recent moves to improve
procedures may help more although that is more
about the timing than it is about——

307. But what do you mean by recent moves to
improve procedures?
   (Sir Bryan Carsberg) I had in mind the
arrangements announced by Sir Leon Brittan as far
as time targets and that kind of thing are concerned.
That suggests that there will be a more systematic
approach to putting cases through stages.

308. Do you think that those time rules will work
unless they are made binding or enforceable?
   (Sir Bryan Carsberg) Given the difficulty that
there is bound to be in reaching agreement on a
revision to the regulations and making formal change
and given also, my Lord Chairman, that our own
position is that although perhaps one can see that
there are procedural weaknesses there, in practice
our experience—and I emphasise our experience—
has not been that these have caused material
difficulty. We have not found ourselves with
particular cases where we have felt that the outcome
has been unfortunate and linked that in our minds to
procedures. My attitude therefore from my
perspective would be, let us give them a chance to
make it work with the new procedures and see how
that works out.

309. Yes, thank you. The atmosphere, as it were,
of .your memorandum I think is less troubled by
Commission procedures than the evidence of other

people. As you have mentioned procedural
weaknesses would you care to indicate specifically
the sort of things that you would regard as
procedural difficulties?
   (Sir Bryan Carsberg) I was responding to the
things that you mentioned, my Lord Chairman. I say
again that in practice they have not been a real
problem for us. If one were sitting down to design a
theoretically ideal procedure, as I say, I think that
one might do it differently, but I am rather inclined
when one has living organisations like the
Commission which is, I think, broadly on the right
track and which has a good competition policy, the
development of which we want to encourage, to say,
well, if in practice it is working pretty well on the
whole, as I think it is, and if there is also an internal
wish, as I see that there is, to improve things further,
let us give it the chance to develop in that way.

310. You would not like to tear up the whole
scheme and start with new legislative frameworks
and a new Regulation 17, which everyone has come
to regard as written in tablets of stone?
   (Sir Bryan Carsberg) That is, I suppose, partly
because of the enormous difficulty of getting
agreement on changes at the European level. I should
not want to do that, no, my Lord Chairman.

311. I get the impression, Sir Bryan, that you do
not think it is necessary to separate out the
investigative function from the prosecuting function
from the decision making function?
   (Sir Bryan Carsberg) No.

312. They can all stay under the one umbrella, is
that your view?
   (Sir Bryan Carsberg) Yes. There are, of course,
routes of appeal, and again in theory one might
question whether there should be more. As I say, my
Lord Chairman, my view is that it should be allowed
to develop and that one should give things a chance
to develop before trying to interfere.

313. I should perhaps have indicated at the
beginning that you, Sir Bryan, as Director General,
will of course answer some of the questions, but if Mr
Whitehorn or Dr Howe want to add anything do not
wait to be asked, just jump in.
   (Sir Bryan Carsberg) Thank you, my Lord
Chairman. I chanced my arm and told them that I
should like them to do that at the beginning,
assuming your permission.

314. Let us specifically think now of Regulation 17.
It has been around now for 31 years. Is it time for a bit of
a revision?
   (Sir Bryan Carsberg) I think that my answer is
really the same, my Lord Chairman. I have not felt in
the matters that have concerned me from the
perspective of one of the United Kingdom
competition authorities that there are sufficiently
serious shortcomings in the present system to
warrant a formal change. With the improvements in
procedures in respect of timing of handling of cases

[Chairman *Contd*]

and so on that the Commission is now introducing one could look for formal rules to enforce those, but in my view these things often work well without formal enforcement rules.

315. What is the route in your view and experience to keep the pressure on the Commission to revise their procedures and get rid of the defects without doing it in a formalistic way?

(Sir Bryan Carsberg) It comes through good and constant contact with the Commission in my view, and in certain parts of my Office we do have a very close working relationship with the Commission. I have already met Mr van Miert, the new Commissioner, and I had very interesting exchanges with him about these new procedures. They are early days, of course, but they are early days as far as the timing of things is concerned and they have to work that through in the context of the resources that they have. I detected a real determination on his part to try to make them work.

316. We have Dr Ehlermann coming next week, and if you have any suggestions about things that we might put to him you might let us have them in a letter—which we will not quote!

(Sir Bryan Carsberg) No doubt you will put to him some of the very interesting questions that you are putting to me.

317. We will certainly probe a bit. Dr Howe, you wish to comment, and would you mention your title or official function?

(Dr Howe) I am head of the Competition Policy Division within the Office of Fair Trading and within that division there is a section that looks after the European Community angle, of which Mr Whitehorn is the head. My Lord Chairman, I wanted only to add that the development of a fairly large series of block exemptions over the last few years into increasingly sophisticated types of agreement perhaps has been stimulated by the sheer volume of work. As another agency in this area I fear that it is often the pressure of work, the backlog of cases, that forces an institution to examine its processes and procedures, and it is clear that there has been some of that within the Commission.

318. Are you in favour of the use of block exemptions?

(Dr Howe) Given Article 85, my Lord Chairman, I think that the answer has to be yes. Article 85 catches so many business agreements and arrangements which the competition authority then has to bless somehow.

319. It is very convenient to reduce the number of cases and areas that have to be probed. Are there relative snags in block exemptions?

(Sir Bryan Carsberg) My Lord Chairman, I think that we should take the view that the answer is yes, provided that decisions are well made. That is bound to be the case when——

320. The answer is yes to what, that it is a good idea to have block exemptions?

(Sir Bryan Carsberg) Yes, that it is a good idea to have block exemptions provided that the decisions

applying them are well made, and I have no doubt that they will be. Block exemptions have the merit that they are given for a relatively short time period and are then reviewable. I think that that is very helpful. One of the problems with the work of a competition authority is that the things that you might do are always very large in relation to what is likely to be regarded as a reasonable expenditure on the activity, and to some extent people have to exercise controls by setting a limit on the resources that one has, it seems to me; and one can argue about whether that should be a bit more or a bit less. Within any practical limit one is going to have to set priorities and that is a perfectly reasonable part of the process, it seems to me.

321. Are there any areas where you think that the Commission ought to introduce now block exemptions where it has not where this would be beneficial to companies?

(Sir Bryan Carsberg) No, I do not think so. I do not know whether Dr Howe is aware of any?

(Dr Howe) My Lord Chairman, I suspect within the intellectual property rights area there may be rather more work still, but the main areas are distribution and purchasing agreements.

322. Across the board or in relation to specific projects?

(Dr Howe) That, I think, is the interesting question, my Lord Chairman, because, as you know better than anyone here, there are the generalised block exemptions and then with footnotes provisions for beer or petrol or whatever, which in a way illustrates the dilemma. They seek to devise some generalised rules to apply to a particular type of business practice and then because beer or petrol or whatever is a bit special they have to devise some rather special arrangements for that product.

323. I am sorry, I asked you whether there were disadvantages flowing from the use of block exemption. You have given us the advantages. Do commercial enterprises find snags in this or do they appreciate it?

(Dr Howe) Personally I should not wish to speak for commerce on this. I should have thought, though, that they would value the block exemption technique rather highly, and from our point of view I suspect that the fear might be that the system becomes too permissive because one has to get the agreements of all Member States and one has to cover such a wide tract and hence rather more is allowed than if you were looking at each case individually, albeit that that would be very time consuming.

324. Another matter that has been referred to by a number of witnesses at which we shall have to look is the use of comfort letters. What are your views about comfort letters? Do you find on the whole that they are variable or that they again have snags? There are a lot of legal issues obviously as to how far they are binding under national competition tribunals and so on and how far people can rely on them.

(Sir Bryan Carsberg) My Lord Chairman, my understanding is that they are not legally binding

[*Chairman Contd*]

although one needs to recognise the weight of authority on your side of the house as far as that goes. I think that all of us who are in this business of competition policy recognise that it is often sensible on a cost-benefit basis to have slightly less formal procedures that work in practice. The fact that one can issue a comfort letter in appropriate cases where it would take time to go through the formal procedures to reach a more formal decision and that that does the job to the satisfaction of the people concerned seems to me to be a good reason for saying that they are worth having.

325. Have they ever gone back on a comfort letter as far as you know?

(*Mr Whitehorn*) Every comfort letter says that the Commission can re-open the case if new facts come to light or circumstances change, but I am not aware of a case where the Commission has actually changed its decision without such a change in circumstances.

Lord Colville of Culross

326. You talk about the people concerned. Who are the people concerned? I am very concerned myself about the transparency of that sort of document. I have met it in other fields where you give waivers to rules of one sort or another. It is very difficult to disperse this so that people know what it is that has been allowed. Indeed, one then gets into a position where you may have to consider objections to the comfort letter because the comfort letter applies only to certain people and other people might wish to object to it in terms if they knew about it. How about transparency?

(*Sir Bryan Carsberg*) I think that I should take the view that the procedures on transparency should match those of the more formal procedures. I should not want to see short cuts taken on transparency. I think that I share what I understand to be your view, which is that it is very important to have good transparency. I do not actually know what the position is on comfort letters as regards transparency.

(*Mr Whitehorn*) The Commission's procedure is developing at the moment. In fact, they have recently started to publish notices in the Official Journal effectively to give people notice of their intention to issue a comfort letter; so that provides an opportunity to, say, competitors to make representations about the matter concerned.

Chairman

327. Do they publish the ultimate decision to issue a comfort letter? Do they actually say: we have issued a comfort letter to X, Y and Z?

(*Mr Whitehorn*) They say: we propose to issue a comfort letter.

328. But after they have done it do they issue a negative notice?

(*Mr Whitehorn*) Not that I am aware of.

329. Should they?

(*Mr Whitehorn*) I think that it is a difficult question.

(*Sir Bryan Carsberg*) I think that our off-the-cuff reaction is, yes, they should. We have not, as you detect, my Lord Chairman, thought about this issue in great depth, but my instinct is to say yes.

Baroness Elles

330. Perhaps I may ask this, my Lord Chairman. Do you find that the commercial enterprises that receive these comfort letters are satisfied or have you had complaints or anxieties expressed to your Office?

(*Sir Bryan Carsberg*) In a sense I think that the position is that if they are not satisfied they can insist on going through the full procedures and get something more formal. I should take it that the way that it works in practice is that there is a mutual convenience in having a comfort letter sometimes and where that is the case, it is what happens. I think that is right, is it not, Mr Whitehorn?

(*Mr Whitehorn*) Yes.

331. Yes, I understand the procedure. I was just wondering whether you have had any evidence or examples of problems arising as a result of comfort letters to people who come to your Office and whether third parties have been affected by comfort letters in this country as a result of the Commission's decisions?

(*Dr Howe*) I cannot think of a case. This is not to say, my Lord Chairman, that we have never had one, and maybe we could just check the records. However, I am not aware of that. Complaints that have been brought to us by companies who have been through the procedure have been more to do with the conduct of a hearing or perhaps the general sort of issue to which the Chairman was alluding, about the same people deciding what the fine shall be as those who have done the investigations. It is that sort of matter that is brought to our attention rather more than individual comfort letters.

Chairman] The evidence that we have had so far, I think, is that really comfort letters do comfort even though people might prefer a speedier final decision.

Lord Holme of Cheltenham

332. My Lord Chairman, I was wondering within your jurisdiction, as it were, or where jurisdictions overlap how you would treat the existence of a comfort letter from the Commission issued to a commercial enterprise in this country? How conclusive an effect would this have on your own deliberations?

(*Sir Bryan Carsberg*) That is an interesting question, my Lord Chairman. I do not think that I have had to face that exactly in those terms. One does, of course, want to accept not only the letter of the law as regards the common market but also the spirit of it. I do support that very much. That would be a factor in my judgment. At the same time I have an important job to do in the United Kingdom and I attach great weight to that as well. In an actual case I think that it might well turn out that the real issue was perhaps about the extent of the coverage of the letter.

[Lord Holme of Cheltenham *Contd*]

It is often not an all or nothing issue, but it might be a question as to whether there were detailed points within the spirit of the approach that needed finer definition or something like that, and one might feel that it would be appropriate for a national authority to take some action in that direction even though one accepted the broad direction of the comfort letter. There was a case a bit like that, though not exactly the same, when I referred not all that long ago to the Monopolies and Mergers Commission the matter of fine fragrances in the United Kingdom. There we had individual exemptions as opposed to block exemptions given to, I think, two perfumiers, so there were individual exemptions, if I remember correctly, and not comfort letters though we understood that the Commission might well proceed by issuing comfort letters to others in the industry. There I thought it right to make a reference notwithstanding the existence of the European position because I was concerned about not the principle really but rather the details of the application, and the perfumiers were being allowed to apply a selective distribution policy broadly defined and I wondered whether perhaps it needed defining a bit more precisely or whether it was being provided evenhandedly. I think that it often turns on that kind of an issue.

Chairman

333. We heard some evidence about the two cases to which you refer and a certain amount of disquiet about the way that it has been done. Are you aware of the extent to which other national authorities would respond to Lord Holme's question? Do other national authorities give full effect to comfort letters or do they regard this as something that because it is not legally binding they can go behind?
(Sir Bryan Carsberg) I do not know, my Lord Chairman. I do not know whether Mr Whitehorn does. Mr Whitehorn worked for the Commission for a period on secondment so he often knows things from an inside point of view, but on this occasion I am afraid that we do not know.

334. Do national authorities themselves issue comfort letters?
(Sir Bryan Carsberg) No, not exactly as such. Someone who is proposing a merger, of course, can obtain confidential guidance on that merger, which is a somewhat similar procedure really, I suppose. We do not call it a comfort letter, but it is guidance rather than a binding decision because, being confidential, it has to be undertaken without the benefit of public consultation. It is a matter where the Secretary of State for Trade and Industry makes the decision although we in fact communicate it to the authorities concerned. I suppose that you could say that is an analogy.

335. It is an equivalent really or comparable.
(Sir Bryan Carsberg) Yes.
(Dr Howe) There is, I suppose, a more formal analogy in the United States and Canada which have business review programmes or advance clearance certificates in the Canadian setup which are akin to comfort letters. These are all systems where the law prohibits certain kinds of behaviour and one is in a more legalistic scenario system from the word go whereas our system is administrative in effect from the word go.

336. Is there any place for discomfort letters?
(Sir Bryan Carsberg) I think that might be the reference, yes!

337. Is there room in your view for a halfway house between the comfort letter and a final commission full decision? Do you think that it would be possible and would it be worthwhile to have a procedure whereby once an agreement had been notified and published so that third parties could comment that should be given binding clearance unless there was a challenge within a fixed period of time?
(Sir Bryan Carsberg) I think that my reaction to that would be one of some caution, my Lord Chairman. I can see that it would be valuable as part of a plan to make sure that time limits were stuck to. I think that I should prefer though that the normal outcome would be expected to be a positive statement of decision rather than allowing time to pass because that would give one more assurance that the thing was decided on good analysis, and that is really what one wants.

338. On the other hand if there were no objections maybe in order to speed things up and get through some back log this would be helpful in a simple case?
(Dr Howe) My Lord Chairman, if Article 85(1) is interpreted very narrowly so that it catches various agreements which on some rather broader analysis of their effects you would have thought did not have any adverse effects on competition, on a hypothesis like that, then it seems to me that there is quite a lot of merit in some proposal of the kind that you outline. Take our own Restrictive Trade Practices Act, for instance, which catches a lot of agreements that frankly the Office of Fair Trading would rather not have to deal with; it would be rather a neat solution if one could say that if nobody had objected within X weeks or X months and nothing had been brought to our attention they should automatically be allowed without any further process. If, however, the law is more focused on anti-competitive arrangements then I think that our Director General's concerns become much more important. Article 85 is a very widely drafted provision.

339. So there might be a limited scope for using this halfway house procedure?
(Dr Howe) Exactly.

340. Unless any of their Lordships have further questions on this aspect, may we perhaps go back to procedural matters. We have heard quite a lot about the hearing officer so far and we are getting rather interested not only in what he does but perhaps also in what he ought to do. Would you like to comment on his function? Do you see ways of improving it? Should he be given a different status? Should he be

[Chairman *Contd*]

made independent of DG IV? Does he need to multiply so that there is more than one hearing officer?

(*Sir Bryan Carsberg*) Broadly, my Lord Chairman, we think that it has been a useful development and that it has worked quite well. There is the question of transparency that we have already discussed in a different context. We have some feeling that there should be transparency for the report of the hearing officer. I do not in fact know how the resources problem bites. I am aware that it is a pretty small operation, though I think a valuable one; and whether or not they have the resources to do what is set out for them I am not really in a position to comment on authoritively. I do not know whether Edward Whitehorn may know more about that.

341. Mr Whitehorn, what do you see as his real value?

(*Mr Whitehorn*) My Lord Chairman, at the moment his role is largely restricted to the oral hearing and he acts there as a kind of referee to ensure that the parties have a fair hearing. In so far as that is his rather restricted role I think that he performs that function well. If I may return to Sir Bryan's point, I think that the resources are sufficient to enable him to carry out that function adequately.

342. I take it that he makes a report?

(*Mr Whitehorn*) He does make a report, yes, my Lord Chairman.

343. Do the parties see that?

(*Mr Whitehorn*) No, they do not, my Lord Chairman.

344. Should they?

(*Mr Whitehorn*) Yes, I think they should. I think that is the point that Sir Bryan made about transparency.

345. And in your view?

(*Mr Whitehorn*) Yes, I think it should be made available.

346. Do you think that there is a need to extend his function so that he does not just concern himself with the oral hearing? Ought he to be supervising the whole process of the enquiry taking decisions on any procedural issue that arises between the parties and the Commission?

(*Mr Whitehorn*) My Lord Chairman, I think that you have to look at that question in the context of the whole procedure. If you were to propose a radical reform of the Commission's procedure, there might indeed be a place for the hearing officer to have a much wider role. Looking at it in isolation, I think that it is rather difficult to see that he should be grafted on to the existing procedures. That might be quite difficult in practice:

Chairman] But some of the witnesses who have come before the Committee have suggested that there is a serious need for somebody to be able to say to the Commission, yes, you must produce this document, yes, you must give this kind of access, yes, you must do.this, that or the other, that is, done by someone at a certain level with a certain independence and

a certain status who would be obeyed by the Commission. It would be a new role for the hearing officer?

Lord Colville of Culross] It is the analogy of the master, is it not?

Chairman

347. Indeed, the analogy of the master?

(*Mr Whitehorn*) I think that there is certainly an argument to be made for that, although I should doubt whether there are a large number of those sort of disputes which need to be solved during the course of proceedings before the Commission. There is, of course, always recourse to the court in Luxembourg although that is limited.

348. Yes, but that takes a long time.

349. One or two of our witnesses have seen that he could have a function, as Lord Colville said, similar to that of a master with the right of appeal by the court of appeal or a right of review by the court of appeal, by the court of first instance. Do you think that there is a need for that or do you think that the evidence perhaps was exaggerating the problems?

(*Mr Whitehorn*) My Lord Chairman, I can think of cases where I think that it would have been useful from the parties' point of view and might have facilitated the procedure, but I should hesitate to say that I think that there is a general need in so far as most cases would benefit from that sort of facility.

350. What he does I think would be very much linked with supervision by the court of first instance. We put to some of the witnesses the question, should there be a special procedure devised to have a rapid interlocutory appeal to the court of first instance from the hearing officer. This is moving into a new area of supervision to get rid of the criticism that people are making about the way that the Commission conducts these enquiries. It is no use having an interlocutory appeal that is going to take a year or two years and that is going to hold everything up; what you want is rather like an appeal to a judge in chambers.

(*Sir Bryan Carsberg*) I was going to say, my Lord Chairman, that it is the sort of thing that is covered in British procedures, is it not? My view rather is that some extra procedural safeguard in that area is the kind of thing one might well think of putting in if one were designing a system from a blank sheet and trying to get the best possible system. If one looks at it rather as a question of how serious have the actual experiences been in terms of shortcomings in this area and is it a high priority, indeed, I think from our own experience we should say that we have not seen evidence to show that there are many serious problems at the moment.

351. Perhaps it is the customers that would?

(*Sir Bryan Carsberg*) Yes, perhaps it is for them to make the case to you, my Lord Chairman.

352. Yes, I realise that, Sir Bryan. I just wondered whether you had any view.

(*Sir Bryan Carsberg*) I did emphasise, from our point of view.

Baroness Elles

353. My Lord Chairman, I was just going to ask Sir Bryan this. There will possibly be many cases of firms who have had problems of access to files but this would not necessarily come across his desk or those of his Office?

(*Sir Bryan Carsberg*) Indeed, my Lord Chairman, I acknowledge that.

354. I thought that would probably be an element that would not come within your purview.

(*Sir Bryan Carsberg*) Indeed.

(*Dr Howe*) I think that firms widely appreciate that we are not there as a court of appeal in any sense to the Commission so they may well not bring these matters to us.

Chairman

355. That is precisely why I put the question.

(*Dr Howe*) I guess that we should also have a certain sympathy for the case officer who is pursuing the case with the hearing officer looking over his shoulder at every step that he takes trying to develop the case. We have a bit of sympathy for him, I think!

Lord Holme of Cheltenham] My Lord Chairman, I think that we are interrogating very proficient gamekeepers on improved rights for poachers!

Chairman

356. If they had a more effective system of gamekeeping in the Commission it might be something that we could learn by. What about the Advisory Committee, Sir Bryan? This is another organisation that we have been asking about. Do you feel that it has a useful role, and should it be improved? ·

(*Sir Bryan Carsberg*) Oh, yes, my Lord Chairman.

357. What is its value?

(*Sir Bryan Carsberg*) Its value is that it is one important means by which the authorities in the Member States can establish communication with the Commission and by which they have the opportunity to express views, including views on the extent to which there may be special considerations that come up from the national market. Its existence makes it more certain that the Commission will give weight to the views of Member State authorities, and that I think is very important because we have an element of expertise in the conditions in our local market.

358. From your point of view, Sir Bryan, I can see the value of this. There has been a lot of criticism about the fact that the Advisory Committee report is not published or even produced to the parties. Do you think that it should be in the interests of transparency?

(*Sir Bryan Carsberg*) I should favour publication, my Lord Chairman, yes.

359. General publication?

(*Sir Bryan Carsberg*) Yes.

360. Or publication to the parties?

(*Sir Bryan Carsberg*) Yes.

361. Which?

(*Sir Bryan Carsberg*) General publication.

Baroness Elles

362. Do you think that Member State governments would really wish their officials on the Advisory Committee to be felt to be tied down to having their reports published when in some cases, I should imagine, they are dealing with confidential matters as far as the Member State in question is concerned as opposed to the client?

(*Sir Bryan Carsberg*) Oh, I see, as opposed to the client. I think that there is an understanding between the authorities and governments—and in a sense government is one of the authorities—that there are different kinds of issues: on the one hand there are cases that concern the behaviour of companies or whatever and on the other hand there are matters of national policy. I should take the view that as far as matters of national policy are concerned, although I might want to give advice to our Government from the perspective of the competition authority, the final decision there must be for the Government. That is the way that our system works, and I accept that readily. That kind of decision is not something for the Advisory Committee, although the Advisory Committee is there to give views on cases. Where it comes to cases, I think my view there would be that the idea that one is a professional in the field of competition policy doing one's job independently of day to day political issues is very important—it is a principle to which I attach very great importance. While I recognise that it is sometimes difficult to draw the dividing line it seems to me that on the whole it can be drawn and I believe in openness in that area. Therefore, I think that on that side of things—the side with which I am concerned, that is, looking at cases—one should have transparency, and any slight difficulty at the margin is slight enough that the need for transparency would override it.

363. I realise the position of your Office of course, Director General, but I am just wondering from the point of view of an official coming from the Department of Trade and Industry, who would presumably be the person on the Advisory Committee, whether there would be some sort of constraint where a government position would be discussed in the Advisory Committee meeting and whether those people would feel that it was right that you could have a full and frank discussion and know that this was going to be reported in public as a result. That is my only concern.

(*Sir Bryan Carsberg*) It would be for the Department of Trade and Industry to express their side of the view; I have given you mine.

(*Mr Whitehorn*) My Lord Chairman, may I just add a word. I think that it is important to distinguish between publishing the opinion of the Committee and publishing the whole proceedings. If it is in fact only the opinion which is published (I am sure that you have seen the opinions published from the mergers Advisory Committee) it does not necessarily reveal very much about the stand taken by a particular government on a particular issue. I am sure that the Advisory Committee itself, if it were aware of the fact that it was to be published, would

[Baroness Elles *Contd*]

fashion it in an appropriate way to avoid those conflicts.

364. That is a restriction on transparency, putting up a curtain over the window?

(Mr Whitehorn) It is in a way, but it is necessary for just the reasons that you were outlining. It is an improvement on not saying anything at all.

365. Better than nothing, but not as good as it could be?

(Sir Bryan Carsberg) My Lord Chairman, let me just add to that that one would wish to see a good indication given of the analysis that was in the minds of people who contributed to the decision making.

Lord Skidelsky

366. My Lord Chairman, this is only a very marginal point at this stage. Sir Bryan, you used the tantalising phrase "professional in competition policy". What sort of individual would that be? What sort of qualifications would he have?

(Sir Bryan Carsberg) I hope me and my staff, my Lord Chairman.

367. It relates to something that has been mentioned in some of the evidence that we have heard about economic criteria. We are talking really about legal processes here. What would a professional in competition policy have had in the way of training?

(Sir Bryan Carsberg) You must forgive me, my prejudices will show——

368. Well, I should like them to show!

(Sir Bryan Carsberg)—and they may be similar to yours. I think it is the training in economics that is fundamental to what I have in mind. Of course, I do not pretend, especially when talking to you, that the outcome is at all simple or that many economists would necessarily agree on a particular case, but I do believe that the process of thinking about a competition policy problem employs economic analysis and is the main structure that one should use in what I characterised as a professional approach to competition policy.

369. If I may just follow up on that, my Lord Chairman, do you believe that that view is generally accepted in Directorate General IV?

(Sir Bryan Carsberg) I have never actually discussed it with them in these particular terms. I said earlier that I have a high regard for competition policy as an element of the things that we do in the European Community and my impression in my own contact with members of DG IV has been that they are professional in their approach in the sense that I have described it.

(Dr Howe) My Lord Chairman, I think that it is more common on the continent for officials working in this area to have some grounding both in economics and in law. That is relatively unusual here, although Mr Whitehorn, if I may say so, is an example. When we look at the European Commission's draft decisions or, indeed, final decisions, I think that it could be said that where we

have reservations they have often been on the sort of underlying economic analysis such as defining the market and this sort of thing which concerns us much more than an anxiety about the legal process, for instance. Most of our work is looking at these early draft decisions. That is where the economic approach perhaps comes in.

Chairman

370. The usual complaints that I hear are that it is judges who do not understand economics.

(Sir Bryan Carsberg) And no doubt they have a criticism of their own of economists, my Lord Chairman.

371. One of the points that you make in your submission is that you think that it is a good idea to authorise Member States to use Article 13 of Regulation 17 in order to carry out investigations. I wonder, Sir Bryan, whether you or one of your colleagues would like to elaborate on that? What are the benefits of this?

(Sir Bryan Carsberg) Perhaps I may begin, my Lord Chairman, and then see whether my colleagues wish to add anything. The first thing to say, I think, is that we did not see this as a profound issue of principle but rather more one of practice. It works well. For one thing it is a way of effectively increasing our involvement in the work of the Commission, which is valuable in its own way. It is also, of course, a way of allowing for troughs and peaks in demands on Commission resources in that if they are conducting an investigation that requires simultaneous action in several Member States at once it may be a strain on their resources over a very short time period where bringing in the Member States can help to ease things. From that point of view, therefore, we think that it is a beneficial procedure, but, as I say, it is not something of great dramatic significance.

(Dr Howe) We have, of course, my Lord Chairman, I think since this Committee's 1982 report, always accompanied European Commission officials on inspections within the United Kingdom. There was a feeling in those early days that this was another referee role, rather like the hearing officer role. There is, therefore, quite a lot of expertise within the Office as far as these sorts of inspections and investigations are concerned which we cannot conduct under domestic law, of course, so that it is relatively easy for my colleagues to embark on one of these investigations on behalf of the Commission on our own because we have been accompanying these officials from Brussels.

Chairman] Do you have any feeling as to whether this could be done equally well or could be done at all in other Member States?

Lord Colville of Culross

372. My Lord Chairman, that is the question that I was going to ask.

(Sir Bryan Carsberg) I think that it would vary from Member State to Member State and that is

[Lord Colville of Culross *Contd*]

something which the Commission can adapt to in its procedures. It does not have to behave in exactly the same way in all cases.

Chairman] Thank you. I should like now to turn to a different subject, that is, mergers. Lord Holme, I do not know whether you have any questions that you would like to put to the witnesses before you leave in relation to mergers?

Lord Holme of Cheltenham] My Lord Chairman, no, thank you.

Chairman

373. May we perhaps talk about the lowering of the thresholds, which, as you know, has been discussed. Can you tell us what your views are about that, Sir Bryan?

(Sir Bryan Carsberg) My Lord Chairman, I said in the paper that in principle I was not opposed to a lowering of thresholds. I did not say that I was shouting for a lowering of thresholds as a strong matter of principle. I think that the present arrangements have worked well. One can see that there are certain advantages in the lowering of the threshold. One can see that it might increase the benefits of the so-called one-stop-shop for companies in that it would reduce for them the costs of the undertaking because they would go to the Commission and have it all dealt with there rather than perhaps going to several authorities separately. One gathers that there are not enormously strong pressures on the part of industry for a change in the thresholds. One can also see the case for a change in terms of the concept of the single market because there may be other cases which should be caught and the present tests do not necessarily capture all the cases that one thinks might be caught. On the other hand, of course, the more one extends the coverage of the Regulation, the more the danger that things with a very high proportion of local content would actually be caught, and one would want to see procedures for making sure that things with substantial local content are appropriately dealt with.

374. Can you give the balance between what is done nationally and what is done in the Community right other than by thresholds? Are there other delimiting or other lines of demarcation that could be used?

(Sir Bryan Carsberg) My Lord Chairman, I should have thought that perhaps thresholds would be a sensible way to do it in practice in terms of practicability and so on, although, of course, there are various ways that one can juggle the balance of the overall size test and the test in relation to how much happens in the Community and in the individual Member States of the Community. There are various ways that one could construct size tests there. I just wanted to conclude the general observation, my Lord Chairman, by saying that of course what I have said is my view from the point of view of a competition authority, and I should want to recognise that this is very much a matter for Government in the context of their having a political agenda which is for them and not for me.

375. This in a way links with the idea of a split jurisdiction, which can happen if you get more than one bid?

(Sir Bryan Carsberg) Yes, my Lord Chairman.

376. Do you find that that is a problem or not?

(Sir Bryan Carsberg) People say that it is a problem. I am not sure that I am really convinced that it is a problem. People said that it was a problem in relation to the well known recent case of the Midland Bank where we had the Lloyds bid that fell under United Kingdom jurisdiction and the Hong Kong and Shanghai bid that fell under EC jurisdiction. There we saw the process working effectively, I thought, and producing a not unreasonable decision. It seems to me that if both parts of the procedure are working as they should then the chance that one will get bad decisions coming out is perhaps rather slight. I suppose that the only thing that you might say, taking that case further as an example, is that if it had actually gone to the Monopolies and Mergers Commission—that is, the Lloyds bid for Midland—they might have decided that it was in the public interest and because Lloyds were not willing to sustain their bid through a Monopolies and Mergers Commission investigation it did not come to that, so an opportunity was lost.

377. Theoretically there is obviously the possibility of real conflict of jurisdiction here and real difficulty in practice. You do not see that having happened so far?

(Sir Bryan Carsberg) No, my Lord Chairman. It is not the role of the competition authorities to say whether they prefer this bid or that bid. The role of competition authorities is to decide whether one or more of them should be stopped because they fail a go or no go kind of test. If more than one bid passes the test then it is a matter for shareholders to resolve through the way that these things are resolved. That being so, I hope that it is relatively unlikely that there would be a problem coming out of this.

Lord Skidelsky

378. In paragraph 13 of your written evidence you said that the lowering of turnover thresholds would have the effect of bringing more mergers under the Commission's jurisdiction, which is obviously correct. You also said that you would not be opposed in principle to that. Are there any robust economic reasons for lowering the threshold?

(Sir Bryan Carsberg) I think that the argument for it would be that it would achieve greater consistency with greater certainty in the application of policy across the Community, which would be desirable perhaps given the concept of the common market.

379. There are always opportunity costs?

(Sir Bryan Carsberg) Yes, I agree. On the other hand, my Lord Chairman, I should recognise that it is working quite well at the moment. Given what I said about the split jurisdiction you will understand that I do not think that the present system has led to

[Lord Skidelsky Contd]

regrettable decisions in a very obvious kind of way. One would not necessarily have made exactly the same decisions, but the process I think is working well enough and there are no great anomalies coming out of it. One might feel therefore on a cost-benefit basis that there is no very great need for change.

380. Would you say that a lowering of the threshold would in current circumstances be justified if one was trying to apply the principle of subsidiarity seriously or would you regard the principle of subsidiarity in this case as part of those wider political considerations to which you were referring?

(Sir Bryan Carsberg) There may be a political dimension to the concept of subsidiarity, but I think that there is also a dimension that interests me, that is, that it is very possible that given the Community—particularly as we find it today—there will be different conditions in particular markets from country to country and that something that is acceptable in one part of the Community would perhaps not be acceptable in another part. My view of competition policy is that pretty heavy weight must be given to anti-competitive effects or opportunities, if you will, for abuse of a dominant position in large parts of the economic community and often Member States are well placed to be the ones to evaluate those. Therefore, I should certainly be concerned about the subsidiarity dimension of the problem, and it would be a sine qua non in my own mind of any change that there should be adequate protections about that.

381. I have just one last point, if I may, my Lord Chairman. From your knowledge of competition regimes in various member countries do we have one of the more robust regimes? Is part of this attempt to lower the turnover threshold an attempt also to counteract weaknesses in competition policy at the national level?

(Sir Bryan Carsberg) We have perhaps a rather unusual system in some ways though that may be less true of mergers than it is of other aspects of competition policy. In practice I think that our regime is pretty robust even though in effect it involves several people, several players, if you will. The Monopolies and Mergers Commission and the Secretary of State at least have to agree on the outcome, and I am involved in the process at different stages. It is robust I think in the sense that things do not get through that by accident. Different people of course will take different views about the outcome that one should want to see on a particular case. One could imagine more draconian regimes, but I think that ours works pretty well in practice and I should not in fact see any wish to compensate for a weakness there as part of the argument that was relevant in my own mind to the threshold decision.

(Dr Howe) My Lord Chairman, I am sure that it is a relevant fact—I am not sure of its significance—that a number of Member States have adopted domestic merger control since the Regulation came in. As recently as three years ago there were only four countries with merger control, and the British at least is the oldest.

Chairman

382. Do you have much contact with the Commission in regard to merger control regulation?

(Dr Howe) Very considerable, my Lord Chairman. The Office is in the lead, so to speak, in the early days of the processing of any merger case. They are all notified to the Office and colleagues will assess the notification and take a view and consult the Department of Trade and Industry and others. So, yes, we are heavily involved in cases.

(Sir Bryan Carsberg) And cases in general cross my desk as part of the process, of course.

383. Has there been much problem with the claiming of protection of legitimate interests by Member States under the jurisdiction of the provisions of Article 21?

(Sir Bryan Carsberg) My Lord Chairman, I do not think that there have been any cases at all.

(Dr Howe) It has never become a real issue in any case that I am aware of. It is part of our assessment to consider whether there might be, and from time to time the possibility has been aired between officials that some case might raise a legitimate national interest, but it has never come through to the front of any case of which I can think, my Lord Chairman.

384. So at the moment there is no change that you would make in the provisions of the merger control regulation, Article 21, in respect of the right of Member States to claim?

(Dr Howe) Not that I am aware of, my Lord Chairman. It was a matter of high interest at the time that the thing was formulated and I think that there was an assumption that it might well be invoked if not by this Member State perhaps by other Member States, but it has not to my knowledge been a very prominent feature at all.

(Sir Bryan Carsberg) One can see the need for it, my Lord Chairman, but it has not been a practical problem in our experience.

385. So you do not want us to say that it should be changed?

(Sir Bryan Carsberg) No, my Lord Chairman.

386. Let us then get to two last matters. I raised the question of mergers because, as you saw, one of the members of the Committee had to leave. In paragraph 26 in the written memorandum you say that "encourage the Commission to continue with and further develop" the approach of the referring back of cases to you. How does that work in practice?

(Sir Bryan Carsberg) I wonder whether reference back was really the right term, my Lord Chairman. Sometimes it is a matter that they decide not to take action in the knowledge that we are taking action. I had my first experience of this kind of situation when I was Director General of the Office of Telecommunications and a case arose that could have been dealt with under European law and, indeed, the complainants took their case to the European Commission with copies to my Office. I began an investigation because I thought it right to do so and the Commission took the view that in those

[Chairman *Contd*]

particular circumstances, first, there were effective means of dealing with it under national law, and they noted that we were intending to deal with it under national law anyway. They were also in the position where their own resources were such that it would be difficult to fit this in. They did not regard it as a high priority in the context of using their resources so they told everybody, myself included, that they would leave it to us. That seems a sensible and helpful thing to do in a case that is predominantly concerning one particular country perhaps although it could be dealt with under European law, where the country has the means to deal with it, both legal and administrative, and actually intends to deal with it. The Commission is not stopped from coming in and taking action again in the future, it will not have fettered its discretion; it will simply be taking the view that this seems an appropriate way to move things forward.

387. Is this better than the Commission's proposals for co-operation with national authorities? As you know, they have proposed that there should be closer co-operation with the courts of Member States? Do you think this is a substitute for that?

(Sir Bryan Carsberg) I think that they both have a role. I do not see why one would rule out one because one had the other. I am very much in favour of closer relationships between the national authorities and the Commission, and I am confident that that can happen. It has happened to a good extent already and I think that it will continue to evolve. I do not think that the national courts perhaps would play a very big role, and, of course, it would be a matter—at least, as things stand at present—for the individuals concerned in a case to take action rather than for the Office of Fair Trading to take action because we do not have the legal power to do it. I think that there is a role for both, my Lord Chairman.

Baroness Elles

388. My Lord Chairman, perhaps I can come in on Sir Bryan's comment on the case to which he was referring. Would you say, Sir Bryan, that it was in fact because your Office was going to investigate and they knew that it would be done efficiently and competently and this is a matter of practice between yourselves and good relations with the Commission would not necessarily be a ground rule in every case?

(Sir Bryan Carsberg) Yes, I think that the Commission would look for certain conditions to be met and one of them would be the expectation that it could be well handled in the individual country, yes.

Chairman

389. Do you not think that in this country we should adopt Articles 85 and 86 for purely domestic practices or agreements, taking out obviously the reference to affecting trade between the Member States?

(Sir Bryan Carsberg) My Lord Chairman, you will be aware—and you did say for purely domestic purposes?

390. Yes?

(Sir Bryan Carsberg)—that the Government has indicated its intention to reform the restrictive trade practices legislation, the 1989 White Paper, and that is something to which I attach great importance. I think that it will lead to a more efficient procedure. We await eagerly news of when legislative time will be found for that.

391. Would you support the idea of, as it were, adopting Article 85 and Article 86 suitably modified into British legislation? There is a lot already in the Restrictive Practices Act.

(Sir Bryan Carsberg) Development along the lines of the White Paper, which is Article 85 stuff, is very much what we are looking for, my Lord Chairman. As far as Article 86 is concerned, you will be aware also of the government green paper and subsequent announcement of a decision not to move to an Article 86 type system here.

392. Is that right or wrong in your view—or perhaps I should say, good or bad?

(Sir Bryan Carsberg) I think that a competition authority such as us is bound to have mixed views. On the one hand we see the value of the deterrence of a prohibition system like Article 86; on the other hand we see great value in the flexibility of our existing system as far as making complex monopoly references are concerned in particular, and I should have been very reluctant to lose that flexibility. There are some things that one can achieve under that which seem to me to be important that one cannot achieve in practice under a prohibition system. I suppose that a competition authority is a bit inclined to say, I should like the best of both worlds, but one has to recognise the burden that that involves and that it is perhaps politically unrealistic to expect it in present circumstances. Therefore, I am not unhappy—I apologise for the double negative, my Lord Chairman, but it sometimes expresses one's feelings.

393. It is like not proven. Finally as far as I am concerned, Sir Bryan, we have had criticism of the fact that the Commission may change its fining policy and people do not know what sort of level and standard they are going to adopt. It is said to be very much better if people could know in advance what sort of fines they will be liable for. Do you have any views about the Commission's policy here? Do you think that it ought to be made more transparent or do you think that they should retain the right to fine as and when they think fit?

(Sir Bryan Carsberg) It is not an area to which I have given a great deal of thought. That is partly an indication that we think the system works well enough without serious problems, and it would be enormously difficult to define the considerations that would go into setting the sort of scale of penalties.

394. We said in the court that the Commission could change its fining policy without giving notice that it was going to do so subject to a review of the reasons. You accept that, do you?

(Sir Bryan Carsberg) Yes, I need say no more in that case, my Lord Chairman.

[Chairman *Contd*]

395. Is there anything else that any one of you would like to add?

(Sir Bryan Carsberg) No, my Lord Chairman, we are delighted to have had the opportunity to give evidence.

(Dr Howe) No, thank you.

Lord Colville of Culross

396. My Lord Chairman, there is just one matter that I should like to ask, if I may. We have heard from a robust and well established national authority. Would it go too far to ask whether our witnesses have any comments about other national authorities either in conjunction with or separately from the way that their courts function because, after all, we are talking about a system that operates across the Community?

(Sir Bryan Carsberg) Yes.

397. I am very interested in how it works elsewhere.

(Sir Bryan Carsberg) Yes, so am I, my Lord Chairman. It often seems to me when one is thinking about what should be done in Europe at the Commission level and what should be done in the Member State that one is a bit inclined to think, well, it is my show in the Member State to some extent and it will be done well enough therefore. The main purpose of having a European policy is perhaps to encourage good competition policy elsewhere partly for the benefits that it will bring to one's own companies which want to compete fairly in those places, but also, of course, because it is good for consumers in the Community. I think that there is an element of that. It would be quite wrong for me to pick out individual countries and say to you, I think this is a weak one, or, I think that is a weak one. I have not done the kind of work that would justify that kind of pronouncement. We do have a particular working relationship with the Bundeskartellamt and the French authority, and I have established that for myself during the year that I have been in office in the Office of Fair Trading and find it helpful with the exchange of views and so on and I am very encouraged by what I find in those two cases. I do not have a detailed knowledge of the other Member States yet.

398. In so far as the national authorities taking part in these processes, for instance, in investigations are concerned, it would be valuable, would it not, if there was an equivalent of competence and expertise across the country?

(Sir Bryan Carsberg) Yes, my Lord Chairman.

399. Perhaps learning from what happens here and in France and Germany?

(Sir Bryan Carsberg) Yes.

400. So it may be universally applicable?

(Sir Bryan Carsberg) Yes, that would be very valuable. In many ways I think that these things work best if there is an element of growing up from the national level as well as imposition at the European level; and, quite apart from that, there is a need independently. Yes, I agree with you. My Lord Chairman, Dr Howe knows much more about this than I do in detail.

(Dr Howe) My Lord Chairman, there is a process of convergence at work within European countries. Given the European Community law, good or bad, people are converging their national laws on it. I think that there is more similarity of approach to at least case analysis and more similarity of law than is perhaps often perceived, and I think that this process of convergence will accelerate.

Chairman

401. Have we reached the stage where all of them are doing something? At one time it was the Germans and ourselves and maybe one or two others halfheartedly, but the rest were really a very long way behind. Does everybody now have a system?

(Dr Howe) The Italians have now got a very good looking law, my Lord Chairman, very similar to Article 85 and Article 86 and a robust looking competition authority. It will be very interesting to see how they apply themselves.

402. I will not ask you the obvious question! Sir Bryan, Mr Whitehorn and Dr Howe, thank you very much for giving up the time to come and see us. It is very good to have such an authoritative team to help us on what we think is a very important enquiry. We are very grateful to you.

(Sir Bryan Carsberg) My Lord Chairman, thank you for the opportunity. We were delighted to be involved.

WEDNESDAY 16 JUNE 1993

Present:

Allen of Abbeydale, L.
Archer of Sandwell, L.
Elles, B.
Hacking, L.

Holme of Cheltenham, L.
Slynn of Hadley, L. (Chairman)
Wedderburn of Charlton, L.

**Memorandum by Dr Claus-Dieter Ehlermann,
Director-General for Competition, European Commission**

I. INTRODUCTION

I take great personal pleasure in having the opportunity to present evidence to the Select Committee. The 1981–1982 Report on Competition Practice proved to be a very important document and was highly influential in the Commission's thinking during the 1980s, when many of the Committee's recommendations were put into practice[1].

I welcome the fact the Committee has now decided to re-examine this matter. Not only have many of the changes introduced during the 1980s now become an accepted part of the Commission's procedure in competition cases, but many new and, I believe, far reaching reforms have recently been introduced or are now being actively considered by the Commission.

These developments can be classified under three main headings: the rights of defence, procedural efficiency, and subsidiarity in relation to Articles 85(1) and 86. I shall consider these issues separately, and then address the issue of the Review of the Merger Regulation.

II. THE RIGHTS OF DEFENCE

1. *Introduction*

I am pleased to be able to report that almost all of the recommendations of the Select Committee in its 1982 Report have been implemented by the Commission and now form part of its standard procedure in competition cases. This can be seen from the following analysis of the points raised by the Committee in 1982.

2. *Inspection powers of the Commission*

In its 1981–1982 Report the Select Committee recommended that, whilst the "indications are that the Commission's exercise of its power [to adopt a decision pursuant to Article 14(3) of Council Regulation 17/62 to submit to an inspection] has not been unreasonable or injudicious . . . it would no doubt be an improvement if its exercise could be made subject to some appropriate independent authorisation. Article 14(3) of Regulation No. 17 could be amended so as to provide that leave of the President of the European Court or of a judge nominated by him should be obtained before a decision requiring an undertaking to submit to investigation is made".

At present, if an undertaking fails to submit to a Commission decision ordering an investigation, the Commission calls upon the aid of the Competent Authority of the relevant Member State, requesting it to "afford the necessary assistance to the officials authorised by the Commission to enable them to make their investigation"[2]. The procedure for providing this assistance varies from Member State to Member State, as it depends on the national legislation giving effect to this obligation. However, it is clear that in some countries the officials of the Member State concerned must request a Court order from a national judge enforcing the Commission decision. Failure to submit to this court order would constitute contempt, leaving the undertaking concerned open to sanction. The Court of Justice[3] has stated that during such a procedure "it is within the powers of the national body, after satisfying itself that the decision ordering the investigation is authentic, to consider whether the measures of constraint envisaged are arbitrary or excessive having regard to the subject matter of the investigation and to

---

[1]See in this respect the Thirteenth Competition Report, pages 60–67.

[2]Article 14(6), Regulation 17/62.

[3]See Hoechst v Commission, Judgment of the Court of Justice, 21 September 1989, ECR [1989] 2919.

ensure that the rules of national law are complied with in the application of those measures". Although the discretion available to the national court is strictly limited in carrying out this function[1], it is inevitable that it could lead to the application of different standards of review, not least due to possibly differing interpretations of the Court of Justice's judgment. If the European Courts did review a Commission decision adopted pursuant to Article 14(3) of Regulation 17 before the inspection took place, any remaining doubts as to the need for a national court to review it would be removed. For this reason, as well as those regarding the need to make it absolutely apparent that all of the Community's procedures provide the highest possible level of guarantees for the protection of human rights, I would favour a procedure by which the leave of a Judge at the Court of First Instance or the Court of Justice would be obtained prior to carrying-out of inspections[2].

However, it is clear that such a development requires the amendment of Regulation 17, and also probably requires an amendment of the texts defining the responsibilities of the Court of First Instance or the Court of Justice. As the existing systems work, allbeit imperfectly, this change is not, however, presently one of the Commission's highest priorities.

3. *Access to file*

It is a vast over-simplification to state simply that the Commission is both judge and jury in competition cases. This excludes the important and increasing role of the European Courts. However, it is correct that the Commission does have a wide jurisdiction in this area, and, in exercising this jurisdiction, must be absolutely certain that it fully respects the right to be heard, *inter alia,* of companies that are the subject of infringement proceedings. This obligation on the Commission stems from the general principle in Community law of the right to a fair hearing[3]. Article 19 of Regulation 17/62 gives effect to this principle, stating that before taking an infringement decision etc. "the Commission shall give the undertakings or associations of undertakings concerned the opportunity of being heard on the matters to which the Commission has taken objection". The Commission is absolutely committed to ensure that it meets the highest standards in this respect. Not only is this stage of the Commission's procedure necessary to give effect to a fundamental principle of Community law, it is also of benefit to DGIV. Occasionally, the hearing of the parties makes it clear that some or all of our concerns are unfounded, or that it is necessary further to develop our arguments to ensure that they are watertight. Equally, in other cases, the exercise of trying to defend a clear infringement of the competition rules has led companies to accept the existence of the infringement, introducing, for example, a compliance programme.

Access to certain of the documents collected by the Commission during its enquiry is an integral and vital aspect of the procedure that guarantees this right to be heard. As the Court of Justice has stated on a number of occasions, in order to meet its obligations in this respect the Commission is obliged to disclose to the defendants in infringement proceedings all the documents on which it is relying in order to prove its case. It is not obliged to give the companies concerned access to its entire file[4], although it is, I believe, obliged to provide to the companies concerned documents that are manifestly exculpatory in relation to the allegations raised by the Commission[5].

However, recognising that the entire decision-making process benefits from the maximum possible degree of disclosure of the documents that it has available, the Commission announced in its Eleventh Competition Report that it had decided to allow undertakings access to much of its file when preparing their defence to a Statement of Objections[6]. This "access to file" was stated to be subject to the

[1]In fact, the Court's judgment in the Hoechst case should, it is submitted, be read to indicate that although a national court may ensure that the measures that the Member State proposes to take to enforce the Commission decision are not "arbitrary or excessive" it may not review the correctness of the Commission decision ordering the inspection, which is the exclusive competence of the European Courts.

[2]See paragraph 24 of the 1981–1982 Report of the Select Committee.

[3]See the Joint Declaration on Fundamental Rights signed by the Presidents of the European Parliament, the Commission and the Council on 5 April 1977, OJ [1977] C103; Rutili v Commission and Council, Judgment of the Court of Justice of 28 October 1975, ECR [1975] 1219 at 1232, and Van Landewyck v Commission, Judgment of the Court of Justice of 29 October 1980, ECR [1980] 3125 at 3248.

[4]For example, in VBVB and VBBB v Commission, Judgment of the Court of Justice of 17 January 1984, ECR [1984] 19 at 59, the Court stated that "it must be observed that although regard for the rights of the defence requires that the undertaking concerned shall have been enabled to make known effectively its point of view on the documents relied upon by the Commission in making the findings on which the decision is based, there are no provisions which require the Commission to divulge the contents of its files to the parties concerned. It does not appear in fact that the Commission has made use of any document which was not available to the parties and on which they have not had the opportunity to make their views known. This submission must therefore be dismissed".

[5]See Judgment of the Court of First Instance in case T–7/89 S.A. Hercules Chemicals v Commission, Judgment of 17 December 1991, not yet reported.

[6]In S.A. Hercules Chemicals NV v Commission the Court clarified that "the Commission may not depart from the rules that it has imposed on itself" in this respect.

obligation not to divulge business secrets and other confidential documents provided to the Commission, and the need to preserve the confidential character of internal Commission documents and working papers. In the Twelfth Competition Report this procedure was explained in more depth; together with the Statement of Objections the Commission would send a complete list of all the documents on the file to the undertakings concerned, indicating the documents to which they may have access.

Since January 1982 the Commission has adopted almost 90 final prohibition decision, and in only a handful of cases has the question of access to file raised issues leading to conflict between the Commission and the parties on this point.

Nonetheless, it should be noted that from a practical viewpoint, the decision by the Commission to grant access to its files has resulted in an additional and significant administrative workload on the Directorate-General for competition. Preparing the file for examination by the parties is a difficult and time-consuming job, as it involves checking every page of a file that is often thousands of pages in length to ensure that business secrets or documents containing other confidential information are not inadvertently disclosed to the undertakings concerned.

This latter point also highlights the fact that this aspect of guaranteeing the right to a fair hearing also gives rise to difficult questions of substance. There is an inherent conflict between the Commission's desire to allow companies access to all the documents on its file, and its obligation, contained in Article 20 of Regulation 17/62, "not to disclose information acquired . . . as a result of the application of this Regulation and of the kind covered by the obligation of professional secrecy".

On a number of occasions the Court of Justice has stressed the importance of this requirement, and the need for the Commission to be extremely vigilant not to pass on confidential information when providing the undertakings in question access to documents during the procedure guaranteeing the right to a fair hearing.[1] In many infringement cases this gives rise to no great difficulty, particularly where only one or very few companies are concerned by the proceedings. In cartel cases involving a large number of defendants, however, it can present very great problems. In fact this issue often results in procedural issues in such cases that could, if not handled carefully, delay the adoption of a final Article 85(I) decision by the Commission almost indefinitely. The evidence on which such cartel cases are based derives almost exclusively from inspections carried out pursuant to Article 14(3) of Regulation 17/62. The companies concerned have, in many cases, claimed that all of the documents copied during such inspections were confidential in nature and should on no account be disclosed to third parties, particularly their customers and competitors. Once the Statement of Objectives had been sent, however, the companies claimed that they should be given access to the whole of the Commission's file, including the documents of their competitors. Where the evidence contained in such documents is central to the Commission's case, and on which it therefore relies in its Statement of Objections, it may, notwithstanding the claim of confidentiality, disclose these documents to other parties[2]. Where this is not the case, however, it will not permit widespread access to these documents.

This is far from a hypothetical problem; in such cases the Commission's file includes a great deal of highly commercially sensitive information, and in particular, details of the prices charged by the various companies operating in the industry, their sales volumes, and often details of their customers. The Commission must be very careful not to disclose such information by error, not only because doing so could damage the company from which the document originated, but also because if the Commission was responsible for exchanging sensitive price information between competitors it could be promoting and facilitating the very behaviour that it is seeking to detect, prohibit and, above all, deter: price fixing and market sharing.

In the Eighteenth Competition Report the Commission therefore explained these issues, and noted that it "must ensure that the access to files does not lead to an exchange of commercially sensitive information between the undertakings which are the subject of the proceedings. This rule applies even if the undertakings agree to waive confidentiality for such information on a reciprocal basis".

Thus, it is clear that it is not possible to simply adopt a single procedure regarding "access to file" in all infringement cases dealt with by the Commission. Although the procedure set out in the Twelfth

---

[1]See, for example, Van Landewyck v Commission, Judgment of the Court of Justice of 29 October 1980, ECR [1980] 3125 at 3238, and AKZO v Commission, Judgment of the Court of Justice of 24 June 1986, ECR [1986] 1985.

[2]In the Eighteenth Competition Report the Commission stated, at paragraph 43, that "This recognition of extensive protection for confidential information is, however, subject to an important exception justified by the public interest in the enforcement of the EEC competition rules. The confidential nature of documents does not preclude their disclosure where the Commission relies upon the information in question as necessary evidence of an alleged infringement of the EEC competition rules. This applies both to its own proceedings and in court proceedings. When deciding whether such disclosure should occur the Commission will take into account the legitimate interests of the undertaking providing the information, and the rights of defence of the parties who are the subject of the proceedings".

competition report[1] works well in most cases, and in particular to those concerning one or few companies, it is not suited to cartel cases involving a large number of undertakings. In these cases the elements of the file that are accessible varies enormously from company to company. As explained, therefore, in the Eighteenth Competition Report, in such cases the Commission sends each company the documents accessible to it together with the Statement of Objections.

It is important to stress the Commission's continuing determination to afford undertakings involved in infringement proceedings the opportunity to examine all the non-confidential documents in its possession that are relevant to their case, and in particular, all documents that may be construed as unfavourable to the Commission's arguments. In cartel proceedings involving numerous companies this is, as I have explained, a difficult and complicated task and I regret to say that in the past the Commission has made a number, all be it be very limited, of errors in this respect. In particular, in the Flat Glass[2] case, the Commission failed to disclose part of certain documents to the companies concerned and, partly as a result of this, its decision was struck down by the Court of First Instance. This occurred, and I would like to make this point absolutely clear, due to administrative error, not a deliberate attempt to falsify evidence. The does not, however, make the Commission's failure in this case any less important, and we have introduced additional internal safeguards to ensure that companies do receive all the documents that should be made available to them, involving the Commission's Legal Service in the preparation of the documentary evidence to be made available to the parties even more closely than before. We are also examining what, if any, further improvements can be made.

I believe that these procedures, together with the effective system of appeals provided by the Court of First Instance, will ensure that the Commission maintains a procedure that guarantees the right to a fair hearing that compares favourably with any other anti-trust system in the world.

4. *The Oral Hearing*

The post of Hearing Officer[3] was created in 1982[4]. The Officer is within DGIV, but is separate from the operational Directorates that deal with the individual cases. His or her central task is to "ensure that the Hearing is properly conducted and thus contribute to the objectivity of the Hearing itself and of any decision taken subsequently. He shall seek to ensure in particular that in the preparation of draft Commission decisions in competition cases due account is taken of all the relevant facts, whether favourable or unfavourable to the parties concerned"[5]. The Hearing Officer has the right of direct access to the Member of the Commission responsible for competition policy, and in fact gives his views in writing to the Director-General and the Commissioner in each case that a Hearing is held on whether he is content that the rights of defence have been fully respected. Prior to the hearing, either at the request of any of the parties or if the Hearing Officer considers it useful, the parties are invited to a preparatory meeting, at which the Commission Officials dealing with the case are present, to clarify the issues raised and, where possible, to resolve in advance any issues regarding the facts of the case[6].

The present Hearing Officer is Mr Johannes, who moved to this post in 1989 from heading the unit in DGIV dealing with Article 85 and 86 cases principally in relation to manufacturing industry. He has a secretary and one full time plus one part time clerical assistants. In the past, problems did occur when the Hearing Officer was unavailable to chair a hearing, as a replacement had to be found from within DGIV. Whilst I totally reject any suggestion that this resulted in any lack of impartiality, it is inevitable that companies will in such circumstances suspect that the loyalties of an official that also deals directly with individual Article 85 and 86 matters ultimately lies with the Commission team responsible for the case. With the appointment of Mr Gilchrist as Hearing Officer for merger cases and as Security Officer, I am happy to note that this problem has been resolved. When Mr Johannes

[1]The Commission stated that it would send a complete list of all the documents on the relevant file to the undertakings concerned, indicating the documents to which they may have access, and explaining why certain documents cannot be divulged. The parties would then be invited to the Commission's offices to inspect the parts of the file accessible to them, from which they could take copies of documents.

[2]Società Italiano Vetro SpA, Fabbrica Pisana SpA and PPG Vernante Permitalia SpA *v* Commission. Judgment of the Court of First Instance of 10 March 1992, not yet published.

[3]See paragraphs 27–29 of the 1981–1982 Report of the Select the Committee.

[4]See Twelfth Competition Report, paragraphs 36–37, Thirteenth Competition report paragraph 75–76, and Commission Decision of 23 November 1990 on the implementation of hearings in convention with procedures for the application of Articles 85 and 86 of the EEC Treaty and Articles 65 and 66 of the ECSC Treaty, published in the Twentieth Competition Report, pages 312–314.

[5]See Article 2 of the Commission Decision of 23 November 1990, on the implementation of hearings in connection with procedures for the application of Articles 85 and 86 EEC Treaty and Articles 65 and 66 of the ECSC Treaty. Twentieth Competition Report, pages 312–314.

[6]See in this respect the recommendation of the report of the Select Committee of 1981–1982, at paragraph 19.

is unavailable, Mr Gilchrist chairs hearings on his behalf. If, exceptionally, both Mr Johannes and Mr Gilchrist is unavailable and the Hearing cannot be rescheduled, an ad hoc replacement will be appointed from the Advisors to the Director-General, who also do not deal with individual cases. Thus, in all cases the parties will be reassured by the fact that a clearly impartial Official will chair the Hearing.

I consider the creation of the post of Hearing Officer to be a very valuable development because it increases the importance of the Oral Hearing. The Hearing should not be seen as a mere formality, simply giving the undertakings the opportunity to repeat the arguments raised in their written submission. Most importantly, it gives them the opportunity, on the record, to clarify issues relating to the correct interpretation of the documents on which the Commission is relying. I place great importance on this step of the procedure and intend to attend as many future hearings as possible.

5. *The Advisory Committee*

The procedures and responsibilities of the Advisory Committee on Restrictive Practices and Dominant positions are set out in Article 10 of Council Regulation 17/62. Article 10(6) of this Regulation states that the opinion of the Advisory Committee shall not be made public. As a result of this it has not been possible, without amending this Regulation, to take up the recommendation of the 1981–1982 Select Committee that a copy of the opinion of the Advisory Committee on Restrictive Practices and Dominant Positions be provided to the undertakings concerned. Although such a modification would, in my opinion, be welcome, it has as yet not been a sufficient priority for the Commission. On the other hand, the Select Committee's recommendation that the Member States receive a copy of the minutes of the oral hearing has been accepted, and these are forwarded to the Competent Authorities as soon as they are approved. It should also be noted in this respect that the members of the Advisory Committee may also attend all oral hearings in person.

It is notable that the Merger Regulation introduces a number of modifications compared to the system regarding the consultation of the Advisory Committee established by Regulation 17[1]. First, it requires the Commission to take the "utmost" account of the opinion of the Committee, and to inform the Committee of the manner in which its opinion has been taken into account. Second, the Committee may recommend publication of its opinion. The Commission has a discretion whether to accept or reject this recommendation. To date all the opinions of the Advisory Committee on Concentrations have been published. The Commission believes that timely publication of these opinions is essential for the transparency of merger control.

6. *The European Courts*

On October 24, 1988, the Council of the European Communities decided to establish the Court of First Instance, as provided for by Article 168a of the EEC treaty[2]. I always supported the idea of creating such Court, above all because the enormous workload of the Court of Justice gave them insufficient time to examine competition cases in great detail. This has now changed, and this has been reflected in a number of Judgments where the Court examined the Commission's decision in minute detail in relation to both its factual and legal content. I remain convinced that the Court of First Instance is both necessary, and carrying out its task effectively. Not only does this have the effect of assuring companies that any Commission decision will be subject to a full review, it also clarifies for the Commission the standards of proof that it must respect in order to adopt an infringement decision in a contested case. I believe that this has led to an improvement in the standards applied by the Commission when adopting such decisions and will continue to do so. It is, therefore, one of the most important developments in Community competition policy during the previous decade.

III. PROCEDURAL EFFICIENCY

Competition policy is a central part of the Community's industrial policy, as it is for most developed economies. It plays a vital role in ensuring that markets remain open and competitive; cartels and abuses of dominant positions can foreclose markets to new entrants just as effectively as governmental regulatory barriers. Competition policy is of particular importance for the Community at a time when the various national economies are integrating rapidly to produce a single market. By ensuring that our markets remain competitive we contribute to ensuring that the Community's industry remains competitive at a world-wide level.

However, it is equally true that the Commission must continue to ensure that the Community's competition policy does not handicap Europe's industry in either of two ways. First, it must be certain

---

[1] Articles 19(3)–(5) of the Merger Regulation.
[2] as amended by the Single European Act.

not to prohibit deals that are not anti-competitive or allow those that will foreclose markets. Second, it must provide an efficient and rapid decision-making process for beneficial agreements.

Although I would not pretend that the substantive aspect of our competition policy cannot be improved, I do think that its basic approach is correct. Over the past few years we have therefore been concentrating on improving the efficiency of our procedures. In its 1981–1982 Report the Committee identified that the time taken to adopt an exemption or negative clearance decision was unacceptable. I agree with this: one of the essential elements of a competitive industry is its ability to react quickly to market changes. In the Community this often takes the form of agreements between two independent companies: the setting up of a new joint venture company for example. Failure to give a speedy decision in such cases, and one which gives the companies concerned adequate legal security, can only hamper the Community's industry.

I fully supported the strict deadlines for decisions in the Merger Regulation. The Commission has respected these deadlines in every single case and it is clear that a full five-month enquiry has been carried out only in cases where this was absolutely necessary. Furthermore, I think it justified to believe that the standard of substantive analysis achieved in merger decisions has not suffered by the fact that it was carried out over a short period. The reason why the Commission is able to achieve this is two-fold. First, adequate resources were provided to enable the setting up of the Merger Task Force and to provide the necessary back-up services, and in particular fast translation facilities. Second, Regulation 4064/89, and the implementing Regulation No. 2367/90, establishes a procedure that enables rapid decision-making.

The same cannot be said in relation to the other Directorates of DGIV. DGIV has been successful in clearing the backlog of "old" cases over the previous few years, and so at the end of 1992[1] there were 1,562 cases involving Article 85 or 86 that remained open and these cases are now being actively dealt with. This figure includes 399 cases opened in 1992, made up of 246 notifications, 110 complaints and 43 cases opened by DGIV itself.

The number of new Article 85/86 cases continues to follow an upward trend; from 293 in 1981, 313 in 1987, 375 in 1990, and 399 in 1992. At present there are 97 "A" grade officials in Directorates B, C and D, which are directly responsible for dealing with cases falling under Articles 85 and 86. This compares with 26 A grades in the Merger Task Force that dealt with 63 notifications in 1991 and 60 in 1992[2]. This works out at an average of 16 cases per person per annum relating to Articles 85 and 86 compared to 2.4 cases per case handler in the Merger Task Force.

Furthermore, the substantive issues that are raised in cases under Articles 85 and 86 are often more complicated to deal with than merger cases; they involve a wider range of legal issues and problems, particularly in difficult Community-wide cartel cases which also require a much greater level of fact-finding. Merger cases, on the other hand, involve intensive efforts by the staff in order to respect strict deadlines.

It is simply not realistic therefore, to expect the Commission to respect the same or similar deadlines in Article 85 and 86 cases that it achieves in merger cases. Indeed, in many cases where infringement procedures are involved, such deadlines would be wholly inappropriate because the fact-finding process, together with the period necessary to ensure that the rights of defence are fully respected, is necessarily lengthy.

However, it is true that DGIV would like to be able to follow short deadlines for many notifications, particularly cases involving forms of co-operation that have no significant anti-competitive effects. Examples of these include certain research and development, distribution, specialisation, and intellectual property licensing agreements. Most importantly, it includes co-operative joint venture agreements that involve structural change for the companies involved. In such cases, unwinding the joint venture would often be difficult, complicated and expensive.

In the past it has often been argued that DGIV is under-staffed. The European Parliament has stated this on a number of occasions; indeed, the Select Committee found in 1982 that this was a "clear possibility"[3]. This remains the case. In 1981 DGIV had 74 A grade officials dealing with Article 85 and 86 cases. The equivalent figure today is 97. Thus, the number of new cases per case handler has slightly increased over this period. However, I do not believe that it is realistic to expect increases in existing staff levels given the present budgetary restraints on the Commission. We have therefore been examining what can be done with our existing resources to speed up decision-making. Since the 1981–1982 Select Committee report the following measures have been taken:

---

[1] See annex 1 for statistical breakdown.

[2] In 1992 the US the Antitrust Division of the Department of Justice employed 581 full time equivalent employees (including attorneys, economists, other professionals and clerical staff) and the FTC Bureau of Competition employed 222 employees: 156 attorneys, 34 other professionals, and 32 clerical staff. The FTC also employs economists who participate in its antitrust enforcement activities.

[3] See paragraph 38 of the report.

— adoption of additional block exemptions, regulation 2349/84 regarding patent licensing agreements, Regulation 123/85 regarding certain categories of motor vehicle distribution and servicing agreements, Regulation 4087/88 regarding franchise agreements, and regulation 556/89 regarding know-how licensing agreements. Other block exemptions, regarding exclusive distribution and purchasing have been completely revised to make them more effective, whilst others, the research and development, specialisation, know-how licensing and patent licensing regulations, have been widened so that they can cover a number of joint venture agreements previously excluded from their scope.

— the wider use of comfort letters. In 1987, for example, 57 cases were closed by comfort letter, in 1992 the equivalent figure was 176[1].

— promoting the efficient use of resources by encouraging the application of Community law by national courts and by referring complaints that do not raise a significant legal, economic or political issue of importance to the Community as a whole to national courts or competition authorities[2].

— increasing the thresholds in the Commission notice on agreements of minor importance which do not fall under Article 85(1)[3]. This notice states that the "Commission holds the view that agreements between undertakings engaged in the production or distribution of goods or in the provision of services generally do not fall under the prohibition of Article 85(1)" if the agreement concerns companies having a market share for the affected products of less than 5 per cent and that their aggregate annual turnover does not exceed 200 million ECU.

— introducing internal DGIV deadlines for dealing with certain Article 85/86 cases. As can be seen from the above it is not possible to adopt a rapid decision-making system for all notifications. The Commission has therefore decided at present to concentrate its resources in this respect to the area of co-operative joint ventures involving structural change. As announced in a Commission press release of 23 December 1992[4] the Commission has committed itself to providing a first reaction in such cases within two months from its receipt of a complete notification[5]. This first reaction would take the form either of a comfort letter, or of a letter announcing an intention to propose that the Commission adopts a formal exemption or negative clearance decision, or of a "warning letter". Although it is by no means perfect, I believe that this is a significant innovation. After the two month period the companies concerned will know where they stand with the Commission. If they receive a comfort letter they can go ahead with the operation without any appreciable risk that the Commission will object to the operation. It is true that such comfort letters are not legally binding on the Commission, which could in theory change its mind and subsequently prohibit the operation. However, we view comfort letters as a crucial tool that helps the Community's competition policy work in practice, and would only withdraw them in circumstances in which we would also withdraw the benefit of a formally granted exemption decision[6]. Although, therefore, they do not fully resolve the issue of the need for legal security in such cases, which can only be granted by formal decision, they do provide a workable solution to the need to give companies an early, and reliable, view on notified joint ventures. Equally, in the rare cases where the companies receive a "warning letter", which can be seen as being similar to the decision under the Merger Regulation to open proceedings and carry out a full enquiry, they will know, at an early stage, that if they go ahead with the project immediately they face a real risk that the Commission will subsequently oppose the joint venture.

In the period since the last Select Committee Report the combination of these measures has significantly helped to reduce the delays faced by companies where dealing with DGIV. However, I would not pretend that they completely meet the need for rapid decision-making in all cases regarding beneficial co-operation. DGIV is therefore continuing to examine what additional measures can be taken to further improve the situation. We are presently examining:

[1]See annex 1 for full breakdown.

[2]See below, point V.1.

[3]O.J [1986] C231/2.

[4]See annex 2.

[5]This caveat also applies under the Merger Regulation, where, pursuant to Article 4(2) of Commission Regulation 2367/90, time limits do not start to run unless and until a complete notification is received.

[6]Article 8 of Regulation 17/62 enables the Commission to withdraw the benefit of an exemption decision:

"(a) where there has been a change in any of the facts which were fundamental in the making of the decision,

(b) where the parties commit a breach of any obligation attached to the decision,

(c) where the decision is based on incorrect information or was induced by deceit,

(d) where the parties abuse the exemption from the provisions of Article 85(1) of the Treaty granted to them by the decision.".

—   the possibility of adopting still further block exemption Regulations, and widening and simplifying the scope of existing Regulations, for example by making wider use of the market share thresholds contained in the block exemptions on research and development and specialisation.

—   whether it is possible to increase the effectiveness of comfort letters. DGIV is examining whether it would be possible to follow-up each comfort letter with a very short, but formal, exemption or negative clearance decision. This would be a significant, and no doubt welcome innovation. However, it is not possible under the existing procedure that must be followed in order to adopt a decision. A form of simplified procedure, similar to that under the Merger Regulation, will need to be devised in order to make it possible. In particular, it will not be possible to adopt every decision in nine languages. I believe that such a procedure can be devised and am optimistic that such a system will enter into force in the future.

—   whether the "informal" self-imposed DGIV deadlines can be extended to other types of cases aside from co-operative joint ventures that involve structural change. At present DGIV is monitoring closely the effects of the new system. It is important to ensure that the existing system works efficiently and is of real use to notifying companies. It must also be examined whether the introduction of these deadlines leads to an increase in notifications. This is in fact an important point. It is well known amongst practitioners that far from all the agreements that could, and perhaps, should, be notified, are in fact filed with the Commission. This is particularly the case in relation to vertical agreements, such as distribution and licensing arrangements, where companies choose to accept the risks of non-notification rather than the costs of doing so. It is quite possible, particularly in relation to such categories of agreements, that a promise to deal with such cases in short, fixed periods, would significantly increase the numbers of notifications.

Furthermore, we are examining what measures can be taken to enable us to meet these deadlines more easily. In particular, we are preparing a revised version of Form A/B in order to ensure that companies notifying under the accelerated procedure provide us with all the necessary information reasonably available to them on notification[1].

Finally, it should always be borne in mind that DGIV's highest priority remains the detection, prohibition and deterrence of cartels and abuses of dominant positions. It is therefore necessary to maintain the appropriate balance between this function, and that of ensuring the rapid approval of agreements that are not damaging to the Community's competitive structure. I believe that the introduction of such deadlines can only be implemented on an evolving basis, ensuring at each step that the correct balance is maintained between DGIV's prohibition and approbation roles. Notwithstanding this I do believe that it will, over time, be possible to expand these informal deadlines to other cases. Indeed, in principle I fully support the recommendation of the Select Committee in 1981–1982 that a non-opposition procedure be introduced in relation to all notifications. If the above-mentioned bottle- necks could be eliminated, I would be happy to propose it. However, given the existing budgetary constraints upon the Commission, and the need to be certain that DGIV continues to devote much of its resources into cartel detection and prohibition, this option is simply not realistic at the present time.

—   how, through greater co-operation with national courts and national competition authorities, a greater number of cases can be dealt with at the national level[2].

Thus, over the coming years I have no doubt that we will continue to improve the efficiency with which DGIV handles its case-load. I believe that this can be done with our existing resources. It should be made clear, however, that unless and until DGIV does receive significant additional human resources it will not be possible to adopt formal, legally binding decisions in Article 85 and 86 cases within short deadlines similar to those in the Merger Regulation.

IV. SUBSIDIARITY, THE LEVEL OF DECISION-MAKING AND ARTICLES 85 AND 86

Article 3b of the Treaty of Maastricht states that:

"The Community shall act within the limits of the powers conferred upon it by this Treaty and of the objectives assigned to it therein. In areas which do not fall within its exclusive competence, the Community shall take action, in accordance with the principle of subsidiarity, only if and in so far as the objectives of the proposed action cannot be sufficiently achieved by the Member States and can therefore, by reason of the scale or effects of the proposed action, be better achieved by the Community.

---

[1] Although this examination is only at an early stage it is clear that such companies will have to provide a level of information similar to that required in relation to notifications under the Merger Regulation.

[2] See below, point IV

Any action by the Community shall not go beyond what is necessary to achieve the objectives of this Treaty."

Although the word "subsidiarity" did not appear in the Treaty of Rome, nor in the Single European Act, it has underpinned Community competition policy from its inception. It is, I think universally accepted that the enforcement of competition policy at the Community level is vital for two basic reasons, one substantive, one procedural. In substantive terms, competition policy enforcement at the Community level is vital if the single market is to be a level playing field. If different standards of competition policy were applied from Member State to Member State in relation to operations having a cross-border effect, investment decisions would be based at least in part on considerations other than those simply relating to operational efficiency. In procedural terms, it must be noted first that only the Commission, in linguistic terms and in relation to powers of discovery, has the tools to be able to effectively review cross-border agreements and practices. This applies not only to fact-finding, but also to ensuring the respect of the rights of defence: how, for example, could a national competition authority cope with an oral hearing that received evidence from individuals of six or seven different nationalities. Second, there are now national Competition Authorities in almost every EEC Member State. Where operations have an effect on the market of more than one of these countries, it is far better that a single authority, the Commission, examines the operation than all the relevant national authorities undertake concurrent investigations. This concern, multiple regulatory control, was one of the basic reasons why the Merger Regulation was so necessary, and why the "one-stop-shop", established by Articles 21(2) and (3) of the Regulations, has proved to be so popular with Community Industry[1]. It also applies to operations falling under Article 85 and 86: there are many cases in which the Member State Competition Authorities need take no action as the matter is being dealt with by the Commission.

However, this does not mean that all competition policy in the Community should be enforced by the Commission. On the contrary, the Member State Authorities have a major role to play in this respect. Operations that have effects limited to a single country are best dealt with by that country's competition authority. They are closer to the market, making them better placed to deal with the case.

The EEC Treaty recognised the "best level" requirement of the subsidiary principle in relation to the competition rules by limiting the Commission's jurisdiction to cases that effect trade between Member States. Furthermore, subsidiarity has underpinned the developments in this area, and in particular in the Merger Regulation, where a combination of Articles 1, 9 and 22(3) seek to ensure that the Commission has sole jurisdiction to examine concentrations having cross-border effects, whereas the Member State Authorities alone deal with cases of a national dimension[1].

Thus, with respect to competition policy, the application of the subsidiary principle has two basic elements; one substantive, one procedural. In substantive terms, I think, at least with respect to Articles 85 and 86, the current balance is correct; the test of effect on trade between Member States is both logical and effective. In procedural terms, however, the Commission has been examining the question of who should apply these Articles. Although it is imperative that a single test be applied throughout the Community to agreements having an effect on trade, it is not necessarily only the Commission that can enforce this test. In certain cases the various national bodies—Courts or domestic Competition Authorities—may be able to enforce the rules in a uniform manner irrespective of their location in the Community. This is the case with respect to Articles 85(1) and Article 86, which set out straightforward prohibition provisions. On the basis of jurisprudence established by the Court of Justice and the Commission, and through the use by national courts of the possibility of asking for a preliminary ruling from the Court by virtue of Article 177 of the EEC Treaty, these rules can in many cases be effectively applied at the national level. Clearly, this does not apply to Community-wide cartels or abuses of dominant positions, which can only be effectively investigated by the Commission, but it does apply to many agreements and practices that effect trade between Member States and therefore have an impact on the Community as a whole but nonetheless can be dealt with by a national court or competition authority.

It is not surprising, therefore, that the Court of Justice decided, as early as 1962 and 1974 respectively[2], that Article 85(1) and Article 86 are directly applicable and thus enforceable by national courts. The Commission has recognised for some time that there are a number of important advantages to the enforcement of Community competition law at the national level. First, national courts are able to give immediate interim relief[3]. Second, national courts can award damages in favour of undertakings or individuals harmed by conduct that infringes Article 85(1) or 86. Third, national courts have a

---

[1]See below, point V.1.

[2]Bosch v De Geus, Judgment of the Court of Justice, 6.4.1964 ECR [1962] 45, BRT v SABAM I, judgment of the Court of Justice, 30.1.1974, ECR [1974] 51.

[3]The Commission does possess the jurisdiction to award interim measures. Due, however, to the procedure that must be respected before interim measures can be adopted, this takes a period which is substantially longer than the equivalent procedure before national courts.

wider range of remedies that can be applied once an infringement of the competition rules has been established. For example, national courts may be able to order a company to take positive action to remedy an infringement such as a requirement to recommence supplying an undertaking that has been illegally refused supplies by a dominant company. The Commission can only state the existence of an infringement, and, where appropriate, impose fines. Fourthly, the Commission wishes to ensure that Community law is a truly integral part of the national legal systems, so that citizens view it simply, in effect, as one part of their own national law. Application of Community law by national courts on a day-to-day basis plays an important role in this respect. Finally, a national court can consider contemporaneously a claim under Community and national law.

For these reasons, and also because of a desire to make the maximum use of its available resources by concentrating cases that have a real impact throughout the Community, the Commission has for a number of years promoted the enforcement of Articles 85(1) and 86 at the national level. This process has recently received a significant boost, first by the Judgment of the Court of First Instance in the Automec case[1], second by the notice of the Commission, adopted on 23 December 1992, on "co-operation between national courts and the Commission in applying Articles 85 and 86"[2] ("the national courts notice").

The Automec case originated from a complaint received by the Commission from an Italian dealer of BMW cars. BMW had terminated the dealership, and Automec challenged this in the Italian Courts on the basis of Article 85(1) and domestic contract law, and simultaneously lodged a complaint with the Commission. The Commission rejected the complaint stating that:

(1)   if it was to carry out its task it had to set priorities, and should not necessarily deal with every complaint that it receives. Thus, it took the view that its main task is to establish the principles for the application of Community competition policy and to deal with cases that can only be effectively handled at the Community level. Many complaints received by the Commission can be adequately dealt with at the national level and this applied in the present case; and

(2)   in this case the complainant could get effective redress at the national level. Furthermore the complaint raised no issues of significant interest for the Community as a whole in legal, economic or political terms.

Automec appealed the decision rejecting the complaint to the Court of First Instance which confirmed the Commission's jurisdiction to reject complaints on the grounds that they lack a significant Community interest, providing that adequate redress is available at national level. The Court highlighted in particular that the remedy requested by Automec, that BMW be ordered to re-admit it into its dealer network, could in any event be ordered only by the national court.

This provides the Commission with an important tool in promoting the application of Articles 85(1) and 86 at the national level. If the Commission decides to take up a case on the basis of a complaint there are no charges for the complainant aside from his or her legal fees. As the Commission itself carries out much of the fact-finding and legal analysis, the legal fees supported by the complainant are also much lower than those incurred during national court actions. It is not surprising, therefore, that the Commission receives a large number of complaints that could be dealt with perfectly adequately at national level. Given its limited resources, DGIV has to accept that it can only deal with those complaints that involve a significant interest for the Community as a whole. In this respect it will continue, for example, to continue to treat as its highest priority those complaints that involve cartels and abuses of dominant positions that span the Community. On the other hand, on the basis of the Automec II judgment, it will reject complaints that raise no significant Community interest where adequate redress is available at the national level.

This policy will, I believe, lead to a significant increase in actions under Articles 85(1) and 86 in national courts. Complaints, by their very nature, allege that an agreement or practice infringes Articles 85(1) or 86, and, that with respect to Article 85 cases, no exemption is possible. Thus the Commission's exclusive right to grant exemptions need not necessarily prevent a national court from giving judgment in these cases.

However, the Commission fully recognises that the fact that only it can grant an individual exemption can cause real difficulties to a national judge when applying Article 85(1). Partly in order to limit these difficulties, partly in order to clarify its approach to the application of Community competition policy by national judges, the Commission adopted the national courts notice. The first part of the notice sets out clearly and publicly the Commission's approach to dealing with complaints following the Automec judgment:

[1]Automec v Commission II, Judgment of the Court of First Instance, 18 September 1992, not yet published.
[2]O.J. [1993] C39.

"13. As the administrative authority responsible for the Community's competition policy, the Commission must serve the Community's general interest. The administrative resources at the Commission's disposal to perform its tasks are necessarily limited and cannot be used to deal with all the cases brought to its attention. The Commission is therefore obliged, in general, to take all organisational measures necessary for the performance of its tasks and, in particular, to establish priorities.

14. The Commission intends, in implementing its decision-making powers, to concentrate on notifications, complaints and own-initiative proceedings having particular political, legal or economic significance for the Community. Where these features are absent in a particular case, notifications will normally be dealt with by comfort letter and complaints should, as a rule, be handled by national courts or authorities."

The notice then considers how a national judge should deal with cases where the defence is raised against an action based on Article 85(1) that the agreement merits exemption. Commission decisions take precedence over national ones, and the notice therefore states that domestic courts must be vigilant not to hand down judgments that conflict with Commission decisions, even future Commission decisions. Thus, the notice states that "if the national court concludes that an agreement is prohibited by Article 85(1), it must check whether the agreement is or will be the subject of an exemption by the Commission under Article 85(3)". The notice then provides practical guidance how to do this. In effect it clarifies for the national judge the rules that have already been established in this area by the Court of Justice[1]. Thus, for example, it states that where the Commission has already granted an individual exemption decision, or the agreement benefits from a block exemption, the national court must simply follow the exemption decision. If the agreement should have been notified, but the parties have failed to do so, no exemption is legally possible[2] and in such case the court may go ahead and apply Article 85(1). Where, however, the agreement has been properly notified, and the national court believes that real doubts exist whether an exemption is possible, the notice states that the court should "suspend proceedings while awaiting the Commission's decision. If the national court does suspend proceedings, it remains free, according to the rules of the applicable national law to adopt any interim measures it deems necessary".

Finally, the notice deals with cases where the agreement has been validly notified, but after having examined the agreement in the light of Commission and Court Jurisprudence, the national court concludes that it is clear that "the agreement, decision or practice cannot be the subject of an individual exemption". The notice states that in such circumstances the national court may apply Article 85(1).

I believe that this last clarification is of considerable importance. Until the adoption of this notice it was not widely known that the Commission favoured an "acte clair"[3] approach by national courts which are faced with a case in which the defendant argues that an exemption could be granted by the Commission, but in the opinion of the Court, based on previous Commission and Court jurisprudence, this can effectively be excluded. This is the case, for example, for simple price fixing cartels. The notice makes it clear that in such cases the national court need not suspend proceedings, but may go ahead and give judgment.

The Commission recognises, however, that some national judges have neither the experience nor expertise which would enable them to easily carry out this task. The notice therefore announces the establishment of a "co-operation procedure" between the Commission and the courts. The notice states that the Commission will reply to questions posed by national courts that are procedural, legal, and factual in nature.

In relation to procedure, the Court might, for example, wish to know whether a notification has been received, whether proceedings have been opened or whether a statement of objections has been sent. It might wish to know how long the Commission believes will be necessary to decide whether an exemption can be granted in the case in question, so that the national court can decide whether it should grant any interim measures.

Regarding questions of fact, the notice states that the Commission will provide national judges with any data, market studies etc. available to it, subject to the limitation regarding its obligation to protect business secrets and other confidential information.

---

[1]See Stergios Delimitis v Henninger Brau AG, Judgment of the Court of Justice, 28 February 1991, ECR [1991] 935.

[2]Article 4 of Regulation 17/62.

[3]The Court of Justice developed the "acte clair" doctrine in the context of the Article 177 procedure. This Article states in its last paragraph that "Where any such question [on the interpretation of Community law] is raised in a case pending before a court or tribunal of a member-state against whose decisions there is no judicial remedy under national law, that court or tribunal shall bring the matter before the Court of Justice". In Srl CILFIT *et al v* Ministry of Health [1982] ECR 3415 at 3429, the Court clarified that where a party to the proceedings raises a question of Community law in such circumstances which has effectively been already dealt with by the Court in previous decisions, and the answer to the question is therefore evident, there is no obligation for the national court to refer the question to the Court of Justice.

Finally, and, most importantly, the notice states that the Commission will answer questions in relation to its "customary practice in relation to the interpretation of Community law . . . in its replies the Commission does not get into the merits of the case.[1] Furthermore, the notice states that the Commission will give an interim opinion on whether any agreement is likely to be eligible for individual exemption.

This Notice, combined with the Commission's policy of effectively forcing some complainants to seek redress through national administrative or judicial bodies, will increase enforcement of Articles 85(1) and 86 at the national level. In particular, the willingness of the Commission to co-operate with national judges will, I believe, give them the confidence to give judgment in cases before them that concern clear breaches of Articles 85(1) and 86. These developments are significant in themselves, but I believe that they represent but one example of a constantly evolving process whereby the Community's competition policy endeavours to apply the subsidiarity principle in practice, and to come to terms with the need for a rapid decision making process that results in legal security for the companies concerned. This process will continue as we adapt to changes in the market place, and in national legal systems.

In particular, I expect that in future we will see greater enforcement of Articles 85(1) and 86 by national Competition Authorities. The Commission has been attempting in recent years to really improve the quality of dialogue and collaboration between the Commission and the national Competition Authorities. Many official from the national authorities have now worked for the Commission for a number of months, and in some cases, years, before returning to their national Authority. This is very important. The Community market is integrating rapidly, and more and more business operations will have a cross-border effect. In dealing with these cases we will need to continue to develop a system of competition law enforcement that rests on a form of partnership between the Commission, the Member State Competition Authorities and the national courts. The evolution towards this very close relationship is already well under way, and will continue. Thus, for the same reasons that I welcome greater enforcement by national courts, I would welcome, indeed consider vital, greater enforcement of Articles 85(1) and 86 by national Competition Authorities. It is for each Member State to adopt the necessary legislation to enable their Competition Authorities to apply Articles 85(1) and 86 and a number of National Authorities already have such jurisdiction. I believe that it is important that the other Member States adopt similar legislation as soon as possible. Such a move would greatly enhance the move towards the de-centralised application of Community law and should be encouraged.

However, I accept that the Commission's monopoly over the right to grant individual exemptions will remain a real limitation in this respect and many cases will remain to be decided by Brussels. Certain commentators have argued that this monopoly should now be terminated. I do not share this view. This is for two reasons.

Firstly, in many respects, Article 85(3) forms the very heart of the Community's competition policy. By setting the standard regarding which agreements and decisions can be exempted the Commission ensures that the core of Community competition policy remains identical throughout the Community. It is relatively straightforward to determine which agreements or practices are, on balance, anti-competitive, and this analysis involves a rather limited subjective content. On the other hand, the decision whether an anti-competitive agreement should be exempted because it produces overall efficiencies for the Community as a whole that outweigh these disadvantages is a much more difficult exercise, and one that involves an appreciable degree of subjective appreciation. In order to make such a judgment the decision maker must have a wide range of information available, and in particular must be in a position to make a qualified judgment as to the interests of the Community as a whole. This function of the Commission is, therefore, very similar to that which it holds with respect to state aids: what may be good for one individual Member State may be severely damaging for the Community as a whole. I remain to be convinced that national courts and indeed national Competition Authorities will have available to them the information necessary to carry out this finely balanced analysis.

Secondly, if the Member State Competition Authorities or national courts were given the jurisdiction to apply Article 85(3), the question would arise whether they had the power to grant the exemption for the whole of the Community, or would the companies concerned need to get exemption from each competition authority in which their agreement or decision would be likely to have economic effects? If the answer to this question would be the latter of these two possibilities, not only would it result in the creation of additional and highly undesirable multiple Regulatory control with the consequential additional costs for companies in terms of lost management time and legal fees, it would also create enormous confusion in substantive terms: what to do, for example, in the face of conflicting decisions or alternative remedies adopted by two different authorities in the same case.

---

[1]This restrictive wording reflects a recognition that the only correct procedure for addressing novel legal questions of Community law raised during national proceedings is a request for a preliminary ruling to the Court of Justice pursuant to Article 177 of the EEC Treaty.

Finally, I am not convinced that a single approach to the enforcement of competition policy exists throughout the Community, whether this be at the administrative or judicial level. Consequently, if the Commission's monopoly over the grant of individual exemptions was lifted a real risk of differential standards of substantive review throughout the Community would develop, and with this forum shopping and thus artificial distortions of capital flows. This would prejudice the basic aims of the single market, and thus, I believe that the Commission's monopoly over the grant of individual exemptions should remain. As a corollary to this, however, the Commission must, and will, continue to improve the speed at which it deals with cases notified to it with a view to acquiring an individual exemption.

V. THE MERGER REGULATION

1. *Introduction. Jurisdiction allocation under the Regulation*

As explained above, the subsidiarity principle has two aspects, one procedural and one substantive. It was both of these that led the Council to adopt the Merger Regulation. Firstly, in procedural terms, only the Community has the tools, both in terms of linguistic infrastructure and fact-finding powers, to enable it to efficiently investigate and decide upon a cross-border merger. In order to make a reliable assessment regarding the market power that will result from such an operation it is vital to gather information, in particular the views of those affected by the transaction, in all markets where the operation will produce economic effects. When the Merger Regulation was adopted most Member States had some sort of regulatory control of mergers and acquisitions. Almost all 12 countries now have an effective competition policy. Furthermore, cross-border mergers and acquisitions had been increasing for a number of years as companies reacted to the challenges of the single markets. The "1992" process was expected to further accelerate this trend. The problem of multiple Regulatory control—the obligation for European firms to seek the approval of two or more authorities for a single concentration—was therefore, an existing and growing problem.

It was these reasons that led the Council to adopt the Merger Regulation in 1989. However, it was also recognised that individual Member State Authorities are perfectly capable of examining concentrations, the effects of which are limited to their own territory. In many respects, national competition authorities can carry out this task better than the Commission. Thus, the task was to find a mechanism to distinguish between those concentrations having a cross-border economic effect, and those which are purely domestic in nature. After considering a number of different tests, the Council adopted a series of three criteria based on turnover which are all required to be met. Currently, these are:

(a)   Aggregate world-wide turnover of the companies concerned must exceed the main threshold of 5,000 million ECU. This reflects the general economic and financial power of the undertakings;

(b)   Community-wide turnover must be greater than the "de minimis" threshold of 250 million ECU for each of at least two undertakings—this demonstrates significant activity in the Community by two or more parties;

(c)   The Regulation does not apply where each of the undertakings concerned achieves more than two-thirds of its Community-wide turnover in one and the same Member State—this criterion is designed to exclude operations which are primarily of a national nature.

Where these thresholds are met the Commission has exclusive jurisdiction to examine the operation—the "one-stop shop". Where they are not met, the Member State competition Authorities have exclusive jurisdiction.

Clearly, any test based exclusively on threshold criteria will never be able to fully reflect the objectives regarding jurisdiction allocation outlined above, and it was inevitable that the Regulation would therefore catch some operations having purely national, regional or local economic consequences. Equally, some concentrations having significant cross-border effects would fall below one or more of the three criteria.

In order to refine the relative crudity of this test the Council adopted two referral provisions, Article 9 and Article 22(3).

Where a concentration threatens to create or strengthen a dominant position in a distinct market within its territory, a Member State may request referral of the case back to national authorities in accordance with Article 9(2). To date five such requests have been received. In three cases the Commission initiated phase 2 proceedings, in one case the operation was cleared by an Article 6(1)b decision and in the remaining case, there was partial referral and partial clearance (Steetley/Tarmac). Referral to the United Kingdom authorities was particularly appropriate in this case because these were concurrently examining a counter bid by Redland for Tarmac under national legislation.

Under Article 22(3) a Member State may request the application of the Regulation to concentrations having no Community dimension. Over the same period one such request has been received in connection with the acquisition of Dan Air by British Airways. This was cleared by a formal Commission decision.

Although it remains to be seen whether the present thresholds, and indeed the referral provisions, need to be revised in order to best reflect the subsidiarity principle, I believe that the first two and a half years of the operation of the Merger Regulation does lead to the conclusion that the system of thresholds, together with the referral provisions, provides a flexible and appropriate manner in which to allocate jurisdiction between the Commission and the Member States in the field of mergers and acquisitions.

2. Other principles underlying the Regulation

Very considerable sums of money are often involved in cross-border investment. Delay in decision-making by the competent regulatory authorities can aggravate or create uncertainty detrimental to the interests of the employees and the business concerned. Consequently, the Regulation is also based on the principle of *rapid decision-making* where the initial examination is completed in one month. Even in cases where serious doubts arise and further investigation has to be carried out, the final decision is always within five months of the original notification. The Commission has met every deadline in every case.

Another important principle of the Regulation is *legal certainty*. In all cases the notifying parties receive a formal Commission decision. This either clears the concentration, affording legal certainty, or provides a formal decision that can be appealed before the European Courts.

These features of the Regulation have been widely valued by business in the pursuit of cross-border acquisitions.

3. Statistical overview of the operation of the Merger Regulation

	Number of cases	Percentage of all cases notified	Percentage of cases falling under Regulation
Article 6(1)a	17	13	—
Article 6(1)b	108	79	91
Article 6(1)c	11	8	9
	136	100%	100%

Thus, of the 119 cases falling under the Regulation, 91 per cent were cleared by means of an Article 6(1)b decision. Proceedings were initiated in the other 9 per cent of cases. Of the 10 cases where Phase 2 proceedings have been closed, one case has led to a prohibition decision. In one other case the notification was withdrawn. The remaining eight cases were closed by an approval decision. However, in six of these cases the final decision was subject to conditions and/or obligations. In the other two cases no conditions or obligations were attached to the approval.

4. Breakdown of cases according to their geographic impact

The geographical breakdown of operations may be assessed either by reference to the nationality of the undertakings concerned or to the geographical market definition adopted by the Commission in its final decision on the case in question. Both approaches show that a large majority of notified concentrations do have clear economic effects in more than one Member State.

Analysis on the basis of the nationality of the companies concerned:

71 per cent of decisions in the first two years involved either undertakings from different Member States (36 per cent) or operations concerning both Community and extra-Community companies (35 per cent). Only 16 per cent related to firms of the same nationality. 13 per cent of decisions concerned only extra-Community companies.

Analysis on the basis of the geographical market definition adopted in the final Commission decision:

Analysis of the individual Commission decisions shows that 60 per cent of decisions in the first two years involved Community-wide markets and 11 per cent concerned markets extending over more than one Member State. 16 per cent covered national markets and 4 per cent sub-national markets.

The remaining 4 and 5 per cent related to geographical markets wider than the Community or non-classified respectively.

5. *Review of the thresholds*

In order to investigate the practical impact of any threshold reduction the Commission has conducted a survey with approximately 300 of the Community's leading companies. The objective of the exercise was to identify what additional cases would have fallen under the Merger Regulation in 1991 and 1992 if the aggregate world-wide turnover threshold had been lowered from 5 to 2 billion ECU with a corresponding reduction in the threshold requiring a minimum level of activity within the Community from 250 to 100 million ECU. Threshold reduction on these lines was outlined in a declaration by the Commission at the time of the adoption of the Merger Regulation. Based on estimates derived from the survey data, the expected increase in the number of cases brought about by threshold reduction would be about double the existing case load of 50/60 cases per year.

Based on the results of the survey as well as other sources of information available to the Commission, it is clear that:

— subsequent to the implementation of the single market programme the expected increase in cross-border mergers within the Community has occurred;

— the majority of the extra cases that would be caught by a threshold reduction as described above had an impact reaching across two or more Member States;

— the two-thirds rule has largely achieved its objective of filtering out cases of purely national interest. However it tended to over-achieve its objective by also removing from the scope of the Community jurisdiction important cases having a valid Community dimension. Consequently, while the principle of the two-thirds rule achieved a valid and necessary function and should be maintained, the question of the threshold level at which the test was pitched (ie two-thirds) merits further consideration. More precisely, the evidence collected by the survey would suggest that a three-quarters level would be more appropriate in terms of balancing the allocation of jurisdiction between the national and Community levels.

The survey has also indicated that general legal and economic considerations militate in favour of increased Commission jurisdiction for merger control in the Community. The advantages of a rapid "one-stop" shop procedure combined with rapid decision-making has been widely appreciated by the business community. On the one hand, increasing economic integration is sharpening competition in the Community and placing pressure on business to reduce costs and take advantage of the economies of scale made possible by the single market. This acts as a driving force stimulating cross-border merger activity in a widening number of sectors and at a reducing level of activity (ie turnover). On the other hand, the adoption of the Merger Regulation has acted as a spur to a number of Member States which have recently recognised the importance of merger control and have introduced their own national legislation, with the result that for those operations falling outside the single Community jurisdiction, there are now an increased number of potential regulatory hurdles to be cleared in any cross-border merger. Consequently, the pressure on business to engage in cross-border merger activity is increasing whilst at the same time the regulatory costs of doing so have already increased. Moreover, increasing competition brought about by market integration is amplifying the need for uniform merger control policy across the Community (ie a level-playing field) so that all market participants are placed on an equal footing in their acquisition strategies.

6. *Review of the referral provisions*

Whilst the existing system for referral under Article 9 has functioned satisfactorily under the current thresholds, it must be recognised that in the event of threshold reduction, there is a possibility that an increased number of primarily nationally-orientated concentrations may now fall under the scope of the Merger Regulation. Consequently, notwithstanding the legal obligation to review the working of referral to national authorities under Article 9, threshold reduction is closely linked with the modalities of referral, and the Commission is assessing both simultaneously. Indeed, were thresholds to be reduced it is likely that a need for increased flexibility in Article 9 will emerge.

There are also good arguments militating for the retention of the possibility for Member States to refer concentrations without a Community dimension to the Commission. Whatever the level of the thresholds, there will still remain the possibility that a concentration having economic effects throughout the Community falls outside the Regulation. The retention of Article 22(3) would enable the referral of such concentrations to the Commission on an *ad-hoc* basis to prevent multiple regulatory control.

7. *Other aspects of the review*

The main areas where scope for improvement in the operation of the Regulation exists would seem to be the following:

—   Although the acceptance by the Commission of modifications to an original concentration plan is expressly provided for in the second phase of analysis, there are in fact no formal provisions to allow for this in the first phase. In order to avoid unnecessary delay and expense, the Commission has already in a number of generally straightforward cases accepted irrevocable undertakings made by the parties to remedy a specific competition problem. It would seem advisable to formalise this practice.

At the same time, with respect to the general procedures for the acceptance of undertakings provided by the parties, there is currently a lack of transparency, both in the first and the second phase of analysis, towards third parties who are unable to comment on proposed undertakings before acceptance by the Commission. This could be rectified by prior publication although inevitably it would entail some corresponding increase in deadlines.

—   Another important area, but sometimes an extremely complicated one, is the distinction between co-operative and concentrative joint ventures. The distinction is vital as it determines whether or not a joint venture operation falls under the jurisdiction of the Merger Regulation. Undoubtedly, the decisions adopted by the Commission since the implementation of the Regulation have clarified the distinction by establishing principles for the analysis of the nature of a joint venture. In the interests of legal certainty the existing case law could be codified.

—   One difficulty encountered by the Commission with the turnover thresholds is their application to the banking and finance sector. The geographic allocation of turnover for financial institutions is an extremely difficult exercise. It would seem that the application of the banking income concept as referred to in Directive 86/635 could considerably simplify matters. This was in fact envisaged by the Council and the Commission at the time that the Merger Regulation was adopted.

8. *Current position of the Commission*

The Commission is presently examining all these points in preparation of a possible proposal to Council. It is conducting this analysis on the basis of wide-ranging consultation and discussion, and is actively seeking the views of the business community. It is also keeping the Member States fully involved in this process by fully informing their Competent Authorities of the Commission's thinking and analysis. The Commission has requested their comments and suggestions with respect to the subject matter of the review. The consultative process is well under way and will be completed in the next month or two. A multi-lateral meeting with all Member States has been scheduled for 21 June to discuss the review. Consequently, as the consultative process is not yet completed, the Commission has as yet reached no conclusion regarding the proposals, if any, that it will submit to the Council.

VI. CONCLUSION

The preparation of this paper has been instructive. It has demonstrated that Community competition policy has probably developed more in terms of procedure and the level of decision-making since 1981 than it had in the first 20 years of its operation. I believe that these developments stand it in good stead to meet the challenges of the next decade. The Community has to a great extent resolved the difficult issues regarding the rights of defence in contested cases that were of major concern in the early 1980s although it is clear that we must continue to refine our procedures that implement the now established rules in individual cases. Furthermore, we have recognised the legitimate need for European businesses to receive speedy and legally binding replies to notified agreements that involve beneficial collaboration and have gone a long way down the path of meeting this need, first by the successful implementation of the Merger Regulation, second by the continuing reforms regarding Article 85 and 86 cases.

I do not pretend that the existing system is perfect, but I believe that the speed with which the Commission presently treats notifications and complaints, and the legal security that we are able to offer, already stands favourable comparison with almost any other anti-trust system in the world. This is not complacency, we will continue to improve and evolve the existing system, after all "They say best men are moulded out of faults/And for the most, become much more the better/For being a little bad.[1]

[1]Measure for Measure [V.i.(539)].

ANNEX I
Statistics of the activities of DGIV[1]

ARTICLES 85 AND 86

	1981	1982	1983	1984	1985	1986	1987	1988	1989	1990	1991	1992
Number of cases open on 31 December	4365	4199	4138	4194	3313	3622	3427	3451	3239	2734	2287	1682
of which notifications	3882	3715	3654	3708	2878	3032	2919	2909	2669	2145	1732	1064
complaints	250	259	283	314	296	330	344	357	359	345	328	287
ex-officio procedures	233	225	201	172	139	160	168	185	211	244	227	211
of which												
New cases registered during the year	293	322	296	299	304	492	313	503	368	375	388	399
of which notifications	185	256	228	195	213	384	190	376	206	201	282	246
complaints	45	49	58	76	66	75	93	83	93	97	83	110
ex-officio procedures	63	17	12	28	25	33	30	44	67	77	23	43
Thus, numbers of cases closed during the year	131	488	357	243	1185	283	408	479	578	880	835	1124
of which comfort letters	(2)	(2)	(2)	3	2	74	57	36	46	158	146	176
formal decisions	21[3]	13[4]	18[5]	23[6]	18[7]	21	18	26	15	12	17	30

[1] Source: Annual Competition Reports.
[2] no information available.
[3] of which 10 were procedural in nature (Regulation 17/62).
[4] of which 4 were procedural in nature (Regulation 17/62).
[5] of which one provisory measure regarding Article 86 and 2 were procedural in nature (Regulation 17/62).
[6] of which 3 decisions were taken in one single case.
[7] of which 1 was procedural in nature (Regulation 17/62).

ANNEX II
Press Release

COMMISSION ACTS TO FACILITATE CREATION OF CO-OPERATIVE JOINT VENTURES

The Commission has taken a series of major steps to readjust its competition policy in order to encourage co-operation between companies, particularly the setting-up of co-operative joint ventures (JVs).

Co-operative JVs are versatile instruments which help companies to pursue different procompetitive goals such as research and development of new or improved products and processes, acquisition and granting of licences for the use of intellectual property rights, provision of services, penetration of new geographic or product markets, specialisation of production, modernising of equipment and restructuring of sectors in decline. If used for the attainment of such aims, they also substantially contribute to economic integration within the single market and to strengthening the competitiveness of European industries world-wide.

The Commission has taken the view that under these circumstances, co-operative JVs generally deserve favourable treatment under Article 85(1) and (3) of the EEC Treaty and that its future competition policy should more clearly reflect this positive attitude. Such readjustment is also necessary to approximate the treatment of co-operative JVs with that of concentrative JVs which are assessed under the Merger Control Regulation.

The application of different sets of rules to the two types of JVs is consistent with a sound competition policy where both relate to different economic situations. However, where a co-operative JV entails important changes in the structure of the participating undertakings it approaches the situation of a merger. This is true particularly for production JVs and fully fledged JVs. Such cases should therefore be treated similarly to concentrative JVs. This means in substance that they should be judged favourably if they are economically beneficial, if a fair share of these benefits is passed on to the consumer, if no disproportionate restrictions are imposed on the parties and if the maintenance or development of effective competition is not put at risk. It also means that "structural JVs" under Article 85 should benefit from a procedural treatment similar to that of mergers.

To attain the above aims, the Commission—by approving a Communication today entitled "Encouraging co-operation between undertakings: a new policy towards co-operative joint ventures"—has taken three important decisions:

1.   It has *widened the scope of its "block" exemption Regulations* enabling joint ventures to be exempted from the competition rules more often and more swiftly, provided they meet the relevant conditions.

   This involves broadening the Group Exemptions on specialisation (No. 417/85), on research and development (No. 418/85), on patent licensing (No. 2349/84), and on know-how licensing (No. 556/89). The Regulations on specialisation and on R & D have been amended to cover also those co-operations which extend beyond the manufacturing stage by including arrangements on joint sales of the contract products. Both "partial function" and "full function" JVs may therefore enjoy automatic exemption. Production JVs are exempted up to an aggregate market share of 20 per cent. For fully fledged JVs, which usually pose a greater risk for competition because they stretch to the distribution stage, the maximum market share has been fixed at 10 per cent. The turnover threshold in the Regulation on specialisation has been increased from 500 million ECU to one thousand million ECU.

   Furthermore, the Regulations on patent licensing and know-how licensing no longer exclude agreements on the transfer of technology concluded between the parent companies and the JV, even where the parents are competitors, provided that a market share threshold of 20 per cent (in the case of a production licence) or of 10 per cent (in the case of a production and sales licence) is not exceeded. This change of the law relieves industry of a considerable administrative burden, as agreements which fall within a group exemption no longer need to be notified to the Commission.

2.   The Commission has adopted a Notice on the assessment of co-operative joint ventures under Article 85(1) and (3). The purpose of this Notice is to *improve the legal certainty for undertakings* by explaining the legal and economic criteria which will guide the Commission in its future policy towards JVs. Such information is particularly important in cases where a co-operation agreement does not benefit from a group exemption.

3.   The Commission has decided to *speed up its proceedings* in all cases of co-operation which imply important changes of the structure of the participating firms (see speech by Sir Leon Brittan to CEPS on "The Future of EC Competition Policy", IP(92)1009 of December 8). Within two months from the date of the complete notification the Commission services will inform the parties in writing whether or not the agreement concerned gives rise to serious doubts as to its compatibility with the EEC competition rules. The character of this letter will vary according to the circumstances of the case: it may be a "comfort letter" confirming the compatibility of the agreement with Article 85(1) or (3). In other cases it will formally approve the agreement by announcing a negative clearance or exemption decision. Where the compatibility of the agreement with the competition rules is doubtful, the parties will receive a warning letter which informs them of the Commission's intention to launch an in-depth inquiry with a view to adopt an exemption or prohibition decision. In all cases where a formal decision is envisaged, the Commission services will also inform the undertakings concerned in advance of the envisaged final date and of any modification of it. These constitute purely internal instructions for the handling of the so-called "structural" cases, and are not legally binding.

Brussels, 23 *December* 1992

Examination of witnesses

DR CLAUS-DIETER EHLERMANN, Director-General, DG IV of the European Commission (formerly Head of the Commission Legal Service), MR C JONES, and MR J JOSHUA, called in and examined.

Chairman

403. Dr Ehlermann, we are very grateful to you and your colleagues, Mr Joshua and Mr Jones, for coming this afternoon. You are by no means unfamiliar with the work of this Committee, and we have been very conscious for a long time that you have taken its reports seriously, and indeed have been extremely helpful in giving evidence to the Committee before. The fact that you have been many times does not mean that you are any the less welcome; on the contrary, you are the more welcome on this occasion in an area which we think is important to investigate where you obviously have very special experience and knowledge. We decided eventually to look into the Commission procedures and the enforcement of Community competition rules because of a number of representations that were made to us by various bodies, mainly practising lawyers in different roles; and it is for that reason we wanted to look at these things. What I would like to do is indicate one or two of the areas where people have made comments or criticisms simply so that you can comment in your own way about them. Can I begin with a fundamental question, which I think was gone into when the Committee reported last time, and that is the anxiety that some people feel that the Commission should be detective, prosecutor, negotiator and decision maker. That feeling has by no means died away. In evidence which we have heard already it has been suggested, and I give you a few illustrations, that there are no checks and balances within the Commission to deal with the problems which a unitary system causes when the Commission is carrying out all the various functions. It has been said to us, for example, that at one stage it seemed that the inspectors were a separate part of DG IV from those conducting the proceedings, but now everyone seems to be rather involved together. It has been suggested to us that there ought to be a distinction, and one witness said, "I think the fundamental and most important distinction is really between the investigator and the decision to proceed. I think one knows from my experience in other fields that the investigator, especially in a large case, very often regards his work as being an extraordinary investment and is very loth to see it being discarded". There are other examples, but I will not go into them. Would you care to comment on that? Do you think that this is still a valid argument? Does the Commission in fact seek to distinguish these various functions amongst the personnel, or with it?

(*Dr Ehlermann*) First of all, I would like to thank you for the invitation. It is always an honour to be invited by the Lords to give evidence before its Select Committees. You know that I have also appreciated very much the reports which the Lords have given. They have, I think, had a distinct impact on the Commission, or the Community's institutions in general. On your specific question, it is of course true that competition policy is run in Brussels in a way which is somewhat peculiar when you look at it from a British experience, perhaps also the French and Spanish viewpoint, where you have this distinction of functions, but it is in no way unique. The Bundeskartellamt is equally a body which combines in itself investigative and decision-making functions. I do not believe that it is possible to say that the rights of defence of the parties or the complainants necessarily suffer. First of all, there are inbuilt checks and balances within the Commission, and we will have opportunities to come to that later. One also has to take into account the very general powers of the court with respect to everything the Commission does. If you have a system of separated functions it is perfectly possible that the supervisory powers of the judiciary are less than with respect to a system which operates in the Commission. It is true that in the past within DG IV there was a separation of investigative and what you might call prosecution functions, up to 1982/83. There was an inspection directorate, and once the inspection directorate had done its work the matters were taken over by somebody else. That proved to be very inefficient. There are good reasons for that. Competition cases depend very much on the individual facts of the case. When taken over by other people, these other people reinterpret the facts which have been collected by somebody else. In writing a statement of objections, which is really the start of the contentions procedure (the matter you are looking at, and that is the second point), the one who is in charge of writing that piece will find that certain facts are lacking, and therefore he will launch his own investigation. My third point is that I do not believe the quality of the statement of objections or of the draft decision will improve if you have a change of persons—a change of rapporteur, as we say—in the course of events. I, myself, have discussed with very experienced people where it is possible, like Mr Joshua, to separate the investigative phase from what comes later. I have convinced myself that that is not possible. That it is an ongoing process. Finally, with respect to this issue, you know that we have limited resources, we have to make use in the best possible way of our limited resources, and I do not believe the separation in this respect would be helpful. What I do believe would be an improvement would be to put in complicated contentious cases, multi-party contentious cases, a team of rapporteurs so they can discuss amongst themselves the facts, particularly the facts, their interpretation of legal issues, as we have done in the merger task force. That would increase, I believe, objectivity, by providing for a series of checks and balances built into the team which would guarantee continuity and efficiency and would also have some training advantages, but with the caveat that it requires resources which

[Chairman *Contd.*]

are not available in all the directorates which deal with co-operative agreements as opposed to mergers and acquisitions.

404. Suppose the resources were available, would you then be in favour of a more divided system of investigation and decision-making presentation of the case?

(*Dr Ehlermann*) No, I think if there were more resources I would rather like to have more teams or larger teams, but I would not favour the separation of functions. The other mechanisms I believe would bring the objectivity which is useful and necessary, and I am thinking of the oral hearing.

405. You said from the point of view of efficiency you preferred the present system to that which obtained before, but what about the reaction of people outside? Do you not think people would have more confidence in the system if there was this division? This is one of the points which has been put to us. People feel, and this is what I said earlier in reading one of the extracts, that whoever is given the case will come up with a decision at the end and will follow it through and becomes more than an objective outsider, it is his case and he is going to win it.

(*Dr Ehlermann*) I have had the chance of reading briefly some of the evidence which was given to you, and I had the feeling that when you really questioned them how they would like the structure of DG IV to be, the answer was not very clear, and different individuals complaining about the actual functions had quite different ideas about how it should be structured.

406. Yes, I think that is right. I think the view of some of the witnesses was if you could start from scratch you might have a different system, but we have this system and therefore the best thing is to make it work in the most favourable way.

(*Dr Ehlermann*) I may also add with your permission that there are changes which you can operate within the existing institutional structure of the Treaty as it is, and there are changes which you cannot operate without amendment of the Treaty.

407. One of the points which has been made to us which is rather linked to this, and I would like to have your comments on it because we have not formed a view, is that one or two of the witnesses said they felt on the part of the people who were actually investigating and presenting and perhaps even deciding, there was no separation of accountability, which was a phrase frequently used—a lack of accountability of people doing the cases to somebody higher up. This was in no sense a criticism of you as Director-General but in detailed cases there ought to be somebody between you and, if I may use the phrase, people on the ground to whom they were accountable, to whom they would have to explain what they were doing

and who would keep an eye on what they were doing. Would you like to comment on that?

(*Dr Ehlermann*) I think that is a misconception of the way DG IV operates. DG IV has a hierarchy. The rapporteur is controlled by what we call a head of unit, and several units form a directorate, and the directorates are then together shaping the Directorate General. Some people feel there is even too much hierarchy, modern industrial organisations are run sometimes with less rather than more hierarchy. It is simply not true that the hierarchy does not take an interest in what the rapporteur is doing, on the contrary the head of division and the director certainly have to read everything which the rapporteur does. I personally pay great attention to the fact that the oral hearing, about which there are also some misgivings I believe, is attended by the head of unit—directors will not always find the time to attend. As I have explained in the written submission, I myself find the oral hearings so important that I attended one recently and I certainly want in controversial cases to find time to attend more. So it is not right to say the hierarchy is not involved. The hierarchy might also make mistakes, that is human, but the general assumption that the rapporteur might operate on his own is simply wrong, and I would like to reject that.

408. Although I am putting the questions to you, Dr Ehlermann, of course if either of your colleagues feel they would like to come in, would they do so without my specifically asking them. Linked with this very much was a comment by a number of people that the legal service appeared now to have less control, less impact, less relationship with what was happening in DG IV than in the past, and the suggestion was made there should be more consultation with the legal service. Do you think that criticism is valid, or if it has been deliberately changed, what was the reason for it? You, of course, have a special position having been head of the legal services before coming into your present role.

(*Dr Ehlermann*) I am not informed of any change of the fundamental rule that the legal service has to be formally consulted by departments, and of course also by DG IV, before the Commission adopts any act that is legally binding. When I say "legally binding" I refer of course also to preparatory acts, and there are many preparatory acts in the course of a procedure leading up to a formal decision. They are consulted on the statement of objectives, they attend the hearing and they are consulted on the preliminary draft decision which is done in the light of the hearing. This prelimary draft decision, which is only prepared if it is felt there is still room for decision, is then sent to the Advisory Committee, the meeting of which the Legal Service attends. Finally, they are, of course, consulted on the final draft of the decision. Their advice is particularly precious because, as you know from your own experience, my Lord Chairman, they represent the Commission

[Chairman *Contd.*]

before the Court of Justice, so if they make a mistake they have to bear somewhat its consequences. Furthermore, as a result of their direct interface with the European Courts they can advise the departments and also DG IV on how the Court of First Instance or the Court of Justice feels.

409. Although the argument, in a sense, could be turned round against the legal crusade, if you get too involved you become too committed. You would say if the lawyer gets too involved perhaps he becomes too committed and loses his independence when presenting the case before the court. Is that something you see as a problem?

(*Dr Ehlermann*) You cannot really say the legal service is less involved and at the same time say, "but this involvement does not lead to anything because they are contaminated anyway by their level of personal commitment to a case". I find this somewhat contradictory. I would strongly reject the underlying assumption that in any way the quality of the advice (because, as I said, advice is necessary and has to be given and is given) has become less precious than it has been in earlier times. They have the same problems of staffing as we have. There are eight lawyers dealing with 85/86 merger cases and they have 125 cases before both courts, which is a very heavy workload, particularly as we try to increase our efficiency and we are producing more decisions. We will probably come to that later.

Lord Wedderburn of Charlton

410. I thought I heard Dr Ehlermann speak about the checks and balances that could be built within the team, as it were, and forgive me if I misheard. If there were more resources he would strengthen that process. I was not sure how one did that. Could we see how that would work?

(*Dr Ehlermann*) My personal belief is that one of the strengths of the Merger Task Force, which is widely recognised as having done an excellent job, derives from the fact that a case is always looked at by a minimum of two, normally three, exceptionally four rapporteurs sitting on the same case. They, of course, have very short deadlines; one month, and, if the second phase is opened, an additional four months. The simple fact that you have a dialogue amongst several people seems to me to be not an absolute guarantee but better than if you are alone and you look at facts and do not discuss it necessarily immediately with colleagues. Of course you have a dialogue with your hierarchy, but to be several, going over the same facts in complicated issues, seems to me to be very helpful.

411. All the members of the team would have an investigatory role. It does not mean to say with the checks and balances within the team that one or more would have the role more pre-eminently of looking at the interests of one party or another?

(*Dr Ehlermann*) I agree with you. It would mean that everybody is doing the same job. There is not a distinction of functions within the team. All the team members would, for example, be looking at the facts and drawing up the draft statement of objections.

(*Mr Joshua*) I am an English barrister by training, and I am a rapporteur in DG IV and have conducted a number of large cartel and other cases. As I understand it, the objection that has been expressed has been not so much to the combination of functions of the adjudicatory role and the decision-making role in the Commission, it is rather to the combination of functions in the same official.

Chairman

412. I think it is a bit of both.

(*Mr Joshua*) With regard to the first point, I think it would be misleading to draw an exact parallel between a body such as the Commission, which is not a purely judicial body, and the straight courtroom model in a contentious case between two litigants. I do not think that there is anything repugnant in administrative law for a body which is given the task of performing a particular function to have, inside that function, an adjudicatory capacity provided that procedure is fair. I think it is very important in such a procedure for the right to be heard to be fully respected. I do not think there is anything particularly repugnant about the idea of one and the same body hearing and deciding, particularly when it is given the broader task of carrying out a particular policy, the enforcement of competition policy.

413. I do not think there is a dispute about the hearing and the deciding, it is the investigating, on the one hand, and hearing and deciding. You cannot separate hearing and deciding.

(*Mr Joshua*) With regard to the combination of the investigation function and the drafting function, as it were, in the same official, Dr Ehlermann has given you an account of our experience in the past when there was such a distinction of function, and he has explained that. I would like personally, from my experience, to rebut what appears to be a kind of underlying assumption that an official who does have this function, of investigating and being responsible, at least on a day-to-day basis, for the drafting of the decision and the conduct of the case, is inherently biased. I think a heavy burden of proof lies upon those who claim that the rapporteurs are biased and are always under the impression that this is their case and they are going to win it come what may.

414. "Enthusiastic" may be a more accurate word than "biased".

(*Mr Joshua*) Possibly it is a good idea to have enthusiastic civil servants. I would like to say that there is, in the system, a large number of checks and balances.

[Chairman *Contd.*]

415. How is the control exercised to make sure that people who are lower down the hierarchy are really doing their job properly? Who does that?

(*Mr Joshua*) In any case presenting a particular difficulty one always makes sure that one's immediate superior is apprised of the difficulties in a particular case. I do not think that this is a case where one particular official goes into a corner and has untrammelled power to decide a case. The idea of a case team is very important. We should emphasise that the role of the legal service is a very real check. Contrary to the impression that may have been given, I think the legal service is consulted more and more and as often as possible in complex cases.

416. You both reject the suggestion that there is a lack of accountability and a lack of control and a lack of supervision in the Commission? One suggestion put to us was perhaps that, although the Commission should lay down the rules for the competition control, the rules should be administered by some wholly independent body; in other words, you would have a tribunal, not a court but some other kind of investigatory and decision-making tribunal, totally independent of the Commission itself. Is that realistic as an idea, or is it a good idea in theory or a bad idea in theory?

(*Dr Ehlermann*) I think there are two different concepts underlying this debate. One is the German request for an independent cartel office. When the Germans formulate that request I think they are thinking of the Bundeskartellamt, which is not separating the investigator from the prosecution functions and the decision functions. With the Bundeskartellamt you have the same type of decision-making in one administrative body, but independent from a political authority. Then you have a different model, which to a certain extent I would call the British, French and Spanish model, where you have the prosecution in a ministerial body, a ministry normally, and the decision-making body, as in France and Spain at least, in something which resembles a court but which is, in fact, not a court. It is an administrative agency which functions very much to principles close to the court. Both models require Treaty amendment, that is my first point. The Germans moved such a Treaty amendment in the run-up to Maastricht, but no delegation was interested in it. I suppose the idea will come back in 1996 when there is a new intergovernmental conference, and we will see which other Member States attach importance to the proposal. In the German debate of course there is very strong commitment to competition as a principle: the positive experience with the Bundeskartellamt, the idea that this is transposable to the Community, and thirdly the interest in a decision which is motivated exclusively by competition considerations. It is interesting that in the follow-up of one of our decisions which was very controversial, this idea of an independent office was picked up by France. I do not know

exactly the motives behind this move, but I assume that they are not identical to the reasons why the German Government or the Bundeskartellamt promoted the idea. I could go into this in more detail but I have published recently a short paper on this subject and I will let you have a translation to save time.[1]

417. Thank you.

(*Dr Ehlermann*) Why I think there are considerable risks connected with this idea, they are not so much related to your concerns about the separation of functions because once again there is a combination, an amalgam, in the Bundeskartellamt like in Brussels. Something which I have not thought through in the same way is to what extent you can apply the British, French or Spanish model to us, but once again if you take the decision-making function out of the hands of the Commission, you have to change the Treaty.

418. Yes, I follow. It was of course the Bundeskartellamt we had in mind in raising this matter with you, and you have answered the query we all had in mind, whether other Member States would be interested to adopt for the Community the German model, and the answer so far is no.

(*Dr Ehlermann*) I think there is a certain current in France but the motives might be different. The Germans proposed this in order to have less politics and more competition orientated—you might say technically orientated—professional decisions. There is a very strong desire for transparency in the decision-making process. I think that later element is strongly shared probably by everybody but whether the same strong emphasis on competition orientated decision is the main motive for those in France who have advocated this solution, I do not know. It is possible that that is not the case because if you institute such an independent office, you need political supervision. The debate about the European Central Bank has clearly shown that it will not be accepted I think to have an independent office without political control. If you want to create a body controlled by a political body, you have to give this political body political rights of supervision, which means in relation to mergers, for instance, you have to introduce something into the merger regulations which allows such control. Therefore the model is not neutral with respect to the substantive rules. My compatriots have fought for a competition orientated merger control, they will have to introduce something like the "public interest test".

419. We heard quite a lot about the control of independent bodies last week, perhaps we could leave that rather big change and go back to the system we do have. I would like to mention two other points of general importance which have been adverted to by witnesses. The first of those relates to access to the documents in the possession of the Commission. Nobody suggests that you

---

[1] Printed at p.134 below.

[Chairman *Contd.*]

should be required to make confidential documents available, even confidential parts of documents, but there is so far a feeling expressed that parties do need to see more of what you have got, particularly things you have got which may assist them in the preparation of their case. What is your comment on that? I know you have introduced some additional safeguards in the Commission, and the Court of First Instance has recently in one or two cases ordered that documents should be made available to the parties and laid down to some extent the rules. One of the comments made is that in the first place those internal safeguards are not producing the documents, which I would like you to comment on, and secondly, the suggestion that what is indicated by the Court of First Instance is not being carried out by the Commission. That was specifically said by one of our witnesses.

(*Dr Ehlermann*) I think I have explained in the written comments the origin of what is called "access to file" which is really the right to be heard, and the 11th Competition Report which went beyond the requirements of the Court of Justice. Let me just add out of the 90 or so infringement cases adopted since the introduction of the reform, problems with respect to access to file have occurred in only a very small number of cases, but of course these cases are the ones which have given rise to criticism. These cases concern almost exclusively multi-defendant cartels; cartels with a certain number of participants, and in these cases I would like to emphasise that we have a conflict between, on the one hand, the desire to make the file available, maximum disclosure, and on the other hand the necessity to respect the principle of confidentiality and business secrets. Take, for example, a cartel involving 20 defendants. The proof of the infringement results from inspections in all the companies concerned. In order to prove a price-fixing or quota arrangement, it is necessary to analyse the prices and sales of each company over a significant period and to do so a large number of documents must be copied at each company. These documents often are at least company-confidential and may even constitute business secrets, and in many cases they will consist of letters between two of the companies involved and will therefore be confidential vis-a-vis some members of the cartel but not others. The file may be some 60 volumes and more in length. In such circumstances access to the full file in each of the 20 companies involves a task for the Commission which is really of epic proportions. Therefore we have stated in the 18th Competition Report that in those circumstances rather than allowing companies to inspect our file, we send them the documents accessible to them with the statement of objections. That is the only realistic way to carry out this task of what is called access to file in those circumstances. Therefore it is not only one procedure which is possible. I recognise, my Lord Chairman, that there is confusion, and I recognise also, particularly with the *Flat Glass* decision the court found that the Commission had failed to live up to its obligations. That is of great concern to me and my colleagues. What can one do?

420. I suspect that there is not a government in existence, now or in the past, which has not at some stage refused to produce documents and somebody made a mistake and they ought to have been produced. What I think we are particularly interested in is whether the right rules are being laid down for people to follow in the Commission?

(*Dr Ehlermann*) What to do? What have we done already? First of all, I have to say I looked particularly closely into the origin of the *Flat Glass* case and convinced myself that it was a mistake, but it was certainly not anything which was a deliberate attempt to deceive the parties. It is perfectly explainable, but it is a mistake. First of all, I have decided that management, that is the hierarchy, should be involved more than it has perhaps been in the past. Second, we are drawing up an internal manual of procedures which every rapporteur should have. Third, we have asked the legal service to determine together what elements of the file are and what are not accessible so that we have an external element of control. We have done that with respect to the list of documents to be sent, together with the statement of objections. What could be done in the future? After your report of 1982 the Hearing Officer was introduced, an element of internal checks and balances. You know the mandate of the Hearing Officer. The mandate is at least not clear on the question of whether the Hearing Officer has a role to play with respect to access to the file. I think it is advisable to clarify this point, and to make the Hearing Officer a sort of ombudsman.

421. We would like you to deal with the Hearing Officer in some detail.

(*Dr Ehlermann*) Here it really is a point where the Hearing Officer could be somebody to whom the parties would address themselves if they have the feeling that in this dilemma between making documents accessible and protecting confidentiality somebody objective, not involved in the investigative process, is necessary. I do not see any other possibility than to involve the Hearing Officer. I am in favour of clarifying, I would say, the mandate of the Hearing Officer, and establishing for the first time the principle that he has the right to be involved in contentious questions regarding issues relating to access to the file. I also believe that we have to put out a notice in general to clearly set out the rules in order to avoid misunderstandings. As I have explained in the written submission to you, the parties in a contentious case sometimes take a somewhat contradictory attitude. On the one hand, they declare that practically everything they submit is confidential or a business secret, but at the same time they want to have access to the papers of their co-defendants. It is a very, very difficult task and will probably always remain controversial.

Lord Holme of Cheltenham

422. In Dr Ehlermann's very interesting submission on this point, on page 4, the second paragraph towards the ends, he says that the Commission ". . . is not obliged to give the companies concerned access to its entire file . . .", the point with which you have just been dealing, but you go on, ". . . although it is, I believe, obliged to provide to the companies concerned documents that are manifestly exculpatory in relation to the allegations raised by the Commission". Given your own disposition to lean towards making more documents available rather than less and to having normative rules that are widely understood, I wondered about the use of the word "manifestly". If any document tends to be exculpatory, for somebody who, on the whole, who wants to open it up, it seems a very major qualification. I would have thought that natural justice and other considerations, let alone openness, would lead you more in the direction of saying "anything that was remotely exculpatory", rather than "manifestly"? I am unclear whether the word "obliged" is your interpretation of the current legal obligations of the Commission, or whether it is a statement of values; whether it is a statement of what you think should be?

(*Dr Ehlermann*) I understand this to be a fair description of what the court in one of its leading judgments, *Hercules*, has said. I have also looked, before this meeting, at what the jurisprudence of the Supreme Court of the United States says. It seems to me that an investigative agency in the US is not obliged to really make available everything and allow the parties to pick out the most minor details in order to present its case. If one has, in the documents, something which clearly pleads in favour of the company I think that we are obliged to make it available under *Hercules*. I personally feel that it is also possible to go beyond that. I do believe, however, that there are limits. There are also limits for the very simple reason that the more clear-cut the infringement is the more the parties are inclined to use delaying tactics. Therefore, at the end of the day one has to be careful in being too generous.

423. The word "manifestly" is perhaps not over-generous?

(*Dr Ehlermann*) No, but that is, as I said, our way of understanding what the court has requested, and it is always possible to go beyond that.

Chairman

424. I think that in this country lawyers have a very liberal approach towards the discovery of documents and give powers to the courts to order production of a wider range of documents than would normally happen in other countries. There may be two problems here: firstly, to make sure that the right documents are produced; secondly, to make sure that people feel the system is working. Your idea of putting out new guidelines and a new memorandum, and a feeling about the sort of documents that ought to be produced, would seem to go a considerable way to achieving that. Suppose that someone is dissatisfied with a refusal. Let us consider the technicalities of dealing with that. You have mentioned the Hearing Officer as someone to whom they can apply. What happens now if someone is dissatisfied and feels you are hiding something? What do they do about it?

(*Dr Ehlermann*) The problem is of course raised at the latest in the oral hearing. We have had recently a very big case involving some 70 or more parties, the *Cement* case, where the issue of access to files was the object of an application to the Court of First Instance. As you know, the Court of First Instance said this matter had to be looked at in case there was a final decision, and then it had to be determined whether the Commission had violated its obligations or not. So there we had a case where parties made it an issue before the judiciary even before the oral hearing took place, but normally it would be brought out at the oral hearing and there the Hearing Officer would have to make up his mind, in judging the case in the light of the oral hearing, how he felt about it.

425. Is there a case for giving the Hearing Officer or somebody else at sufficient level a power to hear applications of this kind even before the oral hearing?

(*Dr Ehlermann*) That is my idea. When I said I wanted the Hearing Officer to be a sort of ombudsman for specific questions relating to access to file, I thought of applications being made to him or her before the oral hearing instead of going to the Court of Justice.

426. Could that include other interlocutory matters as well so the Hearing Officer would be the equivalent—I am sure you are familiar with our procedure here—of our judicial officer called the Master who deals with interlocutory proceedings in civil cases. One idea we have heard canvassed is perhaps the Hearing Officer should have very much the function, as one of his functions, of the Master, so if a party was dissatisfied with any stage of the proceedings he would go and ask the Hearing Officer to make a ruling. Is that practicable?

(*Dr Ehlermann*) I would have to reflect on it because the only issue I addressed really in preparation for this meeting, and also as a consequence of *Flat Glass*, was access to the file, but I could envisage other complaints, like for instance the duration of the period in which a party has to reply to a statement of objections.

427. Precisely the example we have had put to us.

(*Dr Ehlermann*) I use the opportunity—thank you, my Lord Chairman for allowing me to do this—I have read that somebody has said it is not uncommon they get ten days before Christmas to reply. I do not know when that has happened,

[Chairman Contd.]

certainly not recently. In discussions with the Hearing Officer we have agreed to make the normal period of reply to statements of objections two months.

428. Two issues arise on time. Firstly, the time for parties to do something is too short. Secondly, the parties might feel the Commission was not getting on with the case. Could the Hearing Officer not entertain that kind of complaint before the oral hearing?

(Dr Ehlermann) Let me finish with the deadlines for replying to Statements of Objections. We have two months, in the case of complicated cases it is even more, it is three months. If there is a holiday period we try to take this into account to avoid the argument that we take a lot of time for ourselves and the poor parties do not have time to reply. That is something which is very dear to the Hearing Officer and he has already in representing the interests of the parties achieved some results. Again I would have to reflect on it, but I do not see any difficulty involving the Hearing Officer more than he is in all sorts of procedural difficulties arising before the hearing. That is to a certain extent more economical than to have these issues raised after the hearing. I am sorry, you mentioned a second point?

429. The second point is, if it is felt whoever is dealing with the case is not getting on with it, the Hearing Officer could be asked to tell somebody to get a move on. Is that a possible role for him?

(Dr Ehlermann) There, of course, we are changing completely the problem. I think in contentious cases where practising lawyers have particularly complained bitterly before you about DG IV and the way it operates, they hardly complain that things move too slowly. On the contrary here we move to complaints, and I can very well see the concern of a complainant who has not had the case investigated quickly enough. But there we move into the field of subsidiarity and sharing out responsibilities with national competition authorities—do you want me to go into that?

Chairman] No, we will come on to that later on as a separate issue.

Lord Archer of Sandwell

430. I was wondering how you envisage the function of the Hearing Officer in relation to the disclosure of documents. The problem which every system has is that if you are wondering whether a document should be disclosed, you cannot hear a full argument from both sides as to whether it should be disclosed. Presumably in a number of cases the parties concerned will be told of the existence of the document even if they are not told of its contents? Is that so? They will have the opportunity to make representations about that. Presumably the Hearing Officer will have full information about the contents as well? Is that right?

(Dr Ehlermann) The Hearing Officer being part of the administration is, of course, entitled to see the totality of the file—confidential, business secrets, et cetera. I strongly believe that the Hearing Officer in view of his mandate and in view of his function as a somewhat neutral personality, as you said a sort of administrative Master of the Rolls, will necessarily take a very detached view and judge whether the document after all can be made available, either in full or in part. He might need for that exercise, by the way, resources. There is an argument about his resources but I think for the moment his resources are good enough. But for an enlarged function he may, of course, need more resources.

Chairman

431. But if you expanded his functions to make him more like a Master, you might need more than one Hearing Officer, you might need more staff.

(Dr Ehlermann) In fact today we have two Hearing Officers, one for the ordinary Article 85, 86 business and one for mergers.

432. Yes, you explain this in your written paper.

(Dr Ehlermann) Yes. For the very important case of Cement, I had to appoint even a third person. There is no difficulty to have more than one Hearing Officer, even in the field of 85, 86 cases. What I was thinking of was to give the Hearing Officer appropriate staff to look into the file, if necessary to check if that is beyond his own physical possibilities.

433. May I interpose that witnesses speak very warmly of Mr Johannes personally and his work and what he has sought to do, but there is a feeling that he should have rather more opportunity to control things, and I think you go along with that to a certain extent. You used the word "neutral", does the Hearing Officer have sufficient independence and neutrality to be able effectively to do these jobs? It is not a loaded question, I just ask your opinion.

(Dr Ehlermann) I think that is a perfectly fair question—your questions are always fair. There are three people with a special status in the Commission's administration, there is the financial controller, who has by the way the rank of Director-General, there is an ombudsman for personnel matters in administration, and there is the Hearing Officer. Interestingly enough the Hearing Officer, among these three, has the lowest rank; he is only in our jargon an A3. That is a disadvantage but it also has an advantage because it protects him from any danger, which people in higher positions have, under the staff regulations. That is also a matter for consideration, of course, whether hierarchally it might be useful to upgrade him.

434. This was suggested by some of our witnesses, that he could be upgraded.

[Chairman *Contd.*]

(*Dr Ehlermann*) I am personally not opposed to that. However, as you know, we have major budgetary problems, and budgetary authorities are not very amenable these days to create new posts or upgrade posts. However, that is a matter for consideration.

Lord Archer of Sandwell

435. Before we left the question of disclosure and moved on to the Hearing Officer, I wondered if I could ask a supplementary——

(*Dr Ehlermann*) I have not really answered your question. I feel he is sufficiently independent. I will do everything to maintain his independence. I appreciate the advice of the Hearing Officer greatly in order to avoid the repetition of events which have aroused so much criticism, such as the *Flat Glass* decision.

436. I think I rolled two questions into one earlier. The first part of the question was intended to be whether Dr Ehlermann took the view that, even if a document should not be disclosed, its existence wherever possible should be disclosed to the parties, so that the Hearing Officer would have the advantage of hearing the argument as to whether they should be allowed to see it?

(*Dr Ehlermann*) I do not feel on safe grounds to answer your question as to whether the parties know about the existence. Perhaps Mr Joshua could reply to that.

(*Mr Joshua*) My Lord Chairman, I think it is essential here to get away from the realms of speculation, as it were, because we are often told, "Because we say we are innocent there must be some document somewhere which shows that we are innocent. We haven't got it; you haven't produced it; therefore you must be hiding it". There are a number of non sequiturs in that sort of argument, but we do have it quite often. With regard to the question raised by Lord Holme about manifestly exculpatory documents, I think we have to bear in mind that we are not dealing here with cases of police statements and ordinary street crimes and so on when one has witness statements; we are dealing in many cases with documents which are very, very confidential. We go to economic operators and very large companies, and much of what we obtain is extremely sensitive, and we are very aware of the need to maintain confidentiality in that respect. If, however there were a document which was important for the case, then I think our rapporteurs are all extremely careful to make sure that this document is disclosed. Assume that there is a document which is so important that it is exculpatory or could tend to exculpate in an important fashion, and it is in the possession of one or other of the defendants (and I use the word "defendants" loosely; we do not call them that), were that document to be in his possession then I think it would be quite normal to expect that that document would be produced by him during the proceedings, if it was important.

I think it is necessary here to be a little bit more specific. Often in cases we have been asked for the opportunity for a company to go on a speculative basis through all the documents of its competitors on the basis that there might be some document somewhere which might in some unspecified way help them. We have, for natural reasons, been wary of that; but we have, on several occasions, asked the legal representatives of those companies if they could possibly identify, even in general terms, a possible line of defence and we would then undertake to go back through the documentation of their competitors to see if there was any document which could be relevant to that issue. We have been very ready to do that. I can assure you that we are extremely careful. We bend over backwards if there is a document which is relevant. If it is a question of the conflict between confidentiality and the right to be heard, we are very careful to make sure that the right to be heard is paramount.

Chairman

437. Could we just move on to the oral hearing. Some of our witnesses feel that there is a very strong case for making the Hearing Officer's report at the end of the oral hearing, as I understand it, available either generally to the public or at least to the parties. Would you care to comment on that?

(*Dr Ehlermann*) I think the answer is rather, no. The Hearing Officer clearly is an internal mechanism. He is not something like a judge whose judgment of course has to be made public. The parties have attended the hearing; Member States have attended the hearing; they can all form their judgment about the respective procedural rights and obligations. I do not believe that it would be right to make the Hearing Officer's report public.

438. Any decisions of his on interlocutory matters clearly would have to be reasoned, or might have to be reasoned, and then that could be made public. If the Hearing Officer were given the power to deal with what we have called interlocutory matters, and he gave a decision, that would no doubt either be reasoned or at least have to be notified to the parties; they would obviously know about it. Why should that not be made public?

(*Dr Ehlermann*) I doubt whether the Hearing Officer would issue a decision to the parties. In my mind the Hearing Officer would say, as he or she would say now to the Director General and the Commissioner responsible, "You're making a mistake here". It would be followed up by somebody else's decision. I do not see him making a decision with external effects. I think that would change his role.

439. That is totally in contradiction with the concept of him exercising an administrative quasi judicial function on interlocutory complaints. "You have not given me enough time", why should he

[Chairman Contd.]

not say, "The Commission must give you three months, and not two months"?

(Dr Ehlermann) It depends very much how you can see his role.

440. We are looking to his role in the future. We realise under the present procedure he does not have that function, but why should he not usefully have that function? It would give confidence to the parties, would it not?

(Dr Ehlermann) I would have to reflect on that. I am not sure whether I share this view—that he could act with respect to the parties externally.

441. That then answers the question I was going to lead on to, as to whether there should be some way in which contentions of the parties which deal with interlocutory matters could not be dealt with by some special procedure before the Court of First Instance. Suppose a party is dissatisfied with something that happened along the road, surely it is not very satisfactory, is it, that they should have to wait until they take the final decision to Luxembourg? Do you think it would be possible to adopt a form of what we would call an appeal from a master to a judge with some very speeded up interlocutory procedure?

(Dr Ehlermann) There are really two issues: one is the interlocutory procedure before the Court of Justice; and another thing is the legal status of the Hearing Officer and his decisions.

442. I am talking about a challenge to something that has either been done by your team along the road which, instead of waiting until the final hearing for a decision, could be dealt with earlier. Secondly, if there were to be decisions, if there were decisions of the Hearing Officer which could be challenged before the Court of First Instance. Do you not think it is unsatisfactory to have to wait before the final order is challenged before these interlocutory matters are looked at?

(Dr Ehlermann) On the issue of the status of the Hearing Officer's decision, and to whom they are attributable, I would like to reflect. I do not see the possibility of transforming the Hearing Officer into somebody who takes binding decisions. After all, in the institutional system of the Commission, decisions are attributable to the Commission and only to the Commission, even if the person actually signing a letter representing a decision is a Director or a Director-General. At the end all the powers stem from the Commission. I am not sure whether it would be right to isolate the Hearing Officer in such a way so he takes decisions with external effect and his decisions are attackable. I do not think that is compatible with the system as it now is. I shall now address the question of interlocutory judgments on procedural issues. On strictly procedural issues, if you could separate them from substance, but that is a big "if", I think there is a good argument to deal with them quickly, and even before the case after years comes before the court. However, I would put one proviso to this, and that is the court must

be able to decide quickly. In the Cement case the procedural incident took I believe some 10 months, and we suspended our work during that period, which is not very good for moving cases forward.

443. I quite agree. The concept was that any interlocutory decision taken might be treated by a totally new procedure before the Court of First Instance—you might have one judge sitting or two judges sitting with a much more informal procedure than obtains at the moment. You think if the thing could be done speedily, it might be a useful procedure to adopt?

(Dr Ehlermann) Once again, if we could find appropriate procedures to deal with an issue of that kind quickly, and to avoid delaying tactics, I would not be opposed to that. Let me be precise on one point: I think the jurisprudence of the Court on the statement of objections should by all means be up-held. That is, we are dealing with procedural issues other than for statement of objections—I am thinking of the IBM case—and whether this is well-reasoned and whether the underlying legal doctrines are right. That is not a matter for an interlocutory judgment.

444. I understand that. Because of time, unless my colleagues have other questions, perhaps we could deal with some questions rather more shortly although I realise they may be big issues. Comfort letters appear not to be giving quite the comfort to everybody which the term might suggest. I think you have indicated that the use of comfort letters could be improved?

(Dr Ehlermann) Comfort letters are useful, they should be maintained. Yes, we can improve them with respect to transparency, because we can have short notices when a notification comes in, on the lines of what is done under the merger regulations requesting third party comments. We could also issue notices more frequently—though in both cases we need translations and translation is a problem with administrative delays. We could produce an Article 19 paragraph 3 notice in the Official Journal. We can give greater publicity to the content of the comfort letters. We have decided to distinguish clearly in comfort letters whether they are a substitute for a negative clearance or whether they are a substitute for an exemption. What do we want to do? Thinking seriously about this, where we have a comfort letter in so-called structural cases where a lot of investment is involved and where people like to have legal security (which is another issue for more transparency), a comfort letter has to be followed by a formal decision not for negative clearance but for granting an individual exemption. On decisions, we are thinking very hard about how to overcome the administrative lourdeur which makes it so difficult to issue more than some 20 decisions a year until now. We clearly need the co-operation of the Member States and their representatives in the Advisory Committee.

Lord Holme of Cheltenham

445. I wonder if I could ask Dr Ehlermann a question I was able to ask Sir Bryan Carsberg? Particularly if a comfort letter is now to be followed either by a formal exemption or by a negative clearance, would you expect that to be influential or decisive with national competition authorities?

(*Dr Ehlermann*) That is a very important and difficult issue you raise. I would make a major distinction between two areas. One is the area of exemption, where the Commission has a monopoly according to Regulation number 17. I am convinced that it is indispensable to maintain this monopoly, for a series of reasons. But there is another area where Member States' competition authorities can apply Community law, that is the full range of Article 86 and 85, paragraph 1, and that is the area in which we have complaints. I am convinced that we should share out more and more among national competition authorities and DG IV, the complaints according to the question whether there is sufficient Community interest or there is not. This sharing out of responsibilities between agencies is greatly facilitated if a competition authority, a Member State, is allowed and entitled to apply Articles 85 and 86 directly. More and more Member States are nowadays allowed to do so. I would very much like that Sir Bryan would be among them. That would be, I believe, a major contribution to subsidiarity at the level of enforcement and application of Community law.

Chairman

446. How many Member States do not have the power to apply 85 and 86?

(*Dr Ehlermann*) Those who are ready able and willing to apply at this stage include in particular Germany, and since December last year, France. On my list are also Italy, Spain, Belgium, Greece and Portugal. The four who are not are the United Kingdom, Ireland, Denmark and the Netherlands. I say Germany and France are able and also willing, because in order to apply Community law you need staff. The Belgians have a new authority but they have not got the staff to do so. So that is always a consideration which has to be added. But I would make a strong plea in favour of subsidiarity to have Articles 85 and 86 made applicable not only by the judges but also by administrative authorities charged with the application of Community law.

447. You have of course put out a notice about the application of Articles 85 and 86 by national authorities. We have heard one or two comments about that. Has that notice led to much criticism and comment by Member States other than the United Kingdom as to whether the guidelines are the right guidelines?

(*Dr Ehlermann*) I am aware, of course, of the criticism of this country. Let me just say briefly that the communication of December last year is a sort of belated product of reflections on subsidiary which were undertaken years before the subsidiarity debate became a political issue. I have always felt a grassroots approach to the implementation of Community law is essential if the internal market is going to work. I do not believe the Commission alone is able to control—by the way you do not have central control mechanisms in the Member States, enforcement is done by interested parties whether they are citizens or companies. So the debate is wider than just competition law, but competition law lends itself particularly well to this. With hindsight, it is astonishing that we did not think earlier of national administrative authorities, but started with the courts. I think there were fewer competition authorities able to apply, or really capable of applying Articles 85(1) and 96. We did not yet have confirmation by the court that there was discretion with respect to the acceptance of complaints by the Commission—*Automec II* was not yet decided—and we also had uncertainty as to what extent we could share information with national competition authorities, something which the Court of First Instance clarified in the so-called Spanish banking case. There remain advantages with respect to the courts, that they can give injunctive relief very quickly; they can award damages, and you know these different items. I recognise that there are also disadvantages of applying Community Competition law in national courts. Some of the disadvantages are peculiar to a certain legal system. I understand in the British system there are these disadvantages. I see the biggest disadvantage that applying competition law, at least in certain areas, requires very difficult evaluation of economic factors, a balancing of these facts, and judges might not be all equipped to do that.

448. How far is the difference in remedies a discouragement for use of national courts, or do you think we will be able to move towards some form of harmonised system of remedies in national courts?

(*Dr Ehlermann*) Frankly, I think that the time to harmonise these issues has passed. One might have thought about harmonisation in the 60s. I do not believe that the 90s are a period in which we could successfully and convincingly start a movement of harmonisation. Particularly with respect to remedies, I see differences in our judicial systems which are due to profound historical differences and cultural attitudes. A recommendation might be a perfect instrument in this country but it might not be as efficient in other Member States. Therefore, I do not believe that we should engage in a process of harmonising remedies. We should not do it piecemeal just for one specific economic sector.

449. That obviously creates certain difficulties if you do not have an analogous system of remedies but, despite that, you feel that there is much more

[Chairman Contd.]

scope for use of national authorities and national courts in future?

(Dr Ehlermann) I think we have to use all instances available to make Community law applicable—both courts and, what I see now as much more promising, national competition authorities, provided that they are allowed to apply Community law, or at least they have the equivalent instrument under national law.

450. Perhaps I could just put two questions to you on Articles 85 and 86 and then move over in our remaining minutes to mergers. It does not really give it the appropriate time which it merits. We have heard quite a lot of comments about the Commission's fining policy. It is said that there have been changes and people were not given warning about those changes, and that the policy was not sufficiently transparent. Would you like to comment on that? We are aware of the *Musique Diffusion* case in which the court said you could change the fining levels without giving people warning, but this criticism goes rather further than that.

(Dr Ehlermann) I do not believe that there has been a substantial change in the fining policy in the recent past. I think that a major change occurred at the end of the 70s and the beginning of the 80s with the famous *Pioneer* case. We have adopted some 85 cases since January 1982 in which we have fined. The court has, of course, in the past overturned a certain number of decisions on the grounds that they were insufficiently reasoned, but it has only stated that the reasons for imposing a fine were, as far as I recall, insufficiently reasoned in one case. The court has a tendency to reduce the Commission fines. I am looking forward to the day when the court increases the fines.

451. I remember a shiver in court when Mr Advocate General Verloren Van Themaat read out his opinion reminding the Commission that the Court had power to increase the fine!

(Dr Ehlermann) I do not think there is a change. I think the criticism is mainly that it is not foreseeable what kind of fine comes out of the process, and a practising lawyer would probably like to see a sort of tariff formula where one can calculate in advance. I do not think that is possible or advisable. There has to be an element of deterrence in fines. Anyway the risk of being caught is not that big and people would calculate whether they should or should not violate the law in view of the tariff. It is simply not possible to have a tariff because there have to be wide discretionary powers in order to balance all the different elements—Regulation No. 17 first, the Commission and its practice later, and the court following the Commission. There is simply not one case resembling another one. So I reject the argument that there is arbitrariness. Of course one can always motivate decisions better, and there is a strong pressure from the court to motivate more. I can very well understand that. I do not believe that

you can detect in any way something which is fundamentally flawed, and I can go through the list of criteria but we can forward that to you if you want.

452. I think it is really that people have complained about the lack of transparency. We have put to them the suggestion that if people knew too much about the fining policy they would be able too easily to decide in advance whether it was worth buying their conviction. The element of surprise in fining might be a very important weapon for the Commission. I do not think they necessarily accepted that suggestion! Moving on to something else, one other thing which has been much pressed upon us is that there could be and should be a much greater use of block exemptions. Could you comment briefly on that?

(Dr Ehlermann) I do not think that there is any major difficulty procedurally to issue more block exemptions. For some of them you need an authorisation of the Council, where it does not presently exist. Block exemptions require a sort of "habilitation" by the Council. But what is more important is that in order to issue a block exemption the Commission needs experience, and it needs to have a situation where it can categorise this experience into hard and fast rules—black clauses, white clauses, grey clauses. There are two obvious candidates for further block exemptions which come to mind. One is trade mark licensing, and another is software licensing, but we do not have sufficient experience. A candidate which does not come into my mind, that is it is not a candidate, is joint ventures because they are too different. We should not over-do block exemptions. When we discussed with Member States at the end of last year our improvements with respect to joint ventures, we were criticised by at least one Member State, one competition authority, of becoming too lenient and allowing too many agreements to be white-washed and not being careful under the competition principle. There are inherent limits from the point of view of substance.

453. Something which really qualified you would be in favour of adopting?

(Dr Ehlermann) Yes.

454. But one should not go rushing around looking for block exemptions?

(Dr Ehlermann) Yes. I am in favour because block exemptions clarify the situation. They are applicable by national courts and they reduce the input into DG IV's caseload.

455. A final question on something you said in your paper. Before the Commission carry out inspections on company premises and so on, that the leave of a judge in the Court of First Instance or the European Court should be obtained. Is it not satisfactory to go to a national judge from the point of view of time?

(Dr Ehlermann) I believe that the respect for fundamental human rights requires the green light

[Chairman Contd.]

by a judge. I have always felt that the natural judge for Commission actions or Community actions and decisions is the Court of First Instance. The national courts are natural judges for what national authorities and national officials do. The *Hoechst* case has limited the powers of control of national courts lacking the power of the judiciary in Luxembourg to look in advance at the Commission decision to order the investigation. There are risks under the Hoechst jurisprudence that national courts might not respect these limits. I see advantages of bringing in the Court of First Instance before the Commission decision is implemented; advantages that people see that the Community respects in its own judicial system fundamental rights; that there is a control on the Commission decision (which is really a decisive act) not only at the end of the process when a final decision is produced. I recognise that what is a simple idea, which we have tried to put to the court in the *Hoechst* case, is difficult to achieve because you do not only need an amendment of Regulation 17 but you need to amend the rules which govern the court. I do not know whether you have to amend the Treaty or the statute or the rules of procedure, but you have to open the court to such an application. I would personally be in favour of that.

456. If I remember rightly in the *Hoechst* case, *Solvay* and other cases, the European Court had very much in mind that we might have to use national procedures to get consent to do something, and it would be an advantage in using a national court, in that the national court would have power to grant an injunctive relief, to order a company to produce documents or rely on inspection, which the Court of First Instance would not have unless you gave it specific power?

(*Dr Ehlermann*) It works well in this country. I think, because of the involvement of national officials, it is probably always necessary to have a national judge, but I believe that his role would be clarified if there was an EC Court decision, but I do not know by whom. The President of the Court of First Instance, or a Chamber of the Court of First Instance could clarify the situation, but you need a special procedure.

457. You say that the limits might not be respected in some countries, without mentioning names. It might have the opposite effect that the protection might be extended in a way which you did not like?

(*Dr Ehlermann*) I would like to clarify the situation. I think that is something which is very important for you: justice has not only to be done, but it has to be seen to be done.

458. Unfortunately, we have run out of time. What I would like to suggest is that, instead of moving into mergers at this late hour, what we should do is wait until the Commission's proposals are published and then perhaps we could put some questions to you in writing, if you would allow us, if we have any questions when the new proposals come out to revise the Merger Regulations?

(*Dr Ehlermann*) I could satisfy your curiosity about our thinking with respect to the possible amendments in giving you a document which we have sent to all Member States competition authorities, which we will discuss on June 21st. Of course, that is not the final proposal of the Commission. Once the Commission makes a proposal that would be public knowledge. If you were interested in this I could let you have a copy.

459. We would be very glad to have that. Thank you very much indeed. If we have got any supplementary questions we will come back to you. May I say that when Sir Bryan was here it was obvious he feels he has a very comfortable relationship with the Commission in relation to mergers and other matters with which he is concerned. Unless my colleagues have any other questions may I thank you very warmly for having prepared this excellent and very detailed and helpful paper, and secondly for coming and giving us the benefit of your opinion and advice on these various matters. We could not have had anyone more distinguished in the Community to come and we are very grateful to you and to your two colleagues for the help you have given us.

(*Dr Ehlermann*) Thank you very much. Appearing before the Lords always obliges one to clarify one's mind, and I have gone through this process so it is very helpful to myself.

Chairman] Perhaps I can add from a personal point of view it was very nice to hear you, even in a different capacity!

Translation of Article by Dr Ehlermann, referred to in Q416
(Original published in Handelsblatt 8.6.1993/Nr. 108, at page 7)

An EC Cartel Office:
Will it bring only benefits?

In Germany the call for an EC Cartel Office is currently one of the areas of competition policy with the highest media profile. Elsewhere in the Community, however, it is scarcely mentioned. After all, it cannot become a reality unless the Treaties establishing the Community are first amended; as yet, the Maastricht Treaty has not even been ratified. Amendments to the Treaty do, of course, require the unanimity of the Contracting Parties, something which probably cannot be counted on even for the next Treaty revision (on which negotiations are due to start in 1996).

So why is the subject of an EC Cartel Office so unusually topical among the German public?

The call has been triggered mainly by the fact that, in the next few months, Brussels merger control rules will come up for review. In practice, the question is whether they should be extended to certain mergers which as yet cannot be vetted by the Commission. The call for an EC Cartel Office, which at present cannot be realized, is a convenient way of opposing the lowering of the threshold values for "mergers having a Community dimension".

But the motives for the present German interest in an EC Cartel Office are not just economic. The revival in interest has been sparked off by the merger control rules.

The structural reasons for advocating an independent EC competition authority are:

   (i)   the considerable importance attached to the competition principle in Germany;

   (ii)   the good reputation which the Federal Cartel Office enjoys among the public;

   (iii)   the mistrust felt by the public towards the Commission as the guardian of EC competition rules;

   (iv)   the assumption that the blueprint of the Federal Cartel Office can be transferred to EC level: The advocates of an EC Cartel Office expect it to pave the way for decision-making that will focus on competition. They are willing to put up with any possible risks or disadvantages.

It is worth mentioning that there were recent vociferous calls for an EC competition authority independent of the Commission in another Member State, namely France, in the wake of the decision in the de Havilland case. The reasons for this were, of course, the direct opposite of those given by its German advocates: the objective was no longer the competition principle, but greater room for manoeuvre for industrial policy. This episode should give us food for thought.

There can be no denying that the call for an independent EC competition authority reflects a general trend. All over the world, competition decisions are increasingly being taken by authorities that are independent of government to a greater or lesser extent. The German model, in which prosecution and decision-making functions are combined in a single authority—the Federal Cartel Office—is only one example. The two sets of functions frequently tend to be kept separate from each other. The prosecution function remains with the ministerial bureaucracy; only the decision-making function is entrusted to a kind of independent court (as in France and Spain). It is unusual for effective supervision of competition to be exercised by the government alone (the Commission) supported by its ministerial bureaucracy (the Director-General for Competition). In fact, this happens only in Brussels.

Nor can it be denied that an independent EC competition authority would have a number of advantages. Its mandate would be confined to application of the competition rules and divorced from the sphere of the executive's general political business. By staffing it with experts, the influence of politicians, which is a major source of concern for its advocates, could be mitigated further. The specific nature of the decisions taken, ie the fact that they dealt with the particular circumstances of each case, would help them to be accepted. In any event, the transparency of the decision-making process would be enhanced. The Commission would be relieved of the need to take many decisions that were frequently routine in nature. The responsibility for politically controversial and highly sensitive decisions would lie primarily with the EC Cartel Office.

These advantages are, however, offset by a number of disadvantages and dangers which are not perceived—or at any rate not perceived clearly enough—in public discussion but should not be forgotten.

1. An independent EC competition authority is inconceivable without a political supervisory authority. Anyone who has followed the discussion on the European Central Bank will agree immediately. The candidates for such a role are, of course, the Commission but, in the eyes of Member States more favourably inclined towards an industrial policy, probably (also) the Council.

The example of German ministerial authorization shows that the role of the political supervisory authority cannot be confined to verifying *de facto* and *de jure* basis for the Cartel Office decision, as this is a matter for the Court of Justice in Luxembourg. Rather, political control means verification on the basis of political criteria, ie the introduction into merger control of aspects not purely related to competition. However, the Federal Government has fought against this for years. It has finally succeeded in winning acceptance for its purely competition-oriented approach. Should this now be abandoned?

2. The advocates of an EC Cartel Office are willing to tolerate this drawback because they are counting on transparency and the deterrent effect of a public dispute surrounding ministerial authorization. But can the German experience really be transferred to the Community of Twelve? In no other Member State is the competition principle so deeply rooted in public opinion as it is in Germany: in no other Member State, therefore, can a comparable protest be expected from the media if the Commission were to review a decision by the EC Cartel Office. Conversely, such a review might meet with broad public approval if the Commission were to be held in greater political esteem than the EC Cartel Office.

3. Since the competition principle is not valued as highly in the other Member States as in Germany, the general attitude towards a purely practical, non-political EC Cartel Office will be different from what it is in Germany. What is regarded as an advantage in Germany, eg the fact that competition policy is divorced from other policies and made independent, may actually be seen as a disadvantage in other Member States. This does not exactly increase the acceptability of decisions. On the contrary, there is a danger that it will diminish and, with it, the determination of the EC Cartel Office to take courageous decisions. This is more than ever important in the present stage of development of EC competition policy, when it is frequently a matter of applying EC competition law to as yet unexplored areas.

4. In its most recent report, the Monopolies Commission has indicated a further danger, namely the staffing of the new Office. The more important it appears to political leaders, the keener will become the struggle for posts and hence for influence. As a result, the fair distribution of posts among the different nationalities sometimes overshadows the search for quality. In a small, independent authority, this is far more dangerous than in a large administration with many departments.

Added to this is the danger that the independent authority will become isolated. The Federal Cartel Office has fortunately not suffered this fate. An EC Cartel Office, like other independent EC authorities, will have to defend its role.

5. An EC Cartel Office will not speed up the excessively long decision-making processes outside the merger-control field. On the contrary, the creation of a hierarchical structure leading to the Commission, and possibly even to the Council, would only increase the length of the procedure. A speeding-up of the decision-making process could be expected only if

(i)   the cumbersomeness of the present procedures were attributable to the Commission as a collegiate body and

(ii)   the EC Cartel Office could dispense with the collegiate principle.

Neither condition is met. The causes of the excessively long decision-making process lie essentially in the preparatory, and not in the decision-making phase. And the EC Cartel Office will have to observe the collegiate principle in the same way as the Commission. As things stand, the Member States will probably not agree to a decision being taken in small deliberation rooms as in Berlin or at the Court of Justice in Luxembourg.

6. Transferring the responsibility for policing competition between firms to an EC Cartel Office would have important effects on the organization of Commission departments. What would happen to the monitoring of state aid for industry? No one has ever thought of transferring this task to an EC Cartel Office; it will have to remain with the Commission. But where? With the Directorate-General for Industrial Policy?

Who would take over the horizontal functions of the present Directorate-General IV? Who, for example, would comment in principle on competition matters among the chorus of the different Directorates-General? The Directorate-General for Economic and Financial Affairs?

None of this means that the advocates of an EC Cartel Office are wrong. On the contrary, I feel that in the medium and long term there is no way of avoiding an independent competition authority for the Community. But the time is not yet ripe. Nor, at present, is there really "any concrete need for action. The practice so far reveals that no decisions have been taken which disregard essential aspects in favour of other considerations unrelated to competition". These are the words of the Monopolies Commission in its latest Report. No more need be said.

WEDNESDAY 30 JUNE 1993

Present:

Allen of Abbeydale, L.	Oliver of Aylmerton, L.
Archer of Sandwell, L.	Slynn of Hadley, L. (Chairman)
Colville of Culross, V.	Wedderburn of Charlton, L.
Hacking, L.	

Memorandum by the Department of Trade and Industry

INTRODUCTION

1. This memorandum discusses actual and potential developments in the handling of cases under Articles 85 and 86 EEC; and the EC Merger Regulation (ECMR) (Regulation 4064/89). Annexes consider some of these areas in greater detail and provide factual information which may assist the Select Committee during its enquiry.

2. For the purposes of Articles 85 and 86, the United Kingdom competent national authorities are the Secretary of State for Trade and Industry and the Director General of Fair Trading. In addition, under the ECMR, the Monopolies and Mergers Commission is also nominated as a competent national authority.

GENERAL VIEWS

3. The Commission should carry out its duties in this area effectively and efficiently. Her Majesty's Government attaches particular importance to the business need for legal certainty in respect of both individual cases and overall policy guidance. On the application of *Articles 85 and 86,* Her Majesty's Government has consistently encouraged the Commission towards improving its internal procedures so as: to concentrate resources on priority cases; to give business legal certainty wherever possible; and to decide cases more quickly. In determining its priorities, Her Majesty's Government believes that the Commission should concentrate on major infringements of the EC competition rules such as large cartels which affect a number of EC Member States.

4. On the application of the *ECMR,* Her Majesty's Government wishes to see a firm application of the competition criteria for the assessment of mergers, legal certainty for business and a clear demarcation of jurisdiction between the Commission and Member States.

COMMISSION PROCEDURES

(A description of the relationship between the Commission and Member States, and between the United Kingdom competent competition authorities in respect of EC cases, is at *Annex I.*)

5. We understand that the Select Committee's interest has been prompted in part by an outside report which, *inter alia,* drew attention to findings that certain Commission procedures had in some aspects been flawed. Two Court cases in particular have raised concerns about the Commission's administrative procedures. In one case, *PVC*[1], the ECJ criticised the Commission for failing to follow its own rules of procedure. In the other, *Italian Flat Glass*[2], Commission evidence was found to have been properly presented and in some cases appeared to have been altered after an agreed decision. Such cases are rare, but they suggest that further internal review by DGIV of its procedures may be appropriate to ensure consistency and effectiveness in decision making.

6. DTI is aware from regular contacts with the CBI and legal practitioners in the competition field that, in Article 85 and 86 cases, they are concerned about the frequent use by the Commission of "comfort letters" and the slow timescale for processing cases.

Comfort letters

7. The Commission's competition directorate, DGIV, has introduced a number of significant procedural reforms concerning the handling of Article 85 and 86 cases since the early 1980s (see *Annex II)*. The move to make greater use of "comfort letters" in 1982 was aimed at improving certainty for business on the grounds that although they do not have legal force, they are more helpful to business than

---

[1] *Hoechst AG v Commission,* Cases 46 and 227/87.

[2] *Societa Italiana Vetro SpA, Fabbrica Pisana SpA and PPG Vernante Pennitalia SpA v Commission,* Cases 68, 77 and 78/89.

silence from the Commission. DGIV disposes of about 20 per cent of the total number of cases dealt with annually by means of comfort letters (eg in 1991, out of a total of 839 cases dealt with, 680 files were closed, 146 comfort letters were issued and there were 13 formal decisions). This has helped the Commission to reduce the backlog of outstanding cases; it achieved a reduction of 20 per cent in the total number of cases outstanding in 1991, principally by means of comfort letters and closure of files. The Commission has not greatly increased the number of *formal* decisions taken each year which has fluctuated between 10 and the peak of 26 in 1992.

Timescale for Commission decisions

8. On *timescale,* the average time taken by DGIV to process cases that have gone to full decision is two and a half years. It is not known how long, on average, DGIV takes to dispose of cases by means of closing the file or issuing comfort letters.

9. A difficulty in assessing the significance of the time taken to process cases is that the Commission does not publish a breakdown by category of cases. However, it would undoubtedly be helpful to business if DGIV dealt with applications for negative clearance or exemption under Article 85(3) more quickly. Unlike EC merger cases, there is no legislative timetable for dealing with Article 85 and 86 cases and the turn-round time contrasts with the maximum five month timescale for EC merger cases (most being cleared within one month). Her Majesty's Government has encouraged DGIV to introduce internal procedures on timetabling without the need to amend Regulation 17/62.

10. Recently, DGIV has made efforts to improve its handling times. It has introduced from 1 January 1993 a new maximum turn-round time of five months for all Article 85 joint venture cases. The outgoing Competition Commissioner, Sir Leon Brittan, commented in a speech in December 1992 that DGIV should introduce, from 1 April 1993, an internal timescale of five months for a first sift of *all* Article 85 and 86 cases to decide which should be closed and which needed further investigation. We await the views of the new competition Commissioner Mr Karel Van Miert on whether this policy is to be pursued.

Block exemptions

11. Other procedural reforms introduced by DGIV during the 1980s, such as agreeing new *block exemptions,* have generally been welcomed by business and have been useful in reducing both burdens on business (ie from the need to notify certain agreements individually) and demands on the Commission. As a general policy, Her Majesty's Government welcomes the use of block exemptions when the Commission has built up a sufficient knowledge of the sector or category of activity concerned in order to be able to identify those types of agreement which will not prevent, restrict or distort competition in the common market.

12. The Commission also adopts an *"opposition procedure"* as an accompanying measure for dealing with "grey" zones in certain block exemptions. Under this procedure, agreements containing obligations which are neither explicitly exempted nor expressly prohibited, may gain the benefit of the block exemption provided they are notified to the Commission and no opposition is raised within the given time limit, six months in most cases. The intention of this procedure is to achieve a balance between the need to scrutinise agreements from the competition point of view and the need to provide increased certainty for business in areas where competition concerns are thought less likely to arise. There is some suggestion that some companies have sought to abuse this procedure by notifying potentially anti-competitive agreements which do not fall within the scope of the block exemption in the hope that they would inadvertently gain exemption. Its potential for use in any future block exemptions would need to be assessed on the merits.

Commission Notices

13. The Commission has also increased its publication of *Notices* setting out Commission policy on the operation of agreements or other competition issues (eg the role of intermediaries). A list of Notices is at *Annex III.*

14. The Commission Notice of 13 February 1993 on the application of Articles 85 and 86 by national courts (No 93/C 39/05) is generally welcome guidance. However increased referral by firms of Article 85 and 86 cases to national courts (encouraged by the Commission) is unlikely to assist greatly in reducing the Commission backlog of cases, particularly since the Commission retains exclusivity over the grant of Article 85(3) exemptions. The cost of taking an Article 85 or 86 case before a national court, and the limits of a national court's jurisdiction, will continue to be deterrents in many cases. In framing the Notice, the Commission clearly had in mind civil law systems where the courts play a more active and interventionist role than is the case in the United Kingdom. United Kingdom courts would not be able to hear evidence from the Commission on points of law.

ECMR procedures

(Details on the ECMR are at *Annex IV*).

15. *The procedures regarding the EC Merger Regulation* have generally worked well. In broad terms Her Majesty's Government believes the ECMR has been operated effectively. The Commission has met the tight timescales imposed by the Regulation and has established a good reputation. As with many aspects of competition law, there is a trade-off between establishing transparency and certainty against the need to provide decisions for business at minimum cost and delay.

HER MAJESTY'S GOVERNMENT VIEWS ON FURTHER POSSIBLE PROCEDURAL REFORM

16. Her Majesty's Government attaches importance to the respect of mixed competence between the Commission and Member States in the area of competition law and takes account of this in considering proposals for procedural or legislative reform.

Her Majesty's Government view of possible revision of the EC Merger Regulation

17. The ECMR contains specific provision for the review before the end of 1993 of certain aspects of the regime. These are: the level of the thresholds and the provisions for referral of cases to Member States. The review of these may also give an opportunity to consider some aspects of procedure as well.

18. There are arguments for and against a *reduction in the level of thresholds* which determine whether a case falls within EC or national jurisdiction. The main arguments in favour of lower thresholds are: that it would enhance the principle of "one stop shopping" for merger control in the Community; and it would promote a more consistent competition regime throughout the Community. The main arguments against lower thresholds are: that it would reduce national competence over mergers affecting the United Kingdom; it would increase the likelihood of more cases affecting only national or local markets being caught, which could divert Commission resources away from mergers with truly inter-state trade effects; and it could lead to more cases being referred back to Member States under Article 9 [ECMR] which could lead to greater uncertainty for business. On balance, Her Majesty's Government remains sceptical of the need for lower thresholds. Before taking a final view, Ministers await further information from the Commission on the proportion of mergers falling below the present thresholds which have a significant effect on inter-state trade.

19. The provisions in Article 9 for referral of cases to Member States must also be reviewed before the end of 1993. It is not clear whether the Commission will propose any changes in this area. Any change would require unanimity from Member States. As far as Her Majesty's Government is concerned, Article 9 has operated satisfactorily: and our one request[1] was successful. The gateway for referrals is narrow at present and some have suggested it could be broadened. However, there is a danger that a wider gateway leading to more national referrals would diminish the benefits of the "one stop shop" and would tend to detract from a consistent approach to large scale mergers which involve inter-State trade. Her Majesty's Government is therefore reluctant to see Article 9 opened too widely.

20. If the review is widened, Her Majesty's Government's approach to possible procedural changes would take into account principles of transparency, legal certainty and the avoidance of undue burdens on business.

Commission exclusivity over Article 85(3) exemptions

21. In considering Article 85 and 86 cases, Her Majesty's Government considers the Commission should concentrate its resources on major infringements of the EC competition rules where inter-State trade is affected, that is, those cases where it is the best placed to investigate and impose any necessary remedies. Cases which have effects mainly in one Member State are likely to be best dealt with by the competition authorities in that Member State. However this will not invariably be so: for example, a Member State may not be able to conclude a case under national law where it is not clear whether exemption could be granted under Article 85(3), which is within the Commission's exclusive competence.

22. Nevertheless, in cases which involve trade between Member States, Her Majesty's Government attaches great importance to the even-handed application of EC competition rules throughout the Community. The Commission's monopoly on Article 85(3) exemptions has been an important factor in establishing this, particularly when, until very recently, several Member States did not have comprehensive national competition law and therefore had little experience in handling investigations. The Commission has not shown any inclination to delegate to Member States the power to grant exemptions, which would require amendment to Regulation 17/62. Without prejudging what changes

[1]Proposed joint venture between Tarmac and Steetly (see Annex IV paragraph 8).

might be desirable in the longer term, Her Majesty's Government favours procedural changes to be pursued through non-legislative means in the first instance, for example, in national authorities carrying out more inspections of company premises on behalf of the Commission. In the United Kingdom, the OFT is already developing experience of this. The OFT would see some value in providing other forms of assistance where this did not greatly increase the burden on existing OFT resources, or displace more important OFT priorities.

CONCLUSIONS

23. A number of procedural changes in the handling of cases under Articles 85 and 86 have taken place since the Select Committee last reviewed this subject. Member States and the Commission have also been given cause to consider whether the experience of more rapid handling of cases under the ECMR provides relevant lessons for other competition cases. The drive to consider procedural change comes from a number of sources. Among these are the judgments of the European Court of Justice and the European Court of First Instance; political and administrative trends in the Community, such as subsidiarity and deregulation; and market developments which bring to the fore new methods of doing business, such as franchising. Member States are not complacent about the way in which cases are handled and the Commission has given firm indications that discussion of procedural improvements is on the agenda. In the area of the ECMR, any such discussion will take place against the background of the mandatory review of thresholds and of Article 9 [ECMR].

INDEX TO ANNEXES

(Background material referred to in the memorandum)

I Relationship between the Commission and Member States, and between the United Kingdom competent competition authorities, in respect of EC cases.

II Procedural changes for handling Article 85 and Article 86 cases introduced by the Commission since 1981.

III List of Commission Notices.

IV Details on the EC Merger Regulation.

(Other background material relevant to issues discussed in the memorandum)

V Handling Article 85 and Article 86 cases: options for further reform.

VI Statistics, and interpretation, showing Commission activity on Article 85 and Article 86 cases 1981–1991.

VII List of block exemptions.

VIII Note on the structure of DGIV.

ANNEX I

Handling Article 85 and 86 cases

Relationship between the Commission/Member States on Article 85 and 86 cases

1. The Commission is required by Article 10 of Regulation 17/62 to operate its procedures on Article 85 and 86 cases, "in close and constant liaison with the competent authorities of the Member States". The competent authorities in the United Kingdom for the purposes of Regulation 17/62 are the Secretary of State for Trade and Industry and the Director General of Fair Trading.

2. The Office of Fair Trading handles all the casework, seeking legal and policy input from DTI (and other government departments as appropriate), and has the day-to-day liaison role with DGIV. The Department of Trade and Industry has overall policy responsibility, except for cases in the field of transport where it shares policy responsibility with the Department of Transport.

3. The Monopolies and Mergers Commission is a "competent authority" only for the purposes of EC Merger Regulation but co-operates with DGIV in cases where the MMC may be able to provide relevant information within the bounds of provisions in United Kingdom competition law covering commercial confidentiality and business secrecy.

Operation of liaison between Commission/UK competition authorities in practice

4. OFT receives all papers relevant to an Article 85 or 86 case from DGIV. If the Commission should decide to undertake an inspection of UK companies premises under Article 14 of Regulation 17/62 (or its equivalent in transport cases), it will advise OFT whose officials always accompany Commission officials on such visits. OFT informs DTI officials of unannounced visits (commonly known as "dawn raids") and Ministers are informed. On two occasions to date, OFT has carried out such visits on their own (Article 13), on behalf of the Commission, as part of wider investigations (in July 1992, and in April 1993).

5. On receipt of draft decisions and Article 19(3) Notices (summaries of cases proposed to receive negative clearance or be granted exemption), OFT copies papers to DTI and any other interested departments for comment and advice. Such advice is taken into account in the preparation of the UK line taken by OFT at meetings of the EC Advisory Committee on Restrictive Practices and Monopolies in Brussels. OFT provides UK representation at all meetings where draft case decisions are discussed.

6. Provision by DGIV to OFT of background papers, draft decisions and other draft proposals, and the degree of notice of Advisory Committee meetings on Restrictive Practices and Monopolies are set out in Regulation 17/62. There are occasional administrative lapses where DGIV have not complied with the time limit specified in Regulation 17/62 for giving notice of a meeting but they have not been of a frequency or severity to raise at Ministerial level.

7. There is well-established close liaison between OFT and DTI on all aspects of EC competition policy and casework. Each works to its respective internally agreed procedural guidelines. There is a range of DTI and OFT material available to business and others which explains procedures in handling competition cases, under EC competition law.

8. On receipt of draft Commission proposals for new competition law or Notices, OFT similarly copies papers to DTI and any other interested departments for comment and advice. DTI and OFT officials attend Advisory Committee meetings where draft Commission legislative or policy proposals are discussed and DTI takes the lead in preparing the UK line to take at such meetings. DTI takes responsibility for advising interested business groups or legal practitioners of new policy or legislative proposals and inviting comments on Commission drafts which can be taken into account in formulating the UK response.

ANNEX II

DGIV Internal Review/Procedural Changes since 1981

1. DGIV has launched a number of initiatives to accelerate the handling of cases and generally to improve procedures since the last House of Lords Select Committee enquiry into competition practice in 1981–82. The main areas in which improvements have been sought are:

(i) more rapid handling of notifications of agreements requiring exemption; and, consequently,

(ii) greater legal certainty for businesses entering into agreements.

2. The Commission has also sought to improve procedures relating to oral hearings, access to files and inspections. In pursuing these objectives, the Commission has introduced a number of changes to its procedure and practice. These are outlined below.[1]

Block Exemptions

3. Block exemptions are arrangements whereby all agreements which fulfil certain strict criteria set out in an enabling regulation are automatically exempted from the competition rules under Article 85(3), thereby circumventing the need for individual consideration and exemption. Block exemptions were used for a number of years before the 1982 House of Lords enquiry. However, since 1982 the Commission has increased greatly its use of them in an effort to reduce its backlog of case-work. A list of block exemptions currently in force is attached at *Annex VII.*

Opposition Procedure

4. This procedure brings agreements which fall into the "grey" zone of each respective regulation, in other words agreements containing clauses which are not explicitly exempted but which are not expressly prohibited either, within the scope of the block exemption if they are notified to the Commission and no opposition is raised within six months.

[1]The information in this section was reproduced mainly from the Annual EC Commission Reports on Competition Policy, numbers 11 to 21 (1981–1991), published by the Office for Official Publications of the European Communities.

5. The use of the opposition procedure has increased greatly since 1984, although limited use was made of it prior to that date. It applies under five block exemptions: Patent Licensing (Regulation 2349/84), Specialization (Regulation 417/85), Research and Development (Regulation 418/85), Franchising (Regulation 4087/88) and Know-How Licensing (Regulation 556/89). It also applies to two Council Regulations which contain provision for exemptions: Regulation 1017/68 on road, rail and inland waterway transport agreements and Regulation 4056/86 on maritime transport agreements (under which the time period for raising objections is 90 days rather than six months).

Administrative Letters

6. The Commission makes widespread use of administrative or "comfort" letters. A comfort letter is a letter from the Director-General for Competition stating that the notified agreement to which it pertains is probably acceptable under the competition rules. It does not give legal certainty. However, the Commission makes widespread use of such letters in an effort to avoid unnecessary casework.

7. In 1982 the Commission moved to give comfort letters greater value by publishing the essential content of such letters, so as to give interested third parties an opportunity to make known their views. In appropriate cases a comfort letter is sent after publication and a notice to that effect placed in the Official Journal of the European Communities.

Procedures during inspections

8. In 1982 the Commission announced that it had drawn up an explanatory memorandum on procedures to be followed during inspections. This memorandum was in the form of a document attached to the authorization to carry out an inspection, and outlined the scope and limits of the powers of the officials carrying out the investigations, as well as setting out the rights of the undertakings concerned. In this way, the Commission aimed to give reassurance to the undertakings concerned about the scope of its powers and the procedure to be followed during the investigation.

9. In particular, the document explains that the undertaking may call in its legal advisers for consultation during the investigation (although this is not a legal precondition for the start of the inspection and may not delay it). It also states that the undertakings concerned may draw to the attention of the officials carrying out the inspection factors favourable to them which relate to the purpose of the inspection and which emerge from documents other than those requested. This is intended to ensure that the information collected by the Commission is complete and will be used objectively in the subsequent investigation.

Access to files

10. In 1982 the Commission also announced that it had put into effect a proposal to allow the undertakings involved in a procedure to inspect the file on their case. This measure was intended to improve the exercise of the rights of defence in administrative procedures. Undertakings are invited to consult the relevant documents on the Commission's premises (in the case where the undertakings wish to consult only a few documents the Commission may forward copies). The Commission informs the undertakings beforehand which documents they may examine and which are considered confidential. If the undertaking makes a justified request to see a document which is considered to be confidential, the Commission may make a non-confidential summary available.

Hearing Officer

11. In September 1982, the Commission instituted the post of Hearing Officer within the Directorate-General for Competition. The Hearing Officer's task is to ensure that the oral hearing is properly conducted and thus to contribute to the objectiveness of the hearing itself and of any subsequent decision. In performing his duties he ensures that the rights of the defence are respected, while at the same time taking account of the need for effective application of the competition rules. He also ensures that in the preparation of draft Commission decisions in competition cases due account is taken of all the relevant facts, whether favourable or unfavourable to the parties concerned.

12. In order to ensure the independence of the Hearing Officer in the performance of his duties, he has the right of access to the Member of the Commission with special responsibility for competition policy; if he considers it appropriate he may refer to the Member his comments on the draft decision. In order to make sure that the Commission, when taking a decision on a draft decision on an individual case, is fully informed of all relevant factors, the Member of the Commission with special responsibility for competition policy may also submit it for the Hearing Officer's opinion.

Reorganisation of DGIV

13. In 1984, the Commission announced that it had reorganised that part of the Directorate-General for Competition which dealt with individual cases. Two new directorates dealing with individual cases and organised on a sectoral basis were created. Each of the six divisions in these directorates was made responsible for a number of sectors in which it was intended to build up specialised knowledge. All phases of the procedure would be dealt with by the same team. This reorganisation was intended to reduce administrative delays and to allow the Commission to act more quickly and effectively. At the same time, a new directorate was created, which was responsible for co-ordinating decision making and ensuring consistency, objectivity and fairness across the board in the decision making of the other directorates.

Form A/B

14. In August 1985, the Commission introduced a new form to be used for submitting applications for negative clearance and notifications for exemption (form A/B). This replaced the form used for this purpose since 1968.

15. Form A/B asked for information relating to the economic significance of the participants and to their position in the relevant markets, which the old form did not do. It was considered that the lack of this information was a serious hindrance to adopting a decision within a satisfactory timescale and which would give legal certainty. Form A/B has since undergone minor adaptations to take account of the future entry into force of the European Economic Area.

Obligations of Commission officials and those providing information

16. In 1985, the Commission issued new guidelines to its officials on how to handle documentation covered by the obligation of professional secrecy. This followed the Court's judgment in two cases brought by Mr Stanley George Adams against the Commission.[1] Mr Adams alleged that he had suffered damage because he had been identified as the source of information which ultimately led the Commission to impose a fine on his former employer, Hoffman-La Roche, for violating Article 86.

17. The new guidelines stated that where the identity of the person furnishing the information is known to the Commission, the relevant documents may be shown or returned to the undertaking concerned, within the limits indicated by the provider of the information, only after that person has been warned of the risks that this may entail for him and only on condition that he has given the Commission permission to pursue this course of action. Where the person has not revealed his identity, the documents will not be returned to the firm, and no decision may be taken about whether or not they will be returned, until a detailed examination of the documents has been carried out by the Commission to determine the importance of the information to the investigation and also the risk that the provider of the information may be traced and possibly subjected to legal proceedings.

ANNEX III

Commission Notices

Exclusive dealing contracts with commercial agents (1962)

Co-operation between enterprises (1968)

Imports into the Community of Japanese goods (1972)

Sub-contracting agreements (1979)

Concerning Commission Regulations Nos. 1983/83 and 1984/83 on the application of Article 85(3) to categories of exclusive distribution and exclusive purchasing agreements (1983)

Concerning Commission Regulation 123/85 on the application of Article 85(3) to motor vehicle servicing and licensing agreements (1985)

Agreements of minor importance (1986—replacing 1977 Notice)

Procedures for communications to the Commission under Regulation 2671/88 (joint planning and co-ordination of capacity, sharing of revenue and consultations on tariffs on scheduled air services and slot allocation at airports) (1988)

---

[1]Cases 53/84 and 145/83 *Stanley George Adams v Commission.*

The application of Article 4(1)(a) of Regulation 2671/88 (joint planning and co-ordination of capacity, sharing of revenue and consultations on tariffs on scheduled air services and slot allocation at airports) (1989)

Restrictions ancillary to concentrations (1990)

Concentrative and co-operative operations under the ECMR (1990)

Clarification of the activities of motor-vehicle intermediaries (1991)

Modification of the Notice concerning Commission Regulations Nos 1983/83 and 1984/83 on the application of Article 85(3) to categories of exclusive distribution and exclusive purchasing agreements (including beer supply agreements) (1992)

Co-operation between national courts and the Commission in applying Articles 85 and 86 of the EEC Treaty (1993)

The assessment of co-operative joint ventures (1992)

ANNEX IV

EC Merger Regulation

Background

1. The EC Merger Regulation (Council Regulation 4064/89) was agreed in December 1989 and came into force in September 1990.

Main features

2. Mergers which meet certain turnover thresholds are automatically caught and must be notified to the EC Commission. The turnover thresholds are:

— combined worldwide turnover of all the undertakings concerned over 5 billion ECU; and

— EC-wide turnover of each of at least two of the undertakings concerned over 250 million ECU;

— unless each of the undertakings concerned achieves more than two-thirds of its EC-wide turnover within one and the same Member State.

3. Within one month of notification the Commission must decide *either* that the merger falls outside the Regulation, *or* that it comes under the Regulation but raises no serious competition concerns, *or* that it comes under the Regulation and raises serious competition concerns.

4. Where the Commission decides that there are serious competition concerns it will open proceedings. It then has a further four months in which to take a final decision, *either* to prohibit the merger, *or* to clear it with conditions attached, *or* to clear it unconditionally.

5. As a general rule the Commission has exclusive competence over mergers coming under the Regulation. There are certain exceptions to this rule. Under Article 9, the Commission may refer a notified merger to the competent authorities of a Member State where the merger threatens to impede competition on a distinct market within that Member State. Under Article 21, a Member State may take measures to protect its legitimate interests other than competition. Public security, plurality of the media and prudential rules are specified as legitimate interests. Any other public interest must first be recognised by the Commission.

Notified cases

6. To date (26 April 1993), 154 mergers have been notified to the Commission. Of these, 117 (75.9%) have been cleared after one month, 15 (9.7%) were found to fall outside the Regulation, and 11 (7.1%) have gone to full proceedings. Three notifications have been withdrawn and eight decisions are pending (including one case at full proceedings).

7. Of the 11 cases where proceedings were opened, one merger has been blocked (Aerospatiale and Alenia's joint acquisition of de Havilland), six have been cleared conditionally, two have been cleared unconditionally, one has been withdrawn and one case is pending. .

8. One case has been referred to a national authority under Article 9: a proposed joint venture between Tarmac and Steetley which was referred to the United Kingdom because of concerns in the markets for bricks and roofing tiles. The case was referred by the Secretary of State for Trade and Industry to the Monopolies and Mergers Commission. The reference to the MMC was laid aside after the parties announced they had abandoned the proposal.

Case handling

9. The Commission must carry out the procedures in the Regulation in close and constant liaison with the competent authorities of the Member States. Copies of notifications are sent to the Member States within three working days. Members States may submit comments on notified mergers and on the procedures used by the Commission. In cases which go to proceedings, the Commission must consult an Advisory Committee of Member States before taking a final decision. The Committee may deliver an opinion on the Commission's draft decision. The Commission must take the utmost account of the Committee's opinion but is not obliged to follow it.

10. Within the United Kingdom the three competition bodies play a role reflecting the arrangements for handling mergers under domestic jurisdiction. Thus the Secretary of State for Trade and Industry is responsible for policy and for decisions in relation to the United Kingdom's view on individual cases. The DGFT provides advice on the jurisdictional and competition aspects of cases. The MMC would examine any case referred to it by the Secretary of State after a reference back to the United Kingdom under Article 9 [ECMR].

ANNEX V

Handling Article 85 and 86 cases: Options for Further Reforms

1. DGIV receives around 350 new Article 85 and 86 cases a year and initiates around 20 investigations itself. Only around 15–20 formal decisions are reached each year. The balance of cases are not dealt with by formal decision: instead the files are closed (and the agreements expire in due course with no formal decision having been reached) or they are dealt with by means of an administrative or "comfort" letter (this is a letter signed by the Director-General for Competition giving assurances that the agreement is probably acceptable under the competition rules). The comfort letter does not give legal certainty. DGIV takes on average two and a half years to process each case to a formal decision and there is consistently a backlog—currently around 2,500 cases (cf around 4,500 in 1981).

2. DGIV has made efforts to reduce its backlog of cases and for joint ventures has imposed upon itself the same maximum time limit of five months as for the EC Merger Regulation. Other measures which might affect the backlog include an increased emphasis on decentralisation. There are a number of possibilities for future developments in the area of decentralisation of the application of Articles 85 and 86:

    (i) non-legislative procedural reform, requiring no change to Regulation 17/62;

    (ii) legislative procedural reform, requiring change to Regulation 17/62;

    (iii) increased application of Articles 85 and 86 by national courts (see the recent Commission Notice on co-operation between the Commission and the national courts in the application of Articles 85 and 86 EEC).

Non-legislative procedural reform

3. Non-legislative procedural reform means reform requiring no change to Regulation 17/62 EEC, ie procedural differences which the Commission could introduce with the co-operation of Member States without any change to the legal framework currently used in the implementation of Community competition rules. This could include DGIV inviting Member States to take on aspects of its investigations on its behalf, such as carrying out Article 13 inspections instead of accompanying Commission officials; or in appropriate cases, carrying out an investigation under national laws. Other changes could include DGIV self-imposed time limits for the processing of cases, particularly in deciding which cases should be closed on grounds of insufficient Community interest and thus left to Member States to deal with as appropriate.

4. The United Kingdom has until now taken the line that the objective of achieving more rapid processing of cases without jeopardising even enforcement of competition rules throughout the Community can be met by procedural reforms which do not require legislative changes. However, the United Kingdom has also made clear that Member States should retain discretion to turn down Commission invitations to take on more investigatory case-work on behalf of the Commission. In the United Kingdom, OFT would need to assess the impact on their resources and decide whether or not to take on such cases against other priorities.

Legislative procedural reform

5. This would involve changes to Regulation 17/62 such as an end to DGIV's monopoly on granting Article 85(3) exemptions, the imposition of statutory time limits for all cases or the introduction of a formal system of referral of cases to Member States.

6. These changes would have the advantage over non-legislative reforms of greater legal certainty, which could be welcome to business. However, the possibility of greater certainty could also lead to more notifications being made on a fail-safe basis, which in turn would place greater demands on competition authorities. In addition, the question remains whether even application of the competition rules would be maintained if, for example, power to grant exemptions under Article 85(3) were to be devolved to national authorities. The Commission has so far not indicated a willingness to give up its monopoly of the power to grant exemptions under Article 85(3).

Application of Articles 85 and 86 by national courts

7. On 13 February 1993, the Commission published its "Notice on co-operation between the national courts and the Commission in applying Articles 85 and 86 of the EEC Treaty". This followed a draft notice on the same subject which was circulated for comment from the Member States in March 1992.

8. The Notice sets out the Commission's view on how and why national courts should play a greater part in enforcing Articles 85 and 86 EEC. The main thrust of the Commission proposal is that in view of the Commission's resource constraints, free competition within the Single Market can only be safeguarded if both the Commission and the national courts play a role in enforcing EC competition rules. The Commission indicates that it should concentrate on cases which are of particular political, economic or legal significance for the Community. According to the Notice, there is not normally a "sufficient Community interest" in examining a case when the plaintiff can secure adequate consideration of his rights by a national court. It is not clear what the Commission considers to be adequate consideration of rights by a national court.

9. In setting out the Commission position on this matter, the Notice draws attention to *BRT* v *SABAM*[1], in which the ECJ held that Articles 85(1) and 86 create direct rights in respect of individuals which national courts must safeguard. The Commission also cites *Automec*[2] as part of the rationale underpinning the Notice. In this case, the Court upheld the Commission's decision to decline to take action on a case already before a national court, on the grounds that the latter had the necessary competence to apply Articles 85(1) and 85(2), and the necessary remedies to hand.

10. The Notice lists the advantages of pursuing an action in the national courts (possible award of legal costs and damages, quicker implementation of interim measures, combining of claims under national and Community law). It does not, however, take on board any of the disadvantages (potential cost, difficulty in obtaining evidence, doubts over jurisdiction as regards anti-competitive or abusive practices in another Member State) pointed out in the United Kingdom's reply to the Commission on the draft notice following the consultation period.

11. Another important factor which requires further consideration relates to the application of Article 85(3) EEC. National courts cannot rule against agreements already exempted under 85(3) or a block exemption. Complications arise where an agreement has been notified and the Commission has not yet reached a decision as to whether or not it should be exempt. In such a case, the national court must "assess the likelihood of an exemption being granted" and proceed accordingly. This raises questions of legal certainty.

12. The Notice argues that greater participation by national courts in the application of Articles 85 and 86 will free the Commission to devote more time to the development of competition policy within the Community. There is, however, a risk that, far from having a reduced workload, the Commission could become bogged down in giving advice to national courts inexperienced in dealing with Article 85/86 cases and/or handicapped in terms of the information at their disposal.

13. The United Kingdom response to the Commission initiative has been to give a cautious welcome to Commission efforts to prioritise its workload more effectively, but to invite the Commission to consider how its proposals will work in practice.

[1] *BRT* v *SABAM* Case 127/73.
[2] *Automec* v *Commission* Case T-24/90.

ANNEX VI

Table Showing Commission Activity 1981 to 1991

	1981	1982	1983	1984	1985	1986	1987	1988	1989	1990	1991
1. Incoming cases	293	322	297	289	323	589	312	494	231	381	392
2. Outgoing cases	132	488	358	233	1204	380	407	470	443	886	839
2. Formal Decisions (% age of Row 2)	11 (8%)	9 (2%)	15 (4%)	20 (9%)	17 (1%)	23 (6%)	16 (4%)	25 (5%)	15 (3%)	15 (2%)	13 (2%)
3. Comfort letters (% age of Row 2)	n/a	n/a	n/a	3 (1%)	2	74 (19%)	57 (14%)	36 (8%)	46 (10%)	158 (18%)	146 (17%)
4. Files closed (% age of Row 2)	n/a	n/a	n/a	211 (90%)	1185* (99%)	283 (75%)	334 (82%)	419 (87%)	382 (87%)	713 (80%)	680 (81%)
5. Total informal decisions (Row 3 + Row 4) (% age of Row 2)	121 (92%)	479 (98%)	343 (96%)	214 (91%)	1187 (99%)	357 (94%)	391 (96%)	455 (95%)	428 (97%)	871 (98%)	826 (98%)
6. Outstanding cases	4365	4199	4138	4194	3313	3522	3427	3451	3239	2734	2287
7. Average time (in years) to reach formal decision	2	2.3	2.6	1.8	2.5	2.9	0.9	2.7	2.6	2.8	2.5

*=In 1983 and 1984 six block exemptions were implemented meaning that individual exemptions for many agreements which had already been notified to the Commission were no longer necessary.

Interpretation of Statistical Annex

1. The Commission has received an average of around 350 new cases a year over the period. The vast majority of these are notifications/applications under Article 85. Because the Commission was unable to process cases as quickly as they were arriving a backlog of 4365 cases had built up by the end of 1981. The backlog of Article 85 and 86 cases has been greatly eased by the introduction of block exemptions during the 1980s. The effect of this can be seen by the large reduction in the total number of outstanding cases to around 2,300 in 1991.

2. The effect of block exemptions should be a once and for all decrease in cases in the backlog. However, this was only noticeable in 1985 and not in other years following block exemptions. Block exemptions should also decrease the number of applications received by the Commission but since 1986 this has increased to about 400 per year on average.

3. Since 1989 the Commission has significantly increased the number of files closed. These are informal decisions where the agreements are no longer in force, their impact was too slight to warrant further investigation, the complaints have become moot or because investigation had not received any anti-competitive activity. There is no need in these cases to exempt the agreements. There is no procedural explanation for this increase.

4. Administrative or "comfort" letters are sent by the Commission when it wishes to exempt an agreement without taking a formal decision. The increase in the number of files closed, together with an increase in the use of comfort letters has meant that since 1989 the backlog of cases has decreased from 3,451 to 2,287.

5. The number of formal decisions made has remained steady at about 15 per year, although 26 were made in 1992. Formal decisions are taken where the cases involve an important point of policy which the Commission wish to emphasise or where the parties have specifically requested a formal decision and not a comfort letter. These are the cases where Member States have the most opportunity to make formal representations to the Commission and to influence the decisions made, principally through the Advisory Committee which only meets to discuss formal decisions. A formal decision must be made before a fine is imposed. The proportion of formal decisions to total decisions taken annually has fluctuated between 9 per cent (1984—20 formal decisions) and 1 per cent (1985—17 formal decisions)

6. The average time taken for the Commission to reach a formal decision has remained steady at about two years and six months. The longest time taken by the Commission to reach a formal decision was Vifka in which eight years and eight months elapsed between notification and decision between 1978 and 1986. The shortest delay was in the case of Boosey and Hawkes when the Commission took three months in 1987.

7. The figures have been taken from the annual reports issued by the Commission on competition policy. 1991 is the latest year for which the Commission has published figures.

ANNEX VII

EC Block Exemptions

Number and Date	Subject	Date of Expiry
Exclusive dealing agreements		
Commission Regulation (EEC) No. 1983/83 of 22 June 1983	on the application of Article 85(3) of the Treaty to categories of exclusive distribution agreements	31 December 1997
Commission Regulation (EEC) No. 1984/83 of 22 June 1983	on the application of Article 85(3) of the Treaty to categories of exclusive purchasing agreements	31 December 1997
Commission Regulation (EEC) No. 123/85 of 12 December 1984	on the application of Article 85(3) of the Treaty to categories of motor vehicle distribution and servicing agreements	30 June 1995
Patent licensing agreements		
Commission Regulation (EEC) No. 2349/84 of 23 July 1984	on the application of Article 85(3) of the Treaty to categories of patent licensing agreements	31 December 1994
Specialisation and research and development agreements		
Commission Regulation (EEC) No. 417/85 of 19 December 1984	on the application of Article 85(3) of the Treaty to categories of specialisation agreements	31 December 1997
Commission Regulation (EEC) No. 418/85 of 19 December 1984	on the application of Article 85(3) of the Treaty to categories of research and development agreements	31 December 1997
Franchising agreements		
Commission Regulation (EEC) No. 4087/88 of 30 November 1988	on the application of Article 85(3) of the Treaty to categories of franchise agreements	31 December 1999
Know-how licensing agreements		
Commission Regulation (EEC) No. 556/89 of 30 November 1988	on the application of Article 85(3) of the Treaty to certain categories of know-how licensing agreements	31 December 1999
Regulations in the field of transport		
Council Regulation (EEC) No. 4056/86 of 22 December 1986	laying down detailed rules for the application of Articles 85 and 86 of the Treaty to maritime transport	
Council Regulation (EEC) No. 3976/87 of 14 December 1987	on the application of Article 85(3) of the Treaty to certain categories of agreements and concerted practices in the air transport sector	31 December 1992

Number and Date	Subject	Date of Expiry
Council Regulation (EEC) No. 2411/92 of 23 July 1992	amending Regulation (EEC) No. 3976/87 on the application of Article 85(3) of the Treaty to certain categories of agreements and concerted practices in the air transport sector	
Commission Regulation (EEC) No. 83/91 of 5 December 1990	on the application of Article 85(3) of the Treaty to certain categories of agreements between undertakings relating to computer reservation systems for air transport services	31 December 1992 *temp rollover until end December 1993 while new block exemption is negotiated*
Commission Regulation (EEC) No. 84/91 of 5 December 1990	on the application of Article 85(3) of the Treaty to certain categories of agreements, decisions and concerted practices concerning joint planning and co-ordination of capacity, consultations on passenger and cargo tariff rates on scheduled air services and slot allocation at airports	31 December 1992 *temp. rollover until end June 1993 while new block exemption is negotiated*
Insurance		
Commission Regulation (EEC) No. 3932/92 of 21 December 1992	on the application of Article 85(3) of the Treaty to certain categories of agreements, decisions and concerted practices in the insurance sector	31 March 2003

ANNEX VIII

The Structure of DGIV

1. The Directorate General for Competition (DGIV) is headed by a Director-General, who is a Commission civil servant. It is divided into six main parts: Directorates A–E, and the Merger Task Force. The latter is a recent addition, following the introduction of the Merger Regulation.

2. Directorate A is responsible for general policy and co-ordination, including international relations, relations with other Community bodies, and administrative functions, such as the Registry. It has six divisions.

3. Directorates B, C and D are responsible for implementing Articles 85 and 86 and associated legislation. Divisions 1 and 2 of Directorate D are responsible for the equivalent competition provisions of the Treaty of Paris 1951 (the European Coal and Steel Community).

4. Responsibility for Article 85 and 86 cases is allocated along broad sectoral lines according to the goods or services involved. Directorate B has four divisions, C has three, and D four, of which two are responsible for Articles 85 and 86.

5. Directorate E deals with state aid, and has six divisions.

6. Each Directorate has a Head (and in some cases a deputy Head). Below them come Heads of Division, and below them the "rapporteurs", or case officers, who are responsible for individual cases.

7. For investigations under Article 14 of Regulation 17, staff may be borrowed from other Divisions, usually on the basis of ability in a given language.

8. The Merger Task Force has a Head, and is divided up into three "units", each with its own Head.

9. The Task Force is organised somewhat differently from the other divisions: each merger is dealt with by a team individually set up, and drawn from the three units. The teams are chosen in such a way as to provide a balance of specialities (language skills, accountancy, law, economics, etc) within each.

10. In addition, there are two Hearing Officers, who are independent within DGIV, and are responsible for organising and presiding over oral hearings. The post was created in 1982: formerly hearings were conducted by the Director whose Directorate was dealing with the case. A second Hearing Officer has been appointed to deal with hearings under the ECMR.

11. DGIV was considerably reorganised in late 1984. One of the main changes was that the division between the "inspection" and "examining" Directorates was abolished. What was formerly the administrative unit became a Directorate in its own right.

12. According to the Commission's XXIst Report on Competition Policy, on 31 December 1991, DGIV had a staff of 373. (This represented a 5 per cent increase since 31 December 1990.) Of these 46 per cent dealt with cartels and dominant positions, 14 per cent with merger control, 2 per cent with Article 90, 21 per cent with state aid cases, and 17 per cent with international relations, co-ordination, data processing, documentation and other horizontal duties. (Comparable figures for earlier years are not available.)

13. Although not part of DGIV, (it is independent of the Directorates-General), the Commission's Legal Service plays an important role in competition cases. It must be consulted before any formal act is taken by the Commission, and may be involved in meetings between DGIV and undertakings. It also represents the Commission in proceedings before the Courts of Justice and First Instance. Its staff thus check that Commission procedures are in conformity with Community jurisprudence, and such as to be upheld by the Court.

Examination of witnesses

DR CATHERINE BELL, Head of Competition Policy Division; MR PHILIP BOVEY, Head of Solicitors Division D; MR JOHN ALTY, Head of Competition Policy Branch 1, with responsibility for United Kingdom and EC mergers, MR ALAN COOPER, Head of Competition Policy Branch 2, with responsibility for Monopolies and United Kingdom/EC restrictive trade practices; and MISS SERENA HARDY, Solicitors Division D, Branch 3; called in and examined.

Chairman

460. May I, first of all, thank you very much on behalf of the Committee for your memorandum and for coming along today. We hope that we can cover the ground in a reasonable compass. What I propose to do is just to ask the question to the group; would you decide between yourselves who replies? That is not necessarily confined to one; if anyone wants to add anything, please do not hesitate to do so. We welcome Dr Catherine Bell, Head of Competition Policy Division, Mr Philip Bovey, Head of Solicitors Division D, Mr John Alty, Head of Competition Policy Division Branch 1, with a responsibility for United Kingdom and EC mergers, Mr Alan Cooper, Head of Competition Policy Division Branch 2, with responsibility for monopolies and restrictive trade practices and Miss Serena Hardy from Solicitors Division D. Would you like to begin by making a general statement or would you rather we went straight into the questions?
(Dr Bell) My Lord Chairman, I would like to begin by making an opening statement, if that would be convenient. May I say first, thank you very much; it would be very helpful to be able to draw on my colleagues' expertise in answering your questions. I think the issues in front of the Committee are very closely intertwined between policy and law. Hence, you have before you both administrators and legal advisers. Perhaps I might also say that we would welcome a brief opportunity to make one or two remarks off the record at the end of the session, if that would be convenient. We very much welcome the opportunity to talk to you today. We think that it is very timely. I will have to restrict answers to Ministers' public statements where that is appropriate. The Government welcomes the improvements in EEC competition procedures which have been made since the Committee's last report; for example, the

development of the role of the Hearing Officer but the Government is concerned about the difficulties faced by business and practitioners and that these should be addressed. We look at this very much in the context of the Government's Deregulation Initiative and we are concerned that there should be speedy decisions, but not to the point of sacrificing effective application of the competition rules. The Government does believe that there is scope for improvement by further internal reforms without necessarily entering the area of legislative change. In terms of deregulation, we think that there is scope for quicker case handling and, where appropriate, consideration of further block exemptions which would enhance certainty for business. On decentralisation of case handling, there is certainly something to consider but not at the expense of even application of law throughout the Community. Our third consideration is that of fairness, avoiding procedural irregularities such as those which arose in the *PVC* case and the *Italian Flat Glass* case. That is also an area for concern. I would say those are three themes that we see in the debate about these procedures. I think I would add further that we do have a constant dialogue with DG IV at all sorts of levels very frequently. We discuss with them opportunities to improve procedures from time to time. We welcome the opportunity, given by the Committee's interest in this area, to debate this more fully.

461. That is a very helpful introduction. You said that you thought changes could take place without legislation. What is your view about the changes which the Commission itself has been proposing? Sir Leon Brittan wanted to introduce, as you know, ideas about time and complying with timescales. Do you think that will work unless it is adopted by legislation or without some rather tight supervision?

30 June 1993]

Dr Catherine Bell, Mr Philip Bovey,
Mr John Alty, Mr Alan Cooper
and Miss Serena Hardy

[Continued

[Chairman Contd.]

(Dr Bell) I think that we feel there is quite a wide opportunity to make improvements short of legislative change. We very much welcome, for example, the improvement which has been made in relation to Article 85, structural joint ventures, with the proposal, now adopted, for this two months' timetable for a first sift of cases.

462. Could you elaborate on that a little bit, not in great detail? How does that work? How do you see this as an improvement?
(Mr Alty) Clearly, this is one area where companies have been concerned. Joint ventures which are looked at under the Merger Regulation are dealt with according to very tight timetables. Joint ventures which fall under Article 85 previously were looked at in the standard way for Article 85 cases, which is historically a longer procedure. This was having a distorting effect on the way companies planned their business ventures. What Sir Leon Brittan announced was that he would try to put the procedural arrangements for all joint ventures on a much closer footing. That has only just started this year, so it is a bit early to say whether the Commission are going to be able to stick to it and how successful it would be in practice, but we certainly welcome the recognition that the previous arrangements were causing difficulty.
(Dr Bell) I think we would say further that this is a good example of the sort of improvement that can be achieved, short of legislative change. As Mr Alty says, we wait to see how diligent the Commission is in applying this two month rule but a lot of concerns from business are to do with the speed of decision-making and many of those problems may well be amenable to administrative solutions, in terms of better management of the total case load, speeding the decision-making on the most important cases and prioritising the total case load. We certainly feel that there is considerable scope for improvement in that area.

463. One of the things, as I think Mr Alty said, is that if the Commission sticks to the timetable, how do we ensure that this is carried out, if it is not done by directive or regulation?
(Dr Bell) I understand that they have done so to date. I think it is for the surveillance of the competent authorities in Member States and of businesses who have an interest to see whether they are securing decisions within the timescales which the Commission has specified. There is obviously a very active interest in this area of work from a number of groups which have a great deal at stake.

464. Are you monitoring this and keeping an eye on it?
(Mr Alty) We are aware of the decisions that are going through. So far there has not been a huge number of cases but, yes, the Commission is making available the information on how they are handling those cases and whether they are keeping to time.

465. Apart from those, Sir Leon indicated other deadlines to be followed.
(Mr Cooper) They have been proposed; they have not yet been followed through because, of course, he is no longer the competition Commissioner. He proposed a first sift on all cases, so that the parties would get a letter which may not have the status of a comfort letter but they would get an indication after two months as to whether there was likely to be a problem or not. Clearly, if they got a signal that there was a problem, they would be more hesitant about bringing an agreement into force.

466. You say there has been a change of Commissioner, as indeed there has. Has there been any suggestion from the Commission that what Sir Leon said would not now be implemented?
(Dr Bell) I think it is a point on which we wait to see any further specific proposals from the Commission.

467. They have not overtly gone cool on Sir Leon's ideas, as far as you know, or have they?
(Dr Bell) We wait to see whether the Commission brings forward something specific.

468. Have they expressed this by saying, "We are not going ahead", or, "We may not go ahead on any of these ideas"?
(Dr Bell) No, they have not.

469. Is the one you mentioned the only specific example where they really have started to do something?
(Mr Alty) I think Sir Leon said that the Commission was going ahead with structural joint ventures and he would like to do so more widely. I may be wrong but I think he said that to do that would require, or he thought it might require, additional resources. Therefore, I am not sure that they are automatically extending the changes beyond joint ventures.

470. Do you in principle feel that the procedural changes which Sir Leon announced would be a good thing? Would they achieve what needs to be achieved to speed things up?
(Dr Bell) I think we would like to see them go further. There are these specific proposals on structural joint ventures. We would like to see that general approach extended across the total case load. I think it is as Mr Alty says: the feeling in DG IV is to see how they go on structural joint ventures to ensure they can deliver what they have publicly offered.

471. Did not Sir Leon contemplate going further? To go further would be within the framework of his proposals?
(Dr Bell) He did and certainly it is within the spirit of them.

472. Do you think that as he indicated them, if they were carried out, that they would be

[Chairman Contd.]

sufficient, or do you want to suggest we should recommend even further steps to be taken?

(Dr Bell) I think I would say that we are at this stage agnostic about whether that will achieve a sufficient improvement, together with other aspects of the decision-making which you may wish to discuss in terms of transparency and so on, but that is the agenda on which we would wish to encourage DG IV to concentrate at this present time.

473. Even if they do what Sir Leon says they would do, you would still like them to go further?

(Dr Bell) I would say we are agnostic about whether it would be necessary to go further.

474. It might work but it might not?

(Dr Bell) It might work. It might achieve a more certain timescale for business seeking important decisions. Whether that would be sufficient; we would then wish to look at the situation.

475. At least it would be a start?

(Dr Bell) It would be.

Chairman] What about Regulation 17 as a whole? Some people have said that as long as Regulation 17 is there, you cannot get down to radical reforms; you have got to tinker. Do you think the time has come when the Commission should really start again and have a new Regulation 17, assuming that Member States would agree to it? Do you think we have got to the state when we should do something radical?

Viscount Colville of Culross

476. It is 31 years old.

(Dr Bell) I think our feeling is that it is still possible to make achievements short of amending Regulation 17. I think if the text of Regulation 17 is opened, then a wider agenda is put in front of all the principal interests in the Member States and I believe that we should look at these administrative changes in the first instance to see what can be achieved in that area, and then take another appraisal.

Chairman

477. The trouble is that if you tinker it always puts off the day when you are going to be really radical.

(Dr Bell) On the other hand, we bear in mind very much that once one opens the text on those issues—witness the Merger Regulation—it takes a very long time normally to get consensus among the Member States.

478. We recognise that Member States are totally unwilling to abandon Regulation 17 and begin again but surely quite a lot has been learnt from the Merger Regulation that might be relevant to 85 and 86 procedures?

(Dr Bell) I think I would say that the process of learning is going on at the moment, that indeed a good deal has been learnt in the first couple of years of the operation of the Merger Regulation. I think that is causing DGIV to think carefully about the lessons which may be learnt in terms of changing administrative procedures in other areas of their work. I do not think that the time is now right to contemplate further legislative change by opening Regulation 17.

479. Some changes will take place in the Merger Regulation before too long. They may be very limited but the impression we have from witnesses so far is that the Task Force has done a very good job.

(Dr Bell) Yes, we would certainly agree that that is the case.

480. You do not think that there could be something to be learnt from that, from Articles 85 and 86?

(Dr Bell) I certainly think that there are lessons to be learnt in terms of the speed of decision-making which has been achieved under the Merger Regulation.

481. That is precisely what I had in mind. If you have any positive recommendations that you think we could put forward, we would be very glad to have them either now or in a subsequent memorandum. This is the sort of practical and realistic thing that we can recommend. One thing we have focused on a lot with witnesses, or perhaps they have focused on with us, is the role of the Hearing Officer. We had some witnesses who thought that the Hearing Officer could have a very important role in adjudicating on interlocutory problems which cropped up as an enquiry was progressing, for example, if somebody who is being investigated wanted to complain that the Commission was not getting a move on or they were not being given enough time to put in a document or the converse and a number of other interlocutory proceedings. It was suggested that perhaps the Hearing Officer could occupy a role rather like a Master in the High Court in the United Kingdom. On the other hand, that is not a suggestion which commends itself to the Commission. Do you have any views about this?

(Mr Bovey) I think the Hearing Officer is a role which has no exact analogy in the United Kingdom system. In looking at it, we have questioned what exactly his role is. He is not an adjudicator. He is more like an ombudsman but at the moment a rather partial ombudsman because he is concerned only with the actual formal hearing. If you were to extend it into a role in which he was going to pursue potential irregularities, perhaps at the request of particular parties, you would be giving him a potentially extremely extended role, one which it is by no means clear the two of them could do on their present basis.

[Chairman *Contd.*]

Chairman] The question or idea was that his function should change, as you rightly say, in a very significant way and that would obviously involve giving him more staff.

Viscount Colville of Culross] There are two points about this. First of all, could he do it with the resources which he has at his disposal? Secondly, we are talking about a legal philosophy, are we not, because, as I understand what has been said in evidence, the Hearing Officer is not the same as a Master. He is not somebody who is able to make interlocutory decisions about anything because there are rules within the Treaties which prevent him from doing so. Is there anything within the Treaties that would prevent us from suggesting that he should be given functions of that sort?

Chairman] This is what my question is directed to. It is quite plain at the moment he does not have those functions.

Viscount Colville of Culross] Is there any reason why he should not have them?

Chairman] If Member States decided to give him the functions, there is no reason why he should not.

Viscount Colville of Culross] Without an amendment to the Treaty?

Chairman

482. There would need to be an amendment to Regulation 17 certainly.

(*Mr Bovey*) That could possibly be made under Regulation 17 by amendment to Regulation 99. Under the Treaty, the decision has to be that of the Commission. One of the things the *PVC* case shows is that it has to be the decision of the whole Commission, fully and properly taken and there is no way in which that can be sub-delegated in any formal sense, but the procedure leading up to that can be laid down. It would, I think, be possible to interpose the Hearing Officer in that but then he would be a step in the decision-taking tree more like the American administrative law judge rather than the ombudsman role, the person who comes in at the request of a party to correct the actions of the decision-taker under the present system.

Viscount Colville of Culross

483. I understand that. Could he not actually hear people with points of view to express and then come forward with a recommendation which would go to the Commission.

(*Mr Bovey*) Are you suggesting that he should actually hear the case?

Chairman

484. No. He would deal with procedural things along the road up to final decision. The final decision has clearly got to be taken by the Commission. Quite a lot of procedural things crop up. People turn up at the end of the day and attack the Commission's decision on all sorts of grounds. Some of those have occurred at an interlocutory stage. I think what Viscount Colville is asking and what I am going to ask is: Would it be desirable to change his role so that he would regulate these steps along the road, or is it not desirable? It may be totally undesirable. We recognise it is a complete re-think of his role. Or, could he recommend to the Commission that they should decide this, that or the other, having had the opportunity to hear people discussing the interlocutory matters. I think there is a procedural difficulty.

(*Mr Bovey*) Essentially the interlocutory papers do not go to the full Commission. That decision is taken by the Commission official responsible or case officer responsible for the case. What I could certainly imagine as part of the internal procedure is a case officer having to come before, just as litigants have to come before, a Master and asking for an application to disclose particular material or whatever.

485. This is precisely the sort of point that is being suggested, that instead of the case officer or somebody in the ordinary Commission department deciding this sort of thing, if there was a dispute between the company being investigated and the case officer, they could go off to the Hearing Officer and say, "You decide this", or, "You recommend what ought to be done".

(*Mr Bovey*) He would be hearing and deciding in that case, rather than representing.

486. Would this be a good idea or not?

(*Mr Bovey*) I think you need to look at the overall procedure. I do not think you can take this in isolation from all the rest. If, as part of greater transparency and decision-taking, this were seen as a necessary element, then one can see it as being a desirable objective.

487. Let me take a specific example which the practising lawyers put to us. Suppose they feel that the Commission has some documents which they really want to see and the Commission has taken a wrong decision in refusing access to particular documents. The case officer says no and the Commission officer concerned says no. Would it be practicable to say, "Let them go to the Hearing Officer and let him decide"? It is revolutionary but would it in your view be desirable?

(*Mr Bovey*) In purely legal terms, the thing would lack a further step. It is merely moving it to a different Commission official.

488. Except that the idea is that the Hearing Officer should be regarded as being someone independent of the final decision. He would not be the investigating officer out to get a conviction, as it were. He would not be the final decider. He would be an independent person.

(*Mr Bovey*) This is a separation of functions within an administrative structure.

[Chairman Contd.]

489. I understand the Commission would accept that he might be given a higher status and more independence. They would not go so far as to give him this kind of role because it would be so contradictory to their conception of what he should be.

(Mr Cooper) As I understood the Commission's evidence the other week, they would not go so far as to say, "This person should have the decision-making power". One could conceive of a system where the decision-making power was not vested in the Hearing Officer; it still remained with the Commission in a collective sense but internally the Hearing Officer, having heard the arguments of the parties, would make a recommendation to the Commission which would carry an awful lot of weight, and which the Commission would generally expect to follow. I think there are two points. One, which the Commission made to you, is: If the question is, "We believe there are documents on such and such a date which should be disclosed to us", then it is reasonable to ask for a Hearing Officer to make that judgment. It is perhaps less reasonable for a party to come forward and say, "We think there must be something on the file", which could fill four drawers in a cabinet, "and will the Hearing Officer please go right through the file and see if there is anything the investigating officer has withheld from us?" I think the second point is that obviously what we are talking about is the balance between speed and transparency. If, at the end of the day, the case falls in the European Court of Justice because of procedural mistakes at the beginning, then it is quite right that the Commission have not benefited from having speed at the expense of transparency.

490. One suggestion is that there might be some form of rather speedy interlocutory review by the one single judge of the Court of First Instance.

(Mr Bovey) You may be right that this is to be assimilated to a first instance judicial decision and that that is how it should be regarded, but in structure it is actually an administrative decision equivalent to the regulatory issues that our Department takes on insurance or competition or whatever. The moment that you move towards that sort of structure, you are shifting it across from an administrative decision into a first instance in the curial ladder.

491. But only in respect of procedural steps?
(Mr Bovey) Certainly.

492. We have no views about this.
(Mr Bovey) If the Commission were to move to that extent, it could be confined to such.

Lord Hacking

493. My question is very close to yours. Is there an earlier role for the Court of First Instance on procedural matters? If the case comes to the Court of First Instance and one of the prime matters that is being taken up in the court for adjudication by the court is a procedural matter, would it not be more sensible if that could be resolved—and I take your point about it being an administrative rather than a legal decision—and there was an earlier involvement with the Court of First Instance, the single judge?

(Mr Bovey) We have no firm views on this. We certainly do not rule it out or regard it as being wrong in principle. Again, I think it would change the nature of the system, and therefore it is not a procedure that could be introduced without affecting the rest of it. If one looks at our own decision-taking process, if it is a court decision, then one would expect, at least in some instances, there to be an interlocutory appeal up from the Master to however high in the appeal it is appropriate for it to go. With an administrative decision, on an insurance regulation or something of that kind, one would expect the court, if somebody tried to challenge it half-way through, to say, "Wait, hang on a moment. Wait and see whether you do actually get your licence withdrawn", or whatever it might be. We have both systems in this country and they are there because of the way in which they are characterised. What is actually special about this Commission system is the fact that it is deciding on questions of law. All administrative procedures do so, but it is so expressly and openly deciding on questions of law that what people who propose this are perhaps suggesting is that it ought to be turned into a judicial system at a much earlier stage—that the Commission officials ought to be prosecutors rather than deciders.

Chairman] That is to avoid all these things being thrown into the melting pot once the decision comes three years later; you go to court and something which went wrong at an early stage has to be dealt with.

Lord Archer of Sandwell

494. Theoretically, the difference between the two proposals is that if it is decided administratively, you may not get reasons. No-one would be under an obligation to give reasons. If it is decided judicially in any form, there would presumably be an obligation to give reasons. That is the theoretical distinction. Do you see that being of any importance in practice?

(Mr Bovey) I think increasingly there are obligations to give reasons, even on an administrative side. I think the other side of it—and I do not want to sound as though the machinery is there to do people down—is that anybody who is subject to this sort of procedure has a natural interest in time-wasting, in seeking to exploit the procedural opportunities, and this would be seen as such an opportunity. Our own courts in the Datafin judgment took a view on the

[Lord Archer of Sandwell *Contd.*]

appropriateness of interfering with the procedures of the Takeover Panel, I think for very similar reasons because so much is at stake for the participants that they are going to take any opportunity that is available. They have nothing to lose.

Chairman

495. You are not the first person to suggest that if we recommended a procedure intended to help the parties to get a quick decision on a procedural matter rather than going through the whole process, they would immediately abuse it by making frivolous applications.

496. I am not saying frivolous.

497. I withdraw "frivolous"; making applications simply for the purpose of gaining time, which I regard as probably frivolous anyway. Would you do anything to change the present role and status and independence and resources of the Hearing Officer or are you happy with him as he is?
(*Mr Bovey*) Neither of those.
(*Mr Cooper*) There clearly is scope for increasing the status to get to a position where the view of the Hearing Officer is almost something which other officials will tremble at. If a case gets criticism from the Hearing Officer, then they will be very concerned that they have made a mistake. There must very clearly be a point in the procedure at which the Commission makes wholly certain that its case is on firm ground. There may have been one or two cases that have gone all the way through to the Court where there was more opportunity earlier on for the Commission internally—and it is in their interests to get things right—to highlight the difficulties and either realise that the case was lost from that point or to go back and start again, rather than, as you have just said, wait until three years later and find the case is thrown out.

498. The point is that the practitioners complain that they do not have the feeling that the Commission officials dealing with an enquiry exercise a kind of independence of judgment when deciding procedural matters that the hearing officer would be able to do. That is why we have been following this line of enquiry.
(*Mr Bovey*) I think his most important function, at any rate the way the United Kingdom sees it, is the day of the hearing. It is too easy in a bureaucratic procedure, as Mr Cooper says, for the essential point to be missed, the lack of a step in the argument. The mere fact of having an independent referee before whom the matter has to be argued out may of itself refine the judgment. If he were then empowered, as Mr Cooper says, actually to point it out internally within the Commission, and were seen as having the kind of authority that carried with it, then I think the effect would be a really very radical change without altering the whole character of the system.

Lord Wedderburn of Charlton

499. Would that mean that as work of that sort develops you would need more Hearing Officers with more resources? Would that be a recommendation?
(*Mr Bovey*) I am talking about the role of the Hearing Officer as it is envisaged now. I am suggesting that as it is now we should not underestimate the importance of the day in court and, as Mr Cooper says, of the Hearing Officer's recommendation in consequence.
(*Mr Cooper*) I do not think it is for us to prescribe, as it were, the result, the way in which the Commission should go about ensuring that the status of the Hearing Officer and the Hearing Officer's decisions carry essentially an immense weight throughout.

Chairman

500. What we really want to know is whether we should recommend changes. We feel the Commission is not necessarily going to change things itself. If a Member State feels that something could be improved, we should put forward a suggestion. That is why we are following this line. What about the Advisory Committee? Do you have any views about that? We have heard different things as to what its value is. What are your views about that?
(*Mr Cooper*) As you know, the Advisory Committee has a national expert when it is advising on individual cases. The Office of Fair Trading would lead for the United Kingdom on discussions on individual cases. Our observation is that it is a useful stage in the decision-making process because it provides for just the sort of independent review we have just been discussing of some ways of reviewing a decision before that decision is finalised. It gives an opportunity for Member States to raise questions if the case is not convincing and if the decision is not framed in a way which they think will stand up, either for legal reasons or on economic grounds.

501. You think it has a valuable function?
(*Mr Cooper*) We certainly feel that way, yes.

502. Should its report be published?
(*Mr Cooper*) I doubt that we would have any objection to publication except, of course, that publication at the moment is not permitted under Regulation 17.

503. Under the Merger Regulation I think it is given to the parties. I forget whether it is published generally. Should at least the Advisory Committee report be given to the parties or do you think that is not necessary either?
(*Mr Cooper*) We see no objection to that happening, if it was permissible under Regulation 17.

[Chairman *Contd.*]

Chairman] Certainly all these ideas would need either the Commission to shift or to amend something.

Viscount Colville of Culross] Is it not quite so important? Our witnesses may have their objections. Would they, in fact, resist a recommendation that this should be made public for the sake of transparency? It seems to me it is terribly important that sort of material should be made available to the parties.

Chairman

504. I am going to put the question slightly differently and say: Would you propose yourselves it should be published to the parties?

(*Dr Bell*) I think we can only comment on this particular proposition within the framework of what I said at the beginning about Regulation 17. In principle we are anxious to encourage the Commission to look at all possible options to improve transparency and publication of the Advisory Committee's decision would be a step in the right direction.

505. You would be in favour?

(*Dr Bell*) We would be in favour but subject to my comments about opening Pandora's box on Regulation 17.

506. You have to start somewhere. I understand your caution about this. Is this not something which could be done? Let us ask Viscount Colville's question again. Would you oppose our recommending that it should be published to the parties?

(*Dr Bell*) I think in the context of what we have said about Regulation 17, we would have to say that we saw difficulty in opening Regulation 17.

507. In publishing the Advisory Committee's report exclusively?

(*Dr Bell*) If it were, in practical terms, possible to limit changes to Regulation 17 to this sole proposition, then I think we would say that, yes, there is every reason to do that.

508. To the parties or generally?

(*Dr Bell*) Generally, I would say.

509. As with the Merger Regulation?

(*Dr Bell*) As with the Merger Regulation.

510. You mentioned block exemptions in your opening statement. We have had differing views as to whether it is desirable that the Commission should make more use of block exemptions. Some people think it is a splendid idea and some have reservations about doing it. What is your view?

(*Mr Cooper*) I think generally we are in favour of block exemptions where they are genuinely exempting beneficial agreements and the numbers of agreements are so large as to warrant a block exemption. The negotiation process for block exemptions is fairly resource-intensive itself. Clearly, one would want to know that there were significant numbers of agreements being made exempt. It may

have some slight disadvantage if, as a result of the block exemption being published, legal advisers tend to put agreements into forms which they know will fit very closely the block exemption. You can then find parallel behaviour throughout the market but, providing there is some flexibility to change practice, then we do not think that is too great a disadvantage.

511. You talk in paragraph 12 of your very helpful memorandum about potential for abuse. Could you elaborate on that?

(*Mr Cooper*) The potential for abuse was in the sense of those block exemptions which had an opposition procedure. Certain block exemptions have a black list and a white list of types of restriction which may not or may be incorporated in an agreement. They then have, in addition, an opposition procedure, so that if a firm has an agreement which contains restrictions which are on neither the black nor the white list, they may submit the notification and, provided there is no objection raised by Member States, by the Commission or by interested parties, then, after a given period, an exemption is granted. That was the context in which we said they may be open to abuse. The evidence, based on the Commission's annual reports, is both that this procedure is not greatly used but that also, where it is used, more often than not the cases are not appropriate. I think the first year for which we analyzed figures there were eight such notifications, of which seven were immediately judged inapplicable. In at least one case the reason for the inapplicability was that the agreement was completely outwith the scope of the block exemption. We have some reservations as to whether business and its legal advisers are either seriously misunderstanding the block exemption regulation or wondering whether the opposition procedure is a way of getting around the Article 85 prohibition.

512. To move away from that, what about comfort letters, which is another way in which people avoid going through the whole scale procedure of applying for a specific exemption? Some people find comfort letters very comfortable; some people think they are not quite comfortable enough. Do you have any views about the Commission's use of comfort letters?

(*Dr Bell*) We recognise that they are not totally legally watertight. I think our broad view is pretty positive. They do speed up procedures. They have helped DG IV to reduce the backlog of cases that they need to deal with and they have a good record of reliability. As a practical instrument, we think they have a great deal of virtue. It is open to the applicants to apply for a more formal comfort letter if they so choose. In the majority of cases I understand it is their decision to rest with the more informal comfort letter. Broadly we think it is a reasonably acceptable administrative instrument.

D R CATHERINE BELL, MR PHILIP BOVEY,
MR JOHN ALTY, MR ALAN COOPER
AND MISS SERENA HARDY

30 June 1993]   *[Continued*

[Chairman *Contd.*]

513. You have not found people complaining that this is an unsatisfactory procedure?

(*Dr Bell*) I think the difficulty arises for third parties and there is perhaps a question about whether comfort letters could contain more reasoning so that third parties could consider whether they have a basis to take any challenging action, but I think that is a matter for the Commission to consider as to what difficulties are and where the trade-off is between more reasoning and more speed.

514. Would it be realistic to publish comfort letters? Would commercial people resist that?

(*Dr Bell*) I imagine they would resist it if it contained commercially sensitive information. There would have to be some sort of editing in that respect.

515. That is so with Commission decisions. What about the alternative, the sort of halfway house, that if you publish an agreement which is not the subject matter of a block exemption and an agreement has been notified, and it has given third parties an opportunity to comment, would it be possible then to provide that after a certain period the agreement was cleared, in the absence of any opposition?

(*Mr Cooper*) I think you come back to the point I was just making about the opposition procedure in the context of block exemptions.

516. I was thinking outside the block exemptions.

(*Mr Cooper*) There are two risks to that. One is that the agreement slips through, as it were, unnoticed. The second risk is that the Commission finds itself devoting resources to cases which are about to time-expire, just to make sure that there are no hidden difficulties, rather than focusing on priority cases, either cases which need an individual exemption because a very real judgment has been made as to whether an exemption is appropriate or not—and perhaps a major agreement is pending on this decision—or, alternatively, they would be devoting resources to the urgent but potentially trivial case at the expense of, say, investigating cartels.

517. You would not be in favour of this system then?

(*Mr Cooper*) No, we would not.

Lord Hacking

518. Dr Bell, if I heard her correctly, referred to comfort letters not being watertight. Was she directing our attention to the position of the recipient of the comfort letter and saying that the comfort letter did not give enough reliance for the recipient of the comfort letter or how else was she directing her attention to the leak in the comfort letters?

(*Mr Bovey*) I think they are reliable as far as the Commission is concerned but, as Dr Bell said,

the question is of third parties. In practice there have been remarkably few instances of third parties being interested either way. In that sense they are an effective instrument, in exactly the way that Dr Bell said, but as far as the parties are concerned, they are very close to an estoppel.

Chairman

519. Have you ever heard of the Commission going back on a comfort letter?

(*Mr Bovey*) No, we have not.

(*Dr Bell*) No.

Viscount Colville of Culross

520. There is just one footnote on that. I quite see the commercial sensitivity is different but under the Financial Services Act there are hundreds of rules. What has been built up, even since the thing came in, is that you have guidance; you have various systems whereby people get interpretations and guidance of what the rules mean. They are of commercial sensitivity in fact because they carry a certain amount of weight and they are published. It seems to me that there is no real distinction between what we are talking about here and the system we have built up in this country after the 1986 Act.

(*Dr Bell*) Mr Bovey is more familiar than I am with the Financial Services Act.

(*Mr Bovey*) I think that what that guidance is doing is anticipating a view other than in a particular case and it is genuinely guidance of the kind that anybody is usually driven by, although it may be prompted by a particular case. The comfort letter in the particular cases cannot go further than the formal decisions which the organisation has taken. I think the difficulty with comfort letters is that they are deliberately looser; they are anticipating the direction a formal decision is taking or would take rather than resolving it in terms of legal theory. If you had to reason it and explain it in terms of legal theory, it would produce the kind of guidance you are talking about.

Lord Hacking] Basically a comfort letter is, surely, comfort to the recipient of the letter. There is not a broad statement of policy. The consequence is that it is treated as being an alternative to a decision. That system may surprise us but it is treated as working.

Chairman

521. A comfort letter must reflect a policy, I suppose. If you have comfort letters, you have a fair policy. Under Article 13 of Regulation 17 there is power or an option for the Commission to ask Member States to carry out investigations on its behalf. In your experience is this done very much? Should it be done more?

[Chairman Contd.]

(Dr Bell) I think the Commission have increasingly asked Member States' competent authorities to carry out investigations. I think particularly of OFT and the Bundeskartellamt. That is in respect of the United Kingdom a great tribute to the competence and professionalism of OFT. However, I have to say that one of the benefits we have had from preparing for the Committee is to reflect further on this point and to take Ministers' minds quite specifically to how they see the possibility of the Commission using competent authorities in Member States more. I have to say that Ministers will be wary of a development in that direction because they think that there is a danger that one would see the application of investigative powers becoming more rigorous in those Member States which have a very well developed competition infrastructure and less so in those which do not. I think that causes anxiety in terms of a level playing field and, frankly, the more so in the context of the concerns which are being examined in the Government's Deregulation Initiative about uneven application of EC regulations generally. I think a note of caution basically is required.

522. So you would not encourage them to do this more than they are doing at the moment?
(Dr Bell) No.

523. Do you have any experience or knowledge of how far they are doing it in other Member States than our own?
(Mr Cooper) We believe that they have not yet done it in other Member States.

524. At all?
(Mr Cooper) We are not certain of that. It may not have come to our attention.

525. Is it not an extensive practice for the Commission to go to other Member States, as far as you are aware, not even to Germany?
(Mr Cooper) Our information is that it has happened twice with OFT and not otherwise in the Community. That information may not be accurate. The Commission would obviously be able to tell you.

Viscount Colville of Culross

526. May I deal with the Commission notice on co-operation, questions 9 and 10? Perhaps I should not put it exactly like this. I am puzzled really as to how we amalgamate the system whereby the Commission works and the whole apparatus works with how you then adapt it to individual judicial systems in countries like ours, but not only like ours, so that we have got a similar system throughout the EEC. Goodness, they are very different. One asks, "Can you have the Commission as an amicus curiae in the United Kingdom courts?" Plainly you can because there is no difficulty about that but is that something that could be adapted so that there would be a system whereby they could do it fairly throughout the EEC in other courts?
(Miss Hardy) The problem is that if the Commission is to involve itself in cases in all national courts throughout the EEC and provide information perhaps and instruct counsel to go and argue cases, that would defeat the very object of decentralisation. The Commission would be spending a lot of resources in fulfilling that role. The intention behind the notice is that it will spend more time on priority cases and cases which have a significance for the Community.

527. Simply resources or principle?
(Miss Hardy) I think we see it as a problem in practical terms.

528. Given that there were no resource problem, what is the difficulty in principle?
(Miss Hardy) I think that there are many difficulties in it, with moving an administration system of enforcement to a judicial system of enforcement, for the parties. I think we do not expect that the Commission notice will actually produce many more cases in the United Kingdom courts, for the reasons which I am sure others have addressed to you, particularly the question of costs. At the moment complainants to the Commission do not have to pay any costs of the investigation, whereas, of course, they are at risk for the costs in national courts. The Commission has wide powers of investigation and so on. There are many reasons why it is preferred to bring cases to the Commission at the moment than to national courts. We do not see that the Commission's notice is actually going to overcome those difficulties.

Viscount Colville of Culross] I am unhappy about this because it seems to me that I start off with a very British point of view about this. When somebody says "amicus curiae", it seems to me that I am talking in terms that apply to British courts. I do not think we ought to be thinking in those terms. We ought to be thinking in terms of something that would apply all the way through the judicial system in the Community. I do not think we have applied our minds to this at all. I wonder whether our witnesses could help us to look a little bit broader, beyond resources and so on, in order to see if we could get a little further than this.

Chairman

529. The Commission has already either appeared in or sent statements of advice or opinion, at least to my knowledge, to one national court and it may be to more. I think Viscount Colville is suggesting that could be expanded usefully.
(Mr Bovey) May I try—and I am conscious that this is a public hearing and I am going to speculate and it should be seen as such—and state what Lord Colville's issue of principle is. There are already examples in national courts and in our

[Chairman Contd.]

own courts of the executive assisting the court in drawing out the wider implications. There are practical problems, and if that were overdone it would tend to extend the hearing and incur costs for people: essentially the parties would have to bear the cost of public interest hearings. Where I think the borderline comes is between the executive genuinely trying to draw the wider picture to the court's attention and telling the court what the answer is. I think there may be questions of principle about the executive of any kind coming into a court and saying, "This is the answer. We have decided that this is/is not—"

530. I do not think you can see this simply in United Kingdom terms. We have got to ensure uniformity throughout the Community. The whole object of the 177 reference is to get the court's opinion. On every 177 reference the Commission appears as *amicus curiae* in effect. If now the intention is that national judges should decide competition matters more and more implicitly, without referring the 177 to Luxembourg, what is the difficulty about the Commission playing an analogous role in the national court to that which it plays in the Community?
(*Mr Bovey*) On the 177 reference the Commission is only one among others.

Viscount Colville of Culross

531. It is the only *amicus*. Member States chip in with very much national ideas in mind or national situations in mind.
(*Mr Bovey*) We would rather hope that when a case comes in we look at it genuinely and objectively and would put forward a serious argument.

532. I thought every argument inevitably came out in favour of the United Kingdom! I do not seen any conflict between these two.
(*Mr Bovey*) We do not see the Commission's role on 177 as being unique and special, although obviously it has a different function from Member States. In the way envisaged in the courts here, I think it would be the sole provider of expertise and analysis.

533. But they would not necessarily be going into the facts of the particular case; they would be assisting the court as *amicus* on the development of law perhaps in a way in which a national judge would not necessarily know and even national counsel might not be aware. They would be able to inform the court of parallel problems existing in other countries. You do not like this idea?
(*Mr Bovey*) No. As I said, it is already the case in the United Kingdom. I see no reason in principle why assistance should not be given. The danger I see is dictation rather than assistance, particularly in other Member States where the courts are rather differently structured. We have a uniquely well qualified judiciary, perhaps a uniquely unbiddable judiciary.

Chairman

534. I do not think English judges on the whole react very well to dictation. Perhaps you think other states may not be quite so resistant.
(*Mr Bovey*) They are differently structured. They have a middle ground that we do not have.
Viscount Colville of Culross] Perhaps that is something we ought to consider further.
Chairman] Lord Hacking, I think, wants to ask you a question on mergers.

Lord Hacking

535. I do not know if you want us to continue in open session on this question about the position the Government is currently in of how best to revise Merger Control Regulation so as to achieve the right balance between assessment at Community level and assessment at national level? If you are happy to answer that in open forum, we are happy to receive your answer.
(*Dr Bell*) I am happy to give a very broad answer in open forum. I think our broad answer is that the thresholds are at present at more or less the right level, so we are broadly happy at present with where the jurisdictional boundary is between Brussels and national competition authorities.

536. You have had, I think, a look at the Commission working paper which has recently been distributed on 17 May. They are suggesting, are they not, looking at the summary on page 30, certain changes in the turnover thresholds. Do I understand your reply that you are not persuaded by these proposals?
(*Dr Bell*) That is correct.

Chairman

537. How would you modify them?
(*Dr Bell*) I think for the present we feel the thresholds should remain where they are. Perhaps I should also say that we would also not be sympathetic with the idea of opening what we call the exit provisions back into national jurisdiction, Article 9 of the Merger Regulation—and that is another point which has been raised for debate by the Commission—because we feel that the boundary is broadly right in jurisdictional terms. Moreover, the current exit provisions broadly achieve one-stop shopping, which was the original fundamental intention of the Merger Regulation. It allows exits in certain very limited circumstances. We think that the broad approach and the application by the Commission has been acceptable. The other area which the Commission has raised is what it calls its housekeeping proposals in terms of improvements to the decision-making process to achieve greater transparency in the decision-making process. We would certainly be sympathetic to looking at those proposals. We

Dr Catherine Bell, Mr Philip Bovey,
Mr John Alty, Mr Alan Cooper
and Miss Serena Hardy

[Chairman Contd.]

would particularly like to look at the proposals which might be achievable without amending the text of the Regulation. That is our very broad position.

538. In the light of the questions we have asked you, is there anything you would like to add or any points you feel you have not focused on that you should focus on?

(Dr Bell) I think not in open session, my Lord Chairman.

Chairman] Thank you all very much for coming and giving your helpful opinions. If we have put forward ideas you regard as heretical, they are not firm ideas at all; they are simply questions that have arisen out of the submissions that have been put to us and on which we very much want to have your views. We are very grateful to you all for coming.

WEDNESDAY 7 JULY 1993

Present:

Colville of Culross, V.	Skidelsky, L.
Elles, B.	Slynn of Hadley, L. (Chairman)
Holme of Cheltenham, L.	Wedderburn of Charlton, L.

Memorandum by Mr Jeremy Lever QC

1. In my evidence to Sub-Committee E of the House of Lords Select Committee on the European Communities in 1988 (see Session 1988-89, 6th Report, *Merger Control*, HL 31 of 7 March 1989 at page 110) I drew attention to the fact that Directorate General IV (Competition) of the European Communities Commission lacked the resources to carry out promptly and effectively its then existing functions (ie before the adoption by the Council of the Merger Regulation—Council Regulation 4064/89, OJ [1990] L 257/13) and that it was important to provide DG IV with adequate resources to cope with its pre-existing responsibilities rather than leave it in a chronic state of under provision.

2. In Case T-24/90 *Automec Srl v EC Commission* [1992] 5 CMLR 431 the Commission effectively confirmed that its resources were inadequate to permit it to monitor compliance with the rules on competition of the EEC Treaty and in particular that, having regard to the proceedings pending before it and its limited staff numbers, it could not investigate every complaint that was made to it and had to apply "criteria of priority" ([1992] 5 CMLR, pages 475–476, paragraphs 67–68).

3. In part in an attempt to mitigate that state of affairs, the Commission earlier this year published a *Notice on co-operation between national courts and the Commission in applying Articles 85 and 86 of the EEC Treaty*, OJ No 939/6 of 13.2.93. The intention underlying the Notice is to facilitate the application of Articles 85 and 86 by the national courts so that those whose complaints the Commission cannot handle will not be left without a remedy.

4. Another symptom of the inadequacy of the resources of Directorate General IV is its inability to deal with the applications made to it for exemption, pursuant to Article 85(3) of the EEC Treaty, of agreements which attract the prohibition of Article 85(1) and which, in the absence of exemption, are "automatically void" by virtue of Article 85(2). In order to reduce the legal uncertainty resulting from its inability to deal formally with applications for exemption under Article 85(3), the Commission has adopted the practice of issuing "comfort letters" which provide a substantial measure of *de facto* protection from future attack by the Commission but which are not definitive and leave open the possibility that, following on the opening of a formal procedure, exemption might be refused.

5. It seems difficult to see how, on the basis of a comfort letter, a final judgment could be given by a United Kingdom Court to enforce an agreement which attracts the operation of Article 85(1) (something that the national court is enjoined to apply) and which might thereafter be refused an exemption (something that only the Commission can give) so that the voidness of the restrictive provisions of the agreement would continue unrelieved; and this is especially so, given that the European Court of Justice has held that, with a few historical exceptions, such agreements do not enjoy even "provisional validity" by reasons of an *application* for exemption.

6. In this Memorandum, I discuss first the inadequacies of the Commission's recent Notice; and secondly the steps that might and, in my view, should be taken to enable Articles 85 and 86 to be implemented speedily and effectively as rules of public law. Finally I revert to a theme that I ventured to draw to the attention of Sub-Committee E in 1988, namely that the Commission's procedures in competition cases remain unacceptable and require radical reform.

7. The Commission's recent Notice rightly points out that the national courts can indeed must, themselves apply Article 85(1) and (2) and Article 86 of the EEC Treaty. A national court can therefore decide that the conditions for applying those provisions are *not* met and then properly can deal with the case before it without reference to those provisions. Alternatively, if the Commission has issued a bloc exemption that covers the agreement that is before the national court, the national court can and must apply the bloc exemption and treat the agreement as valid.

8. However a serious problem arises where an agreement which does not enjoy the benefit of a bloc exemption has been notified to the Commission for individual exemption (an application for exemption being a necessary condition for the grant of an individual exemption) but has not been dealt with. Here the Commission says that the national courts may, within the limits of their procedural law, ask Directorate General IV for:—

(i)   information of a procedural nature to enable them to discover the status of procedures before the Commission and likely timetables for completing them;

(ii)   advice on points of law;

(iii)   information of a statistical nature, market studies and economic analyses.

9. With regard to (i), it is difficult to believe that at least most of the relevant information of a procedural nature will not generally be available from the parties themselves in United Kingdom litigation.

10. With regard to (ii), it is not clear to me on what basis a United Kingdom Court could take the opinion of the Commission (rather than the European Court of Justice) on points of Community law, especially since Community law is part of United Kingdom law and therefore not a matter for evidence. I suppose that the Commission's advice might take the form of *amicus* submissions; however, one would want to know the status of the individual who was responsible for the submissions since otherwise what might represent the opinion of a relatively junior official with idiosyncratic views would be liable to be given undue weight. In relation to (ii) the Commission also states:—

> "If the Commission says that the case in question is unlikely to qualify for an exemption, national courts will be able to waive a stay of proceedings and rule on the validity of the agreement, decision or concerted practice."

11. But what would then be the position if the "unlikely" were to occur and the Commission, having subsequently, for the first time, gone through the required procedure, were to conclude that the case in question *did* qualify for an exemption. The judgment of the national court would then have been given on a basis which was known to be uncertain and which in the event had turned out to be false.

12. As to (iii), I would have thought that there would be grave problems relating to the admissibility of evidence of facts collected by or on behalf of the Commission, without regard to the rules of evidence applicable in the United Kingdom Courts. For that very reason it is not clear to me that even a formal decision by the Commission provides evidence admissible in the United Kingdom Courts of the substantive facts recited in the decision.

13. Even if the difficulties to which I have alluded were to prove to be of little practical significance, I would still feel that the Notice was largely misconceived in that it regards private litigation founded on Article 85 and/or Article 86 of the EEC Treaty as an adequate substitute for the administration of those Articles as rules of public law. In my experience that is not so. There are often immense practical problems in the way of successfully invoking Article 85 and/or Article 86 in the national courts at least in the United Kingdom. Those problems arise partly because of evidentiary and procedural difficulties, and partly because the United Kingdom Courts generally lack a grasp of the economic principles which underlie competition law. It is, I believe, because the United Kingdom Courts themselves recognise that lack on their part, that they have been as unwilling as they have been to become involved in any review of the substance of the Reports of our own Monopolies and Mergers Commission and subsequent action or inaction on them by the responsible Secretary of State.

14. The present position with regard to the public law implementation of Articles 85 and 86 of the EEC Treaty by the competent administrative authorities of the Member States (for most practical purposes, the Office of Fair Trading in the United Kingdom) is as follows. Leaving aside the special cases in which Council Regulation 17 does not apply (eg air transport, marine transport, merger control), Article 9(3) of Council Regulation 17 authorises the national competent authorities to apply Article 85(1) and Article 86 of the Treaty "as long as the Commission has not initiated any procedure under Articles 2 [applications for negative clearance], 3 [proceedings to terminate infringements] or 6 [proceedings for exemption under Article 85(3)]."

15. There are thus two important limitations imposed by Community law on the powers that may be exercised by the competent national authorities in this area:

(i)   the Commission has the sole power to grant exemptions under Article 85(3) of the Treaty (this is expressly spelt out in Article 9(2) of Council Regulation 17); and

(ii)   by itself initiating a procedure, the Commission can at any time deprive a competent national authority of proceeding further in a case.

16. Despite those limitations, I understand that the Spanish competent authorities have been regularly applying Articles 85(1) and Article 86 as provisions of directly applicable public law. However, the United Kingdom authorities have never sought to do so and United Kingdom law makes no explicit provision for the direct application of Article 85(1) or Article 86 as rules of public law. In particular there is no specific national law power authorising the Director General of Fair Trading ("the Director") to investigate infringements of either of those Articles (contrast the Competition Act 1980, section 3: preliminary investigation by the Director of possible anti-competitive practices) or for the Director or the Secretary of State to refer such infringements as such to the Monopolies and Mergers Commission

("the MMC") (contrast the Competition Act 1980, section 5—competition references; and the Fair Trading Act 1973, sections 50 and 51: monopoly references by the Director and by Ministers).

17. It is important here to recall the weakness of United Kingdom *national, public* law with regard to the grant of relief to persons injured by monopolistic conduct. No matter how strong the monopoly of the wrongdoer nor how objectionable its conduct, the most that an injured party can hope to obtain from the authorities responsible for the administration of competition law as public law is action which, after, probably, a year or so, will prevent the wrongdoer from continuing or repeating the conduct in question. United Kingdom national law does not provide for the imposition of fines for monopolistic abuse as such nor for the making of interim orders for its control on *prima facie* evidence of its existence. Therefore, leaving aside, as in practice often problematical, expensive and risky, the possibility of civil litigation based on Article 86 of the EEC Treaty as a directly applicable Treaty provision, the victim of monopolistic abuse will frequently turn for help to the European Communities Commission in Brussels even in essentially "local" cases which could be better handled locally. It is difficult to imagine a system more antithetical to the principles of subsidiarity.

18. But now one comes back to the fact that the European Communities Commission does not have the resources to deal with the complaints that are addressed to it (see paragraphs 1 and 2 above). Under Community law, where a public agency enjoys a national monopoly in the provision of services of a particular description, its inability to satisfy the demand for such services provides a reason for treating the continued existence of the monopoly as incompatible with the EEC Treaty: see Case C-41/90 *Höfner and Elser v. Macrotron GmbH* [1991] ECR I-1979. What is sauce for the goose is sauce for the gander: the Commission's inability to provide the public law services required in the field of Community competition law entails the consequence that the Commission's "monopoly" in the provision of such services should be modified.

19. The modification should *at least* enable the national authority of a Member State to notify the Commission that in a case directly involving only citizens of that Member State the national authority intended to apply Article 85(1) and/or Article 86 unless within a limited period of time the Commission itself initiated a procedure and undertook to conduct that procedure with all good speed. Unless the Commission did so within the limited time available for that purpose, it would be precluded from thereafter initiating a procedure and thereby depriving the Member State of continuing competence. Where citizens of more than one Member State were concerned, a similar system could operate if the national authorities of each of the Member States concerned could agree which of them should handle the case. The eventual decisions of the competent authorities within the Member States would have to be subject to judicial review; and, through recourse to the procedure whereby national courts can, and at the level of final appeal must, obtain interpretative rulings from the European Court of Justice, the integrity and internal consistency of Community law would be safeguarded.

20. In my view, a limited reform of that nature would not go far enough since it would preserve the Commission's "monopoly" in the field of exemption under Article 85(3): wherever an infringement of Article 85(1) is alleged—whether in the national courts or in administrative proceedings—and it is not clear that the allegation is unfounded, the ability to take a final decision is liable to be unacceptably delayed because of the possibility of grant of an Article 85(3) exemption; and pending a final decision on the grant or refusal of such exemption, the parties to the agreement act at their peril in implementing it.

21. One could adapt precisely the same new system for the application of Article 85(3) as the new system that I have suggested at paragraph 20 above for the application of Article 85(1) and Article 86. If that were felt to go too far, the new system, as operated for the application of Article 85(3), could provide that when a national authority was seised of a request for exemption under Article 85(3), it would prepare a draft decision, granting or refusing exemption; the draft decision would then go to the Commission in Brussels and, after review by the Consultative Committee, either the draft decision would then be adopted by the Commission and would stand as a Commission decision (which could be attacked in the ordinary way before the Court of First Instance) or the Commission would have to produce its own decision within a limited period of time.

22. I pass now to a brief consideration of the Commission's procedures in contentious competition cases. In previous evidence to Sub-Committee E I explained why I regarded the Commission's procedures as unacceptable (see 6th Report of the House of Lords Select Committee on the European Communities, Merger Control, HL 31, 7 March 1991, at pages 110–112). The position has not improved. On the contrary, the judgment of the Court of First Instance in Cases T-68 and 77–78/89, *Re Italian Flat Glass: Società Italiana Vetro SpA v. EC Commission* [1992] 5 CMLR 302 disclosed serious misuse by the Commission of documentary material as a basis for a decision which imposed on the undertakings concerned fines totalling 13.4 million ECUs.

23. The grave defects in the Commission's *modus operandi* in contentious competition cases prejudices not only the undertakings concerned, but the Commission itself and the wider Community interest since, as Commission officials privately acknowledge, the Commision is finding it increasingly difficult

to uphold its decisions in contentious competition cases when those cases come before the analytical scrutiny of the Court of First Instance. At best, there is a waste of Community resources when, following on an administrative procedure and proceedings before the European Courts, a Commission decision is annulled and the Commission is condemned to pay the costs of the undertakings concerned. At worst, the defects in the Commission's *modus operandi* are liable to result in undertakings that *have* committed infringements of Article 85(1) or Article 86 escaping scot-free.

24. My own past suggestions for reform have been modest and, if implemented would have left the Commission as the body responsible for taking the decisions in contentious competition cases (see my evidence to Sub-Committee E, *op cit* at pages 111–112). In confining myself to such modest suggestions, I was influenced first by the well-known general difficulty of getting new Council Regulations at all, secondly by the possibility that the Commission would effectively prevent the making by the Council of the Regulation that would be necessary for more radical reform but, thirdly and above all, by a belief that the Commission would be amenable to reason and would voluntarily introduce the reforms necessary to remove a blemish on its reputation that has been increasingly bringing it into grave disrepute.

25. It is possible that the shock felt by the Commission at the national reactions to Maastricht will have a salutary effect in this as in other areas. But it may already be too late to still the voices that urge the more radical reform of taking away from the Commission altogether its power to take decisions in application of Article 85(1) and Article 86 and giving the power to an independent Competition Tribunal. As matters now stand, the Commission may not be able to count on many allies amongst the well-informed in any debate on this topic.

21 *April* 1993

Supplementary Letter from Mr Jeremy Lever QC

I now have to hand the comments made by Professor Michel Waelbroek, a distinguished practitioner and academic in this field, at the Fordham Corporate Law Institute last October about the *Italian Flat Glass* case referred to at page 9 of my memorandum and I have his permission to quote from those comments to the Sub-Committee. I do so lest it be thought that my views about the unacceptability of the Commission's procedures in competition cases are idiosyncratic. Professor Waelbroek said:

"[In the] *Italian Flat Glass* case . . . the Commission's decision was based on evidence much of which had been—and I'm sorry to say so, but that's what the Court said—distorted. It was fabricated. There were parts of documents which were blanked out without this being apparent from a reading of the documents, and there were also different documents or different dates which were not true as to the whole facts.

"The Court of First Instance undertook a very detailed and meticulous examination of the evidence. They found out that this evidence had been distorted and that the Commission officials and the members of the Commission had been presented with a case which was not the case which existed in reality. The Court of First Instance annulled the Commission's decision, which I think is quite proper and the way it should be.

"I have the impression that the Commission has not swallowed this defeat. Instead of accepting to revise its methods, it is saying, "Oh, we should be allowed to continue." I am not saying that this is what [the Head of Division, DGIV who has addressed the Conference] is advocating.

"But I would not like the Commission to say, because of these battles between the firms who hide and who deviously destroy evidence—the poor Commission, with its shortness of staff, which in the public interest is trying to make the market remain competitive—that the Commission should be allowed to make decisions which rest on documents which are distorted or fabricated. I think it is in the public interest that even the Commission should adopt a new order."

The Commission official, who had addressed the Conference, replied saying " . . . I cannot accept that the Commission really has fabricated or distorted evidence. This is not correct and this is unfair." The Commission's apparent unwillingness to recognise that something seriously amiss had taken place adds to one's concern.

In any event, what is on any view indisputable is that a reform of the Commission's procedures such as I have consistently advocated would almost certainly prevent the *misuse* of evidence which without any doubt occurred in the *Italian Flat Glass* case.

Jeremy Lever QC

27 *April* 1993

Examination of witness

MR JEREMY LEVER, QC, called in and examined.

Chairman

539. Mr Lever, on behalf of the Committee may I first thank you very much for the paper you have put forward to us and for coming today. It is very valuable that we should have the views of one of the leading and most experienced practitioners in competition law in the country and, indeed, in the Community. I want to begin by picking up one point that you mentioned in the memorandum and that you mentioned in some depth in your written evidence in 1988, that is, the question of the amount of resources that Directorate General IV has to carry out its obligations under Article 85 and Article 86. We have heard divergent views about this: some people think that the lack of resources is very important and some people think that it is not so much the lack of resources as the structural defect in the Commission that are responsible for the failings or the faults that are sometimes alleged against the Commission, particularly of course the lack of a clear division between those who investigate and those who pursue and those who eventually decide. Can you tell which of these in your views is really more significant?
(*Mr Lever*) My Lord Chairman, the two views I think are not mutually exclusive. The defects of the system are in part no doubt attributable to lack of resources and they are in part attributable to the structure. The structure has changed over the years. Your Lordships may recall that just over 12 years ago Dr Pappalardo came and gave evidence to your Lordships' Committee and stressed that the internal structure of Directorate General IV contained a sophisticated system of checks and balances which ensured objectivity, and he attached great importance to that internal structure, in particular the division between the investigator on the one hand and the rapporteur if the case was then taken up and prosecuted on the other hand. That division was scrapped in the interest, it was said, of efficiency.

540. That was when you had different directorates dealing with the investigations, A, B and C, I think?
A. Absolutely, my Lord Chairman, and that was scrapped in the interest of efficiency. One has to ask what efficiency means in this context. One can think of various ways of increasing the efficiency of the administration of justice. If one means reducing the time spent one obvious thing would be to eliminate the cross-examination of prosecution witnesses, but one could not regard that as being conducive to the satisfactory administration of justice.

541. Or removing the jury!
A. I am not satisfied that the change that I over the years have respectfully advocated of dividing the functions would necessarily increase

the number of man-hours required to be spent by officials to deal with any number of cases. It might alter the results fundamentally, but I am not satisfied that it would necessarily in itself require more manpower, so I am not satisfied that, when Mr Tugendhat was a commissioner and I put to him the desirability of the change, he was right in saying that they would not be able to find the required additional resources. One consequence of making the change might be that there would be far fewer appeals and that itself would release resources for other purposes. Another consequence might be that cases that were being looked at would come to an end much more quickly. Therefore, I cannot say whether the division of function within the Commission that I have respectfully advocated would in itself necessitate more manpower or reduce the amount of required manpower. However, I then go on and say that either the Commission's own resources need to be substantially increased in any event to perform all the functions that people look to the Commission at present to perform; or those functions must in part be delegated to others for their performance.

542. Theoretically obviously the idea of the same person being prosecutor and judge is an unattractive one. Indeed, some of the evidence that we had suggests that this works out badly in practice because there is a lack of accountability, a lack of supervision of the people dealing with the cases and that lack of accountability has increased over the years. Would that be your view, Mr Lever?
A. My Lord Chairman, I do not know that I should want to say that there had been a change whether for the worse or for the better. I do recall that in 1976 when it was possible that I might myself have had the honour to join the Commission's services I discussed with the then director of IV B, who as such at that time was effectively what we today call the hearing officer as well as having other functions, whether the arrangements for having the investigator, prosecutor, judge and jury all in one body was satisfactory. We both said with a certain twinkle in our eyes that the arrangement would of course be perfectly all right if we were in charge because we were so completely objective but that we should recognise that it was not satisfactory because our successor could not be counted upon to be as unusual as we were.

543. Yes, I think that probably everybody believes that he is the most fair and objective person in the world. That is always the problem. Dr Ehlermann rejected this criticism that there was a lack of supervision and lack of accountability; he said that this criticism misunderstood the hierarchy of DG IV. Do you have the feeling today that there is a lack of supervision, a lack of accountability, in other words, that the person on the ground just gets on with it without really

[Chairman *Contd.*]

having to account to anyone for what he is doing? A particular aspect of this, it was suggested to us, was that in the past the legal officers of the Commission gave more of a lead, more advice, to the case handler than they do today and there was more supervision by the legal department. What do you think about that.

A. Let me deal first with your question about the legal service. When some years ago I urged on Dr Ehlermann, for whom I have the highest personal regard, the desirability of a division of function, one of the questions that he raised was whether what I was saying was not a criticism of the legal service for failing to perform its proper function. I do not think that it is a criticism of the legal service for having failed then or now failing to perform its proper function. The legal service can indeed identify and should identify errors of law on the face of a decision and evident infringements of essential procedural requirements, but it is not, as I see it, the function of the legal service to seek to answer the question whether the decision is correct in substance, and if the legal service were to cease to do that I think that the services—the people at Directorate General IV—would be entitled to say, that is not your affair, that is ours. So much therefore I think for the idea that the legal service can be a substitute for the kind of reform that over the years I have ventured to ask for.

544. I think that the idea was more this, that if, to take a specific example, a party wanted access to particular documents on the Commission's file the legal officers should be there to tell the Commission, you have simply got to give that, you are not carrying out the decisions of the court, you are not carrying out a fair standard by not doing it, not so much a decision as to whether there was a breach of Article 85.

A. I do not think that the legal service really has the resources or the opportunity to perform that function.

545. Has there been a change in their function in your perception over the years?

A. For myself I should be sorry to see the legal service encumbered with that function in the sense that I believe a division of the functions of the kind that I proposed would be much more satisfactory. You also ask me whether one could reconcile the statements that the Commission was a hierarchical body and yet that there was inadequate supervision of what was done. I think, yes, one can reconcile those two statements, though I have not myself ever put it quite like that. The Commission is a hierarchical body and one of the points when you ask about the hearing officer that I should be bound to make is that the hearing officer has an official grade of A3 and does not have the standing within the hierarchical body to make sure that his views are properly considered. But equally one does find that the Commission often speaks with different voices because of a lack of co-ordination. When you ask about the

possibility of the Commission acting as an amicus in the national court I should have to draw attention to the fact that the amicus may be what is described in the introductions to some foreign language dictionaries as a false friend in the sense that it may be rather misleading.

546. Yes, you mention that, but let us just stay with the hearing for the moment. We know what his present functions are. What we are in part interested in is knowing whether those functions should be changed. One suggestion that was put to us is that interlocutory matters that fall for decision in the course of an enquiry might be looked at by the hearing officer. You do not want yourself for the legal services to be involved in decisions, to use your word, you do not want them to be encumbered with decisions about access to documents and that sort of thing. The question is, should the hearing officer have power to rule on interlocutory matters in the way that he does not at present? It would change his function. Would this be desirable? Should he be rather like a Queen's Bench Master in other words?

A. In the old days, my Lord Chairman, and I am speaking about the period before roughly 1978, the director at IVB was rather in that position. It was a very unusual directorate and Dennis Thompson, a distinguished English lawyer who held the post, I think sought to act in the kind of way that you have described. For various reasons that system did not continue and the hearing officer in a sense is the response to its non-continuance. I do not want to appear to be a single issue fanatic, but what you have suggested would be a kind of watered down version of my division of functions, my separate directorate general, which would be headed by an A1, and one would hope that the A1 would be sufficiently relieved of other functions that he could perform the role you have suggested with great authority. At the moment, my Lord Chairman, it is unlikely that people who may be fined ecu 75 million will ever see an A1. They will be lucky if an A2 looks in.

547. We will come on to the more radical ideas, the alternatives, your idea and the idea that you have someone totally outside the Commission taking these decision. Suppose you stick with the present Directorate General IV, would you make any changes to the role of the hearing officer? In your paper on mergers, for example, you said that the procedural safeguards supposedly afforded by the appointment of the hearing officer now appeared to you to be largely illusory. Is that still your view?

A. I do not believe that you can rely on a hearing officer, but not because he is lacking in independence. In my experience Mr Mussard was not lacking in independence, and Mr Johannes is not lacking in independence. There have been cases where the hearing officer has made comments in the course of a hearing that have been highly favourable to defendants but which find no echo whatsoever in the ultimate decision. I should regard,

[Chairman Contd.]

as a step in the right direction but inadequate, publication of the report of the hearing officer at least to the parties but I recognise that that could simply result in emasculation of the report, turning it into a bland, anodyne document such as could be published without embarrassment to the Commission.

548. Before the oral hearing suppose that there are parties dissatisfied with the way that the investigation is going, either by refusal to give access to documents or by the timetable or for some other reason, should the hearing officer be given a role in resolving that dispute between the party and the Commission or would that in your view not be a satisfactory solution?

A. It would not be an adequate solution.

549. Would it be better than the present position?

A. It might be better than the present position, but you must with respect recall that the hearing officer is an A3.

550. Yes, then you would make him an A1 if necessary.

A. But again with respect if you make him an A1, my Lord Chairman, you are by a back door, I think, coming very close to making the reform that I so greatly favour.

551. I am not sure. I thought that your reform was directed to the final decision making process rather than to control of the interlocutory procedures. That is how I read your paragraphs 19 and 20.

A. If you have a very senior official with adequate resources who himself takes these cases under his wing and has nothing to do with the investigation and the prosecution, you will have gone a long way towards adopting the sort of solution that I favour. It would not have the advantage that I should like to see that that official would also be dealing with anti-dumping cases.

552. But in this suggestion that has been put to us he would not be involved in the final decision as to whether there had been a breach of Article 85.

A. Then in that case I should regard that as being a very grave deficiency.

Chairman] But you might have somebody else who was A1 in a separate directorate general dealing with the final decision making process. The question is whether you should have someone controlling the progress and process of investigation.

Viscount Colville of Culross

553. My Lord Chairman, would this not at least be going back to something that is recognised and precedented in that it was very much what was happening in 1978 to that extent on the procedural side?

A. My Lord Chairman, the trouble was that for various reasons the system broke down. It did not work.

Baroness Elles

554. My Lord Chairman, is not one problem that at present there is nobody but nobody to look after or foresee that the defendants and claimants do have access to the files? The idea of at least having the hearing officer stepping in before the case comes for oral hearing would possibly fill that gap without in any way at the moment discussing changes in the structures and the levels of competence. It is just a search for somebody who can deal with the problem in the Commission, and there is nobody at the moment to deal with it?

A. I should entirely accept that one can identify a number of specific deficiencies in the present system, my Lord Chairman, and one can make suggestions for ameliorating it. That is why I hesitate to appear to be a single issue fanatic.

Chairman

555. What Baroness Elles has been putting to you is the whole point of what I have been trying to put to you. Forget about tearing up Regulation 17 and forget about sending the thing off to some wholly new structure, let us live with the present structure: do we improve it by suggesting that the hearing officer should have an upgraded role? If you do not agree, please say so, Mr Lever. Some people have said that it would be a ridiculous idea; other people who have put up the idea seem to think that it is a good idea. We should like to have your view.

A. One of the advantages of what I was proposing is that it involves no change in Regulation 17. If you then say to me, would it be better to tinker with the present system than radically to reform it, I do not believe that tinkering with the present system will remove the fundamental criticism. I think that there is a cancer and one has to take the knife and wield it pretty drastically.

556. But changing the Commission like politics is the art of the possible. We have to start with what we have. I think that we understand your point of view. Let us move away from the hearing officer to the court of first instance. Is there any way in which these preliminary enquiries can be subject to immediate interlocutory appeal in the court of first instance? For example, suppose that even before the statement of objection is served there is some dispute between the parties, would it be practicable to have a process of application to perhaps a single judge at the court of first instance? Is there room for that? Would it work? Again, would it need a radical change?

A. You, my Lord Chairman, are probably infinitely better equipped by your experience to form a view about that than me. When in one case we sought to establish the principle of early judicial review of Commission administrative procedures—we sought to do that in the upper court because the court of first instance had not at that time come into existence—your Lordship

[Chairman *Contd.*]

may recall that we failed. That was a matter that came before the president of the court as a preliminary matter and he came down fairly decisively against early judicial review, saying that it was only when the Commission's act lacked any semblance of legality that the court might be prepared to intervene. I appreciate the problems that would arise with an on-going administrative procedure if parties could haste away at any moment the requisite number of kilometres to Luxembourg to get the Court of First Instance to interfere with the progress of the procedure, especially because parties are not always anxious to hurry these cases on.

557. But the alternative at the moment is that the parties wait until the Commission issues its decision and then sometimes they succeed before the court of first instance on a purely procedural thing way back in history and it really means then that the decision falls to the ground and the decision but for this procedural defect might have been perfectly good. As you said in your paper, people who ought to be fined may get away with it?

A. If that happens that is a very serious defect. People do not always wait. My recollection is that in the recent cement cases they did go off quickly to Luxembourg, they went to the Court of First Instance and they got nowhere at that stage, so it is not necessarily true that people wait. But what your Lordship says is quite right: it is highly unsatisfactory if the Commission has done something that will vitiate everything that follows for everybody to spend a lot of time and resources on an exercise that is bound in the end to be overturned. In some cases it is impossible to see how going to the courts in Luxembourg could help. I am thinking about the important class of cases of interim measures taken by the Commission because it may be perfectly clear that the Commission has gone wrong in taking interim measures but the only way that you could effectively neutralise those interim measures would be by getting the court at Luxembourg to suspend them by interim measures; and there you have to show that certain rather narrow conditions are satisfied, and however wrong the Commission may be, those conditions may not be satisfied, and by the time that the case comes on to final hearing, of course, the interim measures will have ceased and been replaced by final decision. So you cannot in those cases go to Luxembourg. I think all I can say is that I have no satisfactory answer to the question that you raise, my Lord Chairman. I can only say that because of the problem of on-going judicial control, it is all the more important that the administrative procedure should be properly conducted.

558. Yes, I entirely accept that. The idea that was put to us would involve very substantial procedural changes at the court and you would have to work out a fast track to deal with it. It

may have a limited use, but it could have some use, is that your view?

A. Yes, I should just add this, my Lord Chairman, that every time the court says it has not been established that a procedural irregularity has actually made any difference they are neglecting to do something that could make the Commission more careful in future. Even at the cost of letting guilty people off it may be worth the court striking down decisions where things have been done wrong in order to compel the Commission to do the thing right in the first place.

559. Has it been your experience, Mr Lever, without giving us specific confidential details, that the difficulties of access to the Commission file create problems? Some of our witnesses said that this is really the major problem. On the other hand, the Commission's evidence was that anything that can be given will be given.

A. My Lord Chairman, I think that the situation remains very unsatisfactory. I think that we have reached a position where the Commission says that it is not bound to disclose a very great deal of the documentary material that is available to it but that you can trust it, rely on it, to disclose to defendants material that might assist their defence. But when Commission officials are pressed, as they have been by the Court of First Instance, they admit that it is not possible for them in the course of an administrative procedure to identify what material on the file may be of assistance to the defendant, and with that I should absolutely agree: it is not possible for them to and that makes it to my mind essential that everything that is not a real business secret of somebody else that is on the file should be made available to defendants, and that if it is a real business secret that cannot be disclosed it ought not to be admissible in evidence, and my understanding is that it is not. It is also right to say that the Commission is liable to misconstrue documents that are exculpatory and incriminating and that they are liable to misconstrue documents because they are working on a translation into, for example, French from English and the official in question, who may not be a French language speaker, using the French language version simply gets hold of the wrong end of the stick. I am not in any way underestimating the problems of a multilingual civil service having to operate on a very limited budget as Directorate General IV is, so when I say these things it is not because of a lack of sympathy for Directorate General IV.

Baroness Elles

560. Can you kindly tell us who takes the decision as to the confidentiality of the document to be seen or not seen? Is it just the case handler or does it go higher?

A. My Lord Chairman, I am not a good person to ask that. One of the difficulties is to know who actually takes any decision. Again, it is vastly unsatisfactory that the Commission has never, so

[Baroness Elles *Contd.*]

far as I know, published who has powers of authority and who has powers of signature so you have no idea of the authority that anybody has.

561. Would it be helpful if the Commission—Directorate General IV—were asked to produce rules of procedure by which they run their administrative judicial capacity, the joint capacity that they have in the Commission?

A. It certainly could do no harm, and the need for publication of powers of authority and powers of signature in many fields, and not only this, to my mind is absolutely compelling.

Chairman

562. The Court of First Instance has laid down some guidelines recently I think criticising the Commission for its approach in regard to the access to documents. Do you think that the court of first instance has had any effect on the Commission's conduct of these enquiries in regard to documents?

A. The Commission has lost a number of cases before the Court of First Instance. I cannot say whether that will cause the Commission to alter its procedures.

563. May we turn to the relation between the Commission and the national courts. You have reservations about the role of the Commission as an amicus in the national courts or before national administrative authorities if they are going to deal with more and more competition cases. Would you like to elaborate on that?

A. Yes, my Lord Chairman, and I deal with this, I think, at paragraph 8 of my memorandum to you. I do not myself see that it will be particularly valuable to a High Court judge to obtain information of a procedural nature to enable him to discover the status of procedures before the Commission and likely timetables for completing them. Most of that information should be available anyway. It is possible that it will be useful to know the likely time-table. The idea of the Commission giving the national judge advice on points of law I find to be a rather strange one. The Monopolies and Mergers Commission in the motor car reference not long ago did go to the European Communities Commission for advice on the meaning of a block exemption, and pretty odd advice it got. That is liable to be so because you do not know who has prepared it, and this brings me to the point about the lack of control about which you were asking me. The Court, as I understand it, has recently found that the Commission's agent in different cases has been taking quite inconsistent points—because one agent did not know the points that the other agent was taking it is perhaps inevitable—but, if that is so, I do not know how the national judge would be able to rely on the advice prepared by in effect the Commission's agent.

564. But do you not have to make sure that you have an agent at the right level with the right experience before you let him loose in a national court?

A. Your Lordship has great confidence in the rigour of administration by the Commission.

565. I think that it is always better to be optimistic than over-pessimistic about these things.

A. Your Lordship will know from sitting in the upper Court over many years that the Commission's view of the law is very frequently not accepted by the upper Court. I cannot see myself that a national judge could safely rely upon the views of the Commission. I cannot see why especially in this country where counsel should be capable of being relied upon to have done the necessary research it should be necessary for the national judge to look to the—

566. But the amicus would not be dictating to the judge; obviously he would be saying, look, Mr Lever has submitted this to you, he has got it wrong and this is why in the Commission's submission he has got it wrong. Why would that not be helpful to the judge?

A. I think that it could be profoundly misleading because I think there would be a very serious chance that Mr Lever might have got it right and the Commission might have got it wrong.

567. You say the Court occasionally has not accepted the Commission's submissions about the law. May there not have been occasions when the Commission did not accept Mr Lever's submissions about the law?

A. For my part, my Lord Chairman, I should be sorry to see it happen. I quite believe that you can say to me, the judge is capable of forming his own view about the force of the arguments, whether they are properly founded or not, but I have to confess that I find the idea rather repellent.

568. What about the guidelines that the Commission has issued to national courts and national authorities? Dr Ehlermann suggested that these might perhaps be extended to cover all Article 85 and Article 86 matters. Do you have a view about that? Is this co-operation going to work in the way that it has been indicated or is it not going to work?

A. I think that there is considerable scope for co-operation between a competent authority as opposed to courts and the Commission. But if I may just deal with what I believe to be the real problem for the courts—or one of the problems for the courts—it is when they are confronted with an agreement to which Article 85(1) applies and one of the parties says: "But it is a good agreement, and even though Article 85(2) says that agreements to which Article 85(1) applies are automatically void, this one will in due course gain an exemption from the Commission in Brussels, which is the only body that is entitled to give an exemption, and when that exemption comes through this will be a good agreement." The notice says, well, we are perfectly willing to tell the national judge that we think it is improbable that an exemption will

[Chairman Contd.]

be given, if that will help. I do not see how that might help. What is the national judge supposed to do with the piece of information that an exemption is improbable? The improbable has happened before now. If in three years' time an exemption comes through and the judge has given final judgment on the basis that the agreement is void the situation is not really acceptable.

569. That obviously does open up problems. One of your suggestions, Mr Lever, was that the national authorities should have the priority to grant exemptions under Article 85(3) subject to some overview by the Commission as you outline in your paper?
A. Yes.

570. Does this not open up a spectacle of very different decisions in Member States?
A. I believe that the safeguards that I have suggested would be adequate to prevent that. Of course I understand that wherever there is a division of function there is a risk of inconsistency, hence you find in the United States that the views of one circuit of the federal courts may differ from the views of another circuit of the federal courts.

571. The risk is even greater, is it not, where you are looking at economic appraisal rather than purely legal interpretation?
A. In the case of Article 85(3) there is very little legal interpretation that is required; it is really an appreciation of the factual situation.

572. Precisely, and is that not going to lead to different decisions in different Member States? There may even be political aspects to it?
A. I should have thought that the safeguards I have proposed should look after it, but let it be supposed for a moment that there would be some inconsistency, I think the disadvantage in the Community interest of those inconsistencies would be less than the disadvantages of the present system and that, as your Lordship said earlier, we have to make the best of things and it would be better to get things done subject to the safeguards and risk some inconsistency than for them to go on as they are today.
Chairman] We mentioned economic factors. Lord Skidelsky would like to ask a question here.

Lord Skidelsky

573. In your 1988 memorandum I was very surprised by your remark which is obviously correct that the appreciation of the effect on competition requires considerable judgment and you cannot simply go by a mechanical concentration rule because the problem of a relevant market is a fuzzy area. In a way would you accept that there should be more onus on the part of the Commission to justify its decision in terms of wider economic considerations than there seem to be at the moment so that one can improve decision making not just by improving the legal procedures but also by improving the quality of the argument so that

decisions can be debated in terms of their economic justifications and so we can approach a sensible competition policy by that route? I am quite sceptical of the whole business from the economic point of view. Nevertheless, given the fact that you have this structure in place is not a wide debate on the economic aspects of economic appraisal something that is desirable?
A. There are at least two different kinds of case. In some cases not very much economic analysis is required. The questions are almost jury questions—did A, B and C meet in Rome on a certain date, did they agree certain things, did they go away and implement that agreement or did it all happen coincidentally? In other cases one is concerned essentially with economic analysis, and there I should absolutely accept your Lordship's point that the quality of economic analysis is all important. I do not think that it would follow from that that matters should not be delegated in appropriate cases to the national competent authorities. The man who has just ceased to be the chairman of our own Monopolies and Mergers Commission, Sir Sydney Lipworth, was enthusiastic about the idea of the Monopolies and Mergers Commission, with its considerable experience of investigating complex economic situations, performing functions for the purposes of applying the Community rules on competition. I think that there is a great deal to be said in favour of that. While I absolutely accept the point that you make therefore and that merely improving procedures or making sure that you have your law right will not by itself be enough, and in some cases you will need good economic analysis which we know is quite scarce, I do not think that that militates against the use of national authorities in appropriate cases.

574. The conclusion of your memorandum of 1988 is in fact that unless there is a thorough reform of Directorate General IV's procedures the price of having a Community wide merger control system may be too high, and I suppose that that thorough reform of Directorate General IV's procedures might also include its ability to conduct proper economic analysis of a competence that it does not possess at the moment. Has anything happened since 1988 to alter the conclusion that you reached there?
A. The principal criticism that has been made of the work of the so-called merger task force has been that its decisions did not satisfactorily explain the relevant facts and economic analysis. Mr Dan Goyder is one of the deputy chairmen of our own Monopolies and Mergers Commission and a distinguished writer in the field, and he has expressed that criticism and said that you read the decisions but you cannot really tell whether they are right or wrong because you do not know enough about it. If you accept everything that is said, then of course they are right, but they are not nearly as detailed and illuminating as a Monopolies and Mergers Commission report. That is not to say that our own system is in all respects

[Lord Skidelsky *Contd.*]

ideal, my Lord Chairman; it is not. However, I think that Mr Goyder's criticism is a valid one and it means that one cannot be satisfied that the economic analysis is impeccable.

Lord Holme of Cheltenham

575. If I may, my Lord Chairman, I have a supplementary on Lord Skidelsky's point. It seems to me that the problem is very often the one that you identify as definition of the relevant market and that in many ways it is not so much the question of economic analysis laid on top of that as the premises from which you start—what is the relevant market. Of course, it is a fact that in the European Community relevant markets are often wider than one nation that makes some of these issues by definition Community competition and not just national competition. If I may take your point about national authorities, is not what the Office of Fair Trading here very often does in terms of examining the competitive issues and the definition of markets in a way that is full and transparent and defensible as a piece of analysis quite a tempting analogy? I think very often the companies in front of the Commission are mostly inclined to argue not with the analysis but with the premises—what is the market on which the share is being calculated, on which the index of concentration is being calculated, what is that market.

A. My Lord Chairman, I think that I should not want to draw a hard and fast distinction between the premises, as you call them, and the economic analysis because the definition of a relevant market is nothing other than a tool to help one the better to analyse the economic issues in the case, and the tool itself can only be fashioned using an economic analysis. Having defined the relevant market equally it would be wrong to suppose that you should put on blinkers and not look outside it at all to see whether there is any competition from outside the relevant market. You may want to draw the line in a certain place because you have to draw a line but that does not mean that you then put on blinkers. That kind of question involves, I think, the sort of economic analysis that Lord Skidelsky had in mind, and I do not think that one could say that that is not really economic analysis, that it is choice of premises. I hope that I am right about that, my Lord Chairman.

Chairman

576. At the end of the day does one have to say that either you create a completely new directorate general to do the decision making or you ship the thing off to some new body altogether to take the final decision and leave the Commission with the investigatory, tutorial role? Is this a consequence of all your criticism, that we have to change the whole system?
A. Your Lordship is asking which of the two?

577. No, the consequence of your criticism is that you must do one or the other?
A. Oh, yes.

578. You cannot tinker?
A. That is right.

579. Which of the two then would you choose?
A. I am mindful of the old maxim that the devil you know is better than the devil you do not know. I have always been perfectly willing to accept that the work should be done by the Commission if it was willing to do it in accordance with, as I saw it, proper principles. Perhaps I am rather like Solzhenitsyn in this respect in not having aspired to the abolition of the communist party in the Soviet Union being perfectly satisfied with the introduction of proper principles for the operation of the old regime. Maybe I have been insufficiently ambitious.

580. I think that pragmatically you have been very wise. The chances of getting the Commission and the Community to agree to a whole new setup seem to be very remote. May I ask you just one thing about our own law. Do you see that it would be an advantage if Article 85 and Article 86 were brought more widely into domestic law so that they could be enforced here? You know that the Government has already published its views. What are your personal views on that?
A. My Lord Chairman, I do feel that we should benefit from the national administration of the Community rules on competition as a matter of public law because I believe very strongly that in this area private law is no substitute for public law. I think that that could be done both in the way that I have suggested at paragraphs 18 to 21 of my memorandum and by remodelling our own Restrictive Trade Practices Act so as to "nationalise" Article 85.

Baroness Elles

581. My Lord Chairman, in view of 1996 and the possibility of renegotiation of the treaty and the opening to open up Pandora's boxes would Mr Lever consider that this would be an area that it could be beneficially looked at with a view possibly to changing methods that exist now?
A. My Lord Chairman, yes, I think that, if the Commission continues to resist the idea of internal reform, it then will become necessary to consider very seriously the establishment of a competition tribunal, and I think that that should be on the agenda in 1996.
Baroness Elles] That is very helpful, thank you.

Chairman

582. Mr Lever, we are most grateful to you for coming.
A. Thank you, I am most grateful to your Lordships.

WRITTEN EVIDENCE

Memorandum by Mr August J. Braakman[1]

1. The Dutch Constitution recognises, as a matter of principle, both the supremacy and the direct effect of Community law in the Netherlands. This principle has been laid down in Article 94 of the Dutch Constitution, which reads as follows:

> "Statutory regulations in force within the Kingdom shall not be applicable if such application is in conflict with provisions of treaties that are binding on all persons or resolutions by international institutions".

The supremacy of Community law applies to anterior as well as to posterior national regulations.

2. The application of Community competition rules rests almost entirely with the civil courts. Criminal courts are not concerned with the application of this law since infringements of Articles 85 and 86 EEC Treaty are punished with administrative, and not with penal sanctions. Administrative courts only hear cases concerning decisions of national administrative bodies. It is possible that the Court of Appeal for Trade and Industry (College van Beroep voor het Bedrijfsleven) is asked to adjudicate on an appeal against a decision concerning the application of national competition law in which a decision concerning Article 85 or 86 EEC Treaty is incorporated. However, up until now no such situation has occurred.[2]

3. In civil proceedings, Articles 85 and 86 are applied according to the normal rules of procedure. These rules contain certain limitations for the courts to apply these Articles. The most important limitations are the following.

4. The Courts may only adjudicate on the matter as it was submitted to them. They may not transgress the borders of the dispute between the parties and put forward facts *ex officio*. The Courts may add legal arguments *ex officio*, be it on condition that these arguments fit within the context of the dispute. Secondly, the Court of Cassation is limited to adjudicating on questions of law. Consequently, in appeal proceedings, it is not allowed to raise questions of Community competition law that cannot be answered without an examination of the facts. These limitations are considered to be hindrances to a correct application of Community competition law.

5. The most important hinderance to the application of Community competition law in civil proceedings, however, follows from the fact that these proceedings are rather time-consuming. In cases of an appeal through all three stages, ie Cantonal Court, District Court, which serves as appellate Court for decisions of a Cantonal Court, Court of Appeal, which serves as appellate Court for decisions of a District Court and Court of Cassation which reviews decisions of the lower Courts with respect to questions of law, a period of three to five years is no exception. As in matters where Community competition law is at hand, time is usually of the essence, the plaintiff often decides to have the dispute adjudicated upon in proceedings which are less time-consuming.

6. The first possibility to circumvent main proceedings are the so-called short-term proceedings ("bref delai"). In these proceedings only a statement of claim and of defence are submitted. Thereafter, oral hearings take place. These proceedings are suited to explain to the judiciary matters which are economically and/or legally of a complex nature. However, also these proceedings usually take several months before a decision at first instance is reached.

7. In view of the time-consuming nature of the above proceedings, the plaintiff usually decides to submit the dispute to the judiciary in interlocutory or "kort geding"– procedures. In the following, a brief summary will be given of the disadvantages and advantages of interlocutory proceedings in regard to the application of Community competition law.

8. It is a disadvantage for the application of Community competition law in interlocutory proceedings that, in these proceedings, claims for damages cannot be heard. However, petitions for advance payments to compensate damages due to unfair competition matters are heard, be it with reserve.[3] The most important disadvantage, however, seems to be the rule that the Judge President or the appellate Court may refuse the grant of the required provisions in case he/it is of the opinion that the understanding of the facts in light of Article 85 or 86 which is necessary for a sound decision, cannot be acquired while dealing with the case in interlocutory proceedings or that same would require a too detailed or complex inquiry.[4] The judiciary is free to apply this rule as it seems fit. On the basis of this rule, it may even refuse to refer the case to the European Court of Justice ("ECJ"). There are no rules of

---

[1] Advocate, partner NAUTA DUTILH, Rotterdam, the Netherlands.

[2] Comp Mok, M.R., TVVS 1993, n° 93/5, p. 131.

[3] Comp eg Court of Cassation 29.3.1985 NJ (Dutch Reported Cases) 1986, 84.

[4] Comp Dutch Civil Procedure Law (Burgerlijke Rechtsvordering) (Jansen), aantekening 1 and Article 291; Schenk-Blauw-De Bruyn (1984), p 110/112. See also Court of Cassation 21.4.1978, NJ 1979 194 (WHH).

EC-law that oblige a Judge President or a Court to give a ruling in interlocutory proceedings on the basis of an alleged infringement of Article 85 or 86, or even to obtain the advice of the Commission in such matters.

9. The most important advantages of interlocutory proceedings for the application of Community competition law are:

— judgments in interlocutory proceedings are operative as soon as they have been notified to the other party and regardless any appeal;

— actions are not dismissed on the mere ground that the consequences of the ruling may be reversed. Even in cases where the consequences of an interlocutory ruling cannot (totally) be undone by a judgment in a principal action, the necessity of immediate measures and a fair evaluation of the interests of both parties are considered to be sufficient justification for an interlocutory ruling;[1]

— the requirements for establishing proof are less severe than in the principal action.[2] It is sufficient that the Judge President or the appellate Court is of the opinion that (one of) the parties will be able to prove its assertions.[3] However, in the event of the unsuccessful party starting a principal action, as a rule it will have to bring this action as plaintiff and consequently will have the full onus of proof to substantiate its case;

— in rendering its judgement, the judiciary is not subject to limitations. Orders to reveal the identity of a supplier or to supply a list of third parties to which infringing products have been delivered, may be given. The observation of these rulings may be ensured by the imposition of a penalty;

— the judiciary is prepared to the (partly) allotment of amounts of money the indebtedness of which is not disputed;

— the principle that, in interlocutory proceedings, the judiciary has no competence to decide on questions of law has been softened by the ruling of the Court of Cassation which provides that in these proceedings a provisional interpretation of questions of law may be given and that this will often even be necessary,[4] and, last but not least,

— the time-element. In cases where an interlocutory ruling is required, the case can be submitted to the Judge President on very short notice: the case can even be presented to the Judge President at his residential address.

10. Practice shows that the above advantages outweigh the disadvantages which are inherent to interlocutory proceedings. Notably the necessity of a quick ruling combined with the fact that this ruling is operative as soon as it is notified to the other party, have led to an enormous increase of the number of interlocutory procedures. Usually, the parties accept the interlocutory ruling as final or decide to lodge an appeal in interlocutory proceedings rather than starting a principal action.[5] As a consequence, interlocutory proceedings, although originally meant to result in a provisional Order of Court that does not prejudice the judgment in the principal action and by which it loses its legal force, have gradually developed into autonomous proceedings.[6]

11. Since the entry into force of the EEC Treaty, 130 cases involving Article 85 or 86 have been decided upon by the Dutch Courts. Out of this total of 130 cases, 86 cases were decided in interlocutory proceedings. Out of the total of 130 cases, 15 cases were subject of an Article 177 reference. In four cases such reference was made in interlocutory proceedings.

[1]Court of Cassation 8.2.1946, NJ 1946, 166.

[2]Court of Cassation 31.1.1975, NJ 1976, 146.

[3]Court of Cassation 8.5.1925, NJ 1925, 734.

[4]Court of Cassation 18.4.1913, NJ 1913, 727 and Court of Cassation 11.11.1938, NJ 1939, 396.

[5]Appeals against interlocutory rulings have to be noted to the same Court of Appeal as would have had jurisdiction in the event of the suit starting by way of a principal action. The normal rules of appeal apply unless the special character of the proceedings should necessitate a departure from this principle. (Court of Cassation 9.12.1966, NJ 1967, 76). A subsequent possibility of appeal is limited to questions of law only (not of fact) and must be noted to the Court of Cassation. Apart from complaints regarding the violation or incorrect application of (national or European) law, appeals to the Court of Cassation may also be lodged because of a lack of motivation. This is an issue in approximately 2/3 of the cases. Also in an appeal to the Court of Cassation the normal rules of procedure must be applied, if possible. It is to be noted that only in rare cases will these appeals still have an urgent character. The time-limits for an appeal against an interlocutory ruling to a Court of Appeal are two weeks. However, usually the appeal is lodged in a very elementary manner which only serves to meet the time-limits and is completed in a later stage. The time-limits for an appeal to the Court of Cassation are six weeks. It usually takes 18 months to two years to get an interlocutory judgement that is appealed through two stages.

[6]The autonomous and final character of an interlocutory ruling was even underlined by the Dutch government at the occasion of the preparation of the Hague Convention on the mutual recognition and enforcement of foreign judgments (Haagse Executie Verdrag), Dutch Treaties Journal (Tractatenblad), 1967, 32.

12. Generally speaking, there are three possible situations in which the Dutch Courts are requested to apply Article 85 or 86 EEC Treaty:

— the ECJ nor the Commission has been approached,

— the ECJ has been approached, and

— the Commission has been approached.

13. In cases where the ECJ nor the Commission has been approached, Dutch Courts have few hesitations to apply Article 85 or 86 in cases which concern "classic infringements" of said articles, such as eg export prohibitions. In cases which concern more complex questions of Community competition law, it seems safe to say that the Dutch judiciary tends to follow the "Haecht-II"-rule, ie that an agreement that falls within Article 85(1) is prohibited and, therefore, null and void, unless it is to be expected beyond reasonable doubt that the Commission will as yet give an exemption with retro-active effect.[1]

14. Most cases falling in this category, concern the application of the "acte clair" or "acte éclairé". It is regrettable, however, that Dutch Courts usually do not indicate whether they apply the "acte clair" or the "acte éclairé" and, in the latter case, on which judgment(s) of the Court of First Instance or the ECJ their ruling is based.[2]

15. As has been indicated above, there are very few cases concerning Article 85 or 86 where the Dutch judiciary put preliminary questions to the ECJ under Article 177. This fact may be explained by two factors. First, in most cases the real issue consisted in the appraisal of the facts in light of Article 85 or 86. Secondly, the majority of the cases has been tried in interlocutory proceedings. Judges President have been reluctant to request Article 177 rulings, considering that the time required for such rulings makes them unsuitable for interlocutory-proceedings.

16. In most cases concerning the application of Article 85 or 86, both the Judge President and the Commission are approached. It has become standard practice that a complaint is lodged with the Commission, whether or not accompanied by a request for interim measures, and that at the same time interlocutory proceedings are initiated in order to acquire provisional measures for the time the Commission needs for the preparation of a Decision. In these cases, the Dutch judiciary recognises the fact that the Commission is the chief-responsible for the application of Articles 85 and 86. Furthermore, it is also recognised that in light of its powers under Regulation No 17, on the one hand, and its experience and know-how, on the other, the Commission seems to be better equipped to apply Article 85 and/or 86. However, in these cases the position of the Dutch judiciary is often not an easy one.

Although the Judge President is prepared to be guided by the judgment of the Commission, the time the Commission needs for the preparation of a Decision often makes it necessary to request the Judge President to give a first evaluation of the competition law aspects of the case himself. Especially when complex legal and/or factual questions are at hand, this may be a difficult task. Consequently, justiciables often fear that the Judge President or appellate court will refuse to deal with the Article 85 and/or 86-aspects of a case, thereby referring to the principle that there is no obligation to do so (comp hereinabove sub 8).This may be illustrated by the following two examples.

17. The first example concerns a case where the Judge President of the Almelo District Court awarded a claim for the enforcement of an exclusive licence agreement which existed since 1957 and was not notified until 1978, immediately before interlocutory proceedings were initiated. The Judge President refused to stay the proceedings in anticipation of the Commission's evaluation of the agreement. However, he limited the validity of his judgment by providing that it would be valid until the time that he would reach a different conclusion on the basis of the findings of the Commission. The judgment was delivered one year after the notification.

On appeal, the judgment was upheld by the Arnhem Court of Appeal. The Court established that the Commission had still not defined its position and considered this an indication that the agreement did not constitute a serious infringement of Article 85(1).

One month later the Commission did define its position and held that several provisions of the agreement fell within Article 85(1).

In subsequent interlocutory proceedings before the same Judge President and Court of Appeal the earlier rulings were withdrawn and the claim for enforcement was refused.[3]

---

[1]Comp Pijnacker Hordijk, E. H., De Nederlandse rechter en het Europese Kartelrecht, een inventarisatie, SEW (Magazine on Social and Economic Legislation) 7/8 (1987), p 491.

[2]A favourable exception to this practice is the case Vomar/Bull, judgment of the Court of Cassation of 3.5.1991, not yet reported. In this judgment the Court of Cassation annulled the judgment of the Court of Appeal whereby an incorrect application was given of the "de minimis"—Notice of the Commission. The conclusion of Advocate-General Mok is interesting because it provides ample reference to relevant case-law of the ECJ as well as to literature.

18. The second example concerns the case Van Marwijk c.s./FNK-SCK. In this case FNK and SCK, two sister-associations of crane-undertakings, had notified their agreements to the Commission in order to get negative clearance or an exemption under Article 85(3).

The hard core of the agreements was that SCK-members were not entitled to hire non-SCK members for assistance in the execution of a contract. This provision rested upon the consideration that the undertakings of non-SCK-members, and in particular their materials, were only checked by the national authorities, and not by SCK.

Van Marwijk c.s. had lodged a complaint against the agreements, and, more in particular, against the above provision, with the Commission. At the same time, in interlocutory proceedings, Van Marwijk c.s. requested provisional measures for the time the Commission would need to prepare a Decision. The Judge President was asked to order for this period of time the withdrawal of the above prohibition to hire non-SCK-members.

19. The Judge President of the Utrecht District Court has granted the requested measures stating that, in his opinion, it was highly unlikely that the Commission would grant an exemption under Article 85(3) for the agreements and, more in particular, for the above provision.

In arguing his judgement, the Judge President followed precisely the (then draft-) Notice on co-operation between national Courts and the Commission in applying Articles 85 and 86 of the EEC Treaty.[1]

20. However, the Amsterdam Court of Appeal annulled this judgement. The main arguments of the Court were (1) that the underlying factual situation was too complex to deal with in interlocutory proceedings and (2) that the Commission by not reacting to the notification and the complaint by Van Marwijk c.s. for $1\frac{1}{2}$ years, apparently did not consider the agreements to heavily infringe Article 85(1).[2]

Although in the proceedings before the Court of Appeal Van Marwijk c.s. specifically requested the Court to approach the Commission for information on the probable outcome of the procedure before it, the Court, though implicitly, refused such course of action.

21. The danger of this refusal was demonstrated four months later when the Commission, on 11 November 1992, adopted a Statement of Objections.

In this Statement, the Commission indicated that the FNK/SCK-agreements and, more in particular, the prohibition for SCK-members for the execution of a contract, heavily infringed Article 85(1) and that it was excluded that an exemption under Article 85(3) would be granted. The Commission went even further by stating that the infringement was such that a decision under Article 15(6) Regulation 17 whereby the immunity for fines is lifted, was required.

However, notwithstanding this clear position of the Commission, FNK/SCK refused to adapt their agreements and, more in particular, the hard-core thereof, being the prohibition for SCK-member to hire non-SCK-members.

As it would take considerable additional time for the proceedings before the Commission to come to an end, this attitude obliged Van Marwijk c.s. to again start interlocutory proceedings. In these proceedings, a ruling was asked which required FNK/SCK to withdraw the above prohibition to hire non-SCK-members with immediate effect. The interlocutory proceedings took place on 16 June 1993. At the moment of the writing of this report, the outcome thereof is not known yet.

22. The above two examples are chosen because the first case was tried in the period before the publication of the (draft-) Notice on co-operation between national Courts and the Commission, whereas the second case was tried after the publication of said (draft-) Notice.

In essence, the Notice is a codification of the existing case-law. Therefore, the fact that at the time the case was submitted to the Court of Appeal the Notice was still in its draft stage, cannot not have played a role.

The Amsterdam Court has not indicated why it has refused to approach the Commission for information.

The Court may have been lead by the arguments which are developed in the Netherlands against the Notice and the system of co-operation between the national Courts and the Commission it envisages. The arguments which are most heard are the following.

---

[7]Bijblad Industiële Eigendom (Supplement to the Magazine on Industrial Ownership) 1982, Nos. 84 and 85.

[1]OJ 1993, c. 39/6

[2]Interlocutory Ruling of 11.2.1992, Kort Geding (Magazine of reported interlocutory judgements) 1992, 92; Judgement of the Court of Appeal of 9.7.1992, not reported.

23. The main argument which is invoked against the Notice is that Dutch civil procedure law is not suited for the way the Commission envisages its co-operation with the national Courts.

Reference is made to the principle that the judiciary is passive and bound to the facts put forward by the parties. Although this passiveness does not apply to the legal aspects of the case and the judiciary is entitled to add legal arguments *ex officio*, it is felt that approaching the Commission in order to acquire legal arguments and/or a description of the relevant facts, is a bridge too far. The fear is that in this situation the national judiciary would lose its independency and would become the extension of the Commission in the application of Community competition law.

In addition, it is said that apart from being a judicial body, the Commission is also a policy-making body.

As a consequence, approaching the Commission for information may influence the policy of the Commission. this policy may come down to refraining from dealing with the case on short notice.

A further argument is that an approach of the Commission only makes sense if it is meant to acquire information on facts which are generally known.[1]

The reasoning is that in a situation where the Commission has not yet reacted, the facts are apparently not known (yet), and therefore an approach of the Commission is not in order.

24. In my opinion, the refusal of the Amsterdam Court of Appeal to approach the Commission for information on the probable outcome of the procedure before it, is regrettable for two reasons:

(i) legal certainty

It has been indicated above that the majority of the cases concerning the application of Article 85 or 86 are tried in interlocutory proceedings and that it has become standard practice that the case is submitted both to the Judge President and the Commission.

As the Commission needs (considerable) time to prepare a Decision, the Judge President will usually have to give a first evaluation of the case for the period until this Decision.

It has been indicated hereinabove sub 10 that an interlocutory ruling may permanently alter the legal and factual situation between the parties.

Consequently, it is of the utmost importance that the interlocutory ruling is in line with the Decision of the Commission which is yet to come.

In case the Amsterdam Court of Appeal, in the Van Marwijk-case, would have followed the request to approach the Commission for information, the Commission would undoubtedly have responded along the lines of the Statement of Objection which was being prepared, ie that it considered the FNK/SCK-agreements and, more in particular, the prohibition for SCK-members to hire non-SCK-members for the execution of contracts, to be a heavy infringement of Article 85(1) and not eligible for an exemption under Article 85(3), and

(ii) damages

Everyone who is directly or indirectly affected by an infringement of Article 85 or 86, may claim damages.

As damages economic loss and loss of profit may be claimed. Also a reasonable amount may be claimed for costs that had to be made as a result of the infringement and/or to minimise the financial consequences thereof.

However, especially in cases involving Article 85 and 86 the measurement of the quantum of the damages is difficult.

It seems safe to say that the refusal of the Amsterdam Court of Appeal to approach the Commission for information, has caused a lot of extra-damage to Van Marwijk c.s. The refusal implies that much more time is needed to establish that the FNK/SCK-regulations and more in particular the prohibition to hire non-SCK-members, infringe Article 85(1).

Moreover, as the damage mainly consists in a loss of profit, and as losses of profit are difficult to measure, it seems also safe to say that this extra-time causes extra-damage which can not be fully recovered.

Finally, as has been indicated above, in interlocutory proceedings only petitions for advance payments to compensate damages are heard, and then only with reserve.

Consequently, claims for the recovery of damages must be lodged in main proceedings and these proceedings take considerable time to come to an end.

---

[1] Comp. in this sense also Mok, op.cit., p.131.

25. The Notice on co-operation between the Commission and the national Courts in applying Articles 85 and 86 EEC Treaty, tries to bring a solution to the above problems in regard to a correct and timely application of Articles 85 and 86 EEC-Treaty.

The Notice offers the possibility of a quick indication of the way in which the Commission feels that Article 85 or 86 applies and offers the much-needed legal certainty that the interlocutory ruling of the Judge President is in line with the Decision of the Commission which is yet to come.

The main aim of the Notice is to provide a basis for co-operation between national Courts and the Commission. The above examples demonstrate that this co-operation is necessary. Every assistance in the difficult task of applying Articles 85 and 86 at national level should be welcomed.

I recognise the validity of the arguments sub 23 which plead against the way in which the Notice envisages the co-operation between the national Courts and the Commission.

However, I am of the opinion that these arguments are outweighed by the need for legal certainty and for a true incorporation of Community competition law in the legal orders of the Member States.

Rotterdam, 14 *June* 1993

Memorandum by the Competition Law Association

United Kingdom Section of the Ligue Internationale du Droit de la Concurrence

I INTRODUCTION

European Community competition law enforcement now spans the better part of four decades with United Kingdom experience as a Member State spanning over two. In this time EC competition law and practice has developed apace. Landmark decisions of the Commission and Court have pushed out the boundaries of Community competition law. The greater part of the attention of the institutions has been focused on developing the fundamental concepts of the law and on enforcement action. Less attention has been paid to the internal procedures of the Commission in enforcement and to the overall administration of the competition rules by the Commission. The relative maturity of the EC competition law system does require that these two areas—procedure and administration—should be developed commensurately with the substantive law and with enforcement policy to ensure that the rules are applied evenly, fairly and efficiently.

The development and enforcement of Community competition laws over the life of the ECSC and EEC Treaties have been impressive. There is must to be commended, not least the dedication with which the Commission, and DGIV in particular, generally have acted in pursuing the goals of competition policy. This should not, however, be a cause for complacency. There is scope to adjust Commission practices in ways which will add to, and not detract from, these achievements. Moreover, a number of recent decisions of the ECJ and CFI have highlighted serious cause for concern about aspects of Commission procedures and decision-making, with adverse consequences for the effectiveness of the law and for the regard for which it, and the Community institutions, are held. We outline in this submission some problem areas and identify possible ways forward for consideration by the Sub-Committee.

Cases before the Commission fall into three broad categories—serious infringements of Articles 85 and 86 which the Commission pursues to a final decision; agreements which significantly affect competition but which merit formal exemption pursuant to Article 85(3) and lesser cases, which the Commission may deal with through informal procedures or not deal with at all. This submission considers the quality of Commission decision-making in the first category of cases together with a number of issues arising in the second and third categories from the recent move towards greater decentralisation of enforcement. We conclude with some observations on the current operation and proposed review of the Merger Regulation.

II COMMISSION PROCEDURES

Due Process

As is well known, all stages of the investigation of competition infringements are in the hands of the Commission. Serious infringements can lead to very significant penalties and other severe consequences for the culpable parties. Commission fines have reached multi-million pound levels in several cases. Undertakings may be required to divest property, to terminate or amend contracts and to adhere to or refrain from particular behaviour. Therefore the Commission should ensure that it has procedures which safeguard the rights of defence and which are rigorously adhered to.

A succession of recent cases have raised serious procedural issues. Although the Commission has been vindicated in a number of these, several decisions, particularly over the last 15 months, have given rise to significant concerns. These cases are set out in Annex 1.

The Commission is subject to judicial review under Articles 173 and 175. Judicial review of the Commission is a powerful and important remedy. However, under Article 173, the ECJ and CFI can only review those Commission decisions which create immediately binding legal effects. The Court is powerless to remedy unlawful actions in the course of an investigation, such as a refusal of adequate access to the file, save by possibly quashing the Decision taken by the Commission at the end of the proceeding (see *Cimenteries* (Cases T 10-12/92 and 15/92)). Such controls on the Commission are a blunt instrument and may come too late. If an early procedural flaw can only be remedied by annulment of the final Decision, Commission enforcement effort will have been wasted and, in some cases, competition infringements will go without penalty. Moreover, the parties will have to wait, possibly for years, for the correction of an irregularity which may have taken place very early in the Commission investigation. Neither from the parties' point of view nor in the public interest is this the most effective or efficient means of ensuring that EC competition rules are properly applied and that justice is done in all cases. There are a number of areas in which procedures could be improved:

— *Interlocutory Procedures*

The decision in *Cimenteries* (see above) is particularly unsatisfactory given that undertakings clearly have the ability to challenge certain interlocutory decisions by the Commission (eg decisions on interim measures, and the withdrawal of immunity from fines) there is no sense in denying them the ability to challenge equally important matters, such as rulings on requests for access to the file, whether the statement of objections is adequately framed and whether the timetable for response laid down is reasonable. A more adequate system of interlocutory procedures and adjudication should be developed. There are a number of possible alternatives.

One possibility might be to entrust the role of arbiter on interlocutory issues to the Hearing Officer. This would only be a satisfactory solution if procedures were put in place to ensure that confidence in his impartiality was preserved. This, in turn, requires that the Hearing Officer has adequate and apparent authority to ensure that he is able to act independently and that his decisions are binding on the Commission. This latter objective would be facilitated if the Hearing Officer gave a reasoned opinion or decision after hearing representatives from the Commission and the relevant undertakings. That decision should be made available at least to the parties. Transparency is a great discipline. It may also be facilitated if the Hearing Officer were to be attached to the Commission Legal Service instead of being a member of DGIV.

It might be possible alternatively to introduce a right of interlocutory appeal to the CFI. Any such right could be made subject to a filtering process, similar to those for obtaining leave to appeal or to bring judicial review proceedings in domestic law, so as to ensure that investigations are not unduly delayed by unmeritorious applications. Cases could be dealt with expeditiously by the CFI, perhaps in a similar way to that in which interim measure applications are dealt with.

— *Supervision of Cases*

The issues on which decisions have been annulled or fines reduced by the Court have involved a range of irregularities. This may indicate a lack of adequate supervision of the investigatory process. Matters might be improved if the Commission were to publish a statement in response to each case on which it has been found wanting by the CFI or ECJ indicating the steps that it intends to take to guard against repetition of those events. It might also help if the Advisory Committee on Dominant Positions and Restrictive Practices were, following Merger Regulation practice, to publish, or at least communicate to the parties, their Opinion on cases they have considered.

III DECENTRALISATION

The Commission's case load

It is well recognised that the Commission is unable to cope with its workload of notification, complaints and suspected infringements within Article 85(1). This is largely due to the wide interpretation that has been given to Article 85(1) necessitating application to be made for Article 85(3) exemptions and possibly also to the propensity of Articles 85 and 86 complainants to look to the Commission to intervene on their behalf. The number of Articles 85 and 86 cases pending before the Commission is over 2,000 (Commission's XXIst Report on Competition Policy). In the period covered by the XXIst Report only 13 cases were disposed of with a formal decision. The remainder are dealt with informally, often after very considerable delay. For Article 85 notifications where validity of the relevant parts of the agreement can only come from a formal grant of exemption under Article 85(3), this means that agreements enter into a period of limbo. Legal certainty is not assured nor can it be.

This position continues notwithstanding the successive introduction of a number of measures to ease the Commission's administrative burden, such as block exemptions for broad categories of agreements, the successive Notices on Agreements of Minor Importance, other explanatory notices to clarify the application of the rules, doctrines such as that of "ancillary restraints" and in individual cases the practice of the comfort letter to enable it to take a position without going through the lengthy formalities involved in taking a Decision. Comfort letter have been and continue to be an important and welcome part of Commission practice. They assist, in particular, in reducing and removing concern about fines and possible Commission enforcement action. However, since they are necessarily non-binding, they assist to a lesser degree in actions before the Courts.

The Commission has also developed the idea of prioritising cases, so that only those regarded by it as having "Community interest" are dealt with under the Commission procedures. This approach was approved by the CFI in the *Automec II* case on the basis that the complaint in that case was capable of being pursued through the national courts. Clearly, the Commission should use the resources available to it to maximum effect and some prioritising of cases is necessary. Any ordering of the case load must, however, leave those parties whose cases the Commission does not pursue with effective alternative remedies. Two further initiatives have been taken—the Notice on the application as Articles 85 and 86 on National Courts and proposed new procedures for dealing with co-operative joint ventures and other Article 85 cases.

Notice on National Courts

In the Notice the Commission has sought to emphasise the availability of an alternative channel to deal with those cases it does not deal with itself. The Notice on national courts is helpful as a clear statement of the main principles governing the application of EC competition rules by national courts and the ways in which the Commission and national courts can co-operate.

The effect of the Notice will only be seen in time. Currently, despite earlier attempts by the Commission to encourage them, private actions under Articles 85 and 86 still seem relatively infrequent in any Member State, and probably mainly involve the use of Articles 85 and 86 as a defence rather than as the foundation of a cause of action. We can only speak about the United Kingdom, where there are a number of factors which can make private actions inappropriate in particular cases. We would be concerned if the Commission were too readily to assume that it need not act on a complaint because of the availability of Court actions. Issues in the United Kingdom are:

— Whilst national courts are able to consider actions under Article 85(1) and Article 86, they are unable, at present, to grant exemptions under Article 85(3). This is the exclusive preserve of the Commission as a less consequence of Regulation 17/62. Actions under Article 85 are consequently complicated as, in order to decide on issues concerning agreements which have been notified to the Commission, the court may have to leave a final decision until after the Commission's views on a case are known. Where agreements have been notified the restrictive provisions remain unenforceable unless and until a Commission exemption is forthcoming, in which case the provisions will be valid from the date of notification. The Commission's likely attitude consequently can be central to the validity of terms of agreements before the courts.

— The complexity of issues raised in many Articles 85 and 86 actions (eg market definition, assessment of effect on competition) produces what is probably the what is probably the greatest hurdle of all for litigant: that of cost. In addition, there is the risk of having to pay costs of the other side if the litigation is unsuccessful.

— The complexity of proving the issues raised is not only costly but requires extensive fact finding powers. There are rules for discovery of documents in the course of litigation but these do not match the Commission's powers of search and seizure under Regulation 17. It is for the parties to establish the facts by means of evidence and discovery. Rules of evidence, such as those relating to privilege, may create difficulty.

— The ECJ has given guidance (*Delimitis* Case C-234/89) that in doubtful cases the national court might ask the Commission to assist it with economic and legal information. This assumes an activist role for the national court which United Kingdom courts do not adopt and which fits badly into the framework of adversarial proceedings. It is unclear how a British court should use information provided—what status and weight should it have, and what problems would be encountered when the parties seek to challenge it with other evidence in the national proceedings. In any event the Commission is heavily circumscribed by confidentiality obligations in the information that it can provide (*Dirección General de la Competetencia* v *Associacion Espagnole de Banca Privada* Case C-67/91) and it is unclear to what extent the Commission can pass information obtained under Regulation 17/12 to national courts.

— The issue of a writ, will often not have the deterrent value of an early letter from the its Commission following a complaint. Moreover for a United Kingdom civil action to run full course may take several years, with further delay if there is an Article 177 reference from the British court to the ECJ.

— There are no clear rules on the assessment of damage in these cases. The United States courts have developed principles over a number of years to deal with this. No such principles exist as yet in the United Kingdom or under EC rules.

— The Notice may well have over-estimated the attraction of claim for damages. Leaving aside remaining drafts about the existence of the cause of action, experience under the Restrictive Trade Practices Act testifies to the difficulty of qualifying such claims.

— It does not appear that aggravated or exemplary damages or remedies of unjust enrichment and disgorgement are likely to be available in these actions. The incentive that these might provide is consequently absent.

To abandon those cases in which the Commission has little interest and to leave them to actions before national courts may be to leave undertakings without practical and effective remedies. These are other, as yet untried, methods of resolving this problem. Sir Leon Brittan pointed to one way in his speech to CEPS.

Sir Leon Brittan's Speech

The introduction of the Merger Regulation with its strict time limits has highlighted the ability of the Commission to perform its task expeditiously for all cases subject to the Regulation and contrasts starkly with performance in other competition cases. Annex 2 contains a list of cases notified under the Merger Regulation which were found to be Article 85 cases and then dealt with under Article 85 procedures. In each case the Commission took only one month to decide on whether the Merger Regulation applied. At most it would have had a further four months if the Regulation had applied. The Article 85 decisions, by contrast, have taken considerably longer.

To be able to compete effectively on a world-wide scale, companies need to be provided with a quick and effective system. It is of no benefit to either industry or to competition authorities themselves for unnecessary delays to occur. Indeed, the delays in the Commission's current procedures underline perceptions and prejudices about "Brussels bureaucracy" and can send the wrong signal—that the Commission is not serious about the competition rules in many cases.

The Commission has been reluctant to accept legally binding deadlines. It did so under the Merger Regulation as part of the price to be paid to obtain merger control powers at all. A step forward was made by Sir Leon Brittan in December when he heralded a system of non-binding timetables to apply to co-operative joint ventures notified from 1 January 1993 and for other notifications and complaints from 1 April 1993. However, the effect of these proposed reforms (as yet no Notice has been issued except in relation to joint ventures) remains to be seen. The Commission Notice on co-operative joint ventures issued in February contains no reference to those time limits. The press release on a recent co-operative joint venture decision (*Philips/Thomson CSF* and *Sagem* relating to active matrix liquid crystal displays) indicates that the Commission is trying to meet the new deadlines in structural joint venture cases. Commissioner Van Miert stated in a speech in May his commitment in particular to the procedural reforms on joint venture cases. He also indicated that it would be one of his priorities to extend this to other areas of co-operation. It is unclear whether the reforms that Sir Leon Brittan signalled would commence in April are in fact being put in place.

Sir Leon's proposals would, if implemented, be a welcome step forward. They may be a half-way house between the current situation and a system of binding deadlines. Reinforcement of the move towards tighter timetables would be helped by the publication in the Annual Report on Competition Policy together with the list of cases dealt with informally (146 in the period covered by the XXIst Report) of the time taken to do so. Ultimately, the goal should be to move to an opposition procedure as discussed below.

Other approaches

— *Opposition Procedure*

The most helpful innovation would be the introduction of an opposition procedure for all Article 85 cases, such as exists under the Merger Regulation and in various block exemptions and sectoral regulations. This would require, in the absence of a waiver from the Commission, a complete notification to be submitted. Unless it were challenged within a reasonable period, the agreement could be deemed to be unopposed and therefore cleared under Article 85(3). Such a clearance could be given, as a present, for a limited period and on the basis that it might be reviewed if underlying market conditions changed substantially. Any such procedure would need to make provision for third party comment, probably by the publication of a notice in the Official Journal with a set period for the receipt of comments.

> — *Revised Form A/B*
>   It might be possible, as signalled by Sir Leon, for the Commission to indicate speedily that a case is not within the scope of Article 85(1) if the Commission were in possession of better information on notification. One way of achieving this would be to revise Form A/B. We understand that the Commission is looking at Form A/B in any event. Form A/B requires information relating to the undertakings' turnover in the goods and services affected by an agreement to be supplied where more than a 5 per cent market share exists. In the form for notifying mergers (Form C0) the figure is 10 per cent. A single move of this nature would greatly assist in speed with which cases can be dealt with and the compliance costs for business.

It would also assist if the waiver mechanism available in merger cases were introduced for Article 85 cases. This allows the Commission officially to waive a requirement for information under Form C0 where it considers that provision of the information is unnecessary.

> — *Comfort Letters*
>   The Commission's practice on comfort letters could be revised so that it was clear from each letter whether the Commission, following a preliminary assessment, considered that the agreement notified was within Article 85(1) at all. If it did, the Commission should say so and also indicate whether it would be likely, on the facts known, for an Article 85(3) exemption to be forthcoming. Such an indication could be given without prejudice to the Commission stated intention to further action in relation to the file. The Commission could issue a Notice on comfort letters stating the law and practice and developing the use of this instrument.

> — *Competent Authorities of Member States*
>   Most Member States now have national legislation on competition and administrative enforcement agencies. Many of the Member States have modelled their rules on EC competition law. With this infrastructure it might be possible to look to competent authorities in Member States to adjudicate on Article 85 and 86 issues where the Commission considers that there is no Community interest in intervening. This would require jurisdictional rules or a clearing mechanism for cases to be passed to Member State authorities. The EEA agreement provides jurisdictional rules for the allocation of cases between the Commission and the (proposed) EFTA Surveillance Authority. These may offer a helpful model in developing rules as between the central and national authorities.

> Member States are able under Article 88, when read with Article 9(3) of Regulation 17, to apply Articles 85(1) and 86. It is assumed that to do so national implementing rules would be needed. These have been adopted in several Member States, including Germany and Spain which have both used them. The United Kingdom has not introduced the implementing powers.

> The principal concern with such an approach must be divergent practice and interpretation. The risk here is, however, no greater than relying on national courts to perform this function. It may be possible to institute a system of support for national authorities such as those proposed by the Commission to assist the courts.

> This approach can be adopted without any amendment to EC Regulations. Consideration might be given to amending Regulation 17/62 to allow competent national authorities to grant Article 85(3) exemptions. Concerns over divergence of approach are greater. It may be possible to devise mechanisms to reduce this problem.

All of these solutions offer the prospect of an improvement on the current situation and therefore, deserve consideration.

IV CONCENTRATIONS

The Merger Regulation is to be reviewed in some of its aspects before the end of 1993. The Commission is preparing a consultation paper on this which is yet to be published. A number of issues might usefully be addressed in the review.

Undertakings in the first stage

The Commission has no express power at the first stage to accept legally binding undertakings from those notifying concentrations. A list of the cases where undertakings have been taken to date is at Annex 3. The interests of efficient administration dictate that, subject to appropriate safeguards, the Commission should be able to grant conditional clearances without a full second stage inquiry. Appropriate powers should be taken for this purpose. The safeguards should ensure that third parties are given a period to comment on the proposed undertakings before they are finalised.

Access to the file

Access to the file, even to the non-confidential section, is severely limited in concentration cases. There is no right of access for third parties in the first stage. In the second stage the Commission has a narrow means of entitlement to access. The Regulation should establish that competitors, suppliers and customers should be entitled to access.

Definition of turnover

Special rules currently apply for banks and other financial institutions. These are unavailable for other financial institutions since the rules rely on their business being based on ownership of assets and on making loans and advances. Neither may be true. a relevant definition of turnover is needed in these cases.

Advisory Committee

A welcome innovation under the Merger Regulation is the publication of the Advisory Committee Opinion. The Commission does not as yet publish with the Opinion the draft decision on which the Opinion is based. This would bring meaning to the Opinion and be a useful addition to transparency in decision making.

Form CO

If the threshold under the Merger Regulation is reduced, as many expect, a much greater number of mergers will require reporting and come under scrutiny by the EC. Many of these will raise no material competition issues: the thresholds operate by reference to the parties' turnover not the market shares or other competition criteria. The present notification form CO requires the furnishing of a vast amount of market information, within a very tight time limit, in a form that often does not correspond with the way the notifying undertakings keep such information. A copy of the Form is attached in Annex 4.

Although the Commission has been helpful in allowing dispensation from the obligation to supply some of the information sought under form CO, it remains a substantial burden on the undertakings and their advisers, and therefore adds to the transaction costs. That will be of particular significance if the Merger Regulation is extended to apply to smaller mergers. Accordingly, the Commission should be urged to reduce the scope of the information sought under form CO, at the very least for smaller mergers that are unlikely to give rise to material competition issues.

Many mergers and concentrations that have to be notified to the Commission may also have to be notified to one or more other competition authorities. It would be of substantial assistance and further the objectives of efficiency and co-ordination in the approach to competition policy if the form in which notification had to be given to the various different competition authorities could be harmonised. For example, there could be a "core" common form of request, to which the different authorities appended additional information requests required for the purpose of their own laws and procedures. Such harmonisation and simplification was called for in paragraph 5 of the Resolution passed unanimously at the XXXII Congress of the Ligue Internationale du Droit de la Concurrence (1992). A copy of the Resolution is in Annex 5.

ANNEX 1

Recent ECJ and CFI Decisions revealing serious shortcomings in Commission procedures.

Case		Reference	Date of application to the Court	Date of judgment	Result
1	Royaume de Pays-Bas, Koninklijke PTT Nederland NV et PTT Post BV v Commission (PTT POST BV)	C-48 and 66/90	02.03.1990	12.02.1992	Entire decision annulled for breach of the rights of the defence
2	BASF AG and others v Commission (PVC)	T-79, 84, 85, 86, 89, 91, 92, 94, 96, 98, 102 and 104/89	30.03-25.04.1989	27.02.1992	Decision legally non-existent owing to irregularities in its adoption
3	Societa Italiano Vetro Spa and others v Commission (FLATGLASS)	T68, 77 and 78/89	10-23.03.1989	10.03.92	Decision substantially quashed for inadequate analysis of the market and lack of evidence of infringements
4	Dansk Pelsdyravlerforening v Commission (DANISH FURS)	T-61/89	18.01.1989	02.07.1992	Parts of Decision quashed for error of material fact
5	Ahlstrom and others v Commission (WOOD PULP)	C-89, 104, 114, 116, 117, 125, 126, 127, 128 and 129/85	4-30.04.1985	31.03.1993	Inadequate statement of objections and inadequate access to the file

ANNEX 2

List of cases which were originally notified under the Merger Regulation, then held inappropriate under Article 6(1)(a) of the Regulation and subsequently referred by the Mergers Task Force for investigation under Article 85.

Case		Date of notification under Merger Regulation	Date of Decision of Inapplicability	Date of Article 85 Decision
1	Baxter/Nestlé/Salvia	04.01.1991	06.02.1991	awaited
2	Apollinaris/Schweppes	22.05.1991	24.06.1991	27.09.1991
3	Elf/Enterprise	21.06.1991	24.07.1991	awaited
4	BSN-Nestlé/Cokoladovny	16.01.1992	17.02.1992	awaited
5	Flachglas/Vegla	11.03.1992	13.04.1992	awaited
6	Eureko	20.03.1992	27.04.1992	24.07.1992
7	Herba/IRR	24.03.1992	28.04.1992	awaited
8	Koipe-Tabacalera/Elosua	17.07.1992	28.07.1992	awaited
9	VTG/BPTL	09.09.1992	12.10.1992	12.10.1992
10	Philips/Thomson/Sagem	08.12.1992	18.01.1993	29.04.1993

ANNEX 3

List of European Community Merger Regulation cases where undertakings have been given after a one month enquiry

Case		Date of Notification under Merger Regulation	Date of Clearance
1	Fiat/Ford New Holland	07.01.1991	08.02.1991
2	TNT/Post Offices	28.10.1991	02.12.1991
3	Courtaulds/SNIA	19.11.1991	19.12.1991
4	Ifint/Exor	30.01.1992	02.03.1992
5	Thomson Cook/LTU/West LB	16.06.1992	14.07.1992
6	Elf Aquitaine-Thysson Minol	03.08.1992	04.09.1992
7	Air France/Sabena	07.09.1992	05.10.1992
8	British Airtways/TAT	23.10.1992	27.11.1992

ANNEX 4

FORM C0

The whole of Form C0 (see Regulation 2367/90) is reproduced below. The only change is that the footnotes have been numbered sequentially.

SECTION 1

1.1 Information on notifying party (or parties)

Give details of:

1.1.1 name and address of undertaking,

1.1.2 nature of the undertaking's business,

1.1.3 name, address, telephone, fax and/or telex of, and position held by, the person to be contacted.

1.2 Information on other parties to the concentration[1][2]

For each party to the concentration (except the notifying party) give details of:

1.2.1 name and address of undertaking,

1.2.2 nature of the undertaking's business,

1.2.3 name, address, telephone, fax and/or telex of, and position held by, the person to be contacted.

1.3 Address for service

Give an address in Brussels if available to which all communications may be made and documents delivered in accordance with Article 1(4) of Commission Regulation (EEC) No 2367/90.

1.4 Appointment of representatives

Article 1(2) of Commission Regulation (EEC) No 2367/90 states that where notifications are signed by representatives of undertakings, such representatives shall produce written proof that they are authorised to act. Such written authorisation must accompany the notification and the following details of the representatives of the notifying party or parties and other parties to the concentration are to be given below:

1.4.1 is this a joint notification?

1.4.2 if "yes", has a joint representative been appointed?

— if "yes", please give the details requested in 1.4.3 to 1.4.6 below;

— if "no", please give details of the representatives who have been authorised to act for each of the parties to the concentration indicating who they represent;

1.4.3   name of representative;

1.4.4   address of representative;

1.4.5   name of person to be contacted (and address if different from 1.4.4);

1.4.6   telephone, telefax and/or telex.

SECTION 2
Details of the concentration

2.1   Briefly describe the nature of the concentration being notified. In doing so state:

— whether the proposed concentration is a full legal merger, an acquisition, a concentrative joint venture or a contract or other means conferring direct or indirect control within the meaning of Article 3(3);

— whether the whole or parts of parties are subject to the concentration;

— whether any public offer for the securities of one party by another has the support of the former's supervisory boards of management or other bodies legally representing the party concerned.

2.2   List the economic sectors involved in the concentration.

2.3   Give a brief explanation of the economic and financial details of the concentration. In doing so provide, where relevant, information about the following:

— any financial or other support received from whatever source (including public authorities) by any of the parties and the nature and amount of this support,

— the proposed or expected date of any major events designed to bring about the completion of the concentration,

— the proposed structure of ownership and control after the completion of the concentration.

2.4   For each of the parties, the notifying party shall provide the following data for the last three financial years:

2.4.1   worldwide turnover[3],

2.4.2   Community-wide turnover[3][4],

2.4.3   turnover in each Member State[3][4],

2.4.4   the Member State, if any, in which more than two-thirds of Community-wide turnover is achieved[3][4],

2.4.5   profits before tax worldwide[5],

2.4.6   number of employees worldwide[6].

SECTION 3
Ownership and control [7]

For each of the parties provide a list of all undertakings belonging to the same group. This list must include:

3.1   all undertakings controlled by the parties, directly or indirectly, within the meaning of Article 3(3);

3.2   all undertakings or persons controlling the parties directly or indirectly within the meaning of Article 3(3);

3.3   for each undertaking or person identified in 3.2 above, a complete list of all undertakings controlled by them directly or indirectly, within the meaning of Article 3(3).

For each entry to the list the nature and means of control shall be specified;

3.4   provide details of acquisitions made during the last three years by the groups identified above, of undertakings active in affected markets as defined in section 5 below.

The information sought in this section may be illustrated by the use of charts or diagrams where this helps to give a better understanding of the pre-concentration structure of ownership and control of the undertakings.

SECTION 4

Personal and financial links

With respect to each undertaking or person disclosed in response to Section 3 provide:

4.1 a list of all other undertakings which are active on affected markets (affected markets are defined in section 5) in which the undertakings of the group hold individually or collectively 10 per cent or more of the voting rights or issued share capital. In each case state the percentage held;

4.2 a list of all other undertakings which are active on affected markets in which the persons disclosed in response to Section 3 hold 10 per cent or more of the voting rights or issued share capital. In each case state the percentage held;

4.3 a list for each undertaking of the members of their boards of management who are also members of the boards of management or of the supervisory boards of any other undertaking, which is active on affected markets; and (where applicable) for each undertaking a list of the members of their supervisory boards who are also members of the boards of management of any other undertaking which is active on affected markets;

in each case stating the name of the other undertaking and the position held.

Information provided here may be illustrated by the use of charts or diagrams where this helps to give a better understanding.

SECTION 5

Information on affected markets

The notifying party shall provide the data requested having regard to the following definitions:

Product Markets

A relevant product market comprises all those products and/or services which are regarded as interchangeable or substitutable by the consumer, by reason of the products' characteristics, their prices and their intended use.

A relevant product market may in some cases be composed of a number of individual product groups. An individual product group is a product or small group of products which present largely identical physical or technical characteristics and are fully interchangeable. The difference between products within the group will be small and usually only a matter of brand and/or image. The product market will usually be the classification used by the undertaking in its marketing operations.

Relevant Geographic Market

The relevant geographic market comprises the area in which the undertakings concerned are involved in the supply of products or services, in which the conditions of competition are sufficiently homogenous and which can be distinguished from neighbouring areas because, in particular, conditions of competition are appreciably different in those areas.

Factors relevant to the assessment of the relevant geographic market include the nature and characteristics of the products or services concerned, the existence of entry barriers or consumer preferences, appreciable differences of the undertakings' market shares between neighbouring areas or substantial price differences.

Affected Markets

Affected markets consist of relevant product markets or individual product groups, in the Common Market or a Member State or, where different, in any relevant geographic market where:

(a) two or more of the parties (including undertakings belonging to the same group as defined in Section 3) are engaged in business activities in the same product market or individual product group and where the concentration will lead to a combined market share of 10% or more. These are horizontal relationships; or

(b) any of the parties (including undertakings belonging to the same group as defined in Section three) is engaged in business activities in a product market which is upstream or downstream of a product market or individual product group in which any other party is engaged and any of their market shares is 10 per cent or more, regardless of whether there is or is not any existing supplier/customer relationship between the parties concerned. These are vertical relationships.

I   Explanation of the Affected Relevant Product Markets

5.1 Describe each affected relevant product market and explain why the products and/or services in these markets are included (and why others are excluded) by reason of their characteristics, their prices and their intended use.

5.2 List the individual product groups defined internally by your undertaking for marketing purposes which are covered by each relevant product described under 5.1 above.

II   Market Data on Affected Markets

For each affected relevant product market and, where different, individual product group, for each of the last three financial years:

    (a)   for the Community as a whole;

    (b)   individually for each Member State where the parties (including undertakings belonging to the same group as defined in Section 3) do business;

    (c)   and where different, for any relevant geographic market,

provide the following:

5.3 an estimate of the value of the market and, where appropriate, of the volume (for example in units shipped or delivered) of the market[8]. If available, include statistics prepared by other sources to illustrate your answers. Also provide a forecast of the evolution of demand on the affected markets;

5.4 the turnover of each of the groups to which the parties belong (as defined in Section 3);

5.5 an estimate of the market share of each of the groups to which the parties belong;

5.6 an estimate of the market share (in value and where appropriate volume) of all competitors having at least 10% of the geographic market under consideration. Provide the name, address and telephone number of these undertakings;

5.7 a comparison of prices charged by the groups to which the parties belong in each of the Member States and a similar comparison of such price levels between the Community and its major trading partners (eg the United States, Japan and EFTA);

5.8 an estimate of the value (and where appropriate volume) and source of imports to the relevant geographic market;

5.9 the proportion of such imports that are derived from the groups to which the parties belong;

5.10 an estimate of the extent to which any of these imports are affected by any tariff or non-tariff barriers to trade.

III   Market Data on Conglomerate Aspects

In the absence of horizontal or vertical relationships, where any of the parties (including undertakings belonging to the same group as defined in Section 3) holds a market share of 25 per cent or more for any product market or individual product group, provide the following information:

5.11 a description of each relevant product market and explain why the products and/or services in these markets are included (and why others are excluded) by reason of their characteristics, their prices and their intended use;

5.12 a list of the individual product groups defined internally by your undertaking for marketing purposes which are covered by each relevant product market described;

5.13 an estimate of the value of the market and the market shares of each of the groups to which the parties belong for each affected relevant product market and, where different, individual product group, for the last financial year:

    (a)   for the Community as a whole;

    (b)   individually for each Member State where the groups to which the parties belong do business;

    (c)   and where different, for any relevant geographic market.

In each response in Section 5 the notifying party shall explain the basis of the estimates used or assumptions made.

Section 6

General conditions in affected markets

The following information shall be provided in relation to the affected relevant product markets and, where different, affected individual product groups:

Record of Market Entry

6.1 Over the last five years (or a longer period if this is more appropriate) has there been any significant entry to these markets in the Community? If the answer is "yes", provide information on these entrants, estimating their current market shares.

6.2 In the opinion of the notifying party are there undertakings (including those at present operating only in extra-Community markets) that could enter the Community's markets? If the answer is "yes", provide information on these potential entrants.

6.3 In the opinion of the notifying party what is the likelihood of significant market entry over the next five years?

Factors Influencing Market Entry

6.4 Describe the various factors influencing entry into affected markets that exist in the present case, examining entry from both a geographical and product viewpoint. In so doing take account of the following where appropriate:

— the total costs of entry (capital, promotion, advertising, necessary distribution systems, servicing etc) on a scale equivalent to a significant viable competitor, indicating the market share of such a competitor;

— to what extent is entry to the markets influenced by the requirement of government authorisation or standard setting in any form? Are there any legal or regulatory controls on entry to these markets?

— to what extent is entry to the markets influenced by the availability of raw materials?

— to what extent is entry to the markets influenced by the length of contracts between an undertaking and its suppliers and/or customers?

— describe the importance of licensing patents, know-how and other rights in these markets.

Vertical Integration

6.5 Describe the nature and extent of vertical integration of each of the parties.

Research and Development

6.6 Give an account of the importance of research and development in the ability of a firm operating on the relevant market to compete in the long term. Explain the nature of the research and development in affected markets carried out by the undertakings to the concentration.

In so doing take account of the following where appropriate:

— the research and development intensities[9] for these markets and the relevant research and development intensities for the parties concerned;

— the course of technological development for these markets over an appropriate time period (including developments in products and/or services, production processes, distribution systems etc);

— the major innovations that have been made in these markets over this time period and the undertakings responsible for these innovations;

— the cycle of innovation in these markets and where the parties are in this cycle of innovation;

— describe the extent to which the parties concerned are licencees or licensors of patents, know-how and other rights in affected markets.

Distribution and Service Systems

6.7 Explain the distribution channels and service networks that exist on the affected markets. In so doing take account of the following where appropriate:

— the distribution systems prevailing on the market and their importance. To what extent is distribution performed by third parties and/or undertakings belonging to the same group as the parties as disclosed in Section 3?

— the service networks (for example maintenance and repair) prevailing and their importance in these markets. To what extent are such services performed by third parties and/or undertakings belonging to the same group as the parties as disclosed in Section 3?

Competitive Environment

6.8 Give details (names, addresses and contacts) of the five largest suppliers to the notifying parties and their individual share of the purchases of the notifying parties.

6.9 Give details (names, addresses and contacts) of the five largest customers of the notifying parties and their individual share of the sales of the notifying parties.

6.10 Explain the structure of supply and demand in affected markets. This explanation should allow the Commission further to appreciate the competitive environment in which the parties carry out their business. In so doing take account of the following where appropriate:

— the phases of the markets in terms of, for example, take-off, expansion, maturity and decline. In the opinion of the notifying party, where are the affected products in these phases?

— the structure of supply. Give details of the various identifiable categories that comprise the supply side and describe the "typical supplier" of each category.

— the structure of demand. Give details of the various identifiable groups that comprise the demand side and describe the "typical customer" of each group;

— whether public authorities, government agencies or state enterprises or similar bodies are important participants as sources of supply or demand. In any instance where this is so give details of this participation;

— the total Community-wide capacity for the last three years. Over the period what proportion of this capacity is accounted for by the parties and what have been their rates of capacity utilisation?

Co-operative Agreements

6.11 To what extent do co-operative agreements (horizontal and/or vertical) exist in the affected markets?

6.12 Give details of the most important co-operative agreements engaged in by the parties in the affected markets, such as licensing agreements, research and development, specialisation, distribution, long-term supply and exchange of information agreements.

Trade Associations

6.13 List the names and addresses of the principal trade associations in the affected markets.

Worldwide Context

6.14 Describe the worldwide context of the proposed concentration indicating the position of the parties in this market.

Section 7

General matters

7.1 Describe how the proposed concentration is likely to affect the interests of intermediate and ultimate consumers, and the development of technical progress.

7.2 In the event that the Commission finds that the operation notified does not constitute a concentration within the meaning of Article 3 of Regulation (EEC) No. 4064/89, do you request that it be treated as an application within the meaning of Article 2 or a notification within the meaning of Article 4 of Regulation No. 17, as an application within the meaning of Article 12 or a notification within the meaning of Article 14 of Regulation (EEC) No. 1017/68, as an application within the meaning of Article 12 of Regulation (EEC) No. 4056/86 or as an application within the meaning of Article 3(2) or Article 5 of Regulation (EEC) No. 3975/87?

Section 8

Declaration

The notification must conclude with the following declaration which is to be signed by or on behalf of all the notifying parties.

The undersigned declare that the information given in this notification is correct to the best of their knowledge and belief, that all estimates are identified as such and are their best estimates of the underlying facts and that all the opinions expressed are sincere.

They are aware of the provisions of Article 14(1)b of Regulation (EEC) No. 4064/89.

Place and date:

Signatures:

ANNEX 5

Question No 1

EXTRATERRITORIAL APPLICATION OF COMPETITION LAW TO INTERNATIONAL MERGERS AND ACQUISITIONS

THE INTERNATIONAL LEAGUE FOR COMPETITION LAW (LIDC)

— Noting the increase in legislative control of mergers and acquisitions in many jurisdictions;

— Having regard to the interest of the community of nations in the effective control of mergers and acquisitions in order to further the objective of promoting competition;

— Considering that many legal systems assume jurisdiction to regulate the transfer of control whether directly or indirectly of a company incorporated in or a business established in the territory of the jurisdiction concerned;

— Appreciating that in an international economy such jurisdiction may involve consideration of conduct by foreign undertakings carried out outside the territory of the jurisdiction concerned;

— Recognising that such application of competition law has the potential for the infringement of the sovereignty or important interests of other states;

— In the light of the burden that is placed upon enterprises and undertakings by the multiplicity of different regimes to which an international merger or acquisition may be subject;

— Bearing in mind the principles of international law that require respect for the sovereignty of independent states;

— Noting the revised Recommendation of the Council of the OECD concerning Co-operation between Member Countries on Restrictive Business Practices and the bilateral Agreements and Memorandum of Understanding concluded between the United States and Germany, the United States and Australia, the United States and Canada, Germany and France, and the United States and the Commission of the European Communities;

— Considering that increasing co-operation between competition authorities requires appropriate safeguards for the protection of confidentiality;

RECOMMENDS:

1. That the appropriate authorities should examine the extent to which it is possible to harmonise the forms required for notification of mergers and acquisitions in order to simplify those forms with a view to greater efficiency and a reduction in transaction costs.

2. That where the investigation or control by one jurisdiction of a merger or acquisition involves scrutiny of or interference with conduct carried out in other jurisdictions, the authority concerned should consider whether such investigation or control might affect the important interests or policies of those other jurisdictions where the conduct is carried out:

(i)   before initiating such an investigation;

(ii)   while conducting such an investigation; and

(iii) before the imposition of any remedies.

In doing so, it should notify the governments of those affected jurisdictions.

3. That the laws or procedures that regulate mergers and acquisitions should make provision in a case where the interests of another jurisdiction is so affected to enable the appropriate authority of that other jurisdiction to make representations regarding those interests, at least as *amicus curiae,* to the relevant authority, court or tribunal.

4. That such authority, court or tribunal, should have regard to those representations in deciding what, if any action to take in such cases including, without limitation, the making of orders for the production of documents or the supply of information.

5. That insofar as practicable authorities, courts or tribunals should restrict remedies regarding international mergers and acquisitions, including remedies relating to interim relief, to those elements of the merger or acquisition that are to be implemented within the territory, including in particular the transfer in control of companies incorporated in or establishments based in that territory.

6. That all legal systems should ensure the existence of appropriate safeguards of confidentiality, in particular precluding the relevant authority of one jurisdiction from passing to an authority of another jurisdiction documents or information received in confidence from undertakings and establishments save where such communication is expressly permitted by the law of the first jurisdiction.

7. That all legal systems which regulate mergers and acquisitions should seek to conclude an international convention that incorporates the principles set out in paragraphs 2 to 6 above.

8. That UNCTAD should continue or the OECD should resume its programme of producing and updating a compilation of the competition laws of the world and that competition authorities should assist in that enterprise. This compilation should be published.

Memorandum by the Confederation of British Industry

INTRODUCTION

1. The CBI is pleased to be invited to submit evidence to the House of Lords Select Committee on the EC and supports the decision of Sub-Committee E to undertake an enquiry into the enforcement of Community competition rules at a time when there is increasing dissatisfaction with the current enforcement practices of the European Commission and uncertainty as to how the development of competition policy will be affected by Article 3(b) of the Maastricht Treaty which confirms subsidiarity as one of the basic principles of Community law.

2. Competition policy should be drafted and enforced in such a way that inefficient anti-competitive agreements and exploitative behaviour are dealt with swiftly and effectively but without imposing an excessive regulatory burden upon business or hindering the ability of business to react quickly to competitive pressures. In the context of enforcement procedures and the interface between national and Community regulation the aims should be to:

(i)   provide prompt decisions which are objectively justifiable and afford legal certainty;

(ii)   avoid double jeopardy and multiple notifications; behaviour which has implications for the Community market should be judged according to Community criteria.

DEVELOPMENTS SINCE 1982

3. CBI welcomed the conclusions reached by the Sub-Committee after its investigation into Competition Practice in the EC in 1982. For example, the appointment of a Hearing Officer, as proposed by the Committee, was a welcome development which did improve the Commission's procedures.

4. CBI is however concerned that a shortage of resources within DGIV and an increasing backlog of complaints and notifications, particularly under Article 85, have led the Commission to resort to procedural short-cuts in an effort to speed decision-making. The same shortage of resources may, but should not be responsible for procedural irregularities which have come to light in cases before the CFI and the ECJ, most notably in the *Italian Flat Glass* and *Woodpulp* cases.

5. It is not acceptable that the Commission should jeopardise the rights of parties in this way and it should address urgently problems of procedure, delay and legal uncertainty. Procedural safeguards are particularly important in the enforcement of Community competition provisions as the impact of an adverse finding by the Commission is virtually penal in nature and as there is little separation of powers, with the Commission acting as investigator, prosecutor and judge in competition proceedings.

CONTENTIOUS CASES

6. Where parties fail to settle a case informally with the Commission, it is essential that the semi-penal nature of the consequences of an adverse finding be reflected in the procedural rules and that the rights of parties are adequately safeguarded. In this regard, the appointment of a Hearing Officer is a welcome development as stated at Paragraph 3 above.

7. There is however scope for involving the Officer at an earlier stage in the proceedings; this would allow parties the opportunity to be heard by an alternative official to those who are involved in investigating and prosecuting the case. The status of the Hearing Officer could be enhanced and additional resources made available to allow fulfilment of extra duties; for example he could be called upon to adjudicate on the fairness of procedural deadlines set by the Commission for the production of information by the parties.

8. At present, the Hearing Officer's report to the Commission on the Statement of Objections and the defence is not available to the parties. CBI believes that the transparency and fairness of proceedings would be enhanced if this report was made available to the parties. The Hearing Officer has suggested that this would be a useful development as it would ensure that parties have a more complete record of the procedure.

9. In its 1982 Report, the Committee proposed that undertakings have access, subject to necessary safeguards, to the whole of the Commission's file. This right to information is essential if the undertaking is to have the opportunity to comment on or challenge in a meaningful way the evidence upon which the Commission relies in reaching a decision. The consequences of an adverse judgement under Community competition rules are very serious and make safeguards such as are found in judicial proceedings essential. CBI would urge the Committee to restate the necessity of granting parties access to the file subject to the requirements of commercial confidentiality.

10. In order that the Commission does not abuse this exception to the principle of access to the file, the Hearing Officer could be called upon to give a ruling where access is denied.

11. The establishment of the Court of First Instance (CFI) is a welcome development. The Court has the means and ability to investigate and deal with procedural matters and affords parties ready access to files on appeal. A number of procedural irregularities have been highlighted by the Court and the findings in the *Italian Flat Glass* case verify the necessity of having such a court and evidence the shortcomings of the current procedural rules. In this case the Court found that evidence appeared in the Commission's file in a form substantially different from the original, basic errors of fact had been made and questionable inferences had been drawn on the basis of these facts.

12. It is essential that the CFI continue to be adequately resourced so that failures by the Commission to follow appropriate procedures are remedied. Regulation 17/62 does not demand high standards of fairness and leaves the Commission with much discretion to gather evidence and reach decisions in a secretive way. Aside from a fundamental review of the Regulation, enhancement of the role of Hearing Officer and continued pressure from the CFI should help to ensure that parties rights are better protected and minimise the chances of serious failures, such as occurred in *Italian Flat Glass,* being repeated.

13. The Committee recommended in its previous report that parties be informed of the documents submitted to the Advisory Committee and that the Committee's report be made available to the parties. CBI notes that this proposal has not been implemented but wishes to express its support for such a move as a means of increasing the transparency and fairness of proceedings. Under the EC Merger Regulation, the Committee reports are published; there is no justification for a different procedure under Articles 85 and 86.

14. The need for vigilance in the area of contentious cases is particularly important as pressure on the Commission to produce rapid decisions in non-contentious cases under Article 85 increases. The Commission has set itself time limits for producing an initial decision on the applicability of Article 85(1) and likelihood of an exemption being granted in the case of structural joint ventures. CBI welcomes the intention of the Commission to decrease the delays currently experienced under Article 85. However, there is a danger that rights of defence and procedural correctness will be sacrificed in order to meet the target time schedules. This would not be acceptable.

INSTITUTIONAL REFORM

15. To increase the transparency of competition procedures and minimise the risk of ill-founded decisions, some Member States have suggested that a new independent competition tribunal be established, either to deal specifically with cases falling under the EC Merger Regulation, or to facilitate a general separation of the investigatory, prosecutory and decision-making functions, all of which are currently carried out by the Commission.

16. Under the Merger Regulation, CBI does recognise that there is a lack of transparency in the current procedures. However, the establishment of an independent tribunal would require amendment of the Treaty of Rome and is not, therefore, a realistic option at present. In addition, there is no guarantee that the establishment of an additional tribunal would lead to procedural improvements. CBI believes that transparency could be enhanced within the existing institutional framework; the Merger Task Force should publish its opinion on the application of the Regulation to the specific situation with the full decision of the Commission being published at a later date. This would clarify the influence of political and other considerations on the competition decision.

17. The wider concerns arising from the Commission acting as investigator, prosecutor and judge could also be addressed, at least initially, within the existing institutional framework. The Commission has expressed a commitment to increase the transparency of procedures and this is most welcome. The CBI proposals to enhance the role of the Hearing Officer, publish the recommendations of the Advisory Committee and ensure access to the file could give the expression of intent some substance.

ADMINISTRATIVE ISSUES

18. The Commission has recently announced some changes designed to reduce the current backlog of cases under Article 85. The efficient administration of the Merger Regulation by the Merger Task Force has highlighted the shortcomings of the rest of DGIV and its inability to deal with the volume of work under Articles 85 and 86. CBI recognises that many of the problems and in particular the delays in decision-making under Article 85, can be attributed in part to inadequate resourcing. Two of the possible solutions to the present problems nonetheless contain further problems of their own.

DECENTRALISATION

19. The Commission is very keen to encourage parties suffering loss as a result of breach of the competition rules to seek a remedy in their national courts or to complain to their national authorities. CBI believes that such encouragement will do little to diminish the workload of the Commission and national enforcement of Community competition rules raises a number of issues of concern.

20. The Commission Notice (93/C 39/05) on co-operation between national courts and the Commission in applying Articles 85 and 86 fails to distinguish between the binding and non-binding aspects of Community law in many places; it suggests that decisions, opinions and other unofficial Commission statements are on the same footing as case law of the CFI and ECJ in national court proceedings. This is a misguided assumption and a worrying development given that there are no procedural safeguards where the Commission takes informal decisions.

21. The Notice states that national courts could be made to feel more confident in their enforcement of Article 85(1) by requesting economic and legal information from the Commission. However the Commission would not be a party to the proceedings and would not be providing evidence in any formal sense. It would be unacceptable for the Commission to adopt the role of unaccountable evidence giver and interferer in national court proceedings. Where the Commission provides information as a matter of fact, how is the court to assess the reliability of the information given? If the information relates to matters of law it will be little more than an opinion and not authoritative in any legal sense: nonetheless, it is likely to have a strong influence on the national court.

22. If the Commission is in a position to give a reasoned opinion on a case to the national court, then it should be in a position to issue a decision on the case. National court enforcement will not therefore lessen the workload of the Commission to any great extent.

23. In some Member States, the national authorities have the power to apply Articles 85(1) and 86 and there are suggestions that all national authorities should be given such powers.

24. CBI believes that the Commission is overestimating the extent to which it can reduce its workload through decentralisation, particularly as the Commission would retain its exclusive jurisdiction in relation to Article 85(3). CBI would not support decentralised enforcement of Article 85(3) as it could lead to a fragmented policy with similar agreements being treated differently according to forum.

25. The Commission's use of comfort letters is also inconsistent with a policy of decentralised enforcement; such informal decisions assert the Commission's jurisdiction over the case in question but it is often unable to provide a final, legally certain decision. National courts and authorities would not be bound by such letters but would find them persuasive. Only in very few cases is it likely to be manifestly clear that no exemption would be granted or that Article 85(1) does not apply at all. The likely result is a stay in national proceedings until the Commission reaches a decision.

EXEMPTIONS

26. The long delay which often occurs before the Commission deals with an application for exemption under Article 85(3) or for negative clearance creates great uncertainty for business and often jeopardises

investment in worthwhile commercial ventures. The announcement of time limits for decisions on structural joint ventures is a welcome development but the limits are not binding and ventures not deemed to be structural will not benefit.

27. The Commission Notice (93/C 43/02) on assessment of co-operation joint ventures under Article 85 does extend the scope of the existing block exemptions on specialisation, R&D, know how and patent licensing agreements. These extensions are welcome but CBI regrets that the scope of the regulations was not increased further. The very low market share thresholds: 20 per cent for production joint ventures and 10 per cent if the joint venture extends to distribution/marketing, will necessitate notification of a large number of agreements which do not raise serious competition concerns. It also maintains the discriminatory treatment of co-operative as opposed to concentrative joint ventures and contradicts a 1985 draft Commission communication which suggested 15 per cent market share would be regarded as compatible when co-operation extended to marketing.

28. The turnover thresholds seem to assume that any joint venture between two large companies must be worthy of investigation even although the venture itself is relatively small. CBI would like to see a turnover threshold which addresses the turnover of the joint venture itself rather than that of the parent undertakings.

29. The Commission has announced a number of administrative changes designed to enhance the speed of decision-making under Regulation 17/62 and reduce the backlog of cases. Whilst the CBI welcomes the intention of the Commission to reduce the delays in decision-making, the steps it has so far taken are unlikely to address the issue effectively. Given that additional resources are unlikely to be made available to DGIV, CBI believes that the Commission must adopt a more realistic interpretation of Article 85(1), targeting the prohibition on these agreements and practices likely to have seriously anti-competitive effects. A large number of agreements currently held to fall within the scope of Article 85(1) do not have any significant anti-competitive effects. By limiting the scope of Article 85(1) the Commission could significantly reduce its current workload without relying on decentralised enforcement. There is a lack of coherence between Commission proposals to encourage decentralised enforcement of Articles 85 and 86 and the one-stop-shop under the Merger Regulation. CBI believes that there should be a clear division between the jurisdictions so that transactions which have Community implications are assessed at the Community level and so that it is clear which authority will have jurisdiction in any case. A more pragmatic approach to the "effect on trade between Member States" test and a realistic interpretation of Article 85(1) would be the most effective means of reducing the current backlog of cases under Article 85.

CONCLUSION

30. CBI feels that the investigation by the Sub-Committee into Community competition procedures is timely and could help to remedy the procedural defects which have been highlighted by the serious faults in Commission practice in recent cases; these procedural defects jeopardise the rights of parties and undermine the authority of the Community system. There have been some improvements since the 1982 Report of the Committee. However as pressure on DGIV to produce speedy decisions increases, the temptation to breach procedures will increase.

31. In this paper CBI have suggested some changes which would help to ensure that procedures are fair and due process is followed within the current institutional framework. It would be more appropriate to the penal nature of the remedies which can be imposed under Regulation 17 if the procedures were replaced with completely new rules which enshrined the rights to:

— receive timely notice and adequate formulation of the legal and factual issues involved in the case;

— present oral testimony, documentary evidence and argument;

— rebut adverse evidence by cross-examination or other appropriate means;

— appear with counsel;

— have the decision based exclusively on matters introduced into the record;

— have a complete record consisting of the transcript of the oral stage as well as the documentary evidence and other papers filed in the proceeding.

32. However, initially at least, CBI believes that many of the shortcomings in the procedures could be resolved without the need to undertake a fundamental review which would take some time to achieve and may not be agreed by all of the Member States.

33. The Commission has made clear its desire to increase the transparency of procedures and has taken steps to reduce its workload and speed decision-making. However, CBI believes that many of

the Commission proposals are misguided, do not address the root of the problem and are based upon questionable assumptions.

34. Competition law should be clearly formulated and predictably enforced in accordance with fair and transparent procedures. CBI would therefore urge the Committee to recommend that the Commission reappraise its interpretation of Article 85(1) so that agreements which do not have significant anti-competitive implications are taken outwith the scope of the prohibition altogether. Enhancing the role of the Hearing Officer, publishing the Advisory Committee's opinions and ensuring that the CFI is adequately resourced could help to ensure that the procedural framework more effectively protects the rights of undertakings and ensures that the Commission is more accountable than at present.

35. CBI would be pleased to provide further written or oral evidence to the Sub-Committee should their Lordships find this helpful.

May 1993

Memorandum by Mr Peter Duffy

1. This paper considers some implications of the European Convention on Human Rights in relation to EC Competition investigations and proceedings.

2. The Communities are not a party to the European Convention machinery. Proceedings cannot therefore be brought before the Human Rights Commission and Court to challenge any alleged incompatibility of EC Competition procedure with Convention standards. Further, the European Commission of Human Rights has declared inadmissible an attempt to challenge execution of an EC Competition fine by bringing an application against the State, whose courts permitted execution to occur[1].

3. In 1977, the Community Institutions made a formal joint declaration in which they stressed:

> "the prime importance they attach to the protection of fundamental rights as derived in particular from the constitutions of the Member States and the European Convention for the Protection of Human Rights and Fundamental Freedoms.

In the exercise of their powers and in pursuance of the aims of the European Communities they respect and will continue to respect these rights."

It is well established that fundamental rights, including the European Convention on Human Rights are part of the general principles of law whose respect the European Court of Justice (the "ECJ") enforces. The absence of any redress in Strasbourg makes it all the more important that the Convention's standards should be scrupulously respected in EC Competition procedures and the judicial control of those investigations by the ECJ and the Court of First Instance ("CFI").

(a) *Compliance with Article 6(1) of the Convention*

4. In Cases 209–215 and 218/78 *FEDETAB* [1980] ECR 3125, the ECJ stated:—

> "The Commission is bound to respect procedural guarantees provided for by Community law [but] . . . it cannot be classified as a tribunal within the meaning of Article 6 of the European Convention" (paragraph 81 of the judgment).

Article 6 of the Convention contains the fair trial guarantees of the Convention which must be respected in the determination of criminal charges and of civil rights and obligations. It is correct that, because of its investigative functions, the Commission cannot be regarded as fulfilling the criteria for being a "tribunal" under Article 6(1). On the other hand, it is now plain that companies which are fined in competition proceedings ought to be recognised the guarantees of Article 6.

5. A recent case under the Convention indicates that EC Competition proceedings should be classified as criminal in character. The case of *Stenuit* v *France* (1992) 14 EHRR 509 was struck out by the Court after a settlement. The European Commission of Human Rights, however, had powerfully and unanimously held that a French company fined for anti-competitive behaviour had faced a "criminal charge" within the meaning of the Convention:—

> "In the present case, the penalty imposed by the Minister was a fine of FFr 50,000, a sum which in itself is not negligible. but it is above all the fact that the maximum fine . . . was five per cent of the annual turnover for a firm . . . which shows quite clearly that the penalty in question was intended to be deterrent" (paragraph 64 of the Report).

[1]Application No 13258/87 *CM & Co* v *Germany* unpublished admissibility decision of 9 February 1990.

Under Regulation 17, fines of up to 10 per cent of annual turnover can be imposed for breaches of EC Competition rules by the Commission. It is also clear that EC Competition proceedings[1] involve the determination of civil rights and obligations, thus making the guarantees of Article 6(1) applicable in any event: see, for example *Editions Periscope v France* (1992) 14 EHRR 597.

6. Article 6 does not preclude administrative decisions concerning "civil rights" or investigative procedures concerning possible criminal charges, but—and it is a crucial proviso—only on condition that undertakings retain the right to due process on all aspects of the case before a tribunal fulfilling the standards of independence and impartiality required by the Convention. Clearly no difficulty arises in relation to the composition or functioning of the ECJ or the CFI. Traditionally, however, when exercising judicial control over EC Commission Competition decisions, discretion has been recognised to the Commission in applying the Competition rules. The judicial control by the CFI and, in appropriate cases, the ECJ will only provide the judicial redress required under the Convention if all issues are fully considered and no discretionary reserve is shown in relation to Commission findings of fact and/or economic evidence. Appeals before the CFI need to be equated with a first instance criminal trial incorporating a thorough examination of all the evidence and respect for the presumption of innocence and rights of the defence. The EC Treaty provides a clear legal basis for such an approach[2]. Recent decisions of the ECJ and the CFI show a robust approach towards the examination of evidence[3]. It is important that this practice be continued and strengthened if the standards of Article 6 are to be respected.

7. Article 6 guarantees remain relevant to Competition proceedings before the EC Commission notwithstanding that the Commission does not constitute a "tribunal" within the meaning of Article 6(1) of the Convention. In Case 374/87 *Orchem v Commission* [1989] ECR 3283, the ECJ held that the Commission must not compel an undertaking to provide it with answers to questions which might involve an admission by the undertaking of the existence of an infringement. The ECJ held, however, that Regulation 17 can be used:—

> "to compel an undertaking to provide all information concerning such facts as may be known to it and to disclose to it, if necessary, such documents relating thereto as are in its possession, even if the latter may be used to establish, against it or another undertaking, the existence of anti-competitive conduct" (paragraph 34).

This should be contrasted with the approach recently taken by the European Court of Human Rights in *Funke v France* [1993] 1 CMLR 897. The Court gave a broader interpretation to the right to remain silent, which, under its construction, covered the right "not to contribute to incriminating himself" (paragraph 44). It rejected the Human Rights Commission's view that "neither the obligation to produce bank statements nor the imposition of pecuniary penalties offended the principle of a fair trial". In a fact situation comparable to Competition investigation, on the facts the European Court of Human Rights found a breach and rejected applying a looser standard on the basis of the special features of investigation procedures in business and financial matters.

(b) *Compliance with Article 8 of the Convention*

8. Article 8 of the Convention requires respect for private and family life, home and correspondence. In Cases 46/87 and 227/88 *Hoechst v Commission* [1989] ECR 2859, it was said of Article 8 that:—

> "The protective scope of that article is concerned with the development of man's personal freedom and may not be extended to business premises" (paragraph 18).

The ECJ rejected the applicant company's submission that fundamental rights required that "searches should be carried out only on the basis of a judicial warrant issued in advance". A power of search without prior judicial authorisation was held to be implicit in Article 14 of Regulation 17. It is submitted that the position taken by the ECJ ought now to be reassessed in the light of subsequent Strasbourg case law.

9. In *Niemietz v Germany* (December 1992, to be reported in EHRR) the Court of Human Rights found that a search of a lawyer's office came within the scope of Article 8 and rejected the Government's reliance on the ECJ case law:

> "To interpret the words 'private life' and 'home' as including certain professional or business activities or premises would be consonant with the essential object and purpose of Article 8, namely to protect the individual against arbitrary interference by the public authorities" (paragraph 31 of the judgment).

[1]Including those which do not result in imposition of fines but which nevertheless have serious consequences for the companies concerned.

[2]Article 172 explicitly provides that the ECJ may have "unlimited jurisdiction with regard to penalties".

[3]For example the appointment of experts by the ECJ in the *Woodpulp* case.

In *Niemietz* the Court unanimously found a violation of the Convention because the search was found disproportionate on the facts. See also three judgments against France of 26 February 1993: *Funke*, *Cremieux* and *Miailhe*. Violations of Article 8 were found in relation to searches:—

> "the customs authorities had very wide powers; in particular they had exclusive competence to assess the expediency, number, length and scale of inspections. Above all, in the absence of any requirement of a judicial warrant the restrictions and conditions provided for in law . . . appear too lax and full of loopholes for the interferences in the applicant's right to have been strictly proportionate to the legitimate aim pursued" (paragraph 57 of *Funke*).

10. In the light of the above, it is suggested that a welcome adjustment to EC Competition procedures would be to subject EC Commission search and seizure powers to prior judicial authorisation by the CFI.

May 1993

Memorandum by the Federal Cartel Office

1. INTRODUCTION

Sub-Committee E of the House of Lords Select Committee on the European Communities is carrying out an enquiry into the enforcement of the competition rules of the European Communities (EC), with special reference to the procedures and levels of decision-making. The Committee have focused attention on improvements made since the last enquiry 11 years ago, as well as on recent developments towards increased application of EC competition law by national authorities and courts.

The Federal Cartel Office has been asked to contribute to the Sub-Committee's enquiry. The following remarks will be concentrated on the decentralised application of EC competition law, the Federal Cartel Office's experience to date, the problems encountered so far and solutions envisaged.

2. THE NEED FOR INCREASED APPLICATION OF EC COMPETITION LAW BY NATIONAL AUTHORITIES

There are several reasons why national authorities should have a greater share in the application of EC competition rules. As far as cartel and abuse cases (Articles 85/86 of the EEC Treaty) are concerned, the Commission has long had an excessive workload. Even now there is an enormous backlog of cases, and the number of notifications and complaints is likely to increase as the EC becomes more integrated. Therefore it is absolutely necessary to ease the burden on the Commission. Moreover, the application of EC competition law by national authorities will result in bringing EC decision-making closer to the citizen and—in the long run—contribute to the integration of the European Community and the development of a uniform European competition law.

The Commission for its part has expressed the view that cartels should be dealt with at the most efficient level, which could in fact be that of a particular member state whose territory is mainly affected by the restraint of competition involved. However, what the Commission has in mind at this stage is merely increased application of Articles 85(1) and 86 of the EEC Treaty by the national authorities. By contrast, the Commission considers devolving the power to grant exemptions to the authorities of Member States as premature at this point.

Complaints with (nearly) exclusive national emphasis are to be referred increasingly to national authorities and courts in future. To some extent, this is already being done. Here, the Commission has the backing of the European Court of First Instance which, in its Automec (RS T-24/90) judgment of 18 September 1992, ruled that the Commission had discretion in exercising its powers.

3. CURRENT PRACTICE AND OBSTACLES TO INCREASED APPLICATION OF EC COMPETITION LAW BY NATIONAL AUTHORITIES

In the past, only a small proportion of the application of EC competition law has taken place at national level. There are several reasons:

(a)   Under current law, the national competition authorities' powers to apply EC competition law are limited as such. The authorities of member states are competent to apply Articles 85(1) and 86 of the EEC Treaty only as long as the Commission has not initiated proceedings (Article 9 of Regulation No. 17/62 and similar provisions in specific transport regulations). The Commission has exclusive competence for exemptions under Article 85(3) of the EEC Treaty and for the European Merger Control Regulation.

As a result, cases where an infringement of Article 85(1) is not clear and the possibility of granting an exemption exists cannot be handled by national authorities. However, that issue has to be examined in the majority of cases.

Moreover, the national authorities lack the power to impose sanctions if they find that Articles 85(1) and 86 of the EEC Treaty have been violated, which reduces the effectiveness of enforcement.

What is more, the Commission at present seems to be willing to cede to Member States only "run-of-the-mill" cases, while dealing with all major cases itself. Under the circumstances it is hardly surprising that the national authorities are not too keen to apply EC competition law.

(b)   Application of EC competition law at the national level also requires that each national lawmaker should designate the competent authority in this national territory and grant it the necessary powers. This was done in Germany in 1990 in the Fifth Act to Amend the Act against Restraints of Competition (ARC). Section 47 of the ARC designates the Federal Cartel Office as the competent authority which has powers to apply both the ARC and, with the same instruments, the EC competition law. France adopted such national legislation in January 1993 only, whereas other Member States have so far failed to follow suit. This is another reason why there are still obstacles in the way of EC-wide, decentralised application of EC competition law.

(c)   For the above reasons, the Federal Cartel Office has so far enforced EC competition law only in rare cases since the coming into force of Section 47 of the ARC. The main emphasis has continued to be on the enforcement of national law; as a rule, reference was made to Articles 85(1) and 86 of the EEC Treaty, but no further investigations were conducted.

Only recently has the Federal Cartel Office instituted proceedings exclusively on the basis of EC competition law:

—   The Federal Cartel Office has challenged, under Article 85(1) of the EEC Treaty, the exclusive dealing arrangements applied by the tour operator TUI which deny competing tour operators access to a major part of travel agencies. The exclusive dealing arrangements were initially prohibited under Section 18 of the ARC. That decision was, however, rescinded by the courts, and the attempt to introduce Article 85(1) of the EEC Treaty into the pending proceeding was rejected. Two defendants have lodged an appeal with the Federal Supreme Court against the refusal of leave to appeal on points of law.

Meanwhile, the competent Federal Cartel Office Decision Division instituted a new, independent proceeding under Article 85(1) of the EEC Treaty against TUI and started investigations. In this context, it requested information from TUI and other tour operators. Against the order requesting information, TUI has made an appeal to the Berlin Court of Appeals, which will, however, take a decision only after the ARC proceeding has been finally decided.

—   In another proceeding under Article 85(1) of the EEC treaty, an exclusive dealing requirement in the concession agreement between the energy supply company RWE and the city of Kleve has been challenged. In this case, the Commission had agreed not to deal itself with the case.

In the meantime, however, RWE has announced that it will notify the agreement in Brussels pursuant to Article 5 of Regulation No. 17/62 in order to apply for exemption. Since the Commission is considering initiating proceedings in a similar case, there is a certain probability that Brussels will also handle the RWE-Kleve case.

Several other attempts of the Federal Cartel Office to conduct proceedings under EC competition law based on a consensus with the Commission have failed due to the factual difficulties of the cases concerned.

4. POSSIBLE SOLUTIONS

There are several possible solutions to the problems described under 3. They are discussed in detail in the attached paper of the Federal Ministry of Economics of 16 December 1992, which was prepared in co-ordination with the Federal Cartel Office.

The main points are the following:

(a)   Increased enforcement of EC competition law at national level presupposes that the national authorities may also decide on exemptions under Article 85(3) of the EEC Treaty. It should be possible to set in place appropriate procedures to determine competence and ensure a uniform law enforcement.

(b)   An increased enforcement of Article 85(1) and 86 of the EEC Treaty by the Federal Cartel Office and other national authorities would require a consensus procedure ensuring above all that a decision a national authority may take is not undermined by a contrary decision of the Commission.

(c)   In the area of EC merger control it would be desirable to have more cases referred to the national authorities, which would give sufficient effect to the subsidiarity principle. For this reason, too, the thresholds of the Regulation should not be lowered for the time being.

(d)   The setting up of an independent European competition authority would allow a more efficient protection of competition and in particular shorten decision processes and periods considerably.

5. Conclusion

The Commission and the Federal Cartel Office agree that an increased enforcement of EC competition law by the national authorities is necessary. But opinions differ on how this can be achieved. The Federal Cartel Office experience so far shows that on the basis of the present law there are only limited possibilities of reducing the Commission's workload. In the long run a change in legislation seems therefore unavoidable. But this should not exclude the possibility of achieving a more decentralised practice based on a consensus with the Commission as a continuation of the practice mentioned under 3(c) above.

Dr Von Stoephasius/Müller

Berlin, 6 May 1993

Enclosed Memorandum from the Federal Ministry of Economics

Increased participation by national competition authorities in European competition law enforcement and creation of an independent European competition authority.

I. Preliminary Remarks

As European markets become integrated, the Commission's task of protecting competition is growing steadily. In addition to the instruments available, ie block exemption regulations or comfort letters, DG IV has submitted proposals for ceding cases of limited Community interest. One of the proposals deals with increased application of Articles 85(1) and 86 of the EEC Treaty by the courts of the Member States. The Commission intends to publish a notice on the subject before the end of the year. More recourse to national courts is to be welcomed. However, since a national judge is not competent to decide in the Commission's place whether a cartel agreement can be exempted under Article 85(3) of the EEC Treaty, the workload reduction expected to result from that proposal should not be overrated.

Therefore, other solutions have to be found so that the Commission can focus its scarce administrative resources on proceedings of particular Community importance. This could be achieved step by step. The first step within the existing legal framework should be to pursue further the Commission's proposal of getting national competition authorities more involved in the application of Articles 85(1) and 86 of the EEC Treaty (II.).

The next step should be to create the legal conditions which:

—   would allow the competition authorities of the Member States to grant exemptions under Article 85(3) in cases where the national effect clearly has priority over the Community interest (III.);

—   would give a greater role to the Member States in securing compliance in the area of merger control (IV.);

—   would ease the burden of European competition law enforcement on the Commission by establishing an independent European competition authority (V.).

II. Enforcement of Article 85(1) of the EEC Treaty by Member States

According to Article 9(3) of Council Regulation No 17, the national competition authorities are competent to apply Article 85(1) and Articles 86 and 88 of the EEC Treaty, as long as the EC Commission has not initiated proceedings. Since infringements of Articles 85 and 86 may affect trade in more than one Member State, Article 9(3) of Regulation No 17 provides that the EC Commission and several Member States may be equally competent in a particular case.

Given such multiple competence, assigning national authorities a more active role will only succeed if the Commission and the Member States agree in principle on the assignment of tasks and the reciprocal co-ordinating mechanism. The basic principle would have to be that the Commission should attend to cases of substantial Community interest. All other cases should be handled by the national competition authority whose territory is largely affected by the infringement. Any action by a national competition authority would, of course, presuppose that no investigations have to be conducted in other Member States.

Such a general delimitation would have to be backed up by close co-operation between the Commission and the national authorities. The main point here would be to give any national competition authority certainty that in a particular case its decision under Article 85(1) or Article 86 of the EEC Treaty will be allowed to stand. For no national competition authority will become involved, if it is an open question whether its prohibition decision will be reversed by the Commission which, upon application, grants the firm concerned an exemption under Article 85(3) of the EEC Treaty. Prior to any national prohibition decision being taken, the national competition authority and the Commission, on the basis of the facts found in the investigation, would have to come to an understanding to the effect that no exemption will be granted in the case in hand, if there is no change in the factual situation.

It should be borne in mind that the majority of cases subject to EC competition law are not confined to the question of issuing a prohibition, but, as a rule, involve the granting of an exemption as well, which falls within the EC Commission's exclusive competence. Therefore, the reduction in the Commission's workload that is expected to result from the national competition authorities' participation in the application of Articles 85(1) and 86 of the EEC Treaty should not be overrated. Moreover, many Member States have not even allocated powers nationally.

III. TRANSFER TO MEMBER STATES OF THE POWER TO GRANT EXEMPTION UNDER ARTICLE 85(3) OF THE EEC TREATY

Enforcement of European competition law could become more efficient by far, if the competition authorities of the Member States, in addition to their present power to issue prohibitions, were assigned the power to grant exemption under Article 85(3) of the EEC Treaty in cases where the national effect clearly is given priority over the Community interest. Such a step would presuppose a change in Regulation No 17.

For such an extension of the national authorities' powers it would be necessary, on the one hand, to resolve the question of how to assign powers between the EC Commission and the national competition authorities; on the other hand, arrangements would have to be made to ensure uniform application of the Community competition rules by the EC Commission and the Member States.

1. *Assignment of powers*

The assignment of powers between the Commission and the Member States on the one hand, and among the Member States on the other, calls for a decision in principle to be made as to whether the assignment of competence should result in one specific authority having exclusive competence, or whether the application of EC competition law should be organised on the basis of parallel competence of both the Commission and the Member States. Any decision on the issue of competence assignment should be uniform for proceedings under Article 85(1) and Article 85(3) of the EEC Treaty.

The greatest clarity for all parties concerned, including the business community, could no doubt be achieved by the adoption of legal provisions which—like the EC Merger Control Regulation and EEA Agreement—would lay down exclusive powers and assign them to either the Commission or the Member States concerned. However, such an exclusivity system could only work if the assignment of individual cases was absolutely clear and unambiguous. This would presuppose the use of general criteria of delimitation, eg, turnover figures and thresholds, which do not always reflect economic realities. One serious disadvantage of assigning exclusive competence has to be seen mainly in the fact that it presupposes fully operational competition authorities in all Member States. What is more, conflicts of competence between the Member States and the Commission and the Member States among themselves would be taken to the courts. Owing to the duration of the proceedings involved, legal certainty for the firms concerned would also be affected.

Therefore there is much to be said for modelling the transfer of the power to grant exemption under Article 85(3) of the EEC Treaty to Member States on the principle of multiple competence, with the Commission having priority, under Article 9 of Regulation No 17. Then each Member State would have to decide for itself on the extent to which it wants to become involved in proceedings under Article 85(3) of the EEC Treaty in the interest of maintaining competition and in the interest of its own economy. In the case of Member States without competition authorities of their own, the EC Commission would retain exclusive competence. In this model, conflicts of competence would be resolved co-operatively by consensus. If differences of opinion were insurmountable, it would be up to the Commission to take on responsibility for that particular case.

2. *Ensuring uniformity of law enforcement*

Unlike prohibition case where, given the adversary character of the relationship between the competition authority and the enterprises, uniformity of enforcement is ensured through jurisdiction, ie ultimately through the European Court of Justice, there is the danger in exemption cases that enterprises and national competition authorities pursue similar interests. In situations where an alleged or actual public interest might be involved, it could not be ruled out that an exemption is granted even if the conditions for granting such exemption are not satisfied and that the Commission has not been informed of this. In the absence of a divergence of interests, there would be no review by the courts. If the power to grant exemption were transferred to the Member Sates, it would therefore be necessary to ensure uniformity of law enforcement institutionally at the administrative level.

It would be in line with the proposed consensual procedure regarding the assignment of powers that uniform application of the competition rules were ensured by obtaining the Commission's consent. The competent national competition authority would have to obtain the consent of the EC Commission before granting exemption. The consent could be regarded as given after a certain time-limit has expired. If divergences of opinion between the Commission and a Member State cannot be settled, resort to the Advisory Committee would be conceivable.

Such a consensual procedure would fully satisfy the requirement of uniform law enforcement. On the one hand, the Commission would be informed of all national exemption projects before an exemption is granted. Owing to the consent requirement, the Commission, on the other hand, could influence the national competition authority's decision in the interest of uniform enforcement.

If a great number of exemptions were granted by the national authorities, it is to be anticipated, though, that the Commission will have a considerable workload in examining those cases, which would possibly frustrate the aim of easing its pressure of work. It might therefore be considered whether uniform law enforcement could be sufficiently ensured by the national competition authority forwarding its decision to the Commission immediately after an exemption has been granted. The Commission would then still have the possibility of initiating proceedings itself until that decision becomes unappealable. The Commission would also still have the possibility of instituting proceedings for violation of the Treaty.

Other intermediate solution models between the consent model and an ex-post notification would be conceivable. The Member States could, eg, be granted the power to decide autonomously, but only after the Commission has been informed of the intended decision and has been given sufficient time to present its views or to turn to the Advisory Committee.

The decision as to which of the described or other solutions are chosen should be made dependent above all upon an assessment of whether and how the Commission's workload might be eased whilst at the same time uniform enforcement is ensured.

3. *Outcome*

The transfer of the power to decide on exemption cases under Article 85(3) of the EEC Treaty to the Member States would create the Community conditions for considerably enhancing the efficiency of the application of the EC competition rules in that the resources of the Member States' competition authorities would be utilised. The national competition authorities could become a genuine and competent point of contact for the business community as far as EC cartel cases are concerned. This would be helpful above all for small and medium-sized enterprises which cannot afford to set up their own legal departments that are proficient in foreign languages and familiar with the Brussels situation. Decentralised law enforcement would thus excellently take account of the concept of an administration that is close to its citizens.

The legislative efforts involved would be small. It would only be necessary to revise Council Regulation No 17, Article 9. With a view to clarifying the general assignment of powers, it would, however, moreover be necessary for the Commission to publish a notice, specifying in what exemption cases it will retain exclusive decision competence.

IV. EXTENDED DECISION-MAKING COMPETENCE OF THE NATIONAL COMPETITION AUTHORITIES IN EC MERGER CONTROL CASES

The question of whether the national competition authorities' scope for making decisions in EC merger control cases should be extended also plays a major role in the discussion of the possibilities of improving the enforcement of the EC competition rules. The EC Commission's current practice to decide on cases affecting competition interests in one Member State only seems unsatisfactory. As the national competition authority is closer to the factual situation concerned, it would be more appropriate to leave the decision in those cases to the national authority. Experience so far has shown that enterprises tend to deliberately restructure merger projects in order to escape national merger control. The existing assignment of powers therefore has proved not to be competitively neutral.

In order to remedy those problems it would be expedient to develop Article 9 of the EC Merger Control Regulation to the effect that in EC merger cases a Member State is assigned the merger project if the competition considerations are primarily within its territory. Insofar as critical market share concentrations prevail in one Member State only or the merger poses competitive concerns in the opinion of only one Member State, the case should be referred automatically to that State. However, procedural steps to ensure uniform enforcement should be considered.

V. ESTABLISHING AN INDEPENDENT EUROPEAN COMPETITION AUTHORITY

At Community level, efficient enforcement of the competition principle could ultimately benefit the most from an independent European competition authority (whatever its name). Such an authority should have to be responsible both for the enforcement of the competition rules and for merger control. It would render the protection of competition more efficient and give added weight to the competition principle. Short lines of decision would considerably shorten the process of decision-making and raise the efficiency of enforcement. The burden on the Commission would be eased if there was a separation of legislative tasks from administrative tasks. The European competition authority would be exclusively responsible for enforcement, but it would be subject to control by the Commissioner responsible for competition policy. The legislative power to issue block exemption regulations on the basis of powers delegated by the Council and directives under Article 90(3) of the EEC Treaty would remain with the Commission.

However, the legal basis for an independent European competition authority will still have to be discussed.

VI. FURTHER ACTION

Each of the proposed measures requires a different amount of groundwork. Since the "second-step" measures (powers of national competition authorities to grant exemptions under Article 85(3) of the EEC Treaty, their participation in the area of merger control, or an independent European competition authority) require changes of legislation, they could best be combined with other items on the agenda for an adjustment of the legal framework. Special attention would have to be focused on a balanced approach. Efficient competition law enforcement must be ensured at every stage.

Bonn, 16 *December* 1992

Memorandum by Mr Ian Forrester, QC

INTRODUCTION

1. The EC competition rules do not function as one would assume from reading the relevant regulations and pronouncements of Commission representatives.

2. In theory, the prohibition of Article 85(1) extends to a vast class of agreements which contain provisions deemed to involve a restriction of competition. Agreements caught are void, unenforceable and finable. Only if they are exempted can these dire consequences be avoided. The availability of exemptions is indispensable for the system to function as it was designed. Yet in reality the Commission is able to issue only a few specific exemptions per year.

3. There is thus a structural discordance between the asserted jurisdictional reach of the Commission and its administrative capacity to deliver the legal certainty for which its theory creates a need. For a variety of reasons, the Commission refuses to relax its primacy over the conditions for granting an exemption. In addition, it is reluctant to accept that particular agreements do not restrict competition or do not affect trade between Member States.

4. The Commission has consistently been expansionist in how it interprets Article 85(1), and it has been very reluctant to contemplate any version of a US-style "rule of reason" whereby businesses may conclude for themselves that certain businesses practices, although involving technical restrictions, are nonetheless legitimate when viewed in their totality. It has been notably cautious about following the occasional hints offered by the Court of Justice in the direction of a more relaxed interpretation. Thus, far from limiting the class of agreements to which the competition rules apply, the Commission is if anything encouraging the making of competition law arguments. In effect, it is encouraging undertakings to assert that Article 85(1) may apply to contracts to which they are party or which may affect them; but it is not suggesting any radical changes to cope with the increased demand for legal certainty which might be expected to result therefrom.

5. The recent Notice on Co-operation with National Courts is an interesting and helpful step. However, I would submit that although some valuable initiatives have been taken, the structural problem of the intellectual predominance of the Commission has not changed.

THE NOTICE ON CO-OPERATION WITH NATIONAL COURTS

6. As a matter of policy, the Community Institutions are seeking to promote the assimilation of Community law into the fabric of national rules and practices, and to correct the perception that Community law is the exclusive preserve of a distant and unaccountable bureaucracy located in Brussels. Even if the principle of "subsidiarity" had not recently become fashionable, it is manifest that DG IV cannot possibly, with its present resources, police competition compliance throughout the Community.

7. For parties seeking the protection of the competition rules, the Commission points out in its Notice several reasons why, in its opinion, national courts should be able to provide better protection than the Commission. Although I fully understand, and sympathise with, the Commission's objective of discouraging the impression that it is the sole source of effective competition law enforcement, I am not wholly convinced by the Commission's arguments. In fact, the Commission is today a more attractive interlocutor for a plaintiff than a national court.

8. The Notice attempts to propose solutions for some of the substantial practical problems which have discouraged the national courts from applying the competition rules in the past and therefore discouraged potential litigants from resorting to the national courts for this purpose. This requires defining the respective powers of the Commission and the national courts, and establishing the channels of communication by which the Commission can provide guidance on legal principles and relevant factual or procedural information to the national courts. Although the availability of this information is most welcome. I submit that the underlying difficulties are caused not just by problems of communication but of substance and structure.

SHARED COMPETENCE TO INTERPRET ARTICLE 85(1)

9. Both the Commission and the national courts have the power to declare that an agreement caught by Article 85(1) and not exempted under Article 85(3) is void and unenforceable by virtue of Article 85(2). The powers of the national courts are more extensive in this respect, since Article 85(1) frequently only catches a particular provision of an agreement, and the question whether the prohibited provision may be severed from the remainder of the agreement, leaving the latter enforceable, is a matter for decision by the national courts applying national contract law. Only the Commission has the power to promulgate exemptions under Article 85(3) (although a national court has the power to examine whether an agreement is eligible for the benefit of a group exemption).

10. Both the Commission and the national courts have the power to apply Article 86. Paradoxically, Article 86 cases probably lend themselves least well to handling at national level, since evidence will usually be necessary from several countries.

11. The system of partially shared competence gives rise to two obvious problems. First, there is a general risk that decisions taken by national courts may conflict with decisions taken by the Commission in the same case, or with policies reflected in other decisions or statements of the Commission. The Court of Justice has tried to outline considerations which national courts should bear in mind when applying Articles 85 and 86 so as to reduce this risk, most recently in *Stergios Delimitis* v. *Henninger Bräu*[1]. I consider that some inconsistency between different courts looking at the same regulatory texts is a familiar phenomenon and not a very serious one. A richer crop of decisions, albeit of varying levels of clarity and authoritativeness, would be preferable to the present situation where formal decisions are excessively difficult to obtain because of the Commission's limited resources.

12. Second, there is the problem of defining the principles to be followed by the national courts in dealing with agreements containing a restriction caught by Article 85(1), which the national court may properly apply but which may qualify for an exemption under Article 85(3), which the national court has no power to apply. This is a fundamental issue of principle, where I submit the Commission's policy is not realistic. This problem, which flows from the reservation to the Commission, by the language of the Treaty itself, of the power to grant exemptions, has been one of the main obstacles to the application of Article 85 in the national courts. While the then responsible Commissioner, Sir Leon Brittan, was recently willing to look forward to a time when the problem might be solved by a Treaty amendment extending the power to grant exemptions to national authorities, the Commission still feels that the time is not yet ripe for such a change[2].

13. On the one hand the Commission is encouraging a greater recourse to national courts, and no lessening of the scope of the reach of Article 85(1); but on the other hand, the national courts will not be entitled to grant the exemptions for which parties may have a need.

---

[1] Case C-234/89, *Stergios Delimitis* v. *Henninger Bräu AG*, [1991] ECR I-935.

[2] Sir Leon said that "the time is not right" to allow national courts to grant exemptions, since a "sufficient consensus" on standards of antitrust enforcement "has not yet developed that would justify lifting the Commission's monopoly over Article 85(3). At present, the risk that differential application of Community law and forum shopping would result is too great." However, Sir Leon said it should "not be unduly long" before the Commission's view would change.

THE RARITY OF SPECIFIC EXEMPTION DECISIONS

14. Some startling statistical consequences flow from the Commission's position. Its interpretation of Article 85(1) means that at least hundreds, and probably thousands, of agreements signed every year are caught by Article 85(1), prohibited by Article 85(1), void under Article 85(2) (and—in theory—finable under Regulation 17/62). In order for these numerous agreements to be valid and enforceable, on strict theory, an exemption is necessary. But the Commission rarely issues more than five specific exemptions in a year, and usually less than 50 each decade.

15. Informal "comfort letters" do not bind national courts and do not solve the nullity problem. In a pragmatic way, such reassurance is very helpful in those cases where the parties' main anxiety is the risk of a Commission challenge. However, a letter saying that Article 85(1) applies and that the Commission proposes for various reasons to take no further action may be a source of uneasiness. The status of such a letter is a difficult issue. The letter says the Commission favours the agreement but does not propose to issue a formal exemption. If the letter is regarded institutionally, it looks like a blessing, but regarded legally it seems to be nothing very definite. I submit that it is undesirable for the significance of such an important document to be obscure.

16. The Commission acknowledges the difficulties which national courts may experience in dealing with EC competition law, and has said it will issue an "explanatory booklet" giving further guidelines. According to the draft Notice, the booklet will contain further information on many topics such as sources of legal norms, principles of interpretation, disclosure of documents, damages, interim measures, and so on. These are unquestionably important topics, and the booklet will doubtless convey useful guidance, but it can hardly fill the legal gap between an exemption decision and a comfort letter.

I submit that there must be serious doubts, despite the sincere intentions underlying the Notice, as to how far completion cases can be successfully moved away from the Commission within the foreseeable future without more radical changes.

DISINCENTIVES TO THE USE OF NATIONAL COURTS

17. There are a number of serious obstacles to the application of the competition rules which the Notice does not address, and over which the Commission has no control:

— national courts' lack of experience and expertise in dealing with questions of economic fact, and the corresponding scepticism which judges may harbour about radical and absolute-sounding competition law theories;

— the absence of, or prohibition on, such US features as contingent fees, class actions, and treble damages which make it financially realistic for enterprises or groups of enterprises to pursue difficult cases before the courts;

— the difficulty for private parties of obtaining evidence of infringements of competition rules in proceedings before national courts, even in jurisdictions with relatively far reaching discovery procedures.

By contrast, a well-documented complaint to the Commission can encounter a gratifyingly energetic response, including fact-gathering, convocation of a hearing and the taking of a formal decision, all without court costs. It is natural and understandable that the Commission is a more attractive interlocutor than a national judge.

18. It can be argued that disincentives to litigation are a good thing, and that Europe is better off with only a low level of activity in this field. Although the Commission understandably wishes to see a greater use of the competition rules in actual practice, it is unfortunately true that for many parties, if there was no chance of obtaining the Commission's intervention, correcting an alleged infringement at national judicial level may often seem too difficult, slow, costly, or uncertain.

If the Commission goes ahead with its threat not to act in some cases which could, in theory, be raised in national courts, the result may be in many cases to leave potential complainants without any real remedy at all.

THE COMMISSION'S WISH TO CONCENTRATE ITS RESOURCES ON POLICY QUESTIONS

19. The Commission uses the Notice to emphasise its wish to concentrate its limited resources on policy questions, rather than on serving as the institution of first resort in providing remedies for competition law infringements. The Court of First Instance confirmed in *Automec* v. *Commission*[1] that the Commission may validly take the view that Community interest does not justify the Commission

---

[1] Case T-24/0, judgment of September 17 1992; see below.

examining a complaint where the complainant can secure adequate protection of his rights under EC competition law before national courts.

20. The Notice states that the Commission:

" . . . intends, in implementing its decision-making powers, to concentrate on notifications, complaints and own initiative proceedings having particular political, economic or legal significance for the Community. Where these features are absent in a particular case, notifications will normally be dealt with be means of a comfort letter[1], and complaints should as a rule, be handled by national courts or authorities". (Refusals by the Commission to proceed on complaints may be expected to be challenged before the Court of First Instance and, ultimately, the European Court of Justice.)

This is an understandable objective. However, I submit that the Commission should not give up its traditional enforcement role without taking appropriate steps to establish an appropriate and coherent set of legal remedies by way of alternative.

PROCEDURAL GUIDELINES FOR THE APPROACH TO BE TAKEN BY NATIONAL COURTS IN VARIOUS SITUATIONS WHERE ARTICLES 85 AND 86 ARE RAISED IN PROCEEDINGS BEFORE THEM

21. The case law of the Court of Justice has already established a number of principles intended to permit national courts to apply the competition rules while avoiding conflicts with decisions or policies announced or envisaged by the Commission. The Notice attempts to set out these principles clearly and systematically, and urges national courts to apply them. Some deserve further comment.

22. A common problem for national courts is to determine where a procedure before the Commission stands, and to know what formal or informal position the Commission has taken on a relevant matter. These problems are partially addressed by the Notice, which mentions "comfort letters" issued by the Commission in response to notifications as being a factor which national courts may, and by implication, should, take into account, even though they are not binding on the courts. The Notice also refers to the case law of the Court of Justice, the Commission's own decisions, and the various notices which it has issued. Strangely enough, the Notice does not refer to other sources such as the Commission's Annual Competition Reports or the press releases which the Commission frequently issues upon settlement of the case.

23. Where the national court feels uncertain about the existence of an infringement, either because the Commission has already initiated a procedure in a case relating to the same conduct, or because it considers that the law is unclear and would like to have guidance from the Commission, the Notice suggests that the court put the appropriate questions to the Commission, staying the proceedings before it until the Commission's answer is received. Of course, the court also has the option of referring the matter to the European Court of Justice under Article 177 of the Treaty. This is not a new concept, but the Commission has not hitherto so publicly proposed it.

If the national court concludes that Article 85(1) is applicable, it must says the Notice (paragraph 24), check whether an exemption under Article 85(3) may be available.

24. Since notifications are in the hundreds, comfort letters are in the tens, and exemption decisions are in the units, it will frequently occur that a notification has been made but no formal decision has been taken by the Commission. The Notice, following the Court of Justice, says that "national courts may take account of these letters as factual elements". This formula requires further clarification. Technically, the legal effect of an exemption cannot be achieved without the issuance of a formal decision granting it. The comfort letter cannot legally bind the court to find that the agreement is exempt. It would certainly be grounds for the national court to stay proceedings pending the outcome of a request to the Commission to clarify its position by formally issuing an exemption. It may also provide the court with the possibility of suggesting to the party attacking the agreement under Article 85 that this claim should be abandoned, on the illogical ground that the Commission would grant an exemption if it was obliged to take a formal decision. In this potentially common situation, it is regrettable that a clearer legal solution is not proposed.

25. Commission policy is to encourage the making of notifications; if formal exemption decisions cannot be taken because of the administrative burden involved, alternative means of conferring legal reassurance are necessary. If comfort letters do not give enough reassurance to satisfy litigants or national judges, they should be reinforced, for example by expanding the reasoning, or by publishing in the *Official Journal* the fact that they had been sent. Under existing practice, it is not clear to third parties what the Commission has done; and comfort letters are usually rather brief. They would be more convincing if they carried fuller detail, and were more widely publicised.

[1] A "comfort letter" has been the most usual way of ending competition notifications for many years now. It will usually state that the Commission sees no reason to intervene in a particular case. Such letters may be "formal" and preceded by a notice published in the Official Journal, but more usually are "informal".

26. Where the agreement has been notified to the Commission, which has not yet taken a position by way of a decision or comfort letter, the Notice instructs the national court to assess the likelihood that the exemption will be granted. If it finds that an exemption "cannot" be granted, it may proceed accordingly. If it finds that an individual exemption is "possible", it should suspend the proceedings and await the Commission's decision. A formal decision usually takes 18 months to process from start to finish, so probably a comfort letter will be the most likely disposition of the case by the Commission.

27. *Methods by which the Commission will assist a national court:* the Notice considers the kinds of question a national court may ask it in a particular case, and suggests how the Commission will try to respond. It distinguishes three categories of possible request:

(i)   *Information about procedure.* To comply with many of the guidelines described above, the court must ask the Commission about the procedural status of Commission procedures—matters such as whether a case is pending before the Commission, whether a case has been the subject of a notification, whether the Commission has officially initiated a procedure and whether it has taken a position through a decision or comfort letter. The court may also ask how much time the Commission expects to take before taking a position. The Notice says that the Commission will "endeavour to give priority" to cases where national proceedings are suspended pending the outcome of the Commission procedure. This seems a realistic and welcome commitment.

(ii)   *Consultations on points of law.* Here, the language of the Notice is very cautious. The Notice emphasises that the Commission's answers do not bind the national court and that, at least as regards questions concerning the application of Article 85(1) and Article 86, "the Commission does not consider the merits of the case". This language reflects an evident concern by the Commission not to be seen to interfere unduly in national court proceedings. While this is a legitimate concern, there is a danger that it may cause the Commission to undermine the effectiveness of the proposed procedure by formulating its comments in excessively indirect, Delphic, or abstract terms.

(iii) *Requests for factual data.* The Notice refers to statistics, market studies and economic analyses. Here again, the approach is very hesitant, and the Notice points out that the Commission cannot give information which it does not have, or which is covered by an obligation of confidentiality[1]. It also implies that the Commission may reply by telling the court where information can be obtained, rather than giving the information itself.

28. It is precisely in dealing with the question of how to treat requests for information from national courts, which in real terms is likely to be the point of greatest importance to national courts, that the Notice is most cautious. Apart from sensitivity about appearing to interfere, the Notice also appears to reflect a concern that the Commission may be manipulated by litigants. It says:

"As *amicus curiae*, the Commission is obliged to respect legal neutrality and objectivity. Consequently, it will not accede to requests for information unless they come from a national court, either directly, or indirectly through parties which have been ordered by the court concerned to provide certain information. In the latter case, the Commission will ensure that its answer reaches all the parties to the proceedings."

While this caution would be appropriate if the Commission were a total outsider, it seems unnecessarily timid where the Commission has been seized of a notification to which it has given no formal answer, yet as to which only it can take a formal decision.

CONCLUDING COMMENTS

29. In one sense, the Notice is not novel. It merely brings together and states systematically a number of ideas and policies which have already been expressed, either by the Commission itself or by the European Court of Justice and the Court of First Instance. One may doubt whether the impulse given by the Notice in this direction will lead to anything like a quantum leap. The doctrinal complexities of EC competition law remain dense. The problem of the Commission's continuing exclusive competence to apply Article 85(3) remains a major obstacle to the involvement of national courts. The procedures for resolving these problems are not necessarily easy to apply—as is shown by the fact that, although some of them were already proposed by the European Court more than 20 years ago, little use has actually been made of them. Some of the language of the Notice itself suggests that the Commission may take a very cautious, even timid approach in responding to requests from national courts. To make the Notice work requires a major change, not only in approach of the national courts, but also in the Commission's internal culture.

---

[1] In the *Zwartveld* decision, which dealt with a claim by the Commission that it could not produce certain documents on the grounds of confidentiality, the Court said that the Commission must present "imperative reasons relating to the need to avoid any interference with the functioning and independence of the Communities, justifying its refusal to do so" (paragraphs 25 and 26).

30. The Commission has shown in its handling of cases under the Merger Regulation that it can produce short, workmanlike decisions within one month of receiving a notification. By contrast, decisions in application of Article 85(1) and (3) are major pieces of rule-making in which new points of principle are elaborated. If the traditionally broad interpretation of Article 85(1) cannot be relaxed, the Commission should look for alternative techniques of issuing exemption decisions. These need not be, and should not be, exercises in perfectionism. They should be accurate responses to specific problems; if a decision is too brief or not sufficiently convincing, the European Court can put matters right. That would not be a disaster.

31. It is still true today that, as far as I am aware, although national courts have recognised the availability of damages in competition cases in principle, not a single judgment has yet been given by a national court awarding damages under the EC competition rules. While the use of the competition rules as a defence to contract actions, or as a basis for seeking injunctions, has been more frequent, the scale of this use is still strikingly limited. If application of the EC competition rules by national courts were to become more commonplace, this would mean an important change in the legal and business environment in the Community.

32. I would contend that the Commission would be on surer ground if it were to take yet more courageous steps:

— accept that national courts should be given the power to grant exemptions, accepting the natural imperfections of a richer jurisprudence rooted firmly in the legal traditions of each Member State;

— relax its too-extensive interpretation of Article 85(1), and accept that competition law is now sufficiently mature for the risk to be taken for business to reach their own conclusion about what is or is not an unacceptable restriction of competition, without the formal necessity of requiring an administrative decision to be confident of the agreement's enforceability;

— alternatively, if the traditional interpretation cannot be relaxed, and if national courts cannot be given the power to grant exemptions, then at the least the Commission must develop its comfort letter procedures. It must be possible to issue something akin to an exemption, regularly and frequently, without paralysing the Commission's administrative machinery.

The Notice is a welcome step in the direction of recognising the Commission's duty to tidy up the legal questions presented by its administrative limitations; some further steps are however necessary.

Ian S. Forrester, QC
Brussels, 1 *October* 1993

Memorandum by Mr Nicholas Forwood QC

1. The goals of the Rules on Competition in the EEC Treaty are important: more efficient markets, lower costs to the consumer and increased international competitiveness of Community industry, all of which should lead to greater prosperity and growth in the European Community. If those goals are to be achieved, it is particularly important that the procedures for enforcement of the rules—whether administrative or judicial—be clear and effective. The following observations identify some areas of present and future concern with regard to procedure, and suggest possible solutions; the comments inevitably reflect the perspective of a practitioner regularly advising and representing companies faced with competition law problems, usually of a contentious nature.

PROCEDURES BEFORE THE EC COMMISSION

2. Competition proceedings before the Commission are sometimes classified, at the risk of over-simplification, into "structural" and "behavioural" cases. Structural cases are typically those where companies have entered into some form of long term arrangement, eg a merger, joint venture or other semi-permanent form of co-operation. Such a case, if it does not come within one of the existing block exemptions, will typically come before the Commission at the initiative of the companies concerned with a request for an individual exemption of arrangements under Article 85(3) or under the relevant regulations.

3. "Behavioural" cases, on the other hand, normally involve the classic infringements of Article 85 and 86, ie cartels between producers, or predatory pricing or other exclusionary conduct by a dominant firm. By their very nature, these cases are not brought to the Commission's attention by the companies concerned, but rather by complaints by third parties or even by chance[1]. Such cases typically lead to

[1] A classic example is the Commission's discovery, in the course of an Article 14 investigation of a cartel in the polypropylene sector, of other documents revealing other cartels in the PVC and LDPE sectors.

the issue of a statement of objections and, ultimately, a decision finding an infringement and imposing a fine.

4. By and large, the Commission is thought to deal reasonably well with structural cases. So far as the substance of decisions in such cases is concerned, parties seem generally to accept that the Commission's eventual position on a particular case is reasonable, or at least not obviously unreasonable. The main problem is the difficulty in obtaining a formal decision of exemption under Article 85(3), and the consequent lack of legal certainty. While I have not personally come across a case where this lack of legal certainty alone has caused a prospective agreement to be abandoned, it is clearly a potential stumbling block.

5. So far, the Commission has sought to respond to this particular difficulty by "comfort letters". These are however at best only a partial remedy, and at worst may prove to provide false comfort. An Article 85(3) exemption, once the time for appeal to the Court has expired, provides a substantive legal guarantee. A comfort letter cannot bind the Commission to take a favourable decision; still less can it protect an eventual favourable decision, once taken, from challenge in the Court by a third party. This risk is not insignificant; indeed it is almost axiomatic that if a firm which has accepted a comfort letter returns to the Commission some time later to call for a formal Article 85(3) decision in its favour, it will be because the validity of the agreement has since come under challenge by a third party (eg a competitor) or a customer, or even by the other party to the agreement in the event of a dispute between them[1].

6. One possible solution to this problem would be to extend the opposition procedure, which is already currently available under some sectoral block exemption regulations, to be a provision of general application. This would enable parties to notify agreements in the knowledge that, unless the Commission or others raised a strong objection to the agreement within a certain period, typically three months, the agreement would receive an automatic exemption for a period of, say, five years. There can be no philosophical objection to such an arrangement—since such automatic exemptions are already in force in some sectors. It would also recognise that competition policy needs to be applied pragmatically; and such pragmatism should recognise that, overall, more harm may be done through withholding[2] an individual Article 85(3) exemption than would be done by allowing automatic exemptions to a large number of agreements, all of which appear at first sight not to raise serious competition concerns.

7. There is undoubtedly less satisfaction with the Commission's handling of "behavioural" cases. I do not wish to comment in detail on particular cases in which I have been involved, either before the Commission or before the Court. But there are some matters which, even after making due allowances for "forensic indignation" of those representing defendant companies in such proceedings, I believe the Commission should address. These are:

(a) *Access to file*

Discussion on this subject is complicated by a number of factors. First, lawyers and officials from different backgrounds within Europe have different expectations as to what "access to the file" should mean. For example, there is the issue of what precisely the "file" is, or should comprise.[3] Secondly, the various statements by the Commission on this issue over time have not succeeded in creating in the minds of practitioners a clear idea of precisely what the Commission intends its practice to be. Thirdly, possibly in consequence of the first two factors, there is often a significant variation in what Commission rapporteurs actually do by way of disclosure of the file in different cases.

According to the Court's case law[4], the Commission's undertaking in the Twelfth Report on Competition with regard to access to the file goes appreciably further in this regard than was required by the relevant procedural regulations or by the concept of the "rights of defence" as so far developed by the Court. According to the latter, the Commission's obligation of disclosure is limited to disclosing the documents on which it relies for the conclusions in its statement of objections. However there are a number of decisions by the European Commission and Court of Human Rights which might suggest that, for the purposes of the Convention, this limited obligation of disclosure would not satisfy the requirements of Article 6 in relation to the conduct of "criminal proceedings".[5] This issue will have to be resolved soon.

---

[1]For an example of a party to an agreement subsequently seeking to challenge the grant of an exemption to that agreement, see the *UIP* decision of 12 July 1989, OJ L 226/25, appealed to the Court of First Instance in Case T-157 and 168/89 *MGM* v. *Commission* (the appeal is believed to have since been withdrawn).

[2]Or, which will often come to the same thing, failing to grant an exemption in good time.

[3]eg does the "file" in principle comprise every document which may have been gathered by the Commission in the course of what may have initially been a wide ranging investigation of an industry, or should it include only those documents which are or may be (in its view) relevant to the charges that are eventually formulated in the statement of objections?.

[4]See eg Case T-7/89 *Hercules* v. *Commission* [1991] ECR II–   , [1992] CMLR 84, 265.

[5]It is understood that the Committee will be receiving detailed evidence on this aspect from other witnesses.

Two specific problems need also to be addressed in this context. One is the problem of multiple defendants and multiple charges in a single statement of objections. Is every defendant to be allowed to have access to every part of the file, even to parts that do not concern him? Can this problem be resolved by having the Commission compiling separate "files" for each defendant (and even each charge) or does that simply change the nature of the problem without resolving it? Another problem is the protection of business secrets. In the course of its investigations, the Commission may gather documents from one company containing information which might be of commercial value to its competitors. Even if the Commission does not itself rely on those documents in support of its objections, must they nevertheless be disclosed to all defendants (possibly including competitors) so that they can determine whether or not they aid their defence?

(b) *Treatment of economic issues*

Not all cases raise complex economic issues. However some do, particularly when defining the relevant market for the purpose of assessing dominance or for applying the Merger regulation; economic analysis is also important when determining whether particular market conduct is abusive or likely to have been collusive.

Directorate General IV is notorious for being "lawyer heavy". The ratio of lawyers to economists is high (circa 7 to 1), particularly in comparison with other competition agencies. Moreover, such economists as there are tend to be found either within the economic policy unit DGIVA, or within the Merger Task Force. This means that there are relatively few trained economists working as case handlers.

There is some evidence that this shortage of economists has led on occasion to "economically dubious" reasoning in Commission decisions. The Court of Justice recently annulled one decision in which the Commission's conclusion of concertation between producers had been founded on economic inference from an observed parallelism of prices. On a day-to-day level, some practitioners feel that economic evidence is treated with less respect than it deserves. That attitude is reflected in the remark of a senior DGIV official, who observed in the course of a proceeding that any three economists would probably produce three different hypotheses.

Again, I believe that part of the problem is one of perception. Until recently, economic arguments advanced by defendant firms tended to receive only cursory discussion in the Commission's decisions, even if the merits of the arguments were in fact discussed internally within the Commission's services before the decision was taken. That trend has been reversed in some recent cases, where the economic arguments have been more fully dealt with in the reasoning of the Commission's decision. It can only improve confidence in the Commission's decision making if the economic arguments advanced by the defendant are discussed in the decision, and where appropriate rejected on their merits rather than *sub silentio*.

But there are still a number of cases where the statement of objections, or the preliminary views of the case handler, appear to be economically naive (or worse). In such a case, a firm may feel that involvement of an economist from within DGIV would aid in the understanding of its economic arguments. Until the staffing ratios with DGIV reach a better balance, however, clearly not every case can have an economist assigned to it. There is, however, a practical problem of how the firm can seek such involvement without offending the existing case handler and his superiors (who will feel criticised and that the firm is attempting to go "over their heads"). One solution to this problem could be for the Director General DGIV to announce that in any case where a firm thinks that there are serious or complex economic issues to be considered, it should as a matter of practice notify the Director General at as early a stage as possible so that arrangements can be made within DGIV, and within the constraints of available resources, to ensure that the economic issues are seen to be properly dealt with from as early as possible in the proceedings.

Procedures before the Court of Justice

8. The attachment to the Court of Justice (ECJ) of a Court of First Instance (CFI) with competence in competition (and staff) cases has been an important development. After three and a half years of operation, generalisations are difficult, not least since the average duration of competition cases before the CFI has been some two years or more. Nevertheless, the CFI is regarded as being more willing than was the ECJ to scrutinise critically the details of the Commission's reasoning in competition cases. Whether or not that view is justified[1], what is probably just as important is that the Commission appears to believe that its decisions will be more closely scrutinised.

---

[1]Compare for example the steps taken by the ECJ in its "last" competition case, Case 86/85 *et al. Ahlström* v. *Commission* ("Woodpulp"), judgment of 31.3.93, which included the appointment of two sets of experts to advise the Court.

9. There are however areas where the CFI has not yet fulfilled the expectation for it.

(a) Delay—competition cases in the CFI are still taking a considerable period after close of pleadings to come to an oral hearing (frequently a year or longer), and judgments can be some months after the oral hearing, even though there is not normally an Advocate General's opinion, and therefore no reason for the Court to refrain from immediate consideration of a case after the oral hearing has been concluded. Given that the CFI's judgment to the ECJ may be appealed to ECJ on any point of law, which may take a further two years or so, it is particularly desirable that the CFI should—without prejudicing its reputation for effective scrutiny of the facts—do all it can to accelerate proceedings.

(b) No clear pattern has yet emerged as to whether and how the CFI's procedures will differ appreciably from those of the ECJ in relation to factual issues. In one instance, the CFI required the Commission to specify precisely the documents or other evidence it relied on for each of the material findings in the decision; but this appears to have been an exceptional measure. One matter that has attracted comment[1] is the willingness of the CFI on occasion to embark on factual issues which do not appear to have been raised by the parties.

(c) Even in the more complex economic cases (particularly those involving determination of dominance and relevant market under Article 86), the CFI has not so far resorted to the appointment of economic "experts" to assist it, even though the ECJ did so on occasion, most notably in the recent "Woodpulp" cases. At present, it is unclear how far the CFI will consider it appropriate to substitute its own assessment for that of the Commission on issues that call for a measure of "economic judgment", for example, whether or not there is a sufficient degree of competition between two products for them to be treated as being in the same relevant product market. Traditionally, the European Court has been reluctant to second guess the Commission in its economic assessments. But when such assessments are a part of the process or reasoning that leads to a finding of fact (eg dominance), it is arguable that the CFI should not be constrained in its review and should be free to exercise its own judgment on all aspects of the Commission's reasoning; otherwise, questions may arise as to whether the requirements of Article 6 ECHR are respected.

Procedures before national courts and agencies

10. To date, enforcement of EC Competition law has been seen as the principal prerogative and responsibility of the EC Commission. In part this is because of the latter's exclusive competence in certain areas (eg the application of the Merger Regulation, and the grant of exemptions under Article 85(3)); but even where national courts or agencies have concurrent competence (alleged infringements of Article 85(1) or Article 86) there has in the past been a strong preference on the part of individuals complaining of an infringement of the competition rules to turn first to the Commission. There are a number of possible explanations for this, some of which are discussed below, but the practical consequence has been that there have been relatively few cases at least in the British courts which have proceeded to trial; and no case where the competent authorities in the United Kingdom have sought to apply the EEC's competition rules within the area left to them by Article 88 of the Treaty. The Commission's announcement, following the Court of First Instance judgment in *Automec II,* that the Commission will now decline to act on certain complaints where the Community interest is insufficient, makes it important to review whether, in the United Kingdom at least, adequate alternatives exist for individuals or companies that consider that they are being injured by anti-competitive acts contrary to Articles 85 and 86.

11. Since *Garden Cottage,* there has been little doubt that the English Courts would recognise Articles 85 and 86 as giving rights of action to individuals injured by their breach, including a right to damages. Why then have there been so few claims for damages to proceed to judgment? In my experience, there are a number of factors which have led to this result.

(a) First, if a firm is being seriously injured by anti-competitive conduct, that fact will normally become apparent very quickly. Such plaintiffs are primarily concerned with immediate relief against damage they are suffering from the anti-competitive behaviour. If they obtain interim relief, eg by an injunction, this will often lead to a settlement for the *future.* Compensation for past loss (unless this loss is extremely large) will not normally be thought to justify continuing proceedings.

(b) Since interim relief is granted merely on the basis of an arguable case on the merits *(Cyanamid),* many of the complex factual and economic issues do not need to be investigated fully. However the cost/reward of continuing the litigation may shift dramatically when, after interim relief has been obtained/refused, the decision has to be taken whether to continue to full trial.

---

[1]See, eg *The Court of First Instance: the first three years* by M van der Woude (1992–93), 16 Fordham Int Law J, 412, at 460–2.

(c)   A further factor is that, by its very nature, the damage caused by infringements of the competition rules will normally take the form of purely economic loss (eg reduced turnover and profits). Only in the exceptional case (eg when the loss is so great as to threaten the very existence of the plaintiff, cf. *Garden Cottage*) will damages not appear to be an adequate remedy, and so interim relief be available. This situation contrasts sharply with the conditions for interim relief ordered by the Commission.

(d)   In many cases, the "loss" caused by anti-competitive behaviour is dispersed, so as to make it uneconomic for any one plaintiff to resort to legal proceedings to recover his loss. Consider for example, a cartel between confectionery producers which increases prices of confectionery to consumers by 25 per cent. It is doubtful that even the most avid "chocaholic" would have a damage claim of a few hundred pounds. Even for other higher value consumer products (CDs or petrol) a cartel would be unlikely to lead to losses sufficiently great to justify private litigation.

It was, no doubt, a feeling that companies infringing the competition rules could "get away with" the financial consequences of their actions which led in the United States to the availability of class actions. These have been regarded with suspicion this side of the Atlantic, though the attitude is changing. So far, the Commission has not seen it as part of its role under Regulation 17 to require infringing undertakings to adopt measures to compensate those who had suffered loss as a result; such measures can however be very effective[1]. Unless either the Commission does so, or adequate procedures are available in the national courts, many loss-causing infringements will go unremedied.

(e)   In many cases, the precise amount of financial loss will be difficult to prove. Intermediate users of a product, the price of which is increased anti-competitively, will often find it difficult to show that they have not passed the increased cost on to their own customers.

(f)   There are particular problems in bringing an Article 85 or 86 case to trial, over and above those inherent in "normal" litigation. These include discovery, and the way in which the court will deal with "economic" issues.

  (i)   Following the decision of the House of Lords in *Rio Tinto Zinc* v. *Westinghouse*, defendants can and do resist discovery and interrogatories on the grounds that the relevant documents and materials may "tend to expose [them] to proceedings for an offence or for the recovery of a penalty" within the meaning of s.14(1) of the Civil Evidence Act 1968. This may make it particularly difficult for a plaintiff to prove his case. One way in which the rigour of this rule could be mitigated would be if the fact that the Commission had declined to take proceedings itself, in accordance with the *Automec II* ruling, were regarded by the national courts as indicating that discovery would *not* appreciably increase the risks of the Commission imposing fines. The Commission could reinforce this conclusion by making appropriate disclaimers in any letter by which it declined to act.

  (ii) The Commission, in its notice, indicates a willingness to co-operate with national courts dealing with competition cases, in particular by expressing views on particular cases. This recognises, rightly, that national courts will be unfamiliar with many of the economic principles and concepts involved in applying EC competition law (for example the "rule of reason"), and consequently measures which could assist the national judge should be encouraged. Considerable thought needs to be given, however, as to how this process of "co-operation" might apply in a British court. One possibility might be for the Rules of the Supreme Court to be amended to allow a judge to refer questions to the Commission—in a manner analogous to references under Article 177—but in the hope that answers might be given within a shorter time-frame! Another would be for the Commission to appear, on request, as an *amicus curiae*. Whatever the solution, it would be undesirable that potentially beneficial co-operation should be inhibited by formalistic rules as to the admissibility of any such opinions.

12. The final consideration is whether national agencies may be expected to apply Articles 85 and 86, within the area of their remaining competence. In the United Kingdom, it would not appear that this is a likely option, even if appropriate procedures were available, since if there is anti-competitive behaviour within the United Kingdom that would be caught by Article 85 or 86, it would also be likely to be caught by national competition law.

13. I therefore consider that the Commission may have over-estimated the extent to which, *as a matter of practice*, effective remedies for infringements exist in the national courts. Clearly there are areas where procedural changes could be beneficial; some of which I have mentioned above. But there

---

[1]For example, anti-competitive behaviour by airlines in the United States has led to remedial measures whereby each infringing airline was ordered to pay compensation on a fixed-sum per journey basis to every passenger who could show he had travelled on the airline during the period of the infringement.

will still be many cases where, even if these improvements are made, recourse to national courts, or agencies, is not a viable option. If the Commission, for reasons of limited resources or priorities, declines to pursue complaints made to it, it must realise that often the consequence will be that infringements of the competition rules will go unremedied.

28 *May* 1993

Memorandum by UNICE

Regulation 4064/89 on the control of concentrations between enterprises

Position paper on the revision of certain provisions, in particular the thresholds defining the scope of the regulation

INTRODUCTORY REMARK

1. In line with article 1 paragraph 3, the thresholds defining the scope of the regulation will be reviewed before the end of 1993.

With this exercise in mind, this paper in the first instance takes a position on the question of reviewing these thresholds.

In addition, on the basis of the first few years of application of this regulation, it examines whether other amendments are also desirable.

REVIEW OF THRESHOLDS

2. The scope of the regulation is defined in article 1 paragraph 2 of the Regulation in relation to three thresholds:

— aggregate worldwide turnover of all undertakings concerned in excess of ECU 5 billion,

— aggregate Community turnover of each of at least two of the undertakings concerned in excess of ECU 250 million,

— none of the undertakings in question should have more than two thirds of its Community-wide turnover in one and the same Member State.

UNICE points out from the outset that there is for the time being no need to change the last two thresholds.

The threshold of ECU 250 million effectively excludes from the scope of the Regulation mergers where one of the companies has a relatively modest turnover in the Community. These are mergers involving a shareholding by companies which exercise their main activities outside the Community, and cases where a medium-sized firm is acquired by a large company. Neither of these situations of non-application of the Regulation has given rise to major problems.

In the case of a concentration operation which falls outside the scope of the Regulation because of the ECU 250 million threshold and which raises competition problems in a Member State, the legislation of this Member State can be applied. This also holds true for operations which fall outside the scope of the Regulation because of the third threshold.

3. By contrast, the majority of UNICE's member federations consider that the threshold of ECU 5 billion should be gradually lowered.

The difference of treatment between concentration operations involving turnover in excess of ECU 5 billion and other large operations below this threshold discriminates against undertakings which fall below this threshold. It has furthermore highlighted a major deficiency in Community legislation.

The situation is discriminatory because the large operations not covered by the Community Regulation are subject to various national controls based on different criteria in Member States. Therefore, these operations cannot benefit from the "one-stop shop" approach provided for in the Regulation. This is true for undertakings with activities in several Member States, a condition which is generally met for large operations which would fall within the scope of the Regulation if the ECU 5 billion threshold were gradually lowered.

Discrimination against the operations in question can be eliminated by gradually lowering the ECU 5 billion threshold to include large operations which affect several Member States in the scope of the Community Regulation.

At the same time, lowering the threshold would remove a deficiency in Community legislation. In a true internal market, concentration operations which affect competition in several Member States should be subject to Community legislation and control which alone can take account of the interests of the Community as a whole. National legislation and control cannot perform this function.

4. UNICE is aware of the fact that a lowering of the threshold will place a considerable extra burden of work on the European Commission. The latter will be obliged to take measures to place itself in a position to carry out this work within the time limits currently laid down in the Regulation. In any event, it would be unacceptable for undertakings if the Commission were no longer able to meet the deadlines currently in force.

Lastly, UNICE would like small joint ventures to be excluded from the scope of the Regulation. There is no reason why such ventures should fall within the scope of the Regulation simply because the parent companies which found them are large groups.

OTHER AMENDMENTS TO THE REGULATION

5. Regulation 4064/89 provides that article 9, which deals with referral to the competent authorities in Member States, shall also be reviewed.

In addition, it is probable that other points of the Regulation will be opened to discussion.

However, UNICE generally believes that there is no need to amend the Regulation on points other than the thresholds.

Nevertheless, implementation of the Regulation could be improved either by shifts in some of the Commission's interpretations or by revision of some of the implementing texts.

6. *Referral to competent authorities in Member States*

Under article 9 of the Regulation, the European Commission may, at the request of a Member State, refer a case to the competent authority in the Member State in question if the concentration operation threatens to create or strengthen a dominant position in a market inside this State and which has all the characteristics of a distinct market.

UNICE considers it inappropriate to widen the scope of the provision on referral to the competent authorities in Member States. Inclusion of a provision for automatic referral could give rise to a conflict of competence between the European Commission and the Member State concerned, and could thereby violate the principle of the "one-stop shop" which underlies the Regulation. For this reason, a provision for automatic referral should be rejected.

Similarly, UNICE sees no need to amend other conditions of article 9 which have to be met for a referral to be made.

7. *Definition of concentrative joint venture*

UNICE considers that joint ventures with structural effects should fall within the scope of the Regulation.

In order to achieve this aim, it is not essential to amend the definition of a joint venture given in article 3.2 of the Regulation. It would be sufficient to adapt the Commission communication on concentration and co-operation operations (OJEC C 203/10 dated 14 August 1990) to reflect its recent decisions in this area.

8. *Dominant oligopoly situation*

In the Nestlé/Perrier case, the European Commission interpreted the Regulation as being applicable when the dominant position is formed by a duopoly or oligopoly.

UNICE is not convinced by this interpretation and the economic consequences to which it could give rise are difficult to assess. If the Commission continues to apply this interpretation, UNICE hopes that there will be an occasion to have it vetted by the Court of Justice.

9. *Transparency of decision-making process*

UNICE favours improved transparency in the decision-making process within the European Commission. To this end, it supports calls to communicate the Task Force's interim report assessing the operation in question to the parties to the procedure.

However, such an improvement in the transparency of the decision-making process does not require the Regulation to be amended.

10. *Effective recourse against decisions*

When parties seek clearance for a concentration operation, they must have effective recourse when their application is only partially met, and in particular when the Commission makes its decision subject to conditions and obligations. Such recourse must be possible without jeopardising the positive elements of the decision.

UNICE would like to discuss this point with the Commission and the European Court of Justice.

11. *Imposition of conditions in the initial stage of the procedure*

It would be useful if it were possible for the parties to the procedure to accept conditions in the initial stage of the procedure enabling the Commission to accept the operation at this initial stage.

UNICE would like to exchange views with the European Commission on this problem. However, UNICE does not at the present time call for amendment of the Regulation in order to achieve the desired result.

21 *April* 1993

Encouraging co-operation between undertakings by the extension of group exemptions

UNICE POSITION

GENERAL COMMENT

1. UNICE has noted with great interest the Commission's communication which is designed to encourage co-operation between undertakings via an extension of four group-exemption Regulations. It firmly supports this initiative by the Commission.

UNICE recalls that, in its position of 9 April 1992 on the Commission's draft communication on "Guidelines for assessment of co-operative joint ventures in accordance with article 85 of the EEC Treaty", it has already pointed out that amendment of several block-category Regulations is necessary in order to eliminate the discriminatory treatment of co-operative joint ventures as compared with concentrative joint ventures.

The present communication from the Commission constitutes a large step towards achievement of the objective UNICE advocated in its 9 April 1992 position.

SPECIFIC COMMENTS

A. Specialisation Regulation

2. UNICE vigorously supports inclusion in the Regulation of distribution. Incorporation of this function is necessary for the object of specialisation to be achieved.

UNICE regrets that the Commission proposes to limit agreements on distribution to situations in which the market share of the products in question does not exceed 10 per cent. It considers that this restriction maintains a large discrimination as compared with concentrative joint ventures which, in line with recital 15 of Regulation 4064/89, are regarded as being compatible with the rules of competition when the market share of the undertakings involved does not exceed 25 per cent.

In addition, it should be pointed out that the Commission itself, in its 1985 draft communication, spoke of a figure of 15 per cent which would be regarded as being compatible with the rules of competition when co-operation extends to the marketing of products.

UNICE therefore suggests that the 10 per cent threshold be increased.

3. In the event of the threshold being set below 25 per cent, UNICE suggests introduction of what might be termed an opposition procedure for distribution agreements which exceed the threshold finally chosen but are lower than 25 per cent. This would make it possible to obtain authorisation at short notice.

4. UNICE also supports deletion of article 3(1)(b) of the specialisation Regulation which limits automatic application of the Regulation to agreements involving undertakings whose total turnover does not exceed ECU 500 million. This restriction genuinely discriminates against co-operative joint ventures as compared with concentrative joint ventures.

5. Against this, UNICE finds it difficult to understand the reason for introducing the restriction included in article 2(1)(d) which stipulates that group exemption does not apply when the parties neither produce nor distribute products competing with the contract products.

According to the explanatory memorandum, this restriction should prevent parties from co-ordinating the whole of their marketing policy in the relevant market by entering into a specialisation agreement which concerns only products of limited economic importance.

If such co-ordination were planned, it would fall within the scope of article 85(1) and would only be authorised under the terms of the group-exemption Regulation if all the conditions of this Regulation were met. In this case, an authorisation by the group exemption would not raise any competition problems. By contrast, if co-ordination of marketing policy does not meet the conditions of the specialisation Regulation, it could only be authorised by an individual exemption procedure.

In UNICE's view, this demonstrates that for any situation which might occur the restriction proposed at article 2(1)(d) is not well founded.

B. R&D Regulation

6. UNICE supports the amendments proposed by the Commission for the R&D Regulation.

However, with regard to the 10 per cent threshold proposed for sole distribution, it refers back to points 2 and ·3 of this position paper and considers that the comments made there apply equally to amendments to the R&D Regulation.

C. Patent and know-how licensing Regulations

7. Generally speaking, UNICE would like to point out that, in the medium term, it regards more comprehensive and substantial revision of the patent and know-how licensing Regulations as indispensable. Since adoption of these two Regulations, the legal situation in this area has evolved considerably in the United States and Europe should follow this development.

8. The amendments currently on the table relate only to provisions which are particularly important for co-operative joint ventures.

UNICE supports these amendments and would like them to become reality rapidly, at the same time as the amendments to the specialisation and R&D Regulations.

9. With regard to the 10 per cent threshold for licences covering production and distribution, UNICE considers that its comments under points 2 and 3 above apply *mutatis mutandis* and would therefore like this percentage to be raised.

10. Lastly, UNICE would like to point out that care should be taken to use the same terminology to designate the same things in the two Regulations. The existing texts contain a number of differences which could subsequently give rise to interpretation problems.

8 *July* 1992

Draft Regulation amending Regulations 417/85, 418/85, 2349/84 and 556/89 on the application of article 85-3 of the EEC Treaty to certain categories of specialisation agreements, research and development agreements, patent licensing agreements and know-how licensing agreements

UNICE position

GENERAL COMMENT

1. UNICE has noted with great interest the Commission's communication which is designed to encourage co-operation between undertakings via an extension of four group-exemption Regulations. It firmly supports this initiative by the Commission.

UNICE recalls that, in its position of 9 April 1992 on the Commission's draft communication on "Guidelines for assessment of co-operative joint ventures in accordance with article 85 of the EEC Treaty", it has already pointed out that amendment of several block-category Regulations is necessary in order to eliminate the discriminatory treatment of co-operative joint ventures as compared with concentrative joint ventures.

The present communication from the Commission constitutes a large step towards achievement of the objective UNICE advocated in its 9 April 1992 position.

SPECIFIC COMMENTS

A. Specialisation Regulation

2. UNICE vigorously supports inclusion in the Regulation of distribution. Incorporation of this function is necessary for the object of specialisation to be achieved.

UNICE regrets that the Commission proposes to limit agreements on distribution to situations in which the market share of the products in question does not exceed 10%. It considers that this restriction maintains a large discrimination as compared with concentrative joint ventures which, in line with recital 15 of Regulation 4064/89, are regarded as being compatible with the rules of competition when the market share of the undertakings involved does not exceed 25%.

In addition, it should be pointed out that the Commission itself, in its 1985 draft communication, spoke of a figure of 15% which would be regarded as being compatible with the rules of competition when co-operation extends to the marketing of products.

UNICE therefore suggests that the 10% threshold be increased.

In any event, the text should specify that the threshold finally chosen must refer exclusively to sales to third parties and not include sales to the parent companies of the joint subsidiary.

3. In the event of the threshold being set below 25%, UNICE suggests introduction of what might be termed an opposition procedure for distribution agreements which exceed the threshold finally chosen but are lower than 25%. This would make it possible to obtain authorisation at short notice.

4. UNICE also supports deletion of article 3(1b) of the specialisation Regulation which limits automatic application of the Regulation to agreements involving undertakings whose total turnover does not exceed ECU 500 million. This restriction genuinely discriminates against co-operative joint ventures as compared with concentrative joint ventures.

5. Against this, UNICE finds it difficult to understand the reason for introducing the restriction included in article 2(1d) which stipulates that group exemption does not apply when the parties neither produce nor distribute products competing with the contract products.

According to the explanatory memorandum, this restriction should prevent parties from co-ordinating the whole of their marketing policy in the relevant market by entering into a specialisation agreement which concerns only products of limited economic importance.

If such co-ordination were planned, it would fall within the scope of article 85-1 and would only be authorised under the terms of the group-exemption Regulation if all the conditions of this Regulation were met. In this case, an authorisation by the group exemption would not raise any competition problems. By contrast, if co-ordination of marketing policy does not meet the conditions of the specialisation Regulation, it could only be authorised by an individual exemption procedure.

In UNICE's view, this demonstrates that for any situation which might occur the restriction proposed at article 2(1d) is not well founded.

6. The wording of the various provisions concerning exclusive distribution should be amended to permit the conclusion of exclusive distribution contracts with different contractors where the contracts relate to non-competing products.

These amendments are particularly important for the R&D Regulation. The results of R&D are often applied to totally different and non-competing products. In such situations, a contractor may be interested in distributing products sold only in his branch of activity and wish to leave distribution of non-competing products to one or more other contractors.

The suggested amendment is in line with the provision of article 2, paragraph 1, subparagraph 8 of Regulation 556/98 on know-how.

B. *R&D Regulation*

7. UNICE supports the amendments proposed by the Commission for the R&D Regulation.

However, with regard to the 10% threshold proposed for sole distribution, it refers back to points 2 and 3 of this position paper and considers that the comments made there apply equally to amendments to the R&D Regulation.

Similarly, the comment concerning point 6 above is of special importance for the R&D Regulation.

C. *Patent and know-how licensing Regulations*

8. Generally speaking, UNICE would like to point out that, in the medium term, it regards more comprehensive and substantial revision of the patent and know-how licensing Regulations as indispensable. Since adoption of these two Regulations, the legal situation in this area has evolved considerably in the United States and Europe should follow this development.

9. The amendments currently on the table relate only to provisions which are particularly important for co-operative joint ventures.

UNICE supports these amendments and would like them to become reality rapidly, at the same time as the amendments to the specialisation and R&D Regulations.

10. Which regard to the 10 per cent threshold for licences covering production and distribution, UNICE considers that its comments under points 2 and 3 above apply *mutatis mutandis* and would therefore like this percentage to be raised.

11. UNICE believes it necessary to revise the notion of "parent undertaking" in the Regulations governing patent licensing agreements and know-how licensing agreements. In a group of companies, the parent undertaking of a joint venture is not necessarily the owner of the patent or know-how which is granted to the joint venture. Intellectual property rights often belong to a specialised company or to one of the group's operating companies different from that which owns the stake in the joint venture. The terminology of the two Regulations in question should take account of this situation. For instance, use of the term "company in the parent group" could prevent a problem of unduly narrow interpretation.

12. Lastly, UNICE would like to point out that care should be taken to use the same terminology to designate the same things in the two Regulations. The existing texts contain a number of differences which could subsequently give rise to interpretation problems.

21 *September* 1992

Draft communication concerning application of articles 85 and 86 of the EEC Treaty by national courts (Document IV/1009/91—Rev1)

UNICE POSITION

INTRODUCTION

1. The purpose of the communication is to relieve the Commission from dealing with a number of complaints which it believes should be dealt with by national courts or authorities. The Commission "intends, in implementing its decision-making powers, to concentrate on notifications, complaints and own-initiative procedures having particular political, economic or legal significance for the Community" (point 11 of draft communication).

2. UNICE understands the Commission's concern to relieve itself from dealing with complaints relating to questions which are primarily of importance for the undertakings directly involved in the case and which do not have particularly significant implications for competition in the sector in question as a whole.

At a time when everyone in the European Community is calling for application of the principle of subsidiarity, it could be assumed that the approach envisaged in the communication should not pose major problems.

However, decentralised application of article 85 and 86 is more complex than might appear at first sight.

3. First of all, it is difficult to see where in practice the dividing line would be drawn between the powers of the Commission on the one hand and national authorities and courts on the other.

Second, decentralised application as proposed in the draft communication may be a source of uncertainty detrimental to the legal security of undertakings.

Lastly, there are serious doubts as to whether the objective the Commission has set itself can be achieved via the measures set out in the communication.

Dividing line between powers of Commission and national courts and authorities

4. The draft communication refers principally to national courts. The only references to national competition authorities are in points 1.2 and 11.

By virtue of article 3 of Regulation No. 17, the authorities of Member States remain competent to apply the provisions of Articles 85.1 and 86 as long as the Commission has not initiated any procedure.

A communication on decentralisation can hardly pass over the powers of national authorities in silence.

5. The dividing line between the powers of the Commission and those of national courts and authorities is not drawn very clearly in the draft communication. Point 11 states that cases having no particular political, economic or legal significance for the Community should be dealt with by national courts or authorities.

However, the text fails to demonstrate how this distinction will be made in practice.

Will complaints be examined on a preliminary basis and referred to national authorities or courts? Is there a legal basis for referral? Will it be possible to contest a referral? Evaluation of the political, economic or legal importance of a case is particularly subjective. Would it not be essential to issue more specific criteria so that undertakings can form an idea of the route to be followed if they envisage making a complaint?

Problems arising from application of articles 85.1 and 86 by national courts and authorities

6. While national authorities can be expected to have sufficient knowledge of Community competition law, it is by no means certain that this is also the case for national judges.

Although the Commission intends to "develop as far as possible a more general policy of training and awareness that would enable judges and lawyers to improve and increase their knowledge of Community law and procedures", there is legitimate cause for concern about the length of time that will be needed to arrive at a situation which guarantees legal security for undertakings.

7. The Commission retains exclusive power to apply Article 85.3.

This exclusive power is a serious weakness in terms of decentralised application of Article 85.

The ideas put forward in the draft communication to limit part of this weakness are unsatisfactory and legally contestable.

This is particularly true for the proposal made in points 21 and 22 of the draft communication. UNICE considers that it is not the task of a judge confronted with an agreement notified to the Commission to "assess the likelihood of an exemption being granted in the light of the substantive criteria laid down in Article 85.3, the case law of the Court of Justice and the previous decisions taken by the Commission".

Application of Article 85.3 remains exclusively in the hands of the Commission and it would be incompatible with the division of powers between the Commission and national courts and authorities respectively if the latter could take a decision based on a hypothetical assessment of what the Commission might decide with regard to application of Article 85.3.

In this case, the national judge can only suspend his ruling pending the Commission's decision.

8. One of the risks inherent in decentralised application of Article 85 and 86 lies in the absence of uniform judicial control over decisions made by the courts in Member States.

This would result in considerable legal insecurity for the enterprises in question. The procedure of preliminary rulings laid down in Article 177 of the EEC Treaty would only be a relatively weak means of offsetting the absence of uniform judicial control over decisions.

Can the envisaged communication solve the problem of decentralised application of articles 85 and 86?

9. The communication cannot change an undertaking's right to lodge complaints with the Commission if it believes it has suffered from behaviour of other undertakings incompatible with Articles 85 and 86.

Undertakings which believe they have suffered will only choose to appeal to national courts if they are sure that this route is at least as effective as a complaint to the Commission.

Despite a number of advantages enjoyed by procedures initiated with national courts (point 9 of draft communication), undertakings cannot ignore the weaknesses of an appeal to national courts.

These weaknesses include the legal insecurity of procedures initiated with judges who are insufficiently familiar with Community competition law and the length of procedures in the case of a restriction of competition notified to the Commission where the latter has exclusive power to apply Article 85.3.

In UNICE's view, these weaknesses lead to the conclusion that the envisaged communication will not give rise to much wider application of Articles 85 and 86 by national courts than is already the case at the moment. True decentralisation of application of Articles 85 and 86 would require implementation of much more far-reaching measures. However, a detailed analysis of the risks inherent in such decentralisation is essential before this route is adopted.

7 *July* 1992

Memorandum by Mr Ivo Van Bael

As a legal practitioner in Brussels, regularly involved in EC competition proceedings, I am grateful for the invitation of the European Communities Committee to submit evidence on EC competition practice and procedure.

My comments do not purport to be exhaustive. They are offered in support of the continuing efforts of the House of Lords to suggest ways to improve the situation.

1. DECISION-MAKING PROCESS

a. *Delegation of Authority*

The flaws in the Commission's decision-making process have been exposed in the Judgment of the Court of First Instance in *PVC* of 27 February 1992, which led to the inadmissibility of the appeal on the grounds that it had been filed against a legally "non-existent" decision of the Commission.

In theory, competition decisions are adopted by the full Commission, acting as a collegiate body. In practice, however, due to the heavy workload of the Commission, most of the competition decisions have been adopted by the Commission without much of a debate, if any. Typically, the so-called "written procedure" is followed, a procedure whereby the draft decision is circulated to the cabinet of each Commission member and is considered to be adopted if no objections are raised within a period of a few days.

Needless to say, in the absence of a serious deliberation by the members of the Commission, the real power rests with the casehandlers themselves. They are effectively acting as prosecutor, judge and jury, without much internal supervision, as illustrated, for example, in case 5/85, *AKZO CHEMIE* v *Commission*, 1986 ECR 2585, at 2590, 2592 and 2593.

If reality is such that Commission members are too busy to actually discuss the decisions they are adopting, then a system of checks and balances is needed to prevent them merely rubberstamping whatever a casehandler has prepared.

It is submitted that the problems resulting from the wide delegation of authority are not going to be solved by hiring more staff but by instilling more discipline. A greater respect for law and procedure would, in the end, help the Commission fend off the call for an independent competition agency.

b. *Time Frame*

The first few years of operation of the Merger Task Force show that it has been able to cope with its heavy workload and strict deadlines, notwithstanding its small staff.

This performance of the Merger Task Force should cause the other services of DGIV to reflect on their procedures to see where they could be streamlined further. It is, indeed, unacceptable that parties filing a notification must still be prepared to "wait for Godot".

As announced last year by the outgoing Commissioner in charge of competition, the introduction of time limits within which the Commission Services must determine their position should be considered. Another solution to unclog the pipelines would be to attach fewer conditions to block exemptions and to follow more a "rule of reason" approach.

2. DISCRETIONARY POWERS

a. *Case Selection*

The Commission's discretion in choosing which cases to bring has, over the years, proved to be very wide. This makes any prediction hazardous. For example, in a recent case the Commission had refused to intervene in favour of a complainant, although he was facing the execution of a national court order based on agreements allegedly illegal under EC law, which could have had severe adverse consequences on his operations. Later, after the complainant had been able to redress his situation on appeal, the Commission nevertheless brought proceedings which culminated in its decision of 27 October 1992—*Distribution of package tours during the 1990 World Cup*—OJ (1992) L 326/31. One is obviously at a loss to understand why the case was not opened at the time it mattered and why it was nevertheless started more than one year later when there was no longer any interest on the part of the complainant.

b. *Settlements*

It is not because a case is brought that it will necessarily culminate in a decision. As a matter of fact, every year there are many more settlements than decisions.

It is unquestionable that settlement procedures should be encouraged because they save time and money for both the Commission and the defendant, while at the same time the complainant or public at large enjoy faster relief from the restrictive effects of the violation. However, since the Commission, by entering into settlements, is in fact shaping its policy without any of the procedural safeguards provided by an administrative proceeding, it is imperative that the Commission's actions in this respect be sufficiently transparent so as to remain subject to public and judicial scrutiny.

Perhaps the American Antitrust Procedures and Penalties Act (APPA) enacted by Congress in 1974, may provide a useful frame of reference for increasing the transparency and judicial control of the antitrust settlement practice of the EC.

c. *Fines*

A review of all fines imposed by the Commission in past competition cases reveals that the Commission has not endeavoured to establish a uniform tariff of fines. Yet, the rule of proportionality and the principle of non-discrimination would seem to imply that a greater effort should be undertaken to streamline sanctions instead of following an "à la carte" approach.

d. *Merger Control*

The fact that thus far clearance has only been refused in one proceeding, illustrates the permissiveness with which the Merger Task Force has reviewed the transactions submitted to it. This user-friendly attitude is in contrast with the traditional approach of DGIV in the application of Article 86. In other words, had the classic Article 86 interpretation been followed, a considerable number of clearances could have been denied.

This goes to shows that business is regulated by a rule of men rather than by a rule of law. Hence, there is no guarantee that the current favourable approach of the Commission toward restructuring will continue. Indeed, the same criteria which today allow mergers to be cleared could tomorrow be invoked to block mergers.

In contrast, the United States merger legislation allows for the quantification of business concentrations by way of the Herfindahl-Hirschman index. The advantage of this approach is that it provides greater legal certainty.

3. INCREASED NATIONAL ENFORCEMENT

The Commission's recent emphasis on national enforcement is to be welcomed. If the EEA comes into effect, the Commission's workload will increase substantially. Hence, the importance of following an approach based on the now popular subsidiarity concept.

However, this will require a fundamental change in the attitude of DGIV, known to have favoured a wide interpretation of the required effect on trade between Member States (see, eg *Hugin*, *Michelin*).

Also, in order to build more expertise within the national competition authorities, it is suggested that the national representatives attending the Advisory Committee meetings in Brussels should obtain better documentation about the cases they are being consulted on and their views should be more seriously considered by the Commission. Indeed, one has the distinct impression that the national authorities send no representatives at all or only junior representatives to Brussels because the feeling prevails that for the Commission Services, the consultation process is a mere "ritual", without much impact on the further course of the proceeding.

4. *Procedural Improvements*

By way of a preliminary remark, the Commission should be congratulated for having implemented some self-imposed procedural improvements. It is, indeed, remarkable that the Commission, although it assumes *inter alia* the role of prosecutor, has in several areas of concern proven to be more liberal than the Court of Justice. Nevertheless, certain matters are capable of further improvement.

a. *Access to File*

In infringement proceedings conducted by DGIV there appears to be no fixed scenario nor time frame for granting the defendant access to the Commission's file. Sometimes the person named in a complaint is requested to comment on the complaint from the moment the informal investigation process is started, while in other cases the defendant is only given access to the complaint and to the other documents in the Commission's file at the time a statement of objections is served on him.

b. *Dawn Raids*

In reply to written question No 677/79 of Lady Elles concerning the form the consultations prescribed by Article 14(4) of Regulation 17 should take, the Commission replied:

> "the standard administrative practice which has developed throughout the Community is for the Commission officials responsible for the investigation to visit the national authority concerned, when they produce the full text of the draft decision ordering an investigation and supply any further explanation requested. The facts and findings of consultations are recorded in writing" (OJ (1979) C 310/31).

Yet, in the *AKZO* case, referred to earlier, none of these self-imposed safeguards had been complied with. This underlines the need for procedural reform to be laid down in Regulations rather than in statements of principle, from which the Commission Services feel free to deviate.

In *HOECHST* (1989) ECR 2859, the Court of Justice ruled that in the event of lack of co-operation by a company, the Commission investigators have a right to search, provided that they are assisted by the national authorities who must ensure that national procedural rules of safeguard are complied with, in order to respect the company's right of defence. Since these national rules differ from one Member State to another, it is suggested that an effort be undertaken to harmonise these essential standards of protection.

c. *Self-incrimination*

After pointing out that legal persons cannot invoke a right of non self-incrimination, the Court of Justice ruled that certain limits should nevertheless be imposed on the Commission's powers in order to preserve the rights of defence. Since the burden of proof rests on the Commission to demonstrate the infringement, the Commission should not be permitted to ask questions, the answers to which would oblige the company to admit the existence of the infringement (*SOLVAY* (1989) ECR 3355, *ORKEM* (1989) ECR 3283).

Needless to say, this quasi right of non-self incrimination is in need of further clarification.

d. *Hearing Officer*

The impact of this procedural reform has been more cosmetic than real. It is clear that this is the way the Commission Services want it to be because, except for a secretary, he has no staff to assist him.

It is also suggested that the scope of the Hearing Officer's duties be reviewed in order to make them more meaningful. For example, when disputes arise in connection with access to the file or the confidentiality of documents, the Hearing Officer could play a useful role.

I hope the foregoing comments will be of assistance to the European Communities Committee.

Ivo Van Bael
Member of the Brussels Bar
Professor, College of Europe, Bruges

Printed in the United Kingdom by HMSO
19585　C6　12/93　136084　PP
CRC supplied